HOW ECONOMICS FORGOT HISTORY

Economics today has been widely criticised as being more concerned with mathematical technique than the understanding and explanation of real world phenomena. However, one hundred years ago, in Europe and America, economics was fused with the study of history and its practitioners emphasised the importance of the understanding of specific institutions.

How Economics Forgot History shows how the German historical school addressed a key problem in social science and concerned themselves with the historical specific character of economic phenomena and the need to make economic theory more sensitive to the historical and geographical variety of different socio-economic systems. Examining the nature and evolution of the problem of historical specificity, it shows how this issue was tackled by Karl Marx, Gustav Schmoller, Carl Menger, Werner Sombart, Max Weber, Alfred Marshall, John Rogers Commons and Frank Knight. It is also argued that alongside Lionel Robbins, leading figures such as John Maynard Keynes, Joseph Schumpeter and Talcott Parsons also helped to divert the social sciences away from this problem.

Geoffrey M. Hodgson concludes with some suggestions as to how modern economics can once again begin to take this problem on board, and become more sensitive to the great structural and institutional changes in history, as well as those we have witnessed in recent decades. He argues that disciplinary boundaries have to be re-evaluated, in an effort to re-introduce an adequate historical vision to the social sciences.

Geoffrey M. Hodgson is a Research Professor in Business Studies at the University of Hertfordshire. He has published widely in the academic journals and his previous books include *Economics and Utopia* (Routledge, 1999).

This is a splendid piece of intellectual history. Hodgson breathes new life into past ideas and the issues surrounding them. These revived ideas are terribly important for the current generation of economists, both mainstream and heterodox. It is the first book I have seen that gets the complex story of *historismus* into a proper intellectual context. A major contribution is the demonstration that the victory of the Austrians in the *Methodenstreit* was apparent only and how the problem of historical specificity continues to haunt the literature of economics.

Paul Dale Bush
California State University at Fresno, USA

With *How Economics Forgot History* Geoff Hodgson has gone considerable distance toward closing an important gap in methodological thinking about economics: how to explain the concrete, historically specific dimensions of economic life. Many have criticized the flaws of general theorizing. Many have called for a more historically specific economics. But Hodgson delivers a well thought-out account of how to go forward that recommends judicious recourse to universal concepts with ideas from evolutionary and complexity theory. Building on a careful examination of the German historical school and American institutionalism, Hodgson produces an original contribution that will be important to progress in thinking about economics as a social science.

John B. Davis
Marquette University, USA

In this outstanding, thought-provoking and lucidly written book, Geoffrey Hodgson explores the important relationship between economic theory and history, challenging the universalistic doctrine of neoclassical economics. He succeeds impressively in developing a meta-theoretic platform that integrates general principles with historical specificities as they result from particular spatio-temporal contexts. The book provides effective guidance for economists who are prepared to rethink theory formation in a novel way.

Kurt Dopfer
University of St Gallen, Switzerland

Professor Hodgson is showing the way towards something that has scarcely existed since Marx: a historical economics that reaches beyond mere economic history.

John Maloney
University of Exeter, UK

Hodgson's erudition is deeply impressive. Overall, he must know more than anyone in the world about the roots of historical and institutional economics. In this volume the importance of thinking about institutions comes across extremely clearly, as does the contribution of the old institutional economics to this endeavour. This book clears the ground for a new, constructive approach to economics that can contribute to a deeper understanding of the world in which we live.

Paul Ormerod
Volterra Ltd, UK

This is a book that needed to be written, and Hodgson has done a fine job in ensuring that it will be read. It is an intriguing and fascinating account of the rise and fall of a fundamental question in economics, that of the role and nature of historical specificity. I learnt a great deal about the historically dependent nature of economic theory from this comprehensive and thoroughly researched account of the characters and context of those who made it. Were Umberto Eco to turn to economics, he might write something like this. A fascinating narrative of deception, lost trails, personal intrigue, serendipity and turpitude with a dash of world war and shifting power relations. And, in the final analysis, it is a moral story. Economics cannot have universality without history, nor history without universality. They must learn to co-exist. Hodgson has explained this beautifully.

Jason Potts
University of Brisbane, Australia

Economics has two modes of thought and analysis. In one, the economy is examined as a pure, abstract, a-institutional, transcendent system. In the other, the economy is examined in terms of institutions which have history. In his newest book, Geoff Hodgson explores the history, content and conceptual problems of the latter approach. It is a brilliant presentation and interpretation of very important materials.

Warren Samuels
Michigan State University, USA

By the same author

Socialism and Parliamentary Democracy (1977)

Labour at the Crossroads (1981)

Capitalism, Value and Exploitation (1982)

The Democratic Economy (1984)

Economics and Institutions (1988)

After Marx and Sraffa (1991)

Economics and Evolution (1993)

Economics and Utopia (1999)

Evolution and Institutions (1999)

ECONOMICS AS SOCIAL THEORY
Series edited by Tony Lawson
University of Cambridge

Social Theory is experiencing something of a revival within economics. Critical analyses of the particular nature of the subject matter of social studies and of the types of method, categories and modes of explanation that can legitimately be endorsed for the scientific study of social objects, are re-emerging. Economists are again addressing such issues as the relationship between agency and structure, between economy and the rest of society, and between the enquirer and the object of enquiry. There is a renewed interest in elaborating basic categories such as causation, competition, culture, discrimination, evolution, money, need, order, organization, power probability, process, rationality, technology, time, truth, uncertainty, value etc.

The objective for this series is to facilitate this revival further. In contemporary economics the label 'theory' has been appropriated by a group that confines itself to largely asocial, ahistorical, mathematical 'modelling'. *Economics as Social Theory* thus reclaims the 'Theory' label, offering a platform for alternative rigorous, but broader and more critical conceptions of theorizing.

Other titles in this series include:

HOW ECONOMICS FORGOT HISTORY

The problem of historical specificity in social science

Geoffrey M. Hodgson

London and New York

First published 2001
by Routledge
11 New Fetter Lane, London EC4P 4EE

Simultaneously published in the USA and Canada
by Routledge
29 West 35th Street, New York, NY 10001

Reprinted 2002

Routledge is an imprint of the Taylor & Francis Group

Typeset in Palatino by
Keystroke, Jacaranda Lodge, Wolverhampton
Printed and bound in Great Britain by
MPG Books Ltd, Bodmin

British Library Cataloguing in Publication Data
A catalogue record for this book is available from the British Library

Library of Congress Cataloging in Publication Data
Hodgson, Geoffrey Martin
How economics forgot history : the problem of historical specificity in social science /
Geoffrey M. Hodgson.
p. cm. – (Economics as social theory)
Includes bibliographical references and index.
1. Historical school of economics. 2. Social sciences—Study and teaching.
I. Title. II. Series.

HB97 .H63 2001
330.15′42—dc21
2001019349

ISBN 0–415–25716–6 (hbk)
ISBN 0–415–25717–4 (pbk)

To all in academia who place enquiry, truth
and understanding above their personal ambition

CONTENTS

CONTENTS

ILLUSTRATIONS

FIGURES

TABLE

PREFACE

This book has had a very long inception. It concerns a central problem in social science and some steps towards its resolution. I have believed for over thirty years that the problem of historical specificity was one of the key questions in the social sciences. This problem starts from the presumption that different socio-economic phenomena may require theories that are in some respects different from each other. Essential variation among objects of enquiry may impose limits on successful explanatory unification. An adequate theory of (say) the feudal system may differ from an adequate theory of (say) capitalism. Any common aspects of these theories will reflect common features of the real systems involved. Nevertheless, differences between different systems could be so important that the theories and concepts used to analyse them must also be substantially differ-ent, even if they share some common precepts. A fundamentally different reality may require a different theory. This, in rough outline, is the problem of historical specificity.

Karl Marx made this argument in the 1840s and it was the starting point of his own economic theory. Although my own flirtation with Marxism was relatively brief, and I became a resolute critic of several of his ideas, I remained convinced of the importance of this insight.

In particular, for a long time I have also thought that the recklessly over-general postulates of mainstream economics have weakened, rather than strengthened it as a theoretical system. Universal theories are based on the maxim: 'one theory fits all'. Universal theories can have limitations in dealing with specific, concrete phenomena. As in the case of much mainstream economics, they can be insufficiently sensitive to historical and geographic variations.

In the 1980s I became more familiar with the works of the German historical school. For well over a hundred years, they too had tackled and debated this problem. Furthermore, I realised that Carl Menger's famous attack on the German historical school in the 1880s had not been successful in brushing the problem of historical specificity aside. Moreover, the influence of the German historical school had been so wide that leading British economists, including Alfred Marshall, had taken much of their argument on board. In addition, similar concerns had inspired the emerging American institutional economists in the early part of the twentieth century.

I discovered that there was a Lost Continent of theoretical, methodological and empirical studies in economics, largely hidden under the twentieth-century rubble of fascism and war. It contained important thinkers who should in justice rank among the most important social scientists of the twentieth century. Yet they have no memorials in the technocratic domain of modern mainstream economics. Few from the Lost Continent have escaped this oblivion. Many are absent from the classrooms and the textbooks of modern, global academia.

Today, many pay due credit to a few German-speaking authors such as Joseph Schumpeter, Max Weber and Karl Marx. But these authors were part of a great milieu, and many around them were similar in stature. The few are praised but the majority is forgotten. Yet many of the ideas of the few were borrowed or developed from others who lack the credit. Some examples are given in the present work.

I began making substantial notes for this book in about 1994, when I was at the University of Cambridge. Originally, I planned to write a history of institutional economics. A brief discussion of Marxism and the German historical school was to be the first part of the work. It quickly became clear that the neglected German historical school, and those influenced by them, had much more to say on the problem than others had given them credit. The project expanded and it became clear that the planned work on the history of institutional economics could not be confined to a single volume. Discussion of the German historical school, their successors and the problem of historical specificity would occupy a single volume in itself.

The book evolved into a historical and analytical study in which the problem of historical specificity is the dominant theme. However, no more than three chapters focus directly on the German historical school. This book does not attempt to provide an adequate summary of either the historical school or of institutionalism. Both these schools of economic thought are addressed in terms of their engagement with the problem of historical specificity.

The argument here is largely at the level of meta-theory; an attempt is made to explore how different theories relate to each other and mesh together and whether each may be useful as a means to understand a particular segment of reality. Meta-theory occupies the debatable ground between philosophy and theory itself. Accordingly, there is less detailed discussion here of specific theories. Writing a book of this kind where every theory was elaborated in detail would have been impossible. The reader is referred to appropriate sources where necessary. In facing the thematic problem of this book, the establishment of meta-theoretical co-ordinates is a primary and substantial task.

While the contemporary fixation on general theoretical systems is criticised, it is also argued here that some general principles are indispensable. What are also required are additional levels of theorising, guided by broad, general principles but rooted, both conceptually and empirically, in historically and geographically specific phenomena.

It is my strong conviction that the task of development and reconstruction in economics and the other social sciences cannot be fulfilled without a more adequate knowledge of past intellectual history. Without this knowledge we are condemned to repeat the mistakes of the past. Moreover, the thoughts and debates of past economists form a rich quarry of inspiration and ideas.

Regrettably, however, the history of economic thought is an unpopular sub-discipline. It is widely regarded as irrelevant and arcane. Frank Hahn (1992, p. 165) expressed a prevalent view among economists when he wrote: 'What the dead had to say, when of value, has long since been absorbed, and when we need to say it again we can generally say it much better.' Hahn ignored the possibility that much of value has simply been forgotten. If we consider the problem of historical specificity then we can see how wrong his attitude can be. In fact, discussion of the problem dominated economics for about a hundred years. Yet neither the problem nor any adequate solution to it has been 'absorbed'. Today, we do not 'say it much better'. On the contrary, economists are silent on this topic: the problem is widely forgotten and ignored.

Not only is history of ideas an unfashionable and neglected subject, but even the standard history of economics textbooks do not do justice to the problem of historical specificity. The historical school is typically and hastily dismissed for its alleged 'atheoretical' descriptivism and naïveté.[1] This assessment is not only disproportionately brief but also it is inaccurate. While an over-emphasis on the power of empirical work can be found in the writings of some of its members, the historical school contained theorists such as Friedrich List, Thomas Cliffe Leslie, Gustav von Schmoller, Werner Sombart and Max Weber. All of these made a significant theoretical contribution: they attempted to explain or understand the world, as well as to describe it.

Part II is devoted to the attempts of the historical school to deal with the problem of historical specificity. The action takes place mainly in Germany, Austria and the British Isles. When the history of economic thought is revisited, with the problem of historical specificity in mind, new perspectives emerge. The historical school is revealed as grappling, for a hundred years, with one of the central methodological and theoretical problems of social science. Even Alfred Marshall – too often wrongly depicted as an antagonist of historicism – is unveiled as being highly sensitive to this methodological problem. He aligned himself with Schmoller and was rightly critical of some of the English historicists in their empiricist excesses.

Nevertheless, this is much more a story of failure than success. While important insights have been neglected, treatments of the problem were much impaired by the empiricist illusion that the facts could speak for themselves. It was only with the later historical school that this misconception was dropped and substantial theoretical progress began. But these efforts were overwhelmed with the real historical events of fascism and war. An understanding of the sources of this failure and the reasons why attempts to rectify the situation were terminated, can strengthen any modern effort to deal with the problem. Even out of error, ideas can evolve.

Part III discusses the overall fate and eventual neglect of the problem, as both economics and sociology became immersed in ahistorical generalities. The

---

1   Notable exceptions include Schumpeter (1954), Pribram (1983) and Perlman and McCann (1998). In addition, Hutchison (1953, pp. 293–8) pointed out that the modern Austrian criticism of socialist central planning was anticipated in the work of members of the German historical school.

narrative switches to the United States as well as Britain. Again, the central motif of historical specificity changes previous depictions of the intellectual scene. For example, despite his revolutionary contribution to macroeconomics, John Maynard Keynes is revealed as fostering a neglect of the problem and helping to promote a postwar fashion for general theorising in economics. At about the same time, Lionel Robbins attempted to place microeconomics on ahistorical foundations and Talcott Parsons did much the same for sociology.

What is revealed in parts II and III is a tragi-comedy of errors. The narrative involves misunderstandings, shortcomings, complacency, untimely deaths, suicides, personal rivalries, moral deficiencies, careerist ambitions and deliberate attempts to ignore or rewrite history. It also tells of the accidents and specific historical contexts that led to the claimed universality of modern economic theory. We see the effects of foreign invasion, of crises and famine, of two devastating world wars, of the academic milieus of great universities, of ideologies such as liberalism and totalitarianism, of nationalist movements, of immigration flows, of the rise of English as a world language, and of the changing balance of world power. In truth, there is historical specificity written all over the entire history of ideas, as well as over economic and social theories that acknowledge no real historical specificity.

Part IV departs from the historical narrative. I attempt some provisional and incomplete answers to the thematic questions of this volume. I suggest a conceptual framework in which the problem of historical specificity might begin to be resolved. Overall, an attempt is made to move forward the discussion of the problem of historical specificity from a point where it had been abandoned, more than sixty years ago.

In abandoning its former historical orientation, economics as a whole was radically transformed. It lost its emphasis on the study of real, socio-economic systems, instead to become a deductivist exploration of 'individual choice'. The task of explanation of the choosing agent was consigned to psychology. At the same time, sociology found territory adjacent to the new economics, and then soared skywards in generalising abstraction. This book explores some of the causes and consequences of these developments.

Although the historical and theoretical narrative here centres on economics, there is some discussion of sociology and other social sciences. The problems addressed here are so central and important for social theory as a whole that they are hopefully of interest to all social scientists. This book is written with this wider audience in mind.

It is not the intention of this book to provide a new theory. That would be a major task, requiring several further volumes. Those who expect one will surely be disappointed. They will also be misinformed. Economics has grappled with the problem of historical specificity for more than 160 years and it would be very naïve to expect a single author, in a single part of a single volume, to sort out the problem once and for all. Part IV offers some preliminary suggestions towards a future solution – nothing more.

Instead, the main objective is to restore discussion of the problem of historical specificity to its rightful place, to learn from the achievements and mistakes of the past, and to make some suggestions for reconstruction of the social science agenda. In the view of its author, the book will be a success simply if puts some of these issues in the limelight.

Due to increasing loads of administration and teaching, I was not able to make much progress on this book until I left the University of Cambridge at the end of 1998. I obtained a Research Chair at the University of Hertfordshire and I was then able to devote almost all my time to research. This was a wonderful opportunity. I plan further volumes on the economic thought of American institutionalism, as well as other works on the development of the methodology and theory of institutional economics.

My *Economics and Utopia* (1999a) also raised the question of historical specificity. I expand here considerably upon some of the arguments in that book. There are also links here with some of my earlier works, such as *The Democratic Economy* (1984), *Economics and Institutions* (1988), *Economics and Evolution* (1993) and *Evolution and Institutions* (1999b). The argument here builds on several of my earlier books and a few passages repeat arguments made elsewhere. I have done my best to present a fluent and complete argument and at the same time to reduce such repetition to an absolute minimum.

ACKNOWLEDGEMENTS

The author is extremely grateful to Peter Abell, Glen Atkinson, Jürgen Backhaus, Leonhard Bauer, Markus Becker, Mark Blaug, Paul Dale Bush, Victoria Chick, Ha-Joon Chang, John Davis, Wilfred Dolfsma, Kurt Dopfer, Sheila Dow, Wolfgang Drechsler, Stephen Dunn, Alexander Ebner, Ross Emmett, Mario Graça Moura, John Holmwood, Hella Hoppe, Michael Hutter, Stavros Ioannides, Søren Jagd, Thorbjørn Knudsen, Peter Koslowski, Clive Lawson, Fred Lee, Frans van Loon, Uskali Mäki, John Maloney, Anne Mayhew, Brent McClintock, Robert McMaster, Philip Mirowski, Edward Nell, Richard Nelson, Klaus Nielsen, Ted Oleson, Paul Ormerod, Huascar Pessali, Helge Peukert, Jason Potts, Berger Priddat, Erik Reinert, Norbert Reuter, Bridget Rosewell, Malcolm Rutherford, Jorma Sappinen, Bertram Schefold, Alice Schlegel, Andrew Tylecote, Axel van den Berg, Eric Weede, Richard Whitley and many others for discussions, critical comments and other assistance. Some of these people have been especially helpful – far beyond the call of duty. Thanks are also due to four anonymous referees, nominated by the publisher, for their invaluable comments. I am also highly indebted to Markus Becker, Guido Bünsdorf, Hella Hoppe, Bertram Schefold and Heinz-Jürgen Schwering for substantial help with the translation from the original German of several passages quoted in this work. Additional use has been made of short translated extracts from German sources in Gide and Rist (1915), Herbst (1965), Koslowski (1997a), Krabbe (1996), Menger (1985), von Mises (1960) and Parsons (1928).

The University of Hertfordshire has provided me with the abundant research time and fruitful career circumstances to complete this work. While writing the book I have also benefited from brief research visits to the University of Southern Denmark in Odense and the Max Planck Institute, Jena, Germany. The help and hospitality of all these institutions are gratefully acknowledged. Finally, I thank my family – Vinny, Sarah and Jamie – for their love and support.

Part I

INTRODUCTION

1

THE LIMITATIONS OF
GENERAL THEORY

Science must begin with myths, and with the criticism of myths.
(Sir Karl Popper, 'The Philosophy of Science' (1957))

History is important, partly because every complex organism, every human being and every society carries the baggage of its past. Evolution builds on past survivals that encumber actions in the present. Choices made by our ancestors can be difficult to undo. For example, the standard railway gauge used by modern high-speed trains has its origins in the axle dimensions of horse-drawn carts of over two thousand years ago. We travel on railways that were designed with some dimensions inherited from an ancient and inappropriate means of transport. Other examples of lock-in and path dependence in the evolution of technology and conventions are well known in the social sciences.[1]

If history matters – at least in the sense of social development being path dependent – then our analyses must explore the particularities of the past. While we may retain general principles or guidelines, detailed analyses of particular events, structures and circumstances are required. If history matters in this sense, then general theories have their limits. That is one reason why some of the quoted examples of technological lock-in have been controversial: path dependence dulls the lure of a general theory.[2]

In contrast, if we were to possess an adequate general theory of socio-economic structure and change, then we would use it to understand every kind of circumstance within its broad domain of application. Specific circumstances would enter the theory merely as data. Particular theories would no longer be required. The achievement of a general theory of economic behaviour would make the construction of a historically delimited theory redundant. A single theoretical framework would encompass all possibilities. That is the lure of a general theory.[3]

---

1 See, for example, David (1985, 1994), Dosi *et al.* (1988), Arthur (1989, 1994), North (1990), Hodgson (1993a), H. P. Young (1996).
2 Note the discussion of network externalities, and the controversy over whether the QWERTY keyboard and the VHS video system were in some sense optimal or not (David, 1985; Katz and Shapiro, 1985, 1986, 1994; Liebowitz and Margolis, 1990, 1994).
3 There is a slight difference of meaning between the terms 'general theory' and 'universal theory' in that the latter connotes a wider domain of applicability than the former. Both terms are used in this book. Different possible levels of generality emerge after the introduction of different levels of abstraction. See chapter 21 below.

Nevertheless, it is argued here that such a goal is impossible, at least in the social sciences. The desire for a general theory obliges scientists to simplify and to overturn the very generality for which they strive. The lure of a general theory is in part responsible for a degree of neglect of history in contemporary economics and sociology. This chapter considers the basis of this lure. It argues that general theories can be only of limited use in social science. A place for historically specific theories must remain.

For centuries, however, scientists have admired general theories. The Ancient Greeks sought common patterns and symmetries in nature. Pythagoras observed a blacksmith at work and noticed that iron bars of different lengths gave out sounds of different pitch under the strokes of the hammer. Conceptions of sound and length, of music and measure, were amalgamated. Centuries later, at the beginning of the modern world, Isaac Newton formulated his general laws of motion, explaining both the motion of earthly projectiles and the movements of the planets. In 1820 Hans Christian Oersted saw that an electric current flowing through a wire deflected a nearby compass. He thus discovered the hitherto unrecognised link between magnetism and electricity and inspired the development of the electric motor. Michael Faraday set himself the problem of finding the connections between light, heat, magnetism and electricity, and developed a unified theory of electromagnetic radiation. Energy and matter became later unified in Albert Einstein's theory of relativity. Physics still struggles to capture diverse phenomena within a common explanatory framework. Science tries to unify: it strives for general theories. The goal of unification has endured in the history of science and has inspired many of its achievements.

Much innovation in science comes from combining different phenomena in a more general scientific framework. Philosophers of science have rightly identified the power and value of explanatory unification. For example, Paul Thagard (1978) and Philip Kitcher (1981, 1989) have correctly pointed out that explanatory unification has played a significant role in the development of the natural sciences. Likewise, Clark Glymour (1980, p. 31) has argued that successful explanations in science have the feature that they 'eliminate contingency and they unify'. The importance and possible value of explanatory unifications should not be underestimated.

However, the quest for explanatory unification should not be pushed to the point where the nature and value of the particular explanation adopted are given weak scrutiny. Some explanations may unify, but be of little worth. A theory that every event is caused by the gods is an explanatory unification, but it is of little scientific significance. Likewise, as discussed in chapter 16 below, a non-falsifiable general theory such as 'everyone is a utility maximiser' is also of little explanatory value. This book addresses the limits of explanatory unification in the social sciences.

Some claims of explanatory unification are defective in their failure to consider their ontological presuppositions. Others fail, similarly, to question what is meant by 'explanation', being merely satisfied to point to a theory that seemingly 'fits' every eventuality. The ideas that everyone maximises their utility, or that every event is caused by gods, come into this category. However, once we attempt to build more careful and meaningful explanations, then we are faced with the problem that economic reality changes in a way that physical reality does not. Yet the lure of a general theory has often overcome such critical reflections.

The lure of a general theory pervades the social as well as the natural sciences. Again it is believed that a general theory is always better than one with a narrower domain of analysis. Consequently, it is upheld that to become respectable, economics, sociology and anthropology must also uncover general principles or laws – much in the manner of the natural sciences. The aim is for one theory that fits all circumstances.[4]

This notion emerged in the heyday of classical economics. While Adam Smith attempted judiciously to blend induction with deduction, at the same time he sought general principles and laws. However, his classical successors such as David Ricardo and especially Nassau Senior went much further. They pursued more and more an axiomatic and deductivist method, attempting to derive universal conclusions from a few professedly general and fundamental propositions. Ranged against this Ricardian tendency was Thomas Robert Malthus. Malthus criticised the over-emphasis on deduction and generalisation. He wrote in 1819: 'The principal cause of error, and of the differences which prevail at present among the scientific writers on political economy, appears to me to be a precipitate attempt to simplify and generalize' (Malthus, 1836, p. 4).

Significantly, John Maynard Keynes (1972, pp. 100–1) wrote in his 1933 essay on Malthus: 'If only Malthus, instead of Ricardo, had been the parent stem from which nineteenth-century economics proceeded, what a much wiser and richer place the world would be today!' However, Keynes himself made two crucial mistakes. Both helped the Ricardian rather than the Malthusian stem to triumph and spread across the world. One error was to neglect the German historical school and its alternative to Ricardian deductivism. The other mistake was to recommend a 'general theory' of his own. *The General Theory of Employment, Interest and Money* (1936) is one of the most famous cases of an attempted general theory in economics. Keynes's perceptions in his Malthus essay were right, but – as argued in chapter 15 of this work – he did not do enough to prevent a strain of deductivist general theorising that dominated economics for forty years after his death. The case of Keynes is an object lesson. The search for a general theory is not confined to mainstream or neoclassical economics. All sorts of economists have revered a 'general theory'.[5]

For much of the postwar period, 'general equilibrium analysis' has been in vogue in economics. It has attempted to elaborate the general conditions for the existence and stability of market equilibria (Debreu, 1959; Arrow and Hahn, 1971). This work was at the cutting edge of theoretical economics until it ran into analytical difficulties in the 1970s. It was eclipsed by the rising interest in game theory in the 1980s.

---

4   The classic account of the growth of 'physics envy' in economics is Mirowski (1989). However, some reservations concerning Mirowski's thesis are expressed below and in Hodgson (1999b). Overall, economics suffers perhaps more from mathematics envy rather than physics envy (McCloskey, 1991; Blaug, 1999).
5   For example, a 'general theory' is proclaimed in the titles of Roemer (1982), Nell (1998) and Ormerod (1998).

Likewise, in sociology, there has been a similar reverence for general theory of social action, interaction and structure. Twentieth-century milestones in sociological theory – such as Talcott Parsons (1937a), Robert Merton (1949), George Homans (1961), Peter Blau (1964), Jeffrey Alexander (1982–3), Anthony Giddens (1984), James Coleman (1990), Harrison White (1992) and Niklas Luhmann (1995) – are all general attempts to understand 'society', largely unconfined to any historically specific epoch or type of social structure.[6]

Overall, general theories have pervaded economics and sociology for the second half of the twentieth century. General principles are assumed and their logical consequences are explored. In this respect, at least, the social sciences look to physics and other natural sciences as their role models. The more general and inclusive the theory, the greater its prestige. Universalisations take the accolade.

What characterises a general theory in the social sciences? Here we shall take the term 'general theory' to mean the following: It is any substantial explanation or model of the principal characteristics and behaviour of human economies or societies, *largely or wholly in terms of features that are assumed to be common to most conceivable social or economic systems.*

It is true that modern mainstream economists attempt to tailor their theories to specific situations. There are theories of perfect competition, theories of monopoly, theories of oligopoly, theories of labour markets and so on. Such theories may claim to apply to a specific set of circumstances. In some of their assumptions, these theories differ from one another. Nevertheless, some of their features are like those of a general theory. First, some presumptions – such as rationality, scarcity and fixed preferences – are common to all these theories. These core assumptions are held to apply to all socio-economic systems. Second, it is rarely claimed that the theory involved applies to a specific type of socio-economic system or a limited historical period. In these two senses, ahistorical and acultural generalities pervade even specific modes of theorising in modern mainstream economics.

The goal of a general theory has been pursued to the greatest extent in the type of general equilibrium theory developed by Léon Walras, Kenneth Arrow, Gerard Debreu and others. Significantly, from the 1930s to the 1980s, general equilibrium was one of the most prestigious areas of research in economic theory. Of course, the word 'general' in 'general equilibrium theory' applies to the word 'equilibrium' rather than 'theory'. General equilibrium is thereby distinguished from partial equilibrium. Nevertheless, general equilibrium theorists have used the rhetoric and appeal of general theorising as well, often using the term 'general theory of economic equilibrium'. Attempts have been made to apply this general equilibrium approach to feudalism and socialism, as well as to capitalism (Lange and Taylor, 1938; Rader, 1971). In particular, both Oskar Lange and Joseph

---

6   For overviews and discussions of the character of these general theories in sociology, see, for example, Fararo (1989), Holmwood (1996) and Mouzelis (1995). Notably, several of names of sociological general theorists mentioned here were strongly influenced by Parsons, including Merton and Luhmann (who were his students) and Homans (who was a colleague of Parsons at Harvard).

Schumpeter lauded Walras as the architect of a 'truly general theory' in economics.[7]

Abstraction and simplification are necessary for any theory. General theorists, however, build upon features that are taken as common or universal, rather than historically or culturally specific. Their guiding examples in this respect are the successful explanatory unifications and general theories that are found in the natural sciences. For example, in economics, general equilibrium theorists have made ostensibly general assumptions concerning human agents, their endowments and their interactions. With these they attempt to deduce some general results concerning economic equilibria. Likewise, in social theory, general assumptions are made about social agents, their 'exchanges' and the social structures that they inhabit.

GENERAL THEORISTS, NIHILISTS AND EMPIRICISTS

Nevertheless, general theorising is not universally popular. Ranged against the proponents of general theory, in both economics and sociology, are those that are critical of its operational usefulness, explanatory adequacy and universal claims.

For instance, 'post-modernism' is a major assault on general theorising in the social sciences. Post-modernists emphatically reject grand narratives and totalising theory (Lyotard, 1984). The problem is that they can do this only by means of a totalising, meta-narrative of their own. There is no means by which to dispense with a grand narrative other than by an even grander, universal story. Hence the post-modernists fall into a paradox of their own making. As Andrew Sayer (1995, p. 223) puts it: 'Those who are sceptical of meta-narratives should turn their suspicions on "modernism" and "postmodernism" first.' There is no way of avoiding this paradox: grand theory cannot be dismissed by yet another grand, general discourse, whatever its rhetorical appeal. Post-modernism is further weakened by its abandonment of the search for truth. Post-modernism is a symptomatic but nihilistic reaction against the excessive claims for general theorising in social science.

Logically, any argument against general theories must involve general state-ments or narratives. Although these statements are not necessarily general theories, in the sense defined above, they are nevertheless general in their scope. The rejection of general theories must itself involve generalities. There is no escape.

Post-modernism rightly detects some of the limits of general theorising but veers off in a largely unwarranted and unacceptable direction. These mistakes might have been avoided if post-modernists had some awareness of past debates concerning the limits of general theory in the social sciences. We shall briefly

---

7   See Lange (1938), Schumpeter (1954, p. 1082).

discuss post-modernism again in the next chapter, after the problem of historical specificity has been introduced in more detail.

Other critics of general theories take refuge in empirical work. Empiricism is defined as the broad notion that knowledge is based primarily on experience rather than on any body of theory.[8] Empiricists hold that reality can be understood only by detailed, empirical engagement. It is believed that the search for truth is an empirical matter; it involves the gathering of data rather than the unsupported erection of theoretical postulates. If any theoretical generalisation is possible, empiricists believe that it must emerge on the basis of extensive empirical enquiry.

Today, we find both empiricists and general theorists in university social science departments. For centuries, a version of empiricism has been a haven for critics of general theorising. This type of empiricism is antithetical to all theory. We also find empiricist hybrids, who accept some universal propositions, but also believe that further truths are established on the basis of data alone. These hybrids accept the desirability of universal assumptions and then immerse themselves in empirical work, believing that universal truths can eventually be established by induction.[9]

Over time, the balance of debate has shifted back and forth between these various positions. Intellectual fashions come and go. As both economics and sociology go through periods of theoretical crisis, empiricism is seen as the salvation. Even further, the inadequacies of general theorising sometimes create a reaction against all theory. Theory is abandoned in search of the facts. The anti-theoretical empiricists march forth with their clipboards and computers. But as some cohorts of these empiricists get lost in the analytical swamplands of questionnaires and statistics, new groups of general theorists emerge, promising order and deliverance. And so it goes on, each group ascending then descending.

The truth is that both empiricism and general theorising have their intellectual limitations, as does any hybrid combination of the two. Both empiricists and general theorists place their conceptual weight on universal assumptions, placing less emphasis on concepts and theories that are more appropriate to the specific situation at hand. Although empiricists may sometimes fail to champion an explicit general theory, empiricism always has a hidden general theory of its own. This is because, in attempting to measure any quantity, or trying to establish any empirical regularity, acts of classification or taxonomy are unavoidable. For empirical enquiry, entities are placed into groups. The most important properties

---

8   This is a standard definition of the term. Inductivism and positivism are particular versions of empiricism. Positivism is a version of empiricism that emphasises empirical confirmation – rather than falsification – by observation or experiment. Empiricism has a long history and exists in several different forms. Nevertheless, they all have in common the notion that knowledge is based primarily on experience.

9   Induction refers to the method of generalising from a finite sample. If we observe a large number of white swans we may presume, by induction, that all swans are white. However, it is difficult to be sure that we have observed all existing swans, no matter how many we have seen. Indeed, in this case it turns out that in Australia there are black swans, and the presumption of universality is false.

and relations are identified. Connections are made. Accordingly, all empirical investigation involves prior judgements of sameness and difference. For example, we cannot examine transaction costs in firms without first having a notion of what is, and what is not, a transaction cost and a firm. Classification, by bringing together entities in discrete groups, must refer to common qualities. These qualities themselves have generality: they must be assumed to endure through space and time.

All empirical work thus relies on the principle known as 'the uniformity of nature'. For some types, entities or qualities, it has to be assumed that the type, entity or quality in one place in space and time remains the same type, entity or quality at another place in space and time. Otherwise we are faced with an immense collection of disconnected entities and qualities, and no meaningful empirical or other scientific investigation is possible. This supposition of the uniformity of nature is a highly general theoretical principle. Although empirical work depends upon it, the principle cannot be proven or disproven by the data. It must be assumed at the outset.

The idea that empirical data are sufficient for all knowledge thus founders. The empirical researcher must classify, and classification depends on the metaphysical principle of the uniformity of nature. Any empirical investigation depends on the assumptions of identity, continuity and measurability. These assumptions cannot themselves be derived from empirical data. Pure empiricism is thus incoherent.

In addition, a principal goal of any science is explanation. Explanation involves the suggestion of relationships of cause and effect. Without a presumption of causality, there can be no convincing scientific explanation of any phenomenon. However, no empirical enquiry can itself establish a causal relation. No cause can be perceived. Data cannot show us cause and effect. Correlations between sets of events are not necessarily indications of cause and effect. Correlation is not causation. Since David Hume's discussion of this problem, it has been widely accepted by philosophers that causal relations cannot be discerned in the data themselves. Accordingly, any scientific explanation involves the assumption of causal relationships that are themselves absent in the empirical data: they must be assumed. Empirical data cannot on their own provide causal explanations.[10]

Theory has primacy over facts, because concepts and theories are required to formulate any factual statement. However, this does not mean that science always works by first formulating a theoretical explanation and then testing it. There are many cases in the history of science where facts have first emerged without a theory that explains them. Science may subsequently triumph by supplying a theoretical explanation. In this manner, facts may inform or impel the formation of theories. But this does not negate the proposition that all facts depend upon some theoretical grounding.

Consider, for example, the professedly anomalous fact, noted by Wassily Leontief (1953), that the more developed countries have imported relatively more

---

10 The assumption that every event has a cause is a special postulate concerning the uniformity of nature. Hence the problems of causality and uniformity of nature are closely related.

capital-intensive products than they have exported. Recognition of this 'fact' requires prior theoretical concepts such as 'developed', 'capital-intensity' and 'import'. Second, any explanation of this phenomenon requires a theory that cannot spring from the facts alone. For these reasons an empiricist epistemology is flawed. However, this does not deny the possibility, as in the case of the so-called Leontief paradox, that facts may stimulate the search for new theories.[11]

THE LIMITS TO EXPLANATORY UNIFICATION

By its nature, a general theory achieves some explanatory unification. However, as Uskali Mäki (1990a, 1990b, forthcoming) has shown, there are explanatory unifications of different types. First, logical or derivational unification means that 'more and more statements within a discipline become derivable from the same set of axioms, or when the same set of statements becomes derivable from a smaller set of axioms' (Mäki 1990b, p. 331). This notion of unification involves purely deductive connections between axioms and derived statements. Many of the claims of explanatory unification within economics are of this derivational type. They are deductive accomplishments without ontological grounding.

While derivational unification is based on the inferential capabilities of theories, the contrasting idea of ontological unification is based on their referential and representational capabilities. If an ontological explanatory unification is possible, then it must be based on some underlying, ontological unity among a set of phenomena; they must share some substantial ontic foundations. Any explanatory unity among phenomena must result from investigation and discovery, rather than the mere imposition of assumptions. Priority is given to entities rather than propositions (Mäki, forthcoming).

Accordingly, the nature and location of the limits of general theorising vary in each case. The limits of general theorising by derivational unification result from the lack of ontological grounding to its claims. These limits concern neither the boundaries of unification, nor the number of items that can be unified, but the adequacy of the explanation. A derivational unification may be achieved, but on its own it cannot constitute a causal explanation of real phenomena.

On the other hand, the limits of ontological explanatory unification depend upon existence or otherwise of underlying unities among the phenomena under investigation. While the search for underlying unities behind the diverse appearances of real phenomena is rightly a central aim of science, any absence of recurring elements or similarities poses limits to ontological unification. Ontological explanatory unification requires the identification of similar structures or causal mechanisms. The capacity of a theory to unify in this ontological sense depends not on its axioms or propositions, but on the degree of real, underlying unity or similarity in its domain of application. It is primarily these

---

11 A good critique of positivism and empiricism in the social sciences is Hindess (1977). Bunge (1959) provided an excellent discussion of causality.

possible limits to ontological explanatory unification that concern us in the present work.[12]

We can conceive of reality as consisting of different ontological levels. There may be a level relating to matter addressed by physics, a level relating to molecules addressed by chemistry, a level relating to living organisms addressed by biology, and so on. These levels may themselves be subdivided. Within physics, for example, quantum physics and mechanics address different levels. Accordingly, different scientific theories may relate to different levels of reality.

Although universal laws have both scientific appeal and some explanatory power, they are often of limited use when it comes to the detail of specific contexts and situations, operating at a different ontological level. Einstein's theory of relativity may rule the universe, and its domain of application applies to all physical phenomena, but it tells us little of tomorrow's weather or of the carrying capacity of the Golden Gate suspension bridge. In achieving unification, general theories have an awesome appeal. But neither unification nor generality mean that the theory is sufficient for particular, contingent circumstances at a different ontological level.

Arguably, within the social sciences, there are differences among the real items to be explained that place limits on the scope for any general theory. Long ago, Max Weber reached a similar conclusion. In 1904, Weber (1949, pp. 72–80) wrote that 'the most general laws' are 'the least valuable' because 'the more comprehensive their scope' the more they 'lead away' from the task of explaining the particular phenomenon in question. This argument is similar to Ernest Nagel's (1961, p. 575) 'principle of the inverse variation of extension with intension'. This principle alleges that there is a trade-off between the generality and the informative content of a theory. This argument, developed further by Lars Udéhn (1992), has some force against the claimed universality of some of the assumptions of modern mainstream economics.[13]

It has been suggested that a similar problem may apply to the natural sciences. Physicists are now in hot pursuit of the TOE (Theory of Everything) or the GUT (Grand Unified Theory) that will marry quantum theory with the general theory of relativity. Superstring theory is part of this project. But as Jack Cohen and Ian Stewart (1994, p. 365) put it: 'A Theory of Everything would have the whole universe wrapped up. And that's precisely what would make it useless.'[14]

---

12 Although T. Lawson (1997) provides no extensive discussion of the place, types and limits of explanatory unification, his stress on the need for open-minded investigation into underlying causal mechanisms and structures is also valuable in this context.

13 However, while I concur with much of Udéhn's argument, he credits neoclassical economics with some relative success in explaining market, as opposed to non-market, phenomena. While the genuine achievements of neoclassical economics should not be denied, as Clower (1994, 1999) and others have noted, it concedes too much to suggest that it has an adequate definition and analysis of market institutions.

14 See Cartwright (1994) for a stimulating discussion of the role of allegedly general theories in physics and elsewhere. She argued that physical laws (such as Newton's) would hold only insofar as nothing (such as a wind) interferes with the motion of a body in space (p. 282). However, the wind itself could be regarded as a mass of separate particles, each subject to the same (Newtonian)

Another set of problems arise with some types of general theory that arise in the social sciences. Some of these problems are discussed in more detail in chapter 16 and elsewhere. The general theory that individual behaviour results from the maximisation of individual utility is a case in point. It is argued in chapter 16 that this theory is non-falsifiable and it can apply, in principle, to any behaviour, including the behaviour of non-human organisms. If this argument is valid then there is a crucial difference between theories like Newton's or Einstein's, on the one hand, and the theory of utility maximisation, on the other. The difference is that the laws of physics impose restrictions on the type of supplementary theory that can be accommodated. This is not the case with utility maximisation: *any* behaviour is compatible with it. The reckless pursuit of generality in the social sciences has created theories that are compatible with *any* possible behaviour by *any* possible organism. The same cannot be said for prominent theories in the natural sciences.

Accordingly, much explanatory unification in the social sciences is achieved without a search for recurring elements or similarities in reality. The theory of utility maximisation is a case in point. Instead of the successful identification of similar, underlying causal mechanisms and structures, its proponents simply manipulate this theory to fit any phenomenon. Hence, this theory achieves derivational unification but not ontological unification. In contrast, the Newtonian and Einsteinian theories achieved a high degree of ontological unification.

All sciences have to deal with both sameness and difference. As biologists Richard Levins and Richard Lewontin (1985, p. 141) have put it: 'Things are similar: this makes science possible. Things are different: this makes science necessary.' General theorists sometimes over-emphasise the similarities, neglecting the differences. These problems are particularly acute in the social sciences. A general theory can clumsily obscure all historical and geographical differences between different socio-economic systems.

Nevertheless, there are some important examples of successful general theories concerning complex systems. Charles Darwin's theory of evolution is the most important. However, without diminishing the importance of this great achievement, biology does not confine itself to such generalities. Evolutionary biology has a few laws or general principles by which origin and development can be explained. Analysis of the evolution of a specific organism requires detailed data concerning the organism and its environment, and also specific explanations relevant to the species under consideration. Evolutionary biology requires theories that have both specific and general domains. As Lewontin (1991, pp. 142–3) has argued, the notion that 'science consists of universal claims as opposed to mere historical statements is rubbish' and 'a great deal of the body

---

laws. Contrary to Cartwright, the laws would then remain universal. The problem is that this universal formulation is for practical purposes intractable. To deal with wind friction, we have to focus not on the multitude of wafting particles but on the emergent properties and different laws of wind itself. Only in this way is a tractable solution possible. Universal laws may exist in physics (and even in economics) but if we found them they may for this reason be of limited use.

of biological research and knowledge consists of narrative statements'. Likewise, in economics and the other social sciences, there is a place for both.

Similarly, complex systems theory has established a few general principles. W. Ross Ashby's (1952) 'law of requisite variety' is an example. However, once again, systems theory is unable to deliver very much more than this kind of thing at the general level. It 'works' only when it is augmented by much more specific assumptions. The limited but potentially positive role of such general principles and theories is discussed further in chapter 18 of this work. In chapter 21 an attempt is made to show how a limited general theory can supplement more specific theories and explanations. To this end, some ideas from evolutionary biology and systems theory are applied in chapter 22. But it is recognised these principles are far from sufficient on their own.

GENERAL THEORY AND COMPLEXITY

There are strong reasons why the quest for a substantial, richly textured, general theory of complex systems will always be elusive. Simplification has to be radical, stripping any general theory of its comprehensive, explanatory ambitions. Even with a limited number of assumptions, the chain of deductive reasoning cannot take us very far. Kurt Gödel is famous for his demonstration that the axiomatic method has inherent limitations (Nagel and Newman, 1959). He proved that it is impossible to establish the internal logical consistency of a very large class of deductive systems. It is widely believed that this impossibility result is even more pervasive than Gödel was able to reveal. Proofs may be computationally out of reach. Hence Jack Cohen and Ian Stewart (1994, p. 439) argue:

> sufficiently rich formal systems do obey Gödel's theorem, so they must contain true statements whose proofs are a thousand times as long, or a billion times as long, as the statements are. That is, such systems necessarily possess properties that are far simpler than any route by which you could establish them.

Christopher Cherniak (1986, pp. 79–80) has noted the limits of computation in logical systems. It has been shown that all the possible calculation resources of the entire universe, computing for all of the time that the universe has existed, would be insufficient to determine the logical consistency of more than 138 well-defined propositions. Clearly, the computational capacities of a human agent are much more limited than this. The number of propositions that we can process logically must be much less than 138.

Claude Shannon (1950) pointed out that there are about 30 chess moves that can be made from each position on the chess board. In a typical game each play makes an average of 40 moves. Accordingly, there are about $(30^2)^{40}$ or 10^{120} possible chess moves in a single game. This number is greater than the number of particles in the universe, professedly 10^{80}. Any attempt at a general analysis of chess strategy is thwarted by this problem of combinatorial explosion, despite the fact that the rules of chess are relatively simple.

Consider an attempt to develop a general theory of network structures. A general theory of n points in space would have to embrace the possibility of $n(n-1)/2$ connections between any two points in that space. If n is 1000, then the number of possible connections is close to half a million. If a connection is either present or absent, then each may be represented – as a simple first step – by a binary value. Accordingly, the number of possible structures in this simple model is:

$$2^{n(n-1)/2}$$

If n is 1000, then the value of this expression is greater than 10^{150000}. The philosopher Willard van Orman Quine (1987) has coined the word 'hyperastronomic' to describe numbers greater than the number of particles in the universe. The number we are concerned with is *much* greater: a simple general model of a network, with binary-valued connections and 1000 nodes, has to cover an indescribable scale of mega-hyperastronomic variety.[15]

Combinatorial explosions such as these paralyse attempts to place complex phenomena within a richly textured general theory. Adding new dimensions to the space of possibilities, or new branches to a decision tree, increases the scope of the theory. But the computational mass explodes with devastating effect. To deal with complexity even on this relatively modest scale, simplifying assumptions have to be made. Either we are confined to broad principles governing all such structures, or the theory has to confine itself to a manageable and relatively tiny subset of all possible structures. Indeed, such a small subset may represent the most important or relevant phenomena in the real world. In this case the theory has to cease to be general. Otherwise, the analysis is confined to broad statements that do not explain very much.

GENERAL THEORISING IN ECONOMICS

A central problem with all models in the social sciences is that they have to consider not only the structured relations between agents, but also the computations of the agents themselves, as they react to their changing circumstances. Both the system and the agents must be modelled, where the model of the agent includes its perception of the system. This is a level of tangled complexity that is difficult to put in a general model, at least without the imposition of severe simplifying assumptions.

For example, how does the individual agent deal with multiple markets in a general equilibrium model? Roy Radner (1968) has considered the computational problems involved. The general equilibrium models of the type of Kenneth Arrow and Gerard Debreu assumed that a 'market' existed for the exchange

---

15 Accordingly, general theories of graphs or networks have to concentrate on structural or system level properties rather than detailed comparisons of specific network structures.

of every possible commodity, on every possible date, in every possible state of nature. Hence if there are a thousand types of commodity, a thousand possible 'dates' and a thousand possible 'states' then there will be a billion different markets. Assuming all possibilities and connections, the number of markets explodes beyond the calculating engagement of any human agent. Radner (1968, p. 32) concluded that 'there is a basic difficulty in incorporating computational limitations in . . . equilibrium theory based on optimizing behaviour.'

Overall, general equilibrium theorists have had great difficulty deriving general explanatory principles. As Arrow (1986, p. S388) declared: 'In the aggregate, the hypothesis of rational behaviour has in general no implications.' Within general equilibrium theory, the aggregated excess demand functions can take almost any form (Sonnenschein, 1972, 1973a, 1973b; Debreu, 1974; Mantel, 1974).[16] As S. Abu Turab Rizvi pointed out, the conclusions of Sonnenschein, Debreu, and Mantel are general and devastating. The main result

> is that the hypothesis of individual rationality, and other assumptions made at the micro level, gives no guidance to an analysis of macro-level phenomena: the assumption of rationality or utility maximisation is not enough to talk about social regularities.
>
> (Rizvi, 1994a, p. 363)

Facing such problems, Alan Kirman (1992, p. 118) wrote that 'there is no plausible formal justification for the assumption that the aggregate of individuals, even maximizers, acts itself like an individual maximizer.' Research into the problems of the uniqueness and stability of general equilibria has shown that they may be indeterminate and unstable unless very strong assumptions are made, such as the supposition that society as a whole behaves as if it were a single individual (Arrow, 1986; Coricelli and Dosi, 1988). Not only is it assumed that preference functions are exogenously given, it is also assumed that all these preference functions are exactly the same.

Because general theories become overwhelmed by explosive complexity, all attempts at general theorising have ultimately to abandon many generalities. They simplify, declaring that 'more work remains to be done' to generalise the model. The principal theoretical results of general equilibrium theory have depended on such restrictive assumptions. Truly general theorising has proved to be difficult, if not impossible. It is widely accepted that the only truly general explanatory principle that has been derived from general equilibrium theory is 'everything depends on everything else'. The weakness of the theory derives in part from its wanton pursuit of universality, as well as from the limitations of its basic axioms.[17]

---

16 See also Lavoie (1992, pp. 36–41), Rizvi (1994a), Screpanti and Zamagni (1993, pp. 344–53).
17 Mirowski (1989) and Potts (2000) have characterised general equilibrium analysis as a mathematical 'field theory' where every point in space is connected with every other. Potts argued that, on the contrary, economic reality is characterised by limited interconnectedness, as in a lattice or network. Following the precedents of Kirman (1983, 1987), Bush (1983), Ellerman (1984) and Mirowski (1991), Potts saw mathematical techniques such as graph theory as an appropriate formalisation of the limited interconnectedness of this reality.

In practice, all attempts to erect an all-embracing general theory in economics have been highly limited or have led to failure. Leading general equilibrium theorists have latterly accepted the limitations of their project. For example, Frank Hahn (1980, p. 132) has candidly admitted that the typical Walrasian type of theory excludes time, because it collapses the future into the present. It also excludes money, which is essentially a means of dealing with an uncertain future (Hahn, 1988, p. 972). Robert Clower (1994, 1999) passed a similarly negative verdict. He argued, on similar lines, that the Walrasian theory actually excludes production, markets, competition and real trade. Crucially, Walrasian theory concentrates on the logical existence of equilibrium states, at the expense of the mechanisms of market operation (Costa, 1998). Overall, theories of complex phenomena that aim to be general, typically turn out to be very narrow in their scope.

Nevertheless, Hahn (1984) and others have tried to legitimise general equilibrium theory as an attempt to show 'what the world would have to look like' if markets were to operate properly. The declared aim was to demonstrate that real markets could work only at best under highly restrictive conditions. However, this legitimation of general equilibrium theory is unconvincing, because it is only one of many possible theoretical attempts to represent market mechanisms in the real world. It cannot simply be assumed that general equilibrium theory is the only possible theory. Another (perhaps undiscovered) theory might demonstrate that markets can always operate perfectly. To demonstrate that real world markets could 'work' only under highly restrictive conditions, we would have to look at all possible theoretical representations and formalisations of the market system and show that they too all 'worked' at best only under restrictive conditions. This, of course, is an impossible task for mere mortals. Hahn's argument is invalid. Once again, the problem of intractability confounds the general theorist.

In practice, attempts at general theorising in economics, and in other sciences dealing with complex phenomena, turn out to be restricted in their sweep, and thereby fail to be truly general. Although general principles or laws may exist, general theories are either not so general, or of very limited explanatory value. The elaboration of a truly general theory of complex phenomena can be confounded by severe problems of computation and tractability.

WHY A GENERAL THEORY OF BARTER WOULD LOSE MONEY

To recapitulate: it has been argued above that there are several problems with general theorising in the social sciences. One is of analytical and computational intractability. Facing such computational limits, general theorists typically simplify their models, thus abandoning the generality of the theory. Another related problem with a general theory is that we are confined to broad principles governing all possible structures within the domain of analysis. In practice, a manageable theory has to confine itself to a relatively tiny subset of all possible structures. Furthermore, the cost of excessive generality is to miss out on key features common to a subset of phenomena.

16

To illustrate the latter argument, we shall consider two very simple 'models', of respectively a barter and a monetary economy, and consider which involves fewer assumptions and which is more general. Robert Clower's (1967) theoretical framework is the starting point. In a barter economy, every commodity can in principle be traded for every other commodity. By contrast, in a money economy without barter, commodities are traded for money only. Hence, for Clower (1967, pp. 5–7) in a monetary economy:

> the peculiar feature of money as contrasted with a barter economy is precisely that *some* commodities in a money economy *cannot* be traded directly for all other commodities. . . . *Money buys goods and goods buy money; but goods do not buy goods.*

The following diagrams – taken and amended slightly from Clower (1967) – represent these two contrasting arrangements:

	C_1	C_2	C_3	C_4
C_1	x	x	x	x
C_2	x	x	x	x
C_3	x	x	x	x
C_4	x	x	x	x

Exchange relations in a
barter economy

	M	C_2	C_3	C_4
M	x	x	x	x
C_2	x	x	0	0
C_3	x	0	x	0
C_4	x	0	0	x

Exchange relations in a
monetary economy

Figure 1.1 Exchange relations under money and barter

In Figure 1.1, C_1, C_2, C_3 and C_4 each represent commodities. M is money. The presence of symbol 'x' indicates that an exchange between two commodities is possible; a '0' indicates that no such exchange normally takes place. This restrictive structure of an exchange economy is a necessary but not sufficient condition for the existence of money. In addition, money has other special attributes – such as a store of value and means of dealing with an uncertain future – that are not represented here.[18]

---

18 Accordingly, Clower (1967, p. 5) was wrong to suggest that '*a barter economy is one in which all commodities are money commodities.*' On the contrary, commodities under barter do not possess all the characteristics of money. Clower stressed universal exchangeability to the exclusion of other characteristics. But his identification of the contrasting exchange structures of a barter and a monetary economy was nevertheless correct. It was notably endorsed by Davidson (1978, p. 142 n.). For further discussions of Clower's exchange framework see Hodgson (1982, ch. 12), Mirowski (1986, pp. 212–19) and Potts (2000).

At least at first sight, a barter economy model in which all exchanges are possible involves fewer restrictive assumptions than a model in which there is money. A model of a monetary economy must include *additional* restrictive assumptions in order to obtain the special structure of a monetary economy in Figure 1.1 above. The theoretical representation of a monetary economy requires *more* rather than *fewer* restrictive assumptions.

Which model is 'more general'? Of the two models in Figure 1.1, in a sense the barter economy model is more general. The presence of an 'x' in any cell in a matrix in Figure 1.1 indicates that an exchange is possible, not that the exchange has to take place. In this sense, therefore, a monetary economy is a special case of a barter economy: the barter economy model is more general. However, this gives us a partial and potentially misleading picture and the statement needs to be qualified.

Crucially, the very process of apparent 'generalisation' – from a monetary to a barter model – means that some essential features of a monetary economy are lost. Because everything in a barter economy has the money-like property of being able to exchange with everything else, then nothing has the property of money. If all men are kings, then there are no kings, because kingship implies the existence of non-regal inferiors.

Money exists only because some exchanges are admitted and some are excluded. If all exchanges are admitted, then money is excluded. In this sense the barter model is not general: it excludes money. Hence, from this point of view, neither a barter model nor Walrasian-type theory (which excludes money) is an adequate representation of a monetary economy. For a theory to accommodate money, it has to incorporate the special qualities of money, with some forms of exchange being excluded.

This example shows that, while seeming more general in scope, the barter economy model loses key features of the monetary economy. A general theory of barter would not include money. Greater generality in some respects can be gained at the cost of an ability to discriminate between and explain concrete particulars.

GAME THEORY AND THE ESCAPE FROM GENERALITIES

Without much discussion, mainstream economics quietly dropped the search for a general theory in the 1980s. The general equilibrium theory project had broken down (Kirman, 1989; Rizvi, 1994a, 1994b). Game theory had originally been developed and applied to economics by John von Neumann and Oskar Morgenstern in 1944. But it did not become popular until after the general equilibrium project had stumbled upon intractable problems in the 1970s. The eventual turn to game theory was an abandonment of a general theory of market behaviour. This 1980s' bonfire of former generalities meant an important shift in preoccupation – to use the terms of Franklin Fisher (1989) – from 'generalising' to 'exemplifying' theory. Exemplifying theories are theories that say what might

18

happen under specific conditions; generalising theories are ones that attempt to say what must happen.

In game theory there are few general results. Outcomes depend on the assumed structure and parameters of the game itself. Such theoretical constructions exemplify rather than generalise. However, most game theorists retain ahistorical models of human motivation and agency. The individual remains a payoff or utility maximiser. Payoff maximisation is a general theory of individual behaviour but it does not constitute a complete theory of socio-economic dynamics. Game theory mixes payoff or utility maximisation with specific game structures. Many other generalities have disappeared.

Robert Aumann (1985, p. 35) has claimed that the achievement of game theory would lie in 'organizing in a single framework many disparate phenomena and many disparate ideas'. This amounts to the claim that game theory involves a limited form of derivational unification involving a 'single framework' being used to organise 'many disparate ideas'. But this is a much weaker claim of derivational unification than that of general equilibrium theory. Exponents of the latter made the claim that it was possible to explain or predict many economic phenomena with a single, unifying theory. The shift from the general equilibrium to the game theoretic research programme was thus the replacement of a purportedly unifying theory by a purportedly unifying framework, and the replacement of claims of explanation or prediction by the looser claim of a capacity to *organise* phenomena or ideas.

With the exception of Fisher (1989), the abandonment by game theorists of the historical quest for a comprehensive general theory has occurred with remarkably little comment or reflection by mainstream economists. Nevertheless, the big message behind the abandonment of general equilibrium theory should not be overlooked. The true achievement of all the efforts behind the development of the Walrasian and Arrow–Debreu models is to show the severe limits of general theorising in economics. In addition, developments in computability theory in the 1980s and 1990s have shown that optimisation problems typically involve difficulties not only of specification but also of computability.[19]

Perhaps the greatest overall achievement of mainstream economic theory in the last half of the twentieth century has been to confirm the suspicion that substantive general theorising in economics will always bring highly limited and inadequate results. All substantive general theories in complex systems are characterised by shortcomings.

If we put together the results of Gödel and the computability theorists, and combine these with insights gained from complexity theory and the failure of the general equilibrium project, then there is every reason to suppose that attainable general theories in the social sciences, even if important, are always of limited value. While there is no proof of this proposition, the balance of argument has now shifted. We have very strong reasons to believe that attainable and

---

19 For general statements see, for example, Cutland (1980), M. Davis *et al.* (1984) and Bennett and Landauer (1985). For applications to decision theory and economics see Gottinger (1982), Lewis (1985), Spear (1989), Anderlini and Sabourian (1995) and Velupillai (1996).

substantive general theorising will not take us very far; the onus on any remaining general theorists is to show how the immense problems that have been encountered in the past can be overcome. By embracing game theory, economic theorists have seemingly declined this challenge: they have abandoned generalising theories for specific games that serve as exemplars.

With this statute of limitations we may move on. But our route does not at first take us to the future. Instead, we first turn back to nineteenth century, and move forward from there, in order to retrieve what we have lost from the past – to recover what has been long crushed and discarded by the reckless juggernaut of general theorising in social science.

2

THE PROBLEM OF HISTORICAL SPECIFICITY

It takes a great deal of history to produce a little literature.
(Henry James, *Hawthorne* (1879))

Emphatically, the argument in this book is not against the power or value of generalisation. While general theorising can never be enough, general statements are not only necessary but also unavoidable. Nor does this book underestimate the value of empirical work. The concern, however, is that both empiricism and deductive generalisation have their flaws, and some faulty presumptions are shared in common. Accordingly, any attempt to steer a middle way between these poles is likely to share the limitations of each. A more sophisticated position has to be found, recognising a significant role for general theories but also their limitations. Some kind of middle-range theorising – to use Robert Merton's (1968) term – is required to bridge the general with the empirical. Much valuable work in the modern social sciences is broadly of this kind. The problem, however, is that the methodological underpinnings and meta-theoretical justifications are relatively unexplored.

THE IDIOGRAPHIC AND THE NOMOTHETIC

At the end of the nineteenth century, an attempt was made to resolve some of the problems raised here, by demarcating the sciences. One group of sciences was deemed to deal with universals or generalities, the rest with individuals or particulars. The German philosophers Wilhelm Windelband and Heinrich Rickert thus made a distinction between the idiographic and the nomothetic sciences. Nomothetic sciences are said to look for unifying laws. In contrast, an idiographic approach attempts to gain knowledge of concrete particulars.

For Rickert (1899) the natural sciences were nomothetic. But he also placed political economy (economics) and psychology in the nomothetic group. Other social and human sciences were said to be idiographic, studying individual phenomena by empirical, descriptive and comparative methods. It was claimed that the distinction between these two groups of sciences led to very different epistemologies.

The German philosopher Wilhelm Dilthey criticised the division of the sciences between the idiographic and the nomothetic, arguing that any science might usefully combine both methods (Holborn, 1950). Dilthey argued that the cultural and social sciences were not confined to individual cases, but included as their main problem the relationship between the individual and the general. For Dilthey, the real distinction was between the natural and the cultural sciences, and he made a sharp distinction between the two. He argued that the latter are not simply concerned with causal explanation but also with the understanding of the meanings and symbolic significance of the subject matter.

Rickert's distinction between the idiographic and the nomothetic mirrors the modern division between the general theorists and the anti-generalising empiricists. Each reaches a stalemate. The problem, as always, is that all sciences address both the general and the specific. As the philosopher Mario Bunge (1998, p. 23) put it: 'The nomothetic/idiographic dichotomy is untenable because *all* sciences are nomothetic *as well as* idiographic.' Human society is 'a patterned mess'. General frameworks of ideas may help us discern the pattern, but something more is required to deal with the messy details.

THE NEGLECTED PROBLEM

We have set the stage for a methodological problem, of vital significance for the social sciences. The domination of economics and sociology by general theorists, plus a minority of atheoretical empiricists, has excluded this problem. Methodology has become unfashionable in many quarters. The methodological discussion of the general and the specific, of sameness and difference, is forgotten.

I say 'forgotten' not 'unexplored'. For much of the nineteenth century, economists were concerned with a central theoretical and methodological problem. It continued to be discussed by several leading economists, up until the outbreak of the Second World War. Many pages were filled with thoughts on this topic. It engaged the minds of Karl Marx, Carl Menger, Alfred Marshall, Gustav von Schmoller, Werner Sombart, Max Weber, John Commons, Frank Knight and many others.

Today, however, the problem is largely ignored.[1] Most social scientists are unaware of it. It is absent from the textbooks. Neither neoclassical economists nor post-Keynesians seem conscious of the problem. Although earlier theorists such as Karl Marx and John Commons addressed it, contemporary Marxists and

---

1   A notable modern exception is Hutchison's (1981, ch. 8) discussion of the limitations of general theories in macroeconomics. In philosophy there has been a discussion of the possibility and role of general historical explanations or laws (Hempel, 1942; Popper, 1960; Weingartner, 1961). But this earlier debate concentrated on the question of historical prediction, rather than the identification and explanation of different historical phenomena. More recently, however, the philosophy of science has devoted substantial attention to the limits of explanatory unification in the face of diverse (historical) phenomena (Cartwright, 1994; Dupré, 1993; Kitcher, 1989). Some of this discussion has made its way into the philosophy of economics (Boylan and O'Gorman, 1995; Mäki, 1990a, 1990b, forthcoming).

institutionalists give it little attention. Although Max Weber was preoccupied with the problem, it is absent within much of modern theoretical sociology, except in the shadow play of the modern discourse on ideal types. Yet for about one hundred years this issue preoccupied some of the greatest minds in the social sciences and was central to much social and economic analysis.

This book is devoted to this problem. What is it? I call it the problem of historical specificity. It first acknowledges the fact that there are different types of socio-economic system, in historical time and geographic space. The problem of historical specificity addresses the limits of explanatory unification in social science: substantially different socio-economic phenomena may require theories that are in some respects different. If different socio-economic systems have features in common, then, to some extent, the different theories required to analyse different systems might reasonably share some common characteristics. But sometimes there will be important differences as well. Concepts and theoretical frameworks appropriate for one real object may not be best suited for another. The problem of historical specificity starts from a recognition of significant underlying differences between different objects of analysis. One theory may not fit all.

For instance, the socio-economic system of today is very different from the systems of five hundred, one thousand or two thousand years ago. Even today, despite having some important features in common, existing socio-economic systems in different countries are substantially different from each other in key particulars. There are important variations in the structures, rules and mechanisms of production and allocation. Individual purposes and social norms also vary, relating to differences in culture. These differences may be so substantial that they place limits on ontological explanatory unification. As a result, to some degree, different types of socio-economic system may require different conceptual and theoretical tools. A fundamentally different object of analysis may require a different theory.

To repeat: any common aspects of these different theories might reasonably reflect common features of the systems involved. Historically common phenomena – such as the scarcity of physical resources – may exist. However, when we compare socio-economic systems, there are important differences as well as similarities. Arguably, the theories used to analyse them may also have to be different to a significant degree.

Many such differences cannot be captured by mere differences in parameter values. The complexity of economic phenomena suggests that much more than particular applications of a single, general theory would be required. The problem of historical specificity is concerned with the development of distinctive, particularistic theories, each applicable to a particular kind of socio-economic system. An adequate theory of (say) feudalism may not be completely adequate for (say) capitalism as well. An essentially different reality may require a substantially different theory.

An adequate theory of capitalism must the address the pervasiveness of markets and employment contracts and explain the behaviour of market-oriented, profit-seeking firms. However, markets and market-engaged corporations had a much less significant role under feudalism. Accordingly, concepts that relate exclusively to the market – such as market supply, market demand and market competition – would have much less relevance for a theory of feudalism. Instead, a theory of feudalism would have to be centred on another set of essential phenomena. Other concepts, concerning the nature of feudal hierarchy and power, would assume greater relevance. Of course, there is a possibility that a theory of feudalism and a theory of capitalism may share common features and an underlying theoretical framework. The extent of this possibility is explored in part IV of this work. But it would be mistaken to assume that the common underlying framework would necessarily constitute an adequate or complete theory. The essential differences between capitalism and feudalism place limits on the scope of explanatory unifications that embrace them both.

Note that there is a great deal of openness and flexibility here as to what, for example, may constitute an 'essential' difference between one reality and another, or in what ways a theory may 'differ' from another. There may be different understandings of the ways in which systems 'vary in essence' or of what constitutes a 'core concept' of a theory. These questions cannot be answered without some elaboration of a methodology and a social ontology. But it is neither possible nor necessary at this initial stage to achieve absolute precision in these terms. The point being made is that there is a *prima facie* case to answer, covering a wide range of meanings of phrases such as 'reality may differ in essential respects' and 'core concepts and categories of a theory may have to differ'. Acceptance of the *prima facie* case then requires us, necessarily, to try to be more precise about these statements. Indeed, much of the important detail of the debate concerns these very questions of further examination and precision.

But we are unlikely to raise these questions unless we accept the *prima facie* case. This book is largely about raising these questions. It provides no more than a few tentative answers, principally in part IV. The whole point about the long excursion into the history of economic thought in this volume is to show how some of these questions have been raised in the past and obscured and forgotten in the present. In attempting precision and intellectual progress now, we can learn from those that have raised and debated these questions in the past.

As argued in the preceding chapter, there are problems of complexity and tractability involved in formulating any general model, spanning complex and very different cases. The problem of tractability forces many theorists to make specific assumptions. As a consequence, most theorising that claims to be general is in fact specific in its scope. Furthermore, as the comparison of a barter and a monetary economy shows, a move towards seemingly greater generality can sometimes lose the emphasis on the specific connections and linkages that are important features of specific socio-economic structures. Any attempted resolution to the problem of historical specificity should address this possible trade-off between generality and engagement with specific detail.

However, more accurately, the problem could be rephrased as 'the problem of historical and geographical specificity' as there are differences in socio-economic systems across space as well as time. Particular kinds are not in principle restricted in space or time. It is possible – but unlikely in the social context – that two instances of one kind of socio-economic system could appear in different times or places. Hence it could be rephrased as 'the problem of specificity'. However, the phrase 'problem of historical specificity' is retained here because, in the historical discussions of the problem over more than a century, the consideration of differences of type has been placed principally – but not entirely – in an historical context. Nevertheless, geographical differences are as important as historical ones and the discussion in this book applies to all variations, ranged across terrain as well as time.

Let T represent a theoretical analysis that is in some sense adequate and appropriate in explaining the set of socio-economic phenomena in some real domain of enquiry D. Any adequate and appropriate theory T must address underlying causal mechanisms and structures within the phenomena in D. Of course, the criteria of adequacy and appropriateness are themselves part of the problem, but we do not need to address these at this stage of the examination. D is a set of different – historically and spatially located – socio-economic phenomena that can be explained (adequately and appropriately) in terms of T. Technically, T refers to the explanantia and D the explananda. It is possible for the individual phenomena in D to be historically specific and the theoretical analysis T to be historically sensitive.

To be clear: T is never a simple reflection of D. The construction of any T always requires a process of abstraction and simplification, so that details closely related to D are inevitably ignored. Furthermore, there is no a priori reason why T should not also be capable of explaining some additional phenomena that are not included in the original set D. For this reason, it is not the theories, but the individual phenomena, that generally may be described as historically specific.

A principal and befitting aim of science is to find T that cover as large as possible a domain D. However, the main claim being made here is that there are limits to the expansion of D as the domain of any single T.

If possible, some expansion of D may occur in different ways. We may distinguish between an extensive and an intensive expansion. An *extensive* expansion of D typically involves the expansion of the boundaries of the set D in time or space, by introducing a greater variety of essential types of things to be explained. An *intensive* expansion of D involves bringing more 'detail and outcomes' of existing items into the set of things to be explained. The distinction between an extensive and intensive expansion would depend upon a distinction between essential phenomena, on the one hand, and more superficial and detailed phenomena, on the other. Again, these terms require further clarification, and this must be attempted at some later stage.

Crucially, while unification is an important goal of science, the diverse, complex and changing character of socio-economic phenomena means that reckless attempts to make T universal over all possible D may undermine the adequacy of T. By themselves, the existence of diversity and complexity do not undermine the worthiness and importance of explanatory unification in science. Complexity and unification can go together. But the varieties of structure and causal mechanism involved in the diversity of real phenomena may place real limits on attempts at explanatory unification. An adequate theory T to cover an extensive or universal D may be elusive. In this context, groundless attempts to pursue a general theory at all costs might abandon any focus on underlying structures and causal mechanisms. This does not mean that universal features or concepts should be absent from social science. It means that an adequate theory of complex phenomena is unlikely be composed entirely of such universal features. Some reasons for this claim have been made already. Further reasons are raised throughout this book.

Detrimentally, in the modern social sciences we can find examples of the following syndrome. Attempts to derive a T' that covers a vast and expanding D are associated with claims that T' is a good theory *simply because of* the impressively vast content of the set D. But the vastness of D is not a good criterion, on its own, to evaluate the adequacy of T'. Today we can find theories that seem to address an infinite set D. Such theories are sometimes non-falsifiable and impose few limits on membership of D. In this case, serious and sceptical questions must be raised concerning the adequacy or meaning of the claimed explanation in T'. A pathological oversight of the modern social sciences is that such questions are often ignored.

Recognition of the problem of historical specificity involves asking such questions. In part, the problem of historical specificity helps to demarcate the social from the physical sciences. Socio-economic systems have changed markedly in the last few thousand years, whereas the essential properties and laws of the physical world have not altered since the Big Bang. Accordingly, the methods and procedures of the social sciences must alter to follow the changing subject of analysis. This is not so in the physical sciences.

A partial exception is biology. In the biotic, as in the social world, new species and phenomena arise, and others pass away. Accordingly, biology combines general principles (for example: taxonomy, the laws of evolution) with particular studies of specific mechanisms and phenomena. This is one reason why the social sciences should be closer to biology than to physics: biology has a problem of historical (or evolutionary) specificity.

PAST ENCOUNTERS

Today, it is remarkable that this vital methodological problem is rarely if ever posed in all the modern mainstream economics textbooks, at any level, and is discussed infrequently even in the dissenting or methodologically informed literatures in economics. By contrast, the problem of historical specificity was raised clearly by Marx and his followers, and was explored by the German historical school from the 1840s to the 1930s. Minority groups of economists in Britain and elsewhere were influenced by the German historical school, and took the problem on board. It also appeared in American institutionalism, and the issue affected institutionalist thought. But in theoretical terms – with notable exceptions such as John Commons and Frank Knight – there was a failure in America to develop the topic much further than the earlier, German-speaking, economic theorists.

The neglect of the problem of historical specificity is encouraged by the widespread misconception that the economists who discussed the issue were 'against theory'. But if they were all naïve empiricists, then they would hardly be concerned with deeper theoretical and methodological matters. As an example of this misconception, Richard Langlois (1986, p. 5) wrote: 'The problem with the Historical School and many of the early Institutionalists is that they wanted an economics with institutions but without theory.' On the contrary, the historical school and the institutionalists were responsible for many important develop-ments in economic theory, pioneering such 'modern' concepts as national income accounting, growth theory, the multiplier, transaction costs, information asym-metries, bounded rationality and uncertainty (Häuser, 1988; Hodgson, 1998a; Koslowski, 1995, 1997a; Nardinelli and Meiners, 1988; Rutherford, 1994). Among the theoretical and methodological issues they addressed was the problem of historical specificity.

In sum, the problem of historical specificity was clearly addressed by German-speaking economists in the nineteenth century, but it never appeared as a major issue in the English language literature in economics. However, it will be argued here that the issue must be central, at least to any broadly realist approach to the subject. Indeed, it is one of the most crucial problems in economic and social science, and it is not belittled in stature by its neglect.

If this assessment is correct, then the virtual absence of any discussion of the problem in modern economics has itself to be explained. In part, the explanation lies in the persecution and wartime destruction of the Nazi period – from 1933 to 1945 – and their negative effects on German philosophy and social science. The fact that trained economists are no longer required to read German must also be taken into account.[2]

However, there is more to it than that. Despite raising the problem clearly, both Marx and the German historical school had methodological frameworks that were inadequate to deal with the problem. In particular, the successes of their 'Austrian' opponents, in the controversies of the *Methodenstreit* of the 1880s and thereafter, were partly due to these weaknesses. The first methodological counter-attack by the historically inclined economists was flawed, and an ade-quate methodological response did not emerge. A principal weakness in the earlier historical school tradition was an excessive faith in empiricism and inductive methods.

The later historical school recognised this weakness but had inadequate time to develop an alternative. Nazism and the Second World War intervened.

---

2   In the late 1800s and early 1900s most prominent Anglo-American economists could read German and many visited Germany to receive a training in the most advanced economics of that time (Herbst, 1965). Despite the difference of language, before the First World War connections between American and German economists were more numerous than between the American and the British. The leading American economist Richard Ely wrote to Marshall on 11 October 1901: 'I suppose the connection, today, between the German economists and the Americans is closer than between the American and the English. I am speaking about the personal connection as much as about the connection of thought' (Whitaker, 1996, vol. 2, p. 336). Today, however, fluency in German is much less common among Anglo-American economists. So far, very few of the writings of the German historical school have been translated into English.

By 1945 the problem was buried under the rubble of destruction. The conventional wisdom emerged that the German historical school had lost out in the *Methodenstreit*, and the argument was closed.

It will be argued here that this assessment is wrong, that the problem of historical specificity cannot legitimately be ignored, and that there were serious methodological and theoretical defects on all sides of the debate: in the positions of Marx, the historical school, and their 'Austrian' critics.

It may seem remarkable that it was in economics – yes, economics – that this problem was discussed and widely debated for about one hundred years. Sociology did not fully establish itself in Western academia until the early part of the twentieth century. Both economics and sociology went through a methodological transformation in the 1930s, involving a redefinition of the nature and subject matter of these disciplines. These transformations further explain the dereliction of the problem of historical specificity.

The principal architects of this reconstruction were Lionel Robbins (1932) in economics and Talcott Parsons (1937a) in sociology. Although their stances differed, they reached a territorial agreement concerning the domain of analysis of each discipline. In their accounts, economics would be devoted to 'choice' and sociology to 'action'. What they also did in common was to attempt to bury the problem of historical specificity. With the collapse of German academia in the Second World War, and the defeat of institutionalism in the US in the 1940s, postwar economics left the problem of historical specificity behind. Topics such as 'general equilibrium theory' became pre-eminent. Similarly, postwar sociology also preoccupied itself with grand, general themes. In all the social sciences, the problem of historical specificity was almost entirely forgotten.

An aim here is to recover this lost memory. The historical discussion will take us back into the economics of the nineteenth and early twentieth centuries. The claim is that we have much to learn from these past debates.

As long as general theorists, empiricists and hybrids overwhelm the social sciences, there will be insufficient attention to the problem of historical specificity. General theorists do not recognise the problem of historical specificity because they believe that economics can proceed entirely on the basis of universal and historically unspecific assumptions. In the past, some empiricists have reacted against general theorists, emphasising the specificity of each case. But by failing to establish a prior theoretical framework, empiricists are lost without a system of categorisation. In extreme cases, general theorists see only the similarities – empiricists see only the differences. The problem is about the establishment of appropriate categories and assumptions upon which both empirical and theoretical work must proceed. It is impossible in principle to resolve the problem simply by delving into facts. Neither general theorising nor empiricism can do adequate credit to the problem of historical specificity.[3]

---

3   To his credit, Sayer (1995, p. 28) gives a rare mention of the issue. However, contrary to Sayer, the question of 'historical and geographical specificity' has little or nothing to do with the degree of 'context dependence' of the system in question. A unique type of socio-economic system could

SOME WAYS OF AVOIDING THE PROBLEM

Consider some ways in which the problem of historical specificity has been evaded or ignored.

Evasion 1: *the affirmation of overwhelming common features or pervasive problematics.* It is sometimes claimed that all viable socio-economic systems have common attributes. As it stands, it is reasonable to suggest that they may have something in common. Later in this book, we shall discuss and uphold a restricted version of this postulate. However, the mistake is to concentrate entirely on the commonalities, and forget the differences. The existence of common character-istics in all socio-economic systems does not imply that the particular, different characteristics are of little or no importance. It is necessary to focus on both the particular and the general. The error is to assume that all that matters is that which is general or common to socio-economic systems.

Dismissals of the problem of historical specificity typically exclude the particulars. They assume that the allegedly common attributes of all socio-economic systems (e.g. markets, exchange, choice) are the key phenomena of economic analysis, to the exclusion of other, historically contingent, features. Economics becomes ahistorical by focusing solely on what is presumed to be common to all systems.

The one-sided emphasis on commonalities is related to the particular con-ception of economics as the universal 'science of choice'. Menger, Robbins and others argued that economics should address the common problematic of indi-vidual choice under scarcity, and trace out the consequences of multiple, individual 'rational' choices in terms of their intended or unintended outcomes. Whatever the value of this choice-theoretic approach to economics, it leaves much out of the picture. Insufficient stress is placed on the unique historical circum-stances in which individual decisions always take place. The ways in which institutions or cultures may mould individual preferences are neglected.

On the contrary, it is argued here that all socio-economic systems are neces-sarily combinations of dissimilar elements. These combinations will in turn depend on historical and local circumstances. Once we recognise the unavoid-ability and importance of additional and non-universal phenomena, then a new set of theoretical problems emerge concerning the assumptions that are appro-priate in a given context. How do we ground such assumptions in an appropriate methodology? This is part of the problem of historical specificity.

Evasion 2: *the doctrine of a natural type of socio-economic system.* Another way of avoiding the problem of historical specificity is to assume that one system is 'natural' and all other systems 'unnatural'. This idea is deeply rooted in the more general view that the uniformities and regularities of economic life are determined by nature (C. Clark, 1992).

---

be highly context dependent, or, on the other hand, relatively isolated. The existence of either specific or general features does not necessarily relate to their context. Any transhistorical features of socio-economic systems can be dependent on, or relatively independent of, their context.

Once any given type of socio-economic system is regarded as 'natural', then all deviations are regarded as aberrations to be corrected by an appeal to the singular brute facts or natural laws of economic life. This ancient idea has often been used in attempts to give scientific justification to the *status quo*. Moreover, it encourages the social scientist to focus on one type of system only.

One of the problems in this doctrine is that it takes the concept of the 'natural' for granted. In both society and nature, what is and what is not 'natural' is far from straightforward. Evolution has many examples of quirks and path-dependent outcomes. Are extinct species 'unnatural'? Is all that survives and endures 'natural'? Although the Soviet-type economies have collapsed, does that mean that they were 'unnatural'? If it is argued that the Soviet-type economies were unnatural because they were short-lived, then we are drawn to the conclusion that the slave societies of Antiquity are more natural than modern industrial capitalism: Antiquity lasted for thousands of years whereas capitalism has existed for little more than two centuries. Despite the long lasting persistence of the doctrine of natural types in the social sciences, the criteria for bestowing the term 'natural' on one system rather than another have remained elusive.

Evasion 3: *the view of economics as an expression of human nature or psychology.* A common variant of this doctrine is the idea that the chosen system is an expression of 'human nature'. Many Enlightenment thinkers upheld the view that 'human nature' was constant and universal. Consider this famous passage from *The Wealth of Nations* by Adam Smith:

> The division of labour arises from a propensity in human nature to . . . truck, barter and exchange one thing for another. . . . It is common to all men, and to be found in no other race of animals, which seem to know neither this nor any other species of contracts. . . . Nobody ever saw a dog make a fair and deliberate exchange of one bone for another with another dog.
>
> (Smith, 1976, p. 17)

Note that Smith assumed that the predilection to make contracts was not historically and culturally created but was 'a propensity in human nature'. To sustain this 'natural' view of contract and exchange, they have to be regarded as something separate from specific and historically created institutions, such as property, law and courts. By making it universal and 'natural', Smith was thus inclined to see exchange simply as a flows of goods, services or money between persons. However, when exchange occurs in market economies, it is not simply things that are exchanged, but also property rights. Furthermore, contracts are made in the context of the laws and potential sanctions of the legal system. By seeing exchange and contract as essentially manifestations of 'human nature', Smith downplayed the historically contingent institutions upon which these activities depend. As will be shown later, Carl Menger and members of the Austrian school of economics made a similar error.

This idea that economics is founded largely on 'human nature' or psychology is remarkably persistent. It is not argued here that these factors are irrelevant to the understanding of human societies. The problem arises when it is believed that social and economic analysis stems largely from an understanding of human nature or psychology alone. As an example, it will be shown in chapter 15 that John Maynard Keynes fell back on the assumption that economic analysis was based on supposedly universal 'psychological laws'.

Remarkably, the Enlightenment notion of an individual, with given purposes or preference functions, still pervades modern mainstream economic thought. With the spread of modern rational choice theory to other disciplines, it is also making an appearance in sociology and political science. The research agenda often involves a search for the optimal economic, social or political arrangement on the basis of the assumption that society is a collection of fixed, ahistorical individuals. History is then admitted only insofar as it involves comparisons with a single, optimal system. By making the individual ahistorical, the real history of socio-economic systems is lost.

On the contrary, if we regarded the individual as partially constituted by society and its institutions, then history can be readmitted into the story. The individual and society are mutually constitutive; each forms and reforms the other, in an ongoing process. Neither society nor the individual is fixed. Human nature has real effects but it is not static. Nor is there a single, natural order. Accordingly, recognition of the problem of historical specificity is allied to a view of human nature as moulded and reconstituted by social institutions.

Evasion 4: *the affirmation of the free market as the ideal*. Dismissals of the problem of historical specificity often involve a heavy dose of free market ideology. In the history of the subject since Adam Smith, many economists have attempted to use alleged 'economic laws' to attempt to justify free market policies. Those who advocate free and unfettered markets typically hold them up as a pure and ideal standard by which to judge reality. Of course, they observe many cases of inflexible, regulated, fettered or even missing markets in the real world. These are denounced as deviations from the pure and perfect norm.

It has been said that economic theory demonstrates that free markets are optimal. But any competent economic theorist knows that this claim is based on restrictive and challengeable assumptions. Nevertheless, the belief in optimality persists. Believing that markets are the solution, and that markets will work well if only they are free and unfettered, the cases of imperfect or missing markets are then ignored. If the theory does not fit reality, then reality must be made to fit the theory. Imperfections and restraints in existing markets must be removed, and new markets must be set up in places where they are missing.

Leaving the ideological issues on one side, there are important theoretical implications of this commonplace gambit. In short, economics becomes the study of one ideal, pure market system. It is held that no other system, past or present, needs to be studied because it is deemed to be an aberration from the ideal norm. Economic history becomes the story of the development of all economies towards this ideal. Any impurities or 'imperfections' in existing market systems are regarded as unfortunate hangovers from the past. The theoretical discourse focuses on a single model of an allegedly pure market system.

Of course, not all mainstream economists take this extreme view. Many find good reasons for the survival of market imperfections in the system – such as public goods, externalities, and transaction costs – and advocate some government intervention and some non-market forms of organisation. However, the view previously described is sufficiently powerful to constrain the analysis of non-market forms of allocation. Deviations from the pure market ideal are often addressed largely in terms of the central concepts (exchange, prices, costs, supply, demand) of the market system. They are not treated as separate entities, requiring additional theoretical and conceptual frameworks.

A particular version of this free-market ideology is to assume that the ensemble of institutions in American capitalism is the ideal. When economies elsewhere experience recession, such as in Japan and East Asia, it is then exclaimed that the reason for this suboptimal performance is that the free and competitive economic institutions of American capitalism are not adequately replicated in these economies. Again this gives an excuse for ignoring the specific institutions and structures involved. The possibility that their development may be path dependent, or that they may be capable of consistently outperforming American capitalism in other circumstances, does not appear on the agenda.

A theory of the ideal economy is likely to emerge in periods dominated by a single, successful type of system. Opposition to this ideal is most likely to emerge in contexts where it is deemed imperfect or inappropriate. In the nineteenth century, when British capitalism was the engine of its global power, recognition of the problem of historical specificity was notable in Germany and Ireland. German and Irish economists opposed British economic policies, seeing them as a brake on their own national development. They also developed a distinctive theoretical outlook. These dissenting ideas were imported into the United States and influenced American institutionalism. However, by 1945 Britain was no longer the leading world power, and America saw itself as the model for the world. America had emerged from its isolationism and saw its own institutional structures as models for others to follow. This American intellectual domination endured for the remainder of the twentieth century, except for a brief period in the 1980s when Japan was seen as a rival model in terms of economic growth. Accordingly, the notion of a single, ideal system persists.

NEVERTHELESS, THE PROBLEM REAPPEARS

Despite the evasion of the problem of historical specificity, we are used to terms such as 'capitalism', 'feudalism' and 'socialism' in the discourse of economics and other social sciences. Leading economists such as Joseph Stiglitz (1994) and Oliver Williamson (1985) have written works such as *Whither Socialism?* and *The Economic Institutions of Capitalism*. By using such terms, economists are identifying different types of socio-economic system with a view to understanding how such systems work. Sometimes the perceived merits and demerits of one system are compared with those of another.

Leaving aside any normative comparisons and assessments in the literature, it is obvious that to make such an assessment in the first place there must be some taxonomic classification of different types of economic system. If these differences are to be meaningful, there must be an assumption that different systems behave in different ways. In other words, different systems are subject to 'laws' or principles of operation that differ from one system to another. Even if it is accepted that all socio-economic systems are subject to common 'laws' or principles, then such differences are being accepted as well. Otherwise we would have no basis to suggest that one system functioned in a different way from another.

Yet, strikingly, there is little discussion of the underlying methodological problems in making such comparisons, throughout modern economics. Today the subdiscipline of 'comparative economic systems' is relatively neglected. The relevant methodological issues and problems are rarely taught on the economics degree programmes of leading universities. In-depth taxonomic discussions of different types of socio-economic system, or of different types of firm or market are all notable by their rarity.[4]

In contrast, modern mainstream economics defines itself as the science of choice under scarcity, alleging that its principles can apply to all economies where choice and scarcity exist (Robbins, 1932). Real differences between socio-economic systems are either downplayed or ignored at this conceptual level.

This book is primarily about theoretical rather than policy issues. But it will be clear in some places that the theoretical discussion does inform the policy debate. Nevertheless, the prime concern here is methodological and theoretical: How do we establish a typology of different types of socio-economic system? What criteria do we use to distinguish one system from another, and how are these criteria derived? How do we identify incisive principles of operation of specific socio-economic systems, alongside principles or 'laws' that may be common to a larger set of such systems?

This book starts from the following assumption: that the role of any science is to address a particular segment or level of objective reality and to attempt to understand and explain the phenomena in that domain. Every science, in this view, has a real domain of analysis to which it is related. Hence physics is about the nature and properties of matter and energy, chemistry is about substances, astronomy about heavenly bodies, biology about living things, psychology about the human psyche, and so on.

This does not mean that there is a hermetic seal between ideas about the world and the world itself. The possibility of interaction between the science and its object is not denied. Especially in the social sciences, ideas about the real world may both reflect and affect the world itself. Indeed, ideas and habits of thought themselves make up part of the socio-economic structures and institutions that are the subjects of enquiry. This does not contradict or undermine the view taken here that each science is concerned to understand the domain of objective reality

---

4 Today, modern economists rarely explore even the concept of the market. Taken for granted, as a singular, unalterable and universal datum, it is typically investigated no further. Insofar as the institutional nature of real markets is investigated at all, it is more often by sociologists (Baker, 1984; Ingham, 1996; Lie, 1997; Zelizer, 1988). As we shall see below, this has not always been the case.

to which it is ascribed. On the basis of such an understanding, scientific investigation can provide a grounding for technological innovation and for intervention in the natural or social world.

This is a realist view of science, which would be accepted quite widely, but not universally, among philosophers. To deny that the sciences have a real object is tantamount to a denial of the existence of an objective reality. With the current crisis in the theoretical foundations of the social sciences, it is necessary to defend the existence of such a reality and its place in scientific discourse. It would not have been necessary at the time of Marshall or Marx: they took its existence for granted. Accordingly, before we discuss philosophical realism it is necessary to deal with some of these modern reactions against it.

RELATIVISM AND POST-MODERNISM

Today, philosophical relativism and denials of the reality of an objective social world have become fashionable, especially in the discussion circles of post-structuralism and post-modernism. The loss of faith in scientific certainty has been replaced by a methodological voluntarism in which 'anything goes'. However, contrary to the language and sentiments of much 'post-modernist' discourse, scepticism of the purported certainties of science is a very old disposition. It is traceable through Paul Feyerabend and Friedrich Nietzsche back to the 'sceptical' philosophers of Ancient Greece, well over two millennia ago. The Ancient sceptics argued that knowledge was relative and context dependent, and beyond formal proof. Hence scepticism about the powers of reason or scientific method is not new. Yet such very real difficulties in knowing the world do not provide a good case for denying its existence.

The post-modernist literature includes some useful and sensible arguments. Some post-modernists might be sympathetic to arguments in the present book, in favour of historically sensitive theory. Post-modernist oppositions to over-generalisation, dogmatism, deductivism and reductionism are to be commended. On this basis, methodological individualism and (Marxist) 'economic determinism' are both rightly rejected.[5]

However, these critiques are often combined with extreme and untenable positions. For instance, a commendable critique of reductionist explanations is often combined with a reckless hostility to 'essentialism' in which any essential structures behind appearances are denied. The fact that reductionism is misconceived does not mean that we should not attempt to uncover as much as we can of the essential character of an entity, itself consisting of multiple,

---

5 Reductionism sometimes involves the notion that wholes must be explained entirely in terms of their elemental, constituent parts. More generally, reductionism can be defined as the idea that all aspects of a complex phenomenon must solely be explained in terms of one level, or type of unit. According to this view there are no autonomous levels of analysis other than this elemental foundation, and no such thing as emergent properties upon which different levels of analysis can be based.

irreducible aspects or levels. Without some concept of essence, we are unable to make categorisations of sameness and difference that are basic to science.[6]

One of the areas where post-modernism has an impact is in the history and philosophy of science. Bruno Latour's (1987) work in this area is sometimes placed in the 'post-modernist' category. Significantly, Yuval Yonay (1998, 2000) has applied ostensibly post-modernist precepts to the analysis of the history of American institutional economics.

However, such post-modernist ventures often confuse two vitally different levels of argument and analysis. For example, post-modernists often promote the commendable argument that the progress of science depends on a sufficient degree of variety and conversation between different approaches to similar problems. In other words, the evolution of science requires a pluralism of different schools of thought. This is an admirable sentiment.

But what may apply to science as a whole does not always apply to an individual researcher or research team, aiming at a specific solution to a specific problem. An acceptable policy of pluralism concerns the policy of institutions toward the funding and nurturing of science. Such a policy involves 'pluralism in the academy'. But it would not extend to the individual practices of science itself. This confusion, between encouraging contradictory ideas in the academy and encouraging them in our own heads, is widespread in post-modernism. For instance, Warren Montag (1988, p. 90) approvingly described post-modernism as a 'de facto alliance between irreducibly different theoretical forces'. Such alliances between different researchers might serve the interests of academic diversity and freedom. However, if we hold 'irreducibly different' and contra-dictory ideas in our own heads then we have formulae for nonsense. If we hold the idea that A is B, and also that A is not B, then we can prove any nonsensical proposition that we wish.

There is much to be said for tolerance of many different and even antagonistic scientific research programmes within an academic discipline or university. But we should not tolerate the existence of inconsistent ideas within our own heads. The policy toward science must be pluralistic and tolerant, but science itself must be intolerant of what it regards as falsehood. Perceived error must be exposed and criticised, not by denying the opponent a voice, but by explaining the mistake to the scientific audience. The role of diversity is not to sanctify or foster contradiction. Tolerance of the right of a scientist to practise, even when we may disagree with his or her views, does not imply discursive tolerance of any method and proposition. Any failure of social science to erect an adequate and coherent general theory is not rectified by applauding incoherence.

In recent years, some heterodox economists have been attracted by post-modernism. In particular, some post-modernists have found a refuge in institutionalism. Yet post-modernist statements such as 'everyone creates his or her reality, there being no possibility of adjudicating among the different realities'

---

6 Nevertheless, the concept of 'essence' is problematic. The concept of 'population thinking' (see chapters 7 and 22 below) requires that traditional Platonic and Aristotelian conceptions of essence should be substantially modified.

(Hoksbergen, 1994, p. 683) are not only highly contestable on philosophical grounds but also entirely alien to the institutionalist tradition of Veblen, Commons and Mitchell. Philosophically, if there is no possibility of adjudication, then there is little prospect of establishing any kind of proposition, including those that are proposed by Roland Hoksbergen himself. Historically, Veblen, Commons and Mitchell took a very different position. All these institutionalist authors believed that the goal of economics was to investigate and understand real economic phenomena. They believed in the possibility of a scientific pursuit of truth and in the scope for the agreement of a scientific community to the essentials of that truth, even if any agreement is tentative and provisional.

But, despite these objections, post-modernism does not give up on its efforts to conquer heterodoxy. Robert Garnett (1999), for example, attempted to link post-modernism with some modern institutionalist and rethought Marxist themes. He saw a 'common enemy' in any attempt to develop a value theory on the basis of 'the idea that all market-based production and consumption activities are governed by uniform, self-regulative laws or principles' (p. 819). Instead he applauded attempts to construct historically and institutionally specific studies of market institutions and pricing processes. However, despite commendable sentiments concerning specific studies, there is a measure both of error and of omission here. The error is to assume that historically specific pricing theories necessarily exclude any general or systematic principles concerning markets and prices. On the contrary, a historically sensitive theory always itself requires a more general conceptual framework. Without a more general framework, specific theory is impossible. An omission in Garnett's statement is his failure to note that the development of historically sensitive theory is much older than post-modernism. It dates from the 1840s or earlier, not only from within Marxism but also from the German historical school.

Post-modernists have done much damage. Some have attempted to close down crucial debates, such as the relation between agency and structure, because of their evocation of 'grand themes'. By misrepresenting the themes of post-modernism as entirely novel, they have fostered a neglect of the history of ideas, and eschewed some means of escape from the very dilemmas that they have identified. Alex Callinicos (1999, p. 297) put it well: 'Paradoxically, despite postmodernists' claims to represent intellectual openness and plurality, it is only by resisting their attempts to close this debate that social theory is likely to retain its validity.'

Ironically, within sociology, the post-modernists have joined the rational choice theorists and the empiricists in a tacit alliance against conceptually oriented and non-formal social theory. While these three approaches differ hugely in substance and style, for different reasons they have wished to remove social theory from its traditional position of prestige within academic sociology. Post-modernism rejects social theory as a 'grand narrative', empiricism declares that facts alone are the road to truth, and rational choice theory sees traditional social theory as largely useless for building deductive models of social interaction. If social theory is to rebut this triple alliance it must understand the limits of general theorising as well as its indispensable role.

PHILOSOPHICAL REALISM

Although philosophical realists know of no royal road to truth, they claim that truth, nevertheless, is a primary objective for science. Even if all science is provisional and an infallible methodology is always beyond our grasp, this does not mean that we may abandon the search for truth. This search may reveal multiple and contradictory truth claims. Science should not simply rest there, but it should investigate reality and create dialogue between researchers so that error can be removed and the more viable claims advanced. The central task of science is to advance the understanding of how the real world actually works.[7]

It is not the concern of this work to discuss all the pros and cons of realism in detail. But let us first make it clear what realism is not. Philosophical realism does not amount to the statement that we can directly or ultimately know the world. Philosophical realism does not hinge on whether or not the world is knowable. Philosophical realism is not undermined by the valid observation that culturally formed concepts and categories frame all human perceptions. Above all, philosophical realism is not a theory of truth and does not imply any particular theory of truth. It is more about ontology than epistemology. Hence philosophical realism is less about what is or can be known: it is more about what exists.

Realism, as John Searle (1995, p. 153) defined it, is simply 'the view that the world exists independently of our representations of it'. The confusion of issues concerning our knowledge of the world, on the one hand, with the existence of that world, on the other, amounts to what Roy Bhaskar (1975, p. 36) has dubbed the 'epistemic fallacy'. By this he meant the fallacy that 'statements about being can be reduced or analysed in terms of statements about knowledge, i.e. that ontological questions can always be transposed into epistemological terms'.

The removal of this misunderstanding helps to clear the ground for a realist approach. However, it does not prove the existence of the real world beyond our senses. Realism is instead based on the claim that the acceptance of the existence of a real world beyond our senses makes intelligible such essential scientific concepts as explanation and truth. Science, to be science, must be *about* something; it must have a real object of enquiry.[8]

Realists have a trump card to play in disputes with those that deny the existence of an objective reality. Gaston Bachelard (1953, p. 411) remarked some time ago that 'all philosophy, explicitly or tacitly, honestly or surreptitiously . . . deposits,

---

7   For versions of philosophical realism in the social sciences see Archer (1995), Aronson (1984), Bhaskar (1979), Bunge (1998), Harré (1986, 1993), Kanth (1992), T. Lawson (1997), Mäki (1989, 1990b, 1997a, 1998), Manicas (1987), Sayer (1984) and Searle (1995).
8   C. Clark (1992, p. 26) contended that realism in social theory 'would hold that society and social phenomena are independent and separate from the individuals that make up society and individual social phenomena'. This is too extreme and crude a picture. Realists such as Bhaskar, Bunge, Mäki, Searle and others argue repeatedly that society would not exist without individuals, and that social phenomena are not independent of social actors. What is crucial, however, is the realisation that society does pre-date any given individual. Accordingly, although individuals and social structures are mutually constitutive, they are different things (Archer, 1995).

projects or presupposes a reality.' At about the same time, Willard van Orman Quine (1953) advanced a similar view, arguing that every scientific theory contained an explicit or implicit ontology. Since then, several philosophical realists have shown that discourses involving denials of philosophical realism, themselves have to appeal to 'objective' existences such as 'the text' to make the discourse intelligible. In short, to engage in any discourse – 'post-modern' or whatever – is to presume a real objectivity in the form of the language, medium and substance of the communication. This is philosophical realism's trump card: philosophical realism is unavoidable, even in discourses that deny the existence of an objective reality.[9]

Furthermore, to retain any notion of non-tautological truth we have to retain some idea of what the truth statement is about. Accepting this place for truth admits the possibility of falsity. Those who would deny that truth is a helpful concept are likewise excluding fallibility and giving dogmatism full reign. As Bhaskar (1975, p. 43) put it: 'To be a fallibilist about knowledge, it is necessary to be a realist about things. Conversely, to be a sceptic about things is to be a dogmatist about knowledge.' It has been indicated above that much of the modern resistance to realism is fuelled by the valid insight that we cannot know directly any real world that may exist. But it is a mistake to connect this epistemological insight with an anti-realist stance. The fact that we cannot know the world directly is not a refutation of the existence of the real world.

Some unsophisticated realists, however, have wrongly assumed that a real world exists *and* it is directly knowable. This particular (and unacceptable) version of realism is described as 'empirical realism'. Several examples of empirical realism will be given in this book. It is important to emphasise that the denial of empirical realism does not amount to a denial of realism as such. Indeed, the acceptance of the inevitability of some version of realism in all scientific discourse, far from opening the door to all empiricist and other misconceptions, may actually help prepare us to understand and to reject such unacceptable versions of realist philosophy. In particular, it will be shown below that failures to supersede empirical realism have stunted the development of a critical and historically grounded economics.

Accordingly, philosophical realism does not necessarily involve the imperative that assumptions in science have to be 'realistic'. Indeed, sophisticated realists have argued that no assumption can mirror precisely any aspect of the real world. As the real world is always messy and complex, any such 'realistic' assumption would somehow have to reflect this messiness and complexity. On the contrary, all theory is based on abstractions and simplifications. But this does not give us licence to assume anything. The key question is: what abstractions and simplifications are appropriate? The problem of historical specificity addresses this question.

---

9   A good example of the playing of this trump card is Mäki's (1988a, 1988b) demonstration that the 'post-modernism' of McCloskey (1985, 1988) itself relied on the implicit acceptance of an external reality. In the face of this argument, McCloskey (1988, p. 153) was persuaded to declare: 'I am a realist'. Perhaps we are all realists now.

Uskali Mäki (1989) made a useful distinction between, on the one hand, claims concerning 'realisticness' – that is concerning the attribute of being 'realistic' in some sense – and, on the other, 'realism' as a philosophical doctrine. In general, philosophical realism does not necessarily mean the realisticness of assumptions or outcomes. Broadly, the kind of realism promoted in this book involves some notion of abstraction of the most essential and important structures and causal relationships in any given phenomenon.

But we have been getting ahead of the argument. The starting point here is much more general, and could be accepted by philosophical realists of all varieties. It is a guiding principle of this work that realism, broadly defined, has radical implications for the type of theory and approach that is appropriate for economics and, indeed, for the definition of the subject itself.

I wish to make a further claim, concerning economics and other social sciences. Once we adopt broadly a philosophically realist approach to (say) socio-economic phenomena then we are obliged to address an underlying methodological problem, concerning the role of general and specific assumptions in social and economic analysis.

The question is basically, this: are the core assumptions of economic science appropriate for all types and forms of economy, since the dawn of human history, or appropriate for a (temporal or geographical) subset of them only? For example, are the assumptions of economics appropriate for modern market systems only, or for all types of socio-economic system? Do some assumptions have general and transhistorical applicability, while others are historically specific? If so, how do we establish concepts at each level of generality? This, with all its attendant questions, is the problem of historical specificity.

THE STANDPOINT ADVANCED HERE

Discussions of several of the key problems raised in these two opening chapters are relatively sparse in the recent literature in social science. Accordingly, for purposes of clarification and to avoid misunderstandings, some propositions are listed below. They constitute the standpoint of this work, concerning questions of generality and specificity in economic and social theory. The following propositions are upheld in this book:

1   Science cannot be merely the analysis or description of empirical particulars. Descriptions themselves always rely on prior theories and concepts, either explicit or tacit.
2   Science cannot proceed without some general or universal statements and principles. Explanatory unifications and generalisations that explain real causal mechanisms are worthy goals of science.
3   However, general theories of complex phenomena are always highly limited simplifications, largely because of the complexities and computational limitations involved in attempting any truly general theory.
4   Unifications and generalisations in social science provide powerful

conceptual frameworks, but they often lack the ability to discriminate between and adequately explain concrete particulars.

5   Purportedly general theories have explanatory power in the social sciences only when additional, confining and particular, assumptions are made.

6   In dealing with complex (socio-economic) systems, we require a combination of general concepts, statements and theories, with particular concepts, statements and theories, relating to particular types of system or subsystem.

7   The most powerful and informative statements and theories in the social sciences are those that emanate from particular theorising that is targeted at a specific domain of analysis and also guided by general frameworks and principles.

8   The social sciences must thus combine general principles with theorising that is aimed at specific domains. These operate on different levels of abstraction. A philosophically informed meta-theory must address the relationship between these levels.

An over-emphasis on general theory stems from an endorsement of the first two propositions but from a neglect of the other six. As we shall see in the historical discussion below of attempts to deal with the problem of historical specificity, many attempts have failed because of a denial of the second proposition and a failure to understand the first. The thrust of the argument in this book is to establish and accept the first two propositions but also to move on to enforce the other six. It is in this latter zone that the historical argument has been relatively impoverished.

To some, the above propositions may be relatively uncontroversial. It is openly accepted here that the best of modern social science involves theorising that combines some general principles with a specific domain of analysis. The trouble, however, is that typically the meta-theoretical bases for such combinations are inadequately articulated. Furthermore, many social scientists make unwarranted and exaggerated claims for general theory alone. Some examples of these exaggerated claims are discussed in chapters 16 and 17 below.

At this stage this volume enters the historical narrative. In part II there is a discussion of the contribution of both Marxism and the historical school. This was a time when economics was much broader than the narrow formalism of today. Furthermore, the centre of gravity of social science was in Germany, rather than Britain or America. Part III considers the events that led to the abandonment of the problem of historical specificity and the Great Forgetting of the historical and institutional schools, by economists and sociologists alike.

Part II

THE NINETEENTH CENTURY
The German historical school
and its impact

DRAMATIS PERSONAE

Åkerman, Johan (1896–1982)
Ashley, William J. (1860–1927)
Bagehot, Walter (1826–77)
Böhm-Bawerk, Eugen von
    (1851–1914)
Brentano, Lujo (1844–1931)
Bücher, Karl (1847–1930)
Cairnes, John Elliot (1823–75)
Comte, Auguste (1798–1857)
Cunningham, William (1840–1919)
Darwin, Charles (1809–82)
Dewey, John (1859–1952)
Edgeworth, Francis Y. (1845–1926)
Ely, Richard T. (1854–1943)
Engels, Frederick (1820–1895)
Eucken, Walter (1891–1950)
Fichte, Johann (1762–1814)
Foxwell, Herbert (1849–1936)
Giffen, Robert (1837–1910)
Hayek, Friedrich A. (1899–1992)
Hegel, Georg W. F. (1770–1831)
Hewins, William A. S. (1865–1931)
Hildebrand, Bruno (1812–78)
Hilferding, Rudolf (1877–1941)
Hobson, John A. (1848–1940)
Humboldt, Karl Wilhelm von
    (1767–1835)
Ingram, John K. (1823–1907)

James, William (1842–1910)
Jevons, William Stanley (1835–82)
Jones, Richard (1790–1855)
Kant, Immanuel (1724–1804)
Keynes, John Neville (1852–1949)
Knapp, Georg (1842–1926)
Knies, Karl (1821–98)
Knight, Frank H. (1885–1972)
Lachmann, Ludwig M. (1906–90)
Laveleye, Emile de (1822–92)
Le Play, P. G. Frédéric (1806–82)
Leontief, Wassily W. (1906–99)
Leslie, T. E. Cliffe (1827–82)
Lilienfeld, Paul von (1829–1903)
List, Friedrich (1789–1846)
Loria, Achille (1857–1943)
Malthus, Thomas Robert (1766–1834)
Marshall, Alfred (1842–1924)
Marx, Karl (1818–83)
Menger, Carl (1840–1921)
Mill, John Stuart (1806–73)
Millar, John (1735–1801)
Montesquieu, Charles Baron de
    (1689–1755)
Myrdal, Gunnar (1898–1987)
Nietzsche, Friedrich (1844–1900)
Parsons, Talcott (1902–79)
Peirce, Charles Sanders (1839–1914)

Pigou, Arthur C. (1877–1959)
Polanyi, Karl (1886–1964)
Ranke, Leopold von (1795–1886)
Ricardo, David (1773–1823)
Robbins, Lionel (1898–1984)
Robertson, William (1721–93)
Rogers, James E. Thorold (1823–90)
Röpke, Wilhelm (1899–1966)
Roscher, Wilhelm (1817–94)
Rothacker, Erich (1888–1965)
Salin, Edgar (1892–1974)
Savigny, Friedrich K. von
  (1779–1861)
Schäffle, Albert (1823–1903)
Schelling, Wilhelm Joseph von
  (1775–1854)

Schmoller, Gustav von (1838–1917)
Schumpeter, Joseph A. (1883–1950)
Schütz, Karl von (1811–75)
Smith, Adam (1723–90)
Sombart, Werner (1863–1941)
Spencer, Herbert (1820–1903)
Spiethoff, Arthur (1873–1957)
Takishima, Zenya (1904–90)
Toynbee, Arnold (1852–83)
Uno, Kozo (1897–1970)
Veblen, Thorstein B. (1857–1929)
Vico, Giambattista (1668–1744)
Wagner, Adolph H. G. (1835–1917)
Walras, Léon (1834–1910)
Weber, Max (1864–1920)
Wieser, Friedrich von (1851–1926)

3

KARL MARX AND
THE SPECIFICITY OF THE
CAPITALIST SYSTEM

It is the tension between the scientist's laws and his own attempted
breaches of them that powers the engines of science and makes it
forge ahead.

(Willard van Orman Quine, *Quiddities* (1987))

One of the great intellectual changes of the early nineteenth century was
the realisation that history was a developmental process, rather than a display
of movement to and from a fixed, 'natural' order. Historical evolution and progress are modern ideas. Before the nineteenth century there was limited cogni-
sance of a process of political, economic or technological development. Many
political movements looked back to the past, and aimed for its restoration. They
did not aim to advance beyond that which had gone before. The Renaissance
was itself a notion of a re-birth of the culture of Classical Antiquity. Even the
word 'revolution' originally meant a cyclical return to normalcy, rather that
the construction of something entirely new (Western, 1972, p. 1).

Indeed, as late as the 1790s, many leaders of the French Revolution believed
that they were restoring France to a 'normal' or 'natural' state of affairs, by
replacing the despot by the sovereignty of reason. In architecture and discourse,
they made an appeal to an imagined age of democracy and reason in Ancient
Greece. For many at the time, the French Revolution was not seen as a gateway
to a new and higher order but to an imaginary golden age of the past. It was
regarded as a restoration of what was natural and fundamental, against the
corruption and decay of the present. It was an attempt to retrieve what had been
lost.

However, in the eighteenth century a quite different conception of history,
based on ideas of modernity and progress, had also emerged. Giambattista
Vico attempted in his book *Principi d'una scienza nuova* (1725) to develop a theory
of history, and Charles Baron de Montesquieu had argued in his *L'esprit des
lois* (1748) that societies differed according to the 'humour and disposition' of
their peoples. The Scottish Enlightenment played a vital role in changing prevailing views of history. An idea of ongoing economic development and change
is clearly present in *The Wealth of Nations* (1776) of Adam Smith. Other Scottish
Enlightenment thinkers such as John Millar and William Robertson enlarged

upon this conception. These Scottish thinkers promoted a 'four stages' theory of historical development, involving hunting, pasturage, agriculture and commerce (Meek, 1967, p. 39). On this basis, in 1777 Robertson wrote in his *History of America*: 'In every enquiry concerning the operations of men when united together in society, the first object of attention should be their mode of subsistence. Accordingly as that varies, their laws and policies must be different' (quoted in Meek, 1967, p. 37). This was a forerunner of what Marxists describe as the materialist conception of history. Furthermore, the second sentence in the quotation contains an early statement to the effect that economic theories should be sensitive to different historical circumstances.

Despite its references to Antiquity, the French Revolution stimulated waves of original and radical debate, not least about the nature of human history. In the early 1800s there was a detectable change in thinking, in both France and Germany. A key influence here was Georg W. F. Hegel, who saw history as a progressive but non-linear development, in stages, towards an Absolute Idea, rather than cyclical gyrations or gravitations around a previously-established equilibrium. Repeated revolutionary dislocations in Europe, from 1789 to 1848, gave impetus to new, developmental ideas of history and sustained a belief that historical progress and development were possible. It is thus no accident that socialism and communism emerged, in their modern forms, in this period.

This intellectual ferment was particularly energetic in the states of Germany. Horace Friess (1930, p. 396) identified the 'turning point in the development of German culture' at about 1830. The economy was in the first throes of its Industrial Revolution. In 1835 the first German railway began to operate, between Fürth and Nüremberg. By 1850 there were about 20,000 kilometres of railway in operation in what was later to become a unified Germany. These economic and technological changes amplified the possibility of national integration. Germany was a zone of economic, cultural, political and intellectual agitation.

The idea that the world was in a process of ongoing change, rather than being a fixed natural order, also permeated the natural sciences at that time. In England, Charles Darwin had formulated the outlines of his theory of biological evolution as early as 1838, although it was not published until 1859. Nevertheless, ideas of ongoing historical development took deepest root in Germany, where the Hegelian intellectual legacy was strongest, and where – as in France – the signs of political and economic transformation were clearly visible in the convulsions of revolution and change.

ENTER MARXISM

Karl Marx and Frederick Engels were immersed in these intellectual, political and economic events. Their collaboration began in 1844. They witnessed the revolutionary convulsions in Continental Europe in 1848 and became exiles from their native Germany. Eventually they both settled in England.[1]

---

1 The remainder of this chapter makes use of material from Hodgson (1999a).

In the years 1845–6, Marx and Engels jointly wrote their lengthy volume *The German Ideology*. It was never published in their lifetime. As well as being a critique of the ideas and ideologies of others, this work attempted to set out the analytical principles upon which a historically sensitive social and economic theory should be founded. The following passage took up this theme:

> The premises from which we begin are not arbitrary ones, not dogmas, but real premises from which abstraction can only be made in the imagination. They are the real individuals, their activity and the material conditions of their life, both those which they find already existing and those produced by their own activity. These premises can thus be verified in a purely empirical way. The first premise of all human history is, of course, the existence of living human individuals. Thus the first fact to be established is the physical organisation of these individuals and their consequent relation to the rest of nature.
>
> (Marx and Engels, 1976, p. 31)

Two points in this passage are worth highlighting. The first is one of strength, the second of weakness. First, Marx and Engels sensibly emphasised that the premises of their enquiry must be based on a real object, rather than being arbitrary assumptions. Second, they held to the questionable view that these premises can 'be verified in a purely empirical way', without giving any further clarification of what that means. An empiricist believes that it is possible to verify assumptions 'purely' by an appeal to facts. In truth, the resort to empiricism as an alleged method of resolving the problem of historical specificity became commonplace in nineteenth-century writings on the topic. The limitations of any assumption that premises can be established by an empiricist procedure will be addressed later below.

In a letter to the journalist Pavel V. Annenkov dated 28 December 1846, Marx amplified the first and acceptable point noted above. In his communication, Marx again emphasised that science is concerned with a real object. He criticised the theoretical approach of Pierre-Joseph Proudhon and asserted that:

> Mr Proudhon, chiefly because he doesn't know history, fails to see that, in developing his productive faculties, i.e. in living, man develops certain inter-relations, and that the nature of these relations necessarily changes with the modification and the growth of the said productive faculties. He fails to see that *economic categories* are but *abstractions* of those real relations, that they are truths only in so far as those relations continue to exist. Thus he falls into the error of bourgeois economists who regard those economic categories as eternal laws and not as historical laws which are laws only for a given historical development, a specific development of the productive forces. Thus, instead of regarding politico-economic categories as abstractions of actual social relations that are transitory and historical, Mr Proudhon, by a mystical inversion, sees in real relations only the embodiment of those abstractions. Those

abstractions are themselves formulas which have been slumbering in the bosom of God the Father since the beginning of the world.

(Marx and Engels, 1982, p. 100)

This passage underlines an important difference between, on the one hand, the economics of Marx and, on the other hand, that of his classical precursors and the subsequent neoclassical and Austrian schools. The classical and other economists argued from universal assumptions, such as the ahistorical, abstract individual. Marx's approach was very different. In his view, ahistorical and universal categories cannot capture the essential features of a specific socio-economic system. Recognition of the processes of historical development led him to choose concepts that captured the essences of particular systems. Thus Marx claimed that the core categories in *Capital* are abstract expressions of real social relations found within the capitalist mode of production. Such categories were held to be operational as long as such social relations exist.

In the 'method of political economy' section of the *Grundrisse*, written in 1857, Marx (1973b, pp. 100–1) argued similarly that discussions of concrete socio-economic systems must ascend 'from the simpler relations, such as labour, division of labour, need, exchange value, to the level of the state, exchange between nations and the world market'. This, he saw, was the 'scientifically correct method'. Marx's primary aim was to analyse the type of economy emerging in Britain and Europe in the nineteenth century. Thus in the Preface to the first edition of *Capital* he made it clear that the objective of that work was to examine not economies in general but 'the capitalist mode of production'. It was the 'ultimate aim' of that work 'to reveal the economic law of motion of modern society' (Marx, 1976, pp. 90, 92).

Accordingly, unlike the modern economics textbooks, *Capital* does not start with a general and ahistorical 'economic problem'. This procedure would ignore the historically specific and characteristic structures and relations of the object of study. Instead, Marx's economic analysis in the first volume of *Capital* – originally published in 1867 – started from what he regarded as the essential social relations of the capitalist mode of production. This is clear from the key words in the titles of the opening chapters: commodities, exchange, money, capital, and labour power. Marx did not aim to write a text on economics that would be applicable to all socio-economic systems. No such work, in his view, would ever be possible. He argued that it is necessary to focus on a particular socio-economic system, and the particular relations and laws that governed its operation and evolution.[2]

---

2 Although the basic analytical approach of moving from the key characteristics of a specific mode of production – rather than ahistorical universals – was stated by Marx as early as 1846, it was not until the publication of the *Contribution to the Critique of Political Economy* in 1859 that the concept of the commodity was located as the starting point in the analysis of capitalism. Note the famous transitional passage in the *Grundrisse* (Marx, 1973b, pp. 100–8) which was probably written in 1857, and the important comments by Nicolaus in his foreword (Marx, 1973b, pp. 36–41). By 1859 and the appearance of the first volume of *Capital* in 1867 the concept of the commodity was seen, to use Nicolaus's words, as 'a beginning which is at once concrete, material, almost tangible, as well as historically specific' (p. 38).

Marx considered several types of socio-economic system, such as capitalism, feudalism and Classical Antiquity. In Marx's view, capitalism will eventually be replaced by communism. In specifying such different socio-economic systems, he saw the need to develop particular analyses of the structure and dynamic of each one. For instance, he aimed to show that capitalism had inner contradictions, leading to its breakdown and supersession by another mode of production.

In addition, however, he had a more general theory of socio-economic change and transformation. This is summarised in his famous Preface to the *Contribution to the Critique of Political Economy* of 1859:

> In the social production of their existence, men inevitably enter into definite relations, which are independent of their will, namely relations of production appropriate to a given stage in the development of the material forces of production. The totality of these relations of production constitutes the economic structure of society, the real foundation, on which arises a legal and political superstructure and to which correspond definite forms of social consciousness. The mode of production of material life conditions the general process of social, political and intellectual life. It is not the consciousness of men that determines their existence, but their social existence that determines their consciousness. At a certain stage of development, the material productive forces of society come into conflict with the existing relations of production or – this merely expresses the same thing in legal terms – with the property relations within the framework of which they have operated hitherto. From forms of development of the productive forces these relations turn into their fetters. Then begins an era of social revolution. The changes in the economic foundation lead sooner or later to the transformation of the whole immense superstructure.
>
> (Marx, 1971, pp. 20–1)

Hence Marx's theory of socio-economic change centres on the conflict between the 'material productive forces' and the 'relations of production'.[3]

Marx's statement in the *Preface* also sketches a methodology for taxonomising different socio-economic systems. For Marx, the 'mode of production of material life' conditioned social and intellectual activity. Reigning ideas could not be used to characterise social systems at a fundamental level, because 'social existence' had primacy over consciousness. The characterisation of systems had to start instead from the nature of the 'relations of production' and 'property relations'. We shall return to this methodological problem of classification of different systems at later stages of this book.

Whatever the methodology of classification, the demarcation of different types of system was itself crucial. Writing in the 1870s, Frederick Engels (1962, p. 204) echoed and clarified Marx's methodological approach:

---

3   See Cohen (1978) for an eloquent defence of Marx's theory of historical change.

Political economy is therefore essentially a *historical* science. It deals with material which is historical, that is, constantly changing; it must first investigate the special laws of each individual stage in the evolution of production and exchange, and only when it has completed this investigation will it be able to establish a few quite general laws which hold good for production and exchange in general. At the same time it goes without saying that the laws which are valid for definite modes of production and forms of exchange hold good for all historical periods in which these modes of production and exchange prevail.

Both classical and neoclassical economists have neglected the problem of historical specificity. Although it is discussed insufficiently in modern Marxism, past Marxists have been at the forefront in exposing this error. For example, in his critique of Adam Smith and the classical school, the Russian economist Isaac Rubin wrote in the 1920s of 'counterposing *eternal and immutable economic laws* to historically transient and alterable socio-political conditions' (Rubin, 1979, p. 168). The assumption of a given human nature, 'the naturally-conditioned and immutable nature of man in general' became the individualistic ontological foundation of ahistorical economics:

Once the aspiration of the individual to better his situation is made to flow from the constancy of human nature, it is obvious that it will be operative in *all historical epochs* and under *any social conditions*. . . . Smith explains the origin of the most important social *institutions* . . . by the undeviating nature of the *abstract individual* – his personal interest and conscious striving for the greatest gain. He thereby attributes to abstract man *motives and aspirations* (here, the striving to barter and exchange) that are in fact the *result* of the influence exercised on the individual by these same *social institutions* . . . what he takes as human nature, however, is the determinate nature of man as it takes shape under the influence of the commodity-capitalist economy.

(Rubin, 1979, pp. 169–71)

Crucially, the concept of a historically specific socio-economic system directs us to quite different questions from neoclassical and other ahistorical approaches. For instance, the accent on socio-economic transformation and crises contrasts with the more static neoclassical preoccupation with economic equilibria and the theory of relative prices.

Clearly, in demarcating different types of socio-economic system, the definition of each of these types is crucial. Marx regarded the capitalist mode of production as a socio-economic system in which most production takes place in capitalist firms. He saw the capitalist firm as characterised by the following features: the means of production within them are privately owned, their products are the property of the owners and not of the workers, and these products are sold as commodities in the pursuit of profit (Marx, 1976, pp. 291–2). Clearly, this definition involves an employment relationship and excludes co-operatives and self-employed artisans, as Marx himself made clear on repeated occasions. He understood commodities as goods or services that are destined to be objects of market or other contractual exchange. The products of capitalist firms are commodities. In the third volume of *Capital*, Marx (1981, p. 1019) clearly identified a 'characteristic trait' of the capitalist mode of production as follows:

> It produces its products as commodities. The fact that it produces commodities does not in itself distinguish it from other modes of production; but that the dominant and determining character of its product is the commodity certainly does so. This means, first of all, that . . . labour generally appears as wage-labour . . . [and] the relationship of capital to wage-labour determines the whole character of the mode of production.

The general relations that defined the capitalist system were used by Marx to validate the primary deployment of core concepts such as the commodity, exchange, money, capital, and labour power. For instance, the foremost use of the concept of the commodity was validated by the generality of the commodity-form under capitalism itself.

At least at first sight, such an approach seems eminently reasonable. If capitalism is a specific type of socio-economic system, with its own structural features and dynamics of development, then economics has to identify these specific features and dynamic processes. On the basis of their conceptualisation, a historically sensitive theory – with greater explanatory power than any theory based on universal and ahistorical presuppositions – could be constructed as a result.

The upshot of this methodological procedure is that Marxist economics is distinguished radically from classical, neoclassical and Austrian economics. Unlike the other approaches, Marxist economics is not based on ostensibly universal assumptions. Through this methodology, Marxism is connected with what could be regarded as the structural core of the mode of production that presently dominates our planet. Whatever the merits or flaws of Marx's analysis in *Capital*, no other theoretical system in social science has related itself so closely and directly to the general features of the capitalist socio-economic formation.

Marx's vision of history as a succession of different socio-economic systems was attenuated by his ideological commitment to a socialist future. Marx's strong political belief in the possibility and desirability of the revolutionary overthrow of the existing order, and in the construction of a quite different type of economy and polity, led him to focus analytically on what he thought were the distinctive features of the exploitative capitalist system. But whatever the impulse behind his thinking, his idea that history has been a succession of different socio-economic systems, each to some degree with its own structure and dynamic, can be separated from the ideological energy that fuelled its creation, and even from the contentious question of the feasibility of socialism itself. Even if socialism is unfeasible – or undesirable – Marx's dynamic and segmented vision of history remains. His formulation of the problem of historical specificity remains a major achievement. It does not logically depend on, or relate to, other propositions concerning the feasibility or desirability of socialism.

THE UNDER-THEORISATION OF GENERALITIES

However, despite this achievement, there are major theoretical difficulties with Marx's approach to this problem. While his historically confined procedure may support his key analytical concepts in the above manner, it does not validate its own meta-theoretical apparatus. For instance, in *Capital*, the particular focus on capitalism supports Marx's analytical starting point of commodities and exchange. However, other, more general, concepts also appear in his discourse. Broader concepts such as property rights, forces of production, the labour process and so on, cannot by validated by an appeal to a historically specific social system.

We cannot discuss a particular socio-economic system without making use of some, more general, concepts. Some use of transhistorical and ahistorical concepts is unavoidable. This is shown in Marx's own writing. The problem is that it is not admitted explicitly into his own methodology. Marx failed to theorise the unavoidable use of transhistorical and ahistorical concepts in his own work.

We shall use the term 'transhistorical' for any concept or theory that is held to apply to a multiplicity of different historical periods, or different types of social formation. The term 'ahistorical' applies to any concept or theory that is claimed to pertain to *all* possible socio-economic systems. Both concepts transcend any single social formation.

Close examination of *Capital* indicates that at crucial stages in his argument Marx himself had to fall back on transhistorical or ahistorical concepts. Hence, most obviously, the concept of capitalism itself had to invoke the ahistorical and general concept of the mode of production. But the problem goes further than that. For instance, in the very first chapter, Marx invoked the ahistorical concept of use-value in his discussion of commodities and exchange. It was recognised that particular use-values may be socially and historically conditioned. However, the very concept of use-value, unlike the concept of a commodity, was taken as a universal, common to all possible socio-economic systems. Hence Marx himself did not follow his own blanket methodological injunction cited earlier, seeing *all* economic 'categories as abstractions of actual social relations that are transitory and historical'. Indeed, to regard *all* economic categories as historically specific would be untenable, as there would be no taxonomic or meta-theoretical framework in which to situate the particular concepts of analysis.

Similar examples permeate Marx's analysis. For instance, the analysis of the production process in chapter seven of volume one relies on a crucial conceptual distinction. This is between, on the one hand, labour in general – that is the idea of labour as an activity that permeates all kinds of socio-economic system – and, on the other, the organisation and processes of production that are specific to capitalism. Likewise, the distinction between labour and labour power is conceptually quite general, although the specific phenomenon of the hiring of labour power by an employer is far from universal and is an archetypal feature of the capitalist mode of production. There are many other examples. Consider his twin concepts of forces and relations of production. These appear in Marx's general and transhistorical theory – outlined in his famous Preface to the *Contribution to the Critique of Political Economy* – that socio-economic change is promoted when the developing forces of production come up against and break down supposedly antiquated productive relations.

Indeed, the very generality and universality of the concept of labour in Marx's analysis helped him to sustain a supra-historical picture of labour as the life-blood of all socio-economic systems. As Marco Lippi (1979) perceptively observed, despite the claimed historical specificity of Marx's analysis of 'value' in *Capital* it rests essentially on an ahistorical and 'naturalistic' concept of labour. Similarly, Elias Khalil (1990b) showed that Marx's transhistorical concept of social labour amounts to asserting that the actions of agents can be *ex ante* calculated according to a global rationality. The assumption of global rationality is itself a reflection of the specific Western intellectual culture of the nineteenth century and notably and ironically is prominent in modern neoclassical economic theory as well.[4]

To repeat, Marx is not being criticised here for appealing to universal and ahistorical categories. On the contrary, such an invocation is unavoidable. Any study embracing the sweep of history must invoke such general categories. Any attempt to establish historically specific categories must itself rely on a transcendent imperative. There is no way of avoiding this. However, Marx gave insufficient methodological attention to this problem and provided only a limited discussion of the meta-theoretical issues involved. In one rare passage (1971, p. 214) Marx gave a brief admission of 'general abstract definitions, which therefore appertain in some measure to all social formations'. In another he wrote of the 'simple and abstract elements' of the 'labour process' as being 'common to all forms of society in which human beings live' (Marx, 1976, p. 290).

The problem is not that Marx uses transhistorical or ahistorical categories but that he gave no methodological guidance on their importance, or on the means of choosing or establishing them. Without such guidance, we might stumble instead on the abstract concepts – such as scarcity and utility – pertaining to neoclassical economic theory. Yet Marx criticised these alleged universals. Instead, Marx fell back on another set of questionable and ahistorical categories, without giving us sufficient reason for their use.

Logically, we cannot properly establish any particulars without prior universals. The establishment of particular categories requires a general taxonomy or map that can delimit the domain of the particular. Without this overall map we cannot define their zone of particular applicability. Furthermore, the language and methodology of particulars require a framework of universals. We cannot establish the particular concept of the 'capitalist social formation' without the

---

4   It is thus no accident that Marxist sympathisers have often defended models of socialism using neoclassical theoretical tools. See, for instance, Lange and Taylor (1938), Elster (1985) and Roemer (1988).

prior universal concept of 'social formation'. The methodology of particulars must spring from a universal meta-methodology. No significant attempt is made to elaborate this in Marx's writings.

What Marx required was a developed analysis that operated on at least two levels. One level would deal with the specificities of the capitalist system – this part of the analysis was relatively well developed in Marx's writing. What were less well developed were other, more general, levels of analysis. These would provide a framework within which the more general dynamics and evolution of the system could be considered.

In addition, the analysis would also be more able to address more adequately the transition from one social formation to another. Crucially Marxism lacks an adequate theory of transition. With its methodological and analytical weight on concepts that are specific to one system only, it has not got adequate conceptual materials to address the process of change from one system to another.

Notably, within the Marxist analysis of the development of given social formations – such as capitalism – the structural features of the system dominate the analysis. Although Marx recognised the reality of individual agency, he believed that people acted within the constraints provided by the system. Lacking an adequate theory of agency, the constraints did all the explanatory work. People act, but their scope for action is regarded as severely limited by the given system. The limits are seen to be so severe that the psychological and cultural springs of human action are downplayed in the analysis. Instead, the 'capitalist functions only as *personified* capital . . . just as the worker is no more than *labour* personified' (Marx, 1976, p. 989).

Marx's modern followers will deny that his analysis was deterministic and proclaim that human agency is real and in a sense primary. But this dismissal of one type of determinism brings in another through the back door. Human agency is made the prisoner of the socio-economic structure, so much so, that the walls of the cells determine the outcomes. The problem, then, is to explain how structures change. If the constraints do all the explanatory work, we are especially obliged to explain how constraints shift.

Marx proclaimed that: 'At a certain stage of development, the material productive forces of society come into conflict with the existing relations of production' (Marx, 1971, p. 21). He thus depicted a system about to perish because of its internal tensions or contradictions. But he did not tell us of the transition itself. When he came to discuss the transition from one social formation to another, voluntaristic and political human activity moved suddenly to the fore in the explanation. Social revolution became both the explanation and the outcome of the systemic 'contradictions'. Undetermined agents, who now rise above their circumstances and steer the course of history, fill the partial vacuum left by an inadequate analysis of systemic development. But alas, once their work is done, once the revolutionary transition is over, they again become constrained by the new structure. A general theory is required to explain this transformation in the nature and placement of human agency. As a result, an adequate theory of transition requires a transhistorical methodology and theory spanning different social formations.

THE NECESSITY OF IMPURITIES

There is a further problem in Marx's analysis that is relevant here. When analysing capitalism, Marx ignored all the non-capitalist elements in that system, although he clearly acknowledged their empirical existence. He did not ignore these elements as an initial, simplifying assumption. These non-capitalist elements were assumed away at the outset, never to be reincorporated at a later stage of the analysis. This was because Marx believed that the key features of capitalism – including commodity exchange and the hiring of labour power in a capitalist firm – would become increasingly widespread in reality, and would progressively displace all other forms of economic co-ordination and productive organisation.

For example, in the *Communist Manifesto*, Marx and Engels saw the family as 'a mere money relation' (Marx, 1973a, p. 70). If the family is genuinely 'a mere money relation' then it logically follows that we may analyse money and ignore families in our theory. The statement was clearly an exaggeration for rhetorical purposes, but it clothed a more serious analytical belief in the universal, corrosive power of markets and money. Although Marx acknowledged the existence of the family and mentioned it very briefly in *Capital* (Marx, 1976, pp. 471, 620–1), and – much more significantly – Engels published in 1884 a booklet entitled *The Origin of the Family, Private Property and the State*, both authors saw the family as evolving into a wholly commercial institution. They did not see its lingering, non-commercial features as essential for the survival of capitalism itself.

This exaggerated belief in a process of transformation of all social links into relations of commodity exchange enabled Marx and Engels to ignore important institutions such as the family in their analysis of capitalism. Their confidence in the all-consuming power of capitalist markets was the basis for ignoring impurities within the capitalist system. The family is an impurity because it does not work like a capitalist firm. Its *raison d'être* is not to produce products that are sold for profit. Indeed, families produce children but generally their sale is legally prohibited. Marx regarded all such non-capitalist impurities as doomed and extraneous hangovers of the feudal past, eventually to be pulverised by the ever-expanding market. For this reason the analysis of the family was excluded from *Capital*.[5]

The more general omission was a failure to acknowledge the functional role of structural diversity in socio-economic systems. This is a theoretical rather than an empirical point. Marx recognised the empirical existence of a diversity of modes of production but failed to appreciate its function. To repeat: this is not an argument about the *empirical* existence of impurities. Marx freely admitted that they exist. The argument here is that, contrary to Marx, it is not possible in principle for capitalism to rid itself of substantial impurities. Accordingly, the *theoretical* notion of a pure capitalist system is flawed, even at the most abstract

---

5 Feminists such as Hartman (1979) and Folbre (1982) have rightly objected to the efforts of Marxists to subsume households, patriarchy and gender within the general economic terms of the Marxian analysis of markets and capitalist firms.

theoretical level. This is because a capitalism that was pure and self-contained would be unable to function. A capitalism that moved in the direction of greater purity would be a capitalism that destroyed the very market mechanisms and commodities upon which it depended. There is no point in developing abstract models that in principle cannot ever work.

Many particular arguments support this general thesis. As many writers have subsequently argued, there are general limits to the extension of market and contractual relations within capitalism. For example, Joseph Schumpeter (1976, p. 139) argued persuasively in 1942 that such older institutions provide an essential symbiosis with capitalism, and are thus 'an essential element of the capitalist schema'. Schumpeter saw that capitalism depends on norms of loyalty and trust which are in part descended from a former epoch. The spread of market and contractarian relations can threaten to break up the cultural and other enduring bonds from the past that are necessary for the functioning of the system as a whole. In particular, as Schumpeter and others have emphasised, the state is partly responsible for the bonding of society and the prevention of its dissolution into atomistic units by the corroding action of market relations. Accordingly, Karl Polanyi (1944) showed that even in '*laissez-faire*' Victorian Britain the state was necessarily intimately involved in the formation and subsequent regulation of markets. All markets are themselves socially and culturally embedded. As a result, depending on the differences of social system into which they are embedded, there are many possible manifest forms of markets and exchange.

Once we admit the existence of necessary impurities then it becomes clear that no socio-economic system can be understood in its 'pure' form alone. The notion of a pure system is inadequate, even at the most abstract level of analysis. Systems must be understood in terms of their predominant structure along with necessary impurities. Once this is acknowledged, there is no difficulty accepting the idea that different capitalist systems can develop in different ways, especially in different local circumstances. This is because different combinations of impurities are always possible. Impurities are typically hangovers from a particular past. The evolution of a system depends on both its history and its context. Having established this, the possibility of systemic varieties (of, say, capitalism) and their path-dependent evolution, is admitted.

If we accept that a variety of possible subsystems can play the role of necessary impurity, then the particular subsystem involved will profoundly affect the nature of the specific variety of (capitalist) system. We are led to acknowledge that an immense variety of forms of any given socio-economic system could exist. In particular, an infinite variety of forms of capitalism are possible, depending in part on their unique historical baggage of impurities.

The diversity of socio-economic systems is spatial as well as local. Marxists have often promoted the view that history goes through a sequence of pre-ordained stages. One of the consequences of this misleading view is to neglect the coexistence and interaction of diverse types of economy at different points in time. Again, Marx recognised this diversity in the real world, but gave it little theoretical significance. He saw that Germany was a less developed capitalist system than Britain, so he chose to concentrate his analysis entirely on the latter. What was ignored was the interaction between different systems in the global economy. As a result, and contrary to Marx, Germany would not follow the same path of industrialisation as Britain because its global economic environment would be different at a similar level of development. In Marx's analysis this issue, and the related question of spatial location, were neglected.[6]

CONCLUDING REMARKS

There is also a question mark over Marx's exclusive emphasis on 'relations of production' and 'property relations' in classifying different types of socio-economic system. The question is whether differences in ideology or culture offer supplementary or alternative classificatory criteria. Is the use of different property relations necessary, sufficient or unnecessary to identify different systems? Subsequent discussion of the problem of historical specificity touched again and again on these problems, with some writers arguing that cultural factors were more important than legal property rights. We shall return to this question later.

Overall, Marx's achievement was enormous. He was a guiding inspiration for many others, including the historical school theorists themselves. When these theorists attempted different schemes of historical classification, their flaws were equivalent if not greater to those of Marxism. Despite the aforementioned problems, few subsequent efforts achieved as much as Marx. Marx's theory was an enduring high-water mark in the development of economics and social theory.

---

6   Giddens (1981) gave further reasons why the absence of spatial location and economic geography are weaknesses in Marx's historical materialism. Mann (1986) saw a crucial advantage of Weber over Marx in terms of the recognition in Weber of the geographical and spatial.

4

THE OLDER HISTORICAL SCHOOL
IN GERMANY

When one attempts to explain the features of something that is
the product of evolution, one must attempt to reconstruct the
evolutionary history of this feature.

(Ernst Mayr, 'How to Carry Out the Adaptationist
Program' (1983))

Karl Marx, Frederick Engels and the German historical school were products of
the same philosophical culture. The revolution in German philosophy was crucial
in the emergence of the historical school. Kant had argued that knowledge cannot
have content without reference to experience. Hegel, as noted in the preceding
chapter, had elaborated a whole schema of historical development. Furthermore,
Hegel had attacked the idea of the self-regulating market: he saw the state as
necessary for economic, social and political cohesion.[1]

However, ideas unaided cannot change history. Unless new ideas are
embodied in supportive institutions, they come to little. From 1789 to 1815,
Europe was in revolutionary turmoil. Napoleonic troops occupied Berlin and
much of Prussia from 1806 to 1808. At that time, the Prussian State aligned itself
towards institutional reform. In fact, the Napoleonic intervention greatly accelerated a process of German educational reform that had got under way in the
1780s. In 1807, in the midst of this ferment, Johann Fichte proposed a plan for

---

1 The German historical school was preceded by the so-called 'cameralist' and 'romantic' schools
(Pribram, 1983; Tribe, 1988). Menger (1985, p. 178) saw roots of the German historical school in
the late eighteenth century, particularly in the research by historians in the universities of
Göttingen and Tübingen. Pribram (1983) emphasised the influential role of German idealist
philosophy promoted by Fichte and Schelling as well as German jurists such as Savigny and
historians such as Ranke. Tribe (1988, pp. 205 ff.) argued that Roscher's work was in important
respects a continuation of earlier work by other authors in the 1830s. Krabbe (1996) and Reinert
and Daastøl (1997) explored a wider set of influences, notably including Enlightenment thinkers,
from France, Germany and elsewhere. These include the philosopher Herder and his historical
analysis of social cultures. In contrast, Pearson (1999) went so far as to question whether such an
identifiable 'German historical school' existed. But with the overly strict criteria that he used to
demarcate a 'school', it would be difficult to identify any single school of economics in the entire
history of the subject. Pearson, furthermore, overlooks the fact that the shared concern with the
problem of historical specificity was a common thread in the German historical school from the
beginning.

reorganising the universities. Instead of vocational training, they would offer a general scientific education, linked by an overarching, philosophical discourse (Collins, 1998, pp. 640–50).

Karl Wilhelm von Humboldt was appointed Prussian Minister of Education in 1809. Inspired by Fichte, in two years he enacted lasting educational reforms, at all levels of the education system (Sweet, 1980, pp. 53–71). He raised the standards of teacher training and certification. He founded the University of Berlin in 1810. Prussian universities were given some autonomy from the church and from the state. Significantly, Humboldt opposed a system of specialised professional education on the French *Ecole Polytechnique* model. Instead, the driving ethos would be the expansion of all forms of scientific knowledge. Instead of religion at the apex of learning, Humboldt placed philosophy.[2] All university students were required to understand the philosophical problems of truth and explanation. Each faculty of philosophy received full equality of status with the other faculties. These institutional changes were widely emulated by other German states. Within half a century of von Humboldt's reforms, the German universities would be the model for, and envy of, the world (Lenoir, 1998).

In the early nineteenth century there were about twenty academic chairs in German universities devoted exclusively to the study of national or political economy. The first of these chairs had been founded at the University of Halle in 1727 (Streissler, 1990, p. 154). Accordingly, by the time that the German historical school emerged, Germany had a very strong intellectual tradition in economics and economic methodology. By contrast, although economics was taught in some form in most British universities around 1850, there were far fewer chairs in political economy – yet Britain was the birthplace of Adam Smith and classical political economy (Kadish and Tribe, 1993).

FOUNDATION AND DURATION

In the century or so of its existence and prominence, the German historical school produced an enormous and diverse literature. The school appeared in a period of rapid economic, political and intellectual development. It witnessed the unification of Germany in 1870 and the elevation of the country into a world industrial power. The German historical school is often said to have been founded with the publication in 1843 of the *Grundriss* by Wilhelm Roscher. Widely read, this textbook was regarded as the historical school manifesto. It was reprinted no less than 26 times. In it Roscher claimed to lay out 'the historical method' of research. Roscher (1854, p. 42) saw political economy as 'the science of the laws

---

2 There is an important lesson here. As Mirowski (1994, p. 53) has perceptively observed: 'It is no accident that most of the major characters in the economist's hall of fame – from Adam Smith to Karl Marx, from Francis Edgeworth to Thorstein Veblen, from John Maynard Keynes to Nicholas Georgescu-Roegen – had their initial socialization in the precincts of philosophy, and not in economics.' He could also have added Alfred Marshall and Frank Knight, among several other 'greats' with training in philosophy.

of development of the economy and of economic life'. Hence political economy had a real object of analysis.

However, a clear and widely accepted method was not established. At the analytical level, what united this school was more a reaction against the individualist assumptions and deductivist methods of British classical political economy, and a concern to make economics sensitive to different social cultures and historical periods (Priddat, 1995). Other members of this school included (in chronological order by date of birth) Karl von Schütz, Bruno Hildebrand, Karl Knies, Albert Schäffle, Paul von Lilienfeld, Adolph Wagner, Gustav von Schmoller, Georg Knapp, Lujo Brentano, Karl Bücher and Werner Sombart. The historical school is generally divided into two subsets, the 'older historical school' beginning with Roscher and others in the 1840s and the 'younger historical school' with Schmoller in the 1880s.

It would perhaps be more appropriate, however, to date the inception of the school to 1841. This marks the date of the first edition of the influential classic *National System of Political Economy* by Friedrich List. His contemporaries did not regard List as a member of the historical school, largely because he was not a university academic and he lived much of his life outside Germany. However, his inclusion in the school is appropriate because he focused with acute vision on the contrasts between different types of national economic system (List, 1904). He brought attention to the historical and specific features of national economic development. Like many of the historical school proper, he was also a sophisticated critic of the classical theories of Adam Smith and David Ricardo and an opponent of *laissez-faire* economic policies. The German historical school was born of a period when German-speaking people were seeking national unity and identity, and a path of economic development that would be free from the British dominance of world manufacturing and trade.[3]

It is also important to include Max Weber in the historical school. Indeed, he himself wrote in 1904 that he was one of the 'offspring' of this school (Weber, 1949, p. 106). Others, such as Schumpeter (1954, pp. 815–16), identified him as a leading member. Weber worked closely with Sombart. Although Weber is today labelled as a 'sociologist' in fact he was a professor of political economy, from 1894 at the University of Freiburg. In 1896 he took over the chair of political economy previously occupied by his teacher Knies at the University of Heidelberg. In addition he published much material that is clearly of direct relevance to the study of socio-economic systems (Hennis, 1988; Swedberg, 1998). Weber himself (1949, p. 106; 1978, p. 3) was opposed to the creation of separate professorships of sociology in German universities.[4]

Overall, the era dominated by the German historical school can be taken as the hundred years from the publication of List's *National System* in 1841 to the

---

3   List committed suicide in 1864, for reasons of depression not unconnected with his exclusion from academic and political life in Germany.
4   Schumpeter (1954, pp. 815–16) ranked Weber among the most 'eminent' members of the historical school. However, Schumpeter (1954, p. 819) asserted that Weber 'was not really an economist at all'. But this is possible only because Schumpeter had a narrow definition of 'economic theory', explicitly consigning the 'analysis of economic institutions' to 'economic sociology'.

death of Sombart in 1941. The school was prefigured before, and it lingered on afterwards, but 1841–1941 encompasses its heyday. Few schools of economic thought have had such longevity and prominence, and, by comparison, such subsequent neglect. They raised and addressed some of the key conceptual and methodological problems of social science. Yet today modern economy theory is dominated globally and completely – even in Germany – by a highly formalised technical concerns. The recent heroes of modern, mainstream economics are predominantly American. The historical school has been largely forgotten.

In this work it is neither necessary nor possible to summarise the overall evolution and the varied doctrines of the historical school. Their various ethical and policy ideas, for instance, are important, but far beyond the scope of this book (Koslowski, 1995; Müssigang, 1968). Their political viewpoints ranged from socialism, through liberalism, to conservatism and fascism.

PERSISTENT THEMES

Some commentators have gone so far as to suggest that there is no guiding thread through the historical school literature (Pearson, 1999). Others have gone no further than recognising an eclectic list of common concerns. On the contrary, it is asserted here that there is at least one prominent, common theme. From Roscher and List, to Sombart and Weber, all leading members of the German historical school grappled with the problem of historical specificity. Explorations of this problem appeared prominently in the 1840s and persisted for more than a hundred years.

Clearly, however, the problem is tied up with other issues. In particular, early treatments of the problem are often linked with empiricist claims that mere historical data are the source of truth. Consider the statement of Roscher (1849, p. 182) who wrote: 'We do not hesitate to declare economic science a pure empirical science. For us history is not a means, but the object of our investigations.' Roscher continued:

> in our theory we refrain from the elaboration of ideals. Instead we try our hand at simple description, first of the nature and needs of a people, secondly of the laws and institutions of the latter, and finally of the greater or smaller success enjoyed through these laws and institutions. These are things firmly based on reality. They can be proved or refuted with the usual operations of science.
>
> (p. 186)

Here universal theories are rejected in favour of particular theories based on 'simple description' of specific phenomena. This type of blunt appeal to historical facts, as a basis for a historically confined economic theory, was typical of much subsequent writing by the older historicists. They believed that the theories and generalisations of the British classical economists were too sweeping and inaccurate. Instead, among the older historical school, there was a widespread empiricist faith in the possibility of pure description, as if the facts could speak for themselves (Hüter, 1928). However, this ignored the point that description is impossible without a prior conceptual framework and even elements of theory. A crude form of philosophical realism is manifest in these writings. This empiricist appeal to facts as a prior basis for theory, was rightly described by Carl Menger (1985, p. 60) in 1883 as 'empirical realism'. However, despite the naïveté of Roscher's view, he did at least recognise a need for economics to address specific economic institutions, rather than solely to base itself on universal axioms. The problem was that their insistence that theory had to be built on accumulated facts distracted generations of historicists from building an adequate theoretical framework.[5]

Accordingly, Knies (1853, p. 333) insisted that economic theory must be 'based on the facts of historical life'. Hildebrand (1863, p. 145) also wrote on a very similar theme: 'The history of economic culture in connection with the history of all political and juridical development of nations and statistics is the only sure basis on which a successful development of economic science seems possible.' However, there were differences of view between Roscher and Hildebrand. Roscher believed that it was possible by induction to establish general regularities and laws. He also emphasised comparative methods as means of theoretical discovery. Roscher attempted to root economic laws of development in the study of the phenomena of life of a nation. His legacy on this question, however, is incomplete and fragmentary. In contrast, Hildebrand did not believe that principles or laws could be established in the way suggested by Roscher, and emphasised instead a neo-Hegelian, and teleological, stages theory of history. Disputes over the possibility or nature of economic principles or laws dogged the German historical school from its inception.

Another point of difference between Roscher and Hildebrand was over the periodisation of history (Priddat, 1995). Roscher failed to establish a clear principle for distinguishing different socio-economic systems. On the other hand, he placed supreme emphasis on changes in the institutions of money and credit. He thus distinguished between 'natural economies', 'monetary economies' and 'credit economies'. This typology was not to become the most popular. True to their roots in German idealist philosophy and their concept of society as an organism, several German historicists were to periodise history, largely in terms of the reigning *Geist* or spirit of each age. However, although descriptions of historical stages frequently appeared in the texts, little clarity was achieved on the underlying methodology of periodisation or the processes of change involved.

A characteristic historicist theme also appeared and persisted in those early years. It concerned the historical relativity of theory itself. For example, Knies (1853, p. 19) wrote:

---

5   The words 'historicism' and 'historicist' are used to refer here to the doctrines of the historical school. However, possible confusion exists. Popper (1960) used the word 'historicism' to describe the belief in historical predictability that he famously and rightly criticised. Althusser (1969) used the word in yet another sense, to describe Hegelian versions of Marxism. Despite these different usages, I have resisted the temptation to follow Coats (1992), Koslowski (1995) and others to use the words 'historism' and 'historist' instead, on the grounds that the older terms are already widely established in the Anglophone literature.

> In contrast to the absolutism of theory, the historical conception of political economy is based on the following principle. The theory of political economy is also a result of historical development just as the economic conditions of life are.

Knies and others thus recognised that economic theory is also a product of the socio-economic system, and hence itself is bound to change. The economic theory that was appropriate for one epoch would not necessarily be suited for another. This argument required both a typology of socio-economic systems or stages, and a sketch of the type of economic theory that was appropriate for each. At the outset, List, Roscher, Knies, Hildebrand and others attempted to outline those stages through which each economy must develop. However, no single set of definitions prevailed.[6]

On the question of the relativity of theory, List and others argued that Smithian economic principles were appropriate for a relatively developed and dominant socio-economic system, such as the British, but less so for an emerging nation such as Germany at an earlier stage of industrial and political development. This was a plausible argument, but, like Marx, the members of the historical school failed to acknowledge fully that statements concerning the relativity of theory must themselves rest on more enduring and transhistorical meta-theoretical principles. As with Marx, such meta-theoretical principles were barely explored. In the absence of such a meta-theory, the historicists made do with ideas of historical cycles or stages that were themselves ungrounded in terms of their own methodology.

The German historical school failed to resolve, or even reach a consensus on, these meta-theoretical issues. Nevertheless, there were some common conceptual themes. The emphasis was on socio-economic phenomena at the level of the national economy. List had criticised Smith for neglecting the importance of both non-material and non-exchangeable factors in enhancing the productive potential of a nation. In contrast to Smith, List put much greater emphasis on the importance of mental and educational labour. Intellectual labour was not 'unproductive' but given a central place in the analysis. List contended that considerations of productive potential and – in modern parlance – dynamic efficiency could not be reduced solely to current costs and prices. He argued that the productive powers of a nation are greater than the sum of the productive powers of the individuals within it, considered in isolation, because of the productive benefits provided by the national infrastructure and culture. List's emphasis on learning and the learning environment meant that it was not possible, as in neoclassical economics, to take the individual as given, as a starting point of analysis. Learning is more than the discovery or reception of information: it is the reconstitution of individual capacities and preferences, tantamount to a change in individual personality. List understood that learning *reconstitutes*

6　For discussions of these and other stages theories, especially in German thought and its forerunners, see Ely (1903), Kalveram (1933) and Reinert (2000).

the individual, typically within the context of a national culture and set of institutions.[7]

Although the historical school did not acknowledge List as a member, they repeated very similar points. The national system was widely regarded as having a specific character, and was seen to influence all the elements within it. As Knies (1853, p. 248) put it: 'the economic phenomena of national life are historically inseparably bound to the collective existence of nations.' Individuals and organisations within the national unit were seen by the historical school as affected profoundly by the national culture, making an isolated analysis of each component part impossible. Hence some of the members of the historical school suggested in their writings an organicist ontology, where relations between entities are internal rather than external, and hence the essential characteristics of any element are outcomes of relations with other entities. They thus denied that individuals may be treated as elemental or immutable building blocks of economic analysis.[8]

One reason why the individual was disregarded as the exclusive starting point was, at least for Knies (1853), the existence of 'free will'. For him, 'free will' ruled out the possibility of fixed laws of human behaviour. This made it difficult to build up a composite picture, in a process of aggregation, by starting from the individual. Instead, the analytic locus was the system as a whole. Accordingly, the concept of the 'national economy' did not rule out individuals, nor their choice and creativity. Indeed, it provided individuals with the means and context by which they could communicate and act.[9]

The problem in the approach of the older historical school was not a denial of individuality or free will, but a failure to articulate fully the relationship between actor and structure. We find foreshadowings of the modern conception of the actor–structure problem, but the analyses are not developed sufficiently and satisfactorily for modern eyes. Significantly, although some historical school work contained the possibility of a structural or cultural determinism, this was because of an incomplete account of the actor–structure relationship, rather than a denial of individuality itself. Thus Knies (1853, p. 109) discussed the 'enclosure' or 'unification' of individuality, rather than its rejection or submergence:

a nation is something other than an accidental aggregate of individuals. Its historical existence includes various living spheres through which the

---

7 Despite a century of neoclassical supremacy in economics, this issue remains with us. Vickers (1995, p. 115) rightly identified this as a key 'difficulty that economic analysis has been reluctant to confront'. He stressed that with changing knowledge and learning 'the individual is himself, economically as well as epistemologically, a different individual'.

8 List and the historical school should thus be recognised as the origin of the modern concept of 'national systems of innovation' (Lundvall, 1992; Nelson, 1993; Edquist, 1997). Freeman (1995) and Elam (1997) rightly highlight the crucial influence of List in this respect.

9 Against the view of Knies and others, Menger in his *Principles* (1981) saw the existence or non-existence of 'free will' as irrelevant to the question of the existence of laws of human behaviour. However, Yagi (1997, p. 240) argued convincingly that 'we cannot avoid the problem of free will in the construction of his economic theory.'

same spirit is blowing, enclosing all individuality in a unifying frame, through which the whole develops into a coherent movement.

Like many other historicists, Knies saw the coherence of society as a result of the breath of 'the same spirit'. The concept of *Geist* or spirit carried a heavy analytical burden throughout the historical school. It is discussed further in later chapters.

SOCIETY AS AN ORGANISM

Some members of the historical school went so far as to compare the national economy with a biological organism. Michael Hutter (1993, 1994) has shown that the German roots of such a metaphor go back to the eighteenth century and much earlier.[10] It fitted well with Hegelian ideas of the social organism and spirit. From the 1830s, the influential French philosopher Auguste Comte had also promoted the idea. In the historical school, the analogy of the social system as an organism was particularly evident in the works of writers such as Knies (1853), Roscher (1854), Lilienfeld (1873–81) and especially Schäffle (1881). Biological thinking in the social sciences was given an additional impetus in Germany after the translation of Herbert Spencer's *Study of Sociology* into German in 1875. Leading German historicists such as Schmoller were influenced by Spencer's ideas. Darwin's writings also became popular in some German intellectual circles at about that time.

The organism analogy took a number of forms and linked up with a variety of different propositions. Among these were the idea of an organicist ontology, the recognition of social influences on individuals, proclamations of the systemic interdependence of the whole socio-economic system, and proposals of a 'stages' theory of history, compared explicitly with the growth of an organism.

The organism analogy was also associated with the proposition that the socio-economic system could be analysed as if it had a singular will and mind of its own: surmounting those of the individuals comprising it, just as the brain and nervous system of an organism transcend its individual organs and cells. Others saw the dangers in this argument, taking a more sophisticated position where the social organism had some kind of causal power, but by virtue of its capacity to frame and mould individual opportunities and dispositions.[11]

---

10 The idea of society as an organism is found in the Bible and in the writings of Plato and Aristotle. Aristotelian philosophy was particularly influential in Germany in the nineteenth century. The history of the social organism idea is also discussed in Commons (1934a, pp. 25, 43, 99, 119, 733), Merchant (1983, ch. 4) and Khalil and Boulding (1996, p. 182).

11 Notably, while Lilienfeld (1873–81) had argued that society is *actually* an organism, Schäffle (1875–81) differed, seeing the organism analogy as appropriate but not literal. For Schäffle, society was not an organism in a biological or physiological sense, but its symbolic and technological unity gave it organism-like qualities. On this basis Schäffle applied quasi-Darwinian principles to the socio-economic system, and, like others, saw collectives rather than individuals as the units of selection. Schäffle's important and now-neglected 1881 book was praised as 'brilliant' by Weber (1978, p. 18).

Whatever the flaws in such arguments, they hinted at a conceptual and empirical method of treating economic systems: by focusing on behaviour at the aggregate level. Insofar as other social scientists were disposed to treat the individual as a unit of analysis, the idea of society as a single organism countered this individualism by focusing attention on the systemic properties of the socio-economic whole instead. Accordingly, the German historical school economists made the study of *Nationalökonomie* (national economy) a prominent feature of the discipline, long before the emergence of macroeconomics proper in the Anglo-American world. This idea of treating the economy as an organism persisted through the historical school, and provided an important theme of debate concerning the method of economic enquiry for more than one hundred years.[12]

The notion that the economy was like an organism was, for the historical school, much more than verbal play with biological metaphors. It was a device that addressed the problem of moving analytically from the individual to the whole. Unlike the Austrian school of Menger and his followers, and the mainstream economists of the late twentieth century, the historicists did not believe that it was possible, or analytically appropriate, to explain the whole entirely in terms of individual parts, in the manner of methodological individualism. Their analytical device was instead to treat the whole economy as if it was like an individual, thereby capturing the notion of the dependence of the individual upon the whole. However, this device required refinement and could be taken too far. In some unsatisfactory versions, the individual was dissolved into the organism, and played no analytical role once the organism was in place. The historical school sometimes inverted methodological individualism by proposing a version of methodological collectivism, where individuals are explained entirely in terms of the socio-economic system. In both methodological collectivism and methodological individualism, the viability of multiple levels of analysis is undermined. This key methodological problem, of the relationship between the individual and society, dogged the historical school for its entire existence, and was never satisfactorily resolved.

---

12 Above others, Spencer (1851, 1862) promoted the idea of the socio-economic system as an organism in the English-speaking world. Spencer influenced the following economists, all of whom deployed Spencerian organic metaphors: Hearn (1863) in Australia; J. B. Clark (1885) in America; Bagehot (1869), Mummery and Hobson (1889), and Marshall (1890) in Britain.

5

THE HISTORICAL SCHOOL
IN THE BRITISH ISLES

Bold knaves thrive without one grain of sense,
But good men starve for want of impudence.
(John Dryden, *Constantine the Great* (1684))

Gradually, the ideas of the German historical school made their way into the world beyond. In France, P. G. Frédéric Le Play pioneered historical studies of family structures, social geography and economic development. Historicists in other countries included Emile de Laveleye in Belgium and Achille Loria in Italy. But it was in the British Isles that historicist ideas were to have a more significant impact.

The Reverend Richard Jones has been described as a precursor of the British historical school. In 1833 he was appointed Professor of Political Economy at the newly established King's College in London. In 1835, following the death of Malthus, he succeeded him as the Professor of Political Economy at the East India College at Haileybury, near Hertford. He remained there until his death. Jones criticised the Ricardian theory of rent and the deductivist methods of the Ricardian school, and placed greater emphasis on inductive methods in political economy. He criticised Ricardian theory as ahistorical. It neglected the importance of the stages of economic development in the determination of the forms of rent and the organisation of production. Jones thus promoted a comparative and historical approach to economic analysis. However, his ideas had little impact at the time.[1]

Greater impetus was given to the formation of a British historical school by other events. These circumstances led to the formation of a small group of followers of the German historical school in the British Isles. Just as the German historical school and Marxism were influenced by political and economic developments in Germany, the British group was influenced not merely by intellectual discourse but by incidents in the real world. This group was largely Irish in origin. From the perspective of being simultaneously inside and outside

---

1 Nevertheless, Marx (1972) in his *Theories of Surplus Value* recognised the value and importance of Jones's contribution.

its institutions, they criticised the powers and policies of England and brought new ideas to its theatre.[2]

THE IRISH HISTORICAL SCHOOL

A catastrophic famine ravaged Ireland from 1845–9. Successive potato crops failed and the Irish people lost their principal source of food. About one million died from hunger and disease. Another million emigrated to Britain or North America. The Irish economy suffered a devastation from which it did not recover until well into the twentieth century. Ireland became a land of ingrained impoverishment and desperation. In 1841 the population of Ireland was well over 8 million. 50 years later it was less than 5 million.

For many leading advisors, the remedy to such a disaster was to be found in the policies of *laissez-faire* and free trade, established on the basis of the allegedly natural and immutable principles of political economy (Boylan and Foley, 1992). Since 1801, Ireland had been part of the United Kingdom. At the outset of the Irish famine, free trade and private property were declared in the Westminster House of Lords by Lord Brougham to be a 'sacred right' (Woodham-Smith, 1962, p. 72). As the famine continued, Robert Lowe – eventually to become Chancellor of the Exchequer under Prime Minister Gladstone – urged the Parliament in London to oppose Irish land reform 'with the principles of political economy'.

According to these supposed principles, food aid should be limited because such public aid would crowd out the 'natural' and healthy response of the market system to the shortages. The provision of food would decrease the work incentives of the poor, lower the price of food, and diminish the incentives to produce more. The Irish system of land tenure, it was alleged, was the result of free contract between landlord and tenant. Hence the legislative proposals for land reform had to be resisted. If Irish tenant farmers had voluntarily and extra-contractually made improvements to the land that they rented, then they had no legal claim for compensation for such improvements. In the name of economics, it seemed, the Irish had to starve.

---

2 The terms 'England', 'Britain' and 'British Isles' are frequently confused, yet in fact they each refer to very different political and geographical entities. Accordingly, there is no good excuse for the persistent use of inappropriate descriptive terms such as the 'English historical school' (e.g. Koot, 1987; Moore, 1995, 1996). It is tragic that the more widespread ignorance of the history of ideas among social scientists is paralleled by an ignorance of political geography among some historians of ideas. Neither Dublin nor Belfast is in England. Nor have they ever been in Britain, yet they are both situated in the British Isles. The fact that much of the debate over political economy did occur in London in England is not a sufficient riposte, in view of the Irish origins of many of the most important protagonists. During the nineteenth century, Ireland as a whole was governed from London, but this did not make Ireland part of England. Nor has the Westminster Parliament, at least since the Tudor conquest of Wales, ever been appropriately described as the 'English Parliament'. Nevertheless, for reasons of parochialism, nationalism or ignorance such descriptions are all too common. Yet we cannot deal with the cultural and political nonconformity of the Celtic fringes either by ignoring them or by conjuring up some mythically harmonious and comforting unionism. Scholars should give no solace to such error and insularity.

The Irish historical school, led by John K. Ingram and T. E. Cliffe Leslie, reacted against these prominent theoretical and policy pronouncements.[3] They attacked the idea of natural or universal laws of economic science (Koot, 1975). They argued that the Irish famine had been exacerbated by the mistaken policy of free trade, and that this policy was based on the unfitting principles of classical economics. They argued that the laws of economics were not universal: any principles pertaining a developed market economy did not necessarily apply to Irish institutions and culture.

Ireland was thus the principal birthplace of historicism in the British Isles. From Ireland it spread to England, as several of its leaders took up academic appointments in London and elsewhere.[4] Some of its ideas found the support of John Stuart Mill, who himself endorsed what eventually became the Irish Land Act of 1870. As early as 1843, Mill had written that:

> in Political Economy . . . empirical laws of human nature are tacitly assumed by English thinkers, which are calculated only for Great Britain and the United States. . . . Yet those who know the habits of the Continent of Europe are aware how apparently small a motive outweighs the desire for money-getting, even in the operations which have money-getting as their object.
>
> (Mill, 1843, p. 903)

Accordingly, Mill hinted that some of the assumptions and laws of political economy have a historically specific application, to the commercial world of Anglo-American capitalism only. On this point, his position converged with that of the emerging British historical school.[5]

There are further parallels. Both Mill and Ingram were devotees of the increasingly popular positivism of Auguste Comte (Ingram, 1901; Moore, 1999). In the 1830s, Comte developed positivism as a version of empiricism in which observation and experiment were held to be the means of obtaining and testing knowledge. Comtean positivism involved an emphasis on prediction and a rejection of unobservable entities as 'metaphysical'. Science progressed via 'reasoning and observation, duly combined'. Comte saw the study of history as

---

3 Ingram was an Irish nationalist who penned the words of a popular rebel song in his youth. Note the warning in the previous footnote.

4 Partly because of the enormous influence of Adam Smith and others, Scotland already had a distinctive tradition of political economy, quite different from that prevailing in England (A. Dow et al., 1998). The Scottish tradition pre-dated the historical school and emphasised political economy as an aspect of philosophy. Economics or political economy was not established as a separate university subject in Scotland until well into the twentieth century. This strong pre-existing tradition meant that German historicism had a diminished influence in Scotland.

5 In his 1870 discussion of Leslie's ideas on the land question, Mill took an intermediate position, accepting that political economy did contain universal principles, but that these should not serve as mere 'catch-words' but should be accompanied by empirical investigations into the circumstances that may modify their application (Mill, 1967). Nevertheless, strong axiomatic and deductivist elements remained in Mill's economics, to be developed by his Irish student, Cairnes.

a source of facts, by means of which could be discovered 'historical laws'. Comtean ideas were highly influential, especially from the 1840s to the 1860s.

However, Ingram's enthusiasm for Comte exceeded that of Mill. Ingram rejected abstract economics in favour of an inductive and historical approach, in which the dismal science was subsumed within sociology (Moore, 1995, 1999). Ingram crusaded for Comtean principles in his widely debated presidential address of 1878 to the British Association for the Advancement of Science. Following the older German historical school, Ingram (1878, 1915) claimed that the development of a historically specific economics depended upon an empiricist appeal to the facts. However, after 1870, the Comtean movement began to fall out of favour in Britain. Mill then distanced himself from it. In these circumstances, Ingram's continuing allegiance to Comte's ideas became a growing burden rather than an asset (Koot, 1987; Moore, 1999).

Ingram protested against the individualistic character of much of economics. He wrote in 1888:

> The radical vice of this unscientific character of political economy seems to lie in the too individual and subjective aspect under which it has been treated. Wealth having been conceived as what satisfies desires, the definitely determinable qualities possessed by some objects of supplying physical energy, and improving the physiological constitution are left out of account. Everything is gauged by the standard of subjective notions and desires. All desires are viewed as equally legitimate, and all that satisfies our desires as equally wealth. . . . The truth is, that at the bottom of all economic investigation must lie the idea of the destination of wealth for the maintenance and evolution of a society. And if we overlook this, our economics will become a play of logic or a manual for the market, rather than a contribution to social science; whilst wearing an air of completeness, they will be in truth one-sided and superficial. Economic science is something far larger than the Catallactics [science of exchange] to which some have wished to reduce it.
>
> (Ingram, 1915, p. 295)

Ingram put his finger on a problem at the core of economics that was to remain central in disputes about the character and orientation of the science for another century. In their efforts to deal with the economic problems of Ireland, Leslie and Ingram brought some of the ideas of the German historical school into the English-speaking world:

> At least in the English-speaking world, Ireland was the first country where the universality of the laws of political economy was systematically challenged. Leslie and Ingram were the pioneers of historical economics in the English-speaking world, and the almost inextricable problems of Ireland and land were at its very source.
>
> (Boylan and Foley, 1992, p. 139)

THE CONTRIBUTION OF CLIFFE LESLIE

Of the two leading Irish historicists, Leslie made the more significant theoretical contribution. It was Leslie above all who laid the foundations of British historical economics. In a passage originally published in 1870, he reaffirmed the idea of Karl Knies and others that political economy was itself an object of change, and the development of this science would reflect its own intellectual and cultural environment:

> political economy is not a body of natural laws in the true sense, or of universal and immutable truths, but an assemblage of speculations and doctrines which are the result of particular history, coloured even by the history and character of its chief writers; that, so far from being of no country, and unchangeable from age to age, it has varied much in different ages and countries, and even with different expositors in the same age and country.
>
> (Leslie, 1888, p. 21)

However, having made this general and forceful point, the Irish historicists failed to elaborate the precise variation of economic laws and principles that had to be taken into account. They did not explain in sufficient detail that which remained general or that which was specific. Their intuition was that historically sensitive principles would arise as the result of empirical or investigative research. But ultimately this was not a strong point of defence.

When they argued that the Irish were not accustomed to monetary commerce or wage labour, and had little notion of the rights of absolute private property, then they laid themselves open to a number of powerful counter-arguments. Their opponents retorted that these 'natural' and 'everlasting' arrangements, once established, would teach the Irish that they too had to conform to universal economic laws.

A response more sympathetic to the Irish, but still critical of the historical school, would be that Irish problems derived essentially from inequalities of wealth, power and land tenure; or from potato monoculture, limited resources or overpopulation. These were real problems that had to be addressed. It was not demonstrated that the resolution of these problems required a revolt against the 'immutable' and 'scientific laws' of political economy.

The British historical school did not have adequate responses to such arguments. The Irish Famine had brought their school into being, but it did not provide them with doctrinal victory. When bruised by argument, they reached out for the salve of empirical investigation. In 1875 Leslie surveyed the schism that then divided economic theory:

> Two different conceptions of Political Economy now divide economists throughout Europe; of which, looking to their origin, one may be called English, the other German, though neither meets with universal acceptance in either England or Germany. English writers in general

have treated Political Economy as a body of universal truths or natural laws; or at least as a science whose fundamental principles are all fully ascertained and indisputable, and which has nearly reached perfection. The view, on the other hand, now almost unanimously received at the universities, and gaining ground among practical politicians, in Germany, is that it is a branch of philosophy which has received various forms in different times and places from antecedent and surrounding conditions of thought, and is still at a stage of very imperfect development. Each of these conceptions has its appropriate method; the first proceeding by deduction from certain postulates or assumptions, the second by investigation of the actual course of history, or the historical method. In England it is usual to speak of induction as the method opposed to *a priori* deduction, but the inductive and historical methods are identical.

(ibid., p. 83)

Leslie repeatedly characterised the methodological character of the dispute as being between the methods of induction and deduction, each claiming itself as the means to obtain truth. The historical and inductive method, Leslie argued, was based on facts, and was superior for that reason. Logical deduction had a legitimate place in science, but its prior assumptions required an empirical basis. In 1876 Leslie wrote of 'the *a priori* and deductive method' in the following terms:

The economist 'starts,' according to it, with the assumption of a 'knowledge of ultimate causes,' and deduces the phenomena from the causes so assumed. What has still to be done is to investigate the actual phenomena, and to discover their ultimate causes in the laws of social evolution and national history. The bane of political economy has been the haste of its students to possess themselves of a complete and symmetrical system, solving all the problems before it with mathematical certainty and exactness. The very attempt shows an entire misconception of the nature of those problems, and of the means available for their solution.

(ibid., pp. 188–9)

In a few, prescient passages, Leslie gave a glimpse of the theoretical and methodological issues that had to be raised, in addition to mere questions of empirical enquiry. Leslie went further than the naïve empiricists, to question particular assumptions adopted by those disposed towards the deductive method. Writing in 1879, Leslie (1888, p. 81) understood that 'complexity, incessant change, speculation, and potent influence of chance' undermined the deductive ambitions and neat theories of many economists. He wrote again in the same year, arguing that variety, disruption and uncertainty were themselves a product of an acquisitive market economy:

The desire for wealth, or of its representative – money – instead of enabling the economist to foretell values and prices, destroys the power of prediction that formerly existed, because it is the mainspring of industrial and commercial activity and progress, of infinite variety and incessant alteration in the structure and operations of the economic world.

(ibid., p. 223)

Leslie continued the same vein, arguing that in this turbulent and uncertain world, firms cluster together in a given locality, the reason being 'largely the result of want of information' (p. 234). He thus foreshadowed Marshallian and later theories of industrial clustering, based on locally shared access to knowledge in an overall climate of uncertainty. He saw further, that in this uncertain context, competition does not necessary lead to efficient outcomes:

> Instead of the world of light, order, equality, and perfect organisation, which orthodox political economy postulates, the commercial world is thus one of obscurity, confusion, haphazard, in which, amid much destruction and waste, there is by no means always a survival of the fittest, even though cunning be counted among the conditions of fitness.
>
> (ibid., p. 235)

Above all, Leslie was one of the first economists to emphasise the significance of complexity and uncertainty in economic life, and to recognise the limits it places on economic theorising. Against some theorists who desired to take individual preferences as given, Leslie (1888, p. 72) wrote in 1879 that 'human wants . . . vary under different surrounding conditions and in different states of society.' It was thus in his view theoretically unjustified to take human wants or preferences as immutable. Three years earlier he had observed that:

> The desire of wealth is a general name for a great variety of wants, desires, and sentiments, widely differing in their economical character and effect, undergoing fundamental changes in some respects, while preserving an historical continuity in others. . . . the love of property, or of accumulation, takes very different concrete forms in different states of society. . . . The abstract theory on this subject [of wealth] is of the most fragmentary character. It exists only in the form of a few propositions and doctrines. . . . No such theory . . . respecting the effect of consumption on either the nature or the amount of wealth, can be forthcoming without a study of the history and the entire structure of society, and the laws which they disclose. . . . [The] abstract *a priori* and deductive method yields no explanation of the causes which regulate either the nature or the amount of wealth.
>
> (ibid., pp. 167–74)

Leslie thus developed a theme that had already emerged in the German historical school and was later to become pivotal for American institutional economics. He argued that individuals should not be regarded as social atoms with given preference functions, but as intelligent yet malleable human beings, partly moulded by a specific social culture. His argument was elaborated further in 1879:

> The very wants and aims summed up in 'the desire for wealth' arise not from innate, original, and universal propensities of the individual man, but from the community and its history. . . . Political economy is thus a department of the science of society which selects a special class of social phenomena for special investigation, but for this purpose must investigate all the forces and laws by which they are governed. The deductive economist misconceives altogether the method of isolation permissible in philosophy. In consequence of the limitation of human faculties, not that the narrowing of the field is in itself desirable or scientific, it is legitimate to make economic phenomena, the division of labour, the nature, amount, and distribution of national riches, the subject of particular examination, provided that all the causes affecting them be taken into account. To isolate a single force, even if a real force and not a mere abstraction, and to call deductions from it alone the laws of wealth, can lead only to error, and is radically unscientific.
>
> (ibid., p. 212)

Hence, prior to the opening shots of the *Methodenstreit* in 1883, the historical school had one of its ablest exponents in the British Isles. However, the progress of this school was struck by two tragedies. In 1872 in France, Leslie lost the manuscript of his magnum opus on economic and legal history. Ten years later he died, at a relatively young age. As we shall see later, this was not the first untimely death to affect the historicist movement in economics.

Tragedy was compounded with failure. Despite the efforts of its abler followers, the British historical school was unable to develop an adequate methodological foundation for a historically-oriented economics. They charged against deductivism, with weak and ineffective empiricist armour.

MIGRATION TO ENGLAND

Although Irish by birth, Ingram and Leslie resided for much of their lives in London. For this and other reasons, historicist ideas spread to England, especially in the last two decades of the nineteenth century, and particularly to economic historians. James E. Thorold Rogers – sometime Member of Parliament, and professor at both London and Oxford – had affinities with the historical school (Kadish, 1989, ch. 1). Of greater impact were William Cunningham and Herbert Foxwell of the University of Cambridge. Cunningham and Foxwell emphasised elements of historical school thinking in one of the two ancient English universities, and defended an emphasis on facts against those who had an 'exaggerated estimate of the importance of theory' (Foxwell, 1887, p. 101). But they too were to lose out in the struggles to come.[6]

---

6   Cunningham was not born in England but in Edinburgh. See footnote 2 above.

The historical school in the British Isles came under early methodological attack in the 1870s. One of its foremost and most powerful early critics was Walter Bagehot, sometime editor of *The Economist*. Bagehot (1880) exposed some of the empiricist weaknesses of the historical school. He defended a role for abstract and deductive economic theory (Zouboulakis, 1999). However, Bagehot's defence had interesting features that differentiate him from most deductivist economists of the twentieth century. One of them was ably summarised by his assistant Sir Robert Giffen, shortly after Bagehot's early death:

> What Bagehot has done is not merely, like other writers, to point out the abstract character of the science, but to prove as against the Historical School that there is an age and society – the whole business world of England at the present time, and a large part of other communities – in which the assumptions of English Political Economy are approximately true in the concrete as well as in the abstract.
>
> (Giffen, 1880, p. 559)

A key feature of this defence of the abstract assumptions of classical economics is that it acknowledges the problem of historical specificity. Following Mill (1843, p. 906), Bagehot argued that with the triumph of the institutions of English capitalism in the nineteenth century, the abstract assumptions of classical political economy had found their representation in fact. For Bagehot, the principles of political economy did not have universal validity, but they had become manifest in the English commercial economy of the nineteenth century. For this reason they could be taken as valid.

In this respect the Mill–Bagehot approach foreshadows that of Alfred Marshall, Max Weber, Werner Sombart and Frank Knight, who are all discussed later in this book. All these authors endorsed key arguments of the historical school concerning the problem of historical specificity. However, their common additional argument was that the use of some of the abstract, price-oriented principles of (classical or neoclassical) economics could be justified in the particular case of the modern commercial system, precisely because there was some real correspondence between those assumptions and that particular economic reality. Mill, Bagehot, Marshall, Weber, Sombart and Knight all saw the economic analysis of prices and markets as valid in a historically specific period only. These principles of market analysis were not regarded as universally valid, but of sufficient explanatory power to fit the modern capitalist world. For Weber in particular, the development of the money economy of modern capitalism meant the triumph of calculative rationality. Accordingly, these authors argued that price-oriented economics fitted the competitive market economy, but not necessarily any other type of system.

But many members of the historical school still felt uneasy with those classical or neoclassical assumptions, even in the context of the capitalist or market system. Others noted that the Mill–Bagehot argument conceded a significant part of the historical school case. For example, Leslie (1888, p. 179) wrote in 1876:

Recent apologists for the *a priori* and abstract method of economic reasoning feel themselves constrained to confine its application to the most advanced stage of commercial society; they seem even prepared to concede its inapplicability to every country save England, and to confine it to the latest development of English economy. . . . In modern England, they say, there is such a commercial pursuit of gain, and such a consequent choice of occupations, as to effect a distribution of the produce of industry to which the doctrines of Ricardo respecting wages, profits, prices, and rents may be fairly applied. They thus abandon at once the claim formerly made on behalf of political economy to the character of a universal science founded on invariable laws of nature.

Leslie then referred to Bagehot as an adherent of the view he criticised. Here Leslie did not criticise the idea that the classical doctrines could be used to analyse the modern commercial system. The crucial point is in Leslie's final sentence above. In linking the classical economic propositions to English capitalism alone, Bagehot and others had abandoned any claim to their universality.

What is remarkable, therefore, is the degree to which most of the major protagonists in the nineteenth-century debates on economic method accepted that some economic principles were appropriately confined to historically specific phenomena. This was true for Mill, Bagehot and Marshall, as well as for Leslie, Ingram and Marx. Where they differed more markedly was in their contrasting views on induction and deduction in economic theory. In making excessive claims for the inductive method, leading members of the historical school were at their weakest. On the other hand, deductivism threatened to lead economic theory into remote formalism. Eventually, much later, this unrepaired breach was to prove deadly, not only for the historical school, but also for the survival of serious analysis of the problem of historical specificity.

6

THE METHODOLOGICAL FAILURE
OF THE OLDER HISTORICAL
SCHOOL

Science is built up of facts, as a house is built of stones; but an accumulation of facts is no more a science than a heap of stones is a house.

(Henri Poincaré, *Science and Hypothesis* (1905))

Despite their achievements, the arguments of the pre-1883 historical school – in Germany, Britain and elsewhere – were fatally flawed in methodological terms. Part of the problem was their belief that theory could build on mere data, and that facts could be ascertained independently of concepts or theories. Today, philosophers of science almost universally reject this view. But only in the latter half of the twentieth century, with the decline of positivism, did it become widely recognised by philosophers that all descriptions of facts are theory-laden, and all descriptions are dependent on prior theories and conceptual frameworks. In short, no fact can be identified, nor given any meaning whatsoever without some pre-existing conceptual framework.

The historicist statement that all social or economic theory is confined to specific historical phenomena is itself a universal tenet or meta-theoretical axiom. It cannot itself be established by empirical enquiry. Hence some of the very precepts of historicism are incapable of empirical verification or falsification. The notion that all economic theories should be based solely on the historical facts is incoherent: it itself contains universal presuppositions that do not themselves emerge from empirical investigation.

Accordingly Wilhelm Roscher's idea of a 'pure empirical science' based on 'simple description' is incoherent because neither description nor empirical statement is possible without concepts and theories. Likewise, T. E. Cliffe Leslie's idea of 'investigation of the actual course of history' was not possible without the same.

Some further weaknesses of the empiricist position have already been noted in chapter 1 of this volume. For additional reasons rehearsed above, empiricism always and unavoidably hides general or *a priori* theories of its own. For instance, all empirical enquiry is based on classification, and this involves prior judgements of sameness and difference. To some extent, these qualities must be assumed to endure through space and time. Empiricism thus relies on the principle of the uniformity of nature. Furthermore, without a presumption of causality, there can be no adequate scientific explanation of any phenomenon. But empirical enquiry cannot itself establish a causal relation. The idea that empirical data are sufficient for all knowledge thus founders.

Even those who saw the limits of the extreme empiricism of some of the historicists, such as the great English historian Arnold Toynbee, fell inadvertently into the same trap. Toynbee argued in his lectures of 1881–2:

> Advocates of the Historical Method . . . go too far when they condemn the Deductive Method as radically false. There is no real opposition between the two. The apparent opposition is due to a wrong use of deduction; to a neglect on the part of those employing it to examine closely their assumptions and to bring their conclusions to the test of fact.
> (Toynbee, 1894, p. 29)

Toynbee failed here to elucidate what he meant by 'the test of fact'. The meaning and nature of 'the test of fact' have perplexed philosophers for generations. There is no single, agreed method or meaning of this term. We have a plurality of rival methods, going under such names as verificationism, falsificationism and statistical inference. Toynbee wrongly took 'the test of fact' for granted. Equally problematic is the idea that there is a straightforward 'empirical' way of deriving the basic assumptions upon which any deductive structure can be built. We do not obtain these assumptions simply or unambiguously by wallowing in 'facts'. Furthermore, these facts themselves require prior conceptual systems of identification and classification. In sum, Toynbee's proposed marriage of empiricism and deductivism was itself philosophically flawed. Just as induction and deduction are both limited as means of obtaining knowledge, something more than a combination of these two approaches is required.

THE NEED FOR CAUSAL EXPLANATION

A limitation of both empiricism and deductivism is that neither of these approaches – either singly or in combination – is able to locate the causal mechanisms underlying phenomena. A primary goal of science is causal explanation. As noted above, David Hume realised long ago that no stated sequence of facts could itself verify any causal relationship between the events. Similarly, deductive chains of reasoning cannot on their own establish the existence of causal processes in the real world. In sum, neither facts nor deductive reasoning provide us with the means of obtaining and assessing causal explanations. The historical school had rejected the timeless equilibria of classical economics, focusing instead on the phenomena of historical development. They failed, however, to understand sufficiently that the empirical data alone could not reveal the causal mechanisms involved.

The older historical school wrongly concluded that the diversity of historical phenomena itself placed limits on the desirability or possibility of a general theory. However, the successful pursuit of explanatory unification in science involves precisely the explanation of diverse phenomena by means of a single explanatory framework. Various outcomes at the phenomenal level may be explicable in terms of a single theory. The mere observation of phenomenal diversity itself offers no justification for the eschewal of explanatory unification or general theorising.

What the older historical school failed to appreciate was that the true limits to explanatory unification are ontological, and relate to the recognition of fundamentally different types of structure and causal relationship. But the epistemological method of induction itself offers no means of divination of these underlying structures and causal powers.

Having failed to establish a method of discerning causal relationships, some members of the older historical school abandoned the search for historical principles or laws. The Swedish institutional economist Johan Åkerman (1932, p. 80) saw this clearly:

> The economics of equilibrium attempted to escape the philosophical conflict by speaking only of timeless associations; cause and effect needed no explanation. . . . By ignoring time they succeeded at the same time in eluding the riddles of the problem of causation. The *historical* school . . . saw through the assumption of the economics of equilibrium, which passed over the really important problem of causation and time. . . . Because the historical school distrusted the laws of the economics of equilibrium, they themselves arrived at the point of holding that no laws could be laid down.

The problem of causality could not be tackled adequately within the philosophical frameworks of empiricism or deductivism. Furthermore, a mere mixture of the two methods would be no improvement. It took the work of later philosophers – including Charles Sanders Peirce, John Dewey and Alfred Whitehead – to begin to transcend this classic philosophical dilemma, in part by focusing on the ontological issues underlying any notion of causal explanation.

In particular, as Charles Sanders Peirce argued in the late nineteenth century, neither induction nor deduction is capable of discovering entirely novel facts. Induction involves an attempt to confirm or disconfirm a proposition that is given at the start. With deduction the logical conclusion is already contained in the premises (Peirce, 1958, pp. 123–5). With his concept of 'abduction', Peirce attempted to transcend the limitations of each.

These philosophical perspectives were not available to the older historical school. Accordingly, those historicists who worried about the over-reliance on empirical methods were unable to provide an alternative way forward. Writing in 1888, John Ingram (1915, p. 208) warned against the possibility that the historical school 'might occupy itself too exclusively with statistical inquiry, and forget in the detailed examination of particular provinces of economic life the necessity of large philosophic ideas and of a systematic co-ordination of principles'. Yet Ingram himself failed to describe these 'philosophic ideas and principles', or provide any guidelines for their derivation or deployment. This, indeed, was a crucial task. But it was left undone.

Members of the older historical school did not fully understand these problems. Generally they placed their faith in the philosophical method of induction. The facts, they believed, would be their salvation: theoretical development would come afterwards. They were thus vulnerable to the opening salvo in the *Methodenstreit*, fired in 1883 by the Austrian economist Carl Menger, when he argued that any science must necessarily base itself on some abstract concepts and assumptions. Menger successfully identified the internal inconsistencies in the empiricist stance of the older historical school.

Furthermore, Menger identified the crucial problem of causal explanation. While having a powerful intuition concerning the structured and systemic nature of economic activity, the older historical school were unable to relate this notion to that of the individual, purposeful actor. The problem of the relationship between actor and structure was not posed clearly, let alone resolved. If we are told that the main job is to gather facts, then we have little concern for such philosophical questions. This empiricist bias diverted attention from one of the central problems of social theory. These weaknesses formed the breach into which Menger stormed. Although, as will be argued in the next chapter, Menger's individualist account of causal explanation was itself incomplete and unsatisfactory, nevertheless he identified the key question of causal explanation neglected by the older historicists.

ABIDING VIRTUES

However, weak methodological defences in one area do not imply lack of strength in another. The crucial weaknesses of the older historical school concerned the conception of the human agent and the reliance on a faulty empiricist epistemology. Nevertheless, other historicist virtues remained. The historicists had recognised the problem of historical specificity and had argued that different types of socio-economic system require different theoretical categories and principles. The critics of historicism did not devalue these insights. On the contrary, the opponents of the historical school dealt with these problems largely by ignoring them.

7

OUT OF AUSTRIA

Carl Menger and the *Methodenstreit*

> After all, no one would remember the old German Historical School
> if it were not for the famous *Methodenstreit*. Actually, no one
> remembers them anyway.
>
> (Robert M. Solow, 'Economic History and Economics' (1985))

In 1883 the historical school was in a position of overwhelming influence in the universities of both Germany and Austria. It had also spread elsewhere in Europe. In that year, Carl Menger – with his major work on methodology know as the *Untersuchungen* – launched from Vienna a frontal attack on historicism (Menger, 1883, 1985). Menger (1985, p. 49) identified 'that error which confuses theoretical economics with the history of economy' and tried instead to establish a central place in economics for deductive and abstract theory. Unlike modern and misinformed critics, Menger did not depict the historical school as anti-theoretical. Instead, he argued that their theoretical attempts were misconceived. Within a year of its publication, Gustav von Schmoller responded by publishing an unfavourable review of the *Untersuchungen*, and Menger (1884) counter-attacked with a polemical book on 'the errors of historicism'. The debate became both lively and acrimonious.[1]

In at least one important respect, Menger's criticisms in the *Untersuchungen* hit their target. He rightly insisted that: 'Even the most realistic orientation of *theoretical* research imaginable must accordingly operate with abstractions' (Menger, 1985, p. 80). Menger further argued, quite rightly, that it was impossible to derive social or natural laws solely from observation or description. The reason for this was straightforward:

> Every exact law of nature, for whatever realm of the empirical world it
> may claim validity, is based on two unempirical assumptions. First, that
> all concrete phenomena of any definite type (e.g., all oxygen, all
> hydrogen, all iron, etc. . . . .) are qualitatively identical, and second, that

---

1   And to an unnecessary degree. Given the development of economics over the succeeding century, it is clear that Menger and Schmoller had much more in common with each other than with the empty formalism that has since overtaken the subject.

they can be measured in an exact way. In *reality*, however, the above phenomena are neither strictly typical, nor can they be measured in an exact way.

(Menger, 1985, pp. 214–15 n.)

Empiricism was thus demonstrated to be internally inconsistent. The belief that empirical data are sufficient for all knowledge breaks down, because any empirical investigation depends on the non-empirical assumptions of identity, continuity and measurability. We have to make the universal assumption of uniformity of nature. Without some common types and qualities across time and space, neither meaningful empirical investigation nor prediction is possible. Accordingly, the proposition that economics proceeded to build up theory solely on the basis of induction founders. To be operable, the principle of induction requires a belief in the above principle of uniformity of nature, and this itself cannot be an outcome of inductive reasoning.

Philosophically, Menger was a realist and an essentialist. He maintained, in an Aristotelian manner, that the attempt to understand and explain real economic phenomena must reach behind the superficial appearances and attempt to understand the underlying essences.[2] Further, chosen concepts should represent that which is typical, and exclude the superficial and accidental, in the phenomena under scrutiny. The historical school had also attempted to understand 'types' but by a purely empirical method. Menger (1985, p. 56) argued in the *Untersuchungen* that the empiricist approach to this problem was superficially attractive but fatally flawed in methodological terms:

The most obvious idea . . . is to investigate the types and typical relationships of phenomena as these present themselves to us in their 'full empirical reality,' *that is, in the totality and the whole complexity of their nature*; in other words, to arrange the totality of the real phenomena in definite empirical forms and in an empirical way to determine the regularities in their existence and succession. . . . Close examination, however, teaches us that the above idea is not strictly feasible. Phenomena in all their empirical reality are, according to experience, repeated in certain empirical forms. But this is never with perfect strictness, for scarcely ever do two concrete phenomena, let alone a larger group of them, exhibit a thorough agreement.

Menger thus argued that a purely empirical approach cannot produce adequate or general knowledge of complex phenomena, because, being focused on the flux of superficial appearances, it cannot identify and create knowledge of the enduring and persisting elements. The underlying essences must be enduring rather than accidental.

---

2   Useful discussions of Menger's method include Bostaph (1978), Dopfer (1988), Hutchison (1973), C. Lawson (1996), Mäki (1990a, 1997b), Smith (1990) and Van Eeghen (1996). The prevalent interpretation is that Menger was philosophically an Aristotelian, although there are alternative, less convincing, accounts (Dobretsberger, 1949; Milford, 1990).

So far so good. Menger's critique of the empirical realism of the older historical school was devastating. The historical school had not entirely neglected the need for theory, but generally they had wrongly believed that theory could emerge merely from the study of empirical phenomena. In contrast, Menger rightly argued that theoretical presuppositions were necessary before empirical phenomena could be described or understood. As Menger's fellow Austrian, Eugen von Böhm-Bawerk (1890, p. 260) put it succinctly: 'It is absolutely impossible to make a report upon a question of economics, much less to discuss it, without touching upon general theoretical conceptions and propositions.'

Menger's critique of the inductive, empiricist and descriptive methods of the German and British historicists hit its target. For those who wrongly believe that the historical school were entirely 'atheoretical' or 'against theory' that would be the end of the matter. This, however, is definitely not the case. Once it is realised that Menger's demonstration of the inadequacy of description and induction is only part of the *Methodenstreit*, and on other fronts the battle was much less conclusive, then we can begin to discern the enduring value of the contribution of the historical school through the mists of time.

While the devastating impact of the critique of empiricism has to be acknowledged, it is a serious error to dismiss the historical school on this basis. Regrettably, this is often done. On the rare occasions that the historical school is mentioned, we are typically told that they failed because of their naïve empiricism and their inductivist methods. Their formulation of the problem of historical specificity and their other contributions to social science are sometimes completely ignored.[3]

THE ISOLATION OF THE ESSENTIAL FROM THE ACCIDENTAL

Having demonstrated the impossibility of description without prior theoretical concepts, Menger quite rightly saw the outstanding problem as one of the choice of relevant abstractions, by which to classify, analyse and begin to explain

---

3 See, for example, the account of the historical school in Robbins's 1979–81 lectures at the LSE. Robbins (1998, p. 250) remarked:

> the historical school, in my judgement, had got the logic of scientific discovery wrong. Their emphasis on the priority of induction was surely misplaced. This is not to say that it is not essential that hypotheses should be tested eventually against their correspondence with fact. . . . Schmoller and Schmoller's department and its followers produced interesting historical studies, but they produced no significant theory, no significant laws of development which would stand up to logical and historical analysis.

Here Robbins dismissed the historical school because of their (untenable) inductivist method, and not because of their attention to the problem of historical specificity. Robbins ignored the latter problem. The irony, furthermore, is that Robbins himself embraced an untenable empiricist method in suggesting that theories can be 'tested . . . against their correspondence with fact'. Although empirical data is always relevant in theory construction, it is unclear how 'correspondence with fact' can ever act as a final arbiter in the process, and no philosopher of science has ever explained satisfactorily how it could be so.

phenomena. If data cannot be understood without a set of concepts and theories, then which concepts and theories should be chosen? Menger's attempt to answer this question took up much of the text of the *Untersuchungen*. Within this volume he posed a quite particular solution to the problem, from which we may part company without falling back into the empiricist impasse. In fact, Menger's solution to the problem was one among infinitely many possible non-empiricist solutions.

Menger's particular approach rested on two maxims. The first was the perceived need to isolate the essential aspects of the phenomenon, and to disregard the accidental. Menger (1985, p. 60) wrote in the *Untersuchungen*:

> *whatever was observed in even only one case must always put in an appearance again under exactly the same actual conditions* . . . a circumstance which was regarded as irrelevant only in one case in respect to the succession of phenomena will always and of necessity prove to be irrelevant under precisely the same actual conditions in respect of the same result.

Menger's approach has been described as the 'method of isolation'.[4] His second maxim was to break down the essential reality to its simplest, typical and most enduring components. Menger (1985, p. 60) continued, arguing that 'theoretical research . . . seeks to ascertain the *simplest elements* of everything real, elements which must be thought of as strictly typical just because they are the simplest.'

However, as Clive Lawson (1996, p. 451) has pointed out: 'Menger at no stage explains why the simplest elements must be thought of as strictly typical.' Indeed, Menger's argument itself contains presuppositions that are not spelt out fully. He compounds the debatable assumption that the typical elements are the simplest with the further questionable assumption that the concept of the individual fits the bill.

Menger chose the individual as the fundamental unit of analysis. He proposed that human individuals retain features that endure throughout the stages of history. He observed, furthermore, that socio-economic phenomena were the conscious or undesigned result of the interaction of individual human wills. The attempt to show that socio-economic structures and institutions can and should be explained in terms of the interactions of individual human wills takes up much of the *Untersuchungen*. Menger (1985, p. 87) argued that economics should be concerned with the aspect of human life concerned with economising action, that is 'the manifestations of human self-interest in the efforts of economic humans aimed at the provision of their human needs'. The enduring theoretical foundation, therefore, was the economising individual. For him, no other

---

4   Dopfer (1988, p. 556) has argued succinctly that 'Menger's method was to *isolate the essential features of reality from the accidental*.' He saw 'Menger's methodological plea for isolation, as being the central cause for and cornerstone of the *Methodenstreit*'. For discussions of the method of isolation see Mäki (1992, 1994) and T. Lawson (1997).

fundamental level of analysis was appropriate. Menger (1985, p. 93) thus attacked the concept of the 'national economy' as a sufficient unit or level of analysis:

> Thus the phenomena of 'national economy' are by no means direct expressions of the life of a nation as such or direct results of an 'economic nation'. They are, rather, the *results* of all the innumerable individual economic efforts in the nation, and they therefore are not to be brought within the scope of our theoretical understanding from the point of view of the above fiction. Rather the phenomena of 'national economy,' just as they present themselves to us in reality as results of individual economic efforts, must also be theoretically interpreted in this light.

In this way, Menger denied the necessity of multiple levels of analysis. He rejected the historicist emphasis on 'national economies' – or their *Geist* – as prime analytical units. The role of economics, he thought, was to explain national and institutional phenomena in terms of the purposeful individuals within them. Menger thus argued that it was misleading to conceive of the state or the economy as a whole as a single, indivisible organism. While the organic or biological analogy might have limited uses, it was wrong to presume that independent will or purpose could be attributed to the 'social organism'.

Menger pointed out that while some institutions were deliberately created by individuals, many others were not. He rightly emphasised that social institutions often evolve unintentionally out of the purposeful actions of many interacting individuals. But he went further. Menger discarded explanations of the emergence of social institutions that relied on a 'social will' or *Geist* that could not in turn itself be explained in terms of the purposeful behaviour of individuals. Menger is thus remembered as a critic of methodological collectivism and as an early architect of a version of methodological individualism.

In sum, Menger justified the focus on the individual because he saw the economising action of the individual as the general foundational impulse of all economic activity. Significantly, Menger (1985, p. 84) admitted the possibility of other motives, including 'public spirit' and 'love of one's fellow man'. But he simply consigned the study and incorporation of these other motives to other social sciences. For Menger (1985, p. 86), self-interest was part of 'the most original and the most general forces and impulses of human nature'.

However, in response to this argument, even if the selfish, economising motives in fact dominate over the rest, this would not itself justify an exclusive focus on the individual as the elemental unit of analysis. One has to ask how the characteristic of greed and the propensity to economise emerged within individuals. A reasonable answer to this question would involve a discussion of social institutions and culture. It would involve the analysis of the development of markets and money out of a preceding society, less dominated by pecuniary values. It would consider the possibility that individuals are partly moulded by the incentives and values of a pecuniary culture dominated by acquisitive, business institutions. Just as the nation is a result of individual actions, so too is the individual in part a result of national structures and institutions. The assumption of selfish 'economic man', whether true or false, does not itself justify an initial emphasis on individuals alone.[5]

Furthermore, and crucially, these arguments are not sufficient to disregard the problem of historical specificity. Clearly, no methodologically individualist analysis can entirely dispense with institutions. Furthermore, the evolution of institutions is often dependent upon specific circumstances. Accordingly, even a methodological individualist is obliged to acknowledge specific historical formations and institutions. A variety of concepts or principles would apply to different socio-economic systems, without negating the principle that all explanations were at least in part traced back to the individuals involved. However, Menger wished to go further. He aimed to dispense with the problem of historical specificity and to remove it from the economist's agenda. Consider the following passage from the *Untersuchungen*: 'The phenomena of private property, of barter, of money, of credit are phenomena of human economy which have been manifesting themselves repeatedly in the course of human development, to some extent for millennia. They are typical phenomena' (Menger, 1985, p. 103). According to this argument, the typical and enduring elements of socio-economic systems are not simply 'individuals' but also 'private property', 'barter', 'money' and 'credit'. In other words, these are basic and typical human social institutions that have existed 'for millennia'.

It is interesting to note that in order to establish the claim that private property, money and credit were 'typical', Menger fell back on an empirical claim of historical longevity. He thus impersonated a feature of the historical-empiricist methodology of the historical school that he was so keen to renounce. The problem of historical specificity was first diminished by making the individual effectively an historical invariant, and then collapsed further by suggesting that all socio-economic systems throughout history have had a set of common and typical institutional foundations.

The accuracy of historical statements such as Menger's concerning the existence, as 'typical phenomena', of private property, money and credit 'for millennia' has been widely contested. As noted in chapter 18 below, economic anthropologists such as Karl Polanyi et al. (1957) have argued that property, markets and money have assumed very different scopes and forms in earlier societies. It could also be pointed out that Menger overlooked the importance of other social institutions, such as slavery or vassalage, that were pre-eminent in the historical past, and downplayed the particular historical features of the capitalist era, such as the employment contract and the capitalist corporation.

However, we need not enter further into the discussion of the particular factual issues here. The key point is that Menger's (1985, p. 103) statement provides his

---

5   Note that Menger's Aristotelian position may be relevant here. Aristotle separated the 'final causality' associated with human agency and intention from the 'efficient causality' of mechanisms or machines. On this basis, Menger seemed to refuse any attempt to explain final causality, treating it as if it were an original or uncaused cause. If individual intention is an uncaused cause then it is incapable of any (institutional or cultural) explanation. This would rule out an investigation into the institutional or cultural factors that might mould individual intentions. Menger's argument can be framed in these questionable Aristotelian terms.

questionable excuse to ignore the problem of historical specificity. If scarcity, property, markets and exchange are universal, then economics becomes the universal study of individual choices and valuations under conditions of scarcity, and of the allegedly general and universal forms of supposedly elemental institutions such as private property, markets and money. The apparatus of economic theory becomes preoccupied with these issues, rather than specific historical structures. It may wish to address specific institutions and historic junctures, but it will do so, in the name of getting to the 'essential' and 'under-lying' truth, by means of this universal theoretical apparatus. The empirical realism of the historical school was to be replaced by a philosophical realism of universals. After Menger, this was essentially the approach taken by the Austrian school of economists and a subset of neoclassical economists close to and influenced by them.

Another argument was used by Menger to bolster his position. First, he addressed the allegedly universal laws of supply and demand. He argued that it would be a 'methodological error' to confuse specific historical developments

> with the laws which teach us how supply and demand or the quantity of means of circulation influence the price of goods, how the distance of pieces of land from the market and their differential fertility influence ground rent, how the greater or lesser thriftiness or the more or less active business spirit of the inhabitants of a land influence the rate of interest in it!
>
> (Menger, 1985, p. 12)

In other words, Menger warned against any confusion between, on the one hand, the laws of supply and demand and, on the other hand, their specific parametric manifestations. This was a key part of his argument in favour of general laws.

Menger claimed to find a parallel with this situation in biology. Immediately after the above statement, he argued that the error of the historical school was tantamount to a confusion between, on the one hand, theoretical research into the physiology of specific organisms with, on the other hand, 'the effort to establish laws of development of the organic world or even Darwin's theory'. Menger's invocation of Darwin had some considerable rhetorical force, par-ticularly as the historical school was fond of metaphors taken from biology. Although Menger did not spell out the details, the obvious suggestion was that economists should embrace general laws, just as Darwin established universal laws and principles for the natural world.

On close examination, however, Menger's appeal to Darwin did not work. First, Darwin's theory of natural selection is not on the same explanatory level as the laws of physics. Darwin himself did not claim that it was sufficient. Instead he saw natural selection as 'the main *but not exclusive* means of modification' (Darwin, 1859, p. 6, emphasis added). Darwinian evolutionary biology has a few laws or general principles that help to explain the origin and development of organisms. However, analysis of the evolution and nature of a specific organism cannot be understood without detailed information concerning the organism and its environment, and also particular explanations of specific causal mechanisms relevant to the species under consideration.

As philosophers of biology such as Anthony Flew (1959) and David Hull (1973) have discussed, Darwin's theory has a rigorous deductive core, but it explains or predicts little on its own and it is thus placed in the context of a mass of empirical material. There are deductive arguments combined with contingent empirical premises and conclusions. Darwinian biology requires theories that relate to both specific and general domains. In contrast, in physics there are repeated attempts to formulate the general theory of all material phenomena – the so-called 'theory of everything' (Cohen and Stewart, 1994). If anything, Darwin's approach supports a combination of theories relating to general and specific phenomena, and underlines the importance of historical contingency. It was thus inappropriate for Menger to use Darwinism as part of a rhetorical crusade for basing economics entirely on universal economic laws.

To return to the main argument, Menger had established the case for prior concepts and theoretical frameworks, and argued successfully that the explanation of economic phenomena must probe beneath the superficial and accidental aspects of empirical reality. However, in his quest for the underlying essence he provided us with a weak argument for choosing the individual as the fundamental analytical unit, and an even weaker insistence that such phenomena as private property and markets have endured through much of human history. It is in this region that Menger's argument failed. His rebuttal of empirical realism does not automatically lead to methodological individualism, or the universalisation of the market, as Menger suggested. As Kurt Dopfer (1988, p. 557) has rightly observed:

> Menger's division of real phenomena into essential and accidental is crucial methodologically. . . . The scientific dissension, indeed, does not lie in the methodological proclamation itself, but rather in the views . . . about the *criteria* that allow one to decide whether an empirical case is essential or merely accidental. . . . The quest for isolating the essential from the accidental does *not itself provide epistemic criteria for factual selection.* Nor is it clear which epistemology Menger ultimately emphasized when bestowing upon his method of isolation an epistemic rationale that would allow him to identify his essential rationality.

Not only did Menger emphasise the analytic separation of the essential from the accidental, he also had particular views about what was essential, namely an atomistic and individualistic social ontology. This point can be shown clearly when we examine Menger's favourite example of institutional evolution. This is discussed in the following section.

MENGER'S EXAMPLE OF THE EMERGENCE OF MONEY

Consider Menger's famous argument concerning the emergence of money. In the *Untersuchungen* and elsewhere, Menger countered the view of the historical school that a historical description of the involvement of the state in the evolution of money showed that the state was necessary for the creation of money, and essential to its nature. He attempted to show that institutions such as money could emerge through the interaction of individuals, without the state. Menger (1985, p. 153) accepted that 'history actually offers us examples that certain wares have been declared money by law.' But these declarations are often seen to be 'the acknowledgement of an item which had already become money'. Although cases of the emergence of money by agreement or legislation may be historically important, Menger nevertheless argued that:

> the origin of money can truly be brought to our full understanding only by our learning to understand the *social* institution discussed here as the unintended result, as the unplanned outcome of specifically *individual* efforts of members of a society.
>
> (Menger, 1985, p. 155)

An account of the supposed evolutionary process through which money could emerge is found in his *Principles* of 1871:

> As *each* economizing individual becomes increasingly more aware of his economic interest, he is led by this *interest, without any agreement, without legislative compulsion,* and *even without regard to the public interest,* to give his commodities in exchange for other, more saleable, commodities, even if he does not need them for any immediate consumption purpose. With economic progress, therefore, we can everywhere observe the phenomenon of a certain number of goods, especially those that are most easily saleable at a given time and place, becoming, under the influence of *custom,* acceptable to everyone in trade, and thus capable of being given in exchange for any other commodity.
>
> (Menger, 1981, p. 260)

For various reasons discussed by Menger (1892, pp. 246–7), commodities will differ in their saleability. Some commodities will be widely accepted in exchange, others less so. A commodity that is seen to be accepted in exchange will have its saleability enhanced as individuals act on the basis of such a perception.

Hence the evolution of money begins on the basis of subjective evaluations, and becomes progressively reinforced through action and the perception of this action by other individuals. Money thus emerges as a result of this cumulative process. Apart from the attribute of being 'most marketable', which is a culmination and consequence of individual perceptions and choices, Menger (1985, p. 154) also suggested that the good that emerges as money may be 'the most easily transported, the most durable, the most easily divisible'. Consequently, over time, a single commodity or group of commodities can emerge as money, and without state intervention or state decree.

Menger's theoretical explanation of institutional evolution served a number of purposes. First, it separated what was allegedly essential (interactions between individuals with unintended consequences) from what was held to be accidental (the role of the state). Second, it established the particular explanatory procedure that was later to be described as 'methodological individualism': the explanation of socio-economic phenomena exclusively in terms of given individuals and the interactions between them. It is important to realise that these two outcomes are quite separate, and the second does not necessarily follow from the first. In principle, the isolation of the essential could result in the abstraction of the 'national economy' as much as the concept of the individual. At the very minimum, Menger's analysis required auxiliary arguments to establish his individualist methodology. The particular criteria for separating the essential from the accidental had to be provided. What Menger supplied in this respect was sorely inadequate.

In this context it is extremely ironic that Menger (1909) later modified his argument concerning the evolution of money, and admitted an essential role for the state. The problem in Menger's argument is as follows.

In his theory, the emerging monetary unit is homogeneous and invariant. Although not all persons may recognise (say) gold as the emerging monetary substance, Menger originally assumed that they all know 24-carat gold when they see it. But even gold can be faked or alloyed with inferior metals. Hence there is a possibility of quality variation. The emerging monetary unit can be debased or forged. With potential quality variation, the purity and value of the emerging monetary unit may be in doubt. Some actors may notice the high frequency of the trade in a particular commodity, but in contrast to others, regard the commodity in question as unreliable and thereby avoid it as a medium of exchange. Such problems, arising from potential quality variation, could subvert the evolution of the monetary unit. The bad money could drive out the good.

Menger's Aristotelian ontology is partly at fault here. Aristotle inherited from Plato the notion of 'typological essentialism', in which entities are regarded as identifiable in terms of a few distinct characteristics which represent their essential qualities. This differs from the notion of 'population thinking' in Darwinian biology, in which variety and diversity are all-important (Mayr, 1963, 1964, 1976, 1982, 1985a, 1985b). In typological thinking, species are regarded as identifiable in terms of a few distinct characteristics that represent their essence. Accordingly, all variations around the ideal type are regarded as accidental aberrations. By contrast, in population thinking, species are described in terms of a distribution of characteristics. Whereas in typological thinking variation is a classificatory nuisance, in Darwinian evolution the idea of variation encapsulated in population thinking is of paramount interest because it is upon variety that selection operates.

In at least one passage, Menger raised the question of potential quality variation. But at first he dismissed the problem, saying that money is likely to take the form of precious metals, and these are 'easily controlled as to their quality and weight' (Menger, 1892, p. 255). Later, however, in his article on 'Geld', Menger recognised that the problem of potential quality variation could be so serious that the state had to play a role. Menger (1909, p. 42) thus wrote: 'Only the state has the power to protect effectively the coins and other means of exchange which are circulated, against the issue of false coins, illegal reductions of weight and other violations that impede trade.' Nevertheless, Menger applied this argument to a 'developed economy' only. He was reluctant to admit that the state was necessary to protect the integrity of the monetary unit at earlier stages of economic development, and he still clung to his view that, in essence, money was a phenomenon independent of the state. However, debasement is a potential problem at the inception of money, not merely at its developed stage.

There is an additional reason why the state is likely to play a crucial role. While Menger was right to emphasise that many social institutions emerge and develop without a conscious plan, it is often the case that an institution reaches an important stage of development when it becomes consciously recognised and legitimated by other institutions. Symbol and ceremony play an important role here. Money has self-regulating and spontaneous properties, but typically it is also endorsed by some powerful socio-economic institution. Many social institutions to some degree rely upon such declaratory endorsements. Although state decree alone is far from sufficient to create money, as a powerful social institution representing the apex of the legal system, the state is well positioned to take on this declaratory and legitimising role. The state maintains the worth and value of its monetary unit, as well as creating laws to punish forgers and counterfeiters. In thus legitimating a monetary system and helping to engender trust in the monetary unit, the state relies on its crucial symbolic as well as legislative powers. It is not accidental that the images of monarchs and presidents adorn notes and coin. Menger's account of the origin of money as a purely spontaneous process downplays these declaratory aspects and their symbolic representations. There is a nugget of truth in the 'state theory of money' (Knapp, 1924) that Menger was so keen to reject, even if he rightly criticised those who saw money as *entirely* a result of state decree.

If legal or state instruments are necessary to some degree for the full development of money, then these elements could reasonably account for part of the essence of money itself; they are more than mere accidental, historical appearances. Menger gave us no reason to conclude otherwise. As a result, his argument against the 'state theory of money' loses much of its impact. Moreover, Menger's attempt to establish the individual as the primary and fundamental unit of analysis is further undermined. If the state and other institutions are necessary at the very point of conception of money, then they, along with individuals, have to enter as units in the explanation of the emergence and development of money. Menger's attempt to isolate individuals alone, as the enduring elements of socio-economic reality and the basic units of analysis, thus fails.[6]

THE BIRTH OF THE AUSTRIAN SCHOOL

Overall, after having won one important battle – defeating the 'empirical realism' that prevailed among the historical school – Menger failed to win the war,

---

6 Sened's (1997) forceful argument that a state apparatus is necessary to sustain the institution of property is also a vindication of an aspect of the historical school case. See chapter 20 below.

despite what many of the subsequent and typically all-too-brief accounts of the *Methodenstreit* proclaim. Regrettably, many of the members of the historical school continued to fight the battle that had been lost, and attempted to defend a version of empiricism, rather than to focus on the real weaknesses in Menger's argument. The failure of the historical school to reverse Menger's incursion seriously weakened their position, despite their overwhelming prominence in German academia at the time. And today it is Menger – not Schmoller nor Sombart – who is perceived and remembered as the victor.

The more accurate verdict is that the *Methodenstreit* did not give clear victory to either side. This verdict is supported by the observation that both Menger and his historical school opponents subsequently spent much time in attempting to revise and refine their views in the light of the dispute. Menger did not at all deny that historical research was of value, he simply relegated it to the role of an auxiliary science. He did not regard his *Principles* as a final and complete word. As Karl Polanyi (1977, p. 22) has commented: 'Menger wished to supplement his *Principles* [1871] so as not to ignore the primitive, archaic, or other early societies that were beginning to be studied by the social sciences.' As a result 'Menger became anxious to limit the strict application of his *Principles* to the modern exchange economy.' In other words, he wished to recognise his *Principles* as relating to historically specific circumstances.

For this and other reasons, Menger did not permit a reprint or a translation of the first edition, which he deemed to be in need of revision and completion. He resigned his chair at the University of Vienna, in part to devote himself to this task. He left a revised manuscript that was published posthumously in 1923. Yet when Friedrich Hayek reprinted the *Principles* in German in 1933, he chose the first edition. Only the first edition has been published in English translation. Menger's revised views have thus been kept out of sight of English-speaking economists.

Menger is also commemorated as one of the leaders of the 'marginal revolution' although subsequent scholarship has seen his role in that respect as being very different in substance, and quite independent of, that of Léon Walras, William Stanley Jevons or Alfred Marshall (Black *et al.*, 1973; Howey, 1960; Jaffé, 1976; Streissler, 1972). In reality, the 'marginal revolution' was a disparate, long-lasting, and intermittent process. In England, it had Jevons and Marshall at its head, but there was little unity or collaboration between them.[7] Walras did not have a major influence until, long after his death, his ideas began to permeate the American scene in the 1930s. Much of Menger's contribution to value theory, furthermore, can be interpreted as a development of ideas already present in the German historical school rather than a radical break from them (Priddat, 1998).[8]

---

7   In his 1872 review of Jevons's *Theory of Political Economy*, Marshall declared that he found little in it that was 'new in substance' (Pigou, 1925, p. 93).
8   Compared with later generations of Austrian economists, Reinert (forthcoming) points out that Menger was in some respects closer to the historical school. See also Gloria-Palermo (1999) for a powerful re-evaluation of Menger's original project.

Nevertheless, in other respects Menger's impact was crucial. In his wake the so-called Austrian school of economics developed, mainly in Vienna, and included such luminaries as Friedrich von Wieser and Eugen von Böhm-Bawerk.[9]

Partly as a result of his rhetorical and scholastic success, the individualist thrust of Menger's argument survived all the twists and turns of methodological fashion for the next hundred years. Menger and his followers were able to dismiss the notion that empirical data were a sufficient grounding for theory, and chose the individual as the bedrock unit of analysis. However, when Anglophone economics and sociology took a positivist turn in the interwar period, it was often claimed that the individual was the fundamental empirical unit (Degler, 1991; Ross, 1991). After all, it was said, we look around us in our social world, and all we find is flesh-and-blood individuals. Hence ontological and methodological individualism were able to sustain themselves throughout all the methodological shifts in the social sciences, and the waxing and waning of positivism itself. To the methodological sophisticates, it could always be said that theory could not live by facts alone. To others – especially in empiricist times when it was believed that all sciences must confine themselves to observables – the individual was seen as the observable unit in society. The individualist approach thus managed to sustain itself, in part because of its chameleon-like methodological qualities. Individualism can play to both essentialist and empiricist prejudices.

Ideology was also an important issue. Just as Marx was driven in his endeavours not simply by scientific curiosity but also by his commitment to a socialist future, many in the Austrian school were impelled by an individualistic and pro-market political ideology. Originally this was not so much the case, as both von Böhm-Bawerk and von Wieser opposed *laissez-faire* and supported social reforms. Eventually, however, the Austrian school of von Mises and Hayek became associated with a highly individualist ideology. When living in the USA, von Mises (1957) condemned the historical school in McCarthyist tones – principally for its alleged socialism. Austrian theoretical ideas became popular in the 1970s and 1980s, when extreme pro-market ideas were globally in fashion. By this time, their German-speaking historicist rivals of 1841–1941 had been dismissed or forgotten. For these and other reasons, by the last quarter of the twentieth century, the international reputation among economists of Menger and his students far exceeded that of the entire historical school.

Menger's work on the nature and unfolding of institutions is widely and rightly regarded as thematic for what – since 1975 – has become known as the 'new institutional economics'.[10] Typically, and reasonably, the new institutionalists

---

9   It should be emphasised that the original 'Austrian' group was much broader in conception than it became later, when it was led by von Mises and Hayek. As Endres (1997) has shown, and in contrast to von Mises and Hayek, 'Austrians' such as von Wieser and von Böhm-Bawerk regarded it as legitimate for economists to explore the formation of preferences, using insights from psychology if needed. Furthermore, they included endogenous preference changes precipitated by learning as part of their theory.

10   Williamson (1975) originally coined the term. A vast literature is now involved. A textbook summary is found in Furubotn and Richter (1997). Schotter (1981) was one of the first to note and develop the Mengerian link with the new institutionalism.

define institutions in terms of rules (North, 1990, p. 3). Like Menger, the central project of the new institutionalists is to start with given individuals, in an institution-free 'state of nature', and to proceed to explain the emergence of institutions from that starting point. However, in attempting to explain the origin of social institutions, the new institutional economics has to presume given individuals acting in a certain context or framework. To the assumption of given individuals must be added assumptions concerning the rules and modes of behaviour governing their interaction. For example, in Menger's example of the emergence of money, some form of (signed or linguistic) communication is required between the actors, even for barter to take place. Such communication is always rule-bound. More generally, what is forgotten is that in the original, hypothetical, 'state of nature' from which institutions are seen to have emerged, a number of weighty rules, institutions and cultural and social norms have already been presumed. In particular, some form of language is essential for human interaction. Arguably, these original institutions and rules are unavoidable: we can never properly envisage an original 'state of nature' without them. The idea of starting from given individuals interacting in an assumed institution-free environment is misconceived. Because it excludes the linguistic or other rules that are necessary for human interaction, the Mengerian or new institutionalist project to explain the emergence of institutions fails.[11]

THE NATURAL AND THE SOCIAL

Before we leave Menger, we must address an important sub-plot. Much of the discussion between Menger and the historical school involved a criticism of their fondness for organic analogies. Accordingly, Menger (1985, p. 134) asserted 'the incompleteness of the analogy between social phenomena and natural organisms', as if to draw a division between the social and the natural sciences. That, in substance, is how many mainstream and Austrian economists have interpreted it. In 1883, however, Menger was in some respects removing the methodological differences between the physical and the social sciences, by seeing both as subject to universal laws.

However, by proclaiming the individual as the supreme and indivisible unit in the worldly sphere, Menger established a boundary, between the human individual, on the one hand, and the natural and physical reality, on the other. Consistent with Aristotle's distinction between purposeful (finalist) and causal (efficient) explanations, the attribution of rationality and purpose to humans divided them off from the physical and much of the biological world. Yet even if humanity had evolved powers and capacities above other organisms and physical matter, then this evolution still had to be explained. In Menger's scheme, the human individual had been inexplicably emancipated from the physical and natural laws that governed the rest of reality.

---

11 This critical argument originates in Field (1979, 1981, 1984) and is developed in Hodgson (1998a). Notably, Aoki (forthcoming) abandons the attempt to derive institutions from an institution-free state of nature, instead taking historically derived institutions as given. See also Greif (1998).

Menger and the Austrian school had thus forced a division – concerning both ontology and explanation – between biology and the social sciences. Notably, this move was much against the prevailing opinion of the 1880s and 1890s, in both Europe and America. But it was much more in line with the kind of social science that was to emerge gradually after the First World War. Although their views took a long time to become popular in Anglo-American academia, the Austrian school thinkers were among the pioneers of this enduring division between the sciences.

SUMMARY: THE LEGACY OF THE *METHODENSTREIT*

Clearly, the *Methodenstreit* was a major event in the history of economic thought and it changed the course of development of economic theory. Indeed, it concerned the very nature and scope of economic science. For Menger, economics was no longer concerned with the study of economic systems and processes, but was a discipline focused on the economising aspects of human behaviour. It began the process in which economics was eventually transformed from the science of the economy to the science of choice.

More than a century later, many contemporary accounts give the laurels of victory to Menger. Nevertheless, it has been argued here that a total victory for Menger was far from apparent, and not all of his arguments were convincing. From the point of view of economic methodology, in 1883 Menger attempted to establish four propositions:

1 *Anti-inductivism*. Economics can proceed neither initially nor wholly from facts alone; even description relies on a prior theoretical concepts and description cannot itself lead to an explanation of economic phenomena.
2 *Individualism*. The appropriate starting point for economic analysis is the individual, with given purposes and preferences, rather than the 'national economy' or any other higher level unit.
3 *Universality of economic principles*. Some economic principles, such as those relating to supply and demand, pertain to all economic systems. Economics must focus on the elucidation of such principles.
4 *Relegation of historical specificities*. There is no need for economists to give priority to the problem of historical specificity.

It is probably the case that the majority of modern economists accept all four of the above propositions. Hence Menger has had a major impact. It has been argued and accepted in this chapter that the first proposition is persuasive. However, severe problems arise in the other cases.

As argued above, Menger did not give an adequate argument to establish the second proposition, concerning the individual as the unit of analysis. Indeed, there are severe analytical problems with this proposition, especially when attempts are made to explain all institutions as arising from given individuals.

Concerning the third proposition, it can be accepted that some universal or transhistorical concepts or principles are required for economic theory. But there is no obvious reason why these must be primarily the ideas of rational agency or the 'laws' of supply and demand. The case for such particular universal economic laws is far from complete and should not be taken for granted. Furthermore, as noted above, there is evidence to suggest that Menger himself eventually became reticent about this proposition.

The fourth proposition is even more problematic. Even if universal principles are established for economics there is no good reason to deny that supplementary concepts and theories are required to explain the workings of historically specific socio-economic systems. Quite simply, Menger did not make a substantial case here. He thought that his individualistic premises and his arguments for the universality of economic principles were sufficient to demote the problem of historical specificity, which was central to the concerns of the historical school.

To use an imperfect but provocative analogy: if the *Methodenstreit* had been a game of football, perhaps Menger would have lost the contest, scoring one goal against the three scored by the historical school. Menger's goal would have been the most spectacular, but nevertheless he would have lost the match. Despite subsequent mythology – related by twentieth-century economists – he was not widely perceived as the victor at the time. Yet if we read some accounts of this episode, we are given a false account of an intellectual triumph, supposedly leaving the historical school in retreat. On the contrary, the German historical school survived this encounter and drew theoretical strength from it. The more perceptive of its leaders recognised the force of Menger's first argument, and attempted to develop their own theory accordingly. Their engagement with the problem of historical specificity was never abandoned.

Even Menger's supporters, such as von Böhm-Bawerk (1890, p. 268), called for conciliation, writing: 'I desire no battle between the methods. I desire rather their reconciliation and fruitful coöperation'. The limited impact of Menger's attack can also be assessed by examining the reaction of Alfred Marshall. He followed the *Methodenstreit* closely. But, as we shall see in the next chapter, he was far from giving Menger victory on all points. It took several years to elapse, some time after the death of Marshall in 1924, for the myth of Menger's outright victory in the *Methodenstreit* to become conventional. The real story, however, is quite different.

8

ALFRED MARSHALL AND THE BRITISH *METHODENDISKURS*

> Is it so bad, then, to be misunderstood? Pythagoras was misunderstood, and Socrates, and Jesus, and Luther, and Copernicus, and Galileo, and Newton, and every pure and wise spirit that ever took flesh. To be great is to be misunderstood.
>
> (Ralph Waldo Emerson, *Essays* (1841))

This chapter examines the attitude of Alfred Marshall to the problem of historical specificity. It also shows how his intellectual stance has been misunderstood in some modern accounts of his relationship with the historical school. These misunderstandings are so pervasive that a false account of Marshall's engagements with the historical school has emerged and spread among modern commentators. This false account involves the central proposition that Marshall was an opponent of the historical school. For instance, Robert Skidelsky (1983, p. 43) stated that Marshall 'rejected the main contentions of the German historical school'.

Such statements are difficult to reconcile with the fact that Marshall in several places referred positively to members of the German historical school, in his *Principles* and elsewhere. In his 1979–81 lectures at the LSE, Lionel Robbins (1998, p. 306) attempted to explain away these little known positive comments. Robbins did so on the unsupported and implausible grounds that Marshall 'was in some sense *terrified*' of the German historicists. However, the only instance that Robbins could cite of a disagreement between Marshall and any historicist was his altercation in Cambridge with William Cunningham. Furthermore, Robbins neglected to point out that in his debates with Cunningham, Marshall willingly accepted a core proposition of the historical school case and acknowledged the problem of historical specificity. Robbins blindly ignored the fact that Marshall (1949, p. 31) had openly declared in his *Principles* that 'new . . . economic doctrines' were required in different historical periods. On this issue, Cunningham and Marshall were on the same side, and Robbins on the other. By ignoring this central question and some further evidence discussed below, Robbins managed to rewrite history and infer that Marshall was an antagonist of the historical school.

This false account has survived and prospered because it has fitted into more general conceptions of intellectual history, held by both orthodox and heterodox economists. To many orthodox economists, Marshall was a hero who greatly contributed to the development of neoclassical economic theory, and fought valiantly against the 'atheoretical' historicists at Cambridge. Likewise, to many heterodox economists, Marshall was a villain who greatly contributed to the development of neoclassical economic theory, and machinated against the 'more realistic' historicists at Cambridge. The false account fits the prejudices on both sides.

However, this account does not stand up to minimal critical scrutiny. It is a fact that Marshall openly and repeatedly praised and supported many of the ideas and leaders of the German historical school. Furthermore, he understood and addressed the problem of historical specificity in his writings.

As for the supporters of the historical school in Cambridge, the argument here is that they were at least partly responsible for their own marginalisation. This was especially the case with Cunningham, who took an untenable methodological and theoretical position and alienated himself even from other historicist sympathisers. Herbert Foxwell – the other leading historicist in Cambridge – also does not fit into the account. It is a fact that Foxwell was Marshall's close friend and ally until 1908, when Marshall's decision not to back Foxwell as his successor for the Cambridge chair in economics forced them irrevocably apart.

This 1908 incident reflects upon Marshall's character. Again, he was far from the unprincipled schemer and operator that he has sometimes been depicted. True, he could be selfish, tactless, tiresome, obstinate, vain and humourless.[1] However, when he failed to support his closest friend Foxwell, it was not due to duplicity but on the grounds of his own honestly declared academic judgement. His verdict had some foundation. In about 1906 Marshall had developed serious and ostensibly warranted reservations about Foxwell's academic discernment and his capabilities as a teacher. Furthermore, in 1908, Foxwell's record of academic publications was much inferior to that of the successful candidate for the Cambridge chair.

Some accounts of the period have highlighted the policy disputes of the time, particularly over the issue of free trade. Gerard Koot (1987) for example, in an otherwise useful overview, brought policy controversies over free trade to the fore. For Koot, the 'mercantilism' of the historical school took precedence over their methodology. However, there is neither a necessary nor a logical connection between the methodological standpoints of the historical school and any opposition to free trade. It is true that Marshall supported free trade and that several German historicists were critical of such a policy. Cunningham and Foxwell opposed Marshall on this question. But such policy controversies in Britain were hardly a direct 'clash of methods' of the substance, tone and deep methodological impact of the great Continental battle between Carl Menger and Gustav Schmoller.

---

1   Furthermore, Marshall's attitudes to women were decisively unmodern. He opposed the proposal that the University of Cambridge should begin to award degrees to women. On Marshall's complex and enigmatic character see Groenewegen (1995, ch. 21) and T. W. Jones (1978).

Not only have Marshall's relationships with the historical school been misunderstood; Marshall's times also have been misunderstood. It has become a commonplace to refer to the 1870s as the decade of 'the marginal revolution' in economic thought. Yet the more careful historians of ideas have shown clearly that it was less of a sudden revolution than an intermittent process, traceable back to the writings of a variety of economists working as early as the 1830s (Black *et al.*, 1973; Howey, 1960). Furthermore, its impact was delayed. Prior to 1890, most of the published general histories of economic thought failed to mention the term 'marginal utility'. No written account of this supposed 'marginal revolution' in ideas appeared until well into the twentieth century.[2]

For any informed economist working in the years from 1883 to 1914, the Austro-German *Methodenstreit* was as recognisable and important an event as the latterly so-called 'marginal revolution'. Indeed, in retrospect, the deep methodological issues raised in this celebrated 'clash of methods' are even more momentous than the theoretical shift, pioneered by the marginalists, from cost-based to utility-based theories of price.[3]

IT'S ALL IN MARSHALL: HIS RESPECT FOR THE GERMAN HISTORICAL SCHOOL

Marshall was one of the acknowledged pioneers of marginal utility theory. But it is important to note that this neither placed him in a close alliance with Carl Menger, nor made him an enemy of the German historicists. Marshall was fluent in German. Like many aspiring young economists in the nineteenth century, he went to Germany to study under the tutelage of members of the historical school. He was in Dresden in 1868 and in Berlin in 1870–71. He came into contact with several German economists, including Wilhelm Roscher.

In contrast to modern dismissals, references to the German historical school throughout Marshall's writings are respectful and positive, rather than scornful or dismissive.[4] Emphatically, Marshall absorbed rather than rejected much of the doctrine of the German historical school (Hammond, 1991; Hutchison, 1998). Even in the later editions of his *Principles*, Marshall (1949, p. 634) retained a highly laudatory view of the German historicists:

It would be difficult to overrate the value of the work which they and their fellow-workers in other countries have done in tracing and

---

2 According to the JSTOR database, there is no appearance of the terms 'marginal revolution' or 'marginalist revolution' in any leading English language journal of economics until as late as 1950 (A. E. Burns, 1950). However, the term undoubtedly appeared in monographs before that date. Nevertheless, the evidence is that the term 'marginal revolution' is very much a part of the post-1945 recasting of the history of economic thought. Such misleading narratives have focused on the transition from 'classical' to 'neoclassical' price theory, with sorely insufficient regard to what else was happening in economics, especially in the period from 1870 to 1945.

3 Nevertheless, of course, the methodological and theoretical issues were linked in the discussion. See Seager (1893) for an early account of the context and content of the controversy.

4 See the several positive references to Knies, List, Roscher, Schäffle, Schmoller, Wagner and other German historicists that are indexed in Marshall (1919, 1949), and in Marshall and Marshall (1881).

explaining the history of economic habits and institutions. It is one of the great achievements of our age.

Accordingly, Marshall was not in general opposition to the historical school. On the contrary, he often praised their achievements. Furthermore, despite his controversies with some British historicists, during his lifetime Marshall was not depicted as a general opponent of historicism.[5]

Nevertheless, Marshall's economic thought was more individualistic and utilitarian than that of most German historicists. Many historical school economists had argued against the utilitarian view that human welfare could be equated with the satisfaction of subjective desires. However, even on this point, Marshall's position was characteristically conciliatory. On the one hand, in his *Principles*, he described wealth as 'desirable things . . . which satisfy wants'. But on the other hand he admitted 'those elements of the wealth of a nation which are commonly ignored when estimating the wealth of the individuals composing it', including some of the 'non-material elements' stressed by 'German economists' (Marshall, 1949, pp. 45, 49). Marshall's utilitarianism, like Spencer's, was not purely individualist or subjective. If happiness was conceived as the ultimate end, Marshall was just as interested in the concrete conditions under which happiness could prosper. Furthermore, Marshall was also influenced by the metaphor of the social organism, favoured by both Spencer and the German historical school. This also qualified his individualistic outlook. Marshall (1949, pp. 20–1) wrote, in Spencerian terms, that 'economists, like all other students of social science, are concerned with individuals chiefly as members of the social organism. . . . [T]he life of society is something more than the sum of the lives of its individual members.'

It is useful to compare the methodological attitudes of Marshall and Menger, especially in relation to the older historical school. As we have seen in the preceding chapter, Menger's critique of the historicists boiled down to four propositions. Let us examine these. It will be shown that Marshall and Menger agreed on some points but differed in key respects.

Like Menger, Marshall understood the limits of the inductive method. With regard to the first Mengerian proposition in chapter 7 above, they both agreed that economics cannot proceed from facts alone. With regard to the third proposition, they also agreed that economics cannot avoid making use of some universal principles. Turning to the second proposition, their methodologies both focused primarily on the individual, rather than the system. But there was a

---

5   At the time, Seager (1893, p. 237) quoted Marshall's conciliatory and eclectic methodological statements in his *Principles*, and concluded that: 'What Professor Marshall says in regard to method may be quoted as a very fair summary of contemporary German opinion.' Along broadly similar lines, Shove (1942, p. 309) later remarked: 'If any school of thought outside the Ricardian tradition set its mark on the *Principles* it was the Historical School, rather than the marginal utility school, that did so.' One of the few post-1945 commentators to likewise emphasise Marshall's methodological continuity with the German historical school was Hutchison (1988, p. 529) who wrote: 'Alfred Marshall, under German influence, made a strenuous attempt to re-graft a historical-institutional approach on to the neo-classical abstraction.'

significant difference of emphasis. Although Marshall adopted an individualistic methodology, his individualistic viewpoint was highly qualified. Having made the given, rational individual the universal foundation of economic theory, Marshall (1949, pp. 76, 631) then went on to qualify this in his *Principles*. He wrote of 'new activities giving rise to new wants', noting that human character 'is a product of circumstances' and acknowledging that 'changes in human nature' can be significant and rapid.

Most strikingly, concerning the fourth Mengerian proposition, *Marshall did not reject the problem of historical specificity*: unlike Menger he saw it as a legitimate and important question for economists. Crucially, Marshall acknowledged the principle of historical specificity in his inaugural lecture as Professor of Political Economy at Cambridge. This event was two years after Menger's attack in the *Untersuchungen*. Every informed economist was aware of Menger's controversial challenge to Germanic orthodoxy. Significantly, Marshall did not side with the anti-historicist counter-revolution. In his lecture, taking a historicist view, Marshall criticised the English economists of the early nineteenth century because 'they did not see how liable to change are the habits and institutions of industry' (Marshall, 1885, p. 155). Writing as if he were a card-carrying historicist, Marshall (p. 154) further noted that:

> the mathematico-physical group of sciences . . . have this point in common, that their subject-matter is constant and unchanged in all countries and in all ages. . . . [But in contrast] if the subject-matter of a science passes through different stages of development, the laws which apply to one stage will seldom apply without modification to others; the laws of science must have a development corresponding to that of the things of which they treat.

This is an unambiguous recognition of the problem of historical specificity. Likewise, in his *Principles* – the first edition of which appeared in 1890 – Marshall (1949, pp. 30–1) acknowledged that: 'Though economic analysis and general reasoning are of wide application . . . every change in social conditions is likely to require a new development of economic doctrines.'

By comparison, consider the venom that many economists since the 1930s have directed against the German historical school. Compare Marshall's contrasting sympathy for the ideas and achievements of the historicists. Ironically, in 1985 – one hundred years after his inaugural lecture – anyone with historicist sympathies on the scale of Marshall's would have been barred even from a junior university post in any leading department of economics.

Nevertheless, despite his outstanding achievements, detailed problems remained in Marshall's methodological position. He did not elaborate nor explain how the 'laws which apply to one stage' should be modified and applied to another. He did not show what degree or type of modification he had in mind. To what extent, and in what manner, would economic theory have to change to be applied to a changed economic reality? An answer to this question was not apparent. Marshall's statements, while acceptable to many in the historical school, could be interpreted either in terms of mere parametric adjustment of an universal theory, or that quite different laws would pertain from one historical period to another. Marshall fully acknowledged the problem of historical specificity but he did not make a sustained attempt to resolve it. Instead he concentrated on the formulation of the seemingly universal *Principles*, for which he became famous.

GREEDY FOR FACTS: BUT NOT BY FACTS ALONE

Philosophically, Marshall was an admirer of Immanuel Kant. From a similar perspective, Marshall recognised the limitations of all empirical enquiry. Kant (1929, p. 41) had argued in 1781 that 'though all our knowledge begins with experience, it does not follow that it all arises out of experience'. Accordingly, without dismissing empirical work, Marshall recognised the need for additional, theoretical endeavour:

> Greedy then as the economist must be for facts, he must not be content with mere facts. Boundless as must be his gratitude to the great thinkers of the historic school, he must be suspicious of any direct light that the past is said to throw on the problems of the present.
>
> (Marshall, 1885, p. 171)

For Marshall, historical facts were essential, but they cannot on their own provide us with the answers (Marshall, 1949, p. 32). Thus at once he paid unbounded tribute to the work of the historical school, but simultaneously undermined the naïve empiricist views in their midst. Marshall also explained in his inaugural lecture that the mere observation of sequences of events explained nothing:

> facts by themselves are silent. Observation discovers nothing directly of the actions of causes, but only of sequences in time. . . . In economic or social problems no event has ever been the exact precedent of another. The conditions of human life are so various: every event is the complex result of so many causes, so closely interwoven that the past can never throw a simple and direct light on the future.
>
> (ibid., p. 166)

Not only are facts unable to speak for themselves, but also the method of inductive inference is confounded by the complexity of economic phenomena. However, while showing that economics could not rely on induction alone, Marshall appealed to the authority of a leading and sophisticated member of the German historical school. In the *Principles* (Marshall, 1949, p. 24) he quoted and endorsed Schmoller's statement that: 'Induction and deduction are both needed for scientific thought as the left foot and the right foot are both needed for walking.'[6]

Accordingly, Marshall tried to appeal to both sides in the induction versus deduction debate. Although he accepted deduction, he was quite cautious in introducing deductive arguments based on universal assumptions. The deductive core was to be confined to such universal forces as supply and demand. In his inaugural lecture he saw the central and universal core of economic theory as

> a machinery to aid us in reasoning about those motives of human action which are measurable. . . . But, while attributing this high and transcendent universality to the central scheme of economic reasoning, we may not assign any universality to economic dogmas. . . . It is not a body of concrete truth, but an engine for the discovery of concrete truth.
>
> (ibid., pp. 158–9)

In his *Principles*, Marshall outlined a similar idea. Appealing appropriately to biology, he suggested that amidst the historical or evolutionary variety found in economic and biotic phenomena, common features and principles might exist:

> As, in spite of the great differences in form between birds and quadrupeds, there is one Fundamental Idea running through all their frames, so the general theory of the equilibrium of demand and supply is a Fundamental idea running through the frames of all the various parts of the central problem of Distribution and Exchange.
>
> (Marshall, 1949, p. vii)

For Marshall, some general principles were appropriate, corresponding to the elements that were common to diverse phenomena. He argued that the 'general theory of the equilibrium of demand and supply' formed an essential element of the deductive engine of economic theory. However, he wished to restrain and complement this engine's powers. For instance, Marshall (1949, p. 638) warned that the function of

> analysis and deduction in economics is not to forge a few long chains of reasoning, but to forge rightly many short chains and single connecting links. . . . [A]s surely as every deduction must rest on the basis of inductions, so surely does every inductive process involve and include analysis and deduction.

As a result, deduction had to be restrained and limited by empirical anchors. On the other hand, Marshall argued that the danger in some work of the historical

---

6 A problem with Schmoller's statement, however, is that a mixture of two philosophically unsatisfactory methods – induction and deduction – is unlikely to produce a satisfactory result. The intention here is to show the endorsement of Schmoller by Marshall, rather than to sanction Schmoller's methodological formulation.

school was that, in placing an impossible faith in facts alone, they were inattentive to their own acts of classification and logic; and they ignored their own use of deductive reasoning.

> When therefore it is said that a certain event in history teaches us this or that, an element of deductive reasoning is introduced, which is more likely to be fallacious the more persistently it is ignored. For the argument selects a few out of the group of conditions which were present when the event happened, and tacitly, if not unconsciously, assumes that the rest are irrelevant. The assumption may be justifiable: but it often turns out to be otherwise.
>
> (Marshall, 1885, p. 166)

As a result

> the most reckless and treacherous of all theorists is he who professes to let facts and figures speak for themselves, who keeps in the background the part he has played, perhaps unconsciously, in selecting and grouping them, and in suggesting the argument.
>
> (ibid., p. 168)

Here Marshall turned the argument against the naïve empiricists. By claiming that truth is based on the facts alone, they had concealed the prior and unavoidable task of theory in selecting, understanding and arranging those facts. Empiricism was thus a 'treacherous' doctrine, because it downplayed the necessary role of the theorist and the comparison of different theoretical approaches. Those who claimed to build science on facts alone, deluded themselves and others into the false belief that theoretical preconceptions are avoidable. On this issue, Marshall, like Menger, was on strong philosophical ground. Empiricism is flawed as an epistemology, and induction alone is weak as a method.

Overall, Marshall tried to steer an intermediate position between deductivism and empiricism. Although his philosophical position was underdeveloped, his intuitions were consistent and strong. He was highly sceptical of naïve empiricism, on the one hand, and of excessive deductivism and formalism, on the other. As further evidence of this we can cite an interesting correspondence between him and William A. S. Hewins, a man of historicist sympathies who was the first Director of the London School of Economics. Marshall wrote to Hewins on 12 October 1899, concerning the economics curriculum at the School:

> The fact is I am the dull mean man, who holds Economics to be an organic whole, and has little respect for pure theory (otherwise than as a branch of mathematics or the science of numbers), as for that crude collection and interpretation of facts without the aid of high analysis which sometimes claims to be part of economic history.
>
> (Whitaker, 1996, vol. 2, p. 256)

Clearly, Marshall was trying to steer a middle course between overly mathematical economic theory and banal empiricism. Marshall again wrote to Hewins on 29 May 1900:

> Much of 'pure theory' seems to me to be elegant toying: I habitually describe my own pure theory of international trade as a 'toy'. I understand economic science to be the application of powerful analytical methods to unravelling the actions of economic and social causes, to assigning each its part, to tracing mutual interactions and modifications; and above all to laying bare the hidden *causas causantes*.
>
> (Whitaker, 1996, vol. 2, p. 280)

Along very similar lines, Marshall wrote to Francis Edgeworth on 28 August 1902:

> In my view 'Theory' is essential. . . . But I conceive no more calamitous notion than that abstract, or general, or 'theoretical' economics was economics 'proper.' It seems to me an essential but a very small part of economics proper: and by itself sometimes even – well, not a very good occupation of time.
>
> (Pigou, 1925, p. 437; Whitaker, 1996, vol. 2, p. 393)

Sadly, a century later, the economics profession as a whole, including Marshall's own Faculty of Economics at the University of Cambridge, has become much preoccupied with the 'elegant toying' that Marshall had looked down upon so critically. The study of real causes within socio-economic systems, that Marshall saw as the essence of economic science, has become much less fashionable today than the exhibition of mathematical technique for its own sake.

True to his Kantian affections, Marshall saw the priority of such a theory over empirical enquiry. Rightly recognising the limitations of empiricism, he searched for an over-arching conceptual framework within which he could build his theoretical system. He thought that he had found the answer in the 'synthetic philosophy' of Herbert Spencer. Marshall thus followed Schmoller and others in importing ideas from Spencerian biology and philosophy into economics (Pribram, 1983, p. 217).

Even in biology, in the second half of the nineteenth century, Spencer rivalled Charles Darwin in standing. Trained in physics and mathematics, and being a brilliant polymath and synthesiser, Spencer made a significant contribution to biology and extended evolutionary ideas to ethics and social science. Spencer's unified system of ideas was popular and engaging. It seemed that the natural and social sciences could be unified on the basis of a few universal principles. Spencer too offered the lure of a general theory.

Marshall read his works avidly, incorporating several Spencerian notions into his economics (Hodgson, 1993a; Thomas, 1991). As Peter Groenewegen (1995, p. 167) has remarked: 'The significant influence of Spencer on Marshall's thinking cannot be repeated too often.' Spencer provided the key theoretical, or rather meta-theoretical, framework upon which Marshall attempted to build. It was thus a great tragedy for Marshall that Spencer's influence began to wane rapidly in the early years of the twentieth century (Hodgson, 1993a).

John Neville Keynes was an early pupil and devotee of Marshall. His *Scope and Method of Political Economy* (1891) was largely an attempt to develop Marshall's methodology, particularly by trying to steer between induction and deduction, and between description and formalism. Marshall read the proofs of the book and was quite positive about them, although he urged that more attention should be given to contemporary German economists (Moggridge, 1997, pp. 355–6). In his book, Keynes attempted to combine induction with deduction, arguing (p. 227) that economics 'must both begin with observation and end with observation'. Observation to establish premises, deduction to reach conclusions, observation once more to verify them. This work also claimed a continuity of doctrine between the Marshallians at Cambridge and what had gone before. The text minimised theoretical confrontation and tried to find the best in all points of view. Accordingly, it failed to resolve many of the outstanding questions of methodological controversy.

THE *METHODENDISKURS*: MARSHALL AND THE BRITISH HISTORICISTS

As explored earlier in this book, many in the nineteenth-century British historical school were as misled by an empiricist epistemology, as were their earlier co-thinkers in Germany. Marshall countered them on this issue, promoting an ostensibly balanced position, with a role for both induction and deduction. He was careful to cite the authority of Schmoller on this point, and he recognised the value of the empirical work of the historical school.

But even Marshall's balanced statements went too far for Cunningham. Cunningham had studied briefly in Germany, in Tübingen in 1868 and Mannheim in 1874. He became a scholar at Trinity College in 1869 and was taught by Marshall. From 1878, Cunningham taught or examined history at Cambridge, and was appointed a University Lecturer in that subject in 1884. He was an applicant to the Cambridge chair to which Marshall was appointed in December 1884. To evade Marshall's departmental authority, he resigned his university lectureship in 1888 to take up a fellowship at Trinity College. From 1891 to 1897, Cunningham was also Tooke Professor of Economics at King's College, London.[7] He was an occasional teacher at the London School of Economics, from its foundation in 1895. In 1906 he resigned his Trinity Fellowship. He was ordained in 1873 and was vicar at Great St. Mary's church in Cambridge from 1887 until 1908, when he became Archdeacon of Ely. However, he still continued to give occasional lectures in Cambridge and London.

---

7   Notably, in his successful application for the Tooke Chair, Cunningham secured a positive reference from Marshall (Whitaker, 1996, vol. 2, p. 33).

Foxwell, another Cambridge historicist, was one of Marshall's first pupils. He was elected a fellow of St. John's College, Cambridge in 1868. In 1881 he succeeded Jevons as professor of political economy at University College London, while retaining his fellowship at St. John's. Until 1908 he was a very close friend of Marshall. Foxwell favoured the emphasis on demand in the writings of Malthus and Jevons, over the focus on costs of production in the works of Ricardo and Marx. Foxwell thus prefigured J. M. Keynes's stress on 'effective demand' (Koot, 1987, ch. 6). In 1901 Foxwell emphasised that 'in the economic region, all practical questions should be determined on their merits, after detailed and historical investigation of the particular circumstances, and not by summary reference to maxims or dogmas supposed to be of universal application'.[8]

Nevertheless, this was not so far from the view of Marshall, and the two sometimes expressed their closeness on such matters. In their correspondence of 1897 on matters of method, Foxwell suggested to Marshall that J. N. Keynes's position was midway between that of Marshall and his own. Marshall (1996, vol. 2, p. 179) responded in conciliatory tone to Foxwell on 30 January 1897: 'Most of the suggestions which I made on the proofs of Keynes's *Scope and Method* were aimed at bringing it more into harmony with the views of Schmoller.' Marshall thus emphasised his methodological affinities with a leading member of the younger German historical school. Although Marshall admitted differences of methodological emphasis with Foxwell, he did not make much of them.

Overall, Foxwell was more sympathetic to deductive economic theory than Cunningham. In particular, Foxwell had been a friend of Jevons and was an admirer of his work. Foxwell (1919, pp. 387–8) later documented that Cunningham's 'general depreciation of economic theory' had enticed 'friendly controversy' from Foxwell himself, as well as from other Cambridge colleagues. Although, in this obituary of Cunningham, Foxwell also admitted that he had found himself 'more and more inclined to move in his direction'. Foxwell's doctrinal breach with Marshall had slowly widened. In the late 1890s Marshall criticised the overly descriptive content of Foxwell's teaching. After 1903, Foxwell joined Cunningham in arguing for more study of historical subjects on the Cambridge Economics Tripos.

In contrast, Cunningham had entered the doctrinal battle much earlier and with much greater force, after he had lost against Marshall in the 1884 competition for the Cambridge chair. Like his predecessors in the German historical school, Cunningham (1885) defended the focus on national economic units and aggregates. However, he aligned himself with the extreme empiricist wing of the historical school, thereby to become one of Marshall's foremost antagonists (Maloney, 1985, pp. 99–105). Cunningham resolutely opposed the view, expressed convincingly by Marshall in his inaugural lecture, that theory could not be built on facts alone. In positivist terms, Cunningham defended the primacy

---

8 This is an extract from Foxwell's unsuccessful 1901 application to the chair of commerce at the University of Birmingham, to which Ashley was in fact appointed (quoted in J.M. Keynes, 1972, p. 270).

of the facts. For Cunningham (1887, p. 8) economics should be primarily an empirical science, concerned with description and classification:

> Instead of aspiring to be a sort of Pure Physics of Society which assuming a single force – the individual desire for wealth – states the laws of the operation of this force in the supply and demand of different articles of value, Political Economy might for the present be content to *observe* and *classify* and *describe* and *name* as other sciences have been.... No real advance can come from the statement of laws of phenomena which only hold good when a considerable number of cases are excluded as abnormal; if Political Economy is to rank with other empirical sciences one must try to classify the widely varied phenomena of industrial life ... as an empirical science in its classificatory stage.

Hence, according to the above statement, Cunningham's highly inadequate answer to the problem of historical specificity was that economists should be preoccupied with taxonomy. For Cunningham, the main role of 'theory' was to taxonomise categories for the purposes of empirical research. He objected to the assumptions of neoclassical economics in the following terms:

> The underlying assumption against which I wish to protest is ... that the same motives have been at work in all ages, and have produced similar results, and that, therefore, it is possible to formulate economic laws which describe the action of economic causes at all times and in all places.
>
> (Cunningham, 1892b, p. 493)

Cunningham (1892a, p. 12) also wrote at about the same time: 'We cannot then hope to find any strictly economic doctrine that gives us an adequate explanation of the phenomena of exchange in all times in all places.' Interestingly, Cunningham (1892b, p. 492) saw Spencer's work as an example of the dangers of excessive universality in theory. He dismissed Spencer thus: 'since he professes to know laws according to which all organisms develop, he need not trouble about the actual facts.' But this is a non sequitur. Knowledge of laws does not necessarily obviate the need for parametric and other data. Cunningham's remark was a sideways blow also against Marshall, who greatly admired Spencer.

It is true that Cunningham's insistence that economic theory had to have a strong, historically specific component illuminated Marshall's failure to develop one. However, Cunningham almost completely ruined his case by replacing this by a taxonomic empiricism, and by failing to recognise that even taxonomy requires some universal principles before it can proceed. Cunningham (1892a, p. 2) wrote: 'Economic doctrine about the actual world we live in is all built up as a branch of empirical knowledge; it has no universality.' Cunningham did not seem to realise that the negation of universality is itself a universal statement and that all empirical knowledge requires universal categories. Cunningham's extreme, untenable and self-contradictory empiricist position denied the very conceptual tools upon which all enquiry must proceed. Furthermore, Cunningham's criticisms of Marshall were so overstated and unconvincing that he became 'an outsider even among historical economists' such as Foxwell and William Ashley (Koot, 1987, p. 146).

Marshall (1892) responded to Cunningham. However, the Cunningham–Marshall debate did not go into great methodological depth. Marshall again conceded much of the historical school case: historical enquiry was essential for economic theory. Especially given this concession, Marshall's position was an attractive one, even for those young scholars who saw much of value in the work of the historical school. While valuing historical research, Marshall successfully argued that theoretical analysis was required to make sense of causal processes in history. In a clear reference to Cunningham, Marshall wrote to Foxwell on 27 March 1899 criticising those 'who are studying economic history as a mere series of facts' (Whitaker, 1996 vol. 2, p. 251).

A pale shadow of the Austro-German *Methodenstreit*, this British altercation over methods left Cunningham isolated and Marshall in a much stronger position. On the question of historical specificity, Marshall had conceded to the historical school, but from a philosophical standpoint that was stronger than that of his principal British adversary. Marshall chastised Cunningham for his naïve empiricism, not for his attention to the problem of historical specificity.

The Cunningham–Marshall controversy again came to the boil in the early 1900s. Although the controversy then involved the policy matter of free trade, the focal and decisive issue was the content of the economics curriculum in Cambridge. When the Economics Tripos was established in Cambridge in 1903, two full years of undergraduate study were devoted to economic theory, with only one year remaining for applied economics, economic history and politics. Cunningham protested. In 1905 the Economics Faculty Board posted a notice advising students that Dr. Cunningham, Director of Studies in Economics at Trinity College, 'has publicly declared himself to be out of sympathy with the study of economics under the direction of this Board'. Accordingly, students preparing for the examinations in economics were advised to seek counsel elsewhere (Koot, 1987, p. 149; Kadish, 1989, p. 218). This made Cunningham's permanent position at Cambridge unsustainable, and the following year he resigned his college fellowship. Cunningham's intransigent polarisation of the dispute encouraged a bureaucratic and doctrinal reaction, which led to outcomes opposite to those that he intended.

Like many in the older (but not the younger) German historical school, Cunningham saw the salvation of theory in terms of empirical enquiry alone. He failed to understand Menger's forceful argument that even empiricism requires prior universal assumptions, such as the uniformity of nature. All empirical work requires prior universal concepts, such as units of measure. Taxonomies themselves require classificatory schema. All such concepts are tied up with explicit or implicit theories about the world. Theory is unavoidable, and has epistemic priority over facts. Cunningham did not understand this. Marshall did. It was tragic for the British historical school that some of its exponents fought on such weak methodological ground.

The historical school was not uniform in its methodology. Previous accounts of Marshall's relations with historical school have downplayed the difference between the historicists who developed theory (such as Gustav von Schmoller, Max Weber and Werner Sombart) and the more empiricist historicists (such as Wilhelm Roscher and William Cunningham). Marshall sympathised much more with Schmoller and his followers, although he went further than Schmoller in emphasising the analytical priority of theory.

The philosophical untenability of the empiricist position is not sufficiently emphasised in some modern accounts. Marshall was right to insist that empirical enquiry was impossible without theory, and that theory had priority. Like the astute historicists in Germany, Marshall had assimilated Menger's critique of empiricist historicism. So when he took a dislike to some of the views of some of his historicist critics, it was their naïve empiricism rather than their historicism to which he primarily took exception. There is no major inconsistency between his public and his private persona here. Both his letters and his publications criticise empiricism, on the one hand, and praise the German historicist theorists, on the other. His tributes to the German historical school are repeated in his publications, up to and including the later editions of his *Principles*.[9]

Nor is it accurate to characterise Marshall's methodological views as simply 'eclectic' with Marshall 'prepared to use any method that produced helpful and useful results' (Moggridge, 1997, p. 365). On the contrary, Marshall's criticism of those who believed that theories could be spun from facts was relatively sophisticated for his time. Although Marshall's drive for a robust economic theory was eventually harnessed by his more formalistic neoclassical successors, the choice in 1885 was largely between historically informed theory, on the one hand, and naïve empiricism, on the other. Marshall adopted the stronger philosophical position. The tragedy is that Marshall failed to develop a theoretical framework within which the full sweep of historical development and structural change could be accommodated.

In the 1885–1908 period (from Marshall's inaugural lecture to his retirement) the general mood was one of Marshallian politeness and conciliation, rather than the disharmony of the Germanic *Methodenstreit*. Indeed, it is somewhat misleading to describe the Cambridge arguments of the period as a *Methodenstreit* at all. To repeat, unlike Menger, Marshall had explicitly recognised the problem of historical specificity. Regarding the contest between deductive and inductive methods – the second aspect of the Germanic *Methodenstreit* – a superficial but inadequate resolution had been reached when Marshall, like Schmoller, had accepted that both methods had to be combined: 'as the left foot and the right

---

9   In general, Marshall dealt with his antagonists with civility. Perhaps Marshall's most hostile statement against the empiricist historians was in his letter to J. N. Keynes of 27 May 1889 where he wrote: 'I want however to keep my hold on the Historical men: they are Kittle-Kattle, and yet important' (Whitaker, 1996, vol. 1, p. 290). Yet this statement has an unclear meaning. It does not imply that Marshall was hostile to the historical school as a whole. The phrase 'Kittle-Kattle' could be a reference to the 'Chit Chat Club'. This was a select and exclusive academic circle within the University of Cambridge, limited to 15 members. Cunningham, Foxwell and J. N. Keynes were members but strangely Marshall was never invited to join (Groenewegen, 1995, pp. 110, 444).

foot are both needed for walking'. Remarkably, these methodological discussions reached a high degree of consensus. The fact that a methodological dispute persisted at all was more to do with the relative intransigence of naïve empiricists like Cunningham, who never accepted a major role for economic theory. But the intransigent empiricists were never representative of either the German or the British historical schools in their totality. Compared with the clashes between Menger and Schmoller, the British *Methodenstreit* never reached the same degree of intensity or venom over methodological issues. In the British case, *Methodendiskurs* would be a better term.

Far from Marshall being an antagonist of historicism, it would be better to see Marshall as a representative and extension of the type of historically sensitive and theoretically informed thinking that had emerged in Germany by the end of the nineteenth century. To put it truthfully but provocatively, Marshall himself was a product and part of the historical school tradition.

It may be objected, however, that the net result of Marshall's particular efforts to assert the primacy of theory was to establish a neoclassical tradition that became progressively more formal, more technical, narrower and less historical. There is an element of truth here, but Marshall bears only part of the responsibility for the outcome. Crucially, despite his persistent recognition of the importance of the problem, Marshall never developed an adequate theoretical framework to deal with the issue of historical specificity. But other factors were beyond his control. In particular, the fragmented British historical school was much weaker than the German, and it lacked a sizeable cohort of methodologically and theoretically astute researchers.

Both such factors were in play when Marshall retired in 1908, and he did his best to ensure that the youthful Arthur Pigou got the job. Although Pigou was only 30 years of age at the time of the election of the chair, he had published much more extensively than Foxwell. To Foxwell's chagrin and astonishment, Pigou's application was successful.[10]

Pigou subsequently developed formalistic aspects of Marshallian theory, addressing welfare economics and other matters. Whatever the merits and

---

10 Cannan and Ashley were the other two candidates for Marshall's chair. For discussions of the reasons and processes behind Foxwell's rejection and Pigou's appointment see Coase (1972), Coats (1968, 1972), T. W. Jones (1978) and Groenewegen (1995, pp. 622–7). Coase (1972) points out that in 1900–8, Pigou published no less than ten articles in the *Economic Journal* and five books. In contrast, in the same period, Foxwell published no books and just one substantial article – in the *Palgrave Dictionary of Political Economy*. On the other hand, Foxwell's service to the university was much the greater. Marshall's correspondence reveals his criticisms of Foxwell. In a letter to Foxwell of 12 February 1906, Marshall politely and honestly noted their personal differences in 'ideals in economics' and of academic judgement. The most revealing letter is to J. N. Keynes, dated 13 December 1908. Here Marshall criticised Foxwell as a lecturer who 'imposes his judgement on youth' rather than trying 'to develop faculty, and to leave judgement to be formed later'. Marshall also wrote: 'Foxwell's judgements, while always confident, are likely to be in opposite directions at six months notice, I have fear of his judgements. . . . He seems never to see more than one side of any complex question' (Whitaker, 1996, vol. 3, pp. 126, 215). Notably, Groenewegen (1995, p. 625) argued convincingly that Marshall did not abandon support for Foxwell and support Pigou as his future successor until 1906. In supporting Pigou, Marshall had acted on his academic judgement, but it caused an irreparable breach with his closest friend.

justification of Pigou's appointment to the chair, it is clear in retrospect that the elevation of this brilliant, but very young, theoretical economist marked the end of the period of Cambridge's intensive engagement with the German historical school. The huge generational leap from Marshall to Pigou meant the loss of much of the knowledge and awareness of historicism. If Pigou knew anything much about the German historical school, it is not apparent in his writing. Still a tiny department, with no more than two dozen undergraduate students (Groenewegen, 1995, p. 553), there were few to pass on an oral tradition of Marshallian connections with German historicism. Cambridge economics thus entered a period of relative intellectual isolation.

A PLURALISTIC ACADEMY

Despite the historical caricatures of Robbins and others, the Marshallian period was one in which theorists and historicists worked alongside one another: there were differences of view but never a complete compartmentalisation of viewpoints. For example, the young Ashley – eventually to become a guiding light of the British historical school in the early twentieth century – was critical of aspects of Marshall's *Principles* but concluded with the following significant tribute and concordant evaluation:

> The *Principles of Economics* is a work worthy of its author's reputation, and of his position as the *doyen* of English economists. . . . It is the more welcome because it brings a message of conciliation to divergent schools, and it makes it possible for 'deductive' and 'historical,' 'scientific' and 'ethical' economists to work together in harmony.
>
> (Ashley, 1891, p. 489)

A similarly pluralistic spirit was evident when Edgeworth, the leading neoclassical economist and first editor of the *Economic Journal*, opened the first volume:

> The *Economic Journal* . . . will be open to writers of different schools. The most opposite doctrines may meet here as on a fair field. . . . Nor will it be attempted to prescribe the method, any more than the result, of scientific investigation.
>
> (Edgeworth, 1891, p. 1)

We find clear and plentiful evidence of the implementation of this pluralist policy in the early volumes of the *Economic Journal*. There are signs of the influence of historical school thinking on British economics, including challenges to the atomistic individualism of some economic theorists. In the theory of consumption, for instance, there were attempts to go beyond atomistic individualism and develop the theory of interdependent and socialised consumers. Henry Cunynghame (1892) discussed the interdependence of consumer demands, thus setting the limits of the independent individual. Caroline Foley (1893) went much further. Starting from a recognition of the historical specificity of socio-economic structures and behaviour, she saw the need to study consumption as a real, historically conditioned and socially structured process. Pigou (1903, 1913) subsequently made two attempts to incorporate interdependent and inter-subjective aspects of consumer demand into neoclassical analysis. But Pigou (1913, p. 24) himself came to the conclusion that these attempts were 'wholly inadequate'. Not being readily formalised, these issues were eventually to slip off the agenda of mainstream economists in a later period (Mason, 1995; Fullbrook, 1998).

The failure of the British historicists was in part due to their own conception of scientific advance. None of the leading figures of the British school was able to build an alternative methodology or theory, and they remained largely entrapped by an empiricist epistemology. Largely for this reason, and despite the persistent influence of a few individuals, the historical school failed to establish an enduring bridgehead in the British Isles. Gradually pushed aside in academic argument, several members of the British historical school made their way into the discipline of economic history, embraced empiricism, and abandoned economic theory to the theorists. Crucially, the British historicists were overshadowed in the crucial encounters that occurred during the pro-fessionalisation of economics, and the establishment of distinct economics departments in several British universities in early part of the twentieth century.[11]

In justice, William Ashley and John A. Hobson were probably the two historicists sufficiently well qualified to succeed to Marshall's chair in 1908. Crucially for the fate of English economics, Ashley was away at the universities of Toronto and Harvard in the crucial years from 1888 to 1900. A graduate of Oxford, he returned to become Professor of Commerce at the University of Birmingham in 1901. Ashley disliked the drift towards 'pure theory' and argued for an economics based on history and business experience. His relatively sophisticated brand of historicism had explicit 'evolutionary' connotations, and he had an important influence on the important but fledgling subdiscipline of business economics (A. Ashley, 1932; W. Ashley, 1907, 1908, 1924, 1926).

Hobson (1902, 1911, 1914) openly embraced the metaphor of society-as-an-organism that was so central to German historicism. Fatefully, Hobson (1902) had criticised Marshall's marginal utility theory. Although there are clear flaws in Hobson's argument, Marshall also did not come out of this debate without error (Maloney, 1985). Nevertheless, Marshall and his followers kept Hobson at

---

11 See Kadish (1989), Kadish and Tribe (1993), Koot (1987) and Maloney (1985). However, the growth of economics in Britain as a separate discipline under the leadership of Marshall and his followers, and its separation from economic history, did not amount to a 'disintegration of political economy' as some have suggested. In truth, neither Marshall nor his predecessors had an adequately integrated system of political economy. If there was any 'integration' before (say) 1900 it was more to do with the fact that these subjects were often taught together, rather than the existence of any guiding overall framework or discipline of 'political economy'. Furthermore, the story concerning the relationship between economics and economic history is very different in Germany and the USA, and we cannot generalise from the British experience.

arm's length. The influential American economist Richard Ely wrote to Marshall on 11 October 1901: 'I think that there is a feeling in this country that the English economists have not done justice to Hobson' (Whitaker, vol. 2, p. 336). Indeed, Hobson has never received his due. He authored no less than 53 books and hundreds of articles, and influenced twentieth-century thinkers as important as Lenin and J. M. Keynes. Yet he was denied any university post. He died in 1940 as the last – and most long-lived – of the British historicists. His death marked the end of a tradition that failed to establish an enduring foothold and identity in British universities. This did not mean, however, that it did not make a mark.

The fact that there is no extensive discussion of Ashley and Hobson in the present work does not indicate that they were of little importance. Both were to keep the flame of historicism alight in Britain in the early decades of the twentieth century. It is simply that they did not make a major contribution to the exposition or resolution of the problem of historical specificity. It is also regrettable that their ideas did not find any theoretical movement in Britain that addressed this issue. In Britain after Marshall the problem was forgotten.

9

THE RESPONSES OF THE
YOUNGER HISTORICAL SCHOOL
IN GERMANY

Our aim is the understanding of the characteristic uniqueness of
the reality in which we move.
(Max Weber, '"Objectivity" in Social Science and
Social Policy' (1904))

In the German-speaking countries, Carl Menger's methodological attack on the
historical school stimulated an active, sometimes acerbic, and abiding controversy. In the years immediately after the *Untersuchungen* was published in 1883,
Gustav von Schmoller led the counter-attack. However, well into the twentieth
century, others – notably Max Weber and Werner Sombart – addressed at length
the problems that had been unearthed in the *Methodenstreit*.[1]

THE RIPOSTE OF GUSTAV VON SCHMOLLER

Schmoller was a professor of economics successively in Halle (1864–72),
Strassburg (1872–82) and Berlin (1882–1913). He had an enormous, international
influence (Balabkins, 1988). The leading German economist of his time, he
engaged with Menger in a number of controversies, dating back to the 1870s.
In these debates, Schmoller developed his own position, as well as opposing
Menger's. He defended the historical school's 'organic' notion of 'national
economy' and opposed the view that human nature can be reduced to purely
egotistic motivations (Hutter, 1993).

Schmoller (1883, p. 249) conceded that 'Menger is right in his assertion that
every social structure can be eventually traced back to the mental processes of

---

1 Not all of the German historicists opposed Menger's stand in the *Methodenstreit*. Bücher was a
  prominent example. Incidentally, Bücher (1893) developed a geographically-oriented and
  production-based theory of stages of economic development, involving a transition from
  household economy, to town economy, to national economy (Reinert, 2000). Bücher insisted that
  true exchange was virtually absent in the household economy and had developed fully in the
  stage of national economy. Hence, despite his sympathy for Menger in the *Methodenstreit*, Bücher
  took a position on the concept of exchange that was quite different from that of the Austrian
  economist.

individuals'. But for Schmoller this was not the crucial point. For him, individuals were neither purely egotistical nor entirely co-operative. They were motivated by an 'infinite number' of mixed motives, involving both co-operative and egotistical elements. As Schmoller wrote in 1884:

> in spite of the fact that it is the individual and the family that labour, produce, trade, and consume, it is the larger social bodies which, by their common attitude and action, intellectual as well as practical, create all those economic arrangements of society.
>
> (Schmoller, 1897, p. 77)

Hence the choice of the individual as the basic unit of analysis was criticised by Schmoller on the grounds that individuals were always moulded by historical and cultural circumstances. The isolated individual was a fiction. The individual could not be understood without an appraisal of this historical and cultural context. However, contrary to the impression given by Schmoller, the study of history alone could not demolish the atomistic, individualistic ontology upon which Menger's views were based. Menger knew this, and simply insisted that 'larger social bodies' themselves required explanation in terms of the individuals involved. On the whole, Schmoller's defences of the historical school in the mid-1880s were unsuccessful in overturning the Austrian school argument.

In two major works, published in 1898 and 1900, Schmoller made a more robust attempt to refine the methodology of the historical school and make it less vulnerable to critical attack. He upheld the historical sensitivity of theory by insisting that: 'Scientific method depends on the nature of the subject matter under enquiry' (Schmoller, 1898, p. 229). However, unlike many of the preceding members of the historical school, he admitted the limits of purely empirical work: 'Observation and description, definition and classification are preparatory work only' (p. 277). For Schmoller, science must rely on both induction and deduction, as necessary and complementary aspects of enquiry. In his post-*Methodenstreit* view, science must reach beyond superficial appearances: 'there must remain before our eyes, as the ideal of all knowledge, the explanation of all facts in terms of causation' (p. 277). Schmoller thus gave significantly greater emphasis – compared with several of his historical school predecessors – to the search for causal explanation.[2]

Hence, while retaining the notion of the national economy as a focus of analysis, Schmoller (1898, p. 219) argued that 'if the national economy is considered as a whole, the focus must be placed on the real causes of this unity'. These real causes involved individuals and their natural environment. This was a critique of the

---

2 For discussions of Schmoller's views on causality see Gioia (1993) and Dopfer (1998). Notably, Schmoller (1898, pp. 286–7) wrote: 'There is no science possible outside the range of the universal law of causation – not even in the domain of the spiritual life. But the causes at work in the psychical sequence are essentially different from the mechanical ones.' Hence, like Veblen and others, Schmoller clearly adopted the principle of universal causation: he held that every event has a cause. See (Hodgson, unpublished) for a discussion of this principle.

tendency among some of the older historicists to regard the national economy as itself causally efficacious.

In his *Grundriss* of 1900, Schmoller developed these ideas further. He reiterated the importance of abstraction for any meaningful observation (vol. 1, p. 101). His belief in the historical sensitivity of theory was linked to a pronounced scepticism concerning the possibility of formulating any universal historical laws: 'We have no knowledge of the laws of history, although we sometimes speak of economic and statistical laws' (vol. 1, p. 108). It was not even possible to establish universal measures of progress: 'We cannot even say whether the economic life of humanity possesses any element of unity or shows any traces of uniform development, or whether it is making any progress at all' (vol. 2, p. 653). In his critique of overly deductive theory, Schmoller pointed out that axiomatic theory could point to the possibility of schedules of supply and demand, but it could not explain how these curves took a particular shape. That was, for Schmoller, where institutional or cultural factors entered as part of the explanation. However, Schmoller did not show in detail how these factors affected the outcomes. For all his concern with causal explanation, Schmoller did not paint an adequate picture of how an explanatory theory could be built, or of how its core concepts could be derived.

While recognising a role for deduction as well, Schmoller (1900) still placed too much faith in description and induction as means of building theory. He wrote: 'the main aim of all description is to prepare induction, which is the conclusion from singularities to the fundamental law' (vol. 1, p. 102). Again Schmoller failed to understand that theory had to precede observation, as well as to succeed it. He tried to explain how an understanding of causality could emerge, by way of observation of 'regularly and typical repeating series of phenomena' (vol. 1, p. 109). As Alexander Ebner (2000, p. 358) pointed out, 'he never abandoned the idea that comparative research might uncover a sufficient amount of empirical regularities and thus lead to the formulation of historical laws.'

Nevertheless, Schmoller's (1898, 1900) work is extremely rich in institutional analysis. In these volumes, he also attempted to develop an alternative approach to the theory of value, price and distribution. He also discussed extensively and in detail the costs of contracting and of using the market mechanism. He thus foreshadowed the transaction cost theory hinted at by Thorstein Veblen (1904, pp. 46–8) and developed more explicitly and extensively by Ronald Coase (1937) and Oliver Williamson (1975).

Furthermore, Schmoller generally emphasised the importance of underlying causal processes. Indeed, on the question of causality, Schmoller in a sense went even further than his Austrian school adversaries. He did not take the individual agent as given. For Schmoller, the preferences and purposes of the agents themselves – as well as the institutions that they helped to create or sustain – required causal explanation. Schmoller (1898, p. 287) insisted that the investigation of causal processes in economics must reach into the human psyche: 'it becomes incumbent on the practical science, such as economics, to carry its inquiry, as far as may be needed, into the details of psychological processes.' In the *Grundriss* he reinforced the same theme, admitting that psychical processes were not mechanical, but still were subject to causal explanation: 'We know now that psychical causation is something other than mechanical, but it bears the same stamp of necessity' (Schmoller, 1900, vol. 1, p. 107). Accordingly, socio-economic circumstances affected individuals, just as individuals affected socio-economic circumstances.

In contrast, Menger had emphasised causal explanation in one direction only: from given individuals to the formation of institutions. Although there were important informational feedbacks from institutions to individuals in Menger's analysis of institutions, the received information did not reconstitute or transform the goals or preferences of the individual actor. Instead of this uni-directional emphasis at the constitutive level, Schmoller (1900, vol. 1, p. 107) introduced the idea of 'circular causation' where individuals and structures were mutually constitutive of each other. In the hands of the institutionalist and future Nobel Laureate Gunnar Myrdal and others, amended versions of this phrase were much later to play a crucial role in the development of institutional economics.

Schmoller was thus critical of Menger's attempt to take individual preferences as given. Menger had applied the method of isolation too ruthlessly. For Schmoller, the search for causal explanation should not stop with individual goals and choices, but should go on to explore their foundation in the human psyche. In the terms of the *Untersuchungen*, Menger had little defence against this argument, as he could have hardly claimed that the human psyche was an 'accidental' or 'superficial' matter. In response to Menger, Schmoller (1900, vol. 1, p. 110) argued that the method of isolation must be used in economics with great circumspection and care. For Schmoller, psychology provided the key to the social sciences.

However, while effectively making inroads into Menger's individualistic ontology and methodology, Schmoller failed to build an adequate method-ological and theoretical alternative. In his analysis he fell back on ethical norms and notions of *Geist* or spirit. For Schmoller, ethical ideals shaped institutions, and social institutions shaped human habits and behaviour. Such a conception requires an arbitrary and *a priori* framework of ethical universals. An infinite regress is invoked, requiring an ethical principle to validate an ethical principle, and so on. Another problem with this idealistic demarcation of socio-economic systems is that it is based on a faulty conception of knowledge. Ideas and ethical imperatives are seen as driving all human behaviour, implying that human ends are given at the point of activity, always prior to the means and the activity itself. As discussed in the next chapter, the American pragmatism of Charles Sanders Peirce, William James, John Dewey and others displaced these ideas, and brought about revolution in our conception of knowledge.[3]

---

3   For further assessments of Schmoller's work see the symposia in the *Journal of Institutional and Theoretical Economics* (1988) and the *History of Economic Ideas* (1993), including articles by Betz (1993), Dopfer (1988, 1993), Gioia (1993), Hutter (1993), Meyer (1988), Nardinelli and Meiners (1988), Prisching (1993) and Schneider (1993). See also J. C. O'Brien (1987, 1989), Dopfer (1998), Ebner (2000), Harris (1942), Koslowski (1995) and Pearson (1997).

Well into the twentieth century, the view persisted – including in Austria and Germany – that the *Methodenstreit* was unresolved. For example, although Joseph Schumpeter regarded much of the debate as misconceived, he tried persistently to develop the insights on both sides. For Schumpeter (1908, pp. 6–7) 'both sides are mostly right . . . their sole difference lies in their interests in different problems.' Schumpeter later returned to the methodological problems of the *Methodenstreit*. In an important article he demonstrated the significance of Schmoller's work, largely by reconstructing its foundations and meaning. Schumpeter (1926) argued that Schmoller had been misunderstood by some of his critics; it was quite wrong to caricature Schmoller as being interested only in historical description. Schumpeter acknowledged that Schmoller had defended a role for abstract theory. Rather than caricaturing or dismissing him, Schumpeter argued that Schmoller had made a contribution to 'economic sociology' (*Wirtschaftssoziologie*). He justified a place for the type of historically oriented research that Schmoller had developed. Schumpeter thus retained a place for formal, general theorising within economics, while recognising the value of the historical school legacy in its *Wirtschaftssoziologie*. However, this meant the resettlement of the historical school in 'sociology' and its exclusion from the inner sanctum of 'economic theory'. Nevertheless, strong traces of historical sensitivity persisted in Schumpeter's own work.[4]

HISTORICISM, INDIVIDUALISM AND SUBJECTIVISM IN MAX WEBER'S THOUGHT

In the first third of the twentieth century, the ideas of the German historical school were brought to their supreme point of development (Schefold, 1995). In this process, Weber made a major contribution. As noted above, Weber was a professor of political economy, from 1894 at the University of Freiburg and from 1896 at the University of Heidelberg. From 1903 to his early death from influenza and pneumonia in 1920, Weber created and refined a historical methodology for the social sciences. Weber's ideas were developed in a number of methodological papers, including a long essay published in German in 1904 and an unfinished magnum opus, eventually published in English as *Economy and Society*.[5] Among the influences on Weber were Karl Marx and Friedrich Nietzsche. Like many others in his generation, Weber's methodology also had strong neo-Kantian features. In addition, he was strongly influenced by his colleague Sombart. Although they had fierce disputes, Weber frankly admitted how much he was indebted to 'Sombart's great works with their sharp definitions'.[6]

---

4 For discussions of Schumpeter's methodology and the degree of his affinity with the German historical school see Machlup (1951), Swedberg (1989), Shionoya (1990, 1991, 1995, 1997), Streissler (1994), Chaloupek (1995) and Ebner (2000).
5 Several quotations below are taken from this and other works that were unpublished at the time of his death. Generally the date of first publication has no proximity to the date of composition.
6 Quoted in Brocke (1996, p. 50). Brocke alleged that Weber's *General Economic History* 'is in large parts a compendium of Sombart's thoughts' (ibid.).

Nevertheless, the influence went both ways. Particularly on methodological questions, Sombart often turned to Weber.

Weber avoided some of the methodological errors of the earlier historicists. Unlike members of the older historical school, for Weber all empirical enquiries and all attempts to uncover causal linkages behind surface phenomena must begin from a conceptual framework. Hence Weber faced directly the unresolved question of the construction or choice of the concepts that we are obliged to use to achieve any understanding of socio-economic reality, and the criteria that should be deployed to determine their appropriateness or inappropriateness in any given context.[7]

Weber thus addressed some of the key problems of the *Methodenstreit*. He acknowledged that earlier members of the historical school had failed to develop an adequate theoretical and methodological approach and that Menger and his followers had made several valid points. Although he saw the achievements of the historical school as substantive, Weber nevertheless rejected the notion that the national economy could be compared with a living organism, as found in the writings of several members of the historical school. He wrote in a letter shortly before his death:

> if I have become a sociologist . . . it is mainly in order to exorcize the spectre of collective conceptions which still lingers among us. In other words, sociology itself can only proceed from the actions of one or more separate individuals and must therefore adopt strictly individualistic methods.
>
> (quoted in Mommsen, 1965, p. 25)

Weber thus accepted some of Menger's individualistic strictures. Weber's concern to discover underlying causal relations, and not to shortcut the matter by attributing causal powers to structures or wholes, led him to adopt a relatively individualistic methodological approach that contrasted with his historical school predecessors. Essentially, Weber argued that the ultimate stage of explanation of social or economic phenomena should involve the examination of the purposes and actions of the individuals involved. In contrast to believers in the 'social organism', Weber (1968, vol. 1, p. 13) regarded collectives as 'solely the resultants and modes of organisation of the specific acts of *individual* men, since these alone are for us the agents who carry out subjectively understandable action'. Likewise, Weber (1947, p. 102) insisted that

> for sociological purposes there is no such thing as a collective personality which 'acts.' When reference is made in a sociological context to a 'state,'

7　In the so-called *Werturteilstreit* (the dispute over the role of value-judgements in the social sciences that erupted at the meeting of the *Verein für Sozialpolitik* in 1909), Weber and Sombart criticised earlier historicists who had conflated judgements of fact with judgements of value. But this is not a good enough reason to place Weber and Sombart outside the historical school, as Schneider (1995, p. 175) would have it.

a 'nation,' a 'corporation,' a 'family,' or an 'army corps,' or to similar collectivities, what is meant is, on the contrary, *only* a certain kind of development of actual or possible social actions of individual persons.

For Weber, causal efficacy was located exclusively within the individual. However, this does not mean that Weber was strictly a promoter of methodological individualism. Some definitions of methodological individualism (for example, Elster, 1982, p. 453) have suggested that all explanations of social or economic phenomena should be reduced entirely to individuals. Weber did not go this far. Notably, his statement that individuals alone 'carry out subjectively understandable action' is a version of ontological rather than methodological individualism, concerning action as an aspect of social being. Weber was clearly concerned to make intentional individuals – rather than the 'social organism' or 'social forces' – the causal agents behind socio-economic phenomena. But Weber also examined the way in which social structures and institutions can shape human purposes and beliefs. Hence he did not reduce explanations *entirely* to individuals.

Nevertheless the individualistic thrust of Weber's analysis was in remarkable contrast with the earlier historical school. Notably, both Weber and his historical school predecessors lacked the concept of an emergent property. With the concept of emergence, multiple levels of analysis are possible, based on emergent properties and causal powers at each level. Simultaneously, both individuals and institutions are sustainable as causally effective units of analysis. However, Weber and the historical school lacked the concept of emergence. Unable to sustain multiple levels of analysis, their social theory had to conflate upon one level – upon either the system as a whole or upon the individuals that comprised it. Unlike his historical school predecessors, Weber chose the latter option.[8]

Another fateful consequence of Weber's individualistic approach concerned his notion of the disciplinary boundaries between the social sciences. Weber developed a complex set of criteria to determine whether an act was 'economic' or 'social'. Writing in *Economy and Society*, Weber (1968, p. 9) saw economics as concerned with action that is 'strictly rational, unaffected by errors or emotional factors . . . completely and unequivocally directed to a single end, the maximization of economic advantage'. Whereas: 'The economic activity of an individual is social only if it takes account of the behavior of someone else' (p. 22). This was similar to the distinction between 'economic' and 'non-economic' action proposed in 1910 by Philip Wicksteed (1933). Wicksteed defined an 'economic transaction' as one in which one party did not consider the welfare or desires of the other, merely the object of the transaction itself.[9]

---

8 For the notion of emergence see McDougall (1929), Morgan (1927, 1932, 1933). For discussions of emergent properties in modern social theory see Archer (1995), Bhaskar (1979), Hodgson (1999b), Kontopoulos (1993), T. Lawson (1997), Mayr (1988).
9 For a very useful but rather uncritical presentation of Weber's views in this area see Swedberg (1998).

Note that Weber's (and Wicksteed's) definitions centred on the assumed nature of the inner thought processes of the individual, rather than on the social structures within and through which individuals act. The exclusive use of an individualist and subjectivist demarcation criterion between economics and other social sciences, means that inadequate attention is given to the nature of the social structures and institutions, as objects of analysis, alongside the individuals concerned. Both are important: just as structures are formed and changed by individuals, individuals are also changed by structures. In contrast, the seminal criteria of Weber and Wicksteed put exclusive weight on the subjective interpretations of the given individual.

At the same time, the 'economic' individual was treated as a fictional and 'unreal' being, acting 'as if' he or she was calculating or rational. The outcome is that both individual and structure were simultaneously denuded of much social and psychological content. Hence, despite its subjectivist twist, a further consequence of Weber's argument was the explicit relegation of the relevance of psychology for economic analysis. In 1908, Weber (1975, pp. 31–2) saw economics as concerned with the construction of 'general theorems' on the 'unreal' assumption that people behave 'as if' they were 'under the control of *commercial calculation'*, or 'rationality' in this sense. Accordingly, the investigation of the 'real' motives and behaviour of individuals, informed by psychological and other insights, was irrelevant to economics as Weber saw it. The result of this influential argument was to assist a widespread rejection of psychological insights by both sociologists and economists.[10]

Weber's demarcation between 'rational' and non-'rational' action in humans helped to establish barriers between economics, sociology and history. Economics, following Menger, would consider the rational behaviour of the individual, with given ends and in given circumstances. Sociology would consider the manner in which culture may mould those ends. History, in turn, would consider the spirit of the age and the manner in which the given circumstances had evolved. Weber's attitude to psychology, and his individualist and subjectivist demarcation criterion between economics and sociology, affected Talcott Parsons. Principally through Wicksteed, similar ideas influenced Lionel Robbins.

Eventually, in the 1930s, a truce emerged, where economics concerned itself with the rational choice of means to serve given ends, sociology with the explanation of those ends, and history with their temporal context. This agreement gave significant scope for Austrian and neoclassical economics, at the theoretical core

---

10 Near the end of his life, Weber visited Vienna and became friendly with von Mises (Mises, 1978, pp. 69–70). After his death, Weber's ideas remained 'favourite topics' at the famous Mises seminar of 1920–34, where they influenced Haberler, Hayek, Machlup, Morgenstern, Schutz and others (Swedberg, 1998, pp. 198–204). However, von Mises (1933, 1960) seized upon an ambiguity in Weber's position and accused him of confusing history and economic theory. The latter, von Mises insisted, had to remain a matter of *a priori* deduction from the premise of the rational individual. Schutz in particular made an attempt to amend Weber's methodology by bringing in elements of phenomenology and ideas from the Austrian school of economics (Prendergast, 1986). Nevertheless, like Parsons, Schutz diminished the degree of historical sensitivity in Weber's thought (Zaret, 1980).

of the territory of the queen of the social sciences. It also removed the historical school from its prestigious pedestal, but gave them important complementary tasks: in economic sociology, sociology and history. Lionel Robbins (1932), Talcott Parsons (1937a) and Joseph Schumpeter (1954) endorsed this partial resolution of the conflict, by means of a partitioning of the contested territory. These writers were steeped in the German literature, and were also – in part by exporting German ideas – to have a crucial influence on Anglo-American social science in the coming years. These outcomes are discussed later in this book. The disciplinary demarcation criteria, and the narrowing view of the scope of economics, had major and global consequences for the erection of virtually impenetrable disciplinary boundaries after the Second World War.

Despite its dubious aspects, a positive and worthwhile feature of Weber's analysis was to situate the concept of rationality principally in the real and modern world of pecuniary calculation. Accordingly, the concept of rationality became historically confined. Instead of a potentially universal concept, related to any possible activity, he pointed to a concept of rationality that became linked directly to a society in which markets, money and exchange dominated much human behaviour. The merits and demerits of his rationality concept emerge again below, in the discussion of his methodology of ideal types.

WEBER'S THEORY OF IDEAL TYPES

It is generally agreed that Weber (1978, p. 5) borrowed and adapted the term 'ideal type' from Georg Jellinek.[11] The nature and application of this concept are elaborated at length in Weber's 1904 essay entitled '"Objectivity" in Social Science and Social Policy'. In this work, Weber (1949, pp. 64–5) argued for a *Sozialökonomik* (social economics) in which economic problems were to be researched in a broad manner. In order to study economic phenomena it was necessary to draw on a plurality of disciplines and subdisciplines, including economic theory, economic history, and economic sociology. Weber repeatedly and rightly insisted that prior theoretical concepts were required to understand and explain socio-economic phenomena. His discussion of ideal types is an attempt to develop a methodology to construct, appraise and revise these concepts.

For Weber, the 'ideal type' was not a normative conception. The word 'ideal' in this context, as Weber (1949, pp. 98–9) insisted in 1904, 'has no connection at all with *value-judgements*, and it has nothing to do with any type of perfection other than a purely *logical one*'. Weber insisted that judgements of fact had to be separated from judgements of value. For Weber, the ideal type was 'ideal' because it was an imagined 'pure' form of socio-economic reality. His concept of an ideal type was an essential means to classify, conceptualise and illuminate facts.

---

11 For evidence see Machlup (1978, pp. 236–7). On the contrary, Commons (1934a, p. 721) said that Weber was following the philosopher Rickert. Interestingly, the term 'type idéal' appears in the original French version of Comte (1853). Another possible forerunner of Weber's ideal type is Marshall's idea in his 1890 *Principles* of the 'representative firm' (Finch, 1997; Marshall, 1949). The limitations of these concepts are discussed in Hodgson (1993a) and chapter 22 below.

For Weber, any ideal type was provisional and incomplete; it was the outcome of *verstehen*. It was an attempt to interpret and to categorise, and thereby begin to explain, a complex reality, rather than to dig down and discover its allegedly fundamental building blocks. Weber's methodology, therefore, was different from that of Menger. Weber's position also had strong Kantian overtones. Like Kant, Weber believed that the analyst imposed causal relations upon reality. Hence causal relations were seen as a function of explanatory relations. Weber believed that concepts were primarily interpretative; they did not necessarily refer to underlying essences. For Weber (1949, p. 106) 'concepts are primarily analytical instruments for the intellectual mastery of empirical data.'

In contrast, some subsequent authors have taken ideal types as part of the necessary conceptual apparatus for probing beneath superficial appearances to underlying structures. The trouble is that the term 'ideal type' has taken upon itself such a variety of meanings in the subsequent literature that it is difficult to disentangle them and extricate a single, clear core idea. We must further examine the theoretical context in which Weber used the term.

In social science, Weber accepted at least one universal presupposition. Weber (1949, p. 64) wrote of 'that fundamental social-economic phenomenon: the scarcity of means'. For him, 'the scarcity of means' was a universal feature of human existence. Hence he shared a similar assumption with Menger and with neoclassical economists.

Nevertheless, the methodology of ideal types was an attempt to escape from the universal theory promoted by the neoclassicals and the Austrians, and to incorporate the issue of historical specificity. As Weber (1949, p. 72) wrote in 1904: 'Our aim is the understanding of the characteristic uniqueness of the reality in which we move.' Within this analysis, there would be a place for a general theory of markets and exchange, but this would be incomplete without an analysis of the cultural context in which exchange took place:

> The analysis of the *general* aspects of exchange and the technique of the market is a – highly important and indispensable – *preliminary task*. For not only does this type of analysis leave unanswered the question as to how exchange historically acquired its fundamental significance in the modern world; but above all else, the fact with which we are primarily concerned, namely, the *cultural significance* of the money economy . . . we are concerned with the analysis of the *cultural significance* of the concrete *historical* fact that today exchange exists on a mass scale. . . . We will apply those concepts . . . provided by the investigation of the general features of economic mass phenomena . . . we shall use them as *means* of exposition. The *goal* of our investigation is not reached through the exposition of those laws and concepts, precise as it may be.
>
> (Weber, 1949, pp. 77–8)

For Weber, the expansion of markets and exchanges in a particular type of historical and cultural context meant that the analysis of their general features was indispensable but inadequate for an understanding of the modern socio-economic system. Weber criticised the excessive claims for deductivist and purportedly universal economic theory on the following grounds.

> the fantastic claim has occasionally been made for economic theories –
> e.g., the abstract theories of price, interest, rent, etc., – that they can, by
> ostensibly following the analogy of physical science propositions, be
> validly applied to the derivation of quantitatively stated conclusions
> from given real premises, since given the ends, economic behavior with
> respect to the means is unambiguously 'determined.' This claim fails to
> observe that in order to be able to reach this result even in the simplest
> case, the totality of the existing historical reality including every one of
> its causal relationships must be assumed as 'given' and presupposed as
> known. But if *this* type of knowledge were accessible to the finite mind
> of man, abstract theory would have no cognitive value whatsoever.
>
> (ibid., p. 88)

Hence, according to Weber, such purportedly universal economic theories not only failed to explain all the factors involved in the deductive chain, but also, for reasons of tractability, they could not possibly remain universal and take all those factors into account. However, unlike the members of the older historical school, Weber did not believe that ideal types or other theoretical concepts could be revealed by empirical research alone. In 1904 he declared that the members of the historical school

> still hold in many ways, expressly or tacitly, to the opinion that it is
> the end and the goal of every science to order its data into a system of
> concepts, the content of which is to be acquired and slowly perfected
> through the observation of empirical regularities, the construction of
> hypotheses, and their verification, until finally a 'completed' and *hence*
> deductive science emerges. For this goal, the historical-inductive work
> of the present-day is a preliminary task necessitated by the imperfections
> of our discipline. Nothing can be more suspect, from this point of view,
> than the construction and application of clear-cut concepts since this
> seems to be an over-hasty anticipation of the remote future. . . . The
> function of concepts was assumed to be the *reproduction* of 'objective'
> reality in the analyst's imagination. Hence the recurrent references to the
> *unreality* of all clear-cut concepts.
>
> (ibid., p. 106)

For Weber, the idea that concepts were reproductions of reality was profoundly mistaken, and based on an outdated and untenable 'classical-scholastic epistemology'. Instead, he saw concepts as 'not ends but . . . means to the end of understanding phenomena which are significant from concrete individual viewpoints'. From this viewpoint, conceptual precision was required not despite but because of the tangled and complex nature of socio-economic reality:

Indeed, it is *because* the content of historical concepts is necessarily subject to change that they must be formulated precisely and clearly on all occasions. In their application, their character as ideal analytical constructs should be carefully kept in mind, and the ideal-type and historical reality should not be confused with each other.

(ibid., p. 107)

Accordingly, real world muddle was no excuse for a muddled conceptual model. Clear, fixed concepts were necessary to deal with even a messy and changing reality. The ideal type was, in a sense, a limiting case. It had 'the significance of a purely *limiting* concept with which the real situation or action is *compared* and surveyed for the explication of certain of its significant components' (Weber, 1949, p. 93). But this did not mean that it was something implausible or extreme. Weber wanted any ideal type to be somehow assessed and revised by engagement with the chaotic flux of historical development. Any ideal type is both tentative and provisional. It offered a guide towards theoretical construction. It was not a description of a reality but a framework within which reality can first be ordered and described in outline:

The ideal typical concept will help to develop our skill in imputation in *research*: it *is* no 'hypothesis' but it offers guidance to the construction of hypotheses. It is not a *description* of reality but it aims to give un-ambiguous meaning of expression to such a description. . . . An ideal type is formed by the one-sided *accentuation* of one or more points of view and by the synthesis of a great many diffuse, discrete, more or less present and occasionally absent *concrete individual* phenomena, which are arranged according to those one-sidedly emphasized viewpoints into a unified *analytical* construct (*Gedankenbild*). In its conceptual purity, this mental construct cannot be found anywhere in reality. It is a *utopia*. Historical research faces the task of determining in each individual case, the extent to which this ideal-construct approximates to or diverges from reality.

(ibid., p. 90)

For Weber, an ideal type was neither a hypothesis, nor a description of reality, nor a statement of the empirical average, nor a mere description of traits common to a class of phenomena. Its function was theoretical and heuristic: it was a theoretical instrument to organise, interpret and appreciate the facts.

Weber rightly insisted that the value of ideal types could not be appreciated from a naïvely empiricist perspective. If a theory could be a '"presupposition-less" copy of "objective" facts' then there would be no need for an ideal type. But neither theory nor description is possible without prior assumptions. Consequently, no theoretical mirror of objective facts is possible, because theory is part of the cognition of the facts themselves. If the ideal type was to play the part of a prior and partial conceptual framework for theoretical and empirical research then this raised the question of the adequacy of the choice of ideal type.

How do we know if the chosen ideal type has utility or validity? Weber (1949, p. 92) responded with the following words:

> *whether* we are dealing simply with a conceptual game or with a scientifically fruitful method of conceptualization and *theory*-construction can never be decided *a priori*. Here, too, there is only one criterion, namely, that of success in revealing concrete causal phenomena in their interdependence, their causal conditions and their *significance*. The construction of abstract ideal-types recommends itself not as an end but as a *means*.
>
> (ibid., p. 92)

Consequently, the ultimate fruitfulness of an ideal type must depend on its success in locating and revealing significant causal linkages in the phenomenon under investigation. Each set of ideal types must be deployed and examined with this criterion in mind, and then revised accordingly. Weber (1949, p. 105) thus envisaged 'a perpetual process of reconstruction of those concepts in terms of which we seek to lay hold of reality'. In that sense, the ideal type was 'real' and 'objective'. For an ideal type to be adequate, it had to represent an 'objective possibility'.

However, in the above passage and elsewhere, Weber seemed to suggest that the ideal type was no more than an instrument, or means, towards some 'fruitful' end, somehow defined. This instrumentalist stance would downplay any question of the truthfulness of the ideal type. Weber also argued that the selection of an ideal type depended upon the cultural values associated with the researcher, thus giving his theory a relativist twist. On the other hand, such instrumentalist and relativist interpretations are qualified by his insistence on the importance of uncovering causal relations.

For Weber, ideal types may be more or less useful, but it is not sufficiently clear how they can be judged as more or less valid or true. At this crucial point, failing to provide adequate criteria of revelatory success or significance, Weber's theory of ideal types unveils its own incompleteness and imprecision. As Barry Hindess (1977, p. 39) put it: 'Weber's conception of the use of ideal types in sociological explanation involves an inescapable theoretical arbitrariness.' Overall, Weber did not give us sufficient methodological guidelines on how an adequate ideal type is constructed. He seemed to fall back, when pressed, on some imprecise and inadequate notion of successive approximation to an instrumental ideal, driven by empirical enquiry but also coloured by the preconceptions of the researcher.

In addition, from his relatively individualistic standpoint, Weber attempted to use the concept of rationality to inform the concept of an ideal type. He attempted to deal with the problem of arbitrariness in the choice of ideal type by pinning it to the concept of rationality. Accordingly, Weber (1978, pp. 24–8) argued that the 'unrealistic' economic model of the instrumentally 'rational' agent was sometimes helpful in understanding real motives and actions, even if real-world agents were not always rational in the sense of always choosing 'appropriate means to a given end'. For Weber, an ideal type in which people acted rationally in this sense was therefore an important theoretical benchmark for the study of real societies, especially modern societies in which calculative rationality had become paramount.

A problem, however, is that his notion of rationality begs the question of what is 'appropriate' for a given end. Furthermore, any behaviour could be regarded as 'appropriate' by some reinterpretation of the ends that are imputed to the action. For example, if I do not take the quickest route in travelling from A to B, my action could still be regarded as 'appropriate' and 'rational' as long as my end is defined not simply as reaching point B but also in terms of another objective. For example, I may wish to take a scenic but slower route. At least without an inner knowledge of motives, we have no way of knowing whether an action is 'appropriate' or not. Weber failed to notice that the neoclassical concept of rationality, when defined in terms of utility maximisation, has the potential to encompass every conceivable act. As the subsequent history of neoclassical economics demonstrates, any act can be regarded as appropriate and rational by the manipulation of a chosen utility function.

In contrast, Weber saw rationality as a phenomenon that became prominent in historically specific circumstances. He saw 'formal rationality' as fully developed in a pecuniary culture only. Such rationality was associated with the existence of money and price calculations. Significantly, Weber (1975, p. 33) wrote in 1908 that 'the historical peculiarity of the capitalist epoch, and thereby also the significance of marginal utility theory (as of every economic theory of value) for the understanding of this epoch' was that there existed an increasing 'approximation of reality to the theoretical propositions of economics'. Accordingly, for Weber, rationality found its fullest development in modern capitalism.

This was part of Weber's argument that the concept of rationality leads us to a definite ideal type. However, Weber placed the burden of the analysis on his imprecise definition of rationality rather than on the institutional circumstances in which pecuniary calculation may become paramount. As a basis for determining the capitalist ideal type, the vague and subjective criterion of 'appropriate means' overshadowed objective social relations and institutions. Instead of his indistinct concept of rationality – which does not in fact point to any specific ideal type – Weber should have instead focused on widespread markets and general commodification. By attempting to build the concept the ideal type on the shifting sands of the rationality concept, instead of the firmer rock of economic institutions, Weber did not escape from the problem of arbitrariness that beset his theory from the beginning.

However, whatever its limitations, Weber's theory of ideal types was clearly an attempt to deal with the problem of historical specificity. This is not emphasised sufficiently in some other accounts of his work. Ever since the influential Talcott Parsons abandoned the problem of historical specificity in the 1930s, Anglophone sociologists have typically interpreted Weber's theory in a manner that minimised its author's concern with this problem, and have downplayed Weber's intellectual evolution within the tradition of the German historical school. Inevitably, this led to distortions and misunderstandings concerning his theory of ideal types.[12]

Weber criticised Marxist explanations of historical development and wished to improve on Marx's taxonomy of socio-economic systems. According to Weber's own standards, the development of an alternative set of ideal types depended on a detailed study of causal mechanisms. His *Protestant Ethic and the Spirit of Capitalism* (Weber, 1930) was a part of this historical research.[13]

What specific ideal types did Weber propose for the study of human history? In *Economy and Society* and elsewhere Weber (1978) discussed labels such as 'feudal', 'patrimonial', 'bureaucratic' and 'charismatic'. However, it is doubtful whether such a taxonomy of social systems improved on that of Marx. Marx's typology of Antiquity, feudalism, and capitalism may tell us more about significant and systemic causal linkages than Weber's 'patrimonial', 'bureaucratic' and 'charismatic' societies. Marx's categories focused on relations of power and property surrounding the means of production as a whole. In contrast, Weber directed prime attention to issues of personality, organisation, style and spirit. Weber (1949, p. 103) suggested that Marx's approach could be readily recast within the methodology of ideal types. However, Marx suggested a different set of ideal-typical categories, focusing on property relations rather than *Geist* or leadership.

In summary, Weber did not provide enough clear guidance on how ideal types are to be generated theoretically or sustained empirically. As in the *Protestant Ethic and the Spirit of Capitalism* he embraced a multi-causal picture of socio-economic reality, but one in which the *Zeitgeist*, or spirit of the age, assumed prominence. However, as noted above, this emphasis on the *Zeitgeist* was combined with a belief in the ultimate causal efficacy of the individual. In addition, Weber argued that the consideration of what would be 'rational action' in the circumstances was an important conceptual benchmark in the generation of the ideal type. But rationality is too broad a notion to lead us to a particular ideal type. The problem of arbitrariness in Weber's position remains.

Overall, Weber made a significant contribution to the development of historically oriented theory after the *Methodenstreit*. He emphasised the importance and primacy of theory in any empirical endeavour, while seeing the study of history as an important source of crucial concepts. In the end, however, Weber's methodology remained tragically incomplete, and his failure to establish an adequate meta-theory of ideal types conceded crucial theoretical ground to Menger and other methodological individualists. Moreover, and contrary

---

12 For critical assessments, and varying interpretations or developments, of Weber's theory see Parsons (1936, 1937a), Schutz (1967), Runciman (1972), Hindess (1977), Machlup (1978), Zaret (1980), Burger (1987), Mommsen and Osterhammel (1987), Hennis (1988), Holton and Turner (1989), Kalberg (1994), Ringer (1997) and Swedberg (1998). For an assessment of the relatively limited impact of Weber's theory in France and Italy in the early part of the twentieth century see Steiner (1995).

13 Weber's *Protestant Ethic* follows directly – and after two years – the chapter on 'The genesis of the capitalist spirit' in Sombart's (1902) book *Der moderne Kapitalismus*. 'Weber followed up Sombart's indication that . . . protestantism . . . had essentially promoted the development of capitalism' (Brocke, 1996, p. 49).

to Weber's intentions, it created the basis for a damaging partition between the social sciences that was established within two decades of Weber's death and lasted at least for the remainder of the twentieth century.

THE ACHIEVEMENT OF WERNER SOMBART

Sombart was a student of Schmoller at the University of Berlin. While Sombart (1894) was critical of Marx's theory of value, he was strongly influenced by other aspects of Marx's theory of capitalism. Indeed, Sombart saw his own theoretical work as much an extension and completion of that of Marx. For much of his life he held policy views consistent with a reformist socialism. However, Sombart's socialism was always nationalistic, and in his social theory he emphasised nation as much as class. Instead of seeing history as class struggle, he saw capitalist development as the progressive realisation of its true *Geist*. Eventually, Sombart moved some way politically towards Nazism. However, his political stance should not lead us to overlook his massive analytical and theoretical contribution.[14]

From 1906, Sombart taught at the Berlin Business School (*Handelshochschule*). From 1917 to his retirement in 1931, Sombart was a professor of economics at the University of Berlin. Among his students in Berlin were Ludwig Lachmann and the future Nobel Laureate, Wassily Leontief (Backhaus, 1996, vol. 1, pp. 122–3). A leading thinker of his time, Sombart was a close colleague of Weber. Together, with Edgar Jaffé (and later Schumpeter) they edited the important journal the *Archiv für Sozialwissenschaft und Sozialpolitik*.[15]

During Sombart's lifetime, his fame exceeded that of Weber, in Germany and elsewhere. His books were widely sold and discussed. His earlier works on socialism were especially popular. For example, in three months in revolutionary Russia in 1905, Sombart sold over 24,000 copies of a socialistic political essay (Brocke, 1996, p. 20). This greatly exceeded the Russian sales of works by famous socialists, including Wilhelm Liebnecht, Eduard Bernstein and Franz Mehring. The whole German edition amounted to 33,000 copies. In Germany in the early 1930s, Sombart was also a major figure in the development of Keynesian-style policies to combat the Depression (Backhaus, 1985).

The first priority in his major academic work on *Modern Capitalism* was to construct a theory of the development of this social formation.[16] History and

---

14 In fact, Sombart's attitude towards the Nazis was complex (Harris, 1942; Brocke, 1996; Reheis, 1996; Rieß, 1996). He never became a wholesale enthusiast of Nazism. In the 1920s and 1930s, Sombart combined sympathy for Marx's theory with conservative political views. There is a parallel here with Schumpeter. For much of his adult life, Schumpeter combined his conservative and nationalistic politics with an admiration for Marxist theory (Swedberg, 1991). Furthermore, on occasions, Schumpeter declared some sympathy for Hitler's regime (Swedberg, 1991, pp. 148–9, 216).

15 For discussions and evaluations of Sombart's massive contribution see Appel (1992), Chaloupek (1995), Backhaus (1996) and Mote (1997). Lachmann (1971) later wrote an important book on Weber.

16 Sombart's magnum opus has yet to be published in English, although Backhaus (1996, vol. 1, p. 13) reports that Princeton University Press owns the copyright to an extant, abbreviated translation.

theory had to be reconciled. Therein Sombart (1902, vol. 1, p. 21) reiterated a foundational theme of the historical school:

> If one wants to picture the economy, and to perceive its phenomena in a scientific way, then this can only be conceived of in a social environment which has already come into existence in a historic way, to be understood as a historical picture of a certain shape.

He insisted, before Weber became famous for his development of the same idea, that the rational and quantitatively calculating individual was a historically specific product of the capitalist age, and not therefore an assumption that could be made the universal foundation of all social science. Like Weber and others, he saw the notion of *Geist* or 'spirit' as central and primary in each socio-economic system.

> It is a fundamental contention of this work that at different times different attitudes toward economic life have prevailed, and that it is the spirit which has created a suitable form for itself and has thus created economic organisation.
>
> (Sombart, 1902, vol. 1, p. 25)

Sombart regarded each spirit as thoroughly particular, evolving uniquely in its own history. Rejecting the teleological evolutionism found in Marxism and elsewhere in social science, Sombart argued that there was no necessary progress in social change, rather a succession of types of socio-economic system, each ruled by its own spirit or *Geist*.[17]

Sombart's methodological objective was to resolve the questions raised in the *Methodenstreit*, and to bridge the gap between theoretical and empirical investigation. He rejected the empiricism of the older historical school. Sombart (1929, p. 3) wrote that 'theory is the pre-requisite of any scientific writing of history.' Overall, he went further than his historical school predecessors in dealing with the problem of historical specificity. The methodological influence of Weber was significant here. Sombart's later writings provide some of the best examples of this.

In particular, Sombart (1930a, pp. 163–75) took a view similar to that of Weber when he saw human motive as the 'ultimate cause', taking this principle as 'an *a priori* of the cultural sciences'. Sombart argued that motive 'gives effect to human action'. In taking motive as a sufficient explanation of action, without an attempt to investigate the causes of motives themselves, Sombart was following Weber in diminishing the role for psychology in the social sciences (Betz, 1993, p. 345).

However, Sombart's argument was slightly different from Weber's. Sombart saw many psychological categories as valid only for a specific cultural context.

---

17 Notably, Sombart (1956) attempted to develop and defend the concept of *Geist* in response to its critics.

Unlike the American pragmatists and Thorstein Veblen, Sombart did not use a more general psychological theory to connect social reality with human nature and its evolutionary context. Sombart put less general emphasis on psychology than Schmoller. In Sombart's conception, 'nature' was quite separate from 'society'. In this respect, both Weber and Sombart (as well as Emile Durkheim) influenced Talcott Parsons and thereby contemporary sociology, as explained in chapter 13.

For Sombart (1930b, p. 196), as in his early works, 'there is no economy in the abstract, but a particularly constituted, historically distinguishable economic life.' The major flaw of classical and neoclassical economics was to assume 'economic principles which have a universal and uniform application under every variety of conditions' (Sombart, 1929, p. 8). He urged economists to take account of the manifest variety of actual social systems and of the historical forces that were driving them.

Sombart claimed to be one of the few economists to have provided an extensive analysis of the capitalist economic system. For him, 'capitalism' was an economic system dominated by the specific form of pecuniary 'capital'. Like Aristotle, Karl Marx and Thorstein Veblen, Sombart distinguished between the satisfaction of human needs and the pecuniary pursuit of profit. Under capitalism the profit motive was foremost. Capitalism involved a ubiquity of markets and prices, and the prevalence of a particular 'spirit' and acquisitive culture: 'The spirit of the economic outlook of capitalism is dominated by three ideas: acquisition, competition and rationality' (Sombart, 1930b, p. 196).

Sombart (1902, 1916–27, 1930a, 1930b) divided the capitalist era into three periods. First there was 'early capitalism', lasting from about 1500 to 1760. This early period is marked by a pre-capitalist and 'handicraft' mentality. This was followed by 'high capitalism' from 1760 to 1914. The First World War market the onset of 'late' or 'organised' capitalism, in which the state began to intervene more extensively in the developed economies. He insisted that these different phases of capitalism had to be acknowledged in differences in the economic theory used to analyse them. However, there were common features in all forms of capitalism. For Sombart, the entrepreneur was always the motor of capitalist development (Prisching, 1996). The greater the role played by the entrepreneur in the capitalist economy, the greater the realisation of the capitalist ideal type.

Sombart insisted on the historical specificity of different economic institutions, each affecting the forms and mechanisms of exchange, prices and markets. Different types of market institution are possible, involving different routines, pricing procedures, and so on. Sombart argued, for example, that the concept of exchange depended for its meaning on the social and historical context in which the exchange takes place:

> 'Exchange' in the primitive economy (silent barter), 'exchange' in the handicraft economy, and 'exchange' in the capitalist economy are things enormously different from one another. . . . Price and price are completely different things from market to market. Price formation

in the fair at Vera Cruz in the seventeenth century and in the wheat market on the Chicago Exchange in the year 1930 are two altogether incomparable occurrences.

(Sombart, 1930a, pp. 211, 305)

Sombart argued on this basis that: 'A theory of the formation of markets must precede a theory of price formation' (p. 305). However, in emphasising here the issue of historical specificity Sombart neglected the common generic features of all markets. Nevertheless, his statement is an important corrective to the notion of a pure and undifferentiated market – a notion that is promoted in the ideological doctrines of both its critics and its supporters.

Despite the above defect, Sombart did indeed distinguish, elsewhere in the volume, between generic and specific features of social institutions. Indeed, Sombart (1930a, p. 247) differentiated between

three different kinds of economic concepts: 1. The universal-economic primary concepts . . . which are valid for all economic systems; 2. the historical-economic primary concepts . . . which . . . are valid only for a definite economic system: and 3. the subsidiary concepts . . . which are constructed with regard to a definite working idea.

This threefold categorisation was an important breakthrough, and brought the historical school closer to an adequate solution to the problem of historical specificity. It provided a framework in which general postulates concerning choice and scarcity, for example, could be reconciled with the analysis of markets and capitalist firms, and with their particular manifestations in particular countries. Unfortunately, with some exceptions noted below, Sombart's theoretical schema was little noticed or developed.

Some years later, in an outburst against the German historical school, Ludwig von Mises (1960, p. 138) protested against Sombart's (1930a, p. 247) formulation, quoted above. Von Mises questioned 'whether the assignment of the concepts of exchange and price formation to the second group can be justified. Sombart gives no reason for it.' In response to von Mises, all the justification we require is the possible existence of a viable economic system, or subsystem, without exchange or price. If such a system or subsystem could exist, then exchange and price could not be placed at the universal level of analysis. Against this, von Mises wished to elevate exchange and price to universal categories. For this, von Mises gave no justification.

Sombart's threefold classification does require some further development, however. The second and third levels of analysis are insufficiently well defined. The difference between a 'definite economic system' in level two, and 'a definite working idea' in level three, is not altogether clear. It is necessary to refine the definition of each level so that the conceptual separation is clearer. It is important to show in detail how concepts and principles at one level relate to those of another. It would be useful to explore the possibility or otherwise of further subdivisions additional to the aforementioned three. Overall, it is necessary to give this important analytical skeleton some theoretical and empirical flesh and blood.

THE FINAL ACT

A German economist who made an attempt to develop Sombart's theoretical scheme was Edgar Salin at the University of Heidelberg. Salin (1927, 1929) criticised Schmoller for failing to see the limits of inductive reasoning. Salin was a student of Weber, but he saw a danger in the Weberian approach. Weber's approach was too subjectivist and instrumentalist. If ideal types were made mere instruments of cognition, then any concern for the question of truth might be abandoned. Turning to Sombart's theory, Salin found this to be underdeveloped. Salin himself attempted to develop a concept of 'concrete theory' involving a view of the system as a whole. His work stimulated important debates, involving Sombart and Schumpeter, among others. Salin understood that adequate social theory had to involve both universal and particular statements. However, his argument failed to deal sufficiently with the problem of abstraction in the face of complexity and 'is left with many points of obscurity' (Harada, 1997, p. 379).

Salin was of Jewish descent. He left Germany to take up a professorship in Basle in Switzerland in 1927. This was a foretaste of the catastrophic disruption of fascism and war, which was to destroy almost completely the legacy of the German historical school, tragically at the point where it was engaging with the crucial theoretical issues. Nevertheless, Salin survived the holocaust, and his legacy endures in *Kyklos*, a journal that he helped to found.[18]

Within Germany, Salin's work triggered an important response from historicists such as Arthur Spiethoff at the University of Bonn. Spiethoff had been one of Schmoller's favourite disciples. Schumpeter was a colleague of Spiethoff at Bonn from 1925 to 1932. They worked together on business cycle theory and Schumpeter drew much stimulation from Spiethoff's ideas (Ebner, 2000; Schumpeter, 1954, p. 816). Spiethoff (1932) argued that the limited role of pure theory was as a 'heuristic'. Spiethoff tried to develop a role for theory of a more historically sensitive kind. One of his innovations was to use the insights of Gestalt psychology. Spiethoff also attempted to enlarge on Sombart's three categories of economic analysis and to clear the road for further theoretical

---

18 In addition, Salin's influence extended to Japan. After the Meiji Restoration in 1868, a number of works of the historical school were translated into Japanese. The second edition of Salin's *Geschichte der Volkswirtschaftslehre* was translated into Japanese in 1935 and it influenced a school of Japanese historicists including Zenya Takishima (Harada, 1997). Notably Kozo Uno – the leading Japanese Marxist – studied in Germany for two years in the early 1920s and was also influenced by the historical school as well as by Austrian Marxists such as Hilferding. Uno's work addressed problems of historical periodisation and levels of theoretical analysis, similar to those that concerned Sombart and others (Uno, 1980; Sekine, 1975). Ultimately, however, Uno's proposal relies on a concept of 'pure capitalism' that has the same defects as the equivalent idea in the works of Marx, as criticised already in the present book. Nevertheless, the survival in Japan to this day, of relatively influential historical school ideas, has to be noted.

development. He notably developed the concept of 'economic style' in an attempt to give ideas such as culture or *Geist* a more concrete meaning. For Spiethoff, the 'economic style' of a country included not only the prevailing *Geist* but also the structure and dynamics of the socio-economic system.

Spiethoff openly acknowledged that this work would take 'generations'. But war and holocaust, with the catastrophic collapse of German economic life, was only a few years away. By 1938, Spiethoff felt unable to mention the contribution and inspiration of a Jew such as Salin in his publications, probably because of fear of censorship or of reprisal from the Nazi authorities (Harada, 1997, pp. 391–2).

However, after the Second World War, Salin (1948) edited a collection of articles by Spiethoff. Significantly, in this work, Spiethoff expressed his preference for the term 'real type' over 'ideal type' writing: 'real types represent the regularities of a recurring historical subject purified of its historical uniqueness' (Salin, 1948, p. 614). Like Salin, Spiethoff tried to surpass the subjectivist and instrumentalist aspects of Weber's thought. Notably, there is also a postwar article in English by Spiethoff (1952), where he continued to argue that every type of economic system and every pattern of economic activity, 'demands its own economic theory' (p. 132).

Even in the Nazi period, other important contributions appeared. For instance, Erich Rothacker taught at the University of Bonn and made a significant philosophical contribution to the historical school approach (Koslowski, 1997b). In one sentence he crystallised the ontological insight with which historicism and all social theory had to contend: 'Every historical life is constitutively influenced by the tension between the universal and the particular forces' (Rothacker, 1938, p. 8).[19]

But the combined effects of Nazism and war were to destroy much of the heritage of the historical school. Mere embers of German historicism lingered after the Second World War. Nevertheless, their ideas were an important influence on Walter Eucken and Wilhelm Röpke who helped to develop the concept of the 'social market economy' that emerged in the economic policies of postwar Germany (Tribe, 1995; Nicholls, 1994; Schefold, 1995). But a clear focus on the key problem of historical specificity had gone. For instance, Eucken and others accepted that neoclassical general equilibrium theory and economic rationality were 'always valid' and did have general applicability to all types of economy. While he emphasised the importance of history and institutions, he found a central and universal place for neoclassical general equilibrium theory. As Bertram Schefold (1995, p. 247) elaborated:

> Eucken further maintained that if theories specific to certain times were possible, then they must already exist, and because he found none, he decided that they were illusory. But in this he underestimated the wealth of literature in the history of economic thought.

---

19 Among Rothacker's students was Jürgen Habermas.

As the example of Eucken (1950) testifies, after 1945 the German historical school was little more than a pale afterglow. The problem of historical specificity was no longer at the centre of discussion. Accordingly, it is appropriate to mark the end of the German historical school with the demise of Sombart in 1941. Clearly, whatever the limitations and failures of this school, it is misleading to describe it as anti-theoretical. They were concerned to explore the limits of theory – particularly when unaided by empirical data. They did not reject theory as such. Their misgivings concerned the role of general theory. Some went too far, and believed that empirical work could solve the key problems. At the same time, particularly in the more sophisticated statements of Schmoller, Weber and Sombart, there was a desire to create both a theoretical and meta-theoretical framework in which to accommodate historical analysis. Even if there is ultimate failure, we should not fail to recognise the extent of their achievement. The fact that this achievement is largely ignored today is due much to the rise of Nazism and to the devastation of the Second World War.

Part III

THE TWENTIETH CENTURY

From American institutionalism to the end of history

Adams, Henry Carter (1851–1900)
Alchian, Armen A. (born 1914)
Arrow, Kenneth J (born 1921)
Ayres, Clarence E. (1891–1972)
Becker, Gary S. (born 1930)
Beveridge, William H. (1879–1963)
Boas, Franz (1858–1942)
Böhm-Bawerk, Eugen von (1851–1914)
Brentano, Lujo (1844–1931)
Burns, Arthur F. (1904–87)
Burns, Eveline M. (1900–85)
Cannan, Edwin (1861–1935)
Carnap, Rudolf (1891–1970)
Clark, John Bates (1847–1938)
Clark, John Maurice (1884–1963)
Coase, Ronald H. (born 1910)
Coleman, James S. (1926–95)
Commons, John R. (1862–1945)
Copeland, Morris A. (1895–1989)
Davidson, Paul (born 1930)
Demsetz, Harold (born 1930)
Dewey, John (1859–1952)
Duesenberry, James (born 1918)
Durkheim, Emile (1858–1917)
Eichner, Alfred S. (1937–88)
Einstein, Albert (1879–1955)
Ely, Richard T. (1854–1943)
Fetter, Frank A. (1863–1949)

Fisher, Irving (1867–1947)
Haavelmo, Trygve (born 1911)
Hahn, Frank H. (born 1925)
Hamilton, Walton H. (1881–1958)
Hansen, Alvin (1887–1975)
Harrod, Roy F. (1900–78)
Hayek, Friedrich A. (1899–1992)
Henderson, Hubert D. (1890–1952)
Henderson, Lawrence J. (1878–1942)
Hewins, William A. S. (1865–1931)
Hicks, John R. (1904–89)
Hirshleifer, Jack (born 1925)
Hobhouse, Leonard T. (1864–1929)
Homan, Paul T. (1893–1969)
Homans, George C. (1910–89)
Hoxie, Robert F. (1868–1916)
Hutchison, Terence W. (born 1912)
James, William (1842–1910)
Kaldor, Nicholas (1908–86)
Kalecki, Michal (1899–1970)
Kantor, Jacob Robert (1888–1984)
Keynes, John Maynard (1883–1946)
Knight, Frank H. (1885–1972)
Kroeber, Alfred L. (1876–1960)
Lange, Oskar R. (1905–65)
Laski, Harold (1893–1950)
Löwe, Adolph (1893–1995)
McDougall, William (1871–38)

Machlup, Fritz (1902–83)
Malinowsky, Bronislaw K. (1884–1942)
Mitchell, Wesley C. (1874–1948)
Morgan, Conwy Lloyd (1852–1936)
North, Douglass (born 1920)
Pareto, Vilfredo (1848–1923)
Parsons, Talcott (1902–79)
Peirce, Charles Sanders (1839–1914)
Pigou, Arthur C. (1877–1959)
Polanyi, Karl (1886–1964)
Popper, Karl R. (1902–94)
Rickert, Heinrich (1863–1936)
Robbins, Lionel (1898–1984)
Robinson, Joan V. (1903–83)
Salin, Edgar (1892–1974)
Samuelson, Paul A. (born 1915)
Schäffle, Albert (1823–1903)
Schlick, Moritz (1882–1936)
Schmoller, Gustav von (1838–1917)

Schumpeter, Joseph A. (1883–1950)
Seligman, Edwin R. A. (1861–1939)
Slichter, Sumner H. (1892–1959)
Solow, Robert A. (born 1924)
Sombart, Werner (1863–1941)
Souter, Ralph W. (1897–1946)
Spiethoff, Arthur (1873–1957)
Sraffa, Piero (1898–1983)
Taussig, Frank W. (1859–1940)
Tawney, Richard H. (1880–1962)
Veblen, Thorstein B. (1857–1929)
Vining, Rutledge (1908–99)
Watson, John B. (1878–1958)
Webb, Beatrice (1858–1943)
Webb, Sidney (1859–1947)
Weber, Max (1864–1920)
Whitehead, Alfred N. (1861–1947)
Williamson, Oliver E. (born 1932)
Young, Allyn A. (1876–1929)

10

THORSTEIN VEBLEN AND THE FOUNDATIONS OF INSTITUTIONALISM

With Veblen are introduced for the first time into economics Darwinian ideas of the selection and survival of institutions and patterns of behaviour.

(Radhakamal Mukerjee, *The Institutional Theory of Economics* (1940))

On the first centenary of the American Declaration of Independence, the economist Charles Dunbar (1876, p. 140) of Harvard University confessed that 'the United States have, thus far, done nothing toward developing the theory of political economy'. Harvard, of course, was one of the oldest American universities, dating from the colonial period. But in 1876 it did not have a developed graduate programme of study. The first American university to have a graduate programme was Johns Hopkins, founded in 1876. Stanford University was founded in 1885 and The University of Chicago in 1891. Yale College became a university in 1887, as did Columbia and Princeton in 1896. Overall, the modernised university emerged in America between the 1880s and the First World War (Hofstadter and Hardy, 1952; Veysey, 1965). In the twentieth century, the size of American academia was to be multiplied several times over.

But given the paucity of graduate institutions, until the 1920s the young American scholar would still have to look elsewhere to find the frontiers of learning. Up to the First World War, Germany was the unrivalled intellectual centre for the study of economics. Since the early nineteenth century it had had twenty or more academic chairs devoted to the study of national or political economy. It had developed a strong intellectual tradition in the social sciences, with a huge literature. Until well into the twentieth century, no other country could rival this achievement.

Moreover, before the 1930s, no student of economics could keep up with key debates in the subject without knowledge of the German language. In addition, given that no other country could rival the German intellectual legacy, a lengthy visit to Germany was also desirable in order to complete an academic education (Diehl, 1978). Consequently, as Jurgen Herbst (1965, p. 1) observed: 'Between the years 1820 and 1920 nearly nine thousand American students set sail for Europe to enter the lecture halls, seminars, and laboratories of German universities.'

Leading American economists went to Germany to study under the German historical school. Among these were Henry Carter Adams, John Bates Clark, Richard T. Ely and Edwin R. A. Seligman. All four of them embarked on a period of study in Germany in the 1870s. Clark, Ely and Seligman spent some time abroad studying under Karl Knies in Heidelberg. The German historical school proved to be a formative influence on the emerging American economics in general and Adams, J. B. Clark, Ely and Seligman in particular (Dorfman, 1955). Herbst (1965, pp. 130–1) reported the results of a study conducted by a Yale professor in 1908:[1]

> Of the 116 economists and sociologists responding to Professor Farnham's queries, 59 had studied in Germany between 1873 and 1905, and 20 had returned with the *Dr. phil.* degree. Of the more than 80 who specified what they regarded the most important influence on their thinking, 30 listed the historical school . . . and 8 the theory of state intervention. Fourteen referred to Professor Böhm-Bawerk's Vienna school of marginal utility economics; most of these stressed its resemblances rather than its contrast to the German school. Among the teachers most cited as influential were Wagner, Schmoller, Conrad, Roscher, and Knies.

In 1885 the American Economic Association (AEA) was formed (Coats, 1993, ch. 11). Adams, Clark and Ely issued the call that led to its founding. Because of the influence of the German historical school upon them, the three were nicknamed 'the Germans'. Ely was its Secretary from 1885 to 1892 and its President in 1900–1. Dunbar became its President in 1893, J. B. Clark in 1894–5, Adams in 1896–7 and Seligman in 1902–3.

A strong doctrinal theme in the early years of the AEA was the rejection of *laissez-faire* solutions to economic problems. Socialist and social democratic ideas were prominent. The German historicists had taught that the national economy was a social organism, transcending its constituent individuals and groups. The German nation under Bismarck had pioneered the modern welfare state, establishing state provision in education, social security and elsewhere. These policy stances were combined with a hostility to deductive and general theorising.

Influenced by the German historical school, J. B. Clark (1877, p. 712) warned that the notion of rational economic man 'is too mechanical and too selfish to correspond with reality; he is actuated altogether too little by higher psychological forces'. At the same time, Clark attributed his own version of marginal utility to the inspiration of his teacher Knies. Clark was a neoclassical economist, to be later criticised by Veblen and the institutionalists. Nevertheless, the influence of the German school upon him was clearly apparent.[2]

---

1 See also B. B. Seligman (1962, p. 615).
2 It is also important to stress that leading American economists such as J. B. Clark were much driven by ethical policy concerns (Persky, 2000). Religious views also had a role, notably so in the case of Ely and his collaborators (Bateman and Kapstein, 1999; Gonce, 1996).

One enduring influence of the German historical school on American academia was in the rising business schools. The subdiscipline of business economics (*Betriebswirtschaftslehre*) emerged explicitly in Germany in the early years of the twentieth century (Pribram, 1983, p. 234). Dieter Schneider (1995, pp. 190–1) noted that: 'Those economists and business historians who formed the American business schools between 1890 and 1920 had mainly studied with Schmoller and other representatives of the historical school in German speaking countries.' In particular, Edwin Francis Gay, the Dean of Harvard Business School for ten years and President of the American Economic Association in 1929, had lived in Europe for several years and was a former student of Schmoller. He developed and promoted the famous Harvard case study method (Balabkins, 1988; Jones and Moneison, 1990). Schmoller's innovative ideas on the corporation as a social organisation also proved influential in the American context (Schneider, 1993). In this respect, the unacknowledged influence of the German historical school persists today, in leading American business schools.

In 1886, shortly after the foundation of the AEA, the weekly journal *Science* carried a debate, with Adams, Ely and Seligman on the side of historical economics, ranged against Frank W. Taussig and others in opposition. In that same year, Seligman, then an influential economist at Columbia, outlined some key ideas of the German historical school. Seligman (1925, pp. 15–16) described this intellectual movement in the following terms:

1   It discards the exclusive use of the deductive method, and stresses the necessity of historical and statistical treatment.
2   It denies the existence of immutable natural laws in economics, calling attention to the interdependence of theories and institutions, and showing that different epochs or countries require different systems.
3   It disclaims belief in the beneficence of the absolute *laissez-faire* system; it maintains the close interrelations of law, ethics and economics; and it refuses to acknowledge the adequacy of a scientific explanation, based on the assumption of self-interest as the sole regulator of economic action.

Seligman wished this to be the programme of the new economic movement in the United States. The first two points signal a clear awareness of the problem of historical specificity by a leading American economist. His statement, however, reflects none of the methodological difficulties in the position of the German historical school. To make further progress on American soil, the historical school would have to overcome the methodological problems revealed in the *Methodenstreit*. In fact, American institutionalism would fail to overcome many of these problems.

THE INTELLECTUAL REVOLUTION
OF THORSTEIN VEBLEN

The emergence of some of the core ideas of American institutional economics has been dated to the late 1890s (Samuels, 1998). The role of Thorstein Veblen was seminal. Born in Wisconsin, his parents were Norwegian immigrants. Veblen read widely in the social and natural sciences, and became fluent in French and German. Veblen taught at a number of universities, including Chicago in 1892–1906 and Stanford in 1906–9.[3]

Crucial influences upon Veblen included the philosopher and psychologist William James and the philosopher Charles Sanders Peirce. James and Peirce founded the pragmatist school of philosophy, the significance of which for the problem of historical specificity we shall discuss below. At the time, Herbert Spencer was at the peak of his popularity. However, Peirce and James were critical of Spencer, rejecting his utilitarianism in favour of an activist and reconstructive conception of human agency, founded on habits and instincts. Overall, Peirce and James sided with Charles Darwin rather than Spencer (Peirce, 1923, 1935; James, 1880).

I have argued elsewhere that the years 1896–8 marked a revolution in Veblen's thought (Hodgson, 1998b). Although Veblen did not engage directly with the problem of historical specificity, his work did have major implications for the treatment of this issue. In brief, his intellectual achievement at that time was

(a) to focus on institutions as well as individuals as units of social evolution and analysis;
(b) to point towards causal explanations of both individual agency and emergent social phenomena, consistent with both the natural and social sciences;
(c) to view rational deliberation as an outcome of habituation, thereby establishing the primacy of habit over rational thought;
(d) to escape from the three reductionisms of methodological collectivism, methodological individualism and biological reductionism;
(e) to place learning and knowledge at the centre of technological and economic evolution; and
(f) to posit a non-teleological view of historical development.

No more than a brief summary of this intellectual revolution is possible here, before we link these developments with the question of historical specificity. Some of the links will be made at the end of this chapter. Part IV of this work will also deploy some Veblenian ideas in a further engagement with the problem.

Crucially, in 1897 Veblen formulated a critique of Marxism that was to recur and develop in later essays (Veblen, 1897b; 1919, pp. 313–14, 416, 441–2). Veblen rightly argued that the mere class position of an individual as a wage labourer or a capitalist tells us very little about the specific conceptions or habits of thought, and thereby the likely actions, of the individuals involved. Individual interests, whatever they are, do not necessarily lead to corresponding individual actions.

Veblen's brief 1897 discussion of Marxism had a number of remarkable features. First, Veblen (1897b, p. 137) rejected the proposition that the individual is 'exclusively a social being, who counts in the process solely as a medium for

---

3   For a moving account of Veblen's difficult personal life see Jorgensen and Jorgensen (1999).

the transmission and expression of social laws and changes'. In other words, Veblen dismissed the idea that the individual's actions are explicable *entirely* in terms of socio-economic circumstances. This amounted to a rejection of method-ological collectivism, where individual agency is entirely explained in terms of structures, institutions or culture.

Note, however, that while Veblen rejected explanations exclusively in terms of systemic wholes, he did not attempt to explain socio-economic phenomena exclusively in terms of individuals. For this reason, Veblen did not embrace methodological individualism. Veblen did not deny that a human is 'a social being' or 'a medium for the transmission of social laws and changes'. He simply rejected an *exclusive* stress on social determination, and asserted that the human agent is *'also* an individual, acting out his own life as such' (1897b, p. 137, emphasis added). This suggested that humans mould their circumstances, just as they are moulded by them.

Second, Veblen emphasised the importance of detailed, causal processes that George Romanes (1893) and others had seen as central to Darwinism. The Marxist 'materialistic' interpretation of history lacked an explanation of 'the operative force at work in the process'. It did not explain how social forces impel individual actors to think and act. Addressing this hiatus, Veblen (1919, p. 441) followed the pragmatists and saw Darwinism as implying that 'habit and native propensity', rather than rational calculation of material interest, were fundamental in motivating human beings.

Third, for Veblen in 1897, explanations of socio-economic evolution involved individual agents as well as institutions and structures. However, the evolution of individuality must itself be explained as 'a theory of social process considered as a substantial unfolding of life as well'. Veblen thus argued that utilitarian and hedonistic explanations of human behaviour had to be rejected, in part because they did not contain an evolutionary explanation of the origin of the assumed behavioural characteristics. For example, the neoclassical assumption of given preference functions lacks any explanation of the origin and initial acquisition of those preferences. Likewise, writing in 1898, Veblen (1934, p. 79) took the view that the assumption of 'economic man' requires an explanation of his own evolution. In general, postulates about human behaviour at the socio-economic level themselves require explanation in evolutionary terms (Argyrous and Sethi, 1996).

Fourth, the methodological injunction that a processual explanation of origin is required, led Veblen to conceive the individual in both biological and socio-economic terms. Humans are biotic as well as social beings, so their biology cannot be ignored. A viable social science must be linked with biology. This is another implication of Veblen's imperative that socio-economic evolution must be regarded 'as a substantial unfolding of life as well'. However, in contrast to Spencer's grand synthesis, socio-economic phenomena were not seen as reducible to the biotic substratum. The 'theory of the social process' had to be compatible with, but also more than, the theory of the evolution of human life.

Superimposed upon this critique of Marxism came the influence of Conwy Lloyd Morgan, a British philosopher of biology. Morgan (1927, 1932, 1933) was the first to develop the concept of emergent properties. This concept proved to be crucial, for the problem of historical specificity in particular, and the development of social science in general. Morgan was Professor of Geology and Zoology at the University College, Bristol, in England. In 1896 he visited the University of Chicago, where Veblen was a lecturer (Dorfman, 1934, p. 139).[4]

Morgan's Darwinian understanding of evolution led him to promote the idea of an emergent level of socio-economic evolution that was not explicable exclusively in terms of the biological characteristics of the individuals involved. Evolution occurred at this emergent level as well, and without any necessary change in human biotic characteristics. However, Morgan did not make the objects and mechanisms of socio-economic evolution clear. It was left to Veblen to make the crucial next step: institutions became objects of selection in socio-economic evolution. After Morgan's visit to Chicago, the idea of an evolutionary process of selection of institutions began to develop in Veblen's work. Hence Veblen (1899, p. 188) emphasised the 'natural selection of institutions'. However, he did not make the philosophical concept of emergence explicit and this absence would cause problems for the future development of institutionalism in later years.

For Veblen (1899, p. 190) institutions were 'prevalent habits of thought with respect to particular relations and particular functions of the individual and of the community'. What was crucial for his contemporaries was that Veblen did not accept that institutions or culture could be, or had to be, explained in biological terms. He suggested that if socio-economic phenomena were determined exclusively by biological factors – such as a biologically given 'human nature' – then the concepts of institution and culture would be redundant. He rejected both this premise and its conclusion.[5]

With this implicit concept of emergence, Veblen did not require the idea of society as an organism, which had been thematic for the German historical school. Writing in 1901, Veblen (1919, p. 260) rejected 'a physiological conception of culture after the analogy of the ascertained physiological processes seen in the biological domain' and a 'physiological conception of society', as found in the writings of assorted physiocrats, Hegelians, members of the historical school and Herbert Spencer.

Veblen grappled with the problem of the relationship between actor and structure. As we have seen, Veblen's critique of Marxism was prompted by its apparent over-emphasis on the structural determination of individual agency.

---

4   University College, Bristol became the University of Bristol in 1909. At Bristol, Morgan turned increasingly to philosophical issues. His work also influenced Whitehead (1926) and McDougall (1929) among others. His concept of emergence is cited by modern philosophers of biology such as Mayr (1985a). One of the few commentators to note the vital influence of C. L. Morgan on Veblen is Tilman (1996).

5   See Veblen (1934, p. 143). It is useful to contrast Veblen's position on this point with that of his English contemporary, Marshall, who insisted: 'Economic institutions are the products of human nature and cannot change much faster than human nature changes' (Marshall, 1923, p. 260). Unlike Veblen and like Spencer, Marshall saw the development of human institutions as strictly constrained by the rate of evolution of human nature.

Veblen's attempted solution to this problem was to conceive of both agency and structure as a result of an evolutionary process.

VEBLEN'S CRITIQUE OF ECONOMIC DOCTRINES

Despite its limitations, Veblen's appropriation of Darwinian methodological injunctions led to a powerful critique of the reigning economic theories of his time. Essentially, because the agent was a subject of an evolutionary process, he or she could not be taken as fixed or given. Nor could the opposite error be committed: of subsuming agency under the heading of mysterious social forces. A causal account of interaction had to be provided.

After the classical and Marxist traditions of economic analysis, Veblen (1919, pp. 170–1) recognised three other major schools:

- the neoclassical school,[6] dominated by Alfred Marshall in Britain and John Bates Clark in America;
- the Austrian school, including Eugene von Böhm-Bawerk and Carl Menger;
- the German historical school of Gustav von Schmoller and others.

In some respects, Veblen (1898, p. 375) was critical of the German historical school, declaring that

> no economics is farther from being an evolutionary science than the received economics of the Historical School . . . they have contented themselves with an enumeration of data and a narrative account of industrial development, and have not presumed to offer a theory of anything or to elaborate their results into a consistent body of knowledge. Any evolutionary science, on the other hand, is a close-knit body of theory. It is a theory of process, of an unfolding sequence.

Veblen (1901, pp. 71–2) drew a distinction between the 'elder' historical school and the younger 'modernised' school led by Schmoller. He criticised the older generation for their failure to develop a theory:

> economists of what may be called the elder line of the historical school can scarcely be said to cultivate a science at all, their aim being not theoretical work. . . . The elder line of German economics, in its numerous modern representations, shows both insight and impartiality; but as regards economic theory their work bears the character of eclecticism rather than that of constructive advance. . . . Of constructive

---

6 In 1898, Veblen referred to this group as the 'later' or 'recent' classical school. Two years later, Veblen (1919, p. 171) himself coined the term 'neo-classical' to refer to such economists. See Aspromourgos (1986) and Fayazmanesh (1998).

scientific work – that is to say of theory – the elder line of German economics is innocent. . . . The historical economics of the conservative kind seems to be a barren field in the theoretical respect.

For Veblen (1901, p. 76), one of the serious limitations of the older historical school was its reliance on a Hegelian notion of cultural and economic development, as 'an unfolding (exfoliation) of the human spirit'. The same problem was detected in Marxism and Veblen looked to the possibility of an adequate causal account of economic and institutional evolution. In this respect at least, he saw Schmoller as making a significant advance in the theoretical realm. Veblen (1901, p. 81) praised Schmoller for his 'Darwinistic account of the origin, growth, persistence, and variation of institutions'.

However, Veblen (1901, p. 85) noted that Schmoller in his *Grundriss* eventually abandoned a 'dispassionate analysis and exposition of the causal complex at work' and instead argued 'the question of what ought to be and what modern society must do to be saved'. Veblen judged that Schmoller's 'digression into homiletics and reformatory advice means that the argument is running into the sands just at the stage where science can least afford it'. Veblen (1901, p. 86) similarly criticised Schmoller for sustaining a tendency in much of historical school writing; to pontificate on what was 'more desirable' instead of explaining important causal processes. For Veblen, such normative homilies were 'beside the point so far as regards a scientific explanation of the changes under discussion'. Veblen (1901, p. 90) lamented that Schmoller had harked back 'to the dreary homiletical waste of the traditional *Historismus*'.[7]

Overall, Veblen was influenced by the German historical school but he criticised their limitations.[8] Veblen (1898, p. 386) also devoted critical attention to both the neoclassical and Austrian schools. In the case of Menger and the other Austrians, they 'struck out on a theory of process, but presently came to a full stop because the process about which they busied themselves was not, in their apprehension of it, a cumulative or unfolding sequence'. Like the German historicists, 'the Austrians on the whole showed themselves unable to break with the classical tradition that economics is a taxonomic science. The reason for the Austrian failure seems to lie in a faulty conception of human nature' (Veblen, 1898, p. 389). This criticism was also applied to the neoclassical school:

> In all received formulations of economic theory, whether at the hands of English economists or those of the Continent, the human material with which the inquiry is concerned is conceived in hedonistic terms; that is

---

7 These and other remarks by Veblen should be noted by those modern institutional economists, who, allegedly but mistakenly on the basis of Veblen's writing, make the claim that there is no essential distinction between judgements of fact and judgements of value. In fact, there is no foundation for such a claim in Veblen's work. Veblen (1919, pp. 19, 85–90; 1934, pp. 30–1) consistently emphasised the importance of scientific analysis over normative posturing.

8 Schneider (1995, p. 176) claimed that Veblen was distant from the historical school because, according to Rutherford (1984), Veblen embraced methodological individualism. This interpretation of Veblen is criticised in the following footnote.

to say, in terms of a passive and substantially inert and immutably given human nature.

(Veblen, 1898, p. 389)

Then followed Veblen's famous and often quoted critique of the 'hedonistic' assumptions of classical and neoclassical economics:

> The hedonistic conception of man is that of a lightning calculator of pleasures and pains, who oscillates like a homogeneous globule of desire of happiness under the impulse of stimuli that shift him about the area, but leave him intact. He has neither antecedent nor consequent. He is an isolated, definitive human datum, in stable equilibrium except for the buffets of the impinging forces that displace him in one direction or another.

(ibid., p. 389)

The ironic phrase 'lightning calculator' clearly suggests that there is a problem with the assumption that agents have rapid and unlimited computational abilities. The point that 'economic man' has 'neither antecedent nor consequent' should also not pass unnoticed. It connects directly with Veblen's argument that the requirement of a full evolutionary explanation of origin obliges us to abandon the assumption of the given individual:

> The economic life history of the individual is a cumulative process of adaptation of means to ends that cumulatively change as the process goes on, both the agent and his environment being at any point the outcome of the last process.

(ibid., p. 391)

In place of 'a passive and substantially inert and immutably given human nature', Veblen (1898, p. 389) saw instincts and habits as the dynamic bases of intention and action. Following James and others, instincts and habits were seen as the prime movers, and explicable in terms of both biological and socio-economic processes of evolution. Veblen (1898, p. 393) then laid down his core methodological principle: 'an evolutionary economics must be a theory of a process of cultural growth as determined by the economic interest, a theory of a cumulative sequence of economic institutions stated in terms of the process itself.'

On this basis, Veblen rejected not only biological reductionism but also methodological individualism. In 1898, the term methodological individualism had not yet been coined. But consider Veblen's position in the context of modern definitions of that term. Jon Elster (1982, p. 453) defined it as 'the doctrine that all social phenomena (their structure and their change) are in principle explicable only in terms of individuals – their properties, goals, and beliefs'.

To be consistent with methodological individualism as defined in this way, we must ultimately reach a point where all social phenomena are explained exclusively in terms of individuals. The suggestion that 'all social phenomena' have to be explained 'only in terms of individuals' is untenable if individuals themselves are then to be explained in terms other than individuals alone. The analysis would have to stop somewhere and individuals would then have to be taken as a given, explanatory foundation. Accordingly, the version of methodological individualism discussed here depends upon the assumption of given individuals (Nozick, 1977; Hodgson, 1988).

In contrast, Veblen urged 'evolutionary' and 'cumulative' explanation of individual characteristics and behaviour – involving natural as well as social science – with 'both the agent and his environment being at any point the outcome of the last process'. He thus broke from the idea of the given individual and undermined a precept of methodological individualism. In this respect at least, his criticisms of both neoclassical and Austrian economics retain their force to this day.[9]

VEBLEN'S HISTORICAL FRAMEWORK

Veblen rejected the idea that the individual could be taken as given because he believed that the individual was socially and institutionally formed. The capabilities and attitudes of an individual were congealed in his or her habits, acquired in activity and social interaction with others. Human behaviour is largely a matter of institutional coercion and constraint. 'The situation of today shapes the institutions of tomorrow through a selective, coercive process, by acting upon men's habitual view of things' (Veblen, 1899, p. 190). Habits were regarded as basic propensities. Veblen explained how institutions affected habits, without lapsing into either a methodological individualist or a methodological collectivist mode of explanation. In this respect his position differs profoundly from the idea in much of modern economics of the ahistorical, given individual.

In another regard, however, Veblen's argument differed from much of social science, before and since. Before the First World War it was common for social scientists to see social and economic exchange as explicable largely in terms of biological characteristics. By the 1930s, however, this perspective had fallen out of favour in much of Anglo-American academia. Instead it was held that human dispositions and behaviour could be largely or wholly explained in cultural terms.[10]

Veblen held to neither position. He attempted to explain historical change by examining the interaction between given and largely immutable instincts, on the one hand, and cultural and institutional development, on the other. Rare

---

9 Note that, in describing Veblen as a methodological individualist, Rutherford (1984) used the term in a different way from Elster (1982) and others. For Rutherford, Veblen (1919, p. 243) was a methodological individualist simply because he emphasised that social explanations 'must deal with individual conduct and must formulate its theoretical results in terms of individual conduct'. However, Veblen did not state that explanations must be *exclusively* in terms of individuals.

10 For discussions of the interaction between the social sciences and biology in the history of ideas see Hirst and Woolley (1982), Degler (1991), Wiengart et al. (1997), Hodgson (1999b).

among social scientists, he attempted to work within, and link together, both levels of analysis. As Veblen (1914, pp. 2–3) himself wrote:

> A genetic inquiry into institutions will address itself to the growth of habits and conventions, as conditioned by the material environment and by the innate and persistent propensities of human nature; and for these propensities, as they take effect in the give and take of cultural growth, no better designation than the time-worn 'instinct' is available.

In Veblen's (1914, pp. 13–18) analysis, the instincts provide a set of basic drives or dispositions. They have evolved over tens of thousands of years and are grounded in human biology. The basic components of this instinctive endowment are the instinct of workmanship (a human predilection for worthwhile achievement); the parental bent (expressed as sympathy and caring for other members of family or community), and idle curiosity (involving inquisitiveness and search for explanation). According to Veblen (1914, p. 17), these instincts have endured in human evolution because by 'selective survival' they enhance 'relative fitness to meet the material requirements of life'. Furthermore, as human culture and institutions have evolved and changed, these same instincts enhance the 'economic fitness to live under the new cultural limitations and with the new training which this altered cultural situation gives.'

For Veblen, these instincts are promoted or distorted in any given cultural or institutional integument. While institutional evolution proceeds, this changing institutional and cultural environment moulds each individual's instinctive dispositions. For example, Veblen (1899, p. 270) saw an 'emulative predatory impulse' as a 'special development of the instinct of workmanship' in relatively developed economies and cultures, characterised by competition and rivalry over significant reserves of wealth and means of power. Hence there was an interaction between the evolution of institutions and of instincts. These arguments worked at a very general level. As noted further in chapter 18 below, they pointed towards some general, over-arching principles within which matters of historical specificity could be accommodated.

C. L. Morgan's development of a higher, emergent level of analysis provided Veblen with a more particular framework for addressing the problem of historical specificity. Almost as a paraphrase of Morgan's (1896, p. 340) own words, Veblen (1914, p. 18) wrote:

> What is known of heredity goes on to say that the various racial types of man are stable; so that during the life-history of any given racial stock, it is held, no heritable modification of its typical make-up, whether spiritual or physical, is to be looked for. The typical human endowment of instincts, as well as the typical make-up of the race in the physical respect, has according to this current view been transmitted intact from the beginning of humanity. . . . On the other hand the habitual elements of human life change unremittingly and cumulatively, resulting in a continued proliferous growth of institutions. Changes in the institutional

structure are continually taking place in response to the altered discipline of life under changing cultural conditions, but [biological] human nature remains specifically the same.

Veblen saw the need to explain historical development in terms of the interaction between instincts and institutions. Like the assumption of rationality in neoclassical economics, the inherited instincts were regarded as constant and universal. But instincts were not the only motors of human thought and action. At a higher level, reigning and evolving institutions inculcated new and changing habits of thought and action. This habitual and cultural element was, for Veblen, historically contingent and specific. In short, Veblen's theory of human behaviour involved two levels: one instinctive and universal, the other cultural and historically specific.

Clearly, the next analytical step was to categorise and then analyse different types of institutional structures and cultural systems. This would provide a taxonomy of historically specific social formations. In his long-run view of human cultural development, Veblen adopted the same terminology as the pioneering anthropologist Lewis Henry Morgan (1877). Human civilisation was said to be preceded by 'barbarism' and before that by 'savagery'. For Veblen, each of these stages of human development channelled, distorted and built upon human instincts. He failed, however, to develop an adequate theory of the interaction of the instinctive and the social. Nevertheless, his work establishes some vitally important guideposts.

For instance, while rejecting the notion that the individual could be taken as given, Veblen also made persistent attacks on notions of 'natural order' or 'natural rights' in economic theory.[11] He thus undermined some of the major supports for an entirely general or ahistorical economic theory. On this issue Veblen was on the side of the historical school. On the other hand, unlike the historical school, he failed to address the problem of historical specificity directly. All we can do is glean hints and underdeveloped arguments from his writings.

Contrary to some Marxist and neoclassical thinking, Veblen hinted that multiple futures are possible. Equilibrating forces do not always pull the economy back onto a single track. History has no pre-ordained destination. Although Veblen had socialist leanings, he argued against the idea of finality or consummation in economic development. Variety and cumulative causation mean that history has 'no final term' (Veblen, 1919, p. 37). In Marxism the final term is communism or the classless society, but Veblen rejected the teleological concept of a final goal. Furthermore, for Veblen, socio-economic evolution was idiosyncratic and imperfect; it was path dependent and carried the conservative baggage of its past. This meant a rejection of the ideas of the 'inevitability' of socialism and of a 'natural' outcome or end-point in capitalist evolution. There is no natural path, or law, governing economic development.

---

11 See, for example, Veblen (1914, pp. 258–60, 289–98, 340–3; 1919, pp. 37, 154, 186–202, 280–3, 444; 1934, pp. 33–4).

VEBLEN, PRAGMATISM AND KNOWLEDGE

One of Veblen's most underrated contributions to economics is his recognition of the nature and importance of knowledge in productive activity and economic development. Veblen was one of the first to stress the relative importance of immaterial assets, including the 'knowledge and practice of ways and means' (Veblen, 1919, p. 343). For Veblen (1919, pp. 185–6) writing in 1908, production relied on 'the accumulated, habitual knowledge of the ways and means involved . . . the outcome of long experience and experimentation'. The production and use of all material and immaterial assets depend on elusive, immaterial circumstances and combinations of skills. These capacities are built up over a long period of time and reside in the institutions and culture of the socio-economic system. Veblen inherited his conception of knowledge from pragmatist philosophers such as Peirce and James.

The pragmatist viewpoint has important implications for the understanding of the essential character of the economic system. For Peirce (1878, p. 294) habit does not merely reinforce belief, the 'essence of belief is the establishment of habit'. Veblen (1934, p. 88), who followed the pragmatists, thus wrote in 1898: 'A habitual line of action constitutes a habitual line of thought, and gives the point of view from which facts and events are apprehended and reduced to a body of knowledge.' For Veblen (1899, p. 190) 'habits of thought' are 'points of view, mental attitudes and aptitudes': they are not thoughts as such. For Veblen and the pragmatists, habits of thought accommodate and reproduce the conceptual frameworks through which we understand and attribute meaning to the world. Veblen rejected the continuously calculating, marginally adjusting agent of neoclassical theory and emphasised inertia and habit instead.

Previously, the historical school had typically distinguished different types of economic system principally by their *Geist* or spirit, including dominant mental attitudes, culture and ethical norms. The *Geist* was not simply a property of the mind, but was materialised in the state, religion, the family, social customs, language and other institutions. Each *Geist* was the supreme criterion of historical differentiation between socio-economic systems. However, it was not explained how each *Geist* came into being, how it was transmitted from individual to individual, or how it moulded individual thoughts and activities. For many of the historical school, ethical ideals shaped institutions, and social institutions shaped human habits and behaviour.

A difficulty with this idealistic demarcation of socio-economic systems is that it is based on a faulty conception of knowledge. Ideas and ethical imperatives are depicted as driving all human behaviour. In contrast, the pragmatism of Peirce, James, Dewey and others changed our conception of knowledge, rooting it in habitual propensities rather than seeing it as an accumulation of codified ideas.

Both Marxists and institutionalists have criticised the historical school emphasis on *Geist* as a means of distinguishing different types of economic system. For Marxists, the *Geist* or spirit is secondary to the 'mode of production of material life'. Veblen's institutionalist critique was more radical and it applied to Marxism as well. Veblen indicated that both the *Geist*-based and the Marxist analyses relied on some influence of the social totality upon individuals, but without an adequate explanation of the causal processes involved. In particular, Marxism saw the mode of production as determining human thought and behaviour, without an adequate explanation of the causal links between structures and individuals.

Veblen argued that the inadequacies of both historicism and Marxism in this area were traceable to their common, Hegelian roots. Both Marxism and historicism appealed to a mysterious process of 'cultural exfoliation', as Veblen (1901, p. 76) sardonically put it. Instead, Veblen and the pragmatists sketched in outline a causal explanation of how structure and agency interact. Crucially, they pointed to the inner workings of habit. For them, habits were the basis of thoughts and beliefs; and habits were formed and reproduced through institutional constraints and influences. Accordingly, habits were part of the reconstitutive mechanism through which institutions impinged upon individual preferences and purposes.

VEBLEN'S FAILURE

Despite his achievements, Veblen's legacy in this area is an overall disappointment. In particular, Veblen did not engage explicitly with the problem of historical specificity. Although he developed some key ideas that would have helped to open up a richer theoretical approach, he failed to deploy them in the service of such a sustained project.

Although he read a significant part of their literature, there is no evidence that Veblen took on board the more sophisticated discussion of the relation between theory and empirical investigation in the later historical school. Veblen's (1903, p. 300) review of Sombart's *Der moderne Kapitalismus* declared that the historical school had 'recently entered the theoretical field' but Veblen gave little indication of the theoretical issues involved. Although much of his own work was meta-theoretical in character, he did not discuss the type of general, meta-theoretical framework developed by Max Weber or Werner Sombart as a possible grounding for historically sensitive theory.

Several passages in Veblen's writing indicate that he was against empiricist and positivist conceptions of knowledge.[12] However, while he understood that prior concepts and habits of thought are required to understand facts and events, he did not go far enough in emphasising the role of a theoretical framework in all scientific investigation. Indeed, on one occasion Veblen seemed to dismiss or downgrade the importance and indispensability of any general (meta-)theoretical framework for social science. In 1925 he commented on contemporary developments in economics:

---

12 See, for example, Veblen (1904, pp. 344, 371; 1934, pp. 89, 179).

There is little prospect that the current generation of economists will work out a compendious system of economic theory at large. They go quite confidently into their work of detailed inquiry with little help from general principles, except it be principles of common sense, mathematics, and general information.

(Veblen, 1934, p. 8)

Of course, it was possible that Veblen was being ironic here. But he did little to guide the reader away from any misinterpretation. It is not clear whether Veblen endorsed or resisted any abandonment of 'a compendious system of economic theory' and its intrinsic 'general principles'. Joseph Schumpeter (1926, p. 37 n.) saw Veblen in this passage as approving of 'detailed inquiry with little help from general principles'. Schumpeter rightly pointed out that no 'detailed enquiry' is possible without a general theoretical framework. Empirical work is not possible without a 'system of economic theory'. Schumpeter pointed out that Veblen's *Theory of the Leisure Class* was sufficient proof for that Veblen could 'not escape theory' and that he 'might need more of it'. By his own failure to build a systematic theory, and by ambiguous statements such as the above, Veblen aided and abetted the empiricist drift among institutionalists that was present at that time. Schumpeter had rightly identified a crucial defect, which was to gain significance in the years to come.

Although Veblen accomplished an intellectual revolution and established a foundation for institutionalism in America, and although he read and absorbed key German writers such as Schmoller and Sombart, he overlooked much of the methodological legacy of the German historical school and the *Methodenstreit*. After 1903 he referred much less often to the German academic literature and he seems to have lost interest in its methodological and theoretical debates.[13]

Nevertheless, as the next two chapters reveal, other American institutionalists were to continue their engagement with historicism, and pay more attention to the problem of historical specificity. Overall, and as evidenced on this particular issue, Veblen's theoretical corpus is one of sporadic brilliance but systematic deficiency.

---

13 An exception is where Veblen (1915b, pp. 848–9), in an otherwise positive review, severely criticised Sombart (1913a) for his 'latter-day conceptions of the transmission of racial characteristics, coupled with antiquated notions of racial identity' and for his unwarranted acceptance of national frontiers 'as marking racial distinctions' and 'marking distinct lines of inheritance'.

11

EARLY AMERICAN INSTITUTIONALISM AND THE PROBLEM OF HISTORICAL SPECIFICITY

> American social science bears the distinctive mark of its national origin. . . . Its liberal values, practical bent, shallow historical vision, and technocratic confidence are recognizable features of twentieth-century America. To foreign and domestic critics, these characteristics make American social science ahistorical and scientistic, lacking in appreciation of historical difference and complexity.
>
> (Dorothy Ross, *The Origins of American Social Science* (1991))

Although Thorstein Veblen never attained a senior academic position, he had a number of influential students and his academic reputation grew steadily. One of his students was Wesley C. Mitchell who became, in the interwar years, one of the most influential economists in America. By the end of the First World War, institutional economics had become an identifiable movement.[1] Nevertheless, the treatment of the problem of historical specificity within this movement was patchy at best. Although the influence of the German historical school was acknowledged and discussed (Mitchell, 1969), the problem of historical specificity did not receive so much attention. While in the German historical school it had been a central topic of debate, this was not so within American institutionalism. We are obliged to consider the scattered instances in which the issue surfaced in America.

THE EARLY WORKS OF JOHN COMMONS

John Commons was taught by Richard Ely and thereby made intimately aware of the historical school legacy. Like Ely and Veblen, Commons was fluent in German. However, he was not greatly influenced by Veblen, his personal contacts with Veblen were infrequent and there are important differences of theoretical approach. For some years Commons made no claim to be part of the American

---

1 For discussions of American institutionalism in the interwar years see Morgan and Rutherford (1998), Rutherford (1997, 1998, 2000) and Yonay (1998).

institutionalist movement. It was not until his *Legal Foundations* of 1924 that others recognised him as such (Rutherford, 2000). Commons himself he did not use the term 'institutional economics' prominently until 1931 (Commons, 1931).

His early works covered a variety of themes – political, economic and sociological. Although he occasionally referred to pragmatists such as William James and John Dewey, the influence of the pragmatist school upon him in his early writings was not nearly so strong as it was in the case of Veblen. For example, Commons sporadically mentioned the central pragmatist concept of habit but it acquired no theoretical prominence until his *Institutional Economics* of 1934. It is also in this later work that Commons became more interested in pragmatist philosophers such as Charles Sanders Peirce. The brief remarks in this section are confined to his early writings. Commons's later works are discussed in chapter 12 below.

In a series of articles published in the *American Journal of Sociology* in 1899 and 1900, collectively entitled 'a sociological view of sovereignty', Commons (1965, pp. 3–4) argued that individuals are moulded by institutions: 'Those definite and accepted modes of mutual dealing, handed down from generation to generation, and shaping each individual, are institutions.' Nevertheless, while consistently emphasising the 'coercive' role of institutions, there is no indication of the causal processes involved in the 'shaping' of each individual.

Furthermore, there is neither a clear trace of the concept of emergent properties, nor of individuals and institutions as multiple levels of analysis. When Commons wrote of institutional evolution it was largely a process of conscious legal adjudication rather than the operation of causal powers emanating from institutions themselves. In addition, Commons did not have the enthusiasm for Darwin's ideas that was shared by Veblen, Morgan, Peirce and James. Commons's discussions of social evolution are typically more Spencerian in nature. He also rejected the Darwinian 'natural selection' metaphor on the grounds that what is involved in socio-economic evolution is 'artificial selection'.[2]

On the other hand, Commons's overall contribution to the discourse on the historical specificity of socio-economic systems was much more significant than that of Veblen. Even in his early works he emphasised that different historical and geographical circumstances gave rise to different forms of capitalism. In particular, he argued that the United States was impelled by its own distinct history to evolve organisations and structures quite distinct from those in Europe. Commons observed (1893, p. 59), for example, that:

> The English economists have taken the laws of private property for granted, assuming that they are fixed and immutable in the nature of

---

2 Commons (1897, p. 90; 1965, pp. 7, 8, 10, 30) cited Spencer and repeated Spencerian notions such as the alleged law of increasing complexity of the social organism. Absent is the Darwinian notion that variety precedes, as well as results from, the evolutionary process (Mayr, 1982, pp. 45–7, 354; Hodgson, 1993a). On the idea of artificial selection in society see Commons (1897, pp. 90, 95; 1924, p. 376; 1934a, p. 45) and Ramstad (1994). However, Dennett (1995, pp. 316–17) shows that the concept is highly problematic.

things, and therefore need no investigation. But such laws are changeable – they differ for different peoples and places, and they have profound influence upon the production and distribution of wealth.

In addition, as Dorothy Ross (1991, p. 203) pointed out, in his extensive *History of Labor in the United States* (Commons *et al.*, 1918–35) his 'central argument was that American labor organization was unique, the product of competitive market conditions and America's unique historical circumstances'.

For much of his life, Commons was preoccupied with the empirical documentation and theoretical analysis of the legal and customary foundations of the American industrial and commercial system. His *Legal Foundations of Capitalism* (Commons, 1924) attempted to set out its institutional framework. This analysis had clear affinities with earlier work by the German historical school.[3]

However, it was not until 1934, with the appearance of his *Institutional Economics*, that Commons attempted a general philosophical and theoretical statement. Chapter 12 (below) discusses how Commons engaged at length therein with the problem of historical specificity. The tragedy, however, was that this statement came very late for the institutionalist movement in America. By the 1930s, institutionalism had lost much of its innovative theoretical momentum and was negotiating difficult territory. Developments in American thought had challenged the philosophical and psychological foundations upon which institutionalism had been built. But before we discuss these developments and Commons's later contribution, let us first return to the early years of the twentieth century.

THE TRAGEDY OF ROBERT HOXIE

One of the earliest contributors to what eventually to be called 'institutional economics' was Robert Hoxie. Hoxie was at the University of Chicago for many years and he was strongly influenced by Veblen. In 1901, Hoxie devoted an article to the teaching of economic principles, emphasising that the student must gain 'an intimate knowledge of the economic structure of society'. Furthermore, 'economic instruction must proceed from a knowledge of economic structure to principle rather than from a knowledge of economic principle to structure' (Hoxie, 1901, p. 483). He made reference to the German historical school and took on board the notion that society could be treated analytically as an organism. For Hoxie (p. 492) 'Economics aims to give an account in causal terms of the economic organization as it is in process of becoming.' Hoxie (p. 514) continued: 'The economic structure is composed of economic institutions in organic

---

3 See Biddle and Samuels (1997). Schneider (1995, p. 178) stated that in taking the transaction as the basic unit of analysis Commons was following Voigt (1912–13, p. 311) and Amonn (1927, pp. 286–90). Also, Commons's insistence that exchange essentially involves the transfer of property rights has a precursor in the work of Rau (1835, p. 3). It is not known whether Commons read these German works.

relationship.' Nevertheless, Hoxie had excessive faith in the gathering of facts as a means to discover causal relations.

In a later work by Hoxie there is a very brief discussion of the 'historical method'. In this four-page article, Hoxie (1906, pp. 569–70) wrote that 'social institutions are not merely what they can be shown to be by study of their present structure and functioning, but are also what they are actually or potentially in process of becoming as the result of the operation of forces past as well as present.' Hence economics must be concerned not merely with historical narrative but with the understanding of underlying historical forces. But Hoxie's analysis did not get much further than this.

Events interfered with the further development of Hoxie's ideas on the historical method. In 1914, Hoxie was asked by Commons to write a scientific report for the Federal Industrial Relations Commission on the merits and demerits of the new system of 'scientific management' advanced by Frederick Winslow Taylor (1911). While Veblen supported 'scientific management' on the grounds that it organised production on a rational basis and helped to promote output and higher living standards, Commons took a very different view. Taylor believed that workers and trade unions should participate in the 'scientific' process of the detailed study of working time. However, Commons was strongly against any form of worker or trade union participation in management. For this reason, Commons opposed Taylorism. Indebted to Commons, Hoxie felt obliged to slant his report in this direction. Eventually, Commons persuaded a reluctant and dissatisfied Hoxie to publish his draft report. The published report was an equivocal and unconvincing piece of work, in which the arguments in favour of the Taylorist case were inadequately represented (Hoxie, 1915). Charles Mixter (1916) critically reviewed Hoxie's work in the *American Economic Review*. Distraught by his failure, this review prompted Hoxie to cut his own throat from ear to ear (Nyland, 1996). So died tragically a promising theorist of American institutionalism. Commons subsequently suffered a nervous breakdown and was not able to return to work until 1917 (Commons, 1934b, pp. 179, 182).

THE INAUGURATION OF AMERICAN INSTITUTIONALISM

In the summer of 1918, the then president of the AEA, Irving Fisher, set up a Committee on Cooperation in Economic Research, with Walton Hamilton as its secretary. Its chairman was Allyn Young, 'an admirer of Veblen and an old friend of Mitchell' (Dorfman, 1974, p. 26). Another of its members was Harold G. Moulton, a friend and co-thinker of Hamilton. One concern of this committee was to make economic theory relevant for policy. A prominent aim was to address the key problems of economic development after the First World War. One of its enduring by-products was the tentative creation of an identity for institutional economics in the interwar period.

On 11 November 1918, in the Forest of Compiègne in France, an armistice was signed between Germany and the Allies, ending hostilities in the First World

War. All countries involved in the war faced economic and social problems of demobilisation and reconstruction. A few days after the armistice, in December, across the Atlantic, at the annual meeting of the American Economic Association, the term 'institutional economics' was announced in a paper delivered by Hamilton (1919). Works such as Veblen's *Theory of the Leisure Class* had already achieved a wide popular readership. Commons had advised the US and Wisconsin state governments and had become the foremost authority on American labour organisation. Commons was president of the American Economic Association in 1917. Successive leading institutionalists such as Wesley Mitchell and John Maurice Clark (son of John Bates Clark) had established strong academic reputations. But until 1918 the term 'institutional economics' had not been used to describe their school.[4]

Moulton had already approached Veblen and Mitchell and had adduced their support for an initiative to consolidate support in the AEA for the institutionalist cause. In his December 1918 address, Hamilton attempted to define the characteristics of this emerging paradigm. As Dorfman (1974, pp. 25–6) explained, the meeting 'was a part of the general movement for reconstruction of economics that was demanded by advanced, liberal economists of all kinds, in order to cope effectively with the problems of the war and the subsequent peace'. Among others, Hamilton's presentation drew the support of J. M. Clark and Walter W. Stewart. The initiative to found institutional economics was prompted very much by the concerns of postwar economic development. Institutionalism was thus launched as a movement. Its concerns and debates dominated American economics, at least until the 1940s.

If we can speak then of a dominant school in economics in American universities, for much of the first half of the twentieth century it was the 'old' institutionalism. Mitchell became AEA president in 1924. He was followed in that position by institutionalists such as J. M. Clark in 1935, Frederick C. Mills in 1940, Sumner H. Slichter in 1941, Edwin G. Nourse in 1942 and Albert B. Wolfe in 1943. Other AEA presidents – including Allyn A. Young in 1925 and Edwin Gay in 1929 – were sympathetic to institutionalism.

However, the First World War did not simply lead to the inauguration of American institutionalism. It also signalled the end of almost four decades of numerous close personal contacts between young graduate American economists and the German universities. The outbreak of war in 1914 made the academic trip from America to Germany impossible. When the war ended, some American scholars crossed the Atlantic to study. But the numbers involved were much lower than before. As Jurgen Herbst (1965, p. 203) put it: 'With the opening of The Johns Hopkins University in 1876, the massive influence of the German historical school on American social science began. Thirty-eight years later, with the outbreak of World War I, it came to an end.'

---

4 Hamilton (1916, p. 863, n. 5) mentioned that Hoxie had described himself as an 'institutional economist'. This appears to be the first use of the term 'institutional economist' in print. Following Hamilton (1919) the terms 'institutional economics' or 'institutional approach to economics' gradually came into common use (Rutherford, 1997).

Nevertheless, the influence of German ideas on American academia persisted for a while. This influence is abundantly clear in the case of the economist who is discussed in the next section.

FRANK KNIGHT, INSTITUTIONALISM AND THE PROBLEM OF HISTORICAL SPECIFICITY

Frank Knight went to Cornell University in 1913, at first to study philosophy. He particularly admired Immanuel Kant and he acquired a deep and enduring philosophical awareness. He read widely, including texts in the original German. Throughout his life, Knight paid attention to the German historical school and struggled with the problems that they had raised (Noppeney, 1997).[5]

Knight was once asked which area of research he would like to build upon further. He responded: 'There has been the work of one man whom I have greatly admired. If I were to start out again, I would build upon his ideas. I am referring of course to Max Weber' (quoted in Schweitzer 1975, p. 279). In 1927 – years before the German theorist became well known in America – Knight published an English translation of Weber's *General Economic History* (Weber, 1927). It would be difficult to overstate the importance of Weber for Knight. Schweitzer (1975, p. 280) argued that Knight 'was the first American economist who recognised in Weber's work the foundation for . . . a social economics'. Knight (1928b, p. 96) himself wrote:

> there is no doubt that the capitalistic spirit is the most important fact of modern economic history or even of modern history at large. And it is Sombart's work, along with the strikingly similar utterances of Max Weber, which has taught the reading world to appreciate the importance of *quantitative rationality* as a phase of the modern social mind. This must stand as one of the great intellectual achievements of the age.

Clearly, Knight was an important conduit for some of the ideas of the later German historical school. In the above quotation he drew from both Sombart and Weber. Furthermore, Knight described himself as an institutional economist. This fact is not widely acknowledged today: both supporters and opponents of institutionalism prefer to categorise him differently. However, the connection between Knight and institutionalism is clear.

Knight's PhD dissertation was at one stage supervised by institutionalist sympathiser Allyn Young. It was submitted and examined in 1916. Subsequently it was revised for publication as *Risk, Uncertainty and Profit* under the supervision of the leading institutionalist John Maurice Clark (Knight, 1921a, p. ix). It became a classic, and one of the most important economics monographs of the twentieth century. Above all, it was one of the first works to develop the concept of uncertainty in economic theory.

---

5   This section makes some use of material from Hodgson (2001a).

In a letter to his friend Talcott Parsons, dated 1 May 1936, Knight wrote: 'I came to Chicago expecting . . . "institutionalism" to be my main field of work' (Knight, 1936). While at Chicago, Knight taught that institutional economics and Marshallian neoclassical economics had complementary roles. On this issue, he was far from unique. Leading institutional economists such as John Commons, Wesley Mitchell and J. M. Clark all believed that institutionalism could be made compatible with some elements of Marshallian-type price theory, using such concepts as supply and demand.[6]

In a letter dated 16 February 1937 to the institutionalist and close friend Clarence Ayres, Knight reported that he was giving a course on 'Economics from an Institutional Perspective' at Chicago. In fact, Knight had started giving this course in the summer quarter of 1932. Knight's Reading List for Economics 305, Winter 1937, says: 'The task of institutionalism [is] that of accounting historically for the factors treated as *data* in rationalistic, price-theory economics.' He then lists the topics 'individualism and utilitarianism, wants, technology, resources, organization, economic institutions as embodied in law' (Samuels, 1977, p. 503). In principle, there was nothing in Knight's qualified acceptance of some neoclassical tenets to debar him from institutionalism. He himself made the place of institutional economics explicit and extensive.

Like the German historical school, Knight tried to grapple with the problem of historical specificity. In his *Risk, Uncertainty and Profit*, Knight (1921a, p. 9) tried to elucidate some economic principles that related to 'free enterprise' or 'the competitive system'. The study of this system, according to Knight, should proceed 'as a first approximation' from 'a *perfectly* competitive system, in which the multitudinous degrees and kinds of divergences are eliminated by abstraction'. This approach is clearly redolent of Weber's ideal type methodology.

In subsequent works, Knight tried to answer the more fundamental question, which had been addressed by historical school thinkers such as Max Weber and Werner Sombart. Knight asked if any features, assumptions or laws could be applied legitimately to all economic systems. For Knight, these universal principles concerned the questions of choice and allocation under scarcity. Hence these universal economic problems assured a place for the abstractions of neoclassical economic theory. However, he argued that these principles do not take us very far:

> The problem of life is to utilize resources 'economically,' to make them go as far as possible in the production of desired results. The general theory of economics is therefore simply the rationale of life. – In so far as it has any rationale! The first question in regard to scientific economics is this question of how far life is rational, how far its problems reduce to the form of using given means to achieve given ends. Now this, we shall contend, is not very far.
>
> (Knight, 1924, p. 229)

---

6 See, for example, Commons (1931, pp. 648–56), Mitchell (1937, p. 24), J. M. Clark (1936, p. 421).

Nevertheless, Knight held that viable universal principles should not be disregarded. He alleged that there were universals such as 'the general laws of choice', 'general laws of production and consumption'. In other words, for Knight, all individuals throughout history, in their economic activities, make choices, and the same 'laws' govern these choices. Although Knight did not elaborate much on the nature of these supposedly universal laws, he gave an example: 'in the large the conditions of supply and demand determine the prices of goods' (Knight, 1924, p. 259). He wrote further:

> Institutions may determine the alternatives of choice and fix the limits of freedom of choice, but the general laws of choice among competing motives or goods are not institutional . . . there are general laws of production and consumption which hold good whatever specific things are thought of as wealth and whatever productive factors and processes in use. . . . The laws of economics are never themselves institutional, though they may relate to institutional situations. Some, as we have observed, are as universal as rational behavior, the presence of alternatives of choice between quantitatively variable ends, or between different means of arriving at ends. . . . A large part of the extant body of economic theory would be as valid in a socialistic society as it is in one organized through exchange between individuals.
>
> (ibid., pp. 258–60)

However, when we probe these 'general laws' their content is elusive. If 'rational behavior' is a 'general law', as Knight suggests, then it simply relates to the general description of the problem of choice: between alternative ends and between different means of arriving at ends. As Knight himself insisted, such generalities do not take us very far. At this general level, no particular choice outcome can be explained or predicted. One wonders, therefore, why he was inclined to retain the term 'law' at all. In addition, do 'supply and demand' relate to a *general* 'law'? Arguably, such concepts relate to historically specific institutions, such as markets. Hence they are not so general as choice in the abstract. The 'general laws of production and consumption' cited by Knight may not be so general after all.

Whatever the limitations of his solution, Knight was clearly trying to demarcate universal from non-universal laws. His claim was that any universal 'laws of economics' had to be supplemented by the historically specific study of institutions. Knight clearly pointed out that not all laws are universal, and that different laws had different domains of applicability. He gave the following examples:

> Other laws relate to behavior in exchange relations, and of course have no practical significance where such relations are not established. Still others cover behavior in situations created by even more special institutional arrangements, as for example the differences in business conduct created by the custom of selling goods subject to cash discount

or by the existence of a branch banking system as contrasted with independent banks. An intelligent conception of the meaning of science requires a clear grasp of the meaning of classification and sub-classification, of laws of all degrees of generality. Each law is universal in the field to which it applies, though it may not give a complete description of the cases which it fits. Quite commonly a law has the form 'insofar as the situation is of such a character, such things will happen.'

(ibid., p. 260)

Knight's notion here that an 'intelligent conception of the meaning of science requires a clear grasp of the meaning of classification and subclassification, of laws of all degrees of generality' shows the particular inspiration of Weber and the German historicists. Knight gave this insight an additional, institution-alist twist. Institutions were seen to 'determine the alternatives of choice and fix the limits of freedom of choice'. This, for Knight, was the place for institutional economics. Knight thus insisted that the 'general theory of economics' is valid but it does not get us 'very far'. His writings are admirably consistent on this point.

> The principles of the established economics are partial statements, but sound as far as they go, and they go about as far as general principles can be carried. . . . General theory is a *first step*, but never a very long step toward the solution of practical problems.
>
> (Knight, 1921b, p. 145)

Hence Knight made it clear that general theory is of limited use, and economics is dependent on institutionalist insights. For Knight, without institutions, economic man would exist in a vacuum, without a history or a future. Hence he saw the relationship between neoclassical and institutional economics as one of 'complementarity' (Knight 1952, p. 46). As Knight (1924, p. 262) himself put it: 'deductive theory and "institutional" economics' are both relevant:

> at one extreme we might have a discussion limited to the abstract theory of markets . . . at the other extreme we should have the philosophy of history . . . and that is what institutional economics practically comes to. It should go without saying that all are useful and necessary.

Knight (1924, pp. 265–6) went on, to explain the key role of institutional economics:

> The study of such long-time changes would seem to be the most conspicuous task of institutional economics . . . [n]o one would belittle the importance of studying these historic movements in the general structure of social standards and relations . . . [b]ut neither, we think, can anyone contend that such a study should displace the other branches of economics which either are fairly independent of institutions or take

them as they are at a given time and place and use them in explaining the immediate facts of economic life.

Accordingly, institutional economics focused on long-term changes, alongside the study of more general 'laws' that are 'fairly independent' of particular institutions. For Knight, the use of some of the abstract principles of neoclassical economics could be justified in two ways. First, the general problem of choice under scarcity was allegedly universal. Second, he argued that the 'abstract theory of markets' could be applied to a competitive capitalist system, because he saw a sufficient correspondence between its theoretical assumptions and the reality of competitive capitalism. Hence Knight treated the 'abstract theory of markets' in neoclassical economics as a plausible analysis of a historically specific system. This theory was not universally valid, but of sufficient explanatory power to fit the modern capitalist world. In this respect, as noted in chapter 5, Knight followed John Stuart Mill, Walter Bagehot, Alfred Marshall, Max Weber and Werner Sombart. He accepted the issue of historical specificity but he also argued that the principles of orthodox economics were relevant for the modern socio-economic system.

For Knight (1924, p. 229), it was also necessary for the economist to examine the role of institutions and to also embark on 'an exploration in the field of values'. Institutionalists would agree. Knight should be recognised not simply as an American institutionalist, but one who made a major contribution to the literature on historical specificity. Although he argued that neoclassical analysis had some limited relevance to the analysis of a particular type of socio-economic system, he also emphasised the vital supplementary role of additional institutional enquiry. He thus saw economic theories as related to historically specific real objects and attempted to develop a methodology to demarcate the roles of different types of theory. We can criticise him on the details but the scope of his achievement is immense.

FRANK FETTER AND SUMNER SLICHTER

In the United States, during the 1920s and 1930s, other institutional and allied economists emphasised the importance of historically specific institutions. One of these was Frank A. Fetter. Fetter received his doctorate at Halle in Germany in 1894 and was president of the American Economic Association in 1912. He · was influenced by the German historical school, by Veblen, and by Austrian school economists such as Eugen von Böhm-Bawerk and Friedrich von Wieser. He was an acquaintance of Commons. His research was largely on the theory of value and welfare. He coined the term 'psychic income'.

In his works the impact of historical school thinking is abundantly clear. Two of his essays address the concept of capital. For many modern social scientists, oblivious to the problem of historical specificity, 'capital' is a universal concept, applying to all types of socio-economic system. This is a dangerous elision. Under modern capitalism, 'capital' has measurable and marketable characteristics. It refers to stocks of assets that have a market value. Instead, by making the concept of capital universal, these characteristics are mistakenly attached to other forms of asset, whether or not they are measurable or saleable on the market. Hence today we have objectionable concepts such as 'social capital', attached to phenomena which involve social relationships and institutions that are often neither measurable nor marketable. Long ago, Fetter saw the danger in the widening and abuse of the capital concept. He wrote:

> Capital is essentially an individual acquisitive, financial, investment ownership concept. It is not coextensive with wealth as physical objects, but rather with legal rights as claims to uses and incomes. It is or should be a concept relating unequivocally to private property and to the existing price system. Social capital is but a mischievous name for national wealth.
>
> (Fetter, 1927, p. 156)

Accordingly, for Fetter (1930, p. 190), capital was a historically specific phenomenon: 'Capital is defined as a conception of individual riches having real meaning only within the price system and the market where it originated, and developing with the spread of the financial calculus in business practice.'

This laudable conception echoed that of Sombart (1902, vol. 2, p. 129) who defined capital as 'the sum of exchange value which serves as the working basis of a capitalist enterprise'. From this viewpoint, it is misleading and mischievous to extend the term 'capital' to cover social relations or entities of a non-pecuniary nature. The danger with terms such as 'social capital' is that they refer to things that, in fact, may not be measurable or marketable. Accordingly, policies designed to build up 'social capital' may employ a spurious methodology of measurability and incline towards the inappropriate use of pecuniary or market instruments.[7]

Fetter was on the fringes of American institutional economics and also sympathetic to the Austrian school. In contrast, Sumner Slichter was closer to the mainstream of American institutionalism. Slichter was a student of Commons at the University of Wisconsin. He took his PhD at Chicago. After jobs at Princeton and Cornell he moved to Harvard University in 1930 as a specialist in labour economics. He wrote a widely circulated institutionalist textbook (Slichter, 1931). In true institutionalist form, he objected to the tendency of neoclassical economists to treat as universal those phenomena that in reality were historically specific. Slichter (1924, pp. 304–5) complained of neoclassical economics in the following terms: 'The influence of market organization and institutions upon value is ignored. No distinction, for example, is made between forms of market organization' such as 'the stock exchange or the wheat market' or 'the labour

---

7   Much later Schumpeter (1954, p. 323) was also to warn against the abuse of the term 'capital': 'What a mass of confused, futile, and downright silly controversies it would have saved us, if economists had had the sense to stick to those monetary and accounting meanings of the term instead of trying to "deepen" them!'

market'. Similarly, he lamented: 'Interest theories are constructed without reference to the credit system, to corporate or to governmental saving.' On these points and others, institutionalists held very similar views to their historical school forebears.

THE NEGLECTED EVELINE BURNS

We find a penetrating analytic treatment of the problem of historical specificity in a neglected article by Eveline M. Burns. She was married to the Columbia University economist Arthur R. Burns. They were British by birth and both had been educated at the London School of Economics under Edwin Cannan. They moved to Columbia in 1928, where they loosely identified with American institutional economics.[8]

Eveline Burns (1931) was able to look at American institutionalism with fresh, European eyes. The subject of her article was: 'Does institutionalism complement or compete with "orthodox economics"?' She argued that the answer to this question depended in part on the outcome of the further develop-ment of the inadequate theoretical foundations of institutional economics. She recognised that one of the key questions to be addressed was the relationship between Marshallian-type price theory and historically specific institutional structures.

Ever since its inauguration, institutionalists had argued over the compatibility or otherwise of institutionalism with neoclassical price theory. Some followed Veblen's position and rejected all neoclassical approaches. Their problem was that they had no alternative price theory to put in their place. Others argued that a version of neoclassical price theory might have a place within a wider corpus of institutionalist theory. They upheld, in particular, that institution-alism might be compatible with elements of Marshallian-type price theory. Prominent economists that argued to some degree along these lines included John Commons, Wesley Mitchell, John Maurice Clark, Frank Knight, Allyn Young, Paul Douglas and Arthur F. Burns.[9]

Eveline Burns endorsed this compatibilist position, but also urged institution-alists to face up to the question of their own theoretical essence and identity. For her, one of the 'reasons for the slow realization of the promise of institutionalism'

---

8 Arthur R. Burns should not be confused with Arthur F. Burns, the collaborator of Mitchell, who was also an institutional economist and at Columbia from 1941 until his retirement. Colombia dropped Eveline Burns as an economics lecturer in 1942. However, she became a Professor of Social Work at Columbia in 1946 and made a major contribution to the development of the US Social Security system (E. M. Burns, 1949).

9 For instance, Commons (1931, pp. 618–56) wrote that 'institutional economics . . . cannot separate itself from the marvellous discoveries and insight of the classical and psychological economists. . . . Institutional economics is not divorced from the classical and psychological schools of economists.' For an exposition and discussion of Commons's views on the compatibility of neoclassical and institutional economics see Biddle and Samuels (1998). It should be stressed, however, that there was a multiplicity of views among institutionalists on how Marshallian theory could be reconciled with institutionalism, as well as differences on other matters.

was a 'vagueness of the concept of institutionalism itself' (p. 80). She suggested that:

> Institutionalism can perhaps be defined . . . as a method of approach to economic problems in which prominent place is given to the interaction between social institutions on the one hand and economic relationships and the economic aspects of behaviour on the other.

Burns (1931, p. 82) saw 'Max Weber's study of the genesis of the capitalist system of organization' as a 'superb example' of a 'genetic' study of the development of institutions. She went on to address directly the problem of historical specificity, and the question of categorisation of different economic systems:

> We may hope ultimately to discover categories for characterizing the interrelationships of economic phenomena peculiar to different societies and thus prepare the way for generalizations concerning the various forms of social life comparable to those of the biologist concerning the forms of individual life. We have as yet no criteria appropriate to the classification of economic aspects of social life comparable to those used by the biologist for distinguishing plant from animal life, vertebrates from invertebrates or the viviparous from the oviparous. Attempts to characterize societies by reference to a quality so dominating and fundamental that it appears to determine the main types of relationship existing among the various parts, and the functions they perform, have been made among others, by the economic historians. These efforts have evidenced themselves in the use of such terms as nomadic, settled, feudal, socialist or communistic societies, and in general in the characterization by economic historians of types of economic societies in their discussions of stages of development. But the criteria used as bases of classification hitherto, have received surprisingly little serious consideration and have not always been relevant to economic discussion.
>
> (Burns, 1931, p. 87)

This is an exceptionally clear statement of the problem. Burns here argued for historically sensitive categories and for the development of a methodology to underlie the system of classification. For Burns, the appropriate classification of different socio-economic systems depended upon the identification of 'a quality so dominating and fundamental' that it reflected the essential relationships and functions within the system. She continued:

> Perhaps the efforts to characterize capitalist society have given rise, especially in the work of Weber and Sombart, to the most orderly and penetrating consideration of these problems. It is possible to take issue with Sombart's emphasis upon the spirit of the society as the all-powerful conditioning force, to challenge the specific content with which he endows the capitalist spirit, or to doubt the adequacy of his three criteria

(the spirit, the technique and the form of organization) as dimensions in terms of which to describe and classify societies. It is disconcerting to find so little attention paid to the methodological implications of his work.

(ibid.)

Two further key points emerged here. She doubted the use of *Geist* or spirit as a criterion to classify different socio-economic systems, as in the work of Sombart and others. She also sounded an alarm for American institutionalists, concerning the dearth of methodological discussion of the problem. She thus concluded: 'The extent to which institutionalism will in future be regarded as a rival to so-called orthodox economics will, I submit, depend in large measure upon how successfully institutional economists tackle their methodological problems' (ibid.).

Her verdict was appropriate. It amounted to an urgent call for institutionalism to identify its methodological foundations. When Burns published these lines, Veblen was dead. The task of providing institutionalism with a firmer methodological and theoretical foundation fell to its second great mentor, alas near to the end of his career. The theoretical manifesto of John Commons is the subject of the next chapter.

12

THE THEORETICAL MANIFESTO
OF JOHN COMMONS

> He helped to keep alive, in an age moving towards an opposite
> sentiment, the belief that economics, since it is always teleological
> with respect to man, can never constitute an exact science. Hence
> the human will must always be an important part of economics.
> This may be studied objectively, scientifically, but it cannot be
> built into a predictable system. . . . His second great insight was the
> pervasiveness of collective activity, both in the form of organization
> and in custom.
>
> (Neil W. Chamberlain, 'The Institutional Economics of
> John R. Commons' (1963))

When John Commons began the task of providing institutionalism with its first
systematic theoretical treatise, the intellectual background had already changed
radically, compared with the period before the First World War. By the 1920s,
behaviourism was rapidly surpassing instinct psychology (Curti, 1980; Degler,
1991). In philosophy, positivism was rapidly displacing pragmatism. Before
logical positivism spread to America in the 1930s, earlier forms of positivism
were already well established, and their manifestations were clearly visible in
behaviourist psychology. Furthermore, on liberal ideological grounds, there
was a strong reaction against so-called 'social Darwinism' and the use of biological explanations in the social sciences. Links between the social sciences
and biology were axed, and even biological metaphors became suspect (Degler,
1991; Hodgson, 1999b; Ross, 1991). Crucially, even among institutionalists, faith
was lost in the Veblenian research programme to place economics within an
encompassing Darwinian and evolutionary framework.

A rising generation of positivistic social scientists, established in the rapidly
expanding university system of the United States, challenged the philosophical
and psychological underpinnings of institutionalism that Walton Hamilton,
Wesley Mitchell and others had taken for granted in 1918. Hence Commons had
a doubly difficult task: both to build a structure for the first time and to build it
on foundations that were unstable and shifting rapidly. As a result, some of the
earlier, Veblenian themes were diminished or abandoned. For instance, although
Commons's *Institutional Economics* was sprinkled with biological metaphors,
there was no sustained development of the Darwinian themes that Veblen had

taken up before. Furthermore, although Commons still retained a place for pragmatist philosophy, instinct psychology played a less important role.

Nevertheless, Commons was able to add some important new ingredients in this work. One particularly worth noting is the influence of the philosopher Alfred Whitehead (Commons, 1934a, pp. 17, 96). Whitehead had left Britain for Harvard University in 1924. He was strongly influenced by the European philosophies of Henri Bergson (1911), Samuel Alexander (1920) and Conwy Lloyd Morgan. However, despite the explicit mention of Whitehead, and the link with Morgan, the concept of emergence did not become prominent in Commons's work. The second major chance for American institutionalism to assimilate the concept of emergence was lost.[1]

Whitehead emphasised an organicist ontology, in which the essential charac-teristics of any element are outcomes of relations with other entities. In this respect his philosophy stood against the atomist assumptions of much economics. Whitehead also criticised the naïve faith in induction, as found in much historical school writing. Whitehead (1926, pp. 55–6) wrote:

> Induction presupposes metaphysics. In other words, it rests on an antecedent rationalism. You cannot have a rational justification for your appeal to history till your metaphysics has assured you that there *is* a history to appeal to; and likewise your conjectures as to the future presuppose some basis of knowledge that there *is* a future already subject to some determination.

Whitehead's point was similar to that made by Carl Menger in his *Untersuchungen* in 1883. Both Menger and Whitehead argued that metaphysical presupposi-tions were unavoidable, even in empirical work. Commons seemed to have taken this point on board. Furthermore, Commons was influenced by Whitehead's organicist ontology.[2]

However, the question of organicist ontology is different from the idea of society itself as an organism. Commons eventually rejected this analogy. While in 1899–1900 he had approved of Spencer's view of society as an organism (Commons, 1965, p. 30), in his later writings Commons (1934a, pp. 96, 119) declared that the comparison of society with an organism was a 'false analogy'. In rejecting this analogy, both Commons and Veblen differed from several members of the German historical school.

---

1 Exceptionally among the American institutionalists, Copeland (1927) cited Morgan and his concept of emergence.

2 Sometimes the word 'holism' is used to describe an outlook similar to Whitehead's 'organicism' (Wilber and Harrison, 1978). Notably, Gruchy (1947, p. 4) insisted that the whole is not only greater than the sum of its parts, 'but that the parts are so related that their functioning is conditioned by their interrelations'. Such a view is perfectly compatible with Whitehead's organicism. However, Gruchy's (1947, p. vii) definition of holism is less satisfactory. For him, holism involved 'studying the economic system as an evolving, unified whole or synthesis, in the light of which the system's parts take on their full meaning'. This view is inadequate unless it is added that it is also necessary to examine the parts in order to understand the whole. Without such an addendum, 'holism' becomes a reductionist, inverted image of methodological individualism. Given its multiplicity of meanings, the term 'holism' is best abandoned.

JOHN COMMONS AND THE THEORY OF
IDEAL TYPES

In his *Institutional Economics*, Commons made an important attempt to deal with the problem of historical specificity. His discussion therein of the methodology of ideal types covers no less than thirty pages. However, his ideas and terminology are sometimes idiosyncratic and obscure. Commons (pp. 724–48) tried to consider four different types of ideal type: the 'pedagogic', 'propagandist', 'scientific' and 'ethical' ideal type. However, the definitions and distinctions between these forms of ideal type are vague and inadequate. Nevertheless, these thirty pages represent an important attempt to reconcile elements of Weberian methodology with institutionalism.[3]

Clearly, Commons did not presume that empirical enquiry alone could provide the means to categorise different types of socio-economic system. His approach to the subject was in line with that of Sombart and Weber; it thereby reflected the attempts of the younger German historicists to come to terms with Menger's criticisms of naïve empiricism in the *Methodenstreit*. Commons believed that further progress on this question would build on the Weberian theory of ideal types and the contributions of the later historical school. Commons (1934a, p. 720) acknowledged that 'Menger and Schmoller agreed not only that abstraction was necessary, but also that a great many abstractions were necessary in order to ascertain the whole truth.' However, in Commons's (1934a, p. 721) view, the debate between Menger and Gustav von Schmoller was not resolved: 'The effort . . . seemed hopeless, and the dualism went on between the deductive and historical schools, between economics and ethics, between theory and practice, between science and art.'

Commons moved on to consider subsequent contributions by Weber and Sombart, and their responses to Menger in the *Methodenstreit*. Commons (p. 722) approvingly characterised Weber's stand against Menger's isolated 'individualistic man' in the following terms:

> The criticism [of Menger] by Weber is that, in the social sciences, the parts cannot be isolated, and the ideal type should therefore include *all* of the traits and relations which afterwards are to be combined, and, since all of these can be ascertained only from history, the ideal type must be a historical concept.

Furthermore, Commons (1934a, p. 723) accepted Weber's argument that the social scientist had to take on board the subjective reasoning processes of individuals:

> The subject-matter with which the economist deals . . . is human beings whose activities he can fairly well understand by putting himself 'in their

---

3 Notably, there is no parallel to Commons's lengthy 1934 discussion of ideal types in his final theoretical statement (Commons, 1950). Perhaps this indicates that Commons was unhappy with his 1934 account.

place' and thus constructing 'reasons,' in the sense of motives or purposes, or values, of their activity under all the variable conditions of time and space. This is the fundamental reason set forth by Rickert and Weber which separates social or economic science from the physical sciences.

Hence, for Commons, the social sciences were 'subjectivist', in the limited sense that explanations of social action must in part impute reasons and beliefs to individual actors. However, Commons insisted that individual motives and activity had to be considered in the context of 'all the variable conditions of time and space'. Contrary to the Austrian school, the recognition of 'subjectivism' does not mean that explanations can rely on, or be reduced to, individuals alone. The cultural and institutional circumstances that condition and constrain the reasoning processes have also to be taken into account. Commons (p. 730) thus insisted that subjective and environmental conditions had to be considered: 'beings are both subjective *and* environmental – subjective in their emotions, motives, wishes, pains, pleasures, ideals – environmental in their transactions with others.' This is reminiscent of the organicist ontology of Whitehead. The individual is not regarded as an isolated atom, but socially constituted via relations with others.[4]

Although Commons broadly adopted the Weberian concept of the ideal type, he was not entirely satisfied with Weber's approach. In an attempt to make further scientific progress, he tried to refine some aspects of the Weberian methodology. In the following observation, Commons (1934a, p. 731) identified a key problem:

Weber, followed by Sombart and Tawney, constructs the motive of Capitalism, which he names the 'capitalist spirit.' The capitalist spirit 'creates' capitalism. This is the reverse of Karl Marx whose capitalism created the capitalist spirit.

Commons was thus unhappy with the Weberian emphasis on *Geist* or spirit. Elsewhere, Werner Sombart's prevailing notion of the 'capitalist spirit' was criticised extensively on similar grounds (Commons and Perlman, 1929). Commons pointed out that Weber and Sombart had turned Marx on his head, to give ideas and 'spirit' – instead of property relations – analytical priority. Furthermore, for Commons (1934a, pp. 732–3) the 'ideal type, as formulated by Weber and used by him and Sombart, even though it be made elastic and objective, is not yet transactional'. This, for Commons, seemed to be a crucial defect. Among the stated implications of this defect was a 'failure to start economic theory upon the *economic bond* which ties individuals together, such as transactions, debts, property rights'. This is an important point that will be endorsed later in this book. In addition, for Commons, the analysis of this

---

4   See Winslow (1989) for a discussion of the implications of an organicist ontology in economics.

economic bond required an adequate concept of time, as transactional activity is based on expectations of the future as well as the repetition of the past. Allegedly, Weber and Sombart had 'a mistaken concept of custom as something that comes from the past instead of something that looks to the future'. Here, however, Commons was bending the stick too far. It is not a mistake to understand custom as coming from the past. Furthermore, custom does not literally 'look' to the future – as Commons put it – but it helps to create it, almost blindly, out of the momentum of institutions and acquired habits. Custom is a means by which the past is projected into the future.

Commons moved on to make another important methodological point and to clarify his conception of the ideal type. Significantly, for Commons (1934a, p. 734):

> The ideal type is not a theory – it is a formulation of the problem of relationship between the factors, which problem the theory attempts to solve. Yet it requires a preceding theory in order to formulate it. . . . [T]heory becomes, not only a mental process for investigation of facts, but becomes also an interpretation, correlation, and expectation of facts.

This passage constituted a post-*Methodenstreit* recognition of the priority of theory over data. But Commons then confused Weber's ideal type with a hypothesis. For Commons, the hypothesis should be tested somehow. If it did not 'exactly fit' then it should be changed 'to get a better fit'. He continued:

> Then this fit is another stage of a modified ideal type, and so on. Then, further, if we take into account the variability of the factors themselves and endeavor to construct a formula of a *process*, rather than a structure, we have another ideal type, this time of a moving, changing whole, which we must again repeatedly revise to fit the changes which research brings to light.
>
> (ibid.)

A problem here is that Commons gave us no guidance on how we judge whether a theory 'fits' or not. Among philosophers of science, there is no obvious or agreed way in which we can judge whether one theory or ideal type is closer or more fitting to reality than another. Commons presents us with the intriguing idea that the ideal type itself becomes a '*process*, rather than a structure' but does not elaborate on the process by which the ideal type is refined. Commons also neglected Weber's important argument that a combination of ideal types that do not exactly 'fit' reality may be more advantageous, to serve as limiting co-ordinates to deal with a muddled and confused reality. These are among the critical questions, and Commons gave little guidance on them. He lapsed into a vaguely elaborated methodological procedure of successive empirical approximation.

However, in another respect, his argument was much stronger. Commons (1934a, p. 740) went on to acknowledge that the establishment of the ideal type rests on a 'search for uniformity upon the transactions of many going concerns, instead of individualistic emotions'. Crucially, he continued:

> One of these uniformities is Custom. Although individual emotions, or subjective valuations, or the subjective will, may differ so capriciously that no scientific uniformity can be predicated upon them, yet we do find uniformities of action when we look to transactions, instead of emotions.

Commons then went on to insist that the concept of custom must embody 'the principle of expectation which we name Futurity'. On the one hand, for Commons (p. 740): 'Habit is a repetition of acts'.[5] On the other hand, Commons (pp. 740–1) saw custom as involving capacities concerning the future: 'the binding . . . force of custom is the similarity of expectations of gain or loss imagined in the future.' In this latter case he rightly probed beneath the repetition of events, and considered the causes and structured incentives that impel activity. Hence Commons (p. 741) concluded:

> Therefore, the capricious and lawless subjective value or will of Weber, which is incapable of the uniformities required by science, is displaced by those similarities of valuation and willingness which are the subject-matter of both jurisprudence and economics. But no science requires absolute uniformities in order to be a science. . . . The variabilities may be said to be the, as yet, unsolved cases of functional interdependence of factors.

Commons thus objected to the Weberian starting point of the unpredictable individual will. He argued that behaviour becomes more predictable when constrained and moulded by custom. Hence he further attempted to replace Weber's *Geist* by the institutionalised capacities of social custom. This was a significant and important advance. It involved a partial incorporation of some of the insights of pragmatism into the theory of ideal types.

At the same time, Commons's discussion was too imprecise and incomplete to be satisfactory. The assertion of the primacy of custom was not enough. It was inadequately grounded in the psychology of habituation, as evidenced by Commons's presentation of the concept of habit as repeated behaviour rather than an acquired propensity. Commons laudably stressed the 'economic bond' of transactions that tied individuals together, involving particular social relations such as 'debts' and 'property rights'. But the explanation of the nature of these bonds was inadequate. Commons insisted that custom did not merely come from the past but looked to the future, by creating expectations. But it was not made

---

5   We have noted already that the concept of habit did not play a prominent role in Commons's writing until the 1930s. Observe also that Commons's conception of habit here is one of repeated behaviour. Likewise, Commons (1934a, p. 155) wrote: 'Habit is repetition by one person.' In contrast, Peirce, James and Dewey regarded habit as a propensity to act, rather than manifest behaviour itself. Commons never fully assimilated this pragmatist view. For a further discussion of habit, see chapter 19 below.

clear whether such expectations are tacit or overt, or whether they are formed by rational deliberation or by habitation, or by both. The main problem with Commons's reconstruction of the theory of ideal types was that it was inadequate. Commons replaced *Geist* by habit and custom, but failed to give them a sufficient psychological and explanatory grounding.

Part of the reason for Commons's failure was the difficulty of holding to the pragmatist psychology while it was no longer fashionable. The rapid rise of positivism and behaviourism in the 1920s and 1930s made it exceedingly difficult to develop the theory of ideal types, beyond the point that Weber had brought it, upon pragmatist foundations.

COMMONS AND HISTORICAL PERIODISATION

A final aspect of Commons's theory of ideal types is his own system of historical periodisation. In his *Institutional Economics*, Commons (1934a, pp. 773–88) outlined three 'economic stages' namely

> a period of Scarcity preceding the 'industrial revolution,' the latter beginning in the Eighteenth Century . . . a period of Abundance with its alternations of oversupply and undersupply for a hundred years or more . . . and a period of Stabilization, beginning with the concerted movements of capitalists and laborers in the Nineteenth Century.

Clearly, the basic criteria of demarcation here relate to the relationship between available quantities of goods or services and some unspecified norms of aggregate wants or needs. For Commons, different mechanisms of 'legal control and transfer' arose in each of these three historical periods. Allegedly, in the period of Scarcity 'the community usually resorts to rationing both the input and the output of man-power'. By contrast, in the period of Abundance, 'there is the maximum of individual liberty, the minimum of control through government'. Finally, in the period of Stabilization 'there are new restraints on individual liberty, enforced mainly by government' (p. 774).

Commons then attempted to explain how the three periods each in turn gave rise to differences in the legal system and in the extent of liberty. But at each stage the theoretical account of the mechanisms involved is unclear. What do 'scarcity', 'oversupply' and 'undersupply' mean? From his discussion of the concept of scarcity elsewhere in the book, it is evident that, for Commons (1934a, p. 86), 'the unit of scarcity measurement' is in terms of 'money' and 'price'. Hence Commons seemed to refer to scarcity relative to aggregate demand, rather than relative to human need. In another related work, Commons and Selig Perlman (1929, p. 81) referred to the criterion of 'abundance or scarcity of opportunities for getting profits'. However, profits, prices, money and markets were not fully established in the feudal historical epoch, which Commons included as part of the period of so-called 'Scarcity'. Furthermore, at least on the basis of the relationship between some concept of aggregate demand and aggregate supply, the historical periodisation becomes highly questionable. The so-called 'Scarcity' period before the industrial revolution was marked by lower market demand as well as by lower market supply. Standards of living were lower, but prices also were lower in money terms. In addition, market shortages as well as gluts marked the so-called 'period of Abundance' in the nineteenth century. There was a secular rise in market demand as well as in market supply: overall there was no secular trend for one to outpace the other. Similar remarks apply to the so-called period of 'Stabilization' in the twentieth century. Ironically, Commons published these words when the world economy was going through the most destabilising experience of the Great Depression. If Commons's periodisation of history refers to market conditions then it makes little sense. Alternatively, if 'scarcity' and so on are interpreted as being relative to human need then the periodisation still does not stand up to careful examination. After all, in terms of meeting their needs, the Industrial Revolution could hardly be described as a period of 'Abundance' for most people enduring it. Whether defined in terms of human needs or market conditions, Commons's periodisation of history does not endure critical scrutiny.

Furthermore, and most crucially, Commons failed to give an adequate explanation of how each historical period gave rise to specific legal forms and different degrees of liberty. He stated that in the period of Scarcity 'the community usually resorts to rationing' but this assumed the prior existence of unexplained institutions in which 'the community' somehow formed and enforced its will upon the processes of production and distribution. Not only was the prior existence of such institutions unexplained, no adequate reason was given why they should be eroded during the subsequent period of so-called 'Abundance'. Commons (1934a, p. 775) saw markets as being set up by 'powerful lords' as a result of 'the weakness of government and the violence and perjury of the people'. But it is not clear why these 'powerful lords' could not have continued with some system of direct rationing that was presumed to exist beforehand. Questions such as this arise at every point of Commons's weak and unconvincing discussion. Commons's explanation of how each historical period gave rise to specific legal forms and different degrees of liberty is a complete failure.[6]

Furthermore, it is somewhat ironic that, for all of Commons's (1924, 1934a) emphasis on the role of 'legal foundations' and the role of specific legal institutions, he should have attempted to place these somehow upon a supposedly deeper foundation of scarcity and price. He ended up with a schema of historical stages that was much inferior to that that his teacher Richard Ely (1903) had taken and developed from the historical school.

Overall, to his credit, Commons raised the problem of historical specificity and indicated an important line of possible theoretical advance, particularly by emphasising the concepts of habit and custom. But his discussion was not

---

6   Given this negative judgement, it is somewhat surprising that Keynes (1931, pp. 333–4) endorsed Commons's system of historical periodisation. See chapter 15 below.

sufficiently clear or persuasive. His *Institutional Economics* was an attempt to provide American institutionalism with a systematic theoretical foundation. His subsequent *Economics of Collective Action* was partly a distillation of his *Institutional Economics* and was published posthumously in 1950. Ultimately, however, these works did not provide institutionalism with the theoretical defences required to resist existing and future attacks.

AMERICAN INSTITUTIONALISM IN DECLINE

The reasons why American institutional economics declined after the 1930s are varied and complex.[7] Without going into details, some key issues can be mentioned. First, although institutionalism was highly influential in the interwar period, by the mid-1920s its philosophical and psychological foundations were under assault. As noted above, pragmatist philosophy and instinct psychology were being replaced by versions of positivism and behaviourism. Second, these external circumstances combined with an internal loss of theoretical confidence within institutionalism, leading to a failure to deliver an alternative, systematic theory. Third, by the late 1930s, institutionalism was overshadowed by Keynesianism, which seemed to offer hopeful solutions to the pressing problems of depression and unemployment. Fourth, there was a rising fashion within economics for mathematical modelling and econometrics, in part stimulated by the technocratic culture of rising American capitalism. This gradually displaced the more discursive and historically grounded discourses of many of the institutionalists.

Notably, the problem of historical specificity was eventually neglected by American institutionalism. Commons died in 1945 and Mitchell in 1948. The baton of institutionalist leadership eventually passed to the charismatic Clarence Ayres. He paid no attention to the problem. Instead, he developed a general theory of economic development based on the allegedly universal conflict between (ceremonial) institutions and (progressive) technology (Ayres, 1944). Clearly, this theory of economic change was quite general in its scope. As new generations of American institutionalists came under Ayres's influence, the problem of historical specificity was lost to this dwindling tradition.

However, there is often an exception to prove the rule. Morris Copeland was a rare case of an American institutionalist who continued to embrace Veblenian biological analogies long after they had become highly unfashionable among institutionalists themselves. He also continued to recognise the problem of historical specificity. Copeland (1958, p. 60) wrote:

---

7 See Hodgson (1999b, ch. 5) and Yonay (1998) for analyses of the decline of American institutionalism. In addition, Rutherford (1999, 2000) has emphasised its perceived 'scientific' status in the interwar period and how internal dissension and external developments subsequently challenged this.

Perhaps the most important and far-reaching implication of the view that economics should be approached as an evolutionary science is the implication of the historical relativity of economic truths, the implication that the only economic propositions that can be said to be scientifically valid are historical truths. Every economic generalization that has scientific validity must be limited in its applicability to a specific historical period or to specific historical periods and to a specific culture or to specific cultures; i.e., it must refer to a particular society or societies.

But these words fell largely on deaf ears. American institutionalism was by then enamoured by the Ayresian gospel of technology: the belief that technology offered the progressive driving force of both economic and political change. This fitted well with the postwar technophilia of booming American capitalism.

PAX AMERICANA AND THE END OF AMERICAN EXCEPTIONALISM

On the whole, the twentieth century saw a dramatic change in the image and perception of American capitalism. Originally regarded as an exceptional case, America was transformed into an economic role model for the whole world. At first, by 1945, there was an increasing global faith that, among different varieties of capitalism, the American version was the most viable and efficient. It eventually was enhanced by the further belief that no alternative to capitalism was possible. America became the perceived model for the entire world, despite abundant evidence of capitalist variety and innovative dynamism in parts of Europe and East Asia.

This ideological transformation has had profound consequences for the trend of thinking among economists. In the 1920s, American capitalism had industrialised rapidly, and brought with it new forms of work and corporate organisation, from mass production to the multidivisional firm. Its enduring democratic institutions and high social mobility contrasted with the more aristocratic or oligarchic systems of Europe and East Asia. These economic and political institutions contrasted with those in Europe and elsewhere. Hence America was often regarded as an exceptional case. Furthermore, with its isolationist foreign policy, the United States was less inclined to promote itself as a global model.

When victory came in the Second World War – in the year that Commons died – America acquired a new world role. It was no longer protectionist and isolationist; it became the protector of world capitalism and free markets. The American politico-economic system triumphed on a global scale. This reinforced the questionable view that America was the purist and most developed exemplar of capitalism for the world.

With the outbreak of the Cold War in 1948 – the year Mitchell died – the Soviet Bloc challenged this American hegemony. The ensuing rivalry between the two superpowers further reinforced the notion that America represented capitalism in its purist and most viable form. Typically, the differences between East and West were represented in the economics textbooks as differences between a 'command' and a 'free market' economy, with the United States supposedly near to the 'free market' end of the spectrum. In this bipolar contest, the variations in historical and geographical development between different capitalist countries were overshadowed.

In this context, the problem of historical specificity was lost from view. Western economics became the study of the universal laws of the free market economy. Variations in socio-economic structures, institutions and cultures were regarded as being of lesser importance.

Furthermore, after 1945, English became the dominant world academic language and knowledge of German diminished as an academic requirement. These changing patterns of language use paralleled and reinforced the shifts in the balance of international power. The German contribution to the history of economic thought was gradually forgotten. Two defeats in world wars meant the loss of ideas and traditions, as well as many lives. The right to write history went to the victors. The history of the subject became largely Anglophone. The classical economists, plus Marx, Mill and Marshall, marked the long era of British imperialism up to 1919. Keynes largely filled the interwar gap, and attention after 1945 mostly focused on intellectual developments in America. In this biased bicentennial story, the massive literature in German was entirely neglected, and American institutionalism became regarded as a misguided and embarrassing diversion in the grand ascent of twentieth-century neoclassical theory.

After Marshall, most British economists forgot the problem of historical specificity. After the interwar institutionalists, it was also abandoned in America. After the destruction of the Second World War, it was largely forgotten in Germany. It was also abandoned in postwar sociology. Talcott Parsons was the main author of this transformation. He is the subject of the next chapter. Ironically, Ayres himself, as we shall see, also played a crucial role in the development of Parsons's ideas.

Many economists were dazzled by American economic success in the postwar period. As the American economic model became the envy of the world, discussion of alternatives was undermined. The final phases in the development of the view that American capitalism was the most viable and efficient economic model came in the 1980s and 1990s. Rapid economic growth in East Asia in the 1980s led to a temporary challenge to this view. However, the economic slowdown in Japan in the 1990s and the East Asian financial crisis of 1997, battered the image of an alternative, Asian model of capitalism. Furthermore, the collapse of the Soviet Union in 1991 further reinforced global confidence in the American way. By the end of the millennium, China seemed to be the last refuge from global Americanisation. But China's own markets were also opening up rapidly. The second millennium ended with the ideological supremacy of the American model.

Perhaps a general theory about the adoption of general theories in economics is possible. Two propositions emerge. First, challenges to general theorising are likely to arise in rapidly developing countries establishing their own identities against another global power. For instance, nineteenth-century Germany challenged the British policy of free trade within its empire, and gave rise to the historical school. In the early twentieth century, with lingering British imperial hegemony, the United States began to construct its own distinctive version of industrial capitalism, giving rise to American institutionalism. It is no accident that the problem of historical specificity was given more attention in these two sets of circumstances, where each nation was struggling to form and enhance its own identity and institutions.

The second proposition addresses the type of historical period in which general theorising in economics is more likely to flourish. A global economic hegemon is likely to promote the view that its leading economic theories and policies represent general solutions for the world as a whole. This happened in Britain in the nineteenth century, with its classical and neoclassical economists. Similarly general solutions have been promoted by the United States since 1945, with the development of its formal, technocratic style of mainstream economics. The confidence in general theories and solutions is encouraged by the existence of an assured and dominant politico-economic power.

No doubt, this general theory of general theories is an oversimplification. But there are probably nuggets of truth in the argument. If so, exceptions to the rule become even more striking. The abandonment of general equilibrium theory by avant-garde theorists in the 1980s becomes even more significant. Perhaps also the iron law of general theorising will be relaxed in the twenty-first century to allow a renewed discussion of the problem of historical specificity. That is a matter for speculation. The historical narrative in the present work is not yet complete. We return in the next chapter to a key episode in the past ascent of general theorising in the social sciences.

13

TALCOTT PARSONS AND THE ASCENT OF AHISTORICAL SOCIOLOGY

'Tis a common proof,
That lowliness is young ambition's ladder,
Whereto the climber-upward turns his face;
But when he once attains the upmost round,
He then unto the ladder turns his back,
Looks in the clouds, scorning the base degrees
By which he did ascend.
(William Shakespeare, *Julius Caesar*)

Talcott Parsons is regarded as one of the greatest sociologists of the twentieth century. He was largely responsible for bringing Max Weber to the attention of Anglophone scholars. He also elaborated a distinctive and highly influential school of functionalist sociology. However, one of its features was its neglect of the problem of historical specificity, despite the direct influence upon Parsons of Weber and Werner Sombart. In this manner, a few elements of the German historical school tradition were transferred to the American context. But they were dispossessed of much of their content and meaning. Ironically, Parsons achieved distinction by his creation of an ahistorical school of sociology, partly by rummaging selected material from a historically-oriented intellectual tradition.

Furthermore, as well as the German historical school, another major but largely unacknowledged influence upon Parsons was American institutional economics. However, despite these major injections of historicism and institutionalism, Parsons created a distinctively ahistorical system of sociology. This chapter examines this remarkable and fateful transformation of a social science. We examine Parsons's engagement with key thinkers such as Walton Hamilton, Clarence Ayres, Leonard Hobhouse, Harold Laski, Richard Tawney, Bronislaw Malinowsky, Frank Knight, Alfred Whitehead, Joseph Schumpeter, Lionel Robbins and Ralph Souter.

THE ROLES OF WALTON HAMILTON AND
CLARENCE AYRES

From 1920 to 1924, Parsons was an undergraduate student at Amherst College in Massachusetts. Hamilton, who was a member of its faculty from 1915 to 1923, taught him institutional economics. As noted in chapter 11 above, Hamilton played a decisive role in establishing American institutionalism as a movement at the end of the First World War. Hamilton had a strong grasp of the theoretical essentials of the institutionalist movement and was concerned to promote institutionalism as a viable tool for economic policy making.

Another great influence on Parsons at Amherst was Ayres. Ayres had been appointed as a lecturer at Amherst in 1920. According to Parsons's own account, it was the example of Ayres and Hamilton, alongside the influence of his father, which helped to persuade Parsons to change his studies from biology to social science (Parsons, 1970, p. 877, 1976, p. 176; Camic, 1991, p. xv). Ayres and Hamilton impressed upon the young Parsons that institutions and culture, rather than biology alone, moulded human personality.

Given Ayres's formative role on Parsons's thought, it is necessary to sketch a portrait of the teacher in its intellectual surroundings. A forthright and independent thinker, Ayres was educated in philosophy and deeply interested in economics. His PhD dissertation at the University of Chicago had been on the relationship between ethics and economics (Ayres, 1918). As well as being Hamilton's colleague, Ayres was an enduring friend and correspondent of Knight (Buchanan, 1976; DeGregori, 1977; Samuels, 1977). Ayres did not then identify himself as an institutional economist, but he strongly believed that individuals were conditioned by social, cultural and institutional circumstances. On key questions he held a distinctive position. To understand this, we must briefly examine the intellectual context at the time.

As already noted above, in the early decades of the twentieth century, American social science was going through a massive transformation (Degler, 1991; Ross, 1991; Hodgson, 1999b). Before 1914, many sociologists and economists believed that biological instincts largely or wholly explained human behaviour. Around the beginning of the twentieth century, the leading American anthropologist Franz Boas challenged this biological-reductionist view. Boas did not deny the influence of biology on both physical and mental characteristics. But he saw social culture as far more important. However, Alfred Kroeber, a prolific student of Boas, went further. In a number of articles published in the *American Anthropologist* between 1910 and 1917 he declared that it was culture rather than heredity that determined human nature and behaviour.

Parallel developments occurred in psychology. The instinct psychology of William James and William McDougall, which was so influential in the 1890–1914 period, was subsequently displaced by the behaviourist psychology of John B. Watson, Jacob Robert Kantor and others. Although some behaviourists originally retained a role for instincts, the behaviourist stress on observable behaviour meant that, by the 1920s, many leading psychologists rejected the idea of instincts in human beings. Just thirty years after the heyday of James, the concept of instinct had virtually disappeared from American psychology.

Thorstein Veblen had accepted a role for instinct but stressed also the role of institutions and culture. His position was thus much closer to Boas than Kroeber. In the early interwar period, institutionalists such as Hamilton (1919, p. 318) followed Veblen and endorsed 'the part that instinct and impulse play in impelling . . . economic activity'. At the same time they all accepted that institutions and culture played a huge part in moulding human purposes and dispositions.

Ayres, in contrast, took a position that was close to Kroeber and those behaviourist psychologists who downplayed the role of instincts. Kantor (1922, 1924) in particular emphasised the malleability of human nature and the role of culture and institutions in forming the human psyche. Taking these anthropological and psychological developments to their extreme, Ayres eschewed instincts, to emphasise institutions, culture and the pliability of human nature. Ayres (1921a, pp. 561–5) wrote: 'When instincts fall out, institutions get their due. . . . Yet . . . the social behavior of the civilized adult is a matter of institutions and traditions . . . The social scientist has no need of instincts; he has institutions.'

Like many others in the 1920s, Ayres embraced the rising behaviourist psychology. Furthermore, he became an early enthusiast of a version of behaviourism that had no place for instinct. Ayres (1921b) thus rejected instinct psychology. He saw the individual as largely a social product. Although John Dewey remained an important influence, Ayres's agenda was very different from that of the pragmatists as a whole. Key pragmatist concepts such as habit were not prominent in Ayres's approach. In contrast, leading institutionalists such as Hamilton (1919) stressed a role for both habit and instinct in the explanation of behaviour. Most importantly, throughout his life, Veblen maintained an explanatory role for instincts as well as habits in his theory.[1]

Under intellectual pressure at the time, other leading institutionalists shifted their position. After first endorsing instinct psychology, when it was subjected to intense criticism they began to have doubts. Hence, in his early writings, John Commons (1897, 1965) saw instinct as having a place. However, in the 1930s Commons (1934a, p. 637) seemed to side tentatively with the critics of instinct psychology. Similarly, Wesley Mitchell (1910) had earlier seen instinct as central to the explanation of human behaviour. In the 1920s he began to doubt this, writing later that 'the instinct-habit psychology will yield to some other conception of human nature' (Mitchell, 1937, p. 312).

In the 1920s, Ayres was moving with the thinkers at the cutting edge of American social science. He combined his theoretical iconoclasm with his radical liberal politics. Likewise, the young Parsons held radical and social democratic political views (Brick, 1993). Such opinions were not uncommon in American academia at the time. Liberal academics emphasised the universal potential of human achievement, seeing individuals as largely formed by culture and

---

1 Much later, when Ayres (1958) claimed that his own ideas were a development of those of Veblen, he dismissed Veblen's instinct theory as of little ultimate significance. Although Ayres was right to point out that Veblen failed to define instinct adequately, nevertheless, contrary to Ayres, instinct psychology remained foundational to Veblen's position. See especially Veblen (1914).

unconstrained by biological inheritance. For this reason, the idea of biological determinants of human behaviour was opposed. Notions of instinct or biological determination interfered with the dogma that human nature was highly malleable, and that all individuals had a similar potential to achieve and to prosper.

The force behind this intellectual movement in academia had more to do with ideology than with science. Carl Degler (1991, p. viii) and others have argued persuasively that these developments were largely inspired much more by a politics than scientific evidence: 'The main impetus came from the wish to establish a social order in which innate and immutable forces of biology played no role in accounting for the behavior of social groups.' In the contexts of prevalent racism and interwar fascism, such reactions among liberal academics were understandable. The idea that there were any biological foundations to human behaviour was abandoned in the more liberal and leftist intellectual circles of American academia.

Most institutional economists were in accord with these ideological developments. However, their consequence was that the original foundations of institutionalism, in Darwinism and instinct psychology, were removed. This subsidence in its philosophical and psychological foundations weakened institutionalism at a crucial stage of its theoretical development. Institutionalism was profoundly affected by the concomitant separation of biology and social science. Accordingly, the Veblenian research programme of building a 'post-Darwinian' and 'evolutionary' economics was compromised. Although institutionalism continued to represent many popular themes, it lost its original theoretical mission. For instance, while the increasing emphasis on the role of culture was an asset for institutionalism, the intellectual context in which the shift to culture took place made the further development of a distinctive and systematic institutionalist theory much more difficult. Institutionalism lost its methodological cutting edge.

Ayres was moving with the times, and ahead of many of his institutionalist colleagues. Although Ayres became the leader of American institutionalism after 1945, in the 1920s and 1930s his position was relatively marginalised among institutionalists. Yet even in the early 1920s his radical account of institutional influence proved attractive to some – at least for young iconoclasts such as Parsons.

CONVERSION AT AMHERST

Ayres taught Parsons in a philosophy class at Amherst on 'The Moral Order' – with strong ethical and sociological themes. As Parsons (1959, p. 4) himself recollected:

> We read Sumner's *Folkways* . . . and a whole lot of things like Charles Horton Cooley and Emile Durkheim. We also read a lot of Thorstein Veblen, for Veblen was an important mutual hero of both Hamilton and Ayres. So institutional economics was really my jumping off place.

Parsons (1976, p. 178) later explained that it was Ayres who had introduced him not only to the work of Veblen but also to that of Emile Durkheim. The Durkheimian influence proved to be the more lasting of the two. While both authors stressed that the individual was always conditioned by social circumstances, Veblen had attempted to link the social and the natural sciences under a Darwinian scheme, and had made use of material from psychology. In contrast, Durkheim had stressed the differences between the social and the natural sciences, and insisted that psychology should be separated from the social sciences. At the time, in debates with his fellow students, Parsons used Veblenian language to criticise the 'leisure class motives' of those in America who were opposed to social reform (Brick, 1993, p. 368). In one of his surviving student essays he also embraced Veblenian concepts such as 'cumulative change' and 'habits of thought' (Wearne, 1989, pp. 28–9).

However, in his surviving student essays, Parsons confused a Veblenian emphasis on habits with the behaviourist psychology of conditioned reflex (Wearne, 1989, pp. 28–36). Given that Ayres admired both Veblen and behaviourism, it is likely that this mistaken conflation of two quite different doctrines was also the error of his teacher. Later, Parsons was to reject both behaviourism and the Veblenian emphasis on habit. Hence, without much justification, Parsons (1935, p. 441) dismissed '"instinct" psychology' as 'a twin brother of behaviorism'. It is true that early behaviourist psychologists such as John Watson had admitted notions of both habit and instinct into their theory. However, there was an important shift of meaning. While Watson (1919, p. 273) had defined habit as a 'complex system of reflexes', Veblen and pragmatists (such as James and Dewey) saw habit as something that may exist even if it is not manifest in behaviour. As well as habits of behaviour there are habits of thought. Unlike the behaviourists, the pragmatists saw consciousness as part of the process. Dewey (1922, p. 25), for example, saw habits as 'means, waiting, like tools in a box, to be used by conscious resolve'. Parsons ignored these subtle distinctions.

Parsons ratified the emphasis that American institutionalists had always given to the influence of institutions and culture on human agency and behaviour. From his reading of the works of institutionalists and others, and under the special guidance of Ayres, Parsons concluded that it was culture rather than nature that was the decisive and overwhelming factor in explaining human behaviour. He thus emphasised institutions and culture even more than the average institutionalist. Parsons followed Ayres down the more radical road, initially placing himself as a sympathetic critic of institutionalism. But eventually, for reasons we shall explore in detail below, the sympathy was to wane, and to turn into hostility. Nevertheless, Parsons still emphasised the idea that culture and institutions somehow moulded behaviour.

Ironically, Ayres turned Parsons not simply into a follower of the new doctrine – that culture and institutions alone could explain human behaviour – but also into a critic of the then majority of American institutionalists. Although institutionalism itself was eventually to transform itself and move towards Ayres's position, Parsons's critical stance towards institutionalism was to remain.

In 1923 a doctrinal conflict at Amherst College led to the sacking of its liberal and progressive President. A substantial number of faculty members, including Hamilton and Ayres, resigned *en masse* in sympathy. So ended not only a prominent enclave of institutionalist thought but also one of the most seminal relationships between a student and his teachers in the history of social science.

TALCOTT PARSONS IN EUROPE

From 1924 to 1925, Parsons was at the London School of Economics (LSE). His Amherst teachers had provided him with introductions to LSE socialist thinkers such as Harold Laski and Richard H. Tawney. At the LSE he also came under the influence of the anthropologist Bronislaw Malinowsky who introduced Parsons to functionalist modes of theory. In addition, as Parsons (1959, p. 4) related, at the LSE he 'got a great deal from' Leonard T. Hobhouse. Britain's first professor of sociology, Hobhouse wrote on social evolution but was critical of Spencerism. Influenced both by the German historical school and by the new philosophical ideas on emergence, he developed an 'organic' systems view. One of Hobhouse's theoretical projects was the identification of the social institutions that were necessary to promote freedom and social order.[2] Ever since his class under Ayres at Amherst, the problem of social order was central for Parsons too. At the LSE he found both confirmation and development of some of the ideas to which he had been earlier exposed. Parsons (1976, p. 177) later reflected that: 'Of the intellectual influences to which I had been exposed since leaving Amherst, those at the London School of Economics were the closest to the Hamilton–Ayres point of view.'

Ironically, Parsons was to play a role in the 1930s that would help to change the nature of sociological thought in all Anglophone universities. This would parallel a similar and complementary change in economics, led in particular by Lionel Robbins from the LSE. The combined result of these developments would be to obliterate any traces of institutionalism or historicism at the LSE and elsewhere.

In 1925 Parsons moved to Heidelberg University, from where he obtained a doctorate in economics in 1927. His visit to Germany put him in contact with the historical school: one of his teachers was Edgar Salin. Another was Heinrich Rickert. His doctoral dissertation was on the theories of capitalism in the writings of Werner Sombart and Max Weber, with additional references to Karl Marx. Material from his dissertation was reworked and published in two articles in the *Journal of Political Economy* (Parsons, 1928, 1929). These two essays give clear evidence of the influence of the historical school. In them, Parsons (1928, pp. 652–3) criticised 'Anglo-American economic thought' for failing to recognise the historical specificity of the capitalist system.

---

2 Hobhouse was also a major influence on Hobson, who wrote a biography on his mentor with Ginsberg, Hobhouse's successor at the LSE (Hobson and Ginsberg, 1932). Incidentally, Ginsberg (1932) went against the sociological trend of the time by attempting to retain some links between psychology, biology and sociology. He also maintained a notion of instinct in his analysis.

THE MOVE TO HARVARD

In 1927 Parsons was appointed an instructor in economics at Harvard University. Joseph Schumpeter was a visiting professor in 1927–8. Parsons took Schumpeter's economics classes and discussed a number of issues with him (Brick, 1993). In particular, Schumpeter encouraged Parsons to study the work of Vilfredo Pareto. Importantly for Parsons's line of research, Pareto had attempted a general theory in both economics and sociology, and tried to establish a boundary between the two disciplines. Pareto's work was to have a permanent influence on both authors.

The economics department at Harvard was predominantly neoclassical. There was a growing enthusiasm for mathematical formalisation and general equilibrium theory. With the prominent exception of Sumner Slichter, the department was opposed to institutionalism. Regarded more as a populariser than a theorist, this institutionalist was safely sidelined into the subdiscipline of labour economics. The leading theorists in the department, including the influential Frank Taussig – editor of the *Quarterly Journal of Economics* until 1936 – were then hostile to institutionalism.[3]

Initially placed within this department, the young Parsons would have been in difficulty, had he made any expression of sympathy for institutional economics. Already a critic of institutionalism, Parsons went further. The circumstances prompted him to break entirely his dwindling links with the school. The Harvard environment encouraged Parsons to become more critical and dismissive of both institutionalism and the historical school in the years from 1927 to 1935. The change in attitude is remarkable. In the late 1920s, Parsons (1928, 1929) was still sympathetic to German historicism, but he criticised it a few years later (Parsons, 1935). Eventually, Parsons was to write of institutionalism in critical and dismissive tones. References to his own institutionalist past were omitted or downplayed, despite them having been highly significant in his own intellectual development (Camic, 1992).

However, Parsons was not inclined to follow a career as a neoclassical economist. He was not a mathematician and he remained uneasy with neoclassical ways of thinking. Having specialised in the works of both Sombart and Weber, Parsons took a number of strategic career decisions. The first concerned the possible use of the intellectual assets he had acquired in Europe, particularly his doctoral study of both Sombart and Weber.

Would he promote one of these names, or both? Sombart's name was known among intellectuals in the West and his works were in need of translation. Parsons (1929, p. 34) himself had admitted that: 'Unlike Sombart, Weber never developed a unified theory of capitalism.' For this reason, Parsons could have chosen the role of translator and interpreter of Sombart, rather than of Weber.

But Parsons chose Weber, and did not acknowledge Sombart a great deal in his future writings. Reflecting on this choice, much later in his life, Parsons (1976,

---

3   For a history of the department before the Second World War, see Mason and Lamont (1982).

p. 178) said that he chose Weber because he was allegedly 'by far the most important', compared with Sombart and Marx. Leaving this questionable judgement of intellectual calibre on one side, Parsons's earlier works provide clues to further reasons behind his choice of Weber. In a typically brief and foggy discussion of this issue, Parsons (1937a, p. 499) remarked that Sombart's theory, centred as it is on the concept of *Geist*, 'altogether eliminates the utilitarian factors. Hence Sombart's perfectly logical and definite repudiation of orthodox economic theory.' There's the rub: Sombart repudiated orthodox economics but Weber – in Parsons's interpretation – apparently did not. We are left with the distinct impression, even in Parsons's own account, that he chose Weber over Sombart because Weber could be rendered less abrasive for orthodox economists, thus making Parsons's academic life easier. Weber's social theory, with its individualistic elements, did not threaten orthodox economics as much as that of Sombart.[4]

Alongside Pareto and Durkheim, the prospect existed of using Weber's name as a posthumous 'founder' of Western sociology. In the years 1928–30, Parsons translated Weber's *Protestant Ethic and the Spirit of Capitalism* into English. He also helped to produce an edited version of Weber's *Economy and Society* in 1947. But Parsons downgraded Weber's membership of the German historical school and his engagement with the problem of historical specificity. He exaggerated some aspects of Weber's work, to downgrade Weber's strictures on the limits of general theorising. As David Zaret (1980, p. 1193) rightly argues: 'Parsons's interpretation of Weber is idiosyncratic and unduly stresses normative aspects of meaning.' Parsons attempted a general sociological theory in Paretian spirit, while observing Durkheim's conceptual divide between society and nature.

Although he often toyed with the word 'evolution', Parsons wanted biology to play no explanatory role in the social sphere. He also distanced himself from psychology in all its existing forms. In this respect he followed and exaggerated the hints of Durkheim, Weber and Sombart. All three had been major figures in his intellectual development. Parsons paid lip service to the viability of psychology as a science, but its particular claims to enter the terrain of explanation of human action were opposed. His efforts in these directions were so successful that most modern sociologists take such impervious disciplinary separations for granted.

Parsons had two major intellectual assets. The first was the emphasis he had acquired from Ayres and Hamilton on the over-arching role of culture and institutions. The second was his recognition and possession of the highly marketable intellectual legacy of Weber. Unwilling or unable to follow either the institutional or neoclassical roads within economics, Parsons had to carve

---

4 The choice between Weber, Sombart and Marx must also be placed in the dramatic and global political context of the 1930s. Clearly, of the three, Weber was the closest to an American-style liberal. However, to make him one, his German nationalism and pessimistic views on progress would have to be overlooked (Hennis, 1988; Mommsen, 1984). Nevertheless, Zaret (1980, p. 1193) argued convincingly that Parsons's ideological reaction against Marxism was significant and that 'Parsons saw in Weber's writings a non-Marxian foundation for general theory.'

out a new territory for sociology. His break from economics was his second strategic decision. As Hans Joas (1995, p. 275) put it: 'by dint of the approach he was taking, Parsons realized that he was being forced out of the prestigious discipline he had started his career in.' In 1931 Parsons transferred to a new department at Harvard, in which sociology found its home. 'Sociology offered Parsons a way out of this personal and theoretical crisis as well as a solution to the problem of the definition of the proper field of economics' (ibid.).

In 1932, Paul T. Homan of Cornell University wrote to Parsons, expressing his view that institutional economics was at a dead end (Homan, 1932). Homan urged Parsons to make the work of both Weber and Durkheim known to American social scientists (Wearne, 1989, p. 60). Both Weber and Durkheim were to be major figures in Parsons's *Structure of Social Action*.

Parsons became deeply engaged with the problem of demarcation between economics and sociology. To accommodate culture and institutions while rejecting the role of biology or instinct, sociology itself had to be transformed. Furthermore, it had to reach a new *modus vivendi* with the rising new wave of neoclassical economics and preserve its own intellectual territory. As Parsons (1970, p. 827) himself remarked: 'It gradually became clear to me that economic theory should be conceived as standing within some sort of theoretical matrix in which sociological theory also was included.'

At Harvard, Lawrence Henderson set up the famous 'Pareto Circle' in 1932, of which Parsons and George Homans were members. Henderson (1935) admired Pareto and regarded him as the modern Galileo of the social sciences. This Circle read and discussed Pareto's works in sociology and economics. Historians of ideas such as Barbara Heyl (1968) and Geoffrey Hawthorn (1976) regarded the Pareto Circle as crucially significant in the development of Parsons's sociology. Notably, Henderson was critical of institutionalism, especially if it was based on an empiricist methodology or associated with political radicalism. In his critique of empiricism, Henderson rightly insisted that any discerned fact depended in part on the theory that framed it, and agreed with Weber and others on the need for theoretical abstraction in scientific reasoning. Parsons (1937a, p. xxiii) later thanked Henderson for his extensive critical remarks on an early draft of *The Structure of Social Action*, especially on 'the interpretation of Pareto's work'. Henderson also influenced Parsons in his development of the concept of 'social system' (Parsons, 1951, p. vii).[5]

Like others in that Circle, Parsons was strongly influenced by Pareto's distinction between 'logical' and 'non-logical' actions. Pareto saw 'logical' actions as being those where means were consistent with, and appropriate for, the given ends. For Pareto (1971), the study of such 'logical' actions was the domain of economics. On the other hand, like Weber, Pareto (1935) upheld that the residual class of 'non-logical' actions governed much of human behaviour. Such actions were seen as the subject matter of sociology. Accordingly, economics was a

---

5   In turn, and on this score, Henderson had been influenced by Whitehead, who was also at Harvard, and is widely regarded as a key inspiration in the development of systems theory (J. Miller, 1978).

limiting case of the broader theory of social action that it was the task of sociology to build.

In broad terms, Parsons enthusiastically adopted this approach. He saw 'non-logical' actions, involving ideology and values, as establishing the domain and independence of sociology as a science. This development in Parsons's thinking was outlined in letters to Knight in 1932–3 (Camic, 1992, pp. lii–liii). Like Ayres, Parsons continued to benefit from discussions with Knight, who was widely read in the German and English social sciences and highly useful as a critic and sounding board for their ideas.

THE ROLE AND MANOEUVRES OF JOSEPH SCHUMPETER

At this stage, another digression is in order, in part to understand the context of Parsons's own intellectual evolution, and in part as a relevant example in its own right. It concerns the role and intellectual development of Schumpeter.

Schumpeter attained a permanent post in Harvard in 1932. He had really wanted to get Sombart's former chair in Berlin when it became vacant in 1931 but he was unsuccessful. As in the case of Parsons, Schumpeter's move to Harvard coincided with an increasing hostility, on his part, to institutionalism and historicism. Consider the following evidence. In 1926, Schumpeter published a careful and sympathetic account of the work of Schmoller and other historical school theorists. In this article Schumpeter (1926, pp. 3, 18, 22, 24 n. 46) wrote of Schmoller's 'great achievements', of his 'greatness', of his work being 'the programme for the future', of 'his overall achievements' and of his 'success'. In the same article, Schumpeter saw much merit in the work of the leading American institutionalist Wesley Mitchell. Although he also raised thoughtful criticisms, the disposition was largely positive. Within four years, however, Schumpeter was to shift the balance of his assessment of historicism and institutionalism, towards criticism alone.

After his first visit to Harvard in 1927, Schumpeter became more openly critical of the historical school and highly dismissive of the institutionalist tradition. In the Harvard-based *Quarterly Journal of Economics* Schumpeter (1930, p. 158) referred scathingly to the intellectual capacities of both Schmoller and Veblen, and to 'the serious and even glaring defects in their equipment, both natural and acquired'. This atrocious personal abuse was supplemented with sweeping dismissals of much of historicism and institutionalism. Schumpeter (1930, p. 159) pronounced on the 'unsatisfactory state of economic science in Germany' and how Veblen's erroneous teaching had fortunately been corrected in America by 'a phalanx of competent theorists'. But Schumpeter listed neither Veblen's errors, the corrections nor the 'competent theorists'.

In a talk in Japan in 1931, Schumpeter (1991, p. 292) referred to the 'method-ological errors of German historians'. He also described institutionalism as 'the one dark spot in the American atmosphere'. Overall, there was a remarkable transformation from Schumpeter's sympathetic 1926 article on Schmoller, to the hostile statements of 1930–1, in which Schumpeter was keen to dismiss, and to detach himself from, the entire German historical school and American institutionalism. Fortunately for Schumpeter's career, these negative statements would have aided his application for a permanent post in Harvard in 1932.

Yet the irony is that Schumpeter continued throughout his life to draw on the work of the German historical school. Many of Schumpeter's ideas are traceable to the German historicists. For instance, Nicholas Balabkins (2000) has shown that several of Schumpeter's views concerning entrepreneurship have their origin in the work of Albert Schäffle. Schumpeter's notion of 'creative destruction' also has its precedents. Probably inspired by Friedrich Nietzsche, Sombart (1913b) gave multiple examples of how destruction and shortage can spur economic creativity, and concluded: 'again out of destruction a new spirit of creativity arises' (Sombart, 1913b, p. 207). Even more severely, Michael Appel (1992, pp. 260–2) wrote on Schumpeter's famous book *Capitalism, Socialism and Democracy* (1942) and its relationship with the work of Sombart and others:

> In this context, it is remarkable that Schumpeter, who had so clearly distanced himself from the basic economic theory of Sombart, took over his ideas and perspectives on the development of capitalism almost completely. Without hinting of Sombart and the general literature of the 1920s and 1930s, Schumpeter basically offered only what had already been said and written decades ago in the German discussions of the 'future of capitalism'. . . . In his argument, Schumpeter kept completely to the thought that had been developed in Sombart's time. Schumpeter's analysis is in no way original.

The implication of this allegation is that Schumpeter at Harvard continued to draw from the German historicist legacy but gave an impression that this was largely his own work. This impression would have been aided by increasing Anglo-American ignorance of the German historicism after the 1930s. If this allegation is valid, Schumpeter had something to gain from fashionable dismissals of historicism. Yet he remained a great and original thinker in his own right. In order to establish his reputation, he did not need to connive with any voguish or ignorant reaction against the historical school. The tragedy was that he did. It remains for future scholars to determine in detail how many of Schumpeter's ideas were in fact taken from the German historicical school.

By the end of his career, however, Schumpeter (1954, pp. 12–13, 809–14) was able again to refer to historicism in a more positive manner. Furthermore, in one of his last articles, Schumpeter (1951) was to make an appeal for 'historical or institutional study' and 'detailed historical enquiry' to overcome the then growing and one-sided obsession with econometric techniques.

We are left with a conundrum. On the one hand, Schumpeter (1926, 1954) sometimes gave quite careful assessments of the historical school. On the other hand, in 1930–1 he dismissed both the historical school and institutionalism in acerbic and sweeping prose. He largely and generally ignored the historicist inspirations for his own work. These manoeuvres represent a major problem in understanding Schumpeter's character. Clearly, Schumpeter did not always accommodate to prevailing opinion. He generally showed an independence of thought. His criticisms of the historical school would not have helped him secure the Berlin chair. He continued to praise Marx's theories, thus risking rightist hostility in the USA. He criticised Keynesianism when many other economists were on its bandwagon. Nevertheless, and in particular, the volte-face of 1926–30 and his unscholarly assessments of historicism and institutionalism in 1930–1 have to be explained. The most obvious explanation is that Schumpeter changed his stance and tone in part to please the Harvard faculty.

Crucially, it seems that contact with Harvard caused both Parsons and Schumpeter to change their published views on historicism and institutionalism. We are obliged to consider the unpalatable explanation that that their views were altered in part by career opportunism, although this is difficult to prove.

Both Parsons and Schumpeter emphasised the importance of general theory and neglected the problem of historical specificity. In the early 1930s, Parsons set to task on his general sociological theory. He obtained a grant from Harvard to work on what was to become his *Structure of Social Action*. When it was complete, Schumpeter gave this work a very positive evaluation for the university authorities (Swedberg, 1991, pp. 220–1).

Schumpeter – like Carl Menger, Max Weber and Lionel Robbins – accepted that the role of 'economic theory' was to take the individual as given. Schumpeter (1954, pp. 14–16) argued that economic theory was a 'box of tools' that applied to common features of all economic phenomena. Overall, the combined efforts of Parsons, Schumpeter and their allies at Harvard – including the graduate student and future Nobel Laureate Paul Samuelson – helped eventually to transform this academic institution into a crucial American bridgehead for the Mengerian conception of the nature and scope of economic theory, which hitherto had failed to gain an outright victory in the Germanic *Methodenstreit*.

Throughout his academic life, Schumpeter (1954, p. 827) regarded Léon Walras as the 'greatest of all economists'. There are neglected aspects of dynamism and entrepreneurship in Walras's thought (Currie and Steedman, 1990; Morishima and Catephores, 1988). Schumpeter wished to develop such insights. His move to the USA helped to promote further interest in Walras's work. However, as we shall see in chapter 15 below, Harvard also became the bridgehead of the bowdlerised version of 'Keynesian' economics that established itself – against Schumpeter's advice – in the USA after 1936. Especially through the efforts of Samuelson, a strange and distorted synthesis of Walras and Keynes was born.

PARSONS'S ATTACK ON INSTITUTIONALISM

In the Harvard intellectual environment, Parsons eventually developed a direct attack on the institutional economics upon which he had been reared. Parsons (1935) criticised Veblen, largely for his dependence on the concepts of habit and instinct. Parsons was clearing the theoretical ground for his major work on *The Structure of Social Action*. In sweeping and unjustified phraseology, Parsons (1935,

p. 439) described Veblen's emphasis on 'habit' and 'institutions' as 'one element of psychological anti-intellectualism'. But Parsons failed to explain why an emphasis on habits is 'anti-intellectual'.

Parsons (1935, p. 440) also criticised Veblen's thought for its 'behavioristic stress on "objectivity" and its abhorrence of contact with the "subjective"'. Again this was off the mark. Here Parsons repeated the confusion in his Amherst undergraduate essay between Veblen's psychology and behaviourism. Unlike the behaviourists, Veblen emphasised the importance of intelligence and delib- eration, as well as of instinct. For instance, Veblen (1919, p. 238) acknowledged that it is the 'element of discriminating forethought that distinguishes human conduct from brute behavior'. However, Veblen (1914, p. 6) also believed that 'it is only by the prompting of instinct that reflection and deliberation come to be so employed.' The notion that Veblen was a behaviourist who neglected subjective motives or perceptions is completely false.[6]

Many years later, Parsons (1976, p. 178) gave a different account of his earlier objections to institutionalism:

> I think, in retrospect, that I had two major theoretical objections to the institutional point of view. The first was that, in the name of generalized radical empiricism, it denied the legitimacy of analytical abstraction. . . . The second main objection was the neglect of cultural-normative factors in the larger picture which transcended the economic perspective.

Let us consider each of these two criticisms in turn. In the case of the first, there is a grain of truth here. It is true that there was an empiricist tendency in both institutionalism and the historical school. Wesley Mitchell, for instance, some- times suggested that the way to build a theory was simply to gather facts (Ross, 1991, p. 321). However, no such 'name' as 'generalized radical empiricism' has ever been promoted in institutionalism. Furthermore, leading institution- alists such as Veblen and Commons clearly supported a prominent role for analytical abstraction. For instance, Veblen (1919, p. 176) had promoted the idea of economics as an 'evolutionary science' with 'the preconception constantly underlying the inquiry' of 'a cumulative causal sequence'. Commons (1934a, p. 720) noted approvingly that 'Menger and Schmoller agreed not only that abstraction was necessary, but also that a great many abstractions were necessary in order to ascertain the whole truth.' Parsons's first criticism does not apply to the institutionalism of Veblen, Commons or many others.

Turning to Parsons's second criticism, it is blatantly untrue that institutional economists have neglected cultural and normative factors in the analysis of

---

6 To some considerable degree, however, the allegation was true of Ayres, who embraced behaviourist psychology and twice wrote – albeit with some qualification – that 'there is no such thing as an individual' (Ayres, 1918, p. 57; 1961, p. 175). Again we may point to the likelihood that Parsons's understanding of Veblen's thought was very much the questionable version that had been taught by Ayres. On some of the defects of Ayres's interpretation of Veblen see Hodgson (1998e).

human agency and social structure. Indeed, Commons (1934a, p. 720) complained that Carl Menger had eliminated all 'ethical feelings' from economics. Veblen (1934, p. 30) argued that 'it is through . . . everyday approval or disapproval that any feature of the institutional structure is upheld or altered . . . these categories, with all the moral force with which they are charged, designate the motive force of cultural development.' Clearly, both Veblen and Commons recognised the normative and cultural aspects of all human action.

In short, most of Parsons's criticisms of institutionalism were untenable.[7] Not only were these criticisms off-target, but also Parsons fails to give credit to the influence of institutionalists in his own intellectual development. As Charles Camic (1991, p. xxiv) put it:

> what appears, whenever his early writings speak of 'institutional economics,' is not an approving mention of the ideas of his Amherst mentors, but a critical attack upon the psychologism and biologism of the best-known forerunners of institutionalism, Thorstein Veblen and the quantitative economist Wesley Mitchell.

In attacking institutionalism, Parsons was not simply currying favour with his Harvard colleagues. He was also creating a space for his own brand of sociology (Camic, 1987). Parsons had to counter the institutionalist standpoint and its opposition to the compartmentalisation of the social sciences. Developments were to occur within neoclassical economics, which also would require Parsons's critical engagement.

Veblen and the pragmatists had seen habit as foundational for belief. In contrast, Parsons required a picture of the human agent that was relatively free of psychological and biological substrata (Camic, 1989). Parsons regarded habit not as a rooted propensity, but in phenomenal and behaviourist terms of stimulus and response. Hence, along with behaviourism, he rejected habit as well. Having removed habit from the picture, Parsons saw social norms and values as driving human agents and constituting the relations between them. Into the vacuum created by the removal of the pragmatist conception of action – based on habitual propensities and situated reason – Parsons was obliged to introduce an agent driven largely by values and norms. It became a 'top down' explanation of human agency in which normatively infused social structures did the explanatory work. In ridding sociology of habit, Parsons had denuded the concept of agency and conflated it into the concept of social structure. Contrary to Parsons, Veblen and the pragmatists had recognised the role of norms and values too, but they also tried to explain their grounding in shared habits of thought and behaviour. Parsons, in contrast, stressed the normative content of institutions over their role in shaping cognitive frameworks and habits of thought.

The banishment of the concept of habit from sociology was the key symptom of this disunion between the social and the natural (Camic, 1986; Murphy, 1994).

---

7 See Tilman (1992, pp. 170–4) for a discussion of some more of Parsons's criticisms of Veblen, mainly from the postwar period.

Although the concepts of habit and custom were once central to social science, largely because of Parsons and his followers, they have since been jettisoned. Symptomatically, the 1930 edition of the *International Encyclopedia of the Social Sciences* contains entries on habit and custom. In the next, 1968 edition they had been dropped. Where and when the concept of habit was retained, it was typically interpreted as mere behaviour, rather than a propensity or disposition in the sense of James, Dewey or Veblen.

After his direct attack on institutionalism in the 1930s, Parsons referred to this doctrine less often. An exception was in a footnote to his introduction to a translation of one of Weber's works. Here Parsons made the ludicrous claim that: 'Quite adequate comprehension of all Veblen's real contributions can be found in Weber's work' (Weber, 1947, p. 40 n.). Not only were the contributions of Veblen and Weber different in key respects, but also neither had any significant influence on the other. Having attacked institutionalism in the 1930s, by the 1940s Parsons was making the false claim that everything of relevance was in Weber and the institutionalists could be safely ignored.

A LITTLE PHILOSOPHY IS A DANGEROUS THING

Crucially, although Parsons was acquainted with ethical philosophy, he had little training in the philosophy of science. As a result, his use of philosophical terminology was often awkward and idiosyncratic. He read some of Dewey's works as an undergraduate, but his works show little evidence of the influence of pragmatism. He also read some of Immanuel Kant (Münch, 1981) but there is no more than limited evidence of a Kantian influence (Camic, 1987, p. 433). Despite his absorption of Weber, the traces of Kantianism in Parsons's own work are much less by comparison. At Heidelberg, Parsons read some political philosophy, philosophy of law, and philosophy of religion (Wearne, 1989, p. 44). At Harvard, Parsons came into contact with the British philosopher Alfred Whitehead, who had been there since 1924. This was his first detailed and sustained encounter with the philosophy of science. 'Prior to this point the philosophy of science occupied relatively little of Parsons's attention' (Camic, 1991, p. xxxiii). Partly under Whitehead's influence, terms such as 'organic' and 'emergence' made a confident – if sometimes confused – appearance in Parsons's work. Nevertheless, despite Whitehead, Parsons's general understanding of core philosophical issues remained patchy and incomplete.

As an example of Parsons's obscure and idiosyncratic use of philosophical terminology, consider his unusual definition of 'positivism'. Positivism was a term devised by Auguste Comte (1853) to express his view that all knowledge is based on the observation and comparison of data. The term 'logical positivism' was promoted in the 1920s by Rudolf Carnap, Moritz Schlick and others of the Vienna Circle. Like all versions of empiricism, positivism sees experience as the foundation of knowledge. Success in making prediction is regarded as a key attribute of a science. Positivism contends that observation and experiment are the means of obtaining and testing knowledge. Unobservable entities – such as human consciousness or will – are typically dismissed as 'metaphysical'.

This established meaning of positivism had very little to do with the idiosyncratic definition of the word adopted by Parsons. Parsons (1935, p. 452) wrote: 'The "positivistic" theories tend on the whole to reduce economic activities to terms of biological heredity or the external environment or some combination of both.' A similar formulation appeared later when Parsons (1937a, 490) wrote of the 'positivistic sense of reducing social phenomena causally to terms of the nonhuman environment, as natural resources, or of biological heredity or some combination of both'.

Parsons thus identified positivism as a methodological, rather than an epistemological, doctrine. In particular, Parsons saw 'positivists' as those who would promote a kind of natural science of society. However, contrary to Parsons, positivism (as Comte defined it) does not lead to the idea that economic activities can be explained (partly or wholly) in terms of biological heredity. Such explanations play no significant role in the philosophical literature on either Comtean or logical positivism. Nor does biological reductionism necessarily involve positivism. In cavalier fashion, Parsons attached the term to an opinion that at the time he regarded as pernicious – the idea that biology or psychology can have a major part in the explanation of human behaviour. Parsons was concerned that the purposeful nature of human action should be recognised. But the proper name for a doctrine that denies the importance of purpose or intention is behaviourism, rather than positivism.

Elsewhere, however, Parsons (1937a, p. 63) seemed to have a different definition in mind. He saw the 'positivistic element' as consisting of 'the implication that ends must be taken as given'. This is very different from his other definition, and does not logically flow from it. Again, this is hopelessly remote from the standard use of the term by philosophers. Regrettably, Parsons's confused and philosophically illiterate use of the word 'positivism' has helped to render it virtually useless among social theorists – it now connotes an immense and confused variety of meanings.

Ironically, despite his hostility to 'positivism', Parsons's own work is suffused with positivism in the Comtean sense of the word. He wrote of his efforts 'to verify empirically' his ideas, he believed in the possibility of the 'empirical verification of the propositions' of a theory, he claimed 'empirical demonstration' of his own conclusions and he wrote more generally of the 'empirical proof' of propositions (Parsons, 1937a, pp. 11, 24, 698, 721). An attack on 'positivism', by someone who was unknowingly positivist to the core, can only succeed by redefining the term beyond recognition.

Another example of Parsons's twisted use of philosophical terms is his notion of 'empiricism'. Parsons (1937a, pp. 69–70) defined this as the claim that 'the categories of the given theoretical system are by themselves adequate to explain all the scientifically important facts about the body of concrete phenomena to which it is applied'. This is again hopelessly remote from the standard philosophical meaning of the empiricism, as the doctrine that knowledge is based primarily on experience rather than on any body of theory. In attacking what he described as 'empiricism', Parsons was opposing the idea that any one theory could explain everything. He argued that theoretical systems were limited because they were 'logically closed'. In making this point, Parsons was still able to allow truly empiricist notions – as noted in the preceding paragraph – to permeate his work. In the standard senses of these terms, Parsons's work was in fact both positivist and empiricist (Camic, 1987; Zaret, 1980).[8]

THE QUEST FOR AN AHISTORICAL SOCIOLOGY

It was with such ill-defined terminology that Parsons attempted to dispense with the historical school position. But his critique of their central project was remarkably weak. His dismissal largely consisted of the assertion that such 'historical relativism' must inevitably lead to the vaguely defined sins of 'empiricism' or 'positivism' (Parsons, 1935). However, even with his own definitions of these terms, Parsons failed to show why this was necessarily the case.

In his promulgation of Weber's ideas among an English-speaking audience, Parsons downplayed Weber's engagement with the problem of historical specificity. Instead he emphasised Weber's valid recognition of the indispensability of universal concepts in any theoretical system. Parsons (1936, pp. 677–8) noted that Weber had shown

> the logical indispensability, for empirical demonstration, of *general* concepts – both the general 'elements,' into which the 'historical individual' may be resolved, and the general laws relative to the behavior of these elements. . . . The corollary of this is that the methodology of the social sciences cannot be confined to the 'genetic' tracing of temporal sequences.

So far so good. On this point, both Weber and Parsons had a strong case. But Parsons took his argument much further than Weber. Parsons continued: 'Different historical individuals must be capable of analysis into different combinations of the *same* elements.'

There is a key ambiguity here. If Parsons had meant that different analyses of different historical entities must involve *some* similar elements then he would have been on strong ground. However, if he had meant that all such different historical entities must be capable of analysis *entirely* in terms of 'different

---

8 As another example of Parsons's idiosyncratic use of philosophical terminology, consider the term 'emergence'. Although he used it, Parsons never clearly defined the concept. In a key passage in the *Structure of Social Action* where he came closest to a definition, he saw emergent properties as 'a measure of the organicism of the system' (Parsons, 1937a, p. 749). However, Parsons's notion of emergence as a 'measure' has nothing to do with the concept as it is developed in the works of Whitehead, Lloyd Morgan, William McDougall and others. Their concept of emergence concerns the existence of properties of an entity at one ontological level, which are not reducible to or predictable from the lower-level properties of its components.

combinations of the *same* elements' then it would have been a non sequitur. It simply does not follow from his preceding argument. Weber's valid argument that some general concepts are unavoidable does not mean that all concepts must be general in their scope. Such crucial ambiguities helped Parsons to act as Weber's literary executor in the English-speaking world, while abandoning the problem of historical specificity at the same time.

Parsons's intentions were clear. The social sciences must address 'unique historical' cases but only as a 'means' towards the erection of a general theory (Parsons, 1936, p. 678). His ultimate search was for 'a substantial common basis of theory' that would serve a wide variety of circumstances (Parsons, 1937a, p. 774). As Camic (1991, p. li) puts it, in his 1936 discussion of Weber, Parsons ended up

> entirely abandoning his earlier institutionalist emphasis on the *differences* between historical epochs, the value of the genetic method, and the limitations of abstract theories with universal applicability, Parsons now – in a fateful step that will inhibit his treatment of historical diversity hereafter – champions the search for uniform 'general laws'.

This 'fateful step' meant that Parsons was to break without acknowledgement from the letter and spirit of Weber's work. As Weber had recognised, there is nothing wrong with a judicious search for general principles, as long as we do not lose sight of the additional need to conceptualise historically sensitive levels of analysis. But much of Parsonian and post-Parsonian sociology has overlooked the latter point. Parsons overlooked Weber's strictures on the limits of general theorising. Parsons degraded the historically sensitive approaches of Weber and others into a scheme where 'the historical dimension of social life becomes a fund of empirical data to be used for testing general theoretical propositions' (Zaret, 1980, p. 1198). A similarly relegated role for history can be found in much of post-1945 social science.

However, in striking out for a general sociological theory in the 1930s, Parsons was taking a huge risk. At that time, general theories were not that popular in the social sciences. In this ambitious project, Parsons gained confidence from his reading of Pareto and the crucial support of Schumpeter and others at Harvard. Fortunately for Parsons, however, developments were to take place in economics that made general theorising much more fashionable. Among others, Lionel Robbins played a crucial part.

PARSONS AND LIONEL ROBBINS

In 1932 Robbins – a young Professor at the London School of Economics – published his seminal *Essay on the Nature and Significance of Economic Science*. Greater attention is given to Robbins's argument in the next chapter. We may note briefly here that it involved a major attempt to dismiss the problem of historical specificity. Robbins redefined economics as the universal 'science of choice'. Economics was about the rational choice of means to serve given ends. The 'economic problem' was then to determine the best means available to meet those given ends. It applied to all economic systems, as long as there were choices to be made and a scarcity of resources.

Crucially, Parsons did not reject this redefinition of economics. In fact, it served his purposes. By defining economics narrowly, as the science of rational choice, Robbins conceded a substantial territory to the sociologist. For Parsons, sociology was about the social and normative origin of the ends that Robbins had taken as given.

Parsons raised two criticisms of Robbins. First, for Parsons, ends and means could not entirely be separated. In addition, ends could not always be taken as 'given' because they were likely to be affected by the processes involved in their attainment. Parsons (1934, p. 515) wrote: 'Since they contain a future reference, in the sense of being data of the physical world, they can, unlike the other elements of action, only become "given" after its completion.' This idea of the mutual interaction of ends and means was redolent of Dewey (1922, p. 34) and others. Parsons's point was sound, but not original.

Second, Parsons stressed that social action was always framed and driven by social and institutional norms. Allegedly, these normative patterns 'define what are felt to be, in the given society, proper, legitimate, or expected modes of action or of social relationship' (Parsons, 1940, p. 190). As noted above, Parsons was impelled to put such stress on the determination of meaning and behaviour by social norms because he had removed from sociology any instinctive or psychological grounding. For Parsons (1934, p. 533) the 'system of normative rules' embodied in institutions were a 'specifically *non*-economic factor'. The Parsonian emphasis on norms was the keystone of his autonomous sociology.[9]

In reaction against Robbins, Parsons feared that the emphasis of the English economist on facts and logical relationships, to the exclusion of ends, might lead to a neglect of the role of norms in all social activity. Parsons (1934, pp. 520–1) insisted that the idea of a 'logical gap' between ends and means should not be used to sustain 'the idea that a science dealing with "facts" cannot also deal with "norms"'. Later, Parsons (1940) extended this argument by insisting that self-interest was itself socially formed. Historical school and institutional economists had asserted the same proposition, time and time again. But Parsons gave them no acknowledgement: he took for sociology the wisdom that he had learned from institutionalism.

Parsons's tactic was to show that Robbinsian economics had to be grounded upon a general sociological theory. Economics would focus merely on the examination of the logical relationships between means and given ends.

---

9   Note that Schumpeter (1954, pp. 15, 20–1, 819) endorsed a similar but not identical demarcation between the two disciplines. His definition of 'economic theory' or 'economic analysis' was narrow and similar to that of Robbins, consigning the 'analysis of economic institutions' to 'economic sociology'. For instance, Schumpeter (1954, p. 21) wrote: 'economic analysis deals with the questions how people behave at any time and what the economic effects are they produce by so behaving; economic sociology deals with the question how they came to behave as they do.'

Sociology would then assume its place as the study of the social origin of the ends. Hence, Parsons (1937a, p. 768) defined sociology as 'the science which attempts to develop an analytical theory of social action systems in so far as these systems can be understood in terms of the property of common-value integration'. Notably, this definition of the subject was not in terms of the analysis of 'social action systems' as a whole, but in terms of the impact and integration of common values. Sociology was thus defined as the study of an *aspect* of the social system. It had a delineated domain of enquiry. The study of other features was conceded to economists and others.

An implicit contract emerged between them. Economics was henceforth to concerns itself with the rational choice of means to serve given ends; sociology was to be concerned with the explanation of those values and ends. This was the substance of their 'gentleman's agreement' mapped out in the 1930s (Ingham, 1996, p. 244). This agreement tacitly involved the severance of the social sciences from biology and to some degree also from psychology. Accordingly, philo-sophical questions such as the relationship between causality in the natural sciences and causality in the social sciences were ignored. With Robbins (1932), economics became the 'science of choice' without much consideration of what 'choice' actually meant in philosophical terms. And under Parsons (1937a, p. 768) sociology was reconstructed as 'the science . . . of social action' without much discussion of the materialist causes behind intention or action itself.[10]

Crucially, both Parsons and Robbins avoided any direct and integrated analysis of socio-economic structures and institutions as a whole. Each of them focused on a selected analytical aspect. Neither addressed the structured reality in its totality. Their example became tragically influential for the two subjects involved. Both economics and sociology became redefined in terms of the study of types of analytical problem rather than in terms of the explanation of a distinct reality. They became compartmentalised, self-reflective discourses. After Parsons and Robbins, no social science addressed the study of socio-economic systems as a whole.

PARSONS'S LIBERATION STRUGGLE AGAINST 'ECONOMIC IMPERIALISM'

However, the Robbins–Parsons attempt to redraw the boundaries of economics and sociology received a major challenge. This was from a brilliant young hetero-dox economist, who has since remained largely unknown and unrecognised.

Ralph W. Souter was born in New Zealand and fought in the First World War. A Rockefeller Foundation travelling fellowship brought him to Columbia University in 1928. At Columbia he obtained a PhD, and was a lecturer in economics from 1930 to 1935. In 1936 he obtained a chair in economics at the University of Otago, New Zealand, a position he held until his early death in 1946, at the age of 49.

---

10 Although in the 1950s Parsons became interested in psycho-analysis, he never repaired the breach between psychology and sociology.

Souter was heavily influenced by Whitehead's organicism and by Gestalt psychology. He rejected atomistic assumptions in economics in favour of an organicist ontology. He believed in a synthesis of a type of Marshallian 'evolutionary economics' (Souter, 1930, p. 59) and the best of institutionalism. His PhD dissertation is an innovative and outstanding volume, acutely critical, philosophically well informed, and far ahead of its time (Souter, 1933b). For instance, he acknowledged the origin and significance of the concept of emergent properties and brought it into his own work. Also, decades before Nicholas Georgescu-Roegen (1971), Souter (1933b, pp. 116–18) brought the entropy law into economic theory.[11]

As discussed in more detail in the next chapter, Souter attacked the idea that the social sciences should be compartmentalised. He argued for the integration, rather than the compartmentalisation, of the social sciences. The 'organic' nature of social reality required this. Such a standpoint put him into conflict with both Parsons and Robbins, each wishing to create space and autonomy for their own separate academic discipline. Souter's (1933a) review of Robbins's *Nature and Significance of Economic Science* is discussed in the next chapter. In his PhD dissertation, Souter (1933b, p. 94 n.) argued:

> The salvation of Economic Science in the twentieth century lies in an enlightened and democratic 'economic imperialism', which invades the territories of its neighbours, not to enslave them or to swallow them up, but to aid and enrich them and promote their autonomous growth in the very process of aiding and enriching itself.

This is the first known use of the term 'economic imperialism' to describe an attempt to link up economics with the other social sciences. Both historicists and institutionalists had previously promoted notions of a unified social science. Souter argued for such a unification, in which a form of 'evolutionary economics' would be at its apex. At the same time, Souter insisted that the imperial science should enrich rather than subjugate, and even depend upon other disciplines. For example, Souter (1933a, p. 399) wrote: 'Economics is necessarily and inevitably dependent upon sociology, upon psychology, upon technology.'

Notably, this early use of the term 'economic imperialism' contrasts greatly with the works of 'Chicago' economists Gary Becker, Jack Hirshleifer and others, with which it is associated today (Becker, 1976a; Hirshleifer, 1977, 1985; Lazear, 2000). Modern, Chicago-type 'economic imperialism' involves the swallowing up of other disciplines. Professedly, all social sciences face the common 'economic' problem of competition over scarce resources. Accordingly, they must

---

11 It is clear from both the title and content of Souter's 1933 book that he made extensive use of ideas and metaphors from modern physics. Indeed, it was one of the very few cases of a discussion of Einstein's theory of relativity in the context of economics. The fact that Souter's work was subsequently forgotten seems to counter an extreme version of Mirowski's (1989) argument – that economists have achieved recognition by aping physics at its every turn. This does not seem to be the case. The connection was less frequent and more remote.

all be enslaved by the precepts of a Robbins-type economic science. The following statement by Hirshleifer (1977, pp. 3–4) is representative of this approach:

the domain of economics is coextensive with the total sphere of all the social sciences together . . . As economics 'imperialistically' employs its tools of analysis over a wide range of social issues, it will *become* sociology and anthropology and political science. But correspondingly, as these other disciplines grow increasingly rigorous, they will not merely resemble but will *be* economics.

This is very different from the 'economic imperialism' proposed by Souter in 1933. Hirshleifer proposed the widespread use of economic tools. In contrast, Souter proposed an economics that was conjoined with insights from other social sciences. However, despite this huge difference, both forms of 'economic imperialism' challenged the Parsonian project for a general and autonomous sociological theory.

In his discussion of Robbins's (1932) *Essay*, Parsons engaged with Souter's (1933a) review. Significantly, for Parsons, the greater threat came not from Robbins but from Souter. Parsons's (1934, p. 522) rejected Souter's 'economic imperialism' vehemently, in the same way that he had opposed the idea of unified social science that had been frequently proposed by institutionalists and historicists. For Parsons (1934, p. 535), Souter's 'economic imperialism' was a tendency 'against which the sociologist, as well as other scientists, must stand up and fight for his scientific life'. But Parsons gave little detailed justification for this argument. His response to Souter was opaque and unconvincing.

Souter's post-Marshallian and evolutionary attempt to build a unified social science faced the twin opposition of a leading sociologist and leading economist. However, Souter failed to make an impact. His work is almost completely forgotten.

PARSONS AND ADOLPH LÖWE

In the 1930s and 1940s, thousands of refugees from Nazi persecution fled to the United States (Scherer, 2000). Some of these immigrants brought the ideas of the German historical school to America. One of them was Adolph Löwe. He was influenced by the historical school and wrote a major review of one of Sombart's works (Löwe, 1932). Löwe emigrated to England in 1933 and remained at the University of Manchester until 1940, when he moved on to the United States. In his 1935 book *Economics and Sociology: A Plea for Cooperation in the Social Sciences*, Löwe argued, like many before, that capitalism was only one among several types of economic system, which differed in terms of 'historical structure and historical laws'. Nevertheless, reflecting the work of Weber, Sombart and others, Löwe also saw a place for 'pure theory' addressing universal aspects of all economic systems. It was the role of sociology, according to Löwe, to furnish 'middle principles' to connect 'pure theory' with 'the structure and the regularities of motion of particular "economic systems"' (Löwe, 1935, p. 136).

Regrettably, the substance of Löwe's argument did not get all the attention it deserved. Parsons (1937b) reviewed it in the *American Journal of Sociology*. Two features are notable in this assessment. The first is its concentration on the 'logical lack of symmetry between the two sciences of economics and sociology' in Löwe's scheme. This greatly offended Parsons's attempts to demarcate separate realms for the two sciences, in which each science dealt with 'aspects' of the same phenomenon. Second, is the remarkable neglect in Parsons's review of the theoretical problem of historical specificity, which Löwe had made central to his argument. This too interfered with Parsons's project to establish universal principles for sociology to parallel those already proclaimed by economists.

Löwe, a refugee from Germany, brought with him ideas from a great tradition of economic thought. In Germany this tradition was being hampered by Nazi persecution and crushed by Allied bombs. Any presentation of these ideas to the English-speaking world was potentially of great significance for the future. Unfortunately for Löwe, his ideas did not conform to the rising orthodoxies in economics and sociology. Hence, the legacy was almost completely lost to the post-1945 world. The injurious role of Parsons in this episode was significant.

CONCLUDING REMARKS

In 1937 Parsons published his monumental *Structure of Social Action*. Although it was largely a history of ideas – focusing principally on Marshall, Pareto, Durkheim and Weber – it established Parsons's international reputation. The boundaries between economics and sociology, so carefully drawn by Robbins and Parsons, were widely accepted from the 1940s to the 1970s. The postwar consensus in the social sciences was thus established.

Neither the historical school nor the institutionalists were part of this consensus. Eventually, institutionalists such as Veblen were denied a place in the halls of fame of sociology as well as of economics, thanks to the combined efforts of Parsons, Robbins, Schumpeter and others. Yet Parsons owed much of his own intellectual development to institutionalists, notably to Hamilton and Ayres. As Camic (1987, 1992) has argued at length, Parsons's exclusion of the institutionalists when naming his intellectual predecessors in his books was strongly influenced by their generally faltering reputation and their particularly low standing at Harvard.

Parsons never denied the variation and qualitative historical development of societies. Indeed, much of his postwar work was concerned with these issues (Parsons, 1951, 1966, 1977). But he always treated social change and variation within one, over-arching framework of analysis. The overall thrust of his work was a search for general concepts and principles that pervade all history.[12]

---

12 In this project he developed the opaque and cumbersome style of writing that regrettably has been imitated by succeeding generations of sociologists. Mills (1959, p. 40) made the plausible claim that 'one could translate the 555 pages of *The Social System* into about 150 pages of straightforward English.'

In his 1949 presidential address to the American Sociological Society, Parsons (1950, p. 5) argued for '[g]eneral theory, which I interpret primarily as the theory of the social system, in its sociologically relevant aspects'. For Parsons, there were no longer different social systems, but simply *the* social system. This is a remarkable statement for someone so familiar with the historical school and institutional economics. Although Parsons admitted '[s]pecial theories around particular empirical problem areas' these were seen as a minor and highly subordinate areas, driven by empirical data rather than by theoretical problems. Parsons explained:

> The basic reason why general theory is so important is that the cumulative development of knowledge in a scientific field is a function of the degree of *generality of implications* by which it is possible to relate findings, interpretations, and hypotheses on different levels and in different specific empirical fields to each other.
>
> (ibid.)

The logic here is both opaque and questionable. Although science often advances by unification and generalisation, knowledge also cumulates by particular knowledge of specific phenomena. Furthermore, in arguing for a general theory, Parsons repeatedly fudged an important issue. He made a strong case that some general frameworks and principles were both necessary and unavoidable for any social enquiry. But he then excluded the possibility that particular theories are also required to explain particular types of socio-economic system. This historical school insight was simply bulldozed under a general argument for general theory, ignoring the fact that special theories are required as well.

As a further example, consider his concept of 'evolutionary universals'. Parsons (1964) proposed that in evolutionary processes, specific organisational developments have 'generalized adaptive capacity'. Just as the eye evolved independently in different forms in different species, effective and durable organisational forms will likewise appear in different circumstances. Parsons (1977) believed that political democracy based on universal adult suffrage was such a 'evolutionary universal'. Another was 'institutionalized individualism'. All this began to sound like a celebration of the values of postwar American society. His ahistorical sociology looked at history but it then returned to the American present, as if to declare 'the end of history'. The 'social system' of Parsonian sociology appeared more and more like an Americanised 'ideal type'.

By the 1950s, Parsons had become the most highly regarded living sociologist in the world. In an ironic crossing of paths, he visited Cambridge, England in 1953 and delivered the prestigious annual Marshall lectures in Faculty of Economics. However, there was none of Marshall's sensitivity to the problem of historical specificity. The first three chapters of *Economy and Society: A Study in the Integration of Economic and Social Theory* (Parsons and Smelser, 1956) were based on these lectures. The book attempted to show that theories attributed to economists as diverse as James Duesenberry, John Hicks, Michal Kalecki, John Maynard Keynes and Paul Samuelson could all be placed within a single, general theoretical framework. Hence his sociology victoriously encompassed all of economics. The Parsonian analysis thus claimed to be more general than the *General Theory*. Parsons outbid both Keynes and the Keynesians in the auction of generalising claims. However, Parsons and Smelser failed to persuade many economists of the benefits of their proposed sociological imperialism.[13]

Among many sociologists, Parsons had much greater success. He established a universal and ahistorical mode of sociological theory that was widely followed. In this tradition, the historical specificity of particular social relations was overlooked. For example, the influential 'exchange theory' of George Homans (1961) and Peter Blau (1964) proposed that a wide range of activities – including gift-giving and interpersonal communications – are 'exchanges'. This universal concept of exchange obscured its specific, contractual form in a market society. Mere verbal conversation does not necessarily involve a contract. As Commons (1924) and other institutionalists had insisted, exchange in a market economy involves the contractual exchange of property rights within a legal system of private property relations.[14]

Today, sociological theory is in a state of crisis. A consensus over core concepts and approaches is lacking. Parsons fell out of favour in the 1980s, only to be replaced by a discordant cacophony of post-modernists, empiricists and others. Indeed, one of the principal dangers is to conclude, from the failure of the attempt of Parsons to establish a general sociological theory, that all general theorising is doomed. John Holmwood (1996, p. viii) expressed this mood: 'My basic contention is that Parsons's general theory is fundamentally flawed and, indeed, that the very programme of a general theory in sociology is mistaken.' However, the solution to this malaise is not to abandon entirely any general theory. Such a venture would be both vulnerable and internally inconsistent: the notion that a general theory has to be abandoned is itself a general theory. Any argument for such an abandonment would itself require a general meta-theory. There is no way to escape from this contradiction, without accepting that some kind of general theory must be retained, alongside a more specific, historically-oriented discourse.

Instead of concluding that all general theorising must be abandoned, it would be better to learn the vital and more specific lessons from Parsons's recasting of sociology in the 1930s. Such lessons have major implications for all subsequent sociological theory. Among them is the need to reconcile the more general with the historically confined types of analysis. Parsons himself discarded this project.

---

13 See the highly critical reviews of Parsons and Smelser (1956) by Ayres (1957), Boulding (1958) and Worswick (1957), and the (negative) remarks in Johnson and Johnson (1978, p. 155). In his review, Ayres made no mention of the fact that Parsons was formerly his student.

14 Blau (1964, p. 93) made a distinction between 'social' and 'economic' exchange, where the latter is based on a 'formal contract that stipulates the exact quantities to be exchange'. However, many business transactions in the real world do not involve such an exact specification. This is especially the case with the employment contract, which in general is imperfectly and incompletely specified. Blau passed over this problem, seemingly content to place such business and employment issues outside 'the economy'. This is just one case of the recurring failure within the social sciences to demarcate adequately the boundary between 'economics' and 'sociology'. This should lead us to question whether such a boundary is possible or necessary.

With the help of others he consigned the efforts of historicists and institutionalists who were working on the problem, to the dustbins of postwar social science. As we have seen, one of his abetters was Robbins. He is one of the two main subjects of the next chapter. More than anyone else, Robbins and Parsons are responsible for the wrong turnings taken by economics and sociology in the 1930s.

14

DEATH AND COUNTER-REVOLUTION AT THE LONDON SCHOOL OF ECONOMICS

Truth is the most valuable thing we have. Let us economize it.
(Mark Twain, *Following the Equator* (1897))

Again we cross the Atlantic, to observe in the next two chapters some key events in the development of economics in Britain. The outcome, as in America in the 1930s, was that the heritage of the historical school, and the project to develop more historically sensitive theories, would be lost for the remainder of the twentieth century.

These two chapters are centred respectively on the London School of Economics (LSE) and the University of Cambridge. In the case of the LSE, there was an open critical engagement with the historical and institutional economists. The victorious critics captured the LSE positions of power. In the case of Cambridge, its culture of intellectual isolationism did not encourage the recognition or appropriation of a historicist and institutional legacy from elsewhere. Consequently, after Alfred Marshall's retirement, the problem of historical specificity was largely forgotten. As a result, the general theorists were eventually able to extricate victory from the jaws of their Keynesian defeat. This tale is told in the next chapter. Notably, despite the heterodox reputation gained by Cambridge from the 1930s to the 1980s, conditions at the LSE were originally more fertile for a British institutionalism.

EDWIN CANNAN AND ALLYN YOUNG

The towering influence over British economics, for at least the first half of the twentieth century, was Alfred Marshall. As argued in chapter 8, he praised the German historical school and recognised the problem of historical specificity. Although he was to be remembered for his neoclassical approach to economic theory, his conception of economic analysis could also readily accommodate many historical and institutional ideas.

In 1895 – five years after the appearance of Marshall's *Principles* – the London School of Economics was founded.[1] As founders of the School, Beatrice and

---

1 For the early history of the LSE see Beveridge (1960), Dahrendorf (1995), Hayek (1946) and Winch (1969).

Sidney Webb had tried to ensure that economics at the LSE would be empirically grounded and practically oriented. They strongly supported inductivist methods in science and sided with the historicists. Their academic appointments reflected this policy. William A. S. Hewins was appointed as first Director of the LSE. Educated at Oxford, Hewins was also influenced by the German historical school, although he later distanced himself from it (Koot, 1987, ch. 8).

The correspondence in 1899 and 1900 between Marshall and Hewins has been noted in chapter 8 above (Whitaker, 1996, vol. 2, pp. 256, 280). Marshall advised Hewins that the economics curriculum at the School should not be overly formal or mathematical. Above all, Marshall insisted, 'economic science' was to be 'the application of powerful analytical methods to unravelling the actions of economic and social causes'. Under these injunctions, a more methodologically aware and theoretically astute institutional economics might have grown and prospered.

Another early and influential appointment was Edwin Cannan. At the foundation of the LSE, he was appointed as a lecturer. In 1907 he became a professor of economics. Cannan emphasised the institutional foundation of economic systems and recommended that economists should also study law. In his monograph on *Wealth*, Cannan (1914) devoted a chapter to what he regarded as the fundamental institutions of the capitalist system, particularly stressing three elements: the family, private property and the state.

Another prominent figure was Harold Laski, who moved to the LSE from Harvard University in 1920. 'Laski knew Veblen personally and greatly admired much of his work' (Tilman, 1996, p. 133 n.). This created a further link between the LSE and the institutionalist and historicist traditions.

When Cannan retired in 1926, the search for his replacement reached across the Atlantic to Allyn Young. The Director of the LSE, William (later Lord) Beveridge visited Harvard and Young agreed to take the job (Beveridge, 1960, p. 91). Young became the first American professor in Britain.

When Veblen was at Stanford University (1906–9), Young was the chair of the economics department. He had been one of the very few to defend Veblen when he was fired as a result of allegations of marital infidelity from his estranged wife Ellen. Indeed, Young had testified that Veblen was 'the most gifted man whom I [Young] have ever known' (Dorfman, 1934, p. 299).

In his first major published article, Young (1911) argued that economics should turn away from equilibrium-oriented theorising. He warned against over-simplistic, all-embracing theories. He accepted the institutionalist argument that human motivations were moulded by historically contingent institutions. In particular, he endorsed Wesley Mitchell's thesis that 'the money concept itself has been an active factor in giving purpose, system and rationality to economic activity' (Young, 1911, p. 415). We have already noted that Young was one of the supervisors of Frank Knight's seminal PhD dissertation. Young's reputation quickly grew to the point that he became president of the American Economic Association in 1925.

While he remained sympathetic to institutionalism, Young (1927, 1929) began to be critical of its failure to build up a systematic theoretical approach. Like some other leading institutionalists – notably John Commons, Wesley Mitchell, Frank

Knight, John Maurice Clark, Paul Douglas and Arthur F. Burns – Young saw institutionalism as compatible with a Marshallian type of price theory. However, his interpretation of Marshallian economics was even more dynamic than that of Marshall himself, emphasising the phenomenon of increasing returns that had been consigned an appendix of the *Principles*.

Young was sufficiently immersed in the tradition of historicism and institutionalism to acknowledge the problem of historical specificity in economic theory. Soon after his arrival at the LSE, Young (1927, pp. 6–7) wrote that:

> in the social sciences we must make room for two different general classes or types of investigation. In the first type we concern ourselves with certain aspects of the nature and the operations of a complicated social mechanism. We search for uniform and dependable relations that will help to explain the degree of order that is apparent in our social environment. In the second type of inquiries we seek to get an understanding, not of those general and dependable relations among things which we call 'laws,' but of specific events, particular institutions, and unique situations. We look for explanations of *differences*, of the new forms which our institutions and our activities assume from time to time.

Accordingly, Young recognised a place for both general 'laws' and particular explanations of different 'institutions and activities' in economics. A year later, Young published in the *Economic Journal* his famous article on 'Increasing Returns and Economic Progress'. This work was a continuation of Young's attack on the equilibrium tradition in economic theory. He believed that increasing returns were pervasive in modern, manufacturing economies. Consequently, Young (1928, p. 533) explained in distinctly Veblenian language, 'change becomes progressive and propagates itself in a cumulative way.' The main function of markets, argued Young in a distant echo of Adam Smith, is not merely to allocate but to create more resources by enlarging the scope for specialisation and the division of labour.[2]

Nicholas Kaldor was a student of Young at the LSE. Kaldor saw the obsession with equilibrium and the failure to recognise increasing returns as a crucial weakness of economic theory. Kaldor moved to Cambridge in the 1940s, where he was to marry the theoretical systems of Young and Keynes (Toner, 1999). Young was thus indirectly to make a vital mark on the Cambridge economics of the future.

Tragically, Young (like Max Weber in 1920) became a victim of a severe influenza epidemic, and died in London of pneumonia in March 1929. He was just 52 years of age. This American's death was to be decisive for the fate of British economics.

---

2   For a useful exposition and discussion of Young's contribution to economics see Blitch (1995).

ENTER LIONEL ROBBINS

In 1929, Lionel Robbins was elected to the LSE chair that had been vacated by Young. This youthful appointee was to steer LSE economics in a very different direction. Immediately, Robbins set about the task of ridding it of its institutionalist and historicist ballast. His famous *Essay* was published in 1932. In a masterly stroke, he simply redefined economics in terms that would exclude institutionalism and the historicism from within its disciplinary boundaries. Economics was to be the general 'science of choice', but it would exclude any investigation into the psychological origins or institutional moulding of individual preferences or goals. Economics was no longer to have an institutionally or historically specific domain of analysis.

To achieve this transformation of the subject, institutionalism and historicism had to be thrown overboard. But Robbins wanted to retain a place on board for the Austrian school, largely because of Menger's similar redefinition of the scope of economics. Hence Menger's stand in the *Methodenstreit* was vital ammunition against the German historicists and support for Robbins's claims. However, what Robbins retained within economics alongside neoclassicism was just one strain of 'Austrian' theory. As Anthony Endres (1997) has shown, 'Austrians' such as Friedrich von Wieser and Eugen von Böhm-Bawerk saw it as appropriate for economists to explore the formation of preferences, using insights from psychology and elsewhere. In fact, the Austrian school was not as narrow as Robbins contrived.

Robbins redrew the boundaries of the subject in a way that violated both of the broader Austrian and neoclassical traditions. Included within both these streams of thought were ideas and problematics that Robbins wished to place outside economics. Above all, leading neoclassical economists such as Marshall in Britain and John Bates Clark in America would not have subscribed to such a narrow definition of their discipline.

To succeed in defining institutionalism out of the discipline of economics, Robbins had to establish a new lineage for his ideas. To a significant degree, this had to draw upon the existing intellectual powerhouses of Britain, Germany, Austria and America. In Britain, Marshall could be cited, but only if his admiration for the German historical school could be overlooked. As noted in chapter 8 above, Robbins conveniently ignored Marshall's attention to the problem of historical specificity. Robbins managed to rewrite history, and to make Marshall his ally.

Robbins found a suitable emblem in the pioneering neoclassical economist Philip Wicksteed, and he edited his *Commonsense of Political Economy* (1933). Wicksteed defined an 'economic transaction' as one in which one party did not consider the welfare or desires of the other, merely the object of the transaction itself. This attempted narrowing of the domain of the 'economic' served Robbins's purposes.

The choice in Continental Europe was clear: Robbins chose the Austrian side in the German-speaking *Methodenstreit*. America, with its strong institutionalist tradition, was more of a problem. Robbins had to identify a leading American economist who seemed sufficiently close to him. But institutionalists dominated in that country. Among the well-known American economists, one of the best options was Frank Knight, but only if he could be repackaged as a neoclassical economist and his institutionalist sympathies could be obscured or forgotten.

Robbins thus contrived an Austro-neoclassical tradition, from Carl Menger through Philip Wicksteed to Frank Knight. This created a splendid Germanic-Anglo-American triad for Robbins's project. However, it ignored Knight's sympathies for institutionalism and the historical school, and his repeated view that 'utility is misleading as an explanation of economic behavior' (Knight, 1921b, p. 145). Furthermore, Knight was personally very uneasy about the role that Robbins foisted upon him. For instance, he rejected Robbins's insinuation that he had built upon the work of Wicksteed. He insisted in 1934: 'I never read the "Common Sense" until recently' (Knight, 1956, p. 104). When Knight reviewed Robbins's *Theory of Economic Policy* (1952) he objected to the 'pervasive *ad hominem* type of argument' (Knight, 1953, p. 290) in the book. In a reaction from Robbins's (1952, p. 40) depiction of the 'degrading mystique of historicism', Knight (1953, p. 280) jumped to the defence of the historical school: 'I must say that there is a vast amount of truth in historicism, and also that it affords a sorely needed corrective to the naïve utilitarian individualism of the English Classical economists.'

Despite Knight's remarks, Robbins eventually won the battle of ideas, and economics today follows more closely his methodological guidelines than those of Knight. The irony is that much of Knight's work would be excluded from the narrow definition of economics that Robbins established in the 1930s.

THE NATURE AND SIGNIFICANCE OF ECONOMIC SCIENCE

The basic thrust of Robbins's redefinition of economics is familiar to any student of the subject. What the student is unlikely to be told, however, is that this redefinition required the banishment of the two dominant and prestigious intellectual traditions, in Germany and America, to beyond the boundaries of the discipline.

In his 1932 *Essay*, Robbins criticised institutionalism and the German historical school – for failing to discover general economic laws. Robbins (1932, p. 114) wrote: 'not one single "law" deserving of the name, not one quantitative generalisation of permanent validity has emerged from their efforts.' Yet many institutionalists would be reluctant to admit that many 'generalisations of permanent validity' exist, due to the manifestly varied and changing nature of socio-economic reality. In doubting their existence, they should not be condemned outright for failing to discover them.

For Robbins, the economic problem was one of the allocation of scarce means in the pursuit of given ends. Individuals are assumed to have given utility functions and they exchange resources with each other to maximise their own utility. Such a framework universalises the concepts of 'exchange' and 'price'. It is purported that a wide range of social and economic phenomena, in all types of present, past and future economy, can be analysed in these terms, as long as they are afflicted with the seemingly ubiquitous problem of 'scarcity'. As Robbins (1932, p. 20) himself put it: 'The generalisations of the theory of value are as applicable to the behaviour of isolated man or the executive authority of a communist society, as to the behaviour of man in an exchange economy'. All differences between these systems are 'subsidiary to the main fact of scarcity'.

Robbins saw economics as the *a priori* exploration of deductions from the axioms of rational choice. In the old debate between induction and deduction, he came down on the side of the latter. He made grand claims for the scope of deductive economics: it would apply directly to the pressing problems of economic depression and unemployment. As the world was entering the Great Depression, Robbins (1932, pp. 104–5) conjectured optimistically in the first edition of his *Essay* that 'the despised apparatus of deductive theory' will prob- ably provide 'a complete solution of the riddle of depressions within the next few years'. He was clearly hopeful that a deductive general theory could solve the most pressing economic problems of his time. However, a short while later, it became clear to Robbins that this promise could not be delivered. This passage was removed from the second edition of 1935.

Although Robbins's book was not immediately an outstanding success, it eventually had a huge impact. When Paul Samuelson (1947, 1948) re-laid the foundations of postwar neoclassical economics and published his best-selling textbook, Robbins's definition of economics was adopted. The battle against historicism and institutionalism had been won – but more by act of definition than by force of theoretical argument or achievement.

RALPH SOUTER'S CRITIQUE

Ralph Souter's confrontations with both Talcott Parsons and Lionel Robbins have been mentioned in the preceding chapter. His critique of Robbins is discussed in more detail here. Contrary to Parsons and Robbins, Souter insisted that sharp boundaries between economics and the other social sciences could not be drawn. Referring to Robbins, Souter (1933b, p. 38–9) wrote:

> The idea seems to be that, after an initial and final taking over of an elementary modicum of alleged psychological or other facts from those neighbouring sciences, the economist can therefore proceed with his task in magnificent isolation. And this, it would seem, is possible because he has thereby equipped himself with at least the *general forms* of the demand and supply functions which he thereafter devotes himself to manipulating. . . . [But] it is quite impossible to seek to escape the indefinite and progressive inter-penetration of the 'boundaries' of economics into the 'territories' of all the neighbouring social sciences by alleging that the general forms of the demand and supply functions are ascernable without such exhaustive investigations.

This was very similar to a point made by Gustav von Schmoller (1900). Similarly, Souter argued for the integration, rather than the compartmentalisation, of the social sciences. Souter reviewed Robbins's *Nature and Significance of Economic Science* in the *Quarterly Journal of Economics* in 1933. This critical and perceptive review attacked the very principle of a separate domain of economic science. Souter (1933a, pp. 378–9) wrote of Robbins's work:

> it is somehow assumed that the 'analytical' method of 'defining' special disciplines in terms of their respective distinctive *attitudes* towards a common 'subject-matter' somehow or other justifies a particular science in erecting round itself barbed-wire entanglements which would be thoroly pernicious if erected in the name of a classificatory 'definition' in terms of *different* 'subject matters.' . . . It is in this way that 'economic science' miraculously juggles 'psychology' . . . over the wall and so obtain its 'independence.' . . . in the case of economic science this segregation by means of 'analytical definition' is effected by regarding 'economics' as a *purely formal science of implications*.

Hence Souter was resolutely hostile to Robbins's attempt to define economics in terms of the autonomous, deductive investigation of the relation between scarce means and given ends. In 1933, he perceived correctly that this would eventually lead to an economics most arid and formal. Souter (1933a, p. 387) argued that 'the really appalling danger lies in the inability of the economic formalists to understand that their abstractions cannot be made intelligible except through organic subordination to a concrete social and political philosophy.' The result, Souter (p. 385) argued perceptively, was that 'the abstract formalist, in pursuit of perfect formal precision, fails alike in precision and in formality.'

Souter examined some of the reasons for this failure. Prominent among them was the treatment of time and dynamic change. One the one hand: 'From the standpoint of instantaneous or timeless "statics" . . . rationality has no meaning. It is only when we explicitly introduce the category of Time . . . that the concept of formal rationality becomes intelligible' (Souter, 1933a, pp. 387–8.) On the other hand, however, time and change challenged the 'given' ends upon which Robbins wished to erect the whole of economic science: 'For in a "dynamic" world in which we live, the working out of the "implications" of "given" data itself changes the data' (Souter, 1933a, pp. 394–5).

Souter (1933b, p. 94 n.) thus argued for an 'enlightened and democratic "economic imperialism"' which would enrich both sociology and economics by a mutual fusion and interpenetration of ideas. As noted already, this version of 'economic imperialism' is very different from the modern doctrine of Gary Becker, Jack Hirshleifer and others, where it is held that all other disciplines should be subjugated by neoclassical economic theory.

UNIVERSALISM IN FRIEDRICH HAYEK'S ECONOMICS

On an invitation from Robbins, Friedrich Hayek came to the LSE in 1931, where he was elected to a chair. Although Hayek's theory was not so rationalist and deductivist as that of Robbins, he followed Robbins and his Austrian mentors by insisting that the starting point of economic theory was the supposedly universal features of the economic situation, rather than the essential features of any specific type of socio-economic system. Hayek criticised the historical school in the following terms:

> To start here at the wrong end, to seek for regularities of complex phenomena which could never be observed twice under identical conditions, could not but lead to the conclusion that there were no general laws, no inherent necessities determined by the permanent nature of the constituting elements, and that the only task of economic science in particular was a description of historical change. It was only with this abandonment of the appropriate methods of procedure, well established in the classical period, that it began to be thought that there were no other laws of social life than those made by men, that all observed phenomena were only the product of social or legal institutions, merely 'historical categories' and not in any way arising out of the basic economic problems which humanity has to face.
>
> (Hayek, 1935, p. 12)

Consider some relatively minor points first. Contrary to Hayek, there is no good reason why regularities should be absent in principle from complex systems (Cohen and Stewart, 1994). As a result, empirical observation of complex phenomena would not always fail to reveal regularities, nor necessarily lead to the false methodological claim that the sole task of economic science is description. Furthermore, modern students of complexity are aware that such regularities do not necessarily have to emanate from any presumed 'permanent nature of the constituting elements'.

More importantly, like Robbins, Hayek presumed that 'the basic economic problems which humanity has to face' were the universal dilemmas of choice and scarcity. Be that as it may, the focus on these universal phenomena gets us 'not very far' as Knight (1924, p. 229) had put it. Such a universal focus can tell us very little about specific institutions, such as private property and markets. Yet Hayek assumed that the 'basic economic problems' of choice and scarcity could be realised through the operation of markets and private property only. Attempting to reconcile his universal assumptions and his devotion to the specific institutions of property and markets, Hayek postulated that these institutions have existed, to some degree, since the dawn of humanity. This stance on the question of universal and historically specific phenomena persisted through Hayek's writings, despite some shifts in his methodological position.[3]

---

3 For discussions of Hayek's changing position see Caldwell (1988), Fleetwood (1995) and T. Lawson (1997).

For Hayek, the focus on universal assumptions was combined with a 'compositive' method of analysis, working from the individual to the whole. Much later, Hayek (1967, p. 72) wrote: 'the whole of economic theory . . . may be interpreted as nothing else but an endeavour to reconstruct from regularities of the individual actions the character of the resulting order.' However, if historically specific institutions or circumstances affect the 'regularities of the individual actions' then there is a case for examining these specifics, in addition to the deduction of 'the character of the resulting order'. In addition, human interaction depends on *prior* social structures, such as language, the family and the institutions of socialisation. Any attempt to explain these in terms of individual actions alone would involve an infinite regress. Because institutions such as language are required for all economic and social interaction, we can never, neither historically nor logically, arrive at an institution-free 'state of nature' (Field, 1979, 1981, 1984; Hodgson, 1998a). The same unresolved problem that arose in Carl Menger's attempt to build economics on exclusively individualist foundations recurred again in the work of Hayek.

In most of Hayek's writings the market appears as some vague, universal forum in which individual property owners collide. What Hayek failed to appreciate adequately was that the market itself is not a natural datum but a social institution, governed by sets of rules defining restrictions on some, and legitimating other, behaviours (Vanberg, 1986). Furthermore, the market is necessarily embedded in other social institutions such as the state, and is promoted, or even in some cases created, by conscious design. Given that markets are themselves institutions, then they may grow or decline like other institutions: they are not universal entities.

For much of his time at the LSE, Hayek's writings were preoccupied with his critique of planning and socialism. I have discussed these issues at length elsewhere (Hodgson, 1999a). Even here he could have benefited from the legacies of historicism and institutionalism. His incisive understanding of the market mechanism would have been further enhanced by the consideration of the institutional nature of markets. He could also have benefited from the discussion of the economic role of knowledge and the evolution of institutions in the writings of Thorstein Veblen. He could have also recognised that some elements of his criticism of socialist central planning were anticipated in the writings of some members of the German historical school, notably Albert Schäffle, Lujo Brentano and Erwin Nasse (Hutchison, 1953, pp. 293–8). But any positive mention of historicism or institutionalism would not have pleased Robbins. Although the theoretical approaches of Hayek and Robbins were quite different, what they shared was a common and deep hostility to institutionalism and the German historical school. For this reason, Hayek made little use of, or reference to, their works.

During the Second World War, the LSE was evacuated from its buildings in the centre of London and its offices were temporarily located in Cambridge. Hayek knew John Maynard Keynes well. But in theoretical terms they were permanent antagonists. When the *General Theory* appeared in 1936, the Robbins–Hayek grouping at the LSE was the chief British academic opposition to the rise of Keynesianism. Keynes is the subject of the next chapter. Hayek left the LSE for the University of Chicago in 1949. Later he was awarded the Nobel Prize in economics.[4]

CLEOPATRA'S NOSE

History is full of ironies. What if Cleopatra had not been so beautiful? The tale of love and war, involving Julius Caesar and Mark Anthony, might have been different. As another example, what if it not rained on that fateful night before Waterloo? The ground would have been drier and harder. Napoleon might have been able to move forward his artillery in the early morning, and destroy Wellington before the arrival of Blücher. What if Lenin had not arrived in St. Petersburg in 1917? The Bolshevik Revolution might not have occurred. These 'virtual histories' reveal that tremendous panoply of the potential, even greater than the rich and complex world of the actual.[5]

Given this, we may ask: what if Allyn Young had not died in 1929? Apparently, Young had decided before his death to quit his chair at the LSE and to return to the United States. Robbins might have got his chair anyway. But Young might have changed his mind, or he might have had a decisive influence in the appointment of his successor. If so, the story of the LSE and of British economics as a whole might have been very different. Robbins might not have climbed to power, Hayek may have never come to Britain, and a school of British institutionalists might have developed at the LSE. But it did not happen.

After retiring as LSE Director in 1937, Beveridge (1960, p. 92) wrote that Young 'was just the man to make economics as the Founders and I wished it to be'. However, he argued that after Young died, economics at the LSE took a wrong turning: 'The London School of Economics and Political Science, even after forty-two years, had not achieved the purposes for which Sidney and Beatrice Webb had brought it to birth' (Beveridge, 1960, p. 95). Beveridge desired an economics that was less deductive in character and more based on facts. Clearly this was an implied criticism of the direction in which Robbins had led economics at the LSE.

Of course, Young's death does not completely explain the demise of institutional economics at the LSE. Eventually, Robbins's 1932 *Essay* became popular, in both Britain and the United States. Almost certainly, the book would have been published even if Robbins had not achieved early promotion. It was endorsed by a rising generation of neoclassical economists, who became eager to redefine economics in Robbinsian terms. In any case, it was likely that the

---

4   As Hayek's theoretical position developed, and he emphasised rules and institutions more and more, his work acquired some analytical affinities with institutionalism (Boettke, 1989; Leathers, 1989, 1990; Rutherford, 1989; Samuels, 1989; Wynarczyk, 1992). However, Hayek never adequately acknowledged the problem of historical specificity, even in his later writings. Regrettably, he always dismissed '*historismus*' with disdain.
5   See Ferguson (1998) for historical scholarship in this area.

LSE would have succumbed to the growing forces of the postwar neoclassical revival. Nevertheless, Young's death accelerated a process that took much longer in other institutions. With the precocious rise of Robbins, the development of historicism and institutionalism was blocked at an early stage at the LSE.

While the *Methodenstreit* in Germany was still unresolved as late as the 1930s, Robbins and Hayek played a crucial role in rewarding Menger with an apparent victory. Two factors were critical. The first was the adoption of the Mengerian conception of the nature and role of economics by a number of scholars in the West. The departments of economics in two universities played a major role here. One was the LSE. Allied to this, as we have seen in the preceding chapter, was the migration of Talcott Parsons and Joseph Schumpeter to Harvard. Parsons brought with him Weber's endorsement of Menger's individualistic conception of theoretical economics. Schumpeter brought his own, very similar, views on the nature of economics and its relation to other disciplines. The second factor was the almost complete destruction of the German historical school in the 1933–45 period, as a result of fascism and war. Hence the victory of individualistic and ahistorical economics was as much a result of political and institutional events as of persuasive argument.

By comparison, things were very different at nearby Cambridge. From the beginning, Marshall's conception of the role and scope of economics was significantly different from that of Menger. The role of John Maynard Keynes was also crucial. Just as the neoclassical reign of Robbins succeeded the critical institutionalism of Young, Keynes in Cambridge was establishing himself as the leading theorist of a distinctive approach. Compared with the LSE, from the 1930s to the 1970s, Cambridge had a reputation of dissent from the mainstream tradition of economic thought. Part of the Cambridge story is related in the next chapter.

15

JOHN MAYNARD KEYNES AND HIS DECLARATION OF A *GENERAL THEORY*

> Time is a device to prevent everything happening at once, space is
> a device to prevent it all happening in Cambridge.
> (A paraphrase – attributed to Dharma Kumar
> – of Joan Robinson)

Keynes was a product of his Cambridge surroundings. His father wrote a major
treatise on the methodology of economics. Educated initially in mathematics and
philosophy, his move towards economics placed him under the influence of the
Cambridge Marshallian tradition.

As we have seen in chapter 8, Alfred Marshall had explicitly recognised the
importance and significance of the German historical school. Marshall had also
urged John Neville Keynes to immerse himself in the Austro-German literature
on the *Methodenstreit*. However, after Marshall's retirement in 1908, economists
at the University of Cambridge paid dwindling attention to the German historical
school. Strikingly, John Maynard – Neville's son – paid them little regard.
Maynard Keynes followed Marshall in attempting a general theory but with none
of Marshall's acknowledgement of the problem of historical specificity. Apart
from occasional positive citations of Georg Knapp's (1924) theory of money, there
are very few other references to either the German historical school or to
American institutionalism in Maynard Keynes's works. Overall, and unlike his
predecessors, Keynes made little reference to the German historical school and
he seemed largely unaware of its contribution. In Keynes's *Collected Works* as a
whole, there are only two minor footnote references to works of Gustav von
Schmoller and no reference whatsoever to Werner Sombart.[1]

Keynes candidly admitted (1930, vol. 1, p. 199 n.) that his knowledge of the
German language was 'poor'. But this fact alone cannot explain his minimal
engagement with other schools of thought overseas. It would have been possible

---

1 Keynes had encouraged the translation of Knapp's work into English and he referred to it
  approvingly in his own *Treatise on Money* (Keynes, 1930). Of course, Keynes was more familiar
  with some of the members of the British historical school, particularly those who were friends or
  acquaintances of Marshall. Among these, most notably, was Foxwell. Keynes (1972) wrote a
  lengthy obituary on Foxwell in the *Economic Journal* in 1936.

to obtain linguistic help and to make a determined effort to obtain knowledge of a substantial, thriving and long-lasting community of social scientists situated across the North Sea, just a few hundred miles to the east of Cambridge. Indeed, at least for any economist writing before the Second World War, some knowledge of the German contribution to economics was a scholarly requirement, and not a mere option.

Furthermore, to the west across the Atlantic, institutional economics was then a substantial force in America. In this case there was no language barrier. Nevertheless, there is no evidence to suggest that Maynard Keynes was generally familiar with the works of leading American institutionalists. Keynes never referred in his writings to Thorstein Veblen. He was most acquainted with the ideas of Wesley Mitchell. Keynes (1930) cited Mitchell's work on business cycles several times in his *Treatise on Money*. In May and June 1934 he met Mitchell in New York City and received an honorary doctorate at Columbia University (Keynes, 1973a, p. 456; 1982, p. 320). Despite this, Keynes failed to mention Mitchell in his *General Theory*.

Keynes briefly referred to John Commons. In a talk and in an essay both written in 1925, Keynes (1931, pp. 303–4; 1981, p. 438) acknowledged Commons as an 'eminent American economist' and expressed agreement with Commons's idea that history had passed through 'the era of scarcity' followed by 'the period of abundance' in the nineteenth century and the 'period of stabilisation' in the twentieth. In 1927, Commons sent Keynes one of his short articles on 'Price Stabilization and the Federal Reserve System' (Commons, 1927). As a result, Keynes wrote to John Commons on 26 April 1927: 'Judging from limited evidence and at great distance, there seems to be no other economist with whose general way of thinking I find myself in such genuine accord.' However, the influence of Commons on Keynes was slight at best, for there is no evidence that Keynes turned a single page of such key works as *The Legal Foundations of Capitalism* (1924) or *Institutional Economics* (1934). Robert Skidelsky's (1992, p. 229) description of Commons as 'an important, if unacknowledged influence on Keynes' is an unwarranted exaggeration. The evidence of influence simply concerns Commons's highly questionable scheme of historical periodisation, which for some strange reason Keynes briefly found attractive.[2]

Many other economists who came into contact with Keynes were more aware of the historicist and institutionalist legacy. While Keynes was editor of the *Economic Journal* – from 1912 to 1945 – he saw the publication of a substantial number of articles, notes and reviews that cited the works of leading historicists and institutionalists of his day. Yet Keynes paid relatively little attention to these cited works.[3]

---

2   The idea that history had passed through 'the era of scarcity' followed by 'the period of abundance' and the 'period of stabilisation' is found in Commons (1934a, pp. 773–88). It is not clear how Keynes got sight of an earlier draft of these ideas. Keynes's letter to Commons is found in the Commons Papers, State Historical Society of Wisconsin, 1982. It is quoted in Skidelsky (1992, p. 229) and Whalen (1993, pp. 1175–6).

3   In the complete years from 1912 to 1944 inclusive – while the journal was under Keynes's editorship – the following names were cited by other authors in articles, notes or reviews in the

Joan Robinson (1973, p. ix) famously complained that Keynes 'never managed to read Marx'. This was a serious defect for a theorist of the contemporary economic system. However, the omissions go further. Remarkably, in the *General Theory* – his most important and by far his most widely read book – there are no references in the index to leading institutionalists or historicists such as Commons, Knapp, List, Mitchell, Schmoller, Sombart, Veblen or Weber. Schumpeter also receives no mention. Apparently, their ideas played little part in the development of Keynes's theory.[4]

From a policy point of view, Keynes found many kindred voices in other countries. Yet he made inadequate reference to economists, in Germany as well as the United States, who argued long before 1936 that the stimulation of effective demand was the key to economic recovery from the Depression. In the United States, for example, the idea of using public works to revive the economy and reduce unemployment was widespread among economists by 1935 (J. R. Davis, 1971). Yet these American ideas had little impact on Keynes's writing. Language barriers alone cannot explain Keynes's neglect of closely related intellectual developments elsewhere.[5]

Remarkably, as George Garvy (1975) and Jürgen Backhaus (1985) have shown, in Weimar Germany there was a substantial group of economists – including Sombart – who had developed a sophisticated argument for increased public spending to combat recession. As Backhaus (1985) demonstrates, Sombart's views on this matter were grounded in his theoretical analysis of modern capitalism. Again, this had little impact on Keynes. Overall, as Garvy (1975, p. 393) argued, Keynes was a product of a relatively insular academic environment:

Economic Journal: Commons (30), Mitchell (133), Schmoller (69), Sombart (89), Veblen (39), Weber (104). (The number in brackets is the number of items in which each name appears.) However, none of these names is cited in the *General Theory*. In contrast to Keynes, many contributors to the *Economic Journal* believed that the ideas of these leading institutionalists and historicists were of sufficient interest to be worthy of citation.

4   The omission of Mitchell from the *General Theory* is particularly striking, as he had helped to lay the foundations of national income accounting – a practical requirement for the operationalisation of Keynes's macroeconomic principles (Hodgson, 1999b). However, in the *General Theory* there are singular references to two American institutionalists – Knight and Kuznets – and a substantial acknowledgement of the work of the English historicist and institutionalist Hobson. Nevertheless, by comparison, the following economists received multiple references in the *General Theory*: Cassell, Edgeworth, George, Hawtrey, Hayek, Jevons, Kahn, Malthus, Mandeville, Marshall, Mill, von Mises, Petty, Pigou, Ricardo, Robbins, D. H. Robertson, Say and Smith. This number of citations to other authors would refute the defence that Keynes rarely cited institutionalists and historicists because he rarely cited anyone. Mere citation is a blunt bibliographic measure, but there is clear evidence here of a relative neglect of historicism and institutionalism.

5   From the 1920s on, Keynes declared that a policy of free trade was unrealisable and undesirable. Against him, Robbins was one of the leading academic advocates of free trade. In responding to Keynes in the *New Statesman and Nation* on 4 April 1931, Robbins described: 'The shades of a million dead parrots – the much bewhiskered *historismus* of the past – rise up and hail him [Keynes] as a brother, "recognized at last"' (quoted in Koot, 1987, p. 210). Ironically and unfortunately, Keynes was unable to transform this into a useful compliment and to use the plentiful arguments of the historicists against Robbins. Furthermore – unlike the inert parrot of *Monty Python* fame – the flock of 'dead parrots' described by Robbins was far from deceased at the time.

A simple answer to the question why *General Theory* was written in an intellectual vacuum can be given by referring to the well-known isolation of Cambridge economists within the proverbial insularity of Great Britain. . . . Keynes read little of what contemporary economists had to say . . . [n]or did he dig deeply into the wealth of ideas and analyses of the preceding generations of economists. He largely ignored the contributions of his contemporaries (and the generations preceding them) who published in languages other than English.

To what extent can the insularity of Keynes's intellectual environment explain these defects of omission? Significantly, Marshall was also at Cambridge but he referred repeatedly to leading German economists. However, the Cambridge intellectual atmosphere seemed to change after Marshall's retirement in 1908. His successor Arthur Pigou kept the Marshallian intellectual legacy alive but failed to sustain the momentum of Marshall's curricular innovations and reforms. Pigou was a notoriously shy recluse and had 'a total lack of administrative capacity' (Groenewegen, 1995, p. 755). Crucially, he had no apparent knowledge of, or interest in, the German historicist legacy. With the exception of a positive review of Wesley Mitchell's 1913 work on *Business Cycles* (Pigou, 1914), Pigou made no significant mention of historicism or institutionalism. Overall, despite his own achievements, Pigou was less careful than Marshall in reminding others of the qualified and provisional nature of all economic theory. Although Pigou himself made a major contribution, much of this was completed before 1920. In the 1920s, Cambridge economics seemed to rest on its laurels. Keynes himself was largely responsible for the revival of economics at the university. As Robert Skidelsky (1992, p. 286) put it, following the publication of Keynes's *Treatise on Money* (1930), 'Cambridge economics was coming to life after its long war-induced slumber.'

Keynes had the luck and the brilliance to write the most prominent and important economics text that provided a theoretical justification for government interventions to raise the level of employment in the 1930s. He also played a major role in the planning of the new international economic institutions that were to emerge after the Second World War. Accordingly, the term 'Keynesian' became associated with a number of theoretical and policy ideas, some of which in fact pre-date the *General Theory*. Keynes's outstanding volume codified the macroeconomic ideas of the postwar consensus. It became the bible of macroeconomic theory. However, as a result, the silences and omissions of the *General Theory* became the amnesia of postwar generations of economists and policy makers.[6]

Hence, despite the enormous importance and value of his contribution, Keynes was to play an unwitting role in the Great Forgetting that was to afflict economics

---

6 For a discussion of the historical and institutional context of the rise of Keynesianism see Winch (1969). It is not the intention of this chapter to undermine the importance and genuine value of Keynes's contribution. Elsewhere, however, I have criticised Keynes's overly rationalist conception of action and his neglect of the influence of the historically specific past on the decision making processes of the agent (Hodgson, 1988, ch. 10).

in the years to come. Keynes's work was both a symptom and an additional cause of the abandonment of the heritage of historicism and institutionalism in economics after the Second World War. Of course, Keynes's negative role in this respect must be put alongside his major and revolutionary achievements in economics. Nevertheless, his abandonment of historicism and institutionalism had effects that hitherto have been unappreciated, and it is necessary to discuss them here.

Keynes is rightly credited with furthering a global revolution in economic thought, which radicalised the whole approach to macroeconomic theory and policy. However, the crucial historicist lacuna in his knowledge, combined with his own admiration for general theorising, was eventually to help to obliterate both institutionalism and the historical school from the memories of both mainstream and dissident economists.

HOW GENERAL IS THE *GENERAL THEORY*?

Analytically, we focus on just one aspect of Keynes's contribution. Despite the gigantic secondary literature on Keynes and Keynesianism, it has rarely been discussed. Yet Keynes himself attributed to it much importance. Very near to the beginning of his *General Theory* he wrote:

> I have called this book the *General Theory of Employment, Interest and Money*, placing the emphasis on the prefix *general*. . . . I shall argue that the postulates of the classical theory are applicable to a special case only and not to the general case, the situation which it assumes being a limiting point of the possible positions of equilibrium. Moreover, the characteristics of the special case assumed by the classical theory happen not to be those of the economic society in which we actually live, with the result that its teaching is misleading and disastrous if we attempt to apply it to the facts of experience.
>
> (Keynes, 1936, p. 3)

The first chapter of the *General Theory* consists solely of the single paragraph from which the above quotation is taken. Here Keynes was playing a double rhetorical game. First, the term 'general theory' was used to create a contrast with the special theory of the 'classical' economists. Keynes made the convincing argument that the 'classical' theory was a 'special case': it pertained to a special and limited set of possible outcomes. Keynes enlarged on this point throughout the *General Theory*, arguing that the 'classical' theory encompassed neither uncertainty nor disequilibria. He wanted a 'general theory' that could explain such phenomena.

There is a crucial ambiguity in the above quotation. According to one possible interpretation, Keynes was seeking a theory that could explain more adequately the possible outcomes in *one given type* of 'economic society'. Such a theory would be more general and satisfactory than one that explained less. However, such a theory might not be general in the sense that it could lead to adequate explanations of phenomena pertaining to *other types* of 'economic society'. In the terms introduced in chapter 2, Keynes in the above passage might have sought explanations that were more general in an intensive rather than in an extensive sense. The claim made there by Keynes was that his 'general' theory could embrace and explain more phenomena within the single 'economic society in which we actually live'.

However, as shown below, Keynes also made extensive claims about the generality of his theory. He also claimed in the same work that his theory had sufficient generality to apply to several different types of 'economic society', by virtue of its supposed foundation on universal 'psychological laws'.

If the 'economic society in which we live' is different in one or more important respects from other socio-economic systems, then an attempt at an extensive general theory, embracing all or several such systems, might have difficulty including every possibility. The complexity of reality can place limits on the detailed explanatory power of any general theory. The pursuit of a general theory always involves simplification and loss of specific details. The danger is that we may fail to identify the particular mechanisms that were relatively more important at a specific historical juncture. Keynes did not seem to recognise this dilemma. He did not acknowledge that by trying to make a theory more general we may make it less able to focus on the important aspects of the 'economic society in which we live' and less able to design effective policies to deal with economic problems.

In economics, a theory with sufficient explanatory power would have to focus on the key economic relations and processes that were of importance in understanding the nature and behaviour of the system in question. Keynes did not consider that a theory with substantial explanatory power, that applied to the 'economic society in which we live', might have to be a special theory. Indeed, a 'general theory' might under-emphasise some of the historically specific features of the economic system and the causes of the prevailing unemployment of the 1930s. Keynes overlooked the possibility that a special theory could use some assumptions concerning economic institutions that were limited to a historically specific domain of analysis, and end up with much greater explanatory power.

Keynes was concerned to criticise those 'classical' theories that claimed to show that markets would clear and the economy would automatically reach a full-employment equilibrium. But the fact that Keynes clearly considered disequilibria, and other equilibria below full employment, was not enough to make his theory truly *general*. There were other types of system – such as economies without money – that in fact had no place in Keynes's theory. The classical theory is not general, in part because it assumes price flexibility, excludes radical uncertainty and under-estimates the role of money as a store of value and means of dealing with an uncertain future. Nor, for different reasons, is the *General Theory*. While Keynes dropped several of the classical assumptions, he imposed other restrictive conditions. For instance he assumed a monetary economy, without extensive barter, where money plays a special role. While Keynes made his theory more general with one move, he made it less general with another. Overall, it is difficult to say whether the classical or the Keynesian theory is more general. And if one theory is more general that would not necessarily mean that it is a better theory.

In addition, Keynes did little in explicit terms to ground his theory upon historically specific economic institutions. Although institutions, such as the joint stock company and the stock exchange, inevitably protrude into his narrative, he did not start from the specific institutions of capitalist society and then develop a theory that illuminated their principal causal processes and relations. Instead, Keynes (1936, pp. 246–7) appealed repeatedly to 'fundamental psychological factors' as the foundation for his theory. His invocation of supposed psychological factors in his discussion of economic processes is more prominent than any discussion of historically specific institutions. Specific institutions appear casually in the *General Theory* as the mechanisms through which seemingly ahistorical psychological forces express their power. Keynes attempted to develop a 'general theory' that would apply to a number of different types of socio-economic system. He conceived of this general theory as having a universal and psychological foundation.

A striking piece of further evidence confirms this verdict. As Bertram Schefold (1980) has shown, in his 1936 Preface to the German edition of the *General Theory*, Keynes made the following extraordinary but symptomatic argument:

> This is one of the reasons which justify my calling my theory a *General* theory. Since it is based on less narrow assumptions than the orthodox theory, it is also more easily applied to a large area of different circumstances.[7]

According to Keynes, his *General Theory* applied not only to the 'Anglo-Saxon countries . . . where laissez-faire still prevails' but also to countries with strong 'national leadership' such as Nazi Germany. He made this statement on the basis that his analysis was not based on specific institutions but allegedly on 'the theory of psychological laws relating consumption and saving'. Hence Keynes clearly claimed that his theory was not based on historically specific institutions but on general 'psychological laws'. But Keynes gave little guidance on the psychological literature from which these supposed laws were derived.[8]

---

7   Davidson's (1996) translation of this passage is slightly different. In particular, he translates *weniger enge Voraussetzungen* as 'fewer restrictive assumptions' instead of 'less narrow assumptions'. Both translations are possible, but in personal correspondence Schefold has given reasons why his version is to be preferred. We are unlikely to determine Keynes's intended meaning in more precise terms, because the preface was translated into German from a draft by Keynes, which the editor condensed and has since been lost.

8   Schefold (1980) pointed out that, with the exception of the statement concerning 'the theory of psychological laws', the above words were excluded from the English translation of Keynes's preface to the German edition, in his *Collected Works*, vol. 7. Notably, Davidson (1996) quoted and endorsed the key words from the 'missing' passage quoted here. Hutchison (1981, pp. 261–2) has indicated, however, that in the preface to the French edition of the *General Theory*, Keynes made yet another claim, that his theory was also general in the sense that it applied to the general behaviour 'of the economic system as a whole'.

Furthermore, Keynes did not in fact deliver what he had promised: a general theory. Keynes did make some universal statements. In particular, he stressed aspects of human psychology. But he could not show how psychological propensities worked out in practice except by introducing an explicit or implicit institutional framework. Human psychology had to play out its part on some specific institutional stage. It had to be applied to quite specific institutional structures, such as to financial markets, state money and legal contracts. Hence the famous discussion of the psychology of speculation in chapter 12 of the *General Theory* requires a specific type of institutional framework, principally the stock market. Other parts of the book, such as Keynes's theory of money or interest have a greater degree of generality, although these are not universal to all types of human society. Again they refer to historically specific phenomena.

Consider the specific economic phenomena to which Keynes referred in the title of his book. Even here he did not fulfil the promise of a general theory. The work did not provide a general theory of the nature and level of employment in all past, present or possible human societies. What Keynes analysed was the quite specific relationships in modern capitalism between employment, expectations and effective demand. Rather than providing a truly general theory of interest or money, Keynes explored the quite specific, capitalist type of system in which 'money is the drink which stimulates the system to activity' (Keynes, 1936, p. 173). Money has existed for thousands of years but it did not become such an elixir of production until the rise of modern capitalism. Keynes favoured the 'general theory' rhetoric but always ended up exploring the particular circumstances of the contemporary capitalist system. Absent in the *General Theory* is a truly general theory of employment, interest or money.

In sum, Keynes claimed generality but relied upon the historically specific institutions of modern capitalism. Overall, one wonders why Keynes was inclined to use and emphasise the 'general theory' phrase. He could have easily and concisely called his book *A Theory of Employment, Interest and Money*. The intellectual mood of the times may have been a factor. It may help to explain why Keynes aimed to develop a 'general theory' and neglected the problem of historical specificity. Albert Einstein had developed 'the general theory of relativity'.[9] Physics and biology were both basking in the illuminations of Einstein, Darwin and others, and seemingly making great strides towards the conceptual unification of each discipline. Similarly, in these 'years of high theory' (Shackle, 1967) economists were also striving towards a grand, synthetic explanation of the underlying forces of economic recovery and growth.

---

9 Keynes and Einstein met in Berlin in 1926. Hsieh and Ye (1992) and Skidelsky (1992) have both suggested that Einstein inspired Keynes. Galbraith (1996) made a case that the *General Theory* was Einsteinian rather than Newtonian in its assumptions because Keynes broke from 'Newtonian reductionism and his space-time dichotomy, as both were reflected in the classical economics'. Instead 'Keynes sought to disestablish the absolute space of classical markets, and to end the separation of markets from the world of money'. This does not alter the fact that physics deals with physical constants and laws of nature that are fixed, whereas the subject-matter of economics evolves and changes through history. Even if the Einsteinian parallel has substance, it is does not sustain the possibility of an entirely 'general theory' in the domain of economics.

Notably, Keynes did show some awareness of the philosophical basis of the problem of historical specificity. In a letter to Roy Harrod dated 4 July 1938, Keynes (1973b, p. 296) wrote:

> Economics is the science of thinking in terms of models joined to the art of choosing models which are relevant to the contemporary world. It is compelled to do this, because, unlike the typical natural science, the material to which it is applied is, in too many respects, not homogeneous through time.

However, there is an inconsistency in Keynes's work. In the above letter he implied that economic theory must be related to historically specific material. Yet the *General Theory* was attempted on the basis of universal 'psychological laws'. If Keynes had been aware of the vast historical school literature, which had tried to develop economics in full awareness that economies are 'not homogeneous through time', then he would have been less likely to attempt an entirely *general* theory.

Any analysis in economics that engages with reality is bound to make some assumptions about the institutional make-up of society. The *General Theory* was no exception. But the reckless striving for generality relegates specific institutions to the background, whereas they ought to occupy the centre of the stage. There is not much discussion in the *General Theory* of specific economic institutions that are, in fact, indispensable to his argument. For example, Keynes was concerned to examine the nature of the wage bargain, and the relation between real and money wages. But the institutions of the labour market and employment are not discussed in any depth. In this respect, Keynes attempted the impossible: to draw quite specific conclusions from a theory that purported to be general.

This pretence of generality has widely afflicted economics for much of the twentieth century. Because of Keynes, many of his followers have attempted general theories as well. On the other hand, some post-Keynesians have stressed the importance of history and specific economic institutions, so that the rhetoric of general theorising has been implicitly undermined.

For example, Victoria Chick (1986) has shown that standard assumptions of monetary theory are specific to the financial institutions involved. As these institutions evolve through time, different theoretical principles can pertain. In particular, the nature of money itself changes, from precious metal, to bank deposits, to data in computer memories. Chick argued that because of the institutional realities of pre-industrial capitalism, saving necessarily preceded investment. Subsequently, as soon as banks were able to create credit, saving no longer had to precede investment. As the banking system evolved it enhanced the capacity for the banks to create credit. Hence, by the 1920s and the time of Keynes, banking institutions and the credit system had evolved to the point that investment could and would precede saving. This was the quite specific historic period to which the allegedly *General Theory* applied. Subsequently, as Chick pointed out in her paper, financial institutions have developed further, with massive global speculation in a variety of financial assets. This may mean that Keynesian analyses and remedies can to some extent become obsolete.

Chick's argument underlines the fact that the *General Theory* was not, in truth, a general theory but it applied to a historically specific set of capitalist institutions. Like Chick, other Post Keynesians have explicitly centred their analysis on historically specific institutions. What has been largely unnoticed, however, is the implication that the professedly general theoretical status of the *General Theory* is likely to be undermined as a result.

JOHN MAYNARD KEYNES, JOSEPH SCHUMPETER AND ECONOMIC POLICY

In his extended and generous obituary of Keynes, Schumpeter (1946, p. 514) wrote of the *General Theory*:

> But there is one word in the book that cannot be defended on these lines – the word 'general.' Those emphasizing devices – even if quite unexceptionable in other respects – cannot do more than individuate very special cases. Keynesians might hold that these special cases are the actual ones of our age. They cannot hold more than that.

Schumpeter thus criticised Keynes for propounding a theory that claimed to be general but in fact was not. Similarly, in his earlier review of the *General Theory*, Schumpeter noted the contrast between Keynes's claim to provide a general theory and his keenness to promote specific economic policies. Schumpeter (1936, p. 792) claimed that Keynes had adopted the 'Ricardian' practice of claiming highly specific policies from an allegedly general theory:

> Mr. Keynes underlines the significance of the words 'General Theory' in his title. . . . But . . . everywhere he really pleads for a definite policy. . . . It is, however, vital to renounce communion with any attempt to revive the Ricardian practice of offering, in the garb of general scientific truth, advice which – whether good or bad – carries meaning only with reference to the practical exigencies of the unique historical situation of a given time and country.

This is a valid criticism. Schumpeter (1954, p. 1171) dubbed this defect 'the Ricardian vice'. He thus alleged a parallel between Ricardo and Keynes: 'Keynes . . . was Ricardo's peer also in that his work is a striking example of . . . the Ricardian Vice, namely, the habit of piling a heavy load of practical conclusions upon a tenuous groundwork.'

Schumpeter (1946, p. 514 n.) also noted that Oskar Lange in 1938 had 'paid due respect to the only truly general theory ever written – the theory of Léon Walras'. Lange (1938, p. 20) had argued that 'both the Keynesian and the traditional theory of interest are but two limiting cases of what may be regarded to be the general theory of interest . . . the essentials of this general theory are contained already in the work of Walras.' Later Schumpeter (1954, p. 1082) mistakenly declared Keynes's *General Theory* to be 'a special case of the genuinely general theory of Walras'. Clearly, Schumpeter too was beguiled by the lure of a general theory. That is one reason why he praised Walras throughout his life. Schumpeter rightly pointed out that the *General Theory* was not truly general. Schumpeter's persuasive criticism of Keynes was that instead of attempting to derive specific policies solely from a theory that claimed to be general, Keynes should have analysed a historically specific situation. His unpersuasive criticism of Keynes was that the *General Theory* was not general enough.

Schumpeter's invocation of Walras as a general theorist was also questionable. Contrary to Schumpeter, Walrasian theory is not general. Walras made restrictive assumptions in his model, by excluding out-of-equilibrium trading, for instance (Bertrand, 1883; De Vroey, 1998). It has been admitted by leading practitioners of Walrasian theory – such as Kenneth Arrow (1986) and Frank Hahn (1980) – that it fails to incorporate key phenomena, such as time and money.

Although some of Schumpeter's criticisms of Keynes were on target, others were not. In particular, Schumpeter's attempt to put Keynes in the same camp as Ricardo is misleading. Although Keynes tried to draw out specific policies from something masquerading as a 'general theory', he did this in a manner very different from that of Ricardo. Ricardo was a deductivist theorist *par excellence*. Keynes preferred the more tentative and empirically informed theorising of Malthus and others.

The genuine defect that Schumpeter recognised was that Keynes simultaneously revered a 'general theory' and attempted to derive quite specific policy conclusions from such an edifice. For instance, the scope for governmental management of the level of effective demand would depend crucially on the economic institutions in a particular country and the nature and extent of its engagement with world markets. An entirely 'general theory' can tell us little of these vital but specific details. In this respect, Schumpeter's criticism hit home. It might be possible to regard Keynes's work as a framework for viable analyses that addressed such specific circumstances, but Keynes himself did not lay down guidelines for the development of historically sensitive theories.

THE POSTWAR TRIUMPH OF 'GENERAL THEORY'

Keynes's theory triumphed, at first by capturing, by the end of the 1930s, the two great Anglo-American academic bastions of Harvard and Cambridge. This was an impressive achievement and did a great deal to establish for Keynes a global and deserved reputation. Yet Harvard had been the centre of resistance against interwar institutionalism in the United States. And Cambridge had forgotten the historicist background to its earlier, Marshallian revolution. The price of victory was indeed very dear. Cambridge insularity and Harvard neoclassicism were legitimised. Consequently, the manner and locations of the Keynesian triumph helped to obliterate the memories of historicism and institutionalism on a global scale.

The subsequent story of how the economics of Keynes was transformed and vulgarised into postwar 'Keynesianism' is well known. Like Marshall before him, Keynes was highly critical of the abuse of mathematical and formal methods.[10] Despite this, the rising general of mathematical economists hijacked some of his ideas. Influential academic contributions – including those from Alvin Hansen and Paul Samuelson in America, and Roy Harrod and John Hicks in England – helped to create a mathematical 'Keynesian' system.

Alongside this so-called 'Keynesian general theory', Walrasian micro-economics became widely accepted in the 1940s, particularly as the result of the work of John Hicks (1939) in the UK and Paul Samuelson (1947, 1948) in the USA. As a result, 'general equilibrium theory' became the core of microeconomic analysis.

The attraction of the new 'Keynesian' macroeconomics was partly its claim to generality, partly its technocratic lure, and partly because of its apparent policy solutions to the pressing economic problems of the day. For a rising generation of technocratic economists, the synthesis of Walrasian general equi-librium theory with the Keynesian macroeconomic 'general theory' was all very appealing.

Although Keynes attacked the equilibrium theorising found in the classical and neoclassical traditions, his own announcement of a 'general theory' struck a chord among the rising generation of mathematical, Walrasian economists. If he had addressed the problem of historical specificity and eschewed the 'general theory' label, then the notorious postwar synthesis in economics would have been more difficult to achieve. Hence Keynes must take a small part of the blame for the incorporation of 'Keynesianism' into the postwar, neoclassical, textbook synthesis of microeconomics and macroeconomics.

There were justified protests from some Keynesians that Walrasian micro-economics was incompatible with Keynesian macroeconomics, but the phrases 'general theory' and 'general equilibrium theory' have two out of three words in common. While the word 'general' in 'general equilibrium theory' applies to the word 'equilibrium' rather than 'theory', general equilibrium theorists used the rhetoric and appeal of general theorising. A mathematicised 'general theory' in macroeconomics was placed alongside a mathematical 'general equilibrium theory' as its microeconomic complement. The rhetorical battle was won. As Terence Hutchison (1981, p. 249) put it: 'Keynes's work was treated as, and indeed largely re-established, *general* macroeconomic theory, as complementary with general microeconomic theory.'

The effect of this 'general theory' rhetoric in the literature in economics was dramatic. Prior to 1936, among the leading Anglo-American journals in

---

10 In his letter to Roy Harrod of 16 July 1938, Keynes (1973b, p. 299) wrote: 'In economics . . . to convert a model into a quantitative formula is to destroy its usefulness as an instrument of thought.' For more on Keynes's critical views of econometrics and mathematical modelling see Moggridge (1992, pp. 621–3).

economics, the phrase 'general theory' appeared in the title of two articles only.[11] A few book titles or subtitles carried the phrase, as in Knut Wicksell's *Lectures* (1934). After the appearance of the *General Theory*, these two words appeared in a stream of articles themselves discussing Keynes's book. Subsequently, there appeared a steady flow of mainstream books and articles, each claiming to construct a 'general theory' of some kind or another.[12]

General theorising became the vogue, in economics and elsewhere. Under the leadership of Talcott Parsons, sociology had already taken this road. At an even more abstract level, 'general systems theory' attempted a general theory of all human and non-human systems (Bertalanffy, 1950). In the United States, the Society for General Systems Research was founded in 1954.

Of course, Keynes was not responsible for all these outcomes. Nor were they all of negative worth. It is argued in this book that there is a role for general theorising in the social sciences and much can be learned from systems theory and other developments. The problem was that Keynes's use of the 'general theory' term to analyse what were highly specific historical circumstances helped to obliterate all consideration of the problem of historical specificity from economics. Furthermore, it helped to create the postwar synthesis between neoclassical general equilibrium theory and postwar macroeconomics.

Because of his influence and brilliance, Keynes was a bridge between the interwar and the post-1945 eras. He was associated with postwar policies that were designed to avoid a repetition of the Depression of the 1930s. This span between the interwar and postwar epochs was adorned with his name and shaped by his rhetoric. However, the historicists of Germany and the institutionalists of America were barred entry to the new era. They also became lost from the rewritten history of ideas.

As well as giving unintended succour to the rising neoclassical generation, Keynes's use of the 'general theory' phrase also hindered the critics of mainstream economics. Those heterodox economists, attempting to keep the radical theoretical message of Keynes alive, were also diverted from the problem of historical specificity. This was no less true at Cambridge itself. From the 1940s to the 1980s, Keynes's followers dominated the Faculty of Economics at Cambridge. Nicholas Kaldor, Joan Robinson and Piero Sraffa contributed to the reputation of Cambridge as an international centre for heterodox economics. Despite some significant and enduring recognition of the importance of history and institutions, the particular theoretical and methodological problem of historical specificity

---

11 This search of article titles was done on the JSTOR internet database of leading economics journals. The two pre-1936 articles are Zinn (1927) and Knight (1928a). Among journals of economics prior to 1936, the JSTOR database covers the *Quarterly Journal of Economics* (1886), the *Economic Journal* (1891), the *Journal of Political Economy* (1892), the *American Economic Review* (1911), the *Review of Economics and Statistics* (1919), *Econometrica* (1933) and the *Review of Economic Studies* (1934). (The year of foundation and first inclusion is given in brackets.)

12 For example, Wald (1947), Isard (1949), Hansson (1952), Mishan (1952), Pen (1952), Lipsey and Lancaster (1956), Chamberlin (1957), Debreu (1959), Lange (1965), Harsanyi (1966), Vanek (1966, 1970), Arrow and Hahn (1971), Olson (1986), Day (1987), Ghiselin (1987), Harsanyi and Selten (1988), Lindenberg (1990), Rosser (1991), Woo (1992).

was largely forgotten. Recognition of the importance of history, or even of historically specific institutions, does not amount to recognition of the analytical problem of historical specificity. What the post-Marshall Cambridge theorists failed to address adequately was the methodological problem of building theories that related explicitly to specific historical and institutional circumstances.

Crucially, the legacy of historicism and institutionalism remained largely untouched at Cambridge. Kaldor continued to emphasise the influence of his teacher, Allyn Young, but made little of the fact that Young was a product of a substantial American institutionalist tradition. Long after its heyday, Joan Robinson stumbled belatedly across some remnants of American institutionalism. In her book *Economic Philosophy* (1964, pp. 103–7) there is a positive appraisal of Clarence Ayres's *Theory of Economic Progress* (1944). In about 1970 she came across Veblen's (1919, pp. 185–200) critique of neoclassical capital theory and concluded that Veblen was 'the most original economist born and bred in the USA' (Robinson, 1979, p. 95). It is a pity that earlier generations of students of economics at Cambridge were not pointed in this direction. It is ironic that a university that makes so much of tradition, made so little use of the long and established intellectual traditions that were at hand.[13]

'POST KEYNESIANISM'

When Joan Robinson, Paul Davidson, Sidney Weintraub and Alfred Eichner worked together in the early 1970s to establish an anti-neoclassical stream of economic thought, they chose the label of 'Post Keynesian economics' (Lee, 2001). This label, like Keynes himself, also fostered a neglect of earlier and allied traditions of economics.

Keynes (1936, p. viii) himself wrote of his 'long struggle of escape . . . from habitual modes of thought and expression'. Ironically, Post Keynesianism itself has faced a 'long struggle of escape' from the *General Theory* title, its claimed ahistorical foundation in universal psychological laws, and its problematic first chapter.

Despite the 'general theory' phraseology, several leading Post Keynesians have been instinctively aware of institutional and historical specificities. Robinson (1974) repeatedly emphasised the importance of 'historical time'. Davidson (1980) likewise understood that 'the economy is a process in historical time' and economic and political institutions 'play an extremely important role'

---

13 In his memoirs of the university in the 1940s and 1950s, H. Johnson painted a very critical picture of Cambridge academic life, affected by the arcane and parcellised culture of the system of autonomous colleges, and with consequent and disproportionate institutional bias towards undergraduate teaching rather than postgraduate research. Lively intellectual debates there certainly were, but according to Johnson these were often 'only a tool for furthering left-wing politics at the level of intellectual debate' (Johnson and Johnson, 1978, p. 150). If we place his account alongside the Cambridge neglect after Marshall of entire traditions of economic thought – including historicism and institutionalism – then there is a case to answer of academic deficiency. On the Cambridge environment see also Winch (1969) and Tribe (2000).

in determining real-world economic outcomes. Eichner (1979, p. 172) clearly argued that Post Keynesian economics must concern itself with 'the behavior of the system as a whole, constituted as a set of historically specific institutions'. Indeed, Eichner had a much better acquaintance than most with institutional economics. However, none of this amounted to an explicit recognition of the limits of general theorising or the problem of historical specificity. As elsewhere, there is little discussion of this methodological problem in the Post Keynesian tradition. Praiseworthy historical and institutional instincts would have been enhanced by an awareness of past debates on the problem.

This methodological failure helped to undermine any focus on 'historically specific institutions'. This was particularly the case when leading Post Keynesians endorsed Keynes's generalist methodology. For example, Davidson (1994, p. 15) defended the idea that the work of Keynes and his followers provided 'a more general theory of the economy since it requires fewer initial axioms'. But, as argued in chapter 1 above, such a general theory would necessarily exclude many assumptions that were grounded on historically specific institutions. Davidson (1996, pp. 52–4) argued for 'the minimum axioms needed for the general theory . . . applicable to *all* economic regimes of money-using systems' and for the exclusion of any additional assumptions. Accordingly, the *General Theory* would be so general as it would encompass all monetary economies, spanning the two thousand years or more when money has been in use, and would have no special focus on the key institutions specific to modern industrial capitalism.[14]

In defence of Keynes, Anna Carabelli (1991, p. 116) wrote: 'For Keynes, a . . . theory which, at the beginning of its analysis, avoided introducing limiting assumptions of independence, was truly general.' This argument suggests that everything must be conceived as depending on everything else. However, as we have seen in chapter 1, the assumption of a monetary economy rules out a whole set of pairwise and barter interactions. A key point about institutions is that some interactions or interdependencies are ruled out. For example, a language acquires meaning because it has restrictive rules of utterance and syntax. It is in the nature of specific institutions, laws and rules that some things are restricted, prohibited or unyielding. Accordingly, just as the presumption of a monetary economy would involve more restrictive assumptions compared with a theory of barter, the adequate representation of other institutional specificities may require *more* rather than 'fewer restrictive assumptions'.

Lange and Schumpeter were in error to describe Walras's theory as entirely general, because it included several restrictive assumptions. However, Keynes, Carabelli and Davidson were doubly wrong – in claiming that the *General Theory*

---

14 Davidson endorsed Keynes's attempts at general theorising while he repeatedly emphasised the non-ergodic character of economic processes. In interpretations of this concept of non-ergodicity, reality itself is both changing and mutable (Davidson, 1993; J. B. Davis, 1998). Yet if economic structures can take radically different forms then these could place ontological limits on general theorising; it would also point to a more confined and historically specific domain of analysis, acknowledged insufficiently by Keynes and Davidson alike.

was truly general and in claiming that any form of generality is necessarily a positive attribute. Notably, all five of these economists were misled by the lure of a general theory. They all failed to observe that a theory designed to apply to a more particular real domain may be more adequate in its analysis of the distinguishing characteristics of the type of economy in question. What Keynesians required was not a general theory but a historically sensitive theory of a modern, monetary, corporate capitalist economy.

To some extent, the Post Keynesian label itself encouraged attempts to build a new or extended 'general theory', against the warnings, before and after Keynes, of members of the historical and institutionalist schools. It even became acceptable for those non-mainstream economists attempting to build a rival paradigm to sport the 'general theory' phrase in the titles of their own works. Hence another group of Post Keynesians avoided the institutional specifics and developed ostensibly general theories, professedly to enhance the 'general theory' of Keynes.[15]

Amnesia took hold. The 'Post Keynesianism' label helped to seal off the valuable pre-Keynesian heritage from view. The German historical school was largely forgotten. The history of economic thought was reconstructed largely in Anglophone terms. Clearly, other economists are not exempt from these criticisms. In the latter part of the twentieth century, not only neoclassical and Austrian, but also institutionalist and Marxist economists alike, have generally neglected the problem of historical specificity. What I am concerned to identify here is the crucial failure of Keynes and his Cambridge followers to take the problem on board. In Cambridge after Marshall, the problem was ignored. Given the role that Cambridge played as an international centre for non-mainstream economics, this neglect was disastrous, not only for Cambridge but also for economics as a whole.

Crucially, at least in the early years, Post Keynesianism lacked any developed methodological foundations. In their calls for 'realism of assumptions', leading Post Keynesians were evidently unaware of the twists and turns of the methodological battles on this theme, which had lasted for well over a hundred years. Eichner (1983, p. 211) took the untenable position that all the assumptions of a theory had to be 'empirically validated'. Similarly, Robinson (1964) believed that all 'metaphysical' assumptions had to go, simply because they were 'metaphysical'. This was an empiricist rejection of everything metaphysical – a position that had been increasingly criticised by philosophers of science since the decline of logical positivism in the 1950s. It has been argued already in this volume, when evaluating the weaknesses of the older historical school, that all science

---

15 Notably, Robinson followed Parsons and entered the out-generalising the *General Theory* race, with the publication of a volume including an essay entitled: 'The Generalisation of the General Theory' (Robinson, 1952). However, this essay tells us little of what 'generalisation' might mean. Also in Cambridge, Sraffa (1960) offered a general theoretical foundation for the analysis of profit-oriented, market economies. Post Keynesians who have attempted to develop a general theoretical framework on Sraffian lines include Pasinetti (1981), Eatwell and Milgate (1983) and Nell (1998). In addition, the phrase 'general theory' is symptomatically included in the titles of the following non-mainstream works: Roemer (1982), Nell (1998), Ormerod (1998) and Hunt (2000).

unavoidably depends on some assumptions that are both 'metaphysical' and cannot be 'empirically validated'. Unlike Robinson and Eichner, Marshall understood this very well. Eichner and Robinson fostered a version of empirical realism that could have benefited from an awareness of its trials and severe limitations in past debates, that had already lasted for well over a hundred years.

It would perhaps be an exaggeration to quote Hegel that the only thing that we learn from history is that people do not learn from history. But one thing is tragically clear. Not only was Post Keynesianism originally founded on weak and undeveloped methodological foundations, but also, by the close of the century, 'Post Keynesian' economics had still failed to provide itself with an agreed and sufficient set of common core principles around which dissidents could gather. This omission might well prove fatal.[16]

Since then the lure of a 'general theory' has become almost universal. By the 1980s, general equilibrium theorists such as Frank Hahn were dominating the Faculty of Economics at Cambridge. By the close of the twentieth century, the distinctive Cambridge tradition in economics – stretching from Marshall through Keynes, to Robinson and Kaldor – had dramatically declined in influence. Cambridge no longer regarded itself as the vanguard, and sought instead to emulate the leading neoclassical departments of economics in the United States of America.

---

16 See Harcourt (1982) for a relatively early consideration of this problem. Much later, Walters and Young (1997) claimed that Post Keynesianism lacked a coherent foundation. The responses of Arestis *et al.* (1999) and Dunn (2000) involved a belated and as yet incomplete endeavour to provide Post Keynesianism with a coherent methodological and theoretical core. Notably, this was attempted by excluding approaches – such as Sraffian economics – that were formerly described as Post Keynesian. It also involved the adoption of the 'critical realism' of T. Lawson (1997) and others. But there has been significant disagreement among Post Keynesians on whether Lawson's dismissal of mathematical economics and econometrics should be followed.

16

THE TRIUMPH OF BARREN
UNIVERSALITY

The unities, sir . . . are a completeness – a kind of universal dove-
tailedness with regard to place and time.
(Charles Dickens, *Nicholas Nickleby* (1839))

In preceding chapters we have observed the growing lure of general theorising
in economics in the nineteenth and twentieth centuries. The idea became
established that the principles of economics must be universal in scope: they must
apply to all types of economic system and to all historical periods. As Philip
Mirowski (1989) and others have discussed in detail, the desire of economists to
emulate physics and other seemingly universal 'hard sciences' is part of this story.
Developments in mathematics were also important. The development of the
integral calculus and the ascension of the field theory concept encouraged and
enabled the search for universals (Potts, 2000). These ideas penetrated economics
in the 1870s and began to power an institutionalised engine of formalisation
that accelerated after the Second World War and eventually transformed the
whole subject. Historicism did not survive this transformation. This formalist
revolution eventually converted 'the whole of economics into a branch of applied
mathematics' (Blaug, 1999, p. 276).

There are many examples of attempts to show or claim empirical regularities
in economics, analogous to the fundamental constants of physics. For example,
part of Milton Friedman's (1956) rhetoric for his quantity theory of money was
the assertion of the existence of a stable relationship between the stock of money
and prices (Mayer, 1997). The promise of such a fundamental and transhistorical
regularity in economics was hard to resist for an economics imbued with the
spirit of universalism and the metaphors of physics. Modern monetarism was
thus born.

As the claims of universality for mainstream economics became ever more
forceful, pressure was imposed on any subdiscipline in which some elements
of institutional and cultural specificity had been retained. Postwar economic
history dwindled in independence and stature to the point where it felt necessary
to prove its virility by adopting mainstream econometric techniques. Similarly,
development economics had emphasised the importance of cultural and institutional differences, until it too was taken over by the proselytisers of the 'rational

peasant' as a manifestation of universal 'rational economic man'. The universal-ising thrust has become so powerful that it has affected not only every branch of economics but sociology and politics as well.

At the core of this drive for universality within economics was the idea of the utility-maximising agent. One of the major tools of general theorising in twentieth- century economics has been its concept of rationality. As the scope of the concept has been both broadened and its content refined, the claims of mainstream economics to a general theory have marched forward with increasing confidence, to the point where they lay claim to the territory of the entire social sciences and beyond.

Earlier neoclassical economists, such as Alfred Marshall and Vilfredo Pareto, made it clear that economics was concerned with the more deliberative and calculative aspects of human behaviour. Marshall (1949, p. 17) wrote that 'the side of life with which economics is specially concerned is that in which man's conduct is most deliberate.' Pareto (1971) saw economics as being concerned with 'logical' actions, namely those where means are logically related to ends. Pareto (1935) also devoted himself to a quite separate science of sociology, claiming that this, in contrast, dealt with 'non-logical' action. From both the Marshallian and the Paretian points of view, economics was not an all-encompassing social science. It was concerned with particular kinds of activity or behaviour.

Philip Wicksteed defined the domain of economics differently. He argued that the distinctive feature of 'an economic transaction is that I am not considering you except as a link in the chain' (Wicksteed, 1933, p. 174). In other words, economics was the study of relatively impersonal transactions. However, although the lines of demarcation were different, economics was still confined in its scope. A legitimate place was accorded to other social sciences.

As discussed in chapter 14, Lionel Robbins (1935, p. 16) began to change things radically with his new definition of economics as 'the science which studies human behaviour as a relationship between ends and scarce means which have alternative uses'. This forced sociologists such as Talcott Parsons onto a different tack. Sociology was to be the study of the formation of ends, economics of the means to attain given ends. A key difference in this new demarcation was that there was no longer a domain of social activity that was in principle free from the clutches of 'economics' as Robbins had defined it. Robbins explicitly denied that economics was concerned with specific domains of enquiry, such as money, prices and markets. The perception of a boundary between the 'economy' and 'society' was no more. Henceforth, economics and sociology were both to concern themselves with different aspects of all human activity.

It then became easier to separate completely the concept of utility from the idea of price or monetary value. Although money values could occasionally be used as surrogates for levels of utility (with the assumption of a constant marginal utility of money) this did not have to be so, especially in the field of pure theory. Furthermore, Paul Samuelson (1938) and others insisted for a time that economics could base itself on the claims of 'revealed preference' alone, and did not need to invoke any psychological theory of human behaviour (Lewin, 1996). Following behaviourist psychology, Samuelson argued that all that mattered was the behaviour itself. Explanations of psychological processes were not required. Like sociology under Parsons, mainstream economics then saw itself as largely independent of any psychological postulates.[1]

Similarly, the assumption of deliberate or conscious choice was also regarded by some as inessential and unnecessarily restrictive, and removed from the theory (Machlup 1946, 1978; Friedman, 1953). As Ian Little (1949, p. 90) remarked, as a result of these developments, 'a theory of consumers' demand can be based solely on consistent behaviour' rather than consumer propensities or plans. All that was required was that behaviour appeared to be consistent: in which case a fixed preference function could be imputed that would satisfy the standard axioms of utility theory.

Once the core axioms of mainstream economics were reduced essentially to 'consistent behaviour' then the door was open to the removal, not only of psychology, but also of real economic and social institutions from the picture. By the 1960s this process was largely complete. Not only economics but also sociology was affected.[2] This chapter assesses the consequences of these developments in the social sciences.

The theory of 'rational choice' has been held up as the theoretical jewel in the neoclassical crown. It comes in various versions, but the central idea is that we may model individual behaviour in terms of a given preference function, in which agents maximise their 'utility'. This function specifies the amounts of utility yielded from each combination of specific inputs. Each input enters as an argument in this function. These inputs can be standard consumer goods or services but can in principle include other items, such as the 'human capital' of the consumer, or the utility of others, or the available 'social capital' (Becker, 1996). It is assumed that individuals make the 'rational choice' that maximises their utility according to the options available. The whole approach is to explain human behaviour simply on the basis of such preference functions, given limited resources and other constraints.[3]

Note that this general approach does not even tell us whether the individual will behave in a selfish or altruistic way. In his modern guise, rational economic man is not necessarily a selfish hedonist. The possibility of a type of 'altruism' is admitted because the individual may have a preference function in which extra utility is gained from the enhanced utility of others (Collard, 1978). The giving of a gift can mean a net gain in utility for the giver: the loss of utility resulting from the loss of the gift is compensated by a gain in utility resulting from the observation of the increased utility of the recipient. In this way, 'altruism' can

---

1 Although Samuelson's 'revealed preference' theory is now widely regarded as a failure (Majumdar, 1958; Sen, 1973; Wong, 1978), it nevertheless had this lasting effect.
2 Mouzelis (1995, p. 5) complained of the surfeit of 'transhistorical, universalistic statements' in sociology which do not take into account 'history and context' and 'tend to be either wrong or trivial'. One of his prime exemplars was rational choice theory.
3 In contrast, Buchanan (1969) and others have argued that a choice is only meaningful if there is a possible alternative. We must have been able to 'act otherwise'. According to this view, the utility-maximisers of neoclassical economics are more like programmed automata than real choosers.

be ostensibly 'explained'. Rational choice theorists do not have to confine their models to greedy agents who simply maximise their own assets.[4]

This relentless quest for universality has led to what is described by its practitioners as 'economic imperialism'. This refers to the invasion of other social sciences by utility-maximising 'economic man'. It is argued that the core assumptions of neoclassical economics should be applied to a wide variety of fields of study, including politics, public administration, sociology, anthropology, psychology, history and even biology, as well as economics itself. The case for the conquest of other social sciences and biology by neoclassical economists rests on the presumed universality of such ideas as scarcity, competition and rational self-interest.[5]

However, in their enthusiasm for economic imperialism, the advocates of the universal rational economic organism eventually settled on a definition of rationality that was unfalsifiable. The concept had become so elastic that any circumstance could fit it. This outcome is explored further below.

MAKING PREDICTIONS

Utility theory is often justified on the claim of its capacity to make predictions. According to Milton Friedman (1962, p. 13) 'economic theory proceeds largely to take wants as fixed'. The economist then makes predictions on the basis of this assumption. The legitimacy of this abstraction then allegedly rests on its 'power to predict'. Countless models have been developed on the basis of the utility-maximising or 'rational' choice. Some of these models generate falsifiable predictions. Others do not.

Consider the attempts to apply rational choice models to political phenomena. Some early models in this vein predicted a zero turnout in democratic elections. The reasoning was as follows. With a sufficiently large number of voters, the costs of voting outweigh any positive marginal expected benefit of the electoral outcome to the voter, so there would be no net incentive to vote (Riker and Ordeshook, 1968). The fact is that large numbers of people do vote voluntarily in elections. The prediction of the model is manifestly false.

However, although the particular model may be falsified, this evidence does not in any way refute utility maximisation or rational choice theory. It refutes one model only, which is based on the assumptions concerning the particular specification of the utility function. For instance, it was assumed that people gained utility from political outcomes, and not from simply exercising their duty to vote. Subsequently, political theorists have had little difficulty in constructing

---

4 However, in this formulation, the 'altruistic' agent is still maximising his or her own utility. It could be argued that true altruism would occur only if we gave to others and made ourselves worse off in net utility terms.
5 Prominent extensions to biology include Becker (1976b) and Hirshleifer (1977, 1985). On 'economic imperialism' see also Radnitzky (1992), Radnitzky and Bernholz (1987) and the critiques in Nicolaides (1988) and Udéhn (1992).

different rational choice models that generated predictions that got closer to voting turnouts in the real world. For instance, it could be assumed that people are getting a substantial amount of utility simply from placing their vote. Tune the utility function appropriately, and we get a closer approximation to the empirical data on real world behaviour.

The point being made here is not that rational choice or utility theory is either refuted or confirmed by the evidence. The point is that utility theory can be used to make falsifiable predictions, but only when particular auxiliary assumptions are made. As Mark Blaug (1992, p. 232) observed: 'The rationality hypothesis by itself is rather weak. To make it yield interesting implications, we need to add auxiliary assumptions.' These add-on assumptions may concern the shape and arguments of the utility functions, the nature of the constraints, the existence of uniformities between agents, and so on. It is these additional assumptions that do the predictive work, not the assumptions of rationality or utility-maximisation *per se* (Shaper, 2000). By this argument, utility theory is not necessarily wrong. But it is manifestly inadequate. Utility theorists demonstrate these inadequacies themselves when they always have to bring in additional assumptions to make any meaningful empirical prediction.

Typically, mainstream economists disfavour the use of *ad hoc* assumptions. Their aim is often to remove all *ad hoc* assumptions, in the pursuit of universality. However, it is only with such additional and *ad hoc* assumptions that rational choice theory can become operational and falsifiable.

Take another example. Many economists believe strongly in the 'law of demand' – it holds that demand curves are always downward sloping. However, on its own, utility analysis does not show this. It is a familiar textbook exercise to show, with indifference curves, how demand schedules for goods may slope either upwards or downwards. We have at least the theoretical possibility of 'Giffen goods', of which more is bought as their price rises.[6]

Whether Giffen goods can exist in the real world is in dispute. George Stigler (1987, p. 24) boldly asserted that the 'law of demand' is 'really true of all consumers, all times, all commodities'. Reviewing much of the evidence on this, Blaug (1992, pp. 140–7) likewise showed that no unequivocal case of a positively sloped demand curve has ever been found. However, this is not a triumphant vindication of neoclassical microeconomics, but instead an illustration of its theoretical shortfall. If the empirical evidence is as conclusive as Blaug has suggested, then the theory must be criticised for failing to be so conclusive in explaining it. Without additional assumptions to close off the perceived theoretical 'anomaly' of upward-sloping demand curves, no adequate basis for the 'law of demand' can be found in standard utility theory.[7]

---

6 In addition, Stiglitz (1987) has shown how the introduction of deficiencies of information can overturn the 'law of demand'. General equilibrium theorists have also exposed problems in deriving aggregate demand relationships on the basis of individual preferences (Kirman, 1989; Rizvi, 1994a).

7 In a very interesting but neglected paper, Heiner (1986) criticised mainstream economics for failing to find a theoretical justification for a universal 'law of demand'. Heiner himself provided such

A related case is the tenacious belief that the demand curve for labour is always downward sloping. Not only goods, but also factors of production such as labour, are said to yield to the universal law of demand. But the theoretical arguments in favour of this are again limited. The downward-sloping demand curve for labour is derived in part from the presumption of the diminishing marginal productivity of labour. But again there is no reason given to support the notion that the conditions giving rise to this effect are universal.

Despite this theoretical lacuna, the belief in universal downward-sloping demand curves for labour is often used as a theoretical basis for the ideological pronouncement that wage increases can 'price workers out of a job'. An anecdote shows the tenacity of this belief among economists. In 1995 the economist David Card was awarded the John Bates Clark Medal by the American Economic Association for his detailed empirical work showing that modest increases in the minimum wage had little or no discernible effect on the employment of low wage workers (Card and Kruger, 1995). This evidence undermined the notion of a downward-sloping demand curve for labour. It received hostile and extreme criticism. Card was lambasted in *Business Week*, in the *Forbes* journal, and by leading economists such as Thomas Sowell and Nobel Laureate James Buchanan (Deaton, 1996, p. 13). Card's work was regarded as heresy, and declaimed as scientifically unsound. For a significant group of economists, the sanctity of the allegedly universal 'law of demand' had to be retained, in labour and non-labour markets alike.

THE NON-FALSIFIABILITY OF THE THEORY

Perhaps a fundamental 'predictive' claim of utility theory is that the substitution effect is negative. Again, the detailed argument can be found in the neoclassical textbooks. This shows that if a price increase occurs, and compensation is made for any change of 'real' (i.e. utility) income, then the demand for the good or service will decrease. Conversely, a price decrease will lead to a demand increase, under similar compensatory conditions. The proof of the negativity of the substitution effect follows directly from the assumptions of the theory (Hicks, 1939).

Can the negative sign of the substitution effect be used to predict human behaviour? Is it a falsifiable prediction? Regrettably, the answer to both questions is no. *Any observed behaviour can be fitted into the theory*. If the price increases and demand also goes up, then that does not contradict the theory. In this case it could simply be said that the 'real' income (measured in terms of utility rather than prices) is not constant. If we were to make an adequate income compensation, and assume a sufficiently lower 'real' income before the price change, then the

---

a theoretical justification, using something very different from utility analysis. Another justification of the 'law of demand' without using utility theory is found in Becker (1962). For another novel approach see Hildenbrand (1994). Yet these arguments are rarely cited: they remain neglected and underdeveloped.

apparent anomaly would disappear. We are free to make a wide range of assumptions concerning the imagined compensation. The compensation has to be such as to place the individual at exactly the same utility level, before and after the price change. But we do not know this utility level, or the shape of the indifference curve!

The compensation is thus a thought experiment, rather than an investigation into processes in the real world. It is difficult to make reality an adjudicator in this thought experiment, because we cannot directly measure utility. The high degree of compensatory discretion makes the theory untestable in terms of its behavioural predictions. The result may have the aesthetic appeal and the apparent universality of a mathematical theorem, but it does not enable us to make any prediction that can be falsified by any possible outcome in the real world.

Experimental psychologists such as Daniel Kahneman, Paul Slovic and Amos Tversky (1982) have thrown down experimental challenges to expected utility theory. More broadly, since the 1980s there has been a spectacular growth in interest in 'experimental economics'. Many people have interpreted the behavioural evidence gathered by the experimenters as a violation of the standard axioms of expected utility theory. Much of this evidence, particularly concerning choices under risk, has led some mainstream theorists to reflect critically upon the standard assumptions of their theory. This evidence is important and it should be taken seriously.[8]

However, if we were to think that the evidence itself refutes or falsifies the core axioms of utility theory, then we would be mistaken. The reason is that the standard core of utility theory is *non-falsifiable*. As Sidney Winter (1964, pp. 309, 315) argued in an early and neglected article: 'any behavior can in one way or another be rationalized as maximizing behavior.' Lawrence Boland (1981) expanded on this theme in another important paper. With the provocative title 'the futility of criticizing the neoclassical maximization hypothesis', his essay was first widely misinterpreted as a defence of a theory that the mainstream economists had already accepted and taken for granted. Consequently, Boland's paper is now largely forgotten.[9]

In fact, it is better understood as a *critique* of the maximisation hypothesis. In his paper, Boland asked if any conceivable evidence would refute the maximising assumption. He then showed that such an attempt at falsification could never work:

> Given the premise – 'All consumers maximize something' – the critic can claim he has found a consumer who is not maximizing anything. The person who assumed the premise is true can respond: 'You claim you have found a consumer who is not a maximizer but how do you know there is not something which he is maximizing?'
>
> (Boland, 1981, p. 1034)

---

8   For summaries of the issues and debates in experimental economics see Kagel and Roth (1995). The debate is taken further by Binmore (1999), Loomes (1998, 1999) and Starmer (1999a, 1999b).
9   See Boland's (1996) own later reflections on the misinterpretation of his argument.

Given that we can never in principle demonstrate that 'something else' (perhaps unknown to us) is not being maximised, then the theory is ultimately invulnerable to any empirical attack. To show empirically that nothing is being maximised we would have to measure every possible variable that could impinge upon humanity, from the changing of the weather to the twinkling of the stars. Clearly, this would be an endless and impossible task. As Boland (*ibid.*) concluded: 'The neoclassical assumption of universal maximization could very well be false, but as a matter of logic we cannot expect to be able to prove that it is.' Boland showed that the neoclassical assumption is not falsifiable. But he also rightly points out that it is not a tautology. It is not a tautology because it is *conceivably false*. It might be the case that nothing is being maximised. But we can never know.[10]

The arguments of Winter and Boland have been much neglected. They do not rule out the role of evidence in evaluating the theory, but they show that the evidence alone cannot be decisive. Boland also warns us that utility maximisation is not 'tautological'. Strangely, some critics regard the allegation of 'tautology' as a damning weakness. On the contrary, a tautological theory, whether it is 'empty' or not, must be accepted as valid. By saying that utility maximisation is not a tautology we are admitting the possibility that it is false, although no single piece of evidence can show that it is untrue.[11]

In some respects, Boland's argument resembles the so-called Duhem–Quine thesis.[12] This thesis derives from the work of the French physicist Pierre Duhem and the American philosopher Willard van Orman Quine (Harding, 1976). According to this thesis, it is not possible to falsify a single hypothesis because we are always faced with a tangle of related and connected hypotheses. Consequently, we can never be sure that the main hypothesis is being targeted and tested on its own, and that other auxiliary hypotheses are not complicating the picture. Boland, Duhem and Quine all pointed to the multiplicity and

---

10 Boland can be misunderstood, unless his strong Popperian inclinations are acknowledged. He alleged that it is 'futile' to criticise the theory because it is 'non-falsifiable' and thereby 'metaphysical'. By the famous Popperian criterion, this also means that it is 'non-scientific'. This is the understated and impish outcome to his argument. Where Boland was vulnerable was not in the demonstration of unfalsifiability but in his excessive faith in the Popperian criterion. For Boland, 'criticism' would usefully be directed at falsifiable statements only – and the main means of 'criticism' would be empirical falsification. In response, Caldwell (1982) showed that Boland's demonstration of the 'futility' of criticising the hypothesis rested upon an overly narrow notion of 'criticism'. Caldwell argued convincingly that it is also possible to criticise some non-falsifiable statements, for instance by looking at their underlying assumptions. Caldwell was right to suggest that the appraisal of theories must deploy a number of additional criteria, and not pin everything on falsification. Nevertheless, Boland's central result – that no imaginable evidence can in principle falsify the theory – still stands.
11 Etzioni (1988) made a strong case that commitments to moral values should be considered as part of a theory of human behaviour. However, his allied critique of utility theory was weakened by the allegation that it is 'tautological' (p. 28) and that neoclassical theory applies to market behaviour (p. 3). As noted above, the former proposition is false. In addition, knowledgeable economists such as Clower (1994, 1999) have rightly rejected the latter proposition.
12 Some of the implications of this thesis for macroeconomics were discussed by Cross (1982). Cross usefully reviewed some of the attacks on the Duhem–Quine thesis and concluded that it has 'withstood criticism' (p. 322).

interconnectedness of possible causal influences behind any empirical phenomenon in the real world, and the general difficulty of isolating and testing them all.

Just as we cannot isolate every connected and auxiliary hypothesis, we cannot consider all the possible hypothetical variables that could be maximised. As a result it can be argued that there is no experimental or other phenomenon that cannot in principle be 'explained' by the theory. Nothing lies outside its scope. Even the so-called anomalies revealed by experiments with human subjects can be explained away. If experiments show that some consumers appear to prefer a monetary reward that is less than the expected outcome, or appear to have intransitive preference orderings, then we can always get round these problems by introducing other variables.[13]

For instance, if an experiment shows that option A with an expected value of $4 is preferred to option B with an expected value of $5 then we can simply assume that there are additional attributes of option A (for example, we may enjoy losing, or gain pleasure from seeing others win) that are consistent with the view that it yields higher overall utility for the subject. Likewise, an experiment may seem to reveal preference intransitivity, by showing that while X is preferred to Y, and Y is preferred to Z, Z is preferred to X. Even this result can be explained away by showing that the three pairwise comparisons did not take place under identical conditions, or were separated in time or space. Accordingly, the consumer could have 'learned' more about his or her true tastes during the experiment itself, or other factors may account for the apparent intransitivity. All we have to do is indicate in some way that the two Zs in the above comparisons are not quite identical. The two Zs could be slightly different in timing, substance, or their informational or other contexts. We then get the result: X is preferred to Y, Y is preferred to Z_1, and Z_2 is preferred to X. Transitivity is no longer violated.

It is also claimed that preference reversals are inconsistent with expected utility theory. 'Preference reversals occur when individuals are presented with two gambles, one featuring a high probability of winning a modest sum of money . . . the other featuring a low probability of winning a large sum of money' (Slovic and Lichtenstein, 1983, p. 596). Assume that a subject is faced with a choice between $15 with certainty, and $1,000 with a probability of 2 per cent. Experiments with real subjects indicate that in such situations the first, $15 option is sometimes chosen (Kahneman et al., 1982; Slovic and Lichtenstein, 1983). This is despite the fact that the expected value of the second option is higher at $20. However, preference reversals also fail to falsify expected utility theory, once we accept that utility is not necessarily measured in terms of the monetary payoffs in the experiment. If we assume an added disutility associated with the choice of a risky and low probability outcome, then the theory that people are maximising their utility is not overturned by these experiments. In general, a

---

13 Hausman (1992, ch. 13) documented several attempts to explain the apparent anomalies that have been revealed by the experimenters, notably by pointing to other possible sources of utility.

risk-averse actor may not maximise expected monetary value but still be maximising expected utility. By appropriate functional manipulation, the choice of $15 can be made perfectly consistent with the maximisation of expected utility, rather than the maximisation of the expected monetary value of the payoff.

Experimental economists such as Vernon Smith (1982) and others have add-ressed the problem of the possible absence of a linear correlation between utility and monetary payoff. In particular, the possibility of additional, subjective utilities – unrelated to the monetary payoffs – has to be diminished. The money payoffs have to 'dominate' the decisions of the agents. To make experiments 'work' in the sense of a close presumed correlation between overall utility and monetary payoff, Smith proposed a number of 'precepts' of experimental assumption and design constituting an 'induced value procedure'. These pre-cepts include nonsatiation, sufficiently large and obvious rewards, restriction of communication between subjects, and so on. But Smith (1982, p. 929) himself was the first to admit that these precepts cannot guarantee any correspondence between observable monetary rewards and preferences that, in principle, are 'not directly observable'. In short, we can never know if the precept has been effectively applied. Accordingly, the most judicious application of Smith's precepts will not banish the problem of non-falsifiability. There is no way of showing that a close correlation between utility and experimental reward has been achieved. The idea that Smith's precepts 'work' is an article of faith, placed so far under relatively little methodological scrutiny.[14]

THE BARREN UNIVERSALITY OF RATIONALITY

Accordingly, a problem with the standard rationality assumptions is not that they lack empirical correlation, but that they could cover every conceivable decision situation and every possible causal mechanism underlying choice. Insofar as there may be common features of every decision situation then it may be possible to extract universal and meaningful propositions. Nevertheless, some important and specific features or causal mechanisms may be excluded by concentrating solely on the common features of every decision situation. In fact, the degree of universality involved is so great that it goes beyond the parameters of mere human decision.

Recent theoretical and experimental studies confirm a high degree of universality, beyond the confines of human society. Experimental work with rats and other animals (Kagel et al., 1981, 1995) has 'revealed' that animals have downward-sloping demand curves, supposedly just like humans. Gary Becker (1991, p. 307) has argued extensively that: 'Economic analysis is a powerful tool not only in understanding human behavior but also in understanding the behavior of other species.' Similarly, Gordon Tullock (1994) has claimed that organisms – from bacteria to bears – can be treated as if they have the same

---

14 For a critical methodological discussion of some of Smith's precepts see Siakantaris (2000).

general type of preference function that is attributed to humans in the micro-economics textbooks. They are all regarded as utility-maximisers. Accordingly, core concepts are not only applied to all forms of human society since the origin of our species, but also to a large portion of the animal kingdom as well. Seemingly, we now have 'evidence' of the 'rationality' of everything in evolution from the amoeba onwards. This suggests that such assumptions are telling us very little about specifically human societies, least of all about the unique complexities of modern human civilisation.

For the neoclassical economist, the fact that utility theory can 'explain' a wide variety of types of economic behaviour is regarded as a strong vindication of this general approach. I take a different view. First, the sheer generality of a theory tells us nothing of its explanatory power. We could conceive of different general theories, such as that we all are programmed by aliens from outer space, or that we are all pawns of God. These would be quite general in their scope and could be applied in principle to any behavioural manifestation. But we would rightly be sceptical of their explanatory value. A theory does not explain anything unless it points to an underlying causal mechanism. In the case of individual behaviour, explanations must thus relate to mechanisms of the human psyche and human interaction and perhaps draw upon psychology, anthropology, sociology and other disciplines. This is precisely what many advocates of utility theory refuse to do. They take the utility functions as given and consign the job of grounding them theoretically to somebody else. By this refusal they indicate that utility theory itself cannot provide a real explanation.

Arguably, human societies are partly differentiated from other animals in terms of developed institutions and cultures. If utility maximising behaviour is not confined to humanity, then these uniquely human elements are downplayed within or absent from the universal picture. Furthermore, whether true or false, this picture can tell us relatively little about historically specific human cultures or institutions. That is the unintended achievement of the exponents of ubiquitous rationality and economic imperialism. The specific causal mechanisms through which human culture and institutions mould and constrain human agents remain largely unexplored in this paradigm. Essentially, there is no adequate theory of human agency at the core of the standard theory. It identifies no uniquely human causal mechanism. Its very weakness stems from the universality it has achieved through axiomatics and deduction, rather than an investigation into causal relations in the real world.

It was noted in chapter 1 that while the laws of physics may be general, they impose restrictions on the type of supplementary theory that may be used to explain particular phenomena. This is not the case with utility maximisation, because *any* particular behavioural model is compatible with it. It can be made compatible with both selfishness and altruism, with both calculative and unreflective behaviour, with intelligence and stupidity, with both humans and non-humans. The lure of a general theory has led economists to worship a deductive theory that tells us very little about reality.

WEAK CRITICISM AND FALSE APPROVAL

However, many critics of mainstream economics have taken a different line of attack. In a classic critique of formalism in economics, Terence Hutchison (1938, p. 27) argued that the basic postulates of 'pure theory' necessarily suffered from a 'complete lack of empirical content'. Many similar remarks have been made by heterodox economists, before and since. I take a different view. The problem with these assumptions is not primarily their lack of empirical corroboration. It is that they are vessels into which *any* empirical content can be filled. The problem with the theory is not that it lacks empirical validation but that any conceivable fact about behaviour, from church attendance to suicide, can be fitted into the theory.[15]

Just as some critics of neoclassical theory wrongly claim that its basic postulates have been falsified, some of its exponents misleadingly suggest that they have so far been confirmed. Jack Hirshleifer (1985, p. 59) went so far as to write: 'Ultimately we must be ready to abandon the rationality paradigm to the extent that it fails to fit the evidence about human behavior.' However, this apparent concession to empirical confirmation in fact conceals a methodological mis-understanding. Hirshleifer did not have to worry, because no conceivable evidence can 'fail to fit' some tortured version of the theory. Both Hirshleifer and the critics of the rationality paradigm share the flawed supposition: that evidence can in principle refute the theory. Both supporters and critics of neoclassical theory have perpetuated the myth that it is susceptible to decisive empirical testing.

As a result, the mainstream theory is not wrong because it is empirically inaccurate. It is not unrealistic in the sense that it fails to fit the data. Any data can be fitted into it. Hence no data can refute the theory. It cannot be displaced simply by an appeal to the evidence. The experimental evidence of preference reversals and other choice 'anomalies' may lead us to search for a different and better theory, but it does not in principle refute the old version based on utility and rational choice.[16]

Critics such as Hutchison (1938) and Alfred Eichner (1983) based their criticism on an untenable and empiricist view of science that denies that some non-falsifiable and 'metaphysical' assumptions are essential to any science. In fact, all sciences depend upon some propositions that are untestable. No theory can be composed entirely of empirically validated elements. Prior concepts are required to make sense of any fact. These prior concepts cannot all be 'tested' empirically. In any case, any 'test' itself relies on prior concepts or categories. As a result, all sciences must unavoidably make extensive use of some untestable and metaphysical assumptions.

---

15 This is no joke. See Azzi and Ehrenberg (1975) and Hammermesh and Soss (1974).
16 I am not arguing that evidence is unimportant. Although evidence cannot falsify the theory, the accumulated evidence may provide a context in which the theory is more readily questioned. See Loomes (1998, pp. 485–6).

Immanuel Kant (1929, p. 7) revealed in 1781 that human reason 'begins with principles which it has no option save to employ' but which 'are no longer subject to any empirical test'. Accordingly, he recognised a role for metaphysics. Subsequently, in the heyday of positivism, the idea that metaphysics had any place in science was challenged. But from the 1950s, positivism itself was subjected to strong philosophical attacks. In particular, Willard van Orman Quine (1951) successfully overturned the view that all scientific and meaningful statements had to be based upon empirical experience. The outcome was 'a blurring of the supposed boundaries between speculative metaphysics and natural science' (p. 20). Eventually, Karl Popper also recognised that some metaphysical propositions are essential to science (Ackerman, 1976, pp. 30–1). The indispensable role of untestable and metaphysical assumptions is now widely accepted by philosophers.[17]

For this reason, the Hutchison–Eichner empiricist criticism of mainstream economics is untenable. In practice, furthermore, their denial of the essential role of non-falsifiable assumptions in any theory would disable any of their own attempts at theoretical construction. Given that it is practically impossible to test all assumptions, any theoretical construction – including theirs – would reveal hidden, *ad hoc* assumptions, privileged to lie beyond empirical test. For reasons outlined above, every theory must involve some untestable assumptions. Hence any theory built on the claim of complete testability would be highly vulnerable to critique by its own canon.

However, this does not mean that 'anything goes' and that all criticisms are disabled. There are powerful theoretical criticisms of the rationality assumption (Simon, 1957; Lane *et al.*, 1996). Essentially, the theory lacks adequate theoretical concepts to discriminate, understand and properly explain key phenomena. A problem with the standard assumptions of rationality and expected utility maximisation is their lack of specific theoretical and conceptual content, pertaining to specific causal mechanisms involved in the human psyche and in the structures of specific real world economic institutions.

To repeat: the empirical evidence is valuable and important, but it cannot be used to show that the theory is false. In recent years, there have been attempts to apply models of rational, utility-maximising behaviour to a wide variety of phenomena, even beyond the sphere of commerce and markets. Models of utility-maximising behaviour have been applied to politics, marriage, religion, suicide, and much else. Such attempts have been widely resisted. Many tried to defend their academic discipline or subdiscipline from the 'economic imperialism' of rational choice models. However, the widespread failure to recognise the non-falsifiability of 'rational' maximising behaviour has weakened many such counter-arguments. They appealed to evidence: it was mistakenly argued that rational choice models did not fit the facts. On the contrary, models of utility-maximising behaviour can always be adjusted to fit the facts. The attempt to resist

---

17 In the methodology of economics see, for example, Caldwell's (1982) critical discussion of positivism and Blaug's (1992) account of the role of Lakatosian 'hard core' assumptions.

the incursions of rational choice theory by claiming otherwise was bound to fail. In this instance, appeals to evidence cannot be decisive.

In development economics, for example, there was a debate in the 1970s over whether peasants were or were not 'rational'. Critics of this idea appealed to 'evidence' of 'non-rational' behaviour, without realising that no evidence can strictly falsify the theory. With opponents weakened by their own theoretical position and methodological misunderstandings, the rational choice theorists seemed to win the argument (Popkin, 1979). Similarly weak defences were evident in sociology and political science, as rational choice theorists invaded their territory. Again and again, attempts were made to resist the incursions of utility and rational choice, on the grounds that its assumptions are not 'realistic'. But no theory can employ assumptions that exactly mirror the real world. Such attempted rebuttals of rational choice theory are methodologically flawed and ultimately doomed.[18]

The moral here is that mistaken claims concerning the testability of rational choice theory led its opponents to attack it with weak arguments. It would have been much more fruitful if both sides had admitted that the theory was unfalsifiable and then debated its explanatory value in particular circumstances. Instead, these controversies were entirely confined to claims and counter claims concerning empirical validation. At that primitive level the issue is simple: the assumptions of utility theory cannot be falsified.

Once again the weaknesses of empiricist criticisms of ahistorical theory are underlined. As we have seen, the failures of empiricism have been widely discussed in German economics, at least since the *Methodenstreit*. By contrast, Anglophone social science was overwhelmed by positivism and has been largely unaffected by these issues. As a result, the criticisms of rational choice theory have been severely weakened.

THE DECONSTRUCTION OF RATIONALITY

However, having almost conquered the social sciences, some of the rational choice theorists have become bored with their own weapons of victory. Ironically, it is beginning to be possible, even fashionable, for mainstream economists to question some of these core assumptions. Perhaps because mainstream economists have lost the capacity to police their own disciplinary boundaries, in search of a new separate identity they have begun to question their own *raison d'être*. As the sociologist Kyriakos Kontopoulos (1993, p. 90) has pointed out: 'Ironically, economists become less economistic at a time when sociologists seem to become enamored with rational choice theory.' Accordingly, some economists are now deconstructing rational economic man. As economist Robert Sugden (1991, p. 783) put it:

---

18 A selection of the relevant literature could include: Baron and Hannan (1994), Coleman (1990), Coleman and Fararo (1990), Frank (1992), J. Friedman (1995), Green and Shapiro (1994), Hirsch *et al.* (1987), G. Miller (1997), Orchard and Stretton (1997), Udéhn (1996).

There was a time, not long ago, when the foundations of rational-choice theory appeared firm, and when the job of the economic theorist seemed to be one of drawing out the often complex implications of a fairly simple and uncontroversial system of axioms. But it is increasingly becoming clear that these foundations are less secure than we thought, and that they need to be examined and perhaps rebuilt.

One reason for this change of heart is the rise of game theory. In certain types of game the very definition of rationality becomes problematic. Nevertheless, the response of mainstream economists to these problems has largely been to become immersed in the technicalities, rather than to give the economic agents at the core of the theory of human behaviour some real institutional and cultural flesh and blood. Some still cling tenaciously to the principles of rationality, in a manner that is reminiscent of Ptolemaic astronomers, fitting the evidence of the apparent circular movements of the stars into complicated models (Koestler, 1959). Others are not inclined simply to 'save appearances'; they express their misgivings but fail to look for an alternative paradigm.

For some, the move to game theory has led to the questioning of core assumptions. For others it has reinforced the idea that economics itself is a formal game, with little connection to reality. If a theory makes no claim outside a single domain, then there is no aim to use the theory to explain other real world phenomena. The interest in the theory is typically in its mathematical content, rather than its usefulness to help understand reality. Accordingly, there is a move away from former attempts to build a universal theory (which turned out to be unfalsifiable), to the building of exemplifying theories that are not designed to be put under any empirical scrutiny whatsoever. There is a move from universal to 'what if?' theories. As Donald McCloskey (1991, p. 10) put it, much of modern economics involves 'a search through the hyperspace of conceivable assumptions'. Step by step, much of economics is becoming disengaged with the real world. Instead of looking at real institutional structures and mechanisms, it has become more and more involved in the elaborations of mathematical technique.

For those of us concerned to try to understand the real world, this does not help us get closer to real economic institutions. Even if it has useful applications in this direction (Schotter, 1981), game theory has inherent limitations. Roy Radner (1996) argued that the game-theoretic analysis of institutions is thwarted by problems of uncertainty about the logical implications of given knowledge, and by the existence of multiple equilibria. Furthermore, as Dennis O'Brien (1998, p. 27) has caustically remarked:

> in the intoxication of intellectual knitting patterns for which game theory provides scope, important information has to be pushed to one side . . . because game theory seems to have little capacity for dealing with industrial data. With very limited exceptions, the striking characteristic of game theory treatments of industrial economics is the lack of contact with reality.

This goes not only for the assumptions about the structure of the game but also the conception of the human agent that is found within game theory. Herbert Gintis (2000) has criticised the over-use within game theory of the simplistic assumption of selfish 'economic man'. Even more crucially, as Ariel Rubinstein (1991, p. 923) has argued:

> Deductive arguments cannot by themselves be used to discover truths about the world. Missing are data describing the processes of reasoning adopted by the players when they analyze a game. Thus, if a game in the formal sense has any coherent interpretation, it has to be understood to include explicit data on the player's reasoning processes.

Similarly Cristina Bicchieri (1994, p. 127) observed that 'a description of the players' reasoning processes and capacities as well as a specification of their knowledge of the game situation' was missing in most game-theoretic models. We may draw the inference from these remarks that such processes as cognition and learning – that always take place in, and are moulded by, a specific cultural and institutional environment – are absent from much of game theory. In short, game theory lacks sufficient empirically and historically grounded content. It may develop to overcome these limitations, but there is little sign of this as yet.

What is required to make economic theory sensitive to institutional and cultural realities is the combination of some general, methodological principles to guide analysis, with detailed and empirically grounded theories of how specific types of institution and socio-economic system function. The development of such a theoretical framework is far from complete, but some rudimentary elements will be outlined later in this book.

17

INSTITUTION BLINDNESS AND THE END OF HISTORY

> These are the days when men of all social disciplines and all political faiths seek the comfortable and the accepted; when the man of controversy is looked upon as a disturbing influence; when originality is taken to be a mark of instability; and when, in minor modification of the scriptural parable, the bland lead the bland.
> (John Kenneth Galbraith, *The Affluent Society* (1958))

By mainstream economics we may refer to the type of economics that dominates the modern core journals of the subject. It includes a variety of doctrines and the critic must be careful to distinguish them. But there are particular themes and assumptions that pervade modern mainstream economics. The argument here is that, as a result of an exclusive pursuit of such universal theories, mainstream economics becomes largely incapable of dealing with cultural or historical particularities. As a result – despite the rise of the 'new institutional economics' – mainstream economic theory, in a sense, remains predominantly *institution-blind*. Insufficient attention is given to establishing theories that apply with adequate sensitivity to particular, historically specific, economic mechanisms or institutions.

This is a sweeping condemnation and would seem to ignore the large literature in economics on institutions. It is not that modern mainstream economics is unaware of institutions or is still keen to avoid them. There has been a huge explosion in the literature of attempts to relate economics to institutional phenomena, including the firm, the state, the family and other important economic and social institutions. There has been much important empirical work on institutions in economics, sociology and political science. It is now widely accepted that 'institutions matter' for economic order and development. All these positive achievements should be recognised and commended.[1]

The blindness may be partial, but the impairment is nevertheless serious and disabling. What is meant by this allegation of blindness is that, despite their

---

1 Significantly, the importance of institutions for economic development is now recognised by the World Bank. See, for example, Burki and Perry (1998). Such analyses have their flaws but represent a step in the right direction.

intentions, many mainstream economists lack the conceptual apparatus to discern anything but the haziest institutional outlines. The argument here is that many prominent economists – despite a widespread modern interest in institutions – have not got adequate visual tools to distinguish accurately between different types of institution, nor to appraise properly what is going on within them.[2]

As noted in preceding chapters, we cannot discern or understand phenomena with data alone. Well-chosen concepts and precise theoretical instruments are required. However, as further evidenced below, in its pursuit of theoretical precision, much economics deploys concepts that are too blunt and universal. Without a theory that is both adequate and historically sensitive we remain blind. Such a theory has to be grounded on a well-developed and appropriate methodology.

BUMPING BLIND INTO MARKETS

Despite its limitations, mainstream economics is sometimes forced to engage with institutional realities. At least to maintain some credibility as the science of economic phenomena, economics has to discuss such institutions as markets and firms. Indeed, some consideration of the market is unavoidable, because a legitimate and enduring aim of economic theory is to show how markets allocate resources and how prices are formed. Furthermore, the ideological predisposition of many economists towards markets makes such considerations inevitable.

Given this, it is rather strange that definitions of the market in the textbooks are infrequent and often imprecise. The institutional relations and properties of markets are rarely explored in these texts. For example, Hugh Gravelle and Ray Rees (1992, p. 3) wrote with some vagueness: 'a market exists whenever two or more individuals are prepared to enter into an exchange transaction, regardless of time or place.' There is no mention here of the institutional structure of markets themselves, or of the price mechanism, or of the establishment and enforcement of property rights. Throughout economics, the institutional structure of markets is largely unexplored. As Nobel Laureate Douglass North (1977, p. 710) has remarked: 'It is a peculiar fact that the literature on economics and economic history contains so little discussion of the central institution that underlies neo-classical economics – the market.'

Typically, the market assumes a de-institutionalised form, as if it was the primeval and universal ether of all human interactions. It is believed that when people gather together in the name of self-interest, then a market somehow always emerges in their midst. Mysteriously, the market springs up simply as a result of these spontaneous interactions, as a result neither of a protracted process

---

2 The affliction is not universal and uniform. For instance, the works of Aoki (1990), Chandler (1977), Greif (1998), Hirschman (1986), North (1977, 1990) and others are much better than the norm, exhibiting a deeper awareness of historical change and structural differences in socio-economic systems.

of multiple institution-building, nor of the full development of a historically specific commercial culture.

Related key concepts such as 'exchange' and 'transaction' are also inadequately defined in the mainstream literature. These problems are not confined to economics. Other social sciences fail to come to grips with the institutional and structural realities of the modern world. We have already noted the generalities of 'exchange theory' in sociology (Blau, 1964; Homans, 1961). The concept of 'exchange' therein is so broad that it covers all sorts of social interaction, without being confined to exchanges of property.

In sociology such general theorising has reached its apogee in the work of James Coleman. Following in the tradition of Homans and Blau, Coleman (1990, p. 37) saw exchange as simply a 'pairwise exchange of resources' without the necessity of a reciprocal exchange of property rights. Accordingly, in modern social science, even concepts such as 'exchange' and 'transaction' cannot be taken for granted. Yet they are used habitually and without explanatory ado, as if their meaning is always crystal clear.

In common business parlance, an exchange means something more than the reciprocation of a polite greeting, a wave or a smile. It is even more than a reciprocal transfer of resources. As Karl H. Rau (1835) and John Commons (1924) rightly insisted, exchange proper involves the contractual interchange of property rights, along with the transferred goods and services. Unless a transfer of property rights is involved, it is not properly described as an exchange. Property rights, in turn, are backed up by custom and legal sanctions. These involve other institutions, such as the state. Exchange has to be understood and analysed in terms of the key institutions that are required to sustain it.

Strangely, however, the concept of property rights is also underdeveloped in mainstream economic theory. True, there is a sizeable subdiscipline known as 'the economics of property rights' (Furubotn and Pejovich, 1974). But if we look at this closely then it is clear that the discourse is primarily about individual incentives rather than about property. To the property rights economists, the 'structure of property rights' refers primarily to a set of incentives and dis-incentives for specific individual actions – an amended Benthamite calculus of pleasure and pain – but not essentially to the institution of property itself.

Similarly, Armen Alchian (1977, p. 238) defined the property rights of a person in the universal terms of 'the probability that his decision about demarcated uses of the resource will determine the use'. However, this definition is about control, not ownership, of a resource. The upshot of this definition is that if a thief manages to keep stolen goods then he acquires a substantial property right in them. But on the contrary, legal or normative considerations would suggest that they remain the rightful property of their original owner. Alchian's ahistorical definition of property neglects the essential concept of rightful ownership. It is about mere possession, not property rights.

Crucially, the essence of the right of ownership of a resource is its acknowledgement of that right by others. Yet mainstream property rights economists treat property principally as a relation between an individual and a good, thus downplaying the fact that the institution of property also involves social relations between individuals. Social relations and structures are absent from this conception of property. The primary focus is on the individual, his goods, and his incentives. Any analysis of the construction and nature of the institutions required to sustain and legitimate property is secondary or absent.

For different reasons, sociologists have assumed a de-institutionalised concept of the market. This is partly the result of the influence of Marxism within sociology. Marxists also tend to regard markets as uniform entities, ultimately permeated by just one specific set of pecuniary imperatives and cultural norms. As Viviana Zelizer (1993, p. 193) pointed out, sociologists have become obsessed

> with the cash nexus, with the vision of an ever-expanding market inevitably dissolving all social relations and corrupting culture and personal values. . . . Mesmerized by this vision of inexorable force, sociologists implicitly adopted an extremely simple conception of the process, making it resemble the sweeping away of landmarks by a giant flood. That left unaddressed the crucial question: How do real markets work? Markets were seldom studied as social and cultural arrangements. For if indeed the modern market neutralized social relations and homogenized cultural distinctions, there was nothing much left for sociologists to study. Thus the market was surrendered to economists.

In other words, by seeing the market as a universal pecuniary force, the nature of the market as an institution was neglected. However, economists have had little to say about the nature of markets, other than classifying them by their degrees of competition and the number of buyers and sellers they contain. Beyond this, the institutional aspects of markets are widely neglected. There is little discussion of how specific markets are structured to select and authenticate information, and of how specific prices are actually formed.

In truly biblical tones, influential economists such as Oliver Williamson (1975, p. 20; 1985, p. 143) have proclaimed that: 'in the beginning there were markets'. However, by giving all markets a primeval identity, they are robbed of their historical, structural and institutional characters. This weakness in defining the institutional essence of the market, combined with a mission to spread his concept of 'transaction cost' beyond the market alone, led Williamson eventually to blur his own vital distinction between the market and the firm. We are thus told that hierarchies in the firm are 'a continuation of market relations by other means' (Williamson, 1991, p. 271). The result is that much of the new institutional economics, instead of understanding markets as social institutions, attempts to treat institutions as if they were all markets. But these ubiquitous 'markets' are of a strange, ahistorical and de-institutionalised kind.

The starting point of Williamson's (1985, p. 43) analysis is not historically specific social institutions but 'contractual man'. It is as if all the 'economic institutions of capitalism' are found rolled up inside every single individual human psyche, rather than in the historically contingent social relations. Williamson (1985, p. 3) tried to spin out the analysis from the somehow given 'human nature as we know it' rather than from the specific structures and institutions that constrain and constitute social actors. Similarly, as Michael Magill and Martine Quinzii (1996, p. 11, n.) concurred, 'the transaction costs arguments are derived from basic (universal) attributes of human beings.' Williamson's analysis, which was claimed to apply to 'capitalism' in particular, turned out to be addressed to the universal state of nature. Despite use of the word, there is no focus on the historically specific institutions of capitalism; they are blurred almost beyond recognition. For Williamson and others, 'capitalism' is itself the universal condition, allegedly reflecting the natural and enduring features of 'human nature'.

Indeed, questions are raised about the sensitivity of the new institutional economics to real institutions, particularly when it is claimed that this very same approach can also explain 'the high degree of cooperation and coordination of the activities of honeybees, ants and schooling fish' (Landa, 1999, p. 95). If the core concepts of the new institutional economics have such a wide applicability, then one wonders about their ability to discern the general features of human nature and human institutions, let alone those human institutions with specific features. Human societies and anthills may have some things in common, but the differences are important too. Neither ants, bees nor fish make contracts or exchange property rights. Nor do they reflect on their own society and make conscious plans to sustain or change it. Beyond the realm of human society, there are no genuine organisations or markets.

Loose thinking about key institutions such as the market pervades economics. For instance, in his work on the family, Gary Becker saw no essential distinction between the commercial world of trade and the intimacy of the family. Apart from the duration of the contract, his theory sees little difference between sex with a prostitute and sexual relations between husband and wife. For Becker, they can be analysed with the same theoretical instruments, to the neglect of their distinctive features. Rather than focusing on specific institutions and social structures, his analysis was concerned with abstract allocative choices of a de-institutionalised kind. His work is thus peppered with loose phrases such as 'a market for marriages' (Becker, 1976a, p. 206).[3]

Similarly imprecise habits have spread to sociology. For Coleman (1990, pp. 35–6), markets were simply 'transfers of rights or resources' within 'systems of relations' or a 'system of exchange'. His concept of the market is so general that it can be made up of 'unilateral transfers'. In other words, for Coleman, markets cover a wide range of phenomena including taxation and gift-giving, as well as agreed legal contracts between two parties. Following Becker, Coleman (p. 22)

---

3   Efforts to explain this phrase away as a mere 'metaphor' make matters no better. Becker and Posner (1993, p. 423) explain that the term 'marriage market' means little more than that the matching of partners is 'systematic and structured rather than the result of random shots from Cupid's bow'. But this does not explain the use of the word 'market'. Would the 'metaphor' of a 'central soviet plan for marriages' be any less 'systematic and structured'? Becker and Posner's inadequate explanation gives little recognition either of the institutional character of markets, or of the fact that marriages *per se* are never themselves bought or sold.

asserted: 'It is clear that marriage can be seen as taking place in a kind of market'.[4] Evidently, a near-total blindness regarding different types of social institution afflicts much of modern sociology as well.

However, despite the global march of capitalism, the modern family is still not completely invaded by commercial relations, and strong cultural norms are still sensitive to this fact. Neoclassical economics either ignores the family or tries to force it into a purely contractarian analysis. Becker and Coleman do the latter, making personal relationships within the family conceptually equivalent to commercial contracts, without highlighting the distinctive features of each.

In another context, Becker (1991, pp. 362 ff.) was again sloppy in his use of market language. In some modern societies, babies may be adopted, in return for payment. Becker wrote of babies being sold, when in fact what is involved is the sale of parental rights. However, as Richard Posner (1994, p. 410) rightly pointed out: 'The term *baby selling*, while inevitable, is misleading. A mother who surrenders her parental rights for a fee is not selling her baby; babies are not chattels, and cannot be bought and sold. She is selling her parental rights.' A reckless and imprecise use of terms, along with a neglect of cultural and institutional realities of market economies – especially by those that claim to pursue and admire precision and rigour as well as explanatory scope – combines both tragedy and farce.

THE DANGEROUS IDEA OF THE DE-INSTITUTIONALISED MARKET

We see the tragic side when such versions of economic theory are applied to real-world economic problems. This was illustrated most graphically in the post-1989 economic transformation in the former Eastern Bloc. Since 1989, these Eastern European economies have sometimes been subjected to misguided and unsophisticated economic policies such as 'shock therapy'. A key assumption behind these policies – of which the textbooks give no explanation – was that the market order would rapidly germinate and grow in the primordial soil of human relations, once the old state bureaucracies were swept away. As the influential Western advisor Jeffrey Sachs (1993, p. xxi) contended: 'markets spring up as soon as central planning bureaucrats vacate the field'. In fact, markets did not spring up spontaneously. The requisite commercial rules, norms and institutions were lacking (Kozul-Wright and Rayment, 1997; Grabher and Stark, 1997). As Nobel Laureate Ronald Coase (1992, p. 718) rightly observed: 'The ex-communist countries are advised to move to a market economy . . . but without the appropriate institutions, no market of any significance is possible.'

---

4   Coleman (1990, p. 22) went on to state that marriage involves the 'barter', by each partner, of 'one commodity – himself or herself'. Yet in no legal marriage contract does one person purchase another. Outside of slavery, people are not chattels. Many writers have described marriage using the metaphor of slavery; but Coleman is proposing a structurally impossible kind of slavery where each is equally the owned slave of the other.

Of course, to deny that markets emerge automatically does not mean that they can be instituted simply by decree. Like many institutions, markets involve elements of both spontaneous development and rule design. Both individual initiative and collective decree are ineffective unless there is an adequate cultural and institutional foundation. Lacking an adequate institutional grounding for the growth of market alternatives to state control, many of the Eastern European economies were plunged into years of recession and economic instability (Zecchini, 1997).

It is reported that Alan Greenspan, head of the Federal Reserve Bank in the United States, recognised this mistake after the event. On his own admission, he originally assumed that the collapse of the Soviet regimes 'would automatically establish a free-market entrepreneurial system' believing that capitalism was simply 'human nature'. It turned out, he says, to be 'not nature at all, but culture'.[5] Yet mainstream economists continue to neglect the detailed study of specific cultures. Greenspan's conversion is welcome, but there is a great deal of work to be done to ensure that economics pays recognition to culturally and historically specific institutions.

Understanding the institutional nature of markets is also vital in the context of economic development. This process involves a deeply embedded cultural and moral fabric, involving the behavioural and moral norms that are necessary for the market to function. This fabric does not necessarily emerge spontaneously, from the interactions of given individuals. Essentially, 'the social structure of the society is not a malleable structure that may easily evolve or adjust to accommodate the market and the rules of the game associated with it' (Platteau, 1994, p. 795).

Different types of market institution are possible, involving different routines, pricing procedures, and so on. A growing number of economists have been obliged to notice this. General equilibrium theorists were forced to adopt particular, auxiliary assumptions concerning market procedures in order to obtain a definite outcome. Something special like the 'Walrasian auctioneer' had to be assumed in order to make the model work (Arrow and Hahn, 1971). In other words, some elemental institutional structures had to be brought in to make the model function in its own terms. Again this is confirmation of the argument above, that neoclassical theory works principally through its auxiliary assumptions. But it is widely and wrongly claimed that it is the core theory that is doing all the explanatory work.

As experimental economics has emerged as a major subdiscipline, it has been realised that the simulation of market phenomena necessarily involves the setting out of specific rules and procedures. Modern experimental economists, in simulating markets in the laboratory, have found that they have had also to face the unavoidable problem of setting up its specific institutional structure. Simply calling it a market is not enough to provide the experimenter with the institutionally specific structures and procedural rules. As leading experimental

---

5 Quoted by William Pfaff in the *Boston Globe*, 30 August 1999.

economist Vernon Smith (1982, p. 923) wrote: 'it is not possible to design a laboratory resource allocation experiment without designing an institution in all its detail.'[6]

Each particular market is entwined with other institutions and a particular social culture. Accordingly, there is not just one type of market but many different markets, each depending on its inherent routines, cultural norms and institutional make up. Differentiating markets by market structure according to textbook typology – from perfect competition through oligopoly to monopoly – is not enough. Institutions, routines and culture have to be brought into the picture, otherwise there will not be enough information to determine outcomes. Experimental economists have discovered this truth. Chris Starmer (1999a, p. F13) wrote:

> The results of market experiments show that experimental markets sometimes converge to predicted outcomes, and sometimes they do not. Part of the difficulty in understanding why such differences exist between alternative market institutions derives from the fact that we have a relatively underdeveloped understanding of what determines initial decisions and the dynamics of adjustment.

Although markets have been central to the concerns of mainstream economics for two hundred years, the neglect of real market institutions means that there is still a 'relatively underdeveloped understanding' of the institutional parameters determining market dynamics. The reason for this is that, at least until recently, different types of market institution were rarely examined. If we were to look for the rudiments of a theory of different types of market institution, we would have to look in the very places that many economists have scorned or ignored.

The institutional character of markets was emphasised by German historical economists in the nineteenth century, and by twentieth-century 'old' institutional economists such as John Commons, John Hobson and John Maurice Clark. Long ago Hobson (1902, p. 144) wrote: 'A market, however crudely formed, is a social institution.' Likewise, for J. M. Clark (1957, p. 53) 'the mechanism of the market, which dominates the values that purport to be economic, is not a mere mechanism for neutral recording of people's preferences, but a social institution with biases of its own.' We have also seen how Werner Sombart and others stressed the institutional character of the market. However, these narratives have been dismissed or neglected by most economists.

Significantly, much of the modern analysis of market institutions has taken place on the fringes of economics or sociology. Wayne Baker (1984) made an important study of US financial markets, showing how specific networks and social relationships between actors structured exchanges. Mitchel Abolafia (1996)

---

6   See Holt (1995) and Kagel (1995) for discussions of the evidence from experimental economics of the varying impacts of different market structures or mechanisms.

also researched US financial markets, showing the rules and cultural norms that govern their operation. Jan Kregel (1995) examined the historical evolution of financial markets, relating this history to the different models of market arrangement that are found in neoclassical economic theory. Marie-France Garcia (1986) showed the detailed processes of organisation of a strawberry market in France, involving mechanisms of quality control, information dispersal and pricing by auction. All the studies of real markets indicated that there are different types of market, and that the creation of a market involves a selection from a potentially infinite number of alternative institutional features. Furthermore, markets are often highly organised entities, imposing rules as well as benefits upon their users.

The recognition that (a) the market is an institution and (b) different, institutionally differentiated types of market may exist, has important theoretical and policy implications. Institutionalists start from these very elements that are lacking in the mainstream analysis. Exchange, in the sense of Commons and other 'old' institutionalists, requires, first, a common system of language – or at least mutually understood signs – so that the individuals involved can communicate. Second, an enforceable set of rules or laws must govern the contracts between individuals. Third, there must also be a system of established property rights to make property transfers meaningful and enforceable. There must be laws, and procedures to deal with disputes. In most accounts it is accepted that some of these rules and laws can emerge gradually over time, and possibly – at least in the case of language – without intention or design. The degree to which the state or other powerful organisations have been, or must be, involved in these processes is a matter of important analytical controversy, but it need not concern us in this chapter. The key point here is to notice that all these frameworks are, in an established sense of the word, institutions.

In general, exchange involves contractual agreement and the exchange of property rights. Not all exchanges take place in markets. Markets, where they exist, help to structure, organise and legitimate numerous exchange transactions. A market is an institution in which a significant number of commodities of a particular type are regularly exchanged, and in which market rules and structures pattern these exchange negotiations and transactions. They involve pricing and trading procedures that help to establish a consensus over prices, and often help by communicating information regarding products, prices, quantities, potential buyers or possible sellers.

Markets differ substantially, especially when we consider markets in different cultures. In Japan, for example, selling prices are typically taken as fixed. Any attempt to haggle over prices is regarded as questioning the quality of the goods and insulting the integrity of the seller. On the contrary, in North Africa, extensive bargaining over prices is seen as part of a process of developing a social relationship between buyer and seller. After a long conversation, prices can be reduced by more than a half. Comparing Japan with North Africa, we can see that markets differ not simply on the question of the pricing procedure. They also differ in the very meanings attributed to these processes and in the place of market exchange in social life.

To recapitulate, the market itself is neither a natural datum nor a ubiquitous ether, but a social institution, governed by sets of rules defining restrictions on some, and legitimating other, behaviours. Furthermore, the market is necessarily embedded in other social institutions, such as in some cases the state. It can emerge spontaneously, but it can also be promoted, or even in some cases created, by conscious design. Markets, in short, are organised and institutionalised exchange.

A clear implication of this argument is that the familiar pro- and anti-market policy stances are both rather insensitive to the possibility of different types of market institution. The markets of two thousand years ago were very different from (say) the electronic financial markets of today. In the real world, and even in a single country, we may come across many different examples of the market. We encounter informal markets for second-hand goods, fish and vegetable markets organised and regulated by the local council, and so on. The use of designated tokens to purchase baby-sitting services within an organised baby-sitting collective is also an example of a limited market. There are also markets for the sexual services of prostitutes. Such markets are clearly quite different in substance and connotation. We should thus refrain from treating them all as exactly the same.[7]

Instead of recognising the important role of different possible cultures and trading customs, both the opponents and the advocates of the market have focused exclusively on its general features. Thus, for instance, Marxists have deduced that the mere existence of private property and markets will themselves encourage acquisitive, greedy behaviour, with no further reference in their analysis to the role of ideas and culture in helping to form the aspirations of social actors. This de-cultured viewpoint has difficulty explaining, for example, the high degree of material acquisitiveness and commodity fetishism that prevailed in the planned and allegedly 'socialist' Eastern Bloc before 1989, after decades of extensive official education and propaganda extolling co-operation and shunning greed. This viewpoint has difficulty, furthermore, in recognising the often limited and contrasting versions of consumerism that prevail in different capitalist societies. Obversely, over-enthusiastic advocates of the market claim that its benefits stem simply and unambiguously from the existence of private property and exchange, without regard to possible variations in detailed market mechanism or cultural context. As strange bedfellows, both Marxists and market individualists underestimate the degree to which all market economies are unavoidably made up of densely layered social institutions.

STUMBLING BLIND OVER THE FIRM

Turning to another key institution within modern economies, what is the attitude of most economists to the firm? Clearly, the reality and importance of this

---

7 For discussions of the shared and contrasting features of different markets see K. Polanyi *et al.* (1957) and Callon (1998).

institution have generally been recognised, even if the internal workings of the 'black box' of the firm were widely ignored until the 1970s. However, as with the market, there is a scarcity of precision and an abundance of disagreement on the definition of the firm. There are a variety of views on this issue but generally they fall short of what is required.

Consider an extreme but illustrative case. Discussing 'the economics of religion', Laurence Iannaccone (1991, 1998) described churches as 'firms' that compete on a 'religious market'. True, some churches are registered as legal or corporate entities, but that misses their true essence. Churches are institutions that provide spiritual guidance. Their services are unlike those provided by an insurance company, hairdresser or travel agent. The mistaken idea of a 'religious market' ignores the fact that choice of religious belief is neither necessarily nor principally about buying and selling, nor exchanges of property rights. Crucially, churches do not charge for the spiritual guidance that they dispense. Such services are typically provided without any legal contract or requirement of payment in return. The unqualified description of 'churches as firms' ignores some vital and specific features of church organisation and function. Further-more, it robs the notion of the firm of much necessary precision and institutional specificity. If some economists can, without any qualification, describe 'churches as firms' then that betrays some institutional emptiness in their concept of the firm. If 'churches are firms' and essentially the same 'theory of the firm' can be used to analyse them both, then this suggests some limitations of that 'theory of the firm' when applied to the profit-oriented corporations of the commercial world.[8]

Some economists see little difference between the firm and the market. In their classic article, Armen Alchian and Harold Demsetz (1972, p. 777) wrote: 'Telling an employee to type this letter rather than to file that document is like my telling a grocer to sell me this brand of tuna rather than that brand of bread.' The contractual relationship between shopper and grocer was seen as virtually equivalent to the generally more enduring and complex employment relationship with the organisation of the firm.

The approach of Coase was much better. Generally, he has been much more sensitive to institutional differences than most economists. But he has still tangled with the problem of historical specificity (Hodgson, 1998d). In his early and famous article, Coase (1937) seemed to confine himself to the type of firm that involves employment contracts, that is the capitalist firm. By contrast, half a century later he expressed regret for this earlier emphasis and addressed a much broader conception of the firm (Coase, 1988). Nowhere did he acknowledge that this change in definition may lead to different answers to the classic questions he raised in his 'nature of the firm' article. In short, Coase seemed unsure whether his theory of the firm is universal, covering all possible types of firm, or is confined to a the specific case of the capitalist firm.

---

8 Leathers and Raines (1992) have disputed a claim by Iannaccone (1991) and others that Adam Smith treated churches simply as competitive firms.

Other leading theorists have fared no better. Sanford Grossman and Oliver Hart (1986, p. 692) defined the firm 'in terms of the assets it owns'. Again this focused exclusively on the relationship between persons and things, to the neglect of structured relations between persons. As David Ellerman (1992, p. 12) rightly put it: 'Being the firm . . . is a contractual role, not a property right.' This contractual role is defined and supported by socio-economic institutions. To understand and define the firm, we must look at these specific institutions.

To their credit, some 'new institutional economists' have focused on structured relationships between persons. For instance, Eirik Furubotn and Rudolf Richter (1997, p. 272) wrote: 'A *firm* is understood . . . as a network of relational contracts between individuals . . . with the purpose of efficiently organizing production.' However, this definition is inadequate, because it is unable to make a distinction between a firm and a network, simply because the former is defined as an example of the latter. Yet in the real world there is such a distinction. A network is typically understood as a loosely structured but enduring cluster of several contractors or firms, linked together by ongoing relational and legal contracts, and perhaps also by agreed rules between them. A network is not a single firm. The firm itself is recognised in law as a 'juridical person' or 'legal person', capable of making legal contracts and exchanging its products with others. By these criteria, the firm is a historically specific entity.[9]

As well as confusing the (vaguely defined) 'market' with the (vaguely defined) 'firm', another common error is to confuse the term 'organisation' with 'firm'. This habit is so widespread in business schools that the two terms are often taken to mean the same thing. Yet a firm is a very particular type of organisation that produces, owns and sells goods and services. Not all organisations do this. Furthermore, not all organisations have the status of a singular 'legal person' that is always accorded to the firm. Accordingly, if the terms 'organisation' and 'firm' are conflated then the temptation is to miss out on the key legal and contractual aspects of the firm. Regrettably, the modern economic theory of the firm is pervaded by a quasi-Maoist disregard of the value and force of formal legal relations of contract and ownership.[10]

Overall, in the literature on the theory of the firm, the desire to create a universal theory of the nature and behaviour of the firm gets in the way of the discussion of historical specificities. What is insufficiently prominent is the notion of the firm as a historically specific formation. If we abandon the aim to create a universal and ahistorical concept of the firm, then we can examine its nature by looking at the specific institutional realities.

---

9 For discussions of the role of legal relations in an institutional context see Nutzinger (1976), Bromley (1989) and Pagano (1991).

10 I refer here to the highly limited and circumscribed notion of private property in China and the lack of legal definition and autonomy of Chinese enterprises, especially in the Maoist period (R. O'Brien, 1979). An economic theory that neglects the importance of formal legal relations will be unable to explain the difference in performance between the politically administered Maoist enterprises and firms in a context of more clearly defined legal relations of contract and ownership. Fortunately, the possible differences in both legal substance and economic performance are now better understood in China.

In the modern business world, the firm is treated as an organisation with a defined legal status as a singular 'legal person'. If we enter into transactions with a firm then we deal with individuals within that firm. But we nevertheless understand that those individuals are acting in the name of the firm, and that the firm as a whole is taking upon itself any contractual responsibilities into which we may enter. These responsibilities may outlive the individuals involved. This commonplace idea of the firm as a 'legal person' is in line with its derivation from *firmus*, or legal signature. The idea of the firm as a 'legal person' is widely known and understood, except by many economists and sociologists who refuse to acknowledge historically specific legal realities in their quest for a universal theory.

Even in this restrictive sense of a 'legal person', firms have existed for hundreds or even thousands of years. Originally, one person or a partnership owned the firm. The status of 'legal person' emerged in law as the firm evolved beyond its previously frequent ownership by a single individual or small group (Greif, 1996). The idea of a 'legal person' is now established in modern statutes of corporate law. Hence it is important not to confuse the firm with a network of multiple legal persons, who may have separate ownership of their own products. A network involves multiple 'legal persons'. By contrast, a firm is one 'legal person' capable of owning resources and making contracts as a singular corporate body, despite the fact that it is an organisation composed of several people.

Once the firm has obtained a workforce, it manages the resources in its possession essentially by administrative control rather than by internal contracts of property exchange. Accordingly, one of the key features of a firm is that it is an organised enclave, apart from the market. Failing to recognise this, many observers are unable to draw clear and well-established boundaries around the firm. There is widespread confusion over this issue. This confusion allows economists to ignore the reality of non-market organisation in the private sector and bring everything there under the conceptual umbrella of market analysis. Corporate control and authority are treated purely as a matter of free contract. They can thus ignore the reality of control and authority within the private capitalist corporation but remain critical of public sector bureaucracy and state planning. Such misconceptions are aided by the lack of clear and adequate definitions of 'firm' or 'market' in social science.

Like many economists, Steven Cheung (1983, p. 11) had some difficulty in surveying the boundaries of the firm. He raised this example:

> A landlord, who wants to build a high-rise finds a building contractor. This contractor subcontracts with a hardwood floor contractor on an agreed price per square foot – a piece count. The subcontractor, who imports the wood materials and adds finishing work to the wood on a piece-rate basis, in turn finds a sub-subcontractor, provides him wood, and offers him a price per square foot laid. Finally, the sub-subcontractor hires workers and again pays them per square foot laid.

Such a complex integration of contracts and subcontracts is very common. But, contrary to Cheung, it offers no great taxonomic difficulty. Cheung seemed to think that piece-rate payments imply the existence of 'a "market"' (p. 10). This explains his repeated – but irrelevant – stress on payments per square foot in the above (p. 11) quotation. However, Cheung gave no reason why piece-rate payments imply the existence of 'a "market"'. Cheung also declared (p. 17) that 'economists may well argue that because they are all vertically integrated by contracts, with transfer pricing, only one firm exists.' However, contrary to Cheung, being 'vertically integrated by contracts' is not the same as vertical integration *within* a firm. Blind to this important distinction, Cheung suggested that the hardwood floor example is something with the characteristics of both 'a "market"' and 'one firm'. The myth of the firm–market hybrid was born. It has since become ubiquitous.

In truth, the hardwood floor example involves (market or relational) exchange, between not one but four 'legal persons': the landlord, the contractor, the subcontractor, and the sub-subcontracted firm with its employees. By the legal criterion, four firms or legal persons were clearly present, not one.

In contrast, Cheung argued that the definition of the firm is arbitrary. He wrote: 'according to one's view a "firm" may be as small as a relationship between two input owners or, if the chain of contracts is allowed to spread, as big as the whole economy' (p. 17). He then jumped to the conclusion: 'Thus it is futile to press the issue of what is or is not a firm' (p. 18). Cheung's argument was essentially that: different definitions of X are possible, therefore it is futile to define X. But this is a non sequitur. The problem here is in the eye of the beholder. The taxonomic problem diminishes greatly once we define the firm as a legal and non-market entity.

A genuine query emerges: why do so many economists evade the obvious, everyday, legally grounded, definition of the firm? There are two likely and related reasons. One is the tendency to associate the so-called 'economic' attributes of a social arrangement with specific subjective perceptions of the agents involved, rather than with the character of the social structures or institutions. The other is the related desire to make economics general and ahistorical, rather than to associate it with historically specific institutions.

Some writers repel attempts to define the firm as an identifiable legal and non-market entity. It is suggested, for instance, that the boundaries between the firm and the market are being eroded in modern capitalism. It is claimed that this development undermines the idea of the firm as a non-market entity. Nevertheless, we would still have the problem of defining and identifying the past historical phenomenon of the firm. Even the extinction of a species does not exempt us from the task of taxonomy. The truth, however, is that the firm is not extinct.

It is true that there is a huge variety of possible forms of industrial organisation. Open markets, relational contracts, cartels, networks, joint ventures, strategic alliances and business groups are examples. But these are all different types of relationship between firms, sometimes with the addition of another legal entity set up by the firms involved. These relationships between firms are of constitutional, co-ordinative and behavioural significance for the industry as a whole but they do not necessarily alter the (legal) boundary between the individual firms and the world outside.

A muddled reality is no excuse for muddled definitions. Likewise, a mutable reality is no justification for elastic ideas. Accordingly, even if the boundaries between the firm and the market are breaking down in reality, the conceptual distinction between these two terms is still necessary to make sense of such a statement. In order to describe or understand such a tangled reality we need clear concepts and careful definitions to guide us. Without them we are conceptually blind. Clear and unmuddled concepts are necessary to penetrate a muddled world.[11]

THE MYTH OF THE INTERNAL MARKET

For lack of adequate definitions and concepts, the real boundary around the firm in the real world is often missed, sometimes when writers look inside the firm, and sometimes when they look outside, at relations between firms. From within or without, they fail to see the boundary.

Contrary to much talk in the literature, true markets rarely, if ever, exist within firms. It is true that many modern firms have separate functional or territorial divisions, each with their own accounts and profit targets. A key test is whether or not these divisions have separate legal status, and are recognised as 'legal persons'. If so, these divisions themselves constitute firms, even if they are largely owned by, and subordinate to, another company. There are examples of this, with the modern conglomerate subdividing itself into legally separate units. That means that we must have two words, not one: 'firm' and 'conglomerate'. We can happily use both words, but it is important not to confuse the two, as they refer to different things. Yet in the literature the distinction is rarely made.

Of course, the formal legal status of any organisation tells us far from the whole story. Furthermore, legal formalities can sometimes have a fictional status, masking a different reality. For example, a conglomerate of different firms may in practice act like a single firm, because control of the conglomerate is concentrated in the hands of a single group. In this case, additional criteria come into play. However, a case is made in chapter 19 below in favour of the legal criterion being the primary one in circumstances where the rule of law prevails. In general, legal relations are not mere formalities, but are backed with the powers and sanctions of the legal system of the state. Accordingly, if legal criteria are regarded as less important, then the onus is on the researcher is to identify the powers and forces that are sufficient to counter the sanctions and powers of state authority.

There are often internal negotiations and transfers of resources between divisions of the modern firm. But are there 'internal markets' within firms? Many

---

11 In an excellent discussion of different types of business system, Whitley (1999) made a useful distinction between ownership and non-ownership co-ordination between firms. Ownership co-ordination depends on the exercise of ownership and other contracted rights, such as through strategic alliances. Non-ownership co-ordination depends on more informal relationships. Note that this important distinction is sustained only by recognising – rather than ignoring – the importance of formal ownership, although it is far from the whole story.

firms use price indicators for internal accounting, and products may be 'exchanged' by one internal department with another. It may be concluded that this is evidence of an 'internal market'. But typically these exchanges do not involve the exchange of legal property rights. The objects of 'exchange' remain the property of the firm. These 'exchanges' are not legally enforceable contracts of trade. They are internal measures of organisational procedure and accounting. They are accounting transfers, rather than genuine commodity exchanges. Even if a subdivision of the firm is delegated the power to enter into contracts with outside bodies, then the firm as a whole is legally the party to the contract. The subdivision is merely exercising delegated powers: it acts 'in the name' of the corporation, and the corporation as a whole is legally responsible for its liabilities under the agreed contract. Because the firm is a singular legal entity, trading and contract *within* a firm are highly limited.

There is a widespread supposition that 'internal labour markets' exist inside the firm. Employment contracts may be renegotiated, for example. However, these would be cases of the renegotiation of contracts for *inputs* of goods or services *into* the firm. Even the pioneers of the idea – Peter Doeringer and Michael Piore (1971, pp. 1–2) – admitted that 'internal labor markets' are not governed primarily by the price mechanism but by 'a set of administrative rules and procedures'. David Marsden (1986, p. 162) went further: 'internal labour markets offer quite different transaction arrangements, and there is some doubt as to whether they fulfil the role of markets.' What Doeringer and Piore pointed to was a competitive fluidity of labour within the organisation. They did not show that a true market existed within the firm.

Would a competition between employees for an advertised post within the firm be an 'internal labour market'? Not strictly, because this would not constitute regularised and organised exchange but a series of one-off competitions for advertised internal posts. These would be periodic instances of contract reallocation, rather than a true labour market. The regular, repeated and institutionalised exchange that characterises true markets would be lacking.

As another example, the discussion of the modern multidivisional firm suggests that each division within a firm competes in the firm's 'internal capital market' for the budget allocated by the firm's head office (Williamson, 1975). To be sure, some substantial competition and rivalry is involved, but it is not competition in a market. It is completely different from the true capital market where shares in individual firms are bought and sold. The division of the firm has no independently owned share capital to use as a lever to obtain its own loans from outside agencies. The internal competition to which Williamson refers is not market competition but a struggle over power and resources between different parts of the corporate bureaucracy. This mistaken idea of an 'internal capital market' obscures rather than explains the true corporate reality.

Much of the loose talk about 'internal markets' within firms derives from a sloppy use of the term 'market' which, unfortunately, pervades economics today. In terms of genuine, regular and organised exchanges of goods or services, 'markets' are rarely, if ever, found *within* the firm. This pervasive confusion over the nature of markets and exchange allows free-market and other economists to ignore the reality of non-market organisation in capitalist firms and to understand everything in 'market' terms.

CONFLATING THE FIRM AND THE MARKET

Strikingly, however, a similar but inverted defect is found among some non-mainstream economists. The same lack of a clear and adequate definition of the market and of the firm, allows others, often from a very different ideological perspective, to ignore legal and contracting realities and to focus exclusively on questions of control. As an example, the very idea of 'market hierarchies' (Pitelis, 1991) encapsulates this confusion. As in mainstream economics, 'market' and 'organisation' become conflated. Here, however, instead of seeing every-thing through market lenses, the power relations within organisations become eyeglasses to view the system as a whole. From this particular perspective, the universal conceptual focus becomes one of co-ordination and control. Again, the crucial error here is that legal and historical specificities – particularly concerning markets and contracts – are downplayed. As a result, instead of the 'new institutionalist' mistake of treating institutions as if they were all markets, the inverted error becomes one of treating all markets as if they were non-market organisations, and all contracts as is they were all simply matters of power or administrative control.[12]

Also conflating the firm and the market, Ken-ichi Imai and Hiroyuki Itami (1984) discussed the supposed 'interpenetration of organization and market' in Japan. However, they defined both market and organisation without any reference to property rights or contracts, referring instead to factors such as the degree of durability of the relationship and the use or otherwise of price as a major information signal. By this flawed methodology it is not difficult to find elements of so-called 'organisation' in the highly structured and regulated 'markets' of Japan, and to find elements of an alleged 'market' inside many firms. These conclusions follow, however, from the inadequate definitions of 'market' and 'organisation' in the first place. In contrast, superior definitions of these terms would lead to the conclusion that markets – in Japan and elsewhere – are often organised to a greater or lesser degree, but that any market is a quite different type of organisation from the property-owning and contracting legal entity of the firm.

As another real-world illustration, consider the case of a large corporation that has a number of smaller subcontractors and suppliers – such as Benetton, or Marks and Spencer. If we mistakenly defined a firm in terms of a broad notion of control, then the large corporation, plus all the subcontracted suppliers, would together be regarded as a single firm. However, this would simply – and confusingly – shift the definition of 'the firm' from one type of phenomenon to another. Clearly, we require two terms. One – the firm – would describe a

---

12 See Cowling and Sugden (1993), Pitelis (1991) and the critical discussion in Hodgson (1999b).

productive organisation constituted as singular legal entity. The other – such as a 'supplier network' – would describe the entire clustered complex of subordinate subcontractors that are dependent on the contracts of a dominant organisation. It is simply confusing to shift the word 'firm' from the former to the latter.

A firm, a conglomerate, and a 'supplier network' are different things. A firm is a single 'legal person'. A conglomerate is a set of firms, wholly or partly owned by a holding firm and acting as a single entity. A supplier network is a set of firms, each of which may be dependent on the contracts of a single firm, without necessarily being wholly or partly owned by the dominant firm. Once we establish legal and historical specificities, then we can be much more careful in our definitions.

In three classic articles, George Richardson (1972), Victor Goldberg (1980) and Ronald Dore (1983) argued that the relationship between a large corporation and its subordinate contractors is often more durable and intensive than a typical market relationship. This valid and important observation does not change the above argument. It is no excuse for fudging the distinction between a firm and a market. Indeed, it points not to two but to three types of institutional relationship: the firm, the market, and relational exchange. An enduring relationship between a dominant firm and a subordinate subcontractor is not an open market relationship, but it is still one of commodity exchange, involving the legal transfer of property rights. It remains a relationship of commodity exchange between two distinct firms. It is not evidence of commodity exchange, nor evidence of a 'market' within a single, encompassing firm. Firms, markets, and relational exchange are three different things.

MORE ON THE MYTH OF THE FIRM–MARKET HYBRID

In modern economies, there are many cases of complex forms of interaction between productive agencies (Cheung, 1983; Ménard, 1996). However, on inspection most of these allegedly 'hybrid' cases turn out to be interlocking relations or networks between multiple and distinct legal firms or legal persons, rather than a single, encompassing firm.

Part of the problem here is a failure to recognise that markets are but one special case of commodity exchange (Hodgson, 1988). As North (1977, p. 710) has rightly observed: 'most exchanges do not take place in markets.' As a result, instead of just firms and markets, there are three possibilities: the firm, market exchange and non-market exchange. If we adhere to the false dichotomy between firms and markets then truly we have some difficulty in classifying the kind of non-market contractual relations between firms, identified by Richardson, Goldberg and Dore. The real-world ensemble of such interactive relations is neither a firm nor a market so – according to the logic of this false dichotomy – it must assume the 'strange' form of a 'hybrid' or a 'quasi-market' or a 'quasi-firm'. The first error here lies in the adoption of a false dichotomy, ignoring the third (Richardsonian) possibility of non-market contractual exchange.

The second error is to have an inadequately precise definition of the firm, even to the extent that the difference between terms such as 'firm', 'organisation' and 'industry' may potentially dissolve. A wide notion of an 'organisation' is adopted, which is then confused and conflated with the firm or corporation.

Williamson's discussion of hybrids is similarly defective. Williamson (1999, p. 1091) saw 'hybrids' as 'long-term contractual relations into which security features have been crafted'. Admittedly, Williamson was attempting to describe a very important set of phenomena within modern capitalism. Much modern contracting is of this 'long-term' type. However, such 'contractual relations' are not themselves firms, nor are they within firms. Furthermore, the long term, relational and 'security' features of the contractual relations mean that they are not markets either. Market relations are generally more impersonal and are typically short term. But Williamson too is a victim of the false dichotomy. He assumed that if long-term contractual relations are neither firms nor markets, then they must be 'hybrids' of the market and the firm. One must ask, however: what agencies make the (long-term) contracts? In fact, these 'contractual relations' are all between, not within, firms. If we accept and understand the third (Richardsonian) possibility, of non-market contracts of a 'relational' type, then the whole picture is one of relational contracts between firms. There is now no 'hybrid' to be seen. By adopting the obfuscatory concept of a firm–market hybrid, Williamson muddles his former claim that the firm is essentially different from the market.

To his credit, Claude Ménard (1995) defined terms such as 'market' and 'organisation' more precisely than most others. In particular, he defined the market as an institution. He rightly pointed to the possibility that markets themselves involve elements of organisation and regulation. He thus argued: 'In all of these situations, the market activities are significantly permeated with organizational factors' (p. 176). So far so good. He then went off the rails. The fact that markets are organisations does not imply that all organisations can be markets. He tried to demonstrate that *'organizations can be internally structured as quasi-markets'*. Ménard considered franchising 'when very strict standards are imposed on independent participants'. He noted that:

> Classification [into markets or organizations] becomes particularly difficult when firms are interconnected by a dense web of transactions, with strong commitments to each other and complementarities of their assets, but without formal agreements and, moreover, with property rights on these firms clearly maintained as distinct. (p. 176)

On this basis he acknowledged intermediate 'forms' between markets and hierarchies. These were his 'hybrids', involving 'specific combinations of markets incentives and modalities of coordination involving some form of hierarchical relationship' (p. 175).

The problems began when Ménard conflated the notions of 'organization', 'firm' and 'hierarchy'. Indeed, he never provided an adequate definition of the latter two terms, and he seemed to use the terms 'firm' and 'organization' interchangeably. Consider his example of strictly monitored and regulated franchising. With a broad definition of 'organization', this could be described as an 'organized' relationship, but between *two or more* firms or 'legal persons'. Although the relationship has an 'organized' character it does not mean that it is a single firm. Once we realise that every firm is a special kind of organisation but not all organisations are firms, then Ménard's problems disappear. The case when 'firms are interconnected by a dense web of transactions, with strong commitments to each other' is a case of relational contracting between multiple firms. Again, the 'organized' character of the relationship does not imply that everything is organised within a single firm. The fact that 'property rights on these firms [are] clearly maintained as distinct' does not create any taxonomic difficulty. It simply underlines the fact that multiple firms may exist within a single organisational network. Essentially, Ménard's primary error was to allow confusion of the broadly defined organisation with the firm. His secondary error was to overlook the fact that relational contracting involves the exchange of commodities between *different* firms but *not* on an open market. It is thus a third option, after a market and a firm.

Recognition of the general absence of markets and commodity exchange inside all firms is important for several reasons. It dispenses with sloppy and confused terms such as 'internal market', 'continuum' and 'hybrid'. It also helps to show the relevance of the boundaries of the firm and the vital interface between non-market and market modes of co-ordination. Any analysis of the formation and role of these boundaries has vital implications for corporate and public policy. To blur these boundaries is both to confuse the analysis and make the policy issues less vital.

Although the purported 'hybrid' cases disappear when we examine them closely, there is one important case where the boundaries are often difficult to draw. This concerns the classic distinction between an employment contract and a contract for services. A firm may change the status of its workers from employed to self-employed, hiring them to do the same work much as before. The key legal and substantive difference here is that, under an employment contract, the employer has the extensive right to control and interfere with the manner and process of work. There is no such right over a self-employed worker: there is simply the right to obtain the contracted good or service at the agreed quantity and quality.

Although the line between employment and self-employment is often difficult to ascertain, the outcome is important for conceptual as well as policy reasons. The determination of the employment status of the worker will affect the boundaries of the firm itself: self-employed workers may contract with the firm but they are not part of the firm. Although the line is difficult to draw, the distinction is still real. Difficulties of demarcation between types do not imply that differences of type are nonexistent.

It is argued here that the firm exists as a distinct legal entity: it is technically a 'legal person'. It owns its products and sells or hires them to others. It enters into contracts with its workforce and its customers. Accordingly, its external relations are dominated by commodity exchanges or markets. Internally, however, the firm is not ruled primarily by prices, markets or commodity exchange. It is essentially a sphere of administration, organisation and managerial direction. Unless we understand that institutional reality we do not understand the firm.

CONCLUSIONS

As Joseph Schumpeter, Karl Polanyi and many others have observed, markets and exchange cannot govern all relations, even in a capitalist society. Hence there is always a boundary between the sphere of exchange and the remainder of the economy. However, neoclassical economics fails to distinguish adequately between commercial and non-commercial relations and thus it sidesteps the problem. Blind to the nature and boundaries of real markets, all relations are treated as if they were market transactions. At the same time there is an inadequate depiction of markets themselves. Yet the distinction between market and non-market relations is both indelible and central to the reality of the modern world. The precise boundaries of the demarcation profoundly affect the nature of the specific variety of the system.

The conflation of the firm with the market has affected the work of authors such as Williamson who have originally made a sharper distinction between the two. Partly as a result, his concept of 'transaction cost' has become broadened not only to cover the costs of trading in markets but also the costs of organising and managing the firm. Having blurred the boundaries between the two entities, the notion of transaction cost has become broadened beyond the sphere of exchange. It has become almost a universal, catch-all phrase, seemingly explaining everything but in substance explaining very little. To restore meaning to this conceptual chaos, a much clearer distinction between the firm on the one hand, and exchange and markets on the other, is required. Accordingly, following Harold Demsetz (1988), it would be useful to use 'transaction costs' to apply to exchange and 'organizational costs' to refer to the cost of managing and organising the firm.[13]

Other problems arise when mainstream economics addresses different economic systems. Generally there is inadequate sensitivity to different cultures and institutional frameworks, involving different structures and combinations, of market and non-market institutions. Accordingly, there is an inadequate understanding of different types of capitalism, say in Britain, Germany, Japan and the USA (Hodgson, 1999a). Especially when this conceptual blindness is combined with a free-market ideology, then an adequate policy analysis is disabled. It is sometimes simply assumed that if an economy is a successful

---

13 Notably, Coase (1937) did not use the term 'transaction cost'. Instead, he used phrases such as 'contract costs', 'marketing costs' and 'cost of using the price mechanism'. For Coase, these costs were found principally outside the firm, and the firm exists to virtually abolish – rather than simply minimise – such costs. In contrast, Williamson accepts in principle that such 'transaction costs' can apply extensively to firms as well as markets.

economy then it must be a market economy, and if it is suffering recession or slow growth, then the 'obvious' remedy is to extend and deregulate the market. There is little discussion of the way in which the market can be helpful in some contexts but harmful in others. The possibility that pro-market policies can be destructive as well as beneficial often escapes notice.[14]

Much of economics starts from the individual, and tries to spin out the analysis of economic institutions from given, ahistorical agents. A remarkably candid admission of the flaw in this approach was by the econometrician Trygve Haavelmo in his 1989 lecture on receipt of the Nobel Prize. He argued that:

> existing economic theories are not good enough . . . We start by studying the behavior of the individual under various conditions of choice. . . . We then try to construct a model of the economic society in its totality by a so-called process of aggregation. I now think this is actually beginning at the wrong end. . . . Starting with some existing society, we could conceive of it as a structure of rules and regulations within which the members of society have to operate. Their responses to these rules as individuals obeying them, produce economic results that would characterize the society.
>
> (Haavelmo, 1997, p. 15)

Haavelmo rightly suggested that historically specific institutions should be brought into the analysis at the beginning. Institutions are not simply human nature writ large. A few years earlier, another Nobel Laureate had made similar points and had drawn attention to the malaise at the core of modern economics. Robert Solow (1985, p. 330) complained:

> My impression is that the best and brightest in the profession proceed as if economics is the physics of society. There is a single universally valid model of the world. It only needs to be applied. You could drop a modern economist from a time machine . . . at any time, in any place, along with his or her personal computer; he or she could set up in business without even bothering to ask what time or place.

Solow (1985, p. 328) also regretted that 'economic theory learns nothing from economic history, and economic history is as much corrupted as enriched by economic theory.' However, the goal that economics has set itself of becoming the universal physics of society is luring the subject into a formalist morass. For Solow, 'the attempt to construct economics as an axiomatically based hard science is doomed to fail.' From this standpoint, Solow implicitly recognised the problem of historical specificity:

---

14 There is substantial evidence to support the view that the economic crises in East Asia in the 1990s were partly the result of unrestrained free market, deregulatory policies. See the journal symposium in Chang *et al.* (1998).

all narrowly economic activity is embedded in a web of social institutions, customs, beliefs, and attitudes. . . . If economists set themselves
the task of modelling particular contingent social circumstances, with
some sensitivity to context, it seems to me that they would provide
exactly the interpretative help the economic historian needs. That kind
of model is directly applicable in organizing a historical narrative, the
more so to the extent that the economist is conscious of the fact that
different social contexts may call for different background assumptions
and therefore for different models. . . . If the proper choice of a model
depends on the institutional context – and it should – then economic
history performs the nice function of widening the range of observation
available to the theorist. . . . One will have to recognize that the validity
of an economic model may depend on the social context.

(Solow, 1985, pp. 328–31)

Close to the end of the twentieth century, both Solow and Haavelmo pointed to
a line of conceptual and theoretical enquiry that would revive the nineteenth-
century project of the historical school.

A preliminary but important task is to provide social science with the precise
concepts that are required to differentiate different types of institution and
economic system. This is not a task of bland description, because the generation
of adequate concepts requires a secure and prior methodological foundation.
If taxonomies fail to relate to underlying structural differences then they are
without value. Accordingly, conceptual clarification in this vein leads in a
theoretical direction, towards the understanding and explanation of underlying
causal mechanisms.

To build new theories one must necessarily be critical of older theories.
Otherwise the old theory will not give space for the new. Unless the new theory
can make claims of comparative superiority then it will not be graced with a
readership. Science often develops as the result of dispute and debate. In this
manner even wrong theories can be of positive value: they help us clarify what
is required to surpass their defects. It has been argued here that a key problem
of modern social science is its partial blindness to different types of social and
economic institution. This is a chronic inadequacy, disabling adequate analysis.
The problem pervades both economics and sociology. It is this central problem
that must be overcome.

We have to be modest about what we can achieve, but a general direction of
movement has been indicated. To face these tasks, institutional economics must
also understand and build upon its own past. This has involved, without any
apology, some extensive discussion of the history of ideas. From this vantage
point, we may move on to begin to clarify some fundamental principles as a
result. This is the concern of part IV of this work.

Part IV

THE MILLENNIUM
The second coming of history?

18

ARE THERE UNIVERSALS
IN SOCIAL AND ECONOMIC
THEORY?

Every historical life is constitutively influenced by the tension
between the universal and the particular forces.
(Erich Rothacker, 'Historismus' (1938))

The fourth and final part of this volume makes some suggestions for the development of a historically sensitive economics. It must be emphasised that these are
merely preliminary suggestions: no complete theory is provided here. Those who
expect such a theory must have misread the last 15 chapters. The development
of a historically sensitive economics has been a tortuous story lasting more than
160 years, in which the last sixty years involved an almost complete abandonment
of the problem. The first major task is simply to place the problem once more on
the agenda of economics and the other social sciences. Those who expect instant
solutions misunderstand the trials and tribulations required to bring any
fundamentally new theory on the stage. They neglect the weight of history itself.
Nevertheless, in the light of the above historical narrative, an attempt can be
made to move the analysis as far forward as possible, in the limited space that
the remaining pages provide. Given these constraints, it is impossible to discuss
all relevant developments in full, and some parts of the account are inevitably
sketchy or incomplete.

The mistake of much of economics has been to treat the de-institutionalised
fundamentals of a market economy as universal. Market-related ideas such
as scarcity, competition, supply and demand are made foundational for the
analysis of any economic system. The argument in this chapter is that while all
social and economic analysis has to use ahistorical and transhistorical concepts,
we must be careful in choosing them. In particular, historical analysis is distorted
and impaired if we misapply the categories pertinent to one system – such as
a market-based economy – to another when they do not fit so well. Recognising
this, some consideration is given to some basic universal principles and ideas
that may apply to a wide range of socio-economic systems.

We begin by discussing the historically specific character of exchange and
markets. From this vantage point, it is possible to judge the degree of generality
of concepts such as scarcity, competition, supply, demand, and so on.

THE MYTH OF THE UNIVERSAL MARKET

We have noted the tendency in economics to treat the market as universal. Remarkably, however, the market is not often defined in economics. It is taken for granted. To understand the market we must first appreciate the concept of exchange.

As noted in the preceding chapter and elsewhere (Hodgson, 1988), exchange is a necessary but not sufficient condition for markets. The meaning of 'exchange' that concerns us here is one that involves contractual agreement and the exchange of property rights. Such exchanges can be personal or impersonal, immediate or enduring, simple or complex. They may or may not involve money. But, by definition, they all involve contracts and the exchange of property rights. This is narrower than the concept of exchange in 'exchange theory' in sociology.

What is a market? Markets involve multiple exchanges, multiple buyers and multiple sellers, and thereby a degree of competition. A market is an institution in which a significant number of commodities of a particular, reasonably well-defined type are regularly exchanged. They contain rules and structures that pattern these exchange negotiations and transactions. Markets, where they exist, help to structure, organise and legitimate exchange transactions. They involve pricing and trading routines that help to establish a consensus over prices, and help to communicate information regarding products, prices, quantities, potential buyers or possible sellers. Markets, in short, are institutionalised exchange.[1]

With this definition in mind, it is clear that markets have been absent for much of human existence. Goods have changed hands within human societies for hundreds of thousands of years. However, much of this internal circulation was powered by custom and tradition. Transfers of goods often involved ceremony and personal, reciprocal actions. These 'personal and kin-based exchanges' (Harris, 1980, p. 238) contrasted with the potential anonymity of the market. Ceremonial transfers involved 'the continuous definition, maintenance and fulfilment of mutual roles within an elaborate machinery of status and privilege' (Clarke, 1987, p. 4). Most of this internal circulation of goods was devoid of any conception of the voluntary, contractual transfer of ownership or property rights. These reciprocal transfers of goods were more to do with the validation of custom and social rank.

Before the rise of the great civilisations of Antiquity, to find any semblance of contractual trade we have to look to the external fringes of society. While trade of some kind goes at least as far back as the last Ice Age, this trade was largely peripheral and occurred at the meeting of different tribal groups. As Max Weber (1927, p. 195) attested:

> In its beginnings commerce is an affair between ethnic groups; it does not take place between members of the same tribe or of the same community, but it is, in the oldest social communities an external phenomenon, being directed only towards foreign tribes.

---

1   See Rosenbaum (2000) for an incisive and extensive analytic discussion of the nature of the market.

Weber's contention, that trade began externally and between communities rather than within them, has withstood subsequent criticism and scholarly examination. It does not mean that trade was unimportant, simply that the market was not at first a major mechanism for co-ordination, allocation and distribution *within* each socio-economic system. In other words, there was little *intra*-social trade. Trade was typically a collective and *inter*-social enterprise between one tribe and another. 'Trade does not arise within a community; it is an external affair involving different communities' (K. Polanyi, 1944, p. 274).

With the rise of civilisation, both external and internal trade increased substantially. Nevertheless, scholars have warned against the view that these ancient civilisations were predominantly market economies (Finley, 1962; K. Polanyi, *et al.*, 1957; Walbank, 1987). A definable internal market, with multiple buyers and sellers, first appeared in Athens in the sixth century BC (K. Polanyi, 1971; North, 1977). Such ancient markets were quite different from, and economically more peripheral than, the markets found in modern capitalist economies. Ancient markets were economically important, but they were not the dominant form of economic co-ordination. After the fall of the Western Roman Empire, both external and internal trade contracted. It revived haphazardly over the next 1000 years (Hodges, 1988). Nevertheless, external trade dominated internal markets from prehistoric to medieval times. 'Strange though it may seem,' wrote Henri Pirenne (1937, p. 140), 'medieval commerce developed from the beginning not of local but of export trade.' Finally, in the last 500 years, markets have changed in character and expanded enormously in scope, volume and economic importance.[2]

In contrast, the commonplace ahistorical discourse of much modern social science regards all forms of human interaction as 'exchange' and the summation of such 'exchanges' as 'markets'. With an ahistorical definition of these terms, it has no difficulty in applying them to all types of system, from tribal societies through Classical Antiquity to the modern capitalist world. Vague, de-institutionalised and ahistorical definitions are typical tools for the over-zealous general theorist.

However, the case against such ahistorical definitions is that they fail to capture key features of markets and exchange as defined here. These features include contracts and property rights, defined and enactable within a formal or customary legal code. If we choose ahistorical definitions, then we require different, additional words to describe the commercial reality. It is best to give words such as 'exchange' and 'market' a more specific and relevant meaning. In addition, there may be other, more general, concepts. The worst of all theoretical worlds is to use the same words to cover all historical phenomena, from tribal ritual to modern, commercial deals. Even non-market institutions – such as the firm – are sometimes treated mistakenly as if they were markets. Unfortunately, today, many social scientists choose the worst of all theoretical worlds.

---

2   However, as Granovetter (1985, 1993) has pointed out in his critiques of K. Polanyi, this does not diminish the general importance of such phenomena as the forces of supply and demand. Such forces prevail in many or all markets.

Even when we define 'exchange' and 'markets' in a narrower sense, involving contracts and legal property rights, then they have still existed for several millennia. While the concepts are not historically universal, they date from the development of the state and legal systems in the ancient world. Systems of contract and property existed in ancient Sumeria and Egypt. Nevertheless, other systems of economic distribution and co-ordination, based on authority or tradition, were more significant in the economy as a whole. Subsequent economic history charts the complex development of exchange and markets up to the present day. More precise and specific definitions of 'exchange' and 'market' are necessary to discern and track these changes. Upon these definitions a more detailed taxonomy can be erected.

ARE SUPPLY AND DEMAND UNIVERSAL?

If markets are not universal phenomena, then what of the existence of the forces of supply and demand? An argument in favour of the alleged universality of supply and demand came from Hubert Henderson (1921, p. 14):

> The order, which I have sought to reveal, pervading and moving the most diverse phenomena of the economic world, would be a far less noteworthy and impressive thing were it merely the peculiar product of capitalism. Merchant adventures, companies, and trusts; Guilds, Governments and Soviets may come and go. But under them all, and, if need be, in spite of them all, the profound adjustments of supply and demand will work themselves out and work themselves out again for so long as the lot of man is darkened by the curse of Adam.

But this went too far – and included too much. The curse of Adam refers to the necessity of working for a living. Even if is this is a universal affliction, it does not follow that supply and demand are universal.

Henderson and others confuse supply and demand, on the one hand, with production and consumption on the other. Of course, for all human history, there has been a universal need to produce and consume the necessities of life. This is the curse of Adam. But in the technical sense that the terms 'supply and demand' are used in the economics textbooks, production is not the same thing as supply and consumption is not the same thing as demand. Demand refers neither to need nor to consumption, but to the goods or services for which there is a willingness to purchase at a specified price. Supply refers not to production, but to the goods or services for which there is a willingness to sell at a specified price. Supply and demand are measures of exchangeability and thus cannot exist without the institutional prerequisites of property and exchange and some notion of price. Even in the Garden of Eden, it would have taken some time to establish these institutions. Supply and demand are not universal concepts but specific to the world of exchange and markets.

Even in the textbooks, it is often not made sufficiently clear that such terms as supply and demand are measures of exchangeability expressed through the price mechanism, thus requiring the institutional prerequisites of property and exchange. False allusions can thus be made to their universality. On the contrary, it by no means undermines the importance of the mechanisms of supply and demand to relate them specifically and centrally to the world of exchange and markets. An adequate theoretical analysis of these mechanisms acquires its relevance not through any false claim of universality, but through its ability to explain some central and common phenomena in market-based economies.

ARE SCARCITY AND COMPETITION UNIVERSAL?

For Lionel Robbins, the economic problem was the allocation of scarce means in the pursuit of given ends. However, in a direct attack upon Robbins and other neoclassical economists, Marshall Sahlins (1972) showed that tribal economies differ from capitalism in that they do not generate ever-increasing wants.[3] His study of tribal, hunter-gatherer societies in tropical regions showed that they are faced with such an abundance of food and other necessities, that resources are for practical purposes unlimited. This is in clear contrast to modern capitalism. Sahlins thus inverted the neoclassical view: it is possible for there to be vast resources and scarce wants.

Note first that the term scarcity has a number of different meanings. Robbins (1932, pp. 12–16) explicitly related the concept of scarcity to the notion of a resource that is 'limited'. However, several important items in socio-economic systems are not 'scarce' in the Robbinsian sense. For instance, trust, arguably so central to the functioning of an economy, is not a scarce resource in the sense that its supply is limited: trust increases the more it is used or relied upon. Likewise, the reserves of honour or mutual respect do not diminish as they are put to use. Scarcity in the Robbinsian sense is hardly consistent with the enduring phenomenon of mass unemployment; labour power is far from being limited in such circumstances.

A limitation of the Robbinsian principle of scarcity is also exhibited with respect to the issue of information and knowledge. Information is a peculiar commodity, because if it is sold it can be still retained by the seller. In addition, skills and knowledge are not strictly given nor limited, because of the phenomenon of 'learning by doing'. As Albert Hirschman (1985, p. 16) pointed out: 'Use of a resource such as a skill has the immediate effect of improving the skill, of enlarging (rather than depleting) its availability.' Especially in the knowledge-intensive economies of modern capitalism the so-called 'law' of universal scarcity is thus broken. Knowledge and information are not scarce in the sense that they are a fixed resource.

The Robbinsian concept of scarcity as a limited resource is inadequate. We should make a distinction between absolute scarcity, stemming from the

---

3   Sahlins was a pupil of the institutionalist K. Polanyi.

niggardliness of nature, and relative scarcity, describing a situation where some means are not immediately available to a given actor at a given point in time and space. Clearly scarcity, at least in the absolute sense, does not apply to all resources. As noted above, some non-physical resources such as knowledge and trust are not scarce in an absolute sense. However, at least on this Earth, physical resources are limited and the principle of absolute scarcity may apply to them.

In contrast to absolute scarcity, relative scarcity is a ubiquitous and unavoidable problem. No individual or organisation has immediate access to all the physical and non-physical resources it requires to serve its ends. At least in this sense, there is a universal problem. Hence there is some truth in the viewpoint that the concept of scarcity is central to economics. But it is important to recognise that scarcity is universal in limited senses only.

The prominent environmental economist Herman Daly (1974) was one of the few to make a distinction between these two forms of scarcity. Daly pointed out that orthodox economics typically refers simply to 'scarcity' and takes it as constant and universal. It hence pays insufficient attention to the historically contingent and increasing ecological problem of the scarcity of global physical resources in the face of unprecedented levels of world population and economic activity.

Crucially, the problem faced by the choosing agent in obtaining the means to meet given ends is not the only problem that economics has to face. If it is to understand the functioning of any socio-economic system, economics also has to consider how resources are generated in the system as a whole, and also how human purposes and wants may change. The idea that economics should define itself as the science of allocation of scarce resources with given wants, is a particularly narrow and relatively recent conception of the subject. As with the classical, historical and institutional economists of earlier times, economics should be the study of the provisioning of the means of human life, involving the use of resources that are absolutely scarce, relatively scarce and not scarce at all.

In its yearning for universal principles, little effort is made to deconstruct the notion of scarcity in mainstream economics. Scarcity is raised to a universal principle, without much regard to the different types of scarcity and the limitations of each. The concept of competition is made to play a similar role. Since the rise of 'social Darwinism' in the nineteenth century, some economists have claimed that the same principles of scarcity and competition apply to both the human and the natural worlds. Jack Hirshleifer is a prominent recent example. He wrote: 'Fundamental concepts like scarcity, competition, equilibrium, and specialization play similar roles in both spheres of inquiry' (Hirshleifer, 1977, p. 2). This is part of his argument for an 'economic imperialism' where such 'economic' assumptions dominate all the social sciences, and biology as well.

However, biology does not give wholehearted support to the idea that rivalrous competition in the face of scarcity is the universal condition. There is a long tradition of thought in biology that has argued otherwise. Petr Kropotkin published *Mutual Aid* in 1902, and argued that competition is not a universal natural law. He gave plentiful evidence of co-operation in nature. In addition, Herman Reinheimer (1913) rejected the universality of competition in both the social and the natural spheres. Since then, many subsequent studies attest to the view that there are plentiful cases of co-operation in both nature and human society, and relatively limited instances of direct competition over scarce resources. Neither biology nor anthropology gives support to the presupposition of universal competition in the face of scarcity.[4]

Nevertheless, while competition involving mutual rivalry or antagonism is not universal, the absolute scarcity of physical resources means that all organisms are potential 'competitors' for such limited resources. Competition in this restricted sense results from the existence of absolute scarcity. But it does not necessarily result in hostile, unco-operative or greedy behaviour. The concept of competition in this limited sense is nothing more than the concept of absolute scarcity, and it is misleading to infer from it any particular behavioural outcome.

TENTATIVE GUIDEPOSTS IN THE GENERAL DOMAIN

On the other hand, it has been argued in earlier chapters that *some* universal presuppositions are necessary in social science. The existence of relative scarcity, and the absolute scarcity of physical resources, are two such universals. We need to consider the possibility of other transhistorical concepts. Two broad conclusions may be drawn out of the earlier discussion. The first conclusion draws particularly from the discussion of Karl Marx in chapter 2 and of Carl Menger in chapter 6. It is that the theoretical analysis of a specific socio-economic system cannot rely entirely on concepts drawn exclusively from that system. This is because the very organisation and extraction of these concepts must rely on other categories of wider applicability. While analysing specific types of socio-economic system, Marx used universal categories such as 'use-value', 'forces of production' and 'relations of production'. To talk of capitalism we must refer to other socio-economic systems; if we speak of socio-economic systems we are using that transhistorical concept; and so on. The very meta-theoretical terms of this discourse are themselves ahistorical. While historical and institutional specificity is important, we are obliged to rely to some degree on general categories. These general categories and theoretical frameworks operate at an unavoidable and basic level of analysis. What is required is an adequate methodology to guide the construction of these concepts.

The second conclusion is based on the positive achievement of the historical school and on the discussion in the preceding two chapters. It is that the entire analysis of any given system cannot and should not be based on universal concepts alone. The first levels of abstraction must be quite general, but if those universalist layers are extended too far – as in the case of neoclassical theory – then the danger is that we end up with conceptions that are unable to come to

---

4   See, for example, Allee (1951), Augros and Stanciu (1987), Benedict (1934), Lewontin (1978), Mead (1937), Montagu (1952), Wheeler (1930).

grips with reality. The scope of analysis of the more general levels of abstraction should be confined.

A socio-economic system is an example of an open, evolving, complex system. Accordingly, we may look to systems theory, complexity theory and general evolutionary theory for concepts and principles that may apply to all such complex systems. The theoretical trick, at this highest level of generality, is not to expect too much, and to recognise what is useful. Analysis at such a high level of generality and abstraction cannot give us detailed, theoretical or empirical postulates.

Nevertheless, in the first place, systems theory does provide a framework for thinking about these issues (Bertalanffy, 1971; Emery, 1981; Laszlo, 1972; J. Miller, 1978). Systems theory has been applied to economics by Janos Kornai (1971) and Neil Kay (1984), and to sociology by Walter Buckley (1967) and Niklas Luhmann (1982, 1995). However, while Luhmann's work provides important insights concerning the nature of social systems, it remains deliberately confined to the highest level of generality. It suffers, therefore, from the same defects as other exclusively general theories in social science. Systems theory promised solutions to management, social, economic and other problems that a theory at such a high level of generality cannot deliver. The missing link was a connection between different levels of analysis relating to general and specific phenomena.

Likewise, modern complexity theory has tried to adduce some general principles that apply to evolving, complex systems (Cohen and Stewart, 1994; Kauffman, 1995; Holland, 1995). There have been some attempts to bring some insights in this area into economics (Colander, 2000a, 2000b; Louçã, 1997; Potts, 2000). There is much of value in complexity theory but it is again important not to claim too much (Horgan, 1995; Rosser, 1999). Only a little weight can be placed on such a general framework. A crucial general insight of complexity theory is to put limits on general insights; we search instead for specific temporary patterns that may develop spontaneously in complex systems.

In the nineteenth century, Herbert Spencer (1855, 1862, 1880, 1894, 1969) attempted a grand synthesis of the social and the natural sciences on the basis of his general and Lamarckian evolutionary principles. However, his unifying evolutionary principles were substantially flawed and lacked an adequate explanation of the causal links involved (Peirce, 1923, pp. 162–3; 1935, pp. 15–16; Wiltshire, 1978; Hodgson, 1993a). Thorstein Veblen (1898, 1899) argued that the appropriate principles of explanatory unification were to be found at the core of Darwinian, rather than Lamarckian or Spencerian, biology. The American biologist James Baldwin (1909) also argued at some length that the Darwinian principles of natural selection applied not simply to biology but also to mental and social evolution.

Donald Campbell (1965) was one of the first postwar theorists to argue that there are common principles governing the evolution of all complex systems. Richard Dawkins (1983) took up this insight with his idea of 'universal Darwinism'. Some systems theorists have developed the position where the theory of evolution provides a unifying set of principles, under which systems theory is itself subsumed (Laszlo, 1987).

Emphatically, the idea of universal evolutionary principles does not imply that explanations of social phenomena have to be reduced to biological terms. Instead, an appeal to general evolutionary theory provides a very basic transhistorical framework for social science. The basic idea is that complex systems are likely to contain some replicating entities, which are subject to some processes of selection. Clearly, at the biological level, DNA is an example of a replicating entity. But at the social level, the replicating entities are very different. They include social routines and social institutions. However, even if there were a very different system of replication, including one that allowed the inheritance of acquired characters, a coherent account of the evolutionary process would still require the key elements of the Darwinian theory (Dawkins, 1983; Hodgson, 2001b). As long as there is a population of replicating entities that make imperfect copies of themselves, and not all of these entities have the same capacity to survive, then Darwinian evolution will occur. This does not mean that we have a complete explanation of all the evolutionary mechanisms or outcomes. To obtain such explanations we would require, in addition, auxiliary explanations relating to each scientific domain.

Such a general evolutionary schema requires ontological preconceptions. Darwinism is based on the ontological priority of both variation and continuity (Hodgson, 1993a). Upon this ontological foundation the Darwinian principles are established. First, there must be sustained variation among institutions, and the sources and mechanisms of renewal of such variation must be considered. Second, there must be some principle of continuity by which institutions endure and some principle of heredity by which succeeding institutions resemble their precedents or ancestors. Third, there must be a mechanism of selection and sorting among the population of institutions. The issues here are at root ontological, concerning the sources of novelty and the mechanisms of persistence, and do not themselves involve adherence to a particular evolutionary theory taken from biology or elsewhere (Foss, 1994).[5]

---

5   With little reference to the biological literature, J. Foster (1997, pp. 448–9) rejected the use of 'biological analogies' in economics on the highly mistaken grounds that 'they are timeless . . . they cannot address history except through the contrived use of Newtonian comparative statics, with the force of competition acting as the equilibrating mechanism.' Furthermore: 'Time irreversibility, absence of equilibrium, structural instability and fundamental uncertainty are features of historical processes, as stressed by many evolutionary economists, but they are not to be found in ahistorical biological analogies.' While this description may apply to a subset of the biological literature, modern biology is full of explanations of process, time irreversibility, the importance of history, structural change, non-equilibriating dynamics, non-Newtonian frameworks, fundamental uncertainty and so on. Consider Cohen and Stewart (1994), Dennett (1995), Gould (1985, 1989), Kohn (1985) and Mayr (1988, 1992) as well as Campbell (1965) and even Dawkins (1983, 1986). Bertalanffy (1971) – one of the leading theoretical biologists of the twentieth century – saw time reversibility and equilibrium as the antithesis of evolution and life. These references are from a range of viewpoints within Darwinism. They undermine Foster's blanket mischaracterisation of biology and 'biological analogies'. In truth, the question of the adequacy or otherwise of 'biological analogies' is not the fundamental question, as all social systems are subject to essential evolutionary principles by virtue of the existence of variety, replication, inheritance and selection. These principles have been defined and discussed by Campbell (1965), Dawkins (1983) and Dennett (1995).

Additional principles have been advanced in an evolutionary framework. Some of these will be discussed in chapter 22 below. Inspired by the earlier writings of Jean-Baptiste de Lamarck and Karl Ernst von Baer, the idea of a 'law' of increasing complexity in both natural and social systems is found in the nineteenth-century writings of Herbert Spencer (1862). It has twentieth-century defenders but it has remained highly controversial. There is an important, longstanding and unresolved debate within modern biology as to whether evolution produces increasing complexity.[6]

Another major theme is the paradigm of self-organisation, taken from the works of Ilya Prigogine and Isabelle Stengers (1984) and others. Indeed, some evolutionary economists see self-organisation as its central principle. However, the question remains of the mechanisms of selection between self-organised units. Such units exist in an environment, from which, along with others, they have to obtain resources. Hence some such selection process may occur. On this basis, Stuart Kauffman (1993) took the view that a self-organisation perspective is entirely compatible with a broadly-conceived and over-arching Darwinian theory.

A related possibility is the use of the entropy law in the economic domain (Georgescu-Roegen, 1971; Saviotti, 1996). In this framework, the evolution of complex systems involves a decrease of disorder or entropy – or an increase in 'negentropy' – within the system, while entropy always increases in the global system as a whole. Local complexity is gained at this global cost. In general terms, some progress has been made in integrating entropy concepts within an evolutionary framework (Laszlo, 1987; Brooks and Wiley, 1988). However, problems remain with the importation of these ideas into economics. In particular the mode and units of economic evaluation are difficult to reconcile with natural criteria, such as ecological variety and sustainability, other than by collapsing one mode of evaluation into the other (Khalil, 1990a, 1991; Lozada, 1991). Ecological economists are grappling with this fundamental conceptual problem.[7]

It is impossible to do justice to all these issues here. The present aim is simply to indicate some possible sources of universal principles in economics. These are universals at the most abstract level, concerning features common to all evolving complex systems. The purpose of visiting this most abstract level is to adduce a framework of ideas and principles by which to build something more solid and historically sensitive. These general ideas can act as frameworks or heuristics. They cannot involve detailed predictions or explanations. Nevertheless, they are both useful and necessary, as a meta-theoretical 'scaffolding' for further analyses relating to specific phenomena.

---

6 Those giving some support to the principle of increasing complexity in evolving systems include Morgan (1927), Stebbins (1969) and Saunders and Ho (1976, 1981, 1984). Those against any general evolutionary law of increasing complexity include Williams (1966), McCoy (1977), Levins and Lewontin (1985), and Hull (1988).

7 On the one hand, neoclassical 'environmental economists' typically reduce all ecological and resource problems to the subjective utilities of humans alone. On the other hand, 'deep' ecologists make the survival of the planet and the ecosystem the only criterion of evaluation, neglecting the nuances of economic valuation in the shorter term. See the journal *Ecological Economics* for attempts to transcend these two extreme positions.

THE SCOPE OF ANTHROPOLOGY

We have discussed universals at the highest possible level of abstraction, concerning complex systems in general. At the next level we address the universals of human nature and social culture. It is one of the major tasks of anthropology to examine the universal features of human culture. Clearly, we cannot review its achievements or its failures here. We simply note this agenda.

Some important attempts to set out universal principles of human interaction are found in the work of Karl Polanyi (1977). Polanyi believed that although markets and exchange were not predominant in all human societies, certain fundamental types of integrative arrangement could be found in them all. He identified three principles of behaviour that seem to have universality across all forms of economic and social organisation. One is called *reciprocity*, defined as obligatory and reciprocal gift-giving between persons who stand in some specific social relationship with each other. Another, *redistribution*, involves obligatory transfers to some central and encompassing authority. The third he described as *exchange*. This was a regrettable choice of term because it reinforced confusion between general patterns of interchange, and those involving property rights or markets. According to Polanyi, each of these basic integrative mechanisms can take different forms in different socio-economic systems.

To serve as a source of universal cultural principles, anthropology has to recognise the non-universality of market phenomena. In contrast, if markets are perceived as universal then the task of examining the universal features of all human cultures becomes confused with the different assignment of analysing the features of socio-economic systems in which legal relations of property and contract have become more clearly defined. The latter, more specific, agenda for social science is discussed in the following chapters.

Notably, perspectives from anthropology and evolutionary theory have been combined to provide some general results. Usefully, this work considers mechanisms of selection at both the cultural and the genetic levels (Boyd and Richerson, 1985; Durham, 1991).

THE PROVISIONING PROPENSITY AS
A UNIVERSAL PRINCIPLE

The principle of individual utility maximisation has been criticised already in this work. We now consider the possibility of some alternative general impulses in human society. One such universal principle was first expressed in 1845–6 by Marx and Engels (1976, pp. 41–2):

> men must be in a position to live in order to be able to 'make history'. But life involves before everything else eating and drinking, housing, clothing and various other things. The first historical act is thus the production of the means to satisfy these needs, the production of material life itself.

If this is true concerning individual material needs then it must affect the essential nature of society as a whole. Given a primary need for the material prerequisites of life, it follows that within human society the institutions and routines devoted to such provisioning, would also have some priority. Unless such institutions and routines endure and are effective, society would collapse. Accordingly, located not simply in individuals but also in institutions, there are propensities in all societies to produce, acquire and protect the means of human life.

Arguably, these propensities result from mechanisms of cultural selection and social evolution. Within each society, some institutions and routines are more important for the survival of the society than others. Among those of greatest importance for the survival of the system are those relating primarily to the production, acquisition and protection of the requisites of human life. Some societies will give greater priority than others will to these institutions and routines. Especially when there is competition between different cultures, processes of evolutionary selection work at the institutional level. The evolutionary fitness of each social formation will relate to some degree to the efficiency and viability of its institutions concerned with production, acquisition and military capability. These are institutions associated with the provision and protection of the means of human survival in that society. We refer to them as *provisioning institutions*.

Other institutions are less crucial to the reproduction and survival of the society and can be lost or replaced in the evolutionary process. These are typically the institutions of ceremony or leisure. However, in many societies, the routines of production and acquisition are also infused with traditional customs of cere-mony, and may themselves rely on ritual for their social reproduction and survival (Bush, 1986). Ceremony often protects and sustains productive activity. In this case, such ceremony will not readily disappear. Nevertheless, with these qualifications, provisioning institutions may still have some haphazard but ultimate selective advantage in the evolutionary process.[8]

A key indication of what is involved here is the overall level of productivity of vital goods and services in the particular economy. A society that is more productively efficient has a greater potential to out-compete or overrun its competitors. Although there are exceptions to this rule, a society of greater productive efficiency, in terms of the requisites of human life, will have the greater capacity to expand, by further productive investment or by conquest. Historical studies, at least in the post-medieval period, give broad confirmation of the close parallel between levels of productivity and the capacity for politico-economic expansion (Kennedy, 1988; Maddison, 1991).

If this process of evolutionary selection of the 'fittest' (defined here in terms of the highest level of productivity) takes effect, then social cultures in which the routines of production, distribution and acquisition have cultural weight and durability will be the stronger. There would be a tendency for customs that help

---

8   There is a contrast here with the theory of economic growth by Ayres (1944), in that Ayres simply assumed that *all* ceremony and *all* institutions inhibited production and technological advance.

sustain industriousness and acquisition to assume some cultural prominence. However, the particular customs and routines involved can vary enormously, depending on history and other cultural attributes, and leading to a wide range of possible behaviours. Often the possession rather than the production of wealth will be associated with higher status. In other cultures, higher status will be accorded to the hunter and warrior. In still others, the predominance of agricultural production will support a cult of the Earth. The general principle discussed here is consistent with a wide range of cultural outcomes.

This selection mechanism was particularly effective in the earlier periods of human history, prior to the rise of civilisation, when people lived in numerous competing tribal groups, all close to the brink of extinction. The relative advantage of a provisioning culture would be all the more apparent. However, as civilisations grew, and production provided more than the immediate requisites of human life, then the aforementioned mechanisms of cultural selection could have given less immediate priority to provisioning institutions. Nevertheless, the dependence of each community on the means of human life remained, and a haphazard process of selection of these institutions continued. Furthermore, even in a relatively affluent society, some cultural imperatives of production and acquision can grow and evolve. A cultural outcome, in the modern period, has been the evolution of societies in which production and acquisition have themselves replaced religion as the fount of human beliefs and aspirations.

If cultures that give some priority to provisioning institutions prevail for a very long time then they will affect the evolution of individual human attributes. Recognising that the provisioning of the means of life was essential to all societies, Veblen argued that processes of selection would work not only at the institutional but also at the individual level. Veblen (1899, 1914) saw a propensity for 'effective work' or 'workmanship' as one of the basic human instincts. It evolved over hundreds of thousands of years because of the general importance of provisioning for survival. If Veblen's argument is correct, then the cultural selection of institutions involved in the provisioning of the means of life may have some longer-term parallel in the natural selection of individual human propensities for similarly worthwhile effort. These industrious propensities will exist alongside other individual predispositions.

At neither the cultural nor the individual level does the selection process hone the socio-economic system to its highest productive efficiency. Mechanisms of selection are erratic and imperfect, particularly in the cultural sphere. Inefficient or destructive institutions can become highly tenacious. Furthermore, as noted above, aspects of ceremony and productive efficiency are often combined. There is always the possibility, as Veblen (1914, p. 25) clearly recognised, of 'instances of the triumph of imbecile institutions over life and culture'.

The general impulse to produce and acquire in all human societies is an inherent, cultural propensity, itself a product of cultural evolution and backed by provisioning instincts within individuals. It is a propensity, rather than a universal actuality: like any propensity it is not always realised in outcomes. Other factors may interfere. Nevertheless, if the above argument has some validity, it is an evolutionary principle of some importance, applying to all human societies. From general principles of evolution, applying to all complex systems involving variation and replication, some general principles that are applicable to all human societies may follow. Some further consequences of the provisioning propensity in human social evolution are explored later below.

19

PROPERTY, CULTURE, HABITS AND INSTITUTIONS

Sow an act, and you reap a habit.
Sow a habit and you reap a character.
Sow a character, and you reap a destiny.
(Attributed to Charles Read in *Notes and Queries* (1903))

Abstraction entails the identification of what is essential to, and enduring in, an entity – ignoring the accidental and superficial. The problem is to decide what is enduring and what is superficial. How are the criteria involved in this demarcation derived? This problem can be approached by means of different time-scales, each involving a different level of abstraction. Already, at a very general level we have considered features and principles that are common to all evolving complex systems. The next level concerned the universals of human existence. A third level may address specific types of socio-economic system.

Rather than attempting immediately to taxonomise and classify specific socio-economic systems, we look more fundamentally at some of the key elements and factors that must be involved in such a classification. As established in the preceding chapter, the initial focus is on the key processes of all economic activity: the production and the distribution of the necessary requisites of human life.

A pivotal task is the identification of the relevant features that, more than anything else, characterise the socio-economic system under examination. Taxonomy involves the separation of the essential from the inessential. In his approach to this problem, Karl Marx argued that such systems were largely differentiated in terms of their 'relations of production'. As he wrote in the Preface to the *Contribution to the Critique of Political Economy* of 1859, the totality of the 'relations of production constitutes the economic structure of society, on which arises a legal and political superstructure and to which correspond definite forms of social consciousness'.

Marx then pointed to the key indicators of the type of economic structure. For Marx, 'property relations' were expressions of 'relations of production . . . in legal terms' (Marx, 1971, p. 21). Marx thus suggested that underlying differences in the economic structure gave rise to substantially different systems of property relations. These property relations were expressions of underlying 'relations of production' or 'economic relations'. Likewise, in *Capital* Marx identified 'juridical' relations, such as contracts, as key expressions of underlying 'economic' relations:

> The juridical relation, whose form is the contract, whether as part of a developed legal system or not, is a relation between two wills which mirrors the economic relation. The content of this juridical relation (or relation of two wills) is itself determined by the economic relation.
>
> (Marx, 1976, p. 178)

Clearly, if the 'juridical relation' is determined by the 'economic relation' then the legal form of the contract would give us clues about the underlying economic relation, even if the mirror to which Marx alludes is a distorting one. For Marx, the surface juridical phenomena were closely related to the underlying reality. Accordingly, legal formalities are not mere surface phenomena that can be ignored, but crucial expressions of an underlying socio-economic reality.

The emphasis on 'property relations' in Marxist theory, as means of classification of different economic structures, contrasts clearly with the emphasis on *Geist* in the historical school tradition. Leading historicists such as Gustav von Schmoller, Werner Sombart and Max Weber gave more emphasis to *Geist*, ideology and social culture in their classification of different socio-economic systems. The differences concern the place of property relations and culture in the classification and analysis of different types of socio-economic system. Are such systems distinguished primarily by culture or by property relations? This is a question that has dogged attempts to classify different types of socio-economic system for much of the last two centuries. Adjudication between these two approaches is complex, but some brief suggestions will be offered here.

Although Marx proposed an approach to this problem, unfortunately he did not provide an adequate solution. The nature of the underlying 'economic relations' and 'economic structure' were obscure. Marx was unclear about the nature of the 'relations of production' or 'economic relations' and their precise relationship with 'property relations'. As noted in the preceding chapter, Marx and Engels saw material needs as basic to human existence and the provisioning of goods to meet such needs as basic to society as a whole. But the primacy of material needs itself tells us little of the specific nature of the 'economic relations', concerned with the production and distribution of these essential material goods and services, that are held to be fundamental. The satisfaction of material needs is crucial – but this proposition itself gives us no criterion to distinguish one way of the organising production of needs from another. Marx (1971, pp. 20–1) wrote in 1859: 'The mode of production of material life conditions the general process of social, political and intellectual life.' Here Marx was right to point to the primacy of activities or relations associated with the fulfilment of human needs. But he did not explain the mechanisms of this conditioning and, in particular, how those activities or relations condition the minds and beliefs of human agents.

The way in which 'legal' form and 'economic' content affected each other was also left unexplained. Marx's (1971, p. 21) argument was that: 'It is not the consciousness of men that determines their existence, but their social existence that determines their consciousness.' But he did not explain the nature of 'social existence' or of the chain of causality by which it 'determines . . . consciousness'. The Hegelians and German historicists saw social circumstances as spirit or *Geist*. Instead, Marx saw social circumstances as the 'mode of production of material life'. In both cases, however, the mechanisms by which social circumstances somehow determined individual consciousness were not clearly identified. We are left with two contrasting dogmas: Marx with the primacy of a vaguely defined 'social existence' and the historical school with the elusive and obverse primacy of ideology, culture or *Geist*.

The search for the essential types of social relationship must involve the identification of those forces and constraints that are most important in determining human behaviour. We have to elucidate the nature of the 'social existence' that is alleged to mould consciousness and activity. In and beyond the satisfaction of their needs, are people motivated primarily by 'economic relations', frameworks of property and law, or by ideologies and beliefs? Is culture somehow the overriding factor?

The controversy between Marxism, on the one hand, and the German historical school approach, on the other, is rooted in the differences between the materialist and idealist philosophical traditions. However, as Dewey, Veblen, Commons and others noted, the pragmatist emphasis on habits of thought provides a means to transcend the dichotomy between materialism and idealism. Pragmatism can provide ideas with a materialist foundation and show how material relations can be expressed in ideas. Accordingly, some resolution of this controversy may be possible if the mediating concepts of habit and custom are restored to their proper place in social theory. Without these concepts we do not have an adequate account of the causal relations between human nature, social existence, consciousness and ideas. Hitherto unresolved, the problem continues to haunt the social sciences. Of immense importance, it concerns the very springs of human action.

HABITS AND THE SPRINGS OF REASON AND ACTION

Let us consider habits and their role. Charles Camic (1986, p. 1044) usefully defined habit as 'a more or less self-actuating disposition or tendency to engage in a previously adopted or acquired form of action'. Habits are the basis of both reflective and non-reflective behaviour. Habits are formed through repetition of action or thought. They are influenced by prior activity and have durable, self-sustaining qualities. Through their habits, individuals carry the marks of their own unique history.

Emphatically, habit does not mean behaviour. It is not itself a recurrent or repeated act. It is not the same thing as a conditioned response. On the contrary, the meaning of habit adopted by Veblen, the pragmatist philosophers and instinct psychologists was of an acquired propensity or disposition, which may or may not be actually expressed in current behaviour. If we acquire a habit we do not necessarily use it all the time. It is a propensity to behave in a particular way in a particular class of situations. 'The essence of habit is an acquired predisposition to *ways* or modes of response. . . . Habit means special sensitiveness or accessibility to certain classes of stimuli' (Dewey, 1922, p. 42).[1]

With the insights of pragmatist philosophy, a solution to this problem was in sight by the end of the nineteenth century. A tragic accomplishment of twentieth-century social science was to remove the solution from sight. Economics put the rational individual in the driving seat, making habit merely a behavioural expression of past rational choices. Sociology made individual action the result not of habits, but of cultural values and norms. In both cases, a foundational and operative concept of habit disappeared from view.

Fortunately, however, modern developments in psychology and philosophy have helped to rehabilitate the pragmatist view. A solution to the problem raised at the beginning of this chapter can be attempted. A brief sketch is given here.

A resolution of the problem must address the connecting mechanisms between situation and belief, between action and context. Recent developments in psychology challenge the former idea of the fully deliberative, isolated individual. A point underlined by much modern psychology is that all ideas and beliefs are situated in a context. Over-deliberative conceptions of action overlook the temporal and the situated aspects of human reason (A. Clark, 1997a, 1997b). Faced with scarce time in a world of complexity, individuals rely on external structures and circumstances that act as filters and constraints and provide appropriate cues for action. It was 'Descartes's error' to separate emotion and reason, body and mind (Damasio, 1994). Mind and reason are also inseparable from the natural and social environment. This environment includes the institutions within which people act. Beliefs and intentions are, in part, formed and changed through interactions with others (Lane *et al.*, 1996). We think and act in and through the contexts of our activities. The idea of the human will as the singular source of all intention and belief is untenable.

Accordingly, intelligence is not simply 'in the mind': it is situated and contextual. In addition, Howard Margolis (1987, 1994), Arthur Reber (1993) and others have stressed the role of habits and non-deliberative action. It is difficult to reconcile these modern psychological perspectives with a view of the mind that is driven largely or wholly by deliberation, values or *Geist*. On the contrary, the mind is seen as built upon habits, which are in turn built upon instincts. As Margolis (1987, p. 29) put it: 'There is a natural hierarchy in the three modes (instinct, habit, judgement). Habits must be built out of instincts, judgement must somehow derive from instinct and habits.'

This work in modern psychology is very much a rehabilitation and

---

1 The conception of a habit as a propensity is found in works as diverse as Camic (1986), Dewey (1922, 1938), James (1981), Margolis (1994), Murphy (1994), Peirce (1878), Schlicht (1998) and others. By contrast, Becker (1992, p. 328) defined habit not as a behavioural propensity but as sequentially correlated behaviour.

development of the ideas of the early pragmatist philosophers, and of Thorstein Veblen who was inspired by them. Paul Twomey has explored in detail the parallels between Veblen's 'economic psychology' and the trajectory of much of modern evolutionary psychology and cognitive science. The perspective that Veblen inherited from Peirce, James and others 'stressed the active and multi-tiered nature of the mind in which instincts, habits, and conscious reasoning are all significant for understanding human behaviour' (Twomey, 1998, p. 437). Many of the ideas of the early pragmatists and instinct psychologists have today made a comeback: 'Modern research has tended to lessen the priority of the conscious, deliberating aspect of the mind' (p. 441).

As Veblen (1919, p. 75) put it: 'All economic change is . . . always in the last resort a change in habits of thought.' This does not mean that economic phenomena are reducible entirely to habits, but that habits are a necessary and foundational feature of all economic life. Unless legal or other rules become ingrained in the habits thought or action of the community, then they remain disembodied and unenforced. As James Murphy (1994) and Ekkehart Schlicht (1998) have argued at length, the enforcement of rules and stipulations presupposes the existence of supporting habits and customary norms. This has clear implications, not only for the understanding of the nature of institutions, but also for any policy aimed at institutional change.

The key point is that habits and tacit knowledge are foundational for all thought and activity (Dewey, 1922; M. Polanyi, 1967; Reber 1993; Hodgson, 1997). Reason itself is impossible without prior and habituated concepts and routines of thought. As Dewey (1922, pp. 30–1) put it: 'Ideas, thoughts of ends, are not spontaneously generated. There is no immaculate conception of meaning or purposes. Reason pure of all influence from prior habits is a fiction.'

All conscious deliberation depends upon latent habit and unfathomable tacit knowledge. Many of these habits are themselves acquired tacitly, in interaction with others. In this manner, it may be possible to overcome the apparent dilemma between methodological individualism and methodological collectivism. By acting not directly on individual decisions, but on habitual dispositions, institutions exert downward causation without reducing individual agency to their effects. The addition of the foundational layer of habit, beneath human agency, provides a basis by which institutions can have effects on individuals without destroying their agency and choice. Furthermore, upward causation, from individuals to institutions, is still possible, without assuming that the individual is given, or immanently conceived.

Accordingly, at the level of the human agent, there are no mysterious 'social forces' controlling individuals, other than those affecting the actions and communications of human actors. People do not develop new preferences, wants or purposes simply because 'values' or 'social forces' control them. What does happen is that the framing, shifting and constraining capacities of social institutions give rise to new perceptions and dispositions within individuals. Upon new habits of thought and behaviour, new preferences and intentions emerge. As Veblen (1899, p. 190, emphasis added) put it: 'The situation of today shapes the institutions of tomorrow through a selective, coercive process, *by acting upon men's habitual view of things'.* Stanley Daugert (1950, pp. 35–6) expertly dissected the view that Veblen had developed by 1898 on this question:

> Veblen appears to be using the concept 'habits of thought' as he formerly used the word 'mind' to describe the process by which the adaptation of phenomena takes place. But adaptation is no longer conceived as primarily a logical or transcendental principle or process. Instead it is conceived biologically, as the response an interested being makes to his environment, his method of dealing with phenomena. . . . His solution of these problems may be stated as follows: our knowledge of phenomena is possible through concepts, which may also be regarded as habits of mind or habits of thought, but since phenomena are habitually permitted to guide or coerce our concepts by impinging persistently and unremittingly (that is, cumulatively) upon our consciousness, our concepts may evolve through a change in phenomena or a change in our point of view of regarding phenomena. Ideas or concepts, that is, habits of thought, are thus not merely the passive products of our environment but are active, dynamic, and creative instruments searching for conduct adaptable to changing circumstances.

In other words, for Veblen, habits of thought were active and foundational for knowledge and action. Habits are ways of adapting and dealing with changing circumstances. And knowledge itself consists in the accumulation of such adaptations and propensities. Accordingly, reason and belief are seen as secondary and expressive, rather than foundational for action. Such a view contrasts enormously with prevailing twentieth-century doctrines in both economics and sociology.

On this basis, a resolution is in sight of the debate concerning the relative importance of 'economic relations', of the legal stipulation of property rights, and of culture and *Geist*. As a result of the above analysis, the crucial question becomes: to what extent do these factors themselves lead to the establishment and reproduction of durable habits of thought and action in the community at large?

THE ELUSIVE CONCEPT OF CULTURE

We first examine central concepts such as culture in this light. Culture, like *Geist*, is a slippery word, with a multiplicity of different meanings (Kroeber and Kluckhohn, 1952). Nevertheless, some attempts at classifying different meanings of the concept are helpful. For example, the anthropologist Roger Keesing (1974) distinguished between culture as an 'ideational system' and as an 'adaptive system'. In the former case, culture is treated as a separate system that consists of sets of shared ideas, values, symbols and meanings. An example of this is the notion of 'cultural beliefs' in the work of Avner Greif (1994b). In contrast, in the latter case, culture is treated as enmeshed into a socio-cultural system, a way of life through which communities survive and adapt. Whereas the ideational tradition sees ideas as having a significant influence on social life, the adaptive tradition sees ideas as derived or secondary.

A problem in the ideational conception of culture is that the causal explanation is incomplete. If culture is a shared system of ideas, values, symbols and meanings it is necessary to ask how these are formed, how they endure through time, and how they affect or mould individual behaviour. Culture is an emergent property of social systems. Nevertheless, its capacity to help mould individuals or their behaviour must in principle be explained in terms of causes that impinge upon individuals, not in terms of mysterious 'cultural forces'. For example, if the 'concept of culture is a *value-concept*', as Weber (1949, p. 76) argued in 1904, then it must be explained how those values are carried and reproduced in the culture, and how individuals come to share and be guided by them. On its own, the idea of culture as an ideational system fails to explain the causal powers of the values, symbols and meanings to which it refers. Any theory of culture has to encompass the habitual foundations of shared values and ideas. Once we accept that habits are foundational for all thought and activity, and that reasoning itself depends on prior habits, then the route towards a more adequate conception of culture involves an incorporation of these mechanisms.

Significantly, the idea of culture as an adaptive system can readily accommodate a habit-based explanation of these issues. It is possible to conceive of culture as an 'adaptive system', made up of habitual components at the individual level. If the concept of habit is reinstated in social science, then the modern idea of culture as an 'adaptive system' can be grounded upon habitual propensities. We may thus leave on one side the modern attempts to classify different meanings of culture and instead rebuild the concept on its earlier habitual foundation.[2]

Individual habits help to sustain behaviours that mesh together in a structured social context, thus forming customs and routines. A custom or routine is essentially a social complex of shared habits. Habit relates to one person. Custom involves 'the continuing group of changing persons' (Commons, 1934a, p. 155). In turn, culture may be regarded as a system of interlocking and durable customs and routines. According to the arguments presented above, habit is foundational, whether culture is viewed as an adaptive or an ideational system, based on shared

---

2   Bourdieu (1977, 1990) has notably re-introduced into sociology the concept of *habitus*. Diplomatically refraining from using the word 'habit' in sociological circles that rejected the word in the 1930s (Camic, 1986), Bourdieu defined *habitus* in rather pretentious terms that judiciously avoid giving it any grounding in instinctive propensities or human biology. It seems that the *habitus* is a collection of social and cognitive attitudes, inherent in the social structure, that channel individual activity. However, the causal processes involved are obscure and his writings neglect the actual mechanisms of habituation (Van den Berg, 1997). On the positive side, Bourdieu's *habitus* indicates how the concept of habit can avoid any conflation of individual and role objectives, thus avoiding the Parsonian danger of viewing individuals as puppets of roles or cultural values. A similar conceptual role was played earlier by habit in pragmatist and institutionalist thought. The next step for modern sociology is to look behind the pretentious wordage, recognise the concept of habit for what it is, locate its classic formulation in the pragmatism of Dewey (1922) and others, and rediscover the old sociological wisdom that humans are biological as well as social beings (Hirst and Woolley, 1982; Degler, 1991; Weingart *et al.*, 1997). A useful attempt to reintroduce habit in sociological thought is by Van den Berg (1998).

habits. Similarly, Veblen (1919, p. 39) viewed culture in the following terms: 'The cultural scheme of any community is a complex of the habits of life and thought prevalent among the members of the community.' This can be placed alongside the classic definition of culture by Edward Tylor (1871, p. 1): 'Culture, or civilization, taken in that wide ethnographic sense, is that complex whole which includes knowledge, belief, art, morals, law, custom, and any other capabilities and habits acquired by man as a member of society.'

Tylor's definition ultimately boils down to the 'capabilities and habits' within a social complex. Habits include and reinforce beliefs. If habit is generally interpreted here as a propensity, rather than mere behaviour, then there is a concordance with Veblen's idea of culture. Accordingly, changes in culture are market by changes in the habits of the community. As Veblen (1919, p. 75) argued in 1898: 'All economic change is a change in the economic community, – a change in the community's methods of turning material things to account. The change is always in the last resort a change in habits of thought.' In short, culture and *Geist* are both manifestations of a system of shared habits of thought and behaviour. As habits are foundational for all human activity, they are foundational for culture too.

It is remarkable how the concept of habit has slipped out of the discourse on culture. Until the 1930s, it was prominent in the anthropological and sociological literature (Camic, 1986). Furthermore, culture was frequently conceptualised in terms of social complexes of habituated behaviour. As a typical example, writing in the *American Journal of Sociology*, Malcolm Willey (1929, p. 207) saw culture as 'common and interrelated habits that constitute the mode of life of the people'. However, by the 1940s, with the rise of Parsonian sociology, such a definition was much less common. Culture was then often defined in terms of ideas, values or symbols. To properly understand culture, especially in the light of modern psychology, the concept of habit has to be restored to its proper place.

We are in a position to define culture as a system of shared habits of thought and behaviour that is prevalent in a group or community. Habits are seen as capabilities or dispositions, placing this definition of culture in an older tradition that includes the works of Tylor and Veblen. Part of the problem with other definitions is that they fail to give culture a habitual foundation. However, the definition of culture in terms of habits may seem remarkably similar to the Veblenian description of an institution. Hence it is necessary to make a distinction between these terms, after the concept of an institution is discussed in more detail.

FROM HABITS TO INSTITUTIONS

Consider property rights and other legally stipulated rules concerning contracts or property. These legal rules emerge through custom or decree. A necessary condition for the establishment of property rights is their embodiment in customs and habits. In the case of common law, the custom is established before it is ratified by a legal edict. In the case of statutory law, legislation may sometimes precede the establishment of customs and habits in accordance with the legislation.

Consider an example of statutory law having an effect on custom. Drink-driving and seat belt laws in some countries have led to new habits and norms of behaviour that were not widely established beforehand. The legislation led to these habitual outcomes through a combination of legal sanctions and the legitimation of new habits. By the normative influence of law, or by sanction or by constraint, behaviour was guided into new channels. In this process, new habits of thought and behaviour were established. In contrast, a law that fails to be observed will be ineffective in building up new habits, and may fall into disrespect and disuse. Accordingly, effective legislation concerning property and contract is either based on existing customs and habits, or it has the potential to be underpinned by new custom and habits.

In an excellent study of the relationship between stipulated rules, customs and habits, and human nature, Murphy (1994, p. 549) came to a similar conclusion: 'In short, viewing nature, custom, and stipulation as a progressive hierarchy with ascending and descending moments offers the most comprehensive and logically rigorous framework for social theory.' Although Murphy took his cue from Aristotle, there is also much here that is consistent with Veblen. Human nature and instincts provide the grounding for habits and customs. In turn, habits and customs are the foundation for deliberation and the formation of explicit rules. Institutions are thus formed, which help preserve and reproduce these habits of thought. There is both upward and downward causation. Most obviously and importantly for our purposes: new rules can give rise to new habits.

From this Veblenian perspective, both the property relations criterion (Marx) and the idea of culture or *Geist* (the German historical school) are incomplete as means of identifying the essence of any social formation. Both approaches retain some validity. But they both have to be related to underlying habits of thought and activity in the community. The missing and unstated substrate of 'economic relations' or 'relations of production' in Marx's theory can be nothing else but the tangled complex of habits and customs relating to productive activity. Likewise, culture or *Geist* have no substance unless they are made up of established social habits of thought and behaviour.

This leads directly to the concept of an institution. We shall define an institution and later compare it with the notion of culture. Essentially, institutions are durable systems of established and embedded social rules and conventions that structure social interactions. Language, money, law, systems of weights and measures, table manners, firms (and other organisations) are all institutions. We need to consider briefly why institutions are durable, how they structure social interactions, and in what senses they are established and embedded. In part, the durability of institutions stems from the fact that they can usefully create stable expectations of the behaviour of others. Generally, institutions enable ordered thought, expectation and action, by imposing form and consistency on human activities. They depend upon the thoughts and activities of individuals but are not reducible to them.

Institutions both constrain and enable behaviour. Generally, the existence of rules implies constraints. However, such a constraint can open up possibilities: it may enable choices and actions that otherwise would not exist. For example: the rules of language allow us to communicate; traffic rules help traffic to flow more easily and safely. Regulation is not the antithesis of freedom; it can be its ally.

Within institutions, many rules are potentially codifiable. The members of the relevant community or society share tacit or explicit knowledge of these rules. This criterion of codifiability is important because it means that breaches of the rule can be identified explicitly. It also helps to define the community that shares and understands the rules involved.

As John Searle (1995) has argued, the mental representations of an institution or its rules are partly constitutive of that institution, since an institution can only exist if people have particular and related beliefs and mental attitudes. Hence an institution is a special type of social structure that involves codifiable rules of interpretation and behaviour. Some of these rules concern commonly accepted tokens or meanings, as is obviously the case with money or language. However, as Weber (1978, p. 105) pointed out in 1907, rules are often followed 'without any subjective formulation in thought of the "rule"'. Nevertheless, the rules are in principle codifiable, so that breaches of these rules can be detected.

In part, rules are embedded because people choose to follow them repeatedly. In addition, pragmatist philosophers and 'old' institutional economists argue that institutions work only because the rules involved are embedded in shared habits of thought and behaviour. Hence institutions are emergent social structures, based on commonly held habits of thought. Upon these structures, actual or potential patterns of social behaviour arise. Habits are the constitutive material of institutions, providing them with enhanced durability, power and normative authority. By reproducing shared habits of thought, institutions create strong mechanisms of conformism and normative agreement. Hence 'custom reconciles us to everything' – as Edmund Burke put it – and customary rules acquire the force of moral authority. In turn, these moral norms help to further reinforce the institution in question.

Institutions are the kind of structures that matter most in the social realm: they make up the stuff of social life. They matter most because of their capacity to form and mould the capacities and behaviour of agents in fundamental ways. Institutions have a capacity to mould and change aspirations, instead of merely enabling them. Institutions are social structures embodying *reconstitutive downward causation*, acting upon habits of thought and action.[3]

Because institutions simultaneously depend upon the activities of individuals and constrain and mould them, through this positive feedback they thereby have strong self-reinforcing and self-perpetuating characteristics. Institutions are perpetuated not simply through the convenient co-ordination they offer. They are perpetuated because they confine and mould individual aspirations.

---

3 For a discussion of the original concept of 'downward causation' see Sperry (1991). Reconstitutive downward causation is further discussed in Hodgson (2000, 2001c).

Institutions are simultaneously both objective structures 'out there', and subjective springs of human agency 'in the human head'. Institutions are in this respect like Klein bottles: the subjective 'inside' is simultaneously the objective 'outside'. The institution thus offers a link between the ideal and the real. The twin concepts of habit and institution may thus help to overcome the philosophical dilemma between realism and subjectivism in social science. Actor and structure, although distinct, are thus connected in a circle of mutual interaction and interdependence.

John Commons (1934a, p. 69) noted that: 'Sometimes an institution seems analogous to a building, a sort of framework of laws and regulations, within which individuals act like inmates. Sometimes it seems to mean the "behavior" of the inmates themselves.' This dilemma of viewpoint persists today. For example, North's (1990, p. 3) definition of institutions as 'rules of the game . . . or . . . humanly devised constraints' stresses the restraints of the metaphorical prison in which the 'inmates' act. In contrast, Veblen's (1919, p. 239) description of institutions as 'settled habits of thought common to the generality of men' seems to start not from the objective constraints but from 'the inmates themselves'. However, as Commons argued, behavioural habit and institutional structure are mutually entwined and mutually reinforcing: both aspects are relevant to the full picture. A dual stress on both agency and structure is required.

Nevertheless, the relationship is not symmetrical; structures and institutions typically precede individuals, even if new institutions are created. We are all born into a world of pre-existing institutions, bestowed by history (Archer, 1995). History provides the resources and constraints, in each case both material and cognitive, in which we think, act and create.

INSTITUTIONS AND CULTURE: WHAT IS THE DIFFERENCE?

A fairly obvious question emerges. It has been accepted here that culture is a complex of interlocking and durable beliefs, customs and routines that permeates a group or community. By comparison, institutions are durable systems of established, embedded and potentially codifiable social rules and conventions that structure social interactions. By the above account, both culture and institutions depend upon shared habits of thought and behaviour among the group of persons concerned. Both institutions and culture have a common foundational basis in habits. Clearly, these definitions are similar, but not identical.

Three key differences require emphasis. Culture refers to shared habits of thought and behaviour that are prevalent in an entire group, community or society. On the other hand, institutions are integrated systems of potentially codifiable social rules, built upon and sustained by common habits. Accordingly, the first difference is that culture refers to traits that are prevalent in an entire group or community; while institutions are systems of rules that can span multiple, or divide individual, cultural groups. The second difference is that culture is essentially a complex of shared habits, whereas an institution is a system of rules, which in turn are grounded upon shared habits. The third difference is that an institution has a dimension of rule codification, mental representation and discursive self-reference that is not necessarily developed in a culture. In short, although institutions and culture both share a similar grounding in shared group habits, institutions also embody potentially codifiable rules that may be confined to a subset of that group.

All individuals participate in not one but several institutions. Individuals use language, they relate to families, they may enter markets and a host of other institutions. Individuals build up a repertoire of habits in each institutional context. Particular contexts and circumstances trigger each habit. Hence an individual may acquire quite different sets of habits, and must learn to discriminate carefully between different contexts. At the same time, each habit builds on experience and precedents. For example, language pervades the whole way we understand the world and the nature of a particular language may affect the way in which a habit is built up. Further habits, most notably concerning gender, authority, reciprocity and so on, will also pervade and affect the entire habitual repertoire. Although habits are acquired through repetitive behaviour, they also require prior habits of cognition and action. Accordingly, the habit-based concept of an institution refers to the overlapping but potentially idiosyncratic and variegated dispositions acquired by individuals.

In contrast, the concept of culture refers to more elemental, habitual dispositions held in common with others in a group. These habitual dispositions penetrate all the institutions in which members of the group are involved.

We may thereby distinguish between institutions and culture in a way that retains a commonly accepted meaning of each term. We may regard an institution as a structured entity, or type of social structure. So when we refer to a specific institution we refer to an entity such as the English language, the Federal Reserve Bank, Toyota or the European Monetary System. Institutions may be classified into groups of entities according to essential structures that they may share in common. When we refer to 'money', 'the capitalist firm' or 'the state' we refer to generic groups of institutional entities with shared essential structures.

In contrast, by culture we mean a set of common and prominent features or attributes found in a specific group or society. A culture is not a specific entity, but a set of traits that may be found in several institutional entities that help structure the life of a specific community. For example, the phrase 'Christian culture' refers to a large group of people sharing some of the basic values and dispositions of Christianity. These Christian cultural traits pervade multiple institutions. Recent governments in Britain have attempted to introduce a stronger 'entrepreneurial culture': by this they mean the development of entrepreneurial values within a range of commercial and educational institutions. And so on.

To use rather loosely a biological analogy, an institution is in some ways like a gene: it is a particular system of embedded and durable rules. By contrast, a cultural trait is like an allele: it is a set of particular attributes or traits that are found in more than one institution.

Some institutions may span several different cultures. For example, many transnational firms encompass different national and local cultures, and some global languages – such as English and Spanish – are used in diverse cultural contexts. Obversely, a cultural type may be a feature of several different institutions. For example, the British cultural trait of hierarchical segmentation and deference to the Establishment has been a prominent and enduring feature of many British institutions – including in the polity, industry and education. Similarly, an individualistic culture, in which individual rights and self-gratification are prominent, pervades many institutions in the United States.

If we treat institutions as entities and cultures as features then it is clear that institutions refer to the underlying structures and culture to prevalent common characteristics of different institutions. We may then ask whether institutions or culture are taxonomically more important: are different socio-economic systems distinguished first and foremost by their institutions, or by their culture? In the following sections we address these questions, giving a primary taxonomic emphasis to institutions, but with a secondary but substantial analytical role for culture.

PRODUCTION AND LEGAL RULES

First, some general criteria are necessary to identify the most important institutions in a given system. We need pointers to the more important and hegemonic institutions in any given socio-economic system.

We have argued in the preceding chapter that provisioning institutions have some primacy in the social order. The term provisioning institution refers to those institutions that are directly related to the production, distribution, acquisition, maintenance and protection of the means of everyday life. These include institutions – such as the family and within the education system – that are devoted to the regeneration and development of the human capacity to produce its means of existence. Also included are institutions, such as markets, that are devoted to distribution and acquisition rather than production.

The reason why institutions concerning production and distribution are vital is because production and distribution are themselves vital. In a viable social order these institutions dominate the fabric of social life. They support cultures whereby wealth does not simply maintain life, it also signifies and helps confer privilege and power. These institutions could include firms, markets, the family and the state. Some of these provisioning institutions are discussed in more detail in the next chapter.

This conceptual marriage of Veblen (institutions) and Marx (production) helps us to pick out the kind of institutions that matter most in identifying and classifying each type of socio-economic system. However, we still need to go further. Provisioning institutions, like all institutions, are themselves made up of customary rules. In understanding the character and function of each institution, we have to identify the types of customary rules that matter most. To 'matter most' a type of rule must have a significant general effect on habits of thought and behaviour relating to the production and distribution of vital goods and services, necessary for the reproduction of the social system and the individuals within it. Accordingly, variations in these rules and institutions will have a direct and significant effect on the nature or type of socio-economic system in question.

Rules matter, but they do not all matter to the same extent. Consider language. Searle (1995, p. 60) rightly points out that 'language is the basic social institution in the sense that all others presuppose language, but language does not presuppose the others'. All social interactions depend on some linguistic element. Does this mean that we should understand and classify each socio-economic system in terms of its prevailing language? The answer is no, because variations in language do not have such a significant effect on the nature or type of socio-economic system. German capitalism and Japanese capitalism are at a similar level of development and structurally have much more in common, but their languages are different. Whereas countries such as North and South Korea, or Britain and Jamaica, or Spain and Peru, may share a common language but are very different in terms of their socio-economic structures and capabilities. The existence of a common language does not mean that the socio-economic structures and levels of development are similar. Many chemicals are made up of carbon, hydrogen and oxygen. But this does not mean that we can understand the differences between chemicals largely on the basis of the characteristics of these elements. Language is the basic institution, but differences in language have a secondary place in the analysis of different institutions.

A second proposition is now introduced. In socio-economic systems where the effective rule of law prevails, legal rules have a powerful constraining and legitimising role on habits of thought and behaviour. Competent legal rules constrain behaviour and enable ordered interactions between agents. In this case these rules lead to new or reinforced group habits: institutions are formed or changed. Weber (1947, pp. 124–32) recognised the powerful role of legitimising authority in complex societies. He argued that perceptions of legitimacy can arise from several sources, including the moral force of custom, and the acceptance of its legality. Even those who disagree with particular laws will typically accept them and abide by them, because they regard the procedure by which the law was enacted as legitimate. People in the past have accepted the legitimacy of claims of divine right, or of claims to represent the national will. In many advanced countries today, one of the most important bases of legitimation is the existence of a parliamentary democracy. As long as legal systems are sufficiently well established, legal rules thus provide a very important indication of the type of socio-economic system involved. This is because, in such circumstances, legal rules typically have the power to create accordant habits of thought and behaviour. Where the rule of law prevails, the Veblenian principle of the foundational nature of habits is exercised most strongly in the area of legal legitimacy.

Consider some recent examples. Some laws governing gender and ethnic differences have had a significant impact. Both the United States and Britain have witnessed the economic impact of employment laws prohibiting discrimination according to gender. As a result of equal opportunity legislation in several advanced capitalist countries, more women have become involved in employment and management. In South Africa there have been the dramatic, consecutive effects of changes in laws that first enforced and then banned racial dis-crimination. None of these aforementioned laws has created equal pay or equal advantages for gender or racial groups. Nevertheless, the effects have often been significant. Habits of thought and behaviour concerning the role of women and ethnic groups in the workplace have changed. The institution of the family has adjusted to some degree. Even weak and imperfect laws can have significant effects.

This principle of juridical influence is now combined with the provisioning principle. As Commons (1934a, p. 733) insisted, economic theory must start 'upon the *economic bond* which ties individuals together, such as transactions, debts, property rights'. Accordingly, following Marx and Commons, the laws that matter most in understanding civilised socio-economic systems are those that dominate the production and distribution of vital goods and services. Such laws would concern property rights, contracts, markets, corporations, employment and taxation.

Laws can also have unintended consequences. For instance, they may have a major impact on the structure or performance of a whole industry. For example, in the United States, laws were enacted in an attempt to increase competition and curb any monopoly power in the financial sector. These laws have prevented the development of a completely integrated banking system with a small number of powerful, national clearing banks, as in Britain. Differences in banking law account for a significant part of the difference between the financial sector in the United States and the banking systems in other countries. As Alexander Field (1991) has argued at length, legal rules can differ even when technologies and resources are similar. Furthermore, legal diversity magnifies the diversity of socio-economic structures and performances.

There is another important reason why legal rules are important. In a civilised society, institutions emerge in the context of explicit legal rules. These legal rules are part of the broader system of rules and meanings by which social actors understand and reflect upon the institution in question. As noted above, the mental representation of an institution is partly constitutive of that institution since an institution can only exist if people have the necessary beliefs and mental attitudes (Searle, 1995). Accordingly, legal rules are not merely formal expres-sions of an underlying reality but a major constitutive part of that reality.

This primary focus on legal rules may be questioned. For instance, there is a tradition within Marxism of regarding legal relations as merely formal and epiphenomenal: to focus on legal relations is to fail to address the underlying 'material' conditions or relations. However, it is not clear what these 'material' conditions' are. They must have some social and intersubjective content. Attempts to divide off (legal) form from (socio-economic) content do not work. Both legal 'form' and socio-economic 'content' are important.[4]

---

4   Lenin repeatedly scorned all legal relations as simply expressions of class interests. This anti-legal position within Leninism was further developed in Communist China, which for a long time had a system of justice relying on the decisions of 'people's tribunals' with few codified and guiding laws.

Just as many Marxists see legal forms as mere expressions of class interests, some libertarian philosophers see law as a mere outcome of individual inter-actions. These two positions are strangely similar, and equally at fault. All enduring social relations are both institutional and habitual in character. Furthermore, legal and other mental representations in part constitute these relations and institutions. In the case of institutions, representational forms cannot be divorced from substantive content. In addition, through compliance and constraint, powerful legal structures have a major influence on the habits of thought and behaviour that constitute individual personalities. It is in the character of institutions that the one conditions the other. Legal relations are not mere surface phenomena but part of the essence of institutions.

Other critics may assert that cultures or ideologies are the most important factors in categorising different forms of society. In response, it is argued here that what are truly foundational for all human activity and interaction are ingrained habits of thought. Upon common habits, ideologies, cultures and institutions arise. In turn, such institutions are the basis of social power and control. The stuff of socio-economic reality is institutions. Furthermore, many institutions are constrained by, or partly composed of, legal rules. Legal rules are not themselves foundational, but in a civilised society they are often reliable indicators of what matters most. The ultimately decisive character of the law derives from the coercive power of the state and its monopoly over the use of force. As long as this is the case, legal rules are powerful but not sufficient indicators of the structure of a society.

Of course, there are exceptions. There have been (and still are) many societies in which legal rules were not effective. As Douglass North (1991) has pointed out, the adoption in the nineteenth century of an amended version of the US Constitution by the newly-independent South American countries did not lead to democracy. There was not an adequate civil basis for decrees of popular power. As Schlicht (1998, p. 26) has pointed out, in the former (Communist) German Democratic Republic, the right to free speech was constitutionally guaranteed. Yet the Communist Party could use various sanctions against dissidents that greatly limited the power of free speech. Sometimes the influences of religious and other beliefs are so strong that they negate the formal declarations of the law. In India, for instance, discrimination according to social caste has been illegal since 1948. Yet such discrimination is still widespread and is sustained by Hindu religious beliefs. The formal declaration of a law is not enough to make it a reality. Legal rules and structures have analytical and taxonomic weight only when the laws are effective and enforceable. They do not 'matter most' when they are mere legal declarations, unrooted in the customs and observances of the people.

In summary, differences in systems of legal rules, and in the mode of their operation, provide some of the primary criteria for understanding the varied structures of civilised human society. However, legal rules were either non-existent, or overshadowed by other factors, before the rise of civilisation and the state. Legal structures do not have temporal primacy. What is proposed here is the importance of effective legal structures as means of institutional and systemic classification, but only in civilised societies where the effective rule of law prevails. As Schlicht (1998, p. 26) rightly insisted:

> laws can affect entitlements and obligations only within an atmosphere of generalized law obedience. Such generalized law obedience is established by custom. . . . The law is legitimized by custom, and custom plays a part in prescribing the content of the law.

Clearly and emphatically, this does not mean that the law is the only factor involved. As Richard Whitley (1999, p. 65) has elaborated at length:

> In particular, the significance and importance of ownership in the organizational integration of economic activities differ considerably between, say, post-war Japan and the USA, and are highly contingent upon historical circumstances and current institutional arrangements.

But this does not mean that that we may ignore or downplay legal rules. What it implies is that laws have to be understood in terms of their historical, cultural and institutional context. Laws matter enormously, in both the USA and Japan, as well as elsewhere. But there are always differences of implementation, leniency and interpretation. Several important additional and amending factors are explored below.

LEGAL RULES ARE ALWAYS INCOMPLETE

All legal systems have to cope with complex relationships and with infinite variety. For this reason, the law is typically incomplete. Economists are now familiar with the existence of incomplete contracts (Williamson, 1985; Hart, 1988; Anderlini and Felli, 1994; Cartier, 1994; Foss, 1996). Yet it is difficult in some crucial respects to surpass the earlier arguments and insights of Emile Durkheim on this issue.

Durkheim argued in 1901 that every contract itself depends on factors other than full, rational calculation: 'For in a contract not everything is contractual' (Durkheim, 1984, p. 158). He explained that whenever a contract exists there are factors, not reducible to the intentions or agreements of individuals, which have regulatory and binding functions for the contract itself. These factors consist of rules and norms that are not necessarily codified in law. In a complex world, no complete and fully specified contract can be written. The parties to the agreement are forced to rely on institutional rules and standard patterns of behaviour, which cannot for practical reasons be established or confirmed by detailed negotiation. Typically, each person takes for granted a set of rules and norms, and assumes that the other party does the same.

Durkheim's argument hinges on the question of information. The relevant information pertaining to the typical contract is too extensive, too complex or too inaccessible for anything more than a small part of it to be subject to rational deliberation and contractual stipulation. The more complex the decision situation, the greater amount of information involved, or the more tacit and dispersed the information itself, the more relevant Durkheim's argument becomes.

Even the simplest economic activities rely on a taken-for-granted network of institutional supports. Ludwig Wittgenstein once used the example of signing a cheque. Such an act depends upon the prior existence of many institutions, routines and conventions – banks, credit, and law – that are the antecedents and frameworks of socio-economic action. Without such institutions all human activity would be hopeless. Similar remarks apply to other everyday activities, such as mailing a letter or waiting for a bus. In every case, we habitually and unthinkingly depend upon a dense network of established institutions and routines.

It is widely accepted that in such circumstances there is often a reliance to some degree on trust. By definition, if we trust another party that means we engage voluntarily in a course of action, the outcome of which is contingent on choices made by that other party. Such an outcome is typically beyond our own control. Study after study has shown that trust is vital, even in a cut-throat capitalist world of business and trade. For example, Stewart Macaulay (1963) found that capitalist firms rely on values such as 'common honesty and decency' when making deals. Even when high risks were involved, business people do not necessarily respond by insisting on a formal contract that covers every possibility.

To summarise, legal rules and contracts are always, *and necessarily*, embedded in deep, informal social strata, often involving such factors as trust, duty and obligation. Accordingly, a formal contract always takes on the particular hue of the informal social culture in which it is embedded. As a result, culture re-enters the story as a secondary criterion of classification and explanation.

CULTURE RE-ENTERS AS A SUBSIDIARY CRITERION

What is often neglected is the fact that differences of culture can give rise to nuanced differences in the interpretation and implementation of the same legal rules. For example, different cultures and subcultures have different traditions and expectations concerning the processes of bargaining and contract. In the United States, for instance, it is assumed that the individual is the best judge of his or her interest and will pursue those interests openly. Hence it is typically accepted that a buyer may 'drive a hard bargain' by insisting on the lowest possible price. When the deal is done, however, there is less prospect of renegotiation, because the explicit agreement is taken as sacred. By contrast, in Japan there is a culture of assumed reciprocity and concern. Hence if the buyer were to try to negotiate a lower price the seller may regard this as an insult. It might suggest that the goods are not of high quality and that the seller has not already considered the interests of the buyer by setting the lowest possible price. Furthermore, if the goods or services turn out to be inadequate it is sometimes possible to appeal to the sense of honour of the Japanese trader and obtain some recompense.

Again in the United States, litigation is often regarded as an individual right, fruitfully exercised to keep defaulters in check. In contrast, in Japan, litigation is often regarded as a shameful way of attempting to enforce a contract or gain personal reward. The systems of law and contract in the two countries are quite similar in many respects, but they are overlaid by very different cultural standards. These differences have crucial effects on economic behaviour and performance.

Similar remarks apply to non-legal, behavioural or evaluative norms. In different countries there are different accounting systems in place for calculating corporate profits. Furthermore, there are contrasting modes of perception of the profile of corporate profitability. In the Anglo-American systems, for example, there is a focus on short-term profitability; whereas in Germany and Japan greater emphasis is given to perceived profitability for the long term.

Much of economics (from neoclassicism to Marxism) treats pecuniary incentives as sufficient and self-defining, to the neglect of the necessary and culturally embedded modes of calculation. This leads to an oversight of different varieties of capitalism and of the varying performances and outcomes of different capitalist systems (Hodgson, 1999a). Against this, there is now a substantial literature examining the role of cultural and other differences in explaining the economic performances of advanced capitalist countries.[5]

The cultural heritage of a nation or community also involves subtle and ingrained attitudes that have often persisted for centuries. Symbols of national identity are particularly important in this respect: witness the strong affections for monarchs or national currencies. Religious traditions also matter. Although Weber's idea that the Protestant ethic played a major part in the genesis of capitalism has come under some empirical and theoretical criticism (Lessnoff, 1994), this does not undermine the general importance of religion in influencing economic development. For instance, in Japan, long-standing ethical doctrines – involving Confucianism, Buddhism and Shintoism – have been crucial in engendering high degrees of loyalty both to the capitalist firm and to the nation as a whole. Hence the origins of the Japanese economic 'miracle' have been traced to distinctive cultural traits formed through the interaction of religious, social and technological practices (Morishima, 1982; Dore, 1987; Kim, 1995).

However, we should not go to the opposite extreme. A culture is a complex of shared habits of thought and action within a community. Insofar as legal and other formal rules affect these habits, then they too have to be considered alongside the informal aspects of culture. Furthermore, formal rules can engender and reinforce informal cultural features.

For example, explicit rules and structured incentives back up many of the crucial 'cultural' features of the Japanese economy. Japanese firms do not enter into long-term relations of co-operation with each other simply because of the

---

5   For example, Berger and Dore (1996), Clegg and Redding (1990), Groenewegen (1997), Hampden-Turner and Trompenaars (1993), Hollingsworth and Boyer (1997), Kenworthy (1995) and Whitley (1992, 1999).

high level of trust or loyalty in Japanese culture. They also do so because of the established structures of reciprocal shareholding, in the 'horizontal industrial groups' and between large firms and their suppliers. Because of this reciprocal shareholding, each party has, and is perceived to have, a direct pecuniary interest in the other party's success. These structures promote trust. In Japan, another established shareholding practice promotes a long-term attitude to investment and economic development. This is the 'main bank' system, in part involving 'stable shareholding' in which banks have long-term shareholdings in large firms (Aoki and Patrick, 1994). These long-term shareholdings stimulate and monitor the objective of long-term growth of the value of the company and provide some financial stability to achieve that goal. As a third example from Japan, there is a legally instituted practice of longstanding employment in a single occupation. The Japanese practice of lifetime employment encourages a long-term perspective in the management of relationships between employees and employers. Culture is important, but it is greatly reinforced by collateral patterns of ownership and contract.

The banks in both Germany and Japan are more extensively involved in corporate management than the banks in Britain or the United States. Culture alone cannot explain this. Explanations of this phenomenon have involved legal restraints (Roe, 1990, 1994) and historical path dependence. C. Knick Harley (1991) saw the emergence of the German banks in a context of originally underdeveloped financial markets. Because of this, German firms and banks became dependent on continuing – and path dependent – bilateral and dependent relationships with each other. Unlike the United States, these relationships were not subsequently altered or limited by legislation. On the contrary, German banking laws have remained relatively permissive.

Clearly, the differences between different capitalisms cannot be explained on the basis of culture alone. Many of the differences in both ethos and performance stem from different incentive structures, patterns of ownership and involvement. Many of these reflect particular institutional histories. On the other hand, some of the differences are traceable to deep, enduring, historical cultural roots.

To sum up, the primary criterion for distinguishing between different types of socio-economic system – between capitalism, feudalism and Antiquity, for example – is the legal system relating to the sphere of production. This primary criterion would include the prevailing forms of property and the legal mode of engagement of the workers. However, the differences between varieties of the same type of system also emanate in part from differences in incentive structures, patterns of ownership and social culture.

THE EXAMPLE OF THE EMPLOYMENT CONTRACT

Many of the issues involved in the tangled relationship between social culture and legal rules are illustrated in the complex nature and protracted development of the employment contract under capitalism.[6] Like all contracts, the employment contract involves attempts to define agreed spheres of responsibility. In an employment contract the worker agrees, within limits, to work under the authority of an employer. In return, the employer agrees to pay the worker by the hour, day, week or month, or by the quantity of output produced. A distinctive feature of the employment relationship is the *potential* power of employer control over the manner and pattern of work. Crucially, this power of control is not itself specified in detail; it is implicit and to some extent open-ended. But at the same time there are legal and contractual limits to what the employer may require of the employee.

Production processes involving human beings depend vitally upon dispersed, uncodifiable and tacit knowledge. All production involves learning; and in principle we do not know now what is yet to be learned in the future. It is also subject to disturbances from the outside world. The complexity and inaccessibility of much of this knowledge means that no worker or manager can know fully what is going on.

For these reasons, the employment contract is always flexible and incompletely specified. The terms of the contract cannot in practice be spelt out in full detail because of the complexity of the work process, and the degree of unpredictability of key outcomes. These problems of complexity and uncertainty are found to some degree in other contracts, but with employment contracts they are particularly severe.

Employment contracts are always imperfect and incomplete. Employment contracts often rely on trust and 'give and take' rather than complete or strict legal specification (Fox, 1974). Typically, employment contracts involve intensive social interaction and rely acutely on cultural and other non-contractual norms. The dual dependence upon both formal rules and informal norms is widely accepted in organisation theory (Levitt and March, 1988; Powell and DiMaggio, 1991).

Durkheim's argument concerning *all* contracts is relevant here. The parties to any agreement have no alternative but to rely on some institutional rules and standard patterns of behaviour, which cannot for practical reasons be established or confirmed by detailed negotiation. These problems are greatly enhanced in employment contracts. Accordingly, there is a much greater reliance on inexplicit and semi-explicit norms and rules.

Among others, Joseph Schumpeter (1976) and Karl Polanyi (1944) have noted that relations of employment cannot be completely reduced to explicit contracts. Schumpeter, for example, stressed that employment depends upon norms of loyalty and trust inherited from the former, feudal era. Employment contracts are thus only partially successful attempts to encapsulate a messy and complex situation in contractarian terms. The difficulties outlined by Schumpeter, Polanyi and others cast severe doubt on the possibility of a purified capitalism operating through individual self-interest and explicit contract alone.

---

6 This section summarises a more extensive discussion of the employment contract in Hodgson (1999a).

As noted in preceding chapters, capitalism, like all socio-economic systems, depends on its 'impurities'. These impurities involve ingrained cultural norms and patterns of behaviour. No contract can be understood simply in terms of explicit rules and stipulations. These provide a framework, but they are operational only if embedded in a rich, informal, cultural context.

The employment contract, although central to capitalism, can carry the cultural residues of a feudal past. An illustration of this is Britain, where the explicit legal definition of the employment contract, in terms involving an exchange between consenting parties, is a relatively recent phenomenon. The 'law of master and servant' still carries some of the marks of former servile obligation (Wedderburn, 1971; Kahn-Freund, 1977; Deakin, 1997). Similarly, in other countries, the employment contract did not fully develop in its modern form until well into the twentieth century (Howe and Mitchell, 1999).

The persistence of notions of duty and service in this context is not accidental. To some degree, employment always and necessarily involves hierarchy and duty, as well as contract and agreement. Within limits, employment involves obedience, and authority has to find its legitimacy. Historical notions of social class, duty and service thus play a role. The employment contract depends on informal rules and cultural norms, and takes on their character and hue. Capitalism carries with it the cultural baggage of its historical development in the past. This observation will be extended and generalised in chapter 22.

SUMMARY AND CONCLUSION

This chapter has discussed the attributes that are most important in the classification and analysis of different types of socio-economic system. It asked whether the primary focus should be on economic and property relations (Marx and Commons), or on culture or *Geist* (the German historical school). Discussion of this question has led us to examine the habitual springs of human reason and action. It was argued that habit is foundational both to culture and to institutions such as property.

Culture refers to shared habits of thought and behaviour that are prevalent in an entire group, community or society. In contrast, institutions are integrated systems of potentially codifiable social rules, built upon and sustained by common habits. Accordingly, a culture is an ensemble of shared habitual traits; while an institution is a particular system of potentially codifiable rules. Individuals act out their lives in a multiplicity of overlapping institutions, perhaps conforming to pervasive cultural attributes.

The next problem is to segregate different types of institution in terms of importance and significance for the question at hand. It is argued here that the social institutions of primary importance in this context are those *provisioning institutions* that are directly related to the production, distribution, acquisition and protection of the means of everyday life.

Furthermore, in socio-economic systems where the rule of law has prevailed, effective legal rules have had a powerful constraining and legitimising role on habits of thought and behaviour. Although legal rules are always incomplete, and they never entirely encapsulate the reality, they can involve features that are vital for the recognition and classification of different social formations. Accordingly, the best way to analyse and classify those social formations where the rule of law prevails, is primarily in terms of the effective legal structures associated with their provisioning institutions.

In this way, we can identify several different types of social formation: capitalism, feudalism, and so on. Having done this, culture and other factors re-enter as secondary criteria. Within the basic and incomplete framework of formal law, huge variation is possible. Socio-economic systems with similar legal structures can vary enormously in other respects.

In conclusion, the primary means of demarcating different types of socio-economic system is in terms of different relations of property governing the sphere of production. This particular proposition is in line with Marx's approach. However, the analysis goes further than Marx, by grounding property relations in shared habits and by also emphasising the concept of culture.

This proposed approach – of which no more than a rough sketch is provided here – is an attempt to resolve one of the remaining problems bequeathed by the historical school. It concerns the methods of identification and classification of different socio-economic systems in time and space. Unless we have such a taxonomic system then we are unable to move to the next stage and find theoretical principles that are most appropriate for each system in question.

20

EXCHANGE AND PRODUCTION

Property and firms

> *The causes of wealth* are something totally different from *wealth itself*. . . . *The power of producing wealth* is therefore infinitely more important than *wealth itself*; it insures not only the possession and the increase of what has been gained, but also the replacement of what has been lost.
>
> (Friedrich List, *The National System of Political Economy* (1841))

The previous chapter involved a discussion of whether property or *Geist* is the primary focus of classification. The primary focus on property relations was established and qualified. The purpose of this chapter is to explore the nature of property relations in more detail and to examine some basic provisioning institutions. We start with individual property rights and then move on to consider the firm and other issues.

THE ESTABLISHMENT OF PROPERTY AND CONTRACTS

The development of legally enforceable property rights is a process of such significance that it deserves recognition in terms of the scope and boundaries of the individual social sciences. Without such property rights there can be no exchange, at least in the proper sense of that word. Without exchange there are neither true prices nor established exchange ratios. The proper domain of economics is not universal. It begins with the establishment of legally enforceable property rights, and the discretionary activities of trade and production that depend upon them.

In primitive societies there was no proper ownership, whether by the individual or by the group. As Thorstein Veblen (1934, p. 39) put it in 1898:

> no concept of ownership, either communal or individual, applies in the primitive community. The idea of communal ownership is of a relatively later growth. . . . Ownership is an accredited discretionary power over an object on the ground of a conventional claim; it implies that the owner

is a personal agent who takes thought for the disposal of the object owned. A personal agent is an individual, and it is only by an eventual refinement – of the nature of a legal fiction – that any group of men is conceived to exercise a corporate discretion over objects.

Veblen thus noted that ownership is a 'conventional claim' and applies fully to individuals only. However, some kind of primitive trade was possible before the appearance of a developed concept of ownership. As noted in chapter 18, trade began as external transactions between tribes, rather than within communities. Peaceful trade was based on customary relations and ceremonies between different groups. However, trade and pillage often went together. As Henri Pirenne (1937, p. 21) remarked: 'piracy is the first stage of commerce'. Sometimes trading involved precious metals or even token money. Token money, such as cowrie shells, worked as media of exchange as long as their value was widely acknowledged. The origins of such forms of trade and money are much earlier than that of contracts and property *within* communities (Davies, 1994). However, money did not begin to become established as an *internal* social relation until it developed into a unit of account by which values are measured (Grierson, 1977; Ingham, 2000).

Any form of legal stipulation presupposes established customary norms. Under the influence of growing inter-communal trade, internal transfers of resources also began to assume a different character. Ceremonial, traditional and reciprocal transfers of goods were transformed gradually into discretionary exchanges, with enforceable rights of ownership. Some rudimentary legal rights were established in early territorial chiefdoms, particularly over the tenure of land (Clarke, 1987). The development of substantial individual property rights within communities has always involved a developed set of customs and norms that carry some kind of juridical authority. However, this process was not typically consummated in primitive, tribal societies. Early trade between tribal communities did not involve a developed conception of property. Protracted trade and non-transient contracts required the development of a legal apparatus and a system of law that could recognise 'legal persons' making transactions: who are deemed to have discretion and responsibility, and may enter into contracts with others.

Generally, for a contract to be deemed meaningful, the parties to it must be seen to have a choice over the matter. It is not necessary to go into the old philosophical dispute about 'free will' here. It is merely that societies dominated by custom and tradition allow limited scope for individual discretion. A culture assuming the existence of individual discretion must emerge before the notion of a contract becomes substantial.[1]

When property had developed within communities, there was still a problem of contract enforcement in trade between one community and another. There was often no dominant political power or supra-national authority to resolve

---

1 There are exceptions. For instance, some implicit contracts are recognised in modern law and sometimes the state has the right of compulsory purchase.

disputes. For instance, early medieval international trade depended on reputation and sometimes relied on coalitions, guilds, kinship links or religious ties to sustain enforceability (Greif, 1989, 1993, 1994a; Greif *et al.*, 1994; Landa, 1994; North, 1991). Even in modern times, in the absence of an adequate international political or legal authority, such institutional structures have assumed quasi-legal powers (Clay, 1997). These studies show that in the absence of a strong (inter-national) legal authority, quasi-legal institutions emerged to help police and enforce contracts. The historical evidence shows that quasi-legal institutions such as trading coalitions can develop in the absence of legal and statutory ones. We can conclude that trade generally may rely on extra-legal as well as legal powers of contract enforcement. However, it would be wrong to presume that extra-legal institutions are always adequate or efficient, or that legal authorities generally play a minor or dispensable role in all trade.

Trading coalitions are themselves institutions: they acquire powers and vested interests apart from the mere agglomeration of individuals involved. This is especially the case with large coalitions. Any substantial trading coalition that is formed by individuals has to be kept in check by the individuals who form it, so that its acquired powers are not misdirected by its clerks, bureaucrats or officials. The historical existence of trading coalitions does not point to a purely spontaneous, lasting and individualist solution to problems of contract enforcement.

The emergence of law, including property rights, is never purely and simply a matter of spontaneous development from individual interactions. Something else is involved. As Itai Sened (1997) argues in his decisive critique of the notion of property without law, individual rights are established only when a territorial institution establishes its monopoly over the use of force. Accordingly, indi-vidualist writers from Adam Smith to Friedrich Hayek over-emphasised the spontaneity of law, as essentially an outcome of individual interactions. Marxists, on the other hand, have seen law as an inessential epiphenomenon, which can be stripped away to reveal the 'true' a-legal, social reality beneath. Neither individualism nor Marxism is correct. In civilised societies the law is part of the essential social reality, yet at the same time it is more than the outcome of interactions between individuals. It is also an outcome of a power struggle between citizens and the state. The state benefits by maintaining its power, while citizens benefit from a regime of law and order in which they can produce and trade.

Individual property is not mere possession; it involves socially acknowledged and enforced rights. Individual property, therefore, is not a purely individual matter. It is not simply a relation between an individual and an object. It requires some kind of customary and legal apparatus of recognition, adjudication and enforcement. Such legal systems made their first substantial appearance within the state apparatuses of ancient civilisation. Thus, nearly four thousand years ago, on the famous stone of Hammuraby, the Ancient Babylonians carved their detailed code of laws, prescribing penalties and rights. Since that time, the state has played a major role in the establishment, enforcement and adjudication of property rights.

At the same time, the development of any state apparatus carries the omnipresent danger that individual private property would be wilfully appropriated by the state, perhaps using the ancient norms and precedents of communal tenure. The state has the capacity to appropriate, as well as to protect, private property. Sometimes the state has acted as a 'kleptocracy' (Grossman and Noh, 1990). For private property to be relatively secure, a particular form of state had to emerge, countered by powerful and multiple interest groups in civil society. This meant a pluralistic state with some separation of powers, backed up by a plurality of group interests in the community at large. With such a balance of power, a framework of constitutional law could be established, in which the interests of both the state and the citizenry could be protected to some degree.

After some political convulsions, the Athenians developed a state with some minimal separation of powers in the sixth century BC, but it was not until the rise of Ancient Rome, with its developed system of contract and property law, that individual ownership was substantially defined for its citizens. However, although Roman law encoded absolute individual property rights for the first time, they were hemmed in by practices of taxation and sequestration.

What concerns us more here is the *logical* and *causal*, rather than the *historical* priority of a legal apparatus over contracts and property. Some libertarians and free-marketeers uphold that contract and property are potentially spontaneous developments, not requiring a state. The nugget of truth here is that these institutions always involve elements of spontaneity and social interaction, and outcomes cannot result entirely from decree. The flaw is to fail to recognise that some kind of legal or quasi-legal apparatus, however rudimentary, is necessary to preserve property rights. The preservation of internal property rights requires sanctions against theft or fraud. Furthermore, enduring contracts rely upon systems of adjudication in the case of dispute, often using written records of precedents and rules.

There has always been a spontaneous and informal element in the evolution of property and contract. However, all plausible arrangements for their emergence and sustenance somehow involve some kind of legal or quasi-legal apparatus. Against this, Richard Posner (1980) developed a theory of the emergence of property in primitive societies that depended on elaborate 'insurance' arrangements between parties. But this theory is criticised by Jack Knight (1992, p. 120) who argued convincingly that relatively complex institutional rules concerning property are unlikely to emerge and be widely accepted in such circumstances: 'It is hard to see how such complicated rules could emerge from a decentralized process.' Explanations of the emergence of rule-enforcing institutions purely from optimising individual behaviours are often unconvincing (Field, 1979, 1981, 1984; Hodgson, 1998a).

In terms similar to Posner, Oliver Williamson (1983) wrote of a system of 'hostages', where both parties to an agreement are committed to non-salvageable costs. This argument suggests that a system of contract is possible and sustainable without the intervention of a formal legal system. The morsel of truth here is that it is sometimes more costly for parties to break a contract than to complete it. Accordingly, there can be strong incentives for contract compliance other than legal sanctions alone. Nevertheless, the 'hostages' idea is implausible as a *general* mechanism for governing contracts. Contracts are vulnerable to default when new circumstances, perceptions or information arise. Committed costs are insufficiently substantial and widespread to deal with all such eventualities, many of which are unforeseen.

Williamson rightly emphasised that most contractual disputes are resolved without direct recourse to the courts. However, this does not mean that the legal or quasi-legal institutions have no place in the everyday process of contract. As Avner Greif *et al.* (1994, p. 746) put it, 'the effectiveness of institutions for punishing contract violations is sometimes best judged like that of peacetime armies: by how little they must be used.' Where the rule of law prevails, the mere possibility of access to the courts is sufficient for the legal system to bear down upon contractual agreements. The threat of legal action can be silent. A very small frequency of successful litigations is required to act as a credible check on the dealings of the whole trading population.

In short, the idea that property and contract can emerge fully without the state is untenable. Sened (1997) has provided a formal and forceful argument in support of this view. To accept the role of the state in the evolution of property and contract is not to romanticise this institution. The existence of a state does not automatically give rise to private property. It is a necessary but not sufficient condition for its full development. The legal system has also to be grounded in the customs and practices of civil society. Without other checks, property is always vulnerable to state sequestration. As noted above, a constitutional and plural state is required for property to be more secure.

A central argument in this chapter is that the rise of internal property and contracts relied to some degree on the development of a legal and state apparatus. State bureaucracy is common to all civilisations. Although there is no unanimously accepted definition of civilisation (Daniel, 1968), several prominent definitions involve the existence of a state, internal trade and property. The term 'civilisation' is used here to refer to societies with developed state bureaucracies and codified legal systems, with (at least incipient) legally sanctioned property and exchange.

Clearly, trade will not develop unless there is specialisation in production and a division of labour (Diamond, 1997). In addition, the rise of the state is historically and logically prior to the emergence of exchange and markets: state bureaucracies and codified legal systems are necessary preconditions for developed and enduring markets. Contrary to Oliver Williamson's famous remark that 'in the beginning there were markets', the evolution of the market required the preconditions of a division of labour and a legal system. Hence we may concur with Geoffrey Ingham (1996, p. 264) that 'both historically and analytically speaking, in the beginning there were bureaucracies!'

Once contracts and property became established, regularised internal trade was possible. Markets appeared in places where a number of such exchanges could regularly take place. A market was 'a place set apart' from the traditional, ceremonial and political activities of state or society. But often the local or national state was involved in the creation, organisation and regulation of such markets (K. Polanyi *et al.*, 1957).

PRODUCTION, FIRMS AND ORGANISATIONS

Production is the *intentional* creation of a good or service, by one or more human beings, using appropriate knowledge, skills, organisation, tools, machines and materials. Production may include items that are useful or useless, ceremonial or practical. Production in this sense is universal to all human societies. Hunting and gathering is a form of production. Production was transformed with the beginnings of agriculture about 10,000 years ago. Until the rise of civilisation, the organisation of production has been in family or tribal units.

When did the firm emerge? This depends on the definition of the firm, and there is no agreement on this in the literature. How is a firm to be defined?[2] The answer to this question is partly a matter of analytical usefulness. Definitions, to use Plato's phrase, are for 'carving reality at its joints'. In this realistic spirit, there is a case against an excessively wide definition. Is it meaningful to describe a group of primitive hunters, chasing and slaying animals, and processing their skins and meat, as a firm? Is a small team of Neolithic farmers, sowing their seed and husbanding their cattle, a firm?

These questions are answered here in the negative. A key argument is that in such primitive societies – collectively and strongly regulated by ritual and tradition – it is not obvious what the 'non-firm' could mean. If the firm were defined so broadly, every productive activity in such societies would take place in a 'firm'. The concept of the firm would thus represent everything and mean nothing. Reality would not be carved at its joints. The problem here is to establish the widest possible definition of the firm that retains such a separable skeletal attribute.

Alternatively, a narrow definition of the firm could be adopted. For example, the firm could be defined as equivalent to 'the capitalist firm', or confined to the industrial era, or be restricted only to firms with employment contracts. Against this, however, there is a case for capturing a wide class of entities under the umbrella title of 'the firm' in order to focus on its essential attributes, and to use additional sub-categories such as 'the capitalist firm' to delineate specific types. The latter strategy is embraced here. Because the notion of the firm in the existing literature is both broad and vague, it seems appropriate to rectify the vagueness first.

Etymologically, the word derives originally from the Latin adjective *firmus*, meaning strong, powerful, durable and lasting. As a noun, the word went on to acquire the significant meaning of (legally binding) 'signature', and with this important connotation it survives today in several Romance languages.

---

2 This section reiterates the definitional argument in Hodgson (1999b), where my definition is defended from some criticism.

Accordingly, the *firmus* connotes an organisation acting as a singular 'legal person', able to own and trade property as an entity.

If we take these two arguments on board, then the firm could not exist prior to the development of a legal system. The notion of the firm would apply only to those socio-economic systems involving well-defined contracts and property rights. Notably, such ownership and property are necessary conditions for buying and selling to take place. Also there must be a system of law that recognises 'legal persons' making transactions – individuals or groups that are deemed to have collective discretion and choice, and may enter into contracts with others. Once again, such conditions are associated with the rise of civilisation and the existence of a state with a relatively developed legal apparatus.

Firms of a kind – both agricultural and manufacturing units – existed in Ancient Greece and Rome. It was also in Italy, in the twelfth century and after, with its partially enduring legacy of Roman law, that the medieval family firm prospered and multiplied. Surviving records reveal the legal basis of the medieval firm. As Greif (1996, p. 476) has elaborated: 'The essence of the family firm, as originally developed in Italy, was that several individuals agglomerated their capital by establishing a permanent partnership with unlimited and joint liability.' Greif continues:

> The family firm during the 13th and early 14th centuries was a partnership (*compagnia*) among members of the founding family as well as non-family members. Each partner invested some capital in the company and each one's share in the profit was proportional to his investment.

If ownership and property are essential to the firm, then is it possible to define a firm in terms of the assets it owns? In other words, would a group of assets with a single corporate owner constitute a firm? Such a definition, while having the benefit of sharpness, would be unsatisfactory, as David Ellerman (1992), Richard Langlois (1998) and Louis Putterman (1988) all indicate. Consider a consortium that owns a factory, machinery and raw materials, and hires out these assets to a team of managers who, in turn, produce and sell products in their own right. Would the owners of the assets – the consortium – be the firm? No. They would simply be the providers of the capital goods. In contrast, the team of managers and their employees would constitute the firm. Crucially, this management team would own the produced output of the factory. Their sovereignty over the production process and their contractual role as owners of the product makes this management team, rather than the owners of the capital goods, the firm.

It must be emphasised that the firm is a singular legal person. When they are attached to the firm, the members of a firm act in its name, and not in their own. It is important not to confuse the firm with a network of multiple legal persons, who may have separate ownership of their own products. Networks involve multiple firms and are not to be confused with single firms. The firm is a singular legal person, able to make contracts with others, via networks, markets or other arrangements.

316

One of the key features of a firm is that it is an organised enclave, apart from the market. It has already been argued in chapter 17 of this book that true markets rarely, if ever, exist within firms. Many modern firms, however, have separate divisions with their own accounting procedures and profit targets. A key test is whether these divisions have separate legal status, and are recognised as separate 'legal persons'. If so, they themselves constitute firms, even if they are largely owned by, and subordinate to, another company.

The firm is defined here as a type of organisation. All firms are organisations but not all organisations are firms. In turn, we may define an organisation as a special type of institution involving

- criteria to establish its boundaries and to distinguish its members from its non-members,
- a principle of sovereignty concerning who is in charge, and
- a chain of command delineating responsibilities within the organisation.

This is a definition of an organisation that is broader than some others. For example, for Howard Aldrich (1999, p. 2) 'organizations are goal-directed, boundary maintaining, and socially constructed systems of human activity'. Aldrich then excludes 'families and friendship circles' from the set of organisations. A problem here, however, is precisely what is meant by 'goal-directed'. Many firms act routinely, without explicit goals. If a family or friendship circle met together and declared a common objective, would they then be organisations? Because of the difficulty of defining goal-directed behaviour in crucial boundary cases, it is suggested here that a better criterion is the existence or non-existence of a principle of sovereignty concerning who is in charge. This sovereignty makes possible the declaration of organisational goals, even if they are not made explicit. Organisations are a type of structure with the capacity for goal-directed behaviour, irrespective of whether goals are actually declared. In this sense, an organisation has the capacity to be a 'collective actor'.[3]

Organisations involve both power and control. As one-person businesses are definitionally non-organisations and all firms are organisations, the possibility of a single person acting as a firm is excluded. According to the definition adopted here, a firm is always made up of two or more people. We are now in a position to posit a broad but historically limited definition of the firm:

A firm is defined as an integrated and durable organisation involving two or more people, acting openly or tacitly as a 'legal person', capable of owning assets, set up for the purpose of producing goods or services, with the capacity to sell or hire these goods or services to customers. As a singular 'legal person,' the firm may carry legal entitlements and liabilities in its own right.

---

3   For J. Knight (1992, p. 3) 'organizations are collective actors who might be subject to institutional constraint'. Aldrich (1999) tried unsuccessfully to exclude families and friendship circles from his definition of an organisation because, like many other would-be general theorists, he wished to use the term 'firm' and 'organisation' interchangeably. He then missed some key features of firms, including their legal personhood, and their rights of ownership of, and remuneration from, the goods or services that they provide.

These corporate entitlements include the right of legal ownership of the goods as property up to the point that they are exchanged with the customer, and the legal right to obtain contracted remuneration for the produced services. Corporate legal liabilities may also be incurred in the production and provision of those goods or services. Accordingly, after taxation, the owners of the firm have the legal right to the residual income of the firm. This definition does not exclude the possibility that some goods or services could be donated rather than sold.

Note also that the term 'legal' always has a strong customary element; the phrase 'legal or customary' could just as well replace 'legal' in this definition. As suggested above, a sense in which a firm is integrated is that it is regarded as a 'legal person' owning its products and entering into contracts. Further aspects of integration are explored below. The sense in which a firm is durable is that it constitutes more than a transient contract or agreement between its core members and it incorporates structures and routines of some expected and potential longevity.

An important feature of this definition is that it applies only to socio-economic systems that are regulated to a significant degree by law and contract. The fact that a firm is a historically specific rather than a universal economic phenomenon perhaps accounts for the failure of a standard definition to emerge in the literature. For similar reasons there is no commonly accepted definition of the market (Hodgson, 1988). Economists often shun definitions relating to historically specific phenomena because of their mistaken belief that the core principles of economics must be ahistorical and universal.

Crucially, socio-economic systems that are regulated by law and contract are sufficiently complex to accommodate alternative productive arrangements. Accordingly, the possibility of organising production *outside* the firm exists. This means that products are made not by organisations but by self-employed producers. According to the above definition, self-employed producers acting on their own are not firms. Within a firm, individual workers do not buy and sell part-completed products. This is because the firm as a whole owns the partly and wholly completed products. The firm itself cannot by definition be organised as a market. But there is nothing in principle to preclude the alternative of a market-co-ordinated ensemble of self-employed producers. This is the celebrated thought experiment in Coase's 1937 essay.

Accordingly, with the above definition, there is an exchange- or market-based alternative to the firm. Production can conceivably take place in firms, or be performed by self-employed producers that are co-ordinated by markets. The existence of property and contract are necessary for such alternatives to occur in a sufficiently developed form. The definitional boundaries of the firm are thus stipulated and explained.

THE INTEGRATION OF LABOUR INTO THE FIRM

The firm has been defined as an integrated organisation of people. Consider the possible ways in which the firm may become an integrated entity. In history, several possible such arrangements are found, including the following:

- **Slavery**. Slaves had few legal rights and were not classified as legal persons. The slave was acquired or purchased as a chattel and forced to work. Many slaves were obtained by military conquests or raids.

Slaves had few legal rights of exit. Only in exceptional circumstances could they buy their freedom.

- **Bondage**. Under feudalism, bondage was the principal relationship of subordination. The serf or vassal was obliged to obey and to provide military services to his lord. In return, the lord provided protection and granted the use of land to his serfs (Bloch, 1962).

Feudal serfs were bound by law for a lifetime, to their lord and to his land. They had few possibilities of legal exit from their bondage.

- **Employment**. In an employment contract the worker agrees, within limits, to work under the authority of an employer. This authority involves potential direct or indirect control over the manner and specification of the work to be performed. In return, the employer agrees to pay the worker by the hour, day, week or month, or by the quantity of output produced.

In law, employment relationships provide the right of exit by the employee, after a short period of notice is served. Hence employment contracts can last a much shorter period of time. Nevertheless, employers often have an incentive to retain employees because they have acquired specific skills during their period of employment. However, without additional measures, employment relationships can be casual and not much more integrative than the hiring of self-employed contractors. However, these measures exclude legal compulsion; indefinite legal confinement in an employment contract is 'tantamount to slavery'. Workers are likely to remain with an employer for longer periods when some of the following conditions apply: there is no known alternative employment or income; wages are perceived as higher than elsewhere; working conditions are perceived as better than elsewhere; or there is an effective culture of loyalty and commitment to the firm.

- **Co-operation**. Workers may combine together and form a co-operative; they own in common the firm and its means of production.

Typically, each worker's part-ownership of the firm's capital assets provides a major incentive for each worker to remain with the firm. Other incentives may exist, such as the lack of sufficiently attractive alternative sources of income, and an enhanced culture of loyalty to fellow-workers.

There are many additional and intermediate forms but the above four cases are clearly significant, both conceptually and historically.

Is the household a firm? This is partly a matter of refinement of the definition of the firm given above. As the definition is framed, the typical modern household is not a firm because in most countries it does not act as a legal person. Although households act to sustain and reproduce the capacity to work of the wage-earners, it is typically the individual worker, rather than the household, who receives remuneration for that paid work. A useful line can be drawn between the modern household – typically with one or two wage-earners – and the peasant or other traditional family unit. Here, in contrast, some peasant or other traditional family units do trade as legal persons, perhaps using the legal name of the head of the household. Members of the family may not own property in their own right. Such traditional families would qualify as firms, according to the above definition.

As noted in chapter 3 above, Marx provided a definition of the capitalist firm. This definition is accepted here. The capitalist firm is a specific type of firm whose owners hire employees. In a capitalist firm the means of production are privately owned, the products are the property of the owners – not the workers – and these products are sold as commodities in the pursuit of profit. This definition excludes producer co-operatives and self-employed producers.

The state can act as a firm but it is not necessarily a firm. It may act as a firm if it engages in the production of saleable goods or services. In addition, the state may be the legal owner of a public corporation or a nationalised industry. However, on practical grounds, much of the activity of the state cannot be reduced to saleable goods or services. Many of the legislative and judicial functions of government are not suitable for privatisation. But this is a controversial issue that cannot (and need not) be discussed further here.

A market, as defined above, is an institutionalised form of regular exchange. Some markets emerge spontaneously, others are organised by design. In all cases, markets develop rules to govern the exchange of goods and services. A stock market, for example, is a highly organised market regulated by a corporate body. This corporate body provides services to the users of the market and regulates its operation. In fact, such corporate bodies are often themselves firms. But this is not an excuse to conflate the firm with the market. The legal entity that regulates the market and provides services to its users, is part of the market but it is not itself the market. The market as a whole is the sum total of formal and informal social relationships between traders and others associated with its operation. The corporate body that regulates the market is the central and vital player among several on this field.

There is more work to be done in elaborating these and other related definitions. But this must be postponed to another volume. At this stage it is convenient simply to illustrate the definitions, as in Figure 20.1 on p. 321.

Civilisation is not a universal attribute of all human societies but it provides a legitimate level of abstraction for particular theoretical analyses. Once we confine our analysis to civilised human societies, then concepts such as law, property, contract, exchange, markets, organisations, firms and states become central.

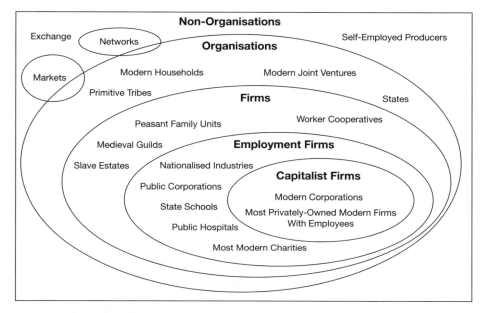

Figure 20.1 Conceptual distinctions between firms and non-firms

At this level of abstraction a substantial general literature has developed. For instance, there is a literature on general principles of organisational or institutional change (Sahlins and Service, 1960; Stinchcombe, 1965). A number of other works, stemming more recently from both sociology and economics, have attempted to apply evolutionary principles to the development of institutions and their 'organisational ecology' (McKelvey, 1982; Nelson and Winter, 1982; Hannan and Freeman, 1989; Baum and Singh, 1994; Aldrich, 1999). Much of this literature operates at a high level of generality. Although this literature is peppered with topical references, it would seem to apply to any system involving markets and firms. Nevertheless, substantial insights can be obtained, even at this level of generality.

21

A NOTE ON SOCIAL FORMATIONS AND LEVELS OF ABSTRACTION

> Grey, dear friend, is all theory, but green is life's golden tree.
> (Johann Wolfgang von Goethe, *Faust* (1808))

In preceding chapters it has been argued that the primary means of demarcating different types of socio-economic system should be in terms of different relations of property governing the sphere of production. When defining key terms in this context, it is important to focus on essential structural characteristics, rather than on contingent functional relationships or outcomes. For example, the employment contract does not necessarily imply the outcome of obedience. Essentially, it invests the employer with limited authority over the worker. The employee may sometimes work voluntarily and without command, in ways that conform to the employer's wishes. Obedience is a possible or likely outcome of this relationship, it is not always actual in fact.

Similarly, capitalism should be defined in terms of its social relations, rather than functional outcomes such as 'the accumulation of surplus value'. Profit is an important outcome of capitalism; but it does not define capitalism. Sometimes, capitalist firms fail to accumulate and make losses: that does not make them any less capitalist. The essence of capitalism is not the outcome of profit but the social structures that create the drive to make profits.[1]

Some different social formations may be briefly defined in the following terms.

- **Classical Antiquity**. This is defined as a civilised society, divided into slaves and citizens, in which most productive workers were slaves. Slave ownership was the core property relation: citizens could own slaves. Citizens, but not slaves, had the legal right to own other property. Two of the most developed examples of this social formation were the Roman and Greek Empires (Anderson, 1974).

---

1 This argument may appear to be undermined by an example from biology. A mammal is defined as a species that suckles its young. This may be a definition in terms of functional outcomes. However, these functional outcomes are not transient and they are pointers to a number of constitutive and structural characteristics that mammals share in common.

- **Feudalism**. Feudalism was a highly stratified social formation, based on land tenure, in which each person assumed specific rights and duties depending on rank. Below the apex of this hierarchy, each person (vassal) had an obligation to provide (primarily military) services to an overlord. In turn, every overlord had a reciprocal obligation to provide protection and the means of maintenance for his subjects. The principal means of maintenance was the fief. This was the part of a landed estate that could be used by the vassal in return for rents and other customary obligations. The right of use of the land could be passed down a multi-layered hierarchy. At the lowest level of the feudal hierarchy, serfs worked the land to produce food and other goods, some of which were consumed directly and some were used to pay rent. The remainder could be sold (Bloch, 1962).
- **Capitalism**. This is a social formation in which markets and commodity production are pervasive, including capital markets and labour markets. Capitalism, in short, is generalised commodity production, where most goods and services are destined to become items of trade. Under capitalism, most production takes place in capitalist firms. A capitalist firm is an institution in which products are made for sale and workers are employed under the supervision of the management. The employment relationship is thus the core relationship of production under capitalism (Marx, 1976).

Some of these definitions are controversial. For example, some broader definitions of capitalism also focus on private property and markets but do make the employment relationship a definitional characteristic (Reisman, 1999). The favoured definition of capitalism above also includes the existence of capital markets. Their absence means that the former Soviet Union was not capitalist. Against this, others centre largely on the employment relationship and thus define capitalism very broadly, to include the former Soviet Union (Cliff, 1955; Screpanti, 2001). In contrast, a case can be made for defining capitalism more narrowly, to identify the powerful and geographically widespread socio-economic system in which both the employment relationship and markets for capital are key, interlinked characteristics.

Markets for capital emerged in England in the seventeenth century, with the emergence of a market for land and the development of a banking system. Limited labour markets developed at the same time. Hence, according to the preferred definition of capitalism here, capitalism emerged in England in the seventeenth century. In most other countries, capitalism did not become prominent until the nineteenth or the twentieth centuries.

Money, markets and competition existed in ancient and medieval societies.[2] But the existence of markets and competition are not sufficient for capitalism proper. Capitalism, as defined here, involves developed capital markets and a predominant form of productive organisation, not based on slavery or serfdom

---

2 Notably, on the basis of an extremely broad and rather vague notion of capitalism, Weber went so far as to describe Imperial Rome as 'political capitalism' (Weber, 1968, pp. 164–6; Love, 1991; Schefold, 1995; Swedberg, 1998, pp. 46–51).

but on the employment contract. Although these have existed in rudimentary forms in earlier societies, their predominance is a modern phenomenon. Prior to the seventeenth century, markets for capital and waged labour were either non-existent or marginal. Capitalism has only a very limited past.

FIVE LEVELS OF ANALYSIS

At this stage it is possible to suggest and outline the different levels of analysis involved in any historically sensitive social science. Werner Sombart's three-tiered system of levels of abstraction was noted in chapter 9 above. In the light of the discussion in chapters 19 and 20, we may now attempt a more extensive hierarchy of levels. This is done in Table 21.1 on pp. 326–7. Five principal levels of analysis or abstraction are involved.

It should be emphasised that nothing here is intended to imply that different types of socio-economic system *necessarily* follow each other in a particular sequence. There is no hint intended here of the kind of 'stages theory' that is found in Marxism and elsewhere. Although each system builds on its own past, its emergence and particular characteristics depend on specific events and contexts. In principle, different outcomes are possible. History can take one of several routes. In particular, at level five in Table 21.1, the possibility of path dependent evolution of different varieties (or styles) of the same type of socio-economic system should be emphasised. Some further observations on this theme will be made in the next chapter.

Table 21.1 is meant to be a preliminary sketch, nothing more. What is suggested, however, is that an adequate analysis of any historically or geographically specific socio-economic phenomenon must involve a combination of theories or concepts taken from all five levels. An analysis that is confined to fewer levels will not provide the required combination of uniqueness and generality.

For example, some theorists analyse specific socio-economic systems chiefly in terms of principles taken from general systems theory or evolutionary theory (level one), others from general psychology or anthropology (level two); still others from the laws of supply and demand (level three). None of these types of analysis, each largely confined to a single level, will be able to discern the detail necessary to establish the key features of the system in question.

Yet remarkably, it is the practice of most social and economic theorists to centre their work on just one level. Neoclassical economics used to be directed at the second level: human society in general. However, in search of greater generalisation, much of neoclassical economics is now addressed to the first level. This is transparently the case with those economists who believe that economic principles apply to ants, bees, pigeons and rats, as well as to humans. Although mainstream economics discusses supply and demand (level three) this is typically treated in an abstract and universal manner, applicable even when markets – or even human societies – do not exist. Much of sociology and anthropology is confined to level two. It addresses the specificities of human society, but the peculiar features of complex human civilisation and of specific social formations are often downplayed. Much work within the old and the new institutional economics, as well as in parts of sociology, is addressed to level three. However, an understanding of the requirements of analysis at this level, and the distinction between it and the more general, lower levels, is typically lacking.

Although Marx's (1976) analysis of capitalism operates at level four – and hence can tell us more of the specific structures and dynamics of that system – it fails to incorporate explicitly and substantiate adequately all the different types of capitalism, especially those that are distinguished by variations in their cultural and institutional integument (Hodgson, 1999a). In other words, Marx failed to deal adequately with the specific forms of social formation at level five. For example, in *Capital* he discussed British capitalism but mainly as a general exemplar of principles at level four. There was little recognition in that work of the possibility that British capitalism might have specific features of importance that might not be readily replicated elsewhere. Hence the nature and behaviour of one capitalist country might differ from another. Furthermore, as argued in chapter 3 above, Marx did not provide an adequate account of the relationship between the entities that he analysed at level four, and the more abstract and general modes of analysis at lower levels.

Much of the past work at level five has been carried out by the historical school and within the old institutionalist tradition. In addition, there are valuable modern studies of different varieties of capitalism. However, the necessary foundational work at lower levels has typically been insufficient. If we concentrate largely on level five, then we commit the error of the older historical school. Lower-level, general concepts and categories, to guide the analysis at this higher level, would be lacking. Without a framework of conceptual coordinates, we would be unable to anchor our categories or taxonomies of analysis. We would be lost in a dark sea of descriptive material.

Two centuries of attempts to deal with the problem of historical specificity, point to the idea that any historically or geographically sensitive analysis must rely on material from all five levels of abstraction. I call this *the principle of five analytical levels*. It establishes five levels of abstraction in social science and insists that historically sensitive analysis must rely on conceptual frameworks drawn from every level.

REALITY AND ANALYSIS: SOME PRINCIPLES OF CONSISTENCY

Note that the five levels here concern levels of analysis or abstraction, rather than ontological levels, in reality. If, in contrast, we were to layer reality in ontological terms then the following four levels might emerge:

(a) the physical, concerning energy and matter;
(b) the chemical, concerning molecules;
(c) the biotic, concerning living things; and
(d) the human, concerning human societies.

Table 21.1 Levels of abstraction in social science

Level of abstraction		Scope of analysis at that level	Examples of possible laws or principles at that level	Key categories or criteria
First	General systems	Features and principles common to all open, evolving and complex systems.	Darwin's principles of evolution; Lamarck's hypothesis of increasing complexity; von Baer's laws; Ashby's law of requisite variety.	Variety, replication, selection, path dependence, scarcity of physical resources, relative scarcity, negentropy, self-organisation, dissipative structures.
Second	Human society	Features and principles common to all human societies.	Human instincts and psychology; general cultural principles derived from anthropology; the provisioning propensity.	Social structure, institutions, culture, language, cognition, instincts, habits, customs, power, human reproduction and socialisation.
Third	Human civilisation	Features and principles common to all civilised and complex human societies.	Institutional self-reinforcement and lock-in; principles of organisational ecology and institutional evolution. Effects of supply and demand on prices; the impurity principle.	Law, property, contract, exchange, markets, organisations, firms, states.
Fourth	Specific types of complex human social formation	Features and principles pertaining to a specific type of socio-economic system, such as:		
		(a) Classical Antiquity,	(a) Dependence on military conquest, slow development of technology.	(a) Slavery, estates, militarised infrastructure, trade, property, contract.
		(b) feudalism,	(b) Rigidly stratified system of land tenure, facing a dynamic intrusion of money, markets and trade.	(b) Inheritance, land tenure, vassalage or serfdom, feudal service, unequal legal rights.

Table 21.1 continued

Level of abstraction	Scope of analysis at that level	Examples of possible laws or principles at that level	Key categories or criteria
	(c) capitalism.	(c) Global spread of commodification, pursuit of profit, capital markets, structural centrality of employer–employee relationship.	(c) Equal legal rights, commodity, money, price, profit, contract, employment, wages.
Fifth	Varieties of each type of complex human social formation	For example, different historical (c.i) or geographical (c. ii) varieties of capitalism	For example: (c.i) mercantile capitalism, agricultural capitalism, industrial capitalism, finance capitalism; (c.ii) American capitalism, German capitalism, Japanese capitalism.	Structural balance between trade, agriculture, industry and services; role of the state and the finance sector; type of social culture – individualist, collectivist or otherwise; degrees of social integration and diversity; level of modernisation of key institutions; nature and role of the family and the sexual division of labour.

The five levels of analysis do not correspond directly with these four ontological levels. For example, the first level of analysis – general systems – applies to subsets of system-type phenomena at ontological levels (a) and (b), and to all phenomena at ontological levels (c) and (d). The second level of analysis – human society – clearly applies to ontological level (d) only. Finally, the third and fourth levels of analysis refer to nested subsets of phenomena at level (d) only. Clearly, there is no one-to-one correspondence between the ontological and the analytical levels.

The different ontological levels each rely on different sets of emergent properties, and will give rise to different analytical principles or theories pertaining to each level. Nevertheless, theories at each ontological level must be consistent with all other theories pertaining to that reality, including those at other levels. Although each theory and mode of theorising is different, no theory can overturn an acceptable theory at another ontological level. For example, reigning socio-economic principles cannot overturn the known and received laws of biology or physics. The theory of capitalist development cannot overturn the principles of Darwinian evolution or the constraints of physical laws. Although a given reality is hierarchically ordered, it is singular. It must therefore be understood in terms of a consistent body of principles or laws. This *principle of hierarchical ontological consistency* – another meta-theoretical principle – is required to avoid contradiction within a theoretical structure. If a theoretical contradiction exists, it must be regarded as a temporary anomaly, requiring intensive theoretical rectification until the principle of consistency is upheld. Any given reality is ruled by consistent laws. Although overall theoretical consistency may sometimes be difficult to obtain, it must be the persistent goal.

However, to some extent, the five levels of abstraction concern different possible realities – not a single, given reality. For instance, at abstraction level four, some of the principles describing the operation of feudalism will differ from those pertaining to capitalism. For example, capitalist corporations are pre-eminently profit-seeking while feudal lords were perhaps primarily concerned with the enhancement of their political power. Different systems can have different and contradictory principles of operation. Likewise, at abstraction level five, the principles of operation of (say) American capitalism will differ from those of (say) Japanese capitalism.

At the same time, the *principle of hierarchical ontological consistency* comes into force in the analytical hierarchy. Any laws or principles pertaining to historically or geographically specific social formation – at abstraction levels four or five – must be consistent with the laws and principles pertaining to all lower levels.

The picture is further complicated by the fact that no social formation exists in a pure form. For example, American capitalism before the civil war contained both capitalist corporations and slave estates. In any given reality, principles governing the operation of one type of provisioning institution may be restricted in their domain of application. Accordingly, dissimilar and even contradictory principles of operation can be found in operation in any given social formation. However, no principle of consistency is overturned here because each set of principles would be restricted in their domain.

The existence of impure social formations relates to what is termed the *impurity principle*. This is one of the issues discussed in the next chapter. This chapter concludes with a brief discussion of another terminological problem that it is convenient to raise at this stage.

THE TERMINOLOGY OF 'REAL' OR 'IDEAL' TYPES

We have already noted that Arthur Spiethoff expressed his preference for the term 'real type' over 'ideal type' (Salin, 1948, p. 614). We have to consider what terminology to use here. If it is retained, the term 'ideal type' has to be used with great caution, even if it is carefully qualified according to Weber's strictures. It encourages a false notion that we are simply dealing with ideas, and not reality. Crucially, any meaningful 'ideal type' involves abstraction from (and simplification of) reality. It refers to the real, as well as being represented by an idea.

Fritz Machlup (1978, p. 213) argued: *'the ideal type is neither ideal nor a type.'* However, Machlup (pp. 213–14) then proposed that the original term should be retained:

> To change its name would not resolve the specific problems in the methodology of the social sciences. If the issues remain with us, we may just as well put up with the ill-chosen name; name-changing this late in the game may make it harder for studious readers to learn from the literary exchanges in the past.

Clearly we must learn from the literary exchanges of the past. But the trouble is that we have been saddled with a misleading Weberian terminology for too long. I am persuaded to follow Spiethoff rather than Weber and use the term 'real type' henceforth. Hence capitalism, feudalism, Classical Antiquity and so on are 'real types'.

22

AN EVOLUTIONARY
PERSPECTIVE ON THE
HISTORICAL PROBLEM

> Every entity . . . is in some measure unique and in some measure
> typical.
>
> (Conwy Lloyd Morgan, 'Individual and Person' (1929))

Having established no less than five levels of abstraction, we are now in a position
to reconsider some principles at level one. It will be argued that at this most
abstract level it is possible to establish some further general principles concerning
the relationship between the other four levels.

Among the possible theories at level one is Darwin's theory of evolution.
Darwin's three principles of variation, inheritance and selection concern the
behaviour of whole, changing populations, not the development of a single
organism or system. In biology, the former type of process (concerning changing
populations) is described as phylogeny. Ontogeny refers to the development of
a single organism or system. As well as developing a (phylogenetic) theory of
natural selection, Darwin and others have hinted at some principles that would
apply to the comparative study of the (ontogenetic) development of organisms.

FUNCTIONAL VESTIGES OF THE PAST

In the *Origin of Species*, Darwin (1859, pp. 450–8) considered rudimentary survivals. Some species of bird, for example, have wings too small for flight. The
snake has a non-functional pelvis, and so on. Some rudimentary human organs
have no remaining functional purpose, such as the appendix. Darwin also
recognised that some rudimentary organs acquire multiple functions, and while
their main function had ceased to be of importance, a secondary function may
be vital. For example, 'in certain fish the swim-bladder seems to be rudimentary
for its proper function of giving buoyancy, but has been converted into a nascent
breathing organ or lung' (p. 452).

Whether they are functional or not, any organism must carry vestigial survivals
of its own evolutionary past. Evolution proceeds incrementally. It is path
dependent and builds efficaciously and sometimes unavoidably on its own
legacy. In his *Descent of Man*, Darwin (1871, vol. 1, p. 211) wrote:

The same part appears often to have been modified first for one purpose, and then long afterwards for some other and quite distinct purpose; and thus all the parts are rendered more and more complex. But each organism will still retain the general type of structure of the progenitor from which it was aboriginally derived.

Hence human evolution bears the indelible stamp of its lowly origins in its bodily form. For instance, human bipedal physiology is built upon the skeletal topology of a quadruped. Here Darwin was building explicitly on much of the argument of the famous Baltic-German embryologist, Karl Ernst von Baer. In 1828, while at the University of Königsberg, von Baer had suggested some laws of development (Gould, 1977). These endured and proved to be widely influential.

Von Baer argued that general features of a large group of animals appear earlier in the embryo than the special features. He also argued that characters of specialist use are developed from those of more general function, thus increasing the degrees of both complexity and specialisation in the organism. Von Baer's laws have been used and refined by the biologists Jeffrey Schank and William Wimsatt (1987) – see also Wimsatt (1986) – and the psychologist Arthur Reber (1993). Reber (1993, p. 85) proposed that: 'Once successful forms are established, they tend to become fixed and serve as foundations for emerging forms.' In addition: 'earlier appearing, successful, and well-maintained forms and structures will tend towards stability, showing fewer successful variations than later appearing forms.' In other words, the more basic structures, once established, stabilise and become less changeable than the layers that are built upon them.[1]

This von Baerian principle is an antidote to any view that evolution is necessarily a royal road to perfection. Evolution always builds on sufficiently successful but imperfect survivals from the past. Hence any complex organism is always a linked structure of imperfect but rigid modular adaptations that were sufficiently successful in a given environment. Even if a modular component was highly efficient in the past, it is unlikely to be as efficient in the changed circumstances of the present. Yet if any imperfect component retains a functional role for the organism, then it may be preserved through natural selection. If the more basic structures of the organism are less changeable than others, then natural selection cannot always readily and incrementally improve each organ or module within the structure.

Evolution is unable to rebuild everything to a near-optimal arrangement. It is not an expert redesigner, somehow understanding the complex interconnections between each part of the system. Such a degree of detailed, complicated and fortuitous re-engineering is unlikely to happen in the haphazard turmoil of nature. Evolution is forced to use the vestigial organs or modules of the past. Hence evolution rarely, if ever, produces an optimal outcome. As Stephen Jay

---

1   Reber (1993, p. 85) warned that: 'These general principles should be viewed as heuristics . . . they are not laws in any strict sense and should not be seen as inviolable.'

Gould (1985, p. 210) remarked: 'Evolution cannot achieve engineering perfection because it must work with inherited parts available from previous histories in different contexts.' In their evolution, complex systems carry the baggage of their own history. Hence to understand the nature of an organism, we must know something about its evolutionary past. As Ernst Mayr (1985a, p. 51) wrote:

> The original physical sciences were time-independent. History plays no role in the laws of physics. Hence when Darwin introduced time into the thinking of biology, this seemed to introduce a new contrast between the two fields. However, the more the physical sciences occupied themselves with systems, and particularly with complex systems as in cosmology and geology, the more it was realized that the past history of a system contributes to its characteristics.

Similar considerations apply to the evolution of the human mind. An important feature of modern evolutionary psychology is its recognition of the essential role of instinct and habit, alongside conscious reasoning, in human behaviour.[2] For instance, Reber (1993) argued that implicit learning of a habitual character is ubiquitous even in humans and higher animals. This is partly because higher levels of deliberation and consciousness are recent arrivals on the evolutionary scene and certainly came after the development of more basic mechanisms of cognition and learning in organisms. There is no good reason for evolution to dispense with habits and instincts once human reasoning emerges. It is much more likely to build upon them, just as humans use the altered skeleton of our four-legged ancestors.

In evolution, primitive organisms first developed heritable traits known as instincts in order to deal with their environment. More sophisticated organisms developed the capacity to learn more through the formation of habits, making them still more adaptable. However, these successful instincts were not dispensed with, and the apparatus of habit was built upon them. Still higher animals, including humans, have developed conscious thought, by means of which they are able to reflect upon the world with which they interact.

Nevertheless, in the human mind, we retain unconscious mental processes that can function independently of our conscious reasoning. Our layered mind, with its lower strata of our unconscious, maps our long evolution from less deliberative organisms. Conscious deliberation builds upon habits and instincts, and depends upon them. By freeing the conscious mind from many details, instincts and habits have an essential role. If we had to deliberate upon everything, our reasoning would be paralysed by the weight of data. Habit is also the basis of our firmly held beliefs. Habits and instincts are highly functional evolutionary survivals of our pre-human past. Hence, although modified, earlier evolutionary forms can retain their use and presence. They do this when they form the building blocks of complex further developments.

---

2 There is now abundant evidence that much of our capacity to learn and use language is an evolved instinct that we inherit from our forbears (Pinker, 1994).

The practice of building on former, successful innovations is also found in the evolution of complex technologies. For example, contemporary Microsoft Windows software carries at its basis some elements of the former MS-DOS software architecture of the 1980s. Software redesign is complex and expensive, so it was expedient to rely on tested and successful modules from former systems.

One of the insights of complexity science has been to suggest that a degree of irreversibility will be inherent in hierarchical organisations such as firms. As Brian Loasby (1998) elaborates, a firm may build on its established 'core' capabilities in ways that rely on past accumulations of experience, and are themselves difficult to reverse.

The implications of these insights are also of extreme importance in socio-economic systems. Because of the complex, interlocking relationship between the substructures within such a system, the processes of adaptation are typically confined to incremental and partial adjustments within an existing configuration. Competitive forces alone cannot always achieve radical, overall redesign. For instance, Ugo Pagano (1991, 2000) has considered the specific relationship between specific technologies and different systems of property rights and labour relations. Each is linked to the other, and each adapts taking the other as given. He argued that the existing technology is a result of preceding social relations and the scope of adjustment is thus confined. Furthermore, existing social relations limit the possibilities of technological change. Because they do not change together, systems of property rights and labour relations do not necessarily adjust towards a configuration that is optimal for them both. Such an outcome might require adjustments that are avoided because they are initially suboptimal. We are dealing with a complex system, involving technology and property in a mutually reinforcing, complementary relation. Evolutionary pressures are unable to redesign radically the whole. If more efficient configurations of technology and property relations exist, then social evolution will typically be unable to find them.

FROM 'POPULATION THINKING' TO THE IMPURITY PRINCIPLE

We now link the above ideas, concerning functional survivals, to Darwinian 'population thinking'. The most fundamental principle of Darwinism is onto-logical. In part it derives from the vision of Thomas Robert Malthus (1798, p. 379) who saw 'the infinite variety of nature' which 'cannot exist without inferior parts, or apparent blemishes'. This ontological diversity is the fuel of Darwinian evolution. Natural selection acts upon this 'infinite variety', selecting and sifting the fitter organisms. In turn, by mutation and recombination, new variety is created.

As Ernst Mayr and others have shown, the ontological primacy of diversity and variety is the basis of a entirely new philosophical outlook. He established the importance of 'population thinking' in which variety and diversity are paramount. This 'population thinking' contrasts with the Platonic notion of 'typological essentialism' in which entities are regarded as identifiable in terms of a few distinct characteristics that represent their essential qualities.[3]

In typological thinking, species are identified in terms of a few essential characteristics. Accordingly, all variations are regarded as accidental aberrations. By contrast, in population thinking, species are described in terms of a distribution of characteristics. In population thinking, variation is not a classificatory nuisance: it is of paramount interest because it is the variety within the population that fuels the evolutionary process.

The core ontological idea is that variety and diversity among members of a type or species are part of its nature. As a result, a type or species has to be understood in terms of that variety. For example, applying this to economics, 'the representative firm' or 'the representative agent' will not do (Hartley, 1997; Hodgson, 1993a; Kirman, 1992). By misleadingly taking a single member as representative of the species of which it is a part, we would be obscuring the variety that is essential to the nature of the population.

One form of variety involves variations within a given species. Another involves variation between different structures in the same organism or system. Darwin had less to say about this. Here an important insight comes from systems theory, with W. Ross Ashby's (1952, 1956) 'law of requisite variety'. This is the idea that a system has to contain sufficient variety to deal with all the potential variation in its environment. Complexity and variety within the system are necessary so that the system can survive and deal with complexity, variety and unforeseeable shocks in the real world.

The 'impurity principle' is the specific application of this more general insight to socio-economic systems.[4] The impurity principle upholds that every socio-economic system must rely on at least one partially integrated and structurally dissimilar subsystem to function. In this book we have described some of the key subsystems in social formations as provisioning institutions. Hence the impurity principle means that there must always be a plurality of provisioning institutions, so that the social formation as a whole has requisite variety to promote and cope with change. Thus if one type of structure is to prevail, other structures are necessary to enable the system as a whole to function.

Capitalism today depends on the 'impurities' of the family, household production and the state. Capitalist economies are never, and never in principle can be, in a 'pure state'. To attempt to make capitalism pure is to make it dysfunctional. Likewise, the system of slavery in classical times depended on the military organisation of the state as well as trade and markets. Likewise, feudalism relied on both regulated markets and a powerful church. Finally, without extensive, legal or illegal markets, long before the 1980s the Soviet-type systems of central planning would have ceased to function. In each of these socio-economic systems, at least one 'impurity' (a non-dominant socio-economic

---

3 See Mayr (1963; 1964; 1976, pp. 26–9; 1982, pp. 45–7; 1985a; 1985b), Metcalfe (1988) and Sober (1985).
4 For convenience, the idea is again summarised here. Earlier presentations of the impurity principle are in Hodgson (1984, pp. 104–9; 1988, pp. 257, 303–4; 1999a, pp. 124–30, 146–7).

structure) has played a functional role in the preservation and reproduction of the system as a whole.

What is involved here is more than an empirical observation that different structures and systems have co-existed through history. What is involved is an assertion that some of these socio-economic structures were *necessary* for the socio-economic system to function over time. The impurity principle is a theoretical guideline, based on ontological considerations. It is not itself a theory and theoretical explanations have to be built upon it. It takes us only so far, and it would be a mistake to claim too much for it. Nevertheless, it is a useful meta-theoretical proposition.

While the impurity principle contends that different kinds of subsystem are necessary for the system as a whole to function, it does not specify the particular kind of subsystem nor the precise boundaries between each subsystem and the system as a whole. Indeed, a variety of types of system and subsystem can feasibly be combined. For example, in many capitalist societies child-rearing is done within the non-capitalist institution of the nuclear family. But, in principle, alternative non-capitalist arrangements are possible for this purpose, such as collective households along the lines of the Israeli *kibbutzim*, or perhaps the rearing of children for sale on the market as child slaves. Some such arrangements may exist in capitalist societies but they are not themselves capitalist. Furthermore, in general – as illustrated by the particular case of subsystems of slavery within capitalism – the boundaries between subsystem and dominant system can be highly variable.[5]

The fact that one or more of a variety of possible subsystems can fulfil the need for a dissimilar subsystem is of particular significance for the argument here. As noted already in this work, the particular subsystem, the nature of the combination, and the precise boundaries of the demarcation profoundly affect the nature of the specific variety of capitalist system. A corollary of the impurity principle is the contention that a huge variety of forms of any given socio-economic system can exist. In particular, an infinite variety of forms of capitalism is possible.

The impurity principle identifies variety both within and between different socio-economic systems. Like 'population thinking' it is an ontological principle, but it goes further, to conceptualise variation within as well as between systems. Furthermore, as shown below, it can dovetail neatly with the Reber–Schank–Wimsatt version of von Baer's laws.

---

5 Is the impurity principle functionalist? Functionalism is typically defined as the notion that the contribution of an entity to the maintenance of a system is sufficient to explain the existence of that entity. However, the impurity principle does not purport to explain why any one given mode of production or subsystem may exist. To say that the household sustains the capitalist system, does not itself give an explanation for the existence of the household. Because the impurity principle does not purport to explain the existence of any one specific system or subsystem, it is not a case of functionalism.

THE PRINCIPLE OF DOMINANCE AND THE IDEA OF PROMINENCE

Before this synthesis is attempted, we must summarise another principle.[6] The *principle of dominance* is the notion that in socio-economic systems some provisioning institutions are more dominant than others. Unlike the impurity principle, in this general form the principle of dominance is compatible with Marxism. Marx (1973b, pp. 106–7) wrote:

> In all forms of society there is one specific kind of production which predominates over the rest, whose relations thus assign rank and influence to the others. It is a general illumination which bathes all the other colours and modifies their particularity. It is a particular ether which determines the specific gravity of every being which has materialized within it.

In any social formation, it is likely that one type of institutional structure, relating to the production and distribution of the requisites of human life, will dominate the rest. However, Marx was again unclear about the precise mechanisms involved. How precisely does dominance occur and by what criteria do we discern its existence and degree? The argument in chapter 19 above points to the nature and extent of shared habits of thought as a possible way of beginning to answer this question. Accordingly, to some degree, the habits of thought and action connected with one type of provisioning institution will influence and pervade the whole society.

For example, the habits and norms of pecuniary calculation associated with the market can dominate a society. The USA is an appropriate example here. Alternatively, nineteenth-century Britain was still dominated by habits of deference, service and obligation that in part were remnants of the earlier, feudal era. The form of dominance entertained here is essentially cultural, understood in terms of shared habits of thought and action in a society.

The outcome of this focus on habits and culture is different from that in the account of dominance in the work of Marx. In contrast, the argument here is that capitalism itself can be dominated by (say) a market culture or by a culture of service and obligation. For Marx, these would both be capitalism, pure and simple.

However, for reasons discussed in chapter 19, culture alone should not provide the primary criteria of classification. On reflection, an additional notion, similar to but distinct from the idea of dominance, is required. We shall refer to this idea as 'prominence'. The initial criteria of classification should be grounded in the legal forms relating to the more common types of provisioning institution. Sometimes this categorisation will be difficult because of the inability to

---

6　This section in part modifies statements in earlier works (Hodgson, 1984, pp. 105–9, 220–8; 1988, pp. 168–70, 256).

determine which types of provisioning institution are more common. Two rival types of provisioning institution might have roughly equal prominence.

The idea of prominence could relate to the greater share of productive activity. If so, some common metric of evaluation of the 'share of production' would be required. Otherwise, the concept of the 'greatest share' of production has no meaning. One possibility is to define prominence in terms of the greatest share of productive employment. Alternatively, prominence could be defined in terms of a price measure of the share of output of goods or services.

Clearly, prominence and dominance are not the same. Any such measure of prominence may not correspond to dominance, in terms of the prevailing cultural values and norms in the society as a whole. For example, familial cultural values and habits may endure even if the greatest share of productive activity takes place in capitalist firms. Alternatively, cultural traits associated with markets, such as habits of pecuniary evaluation, could penetrate all spheres of life, and not simply the market. Habits of deference or bureaucracy, associated with the state, might be pervasive, and so on.

Arguably, different socio-economic systems may first be classified in terms of the idea of prominence. This is the first cut in the determination of the 'real type'. However, this cannot tell the whole story. A secondary and essential sub-classification should occur in terms of the principle of dominance. Given the importance of habits of thought in the minds of the population, this secondary criterion can tell as much, or more, about the character of the society as a whole. Both criteria must be operative. Furthermore, given a possible variety of classified sub-types, in some types of social formation a huge diversity of real outcomes is possible.

THE INITIAL CLASSIFICATION OF SOCIAL FORMATIONS

Consider several provisioning institutions: family structures, inter-social trade, slavery, the state, markets and exchange, vassalage or serfdom, and capitalist firms. For simplicity, we shall exclude other structures and relations. In Figure 22.1, the logical and historical relations between these provisioning institutions are considered in four different types of social formation: tribalism, antiquity, feudalism and capitalism.[7]

There is a key difference between Table 21.1, concerning five levels of analysis, and Figure 22.1, concerning the layering of provisioning institutions. The principle of five analytical levels concerns different levels of theoretical abstraction. In contrast, Figure 22.1 depicts the layering of real world institutions, all at the fourth level of analysis in Table 21.1. Table 21.1 shows an analytical hierarchy.

---

7   Schmoller (1900, vol. 1, pp. 53–7) distinguished three types of social organisation in the national economy: the family, the community, and the firm. According to the argument below, three similar elements appear in capitalism, namely the family, the state and the firm. Along with the market they make up the capitalist 'real type'.

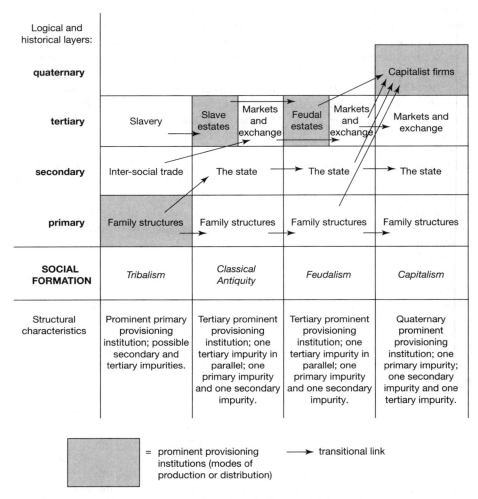

Figure 22.1 Layered provisioning institutions in four social formations

Figure 22.1 shows four ontological structures, each pertaining to a different possible reality.

A primary provisioning institution is not necessarily prominent: primacy and prominence are not the same. If a provisioning institution has primacy, then all others depend upon it. In all four types of social formation, some kind of arrangement for the rearing of children is necessary and primary. Although the nature of the family structure can vary enormously, both between and within these four cases, some kind of family structure is a prior condition for all other provisioning institutions. The term 'primary' refers to the fact that the family is the provisioning institution upon which all others depend for their existence. Like instincts in human evolution, historically the family emerged first, and all other provisioning institutions still depend upon it.

Within tribalism, the family structure is the *primary* and *prominent* provisioning institution. The family is prominent in tribal society because much production takes place in extended family units. Furthermore, familial cultural traits such as status, the seniority of elders, and patriarchy or matriarchy, *dominate* tribal society as a whole. In the other three cases – antiquity, feudalism and capitalism – the family is not prominent but it remains a *primary impurity*.

In all cases in Figure 22.1, a box representing a provisioning institution is secondary to, and dependent upon, the provisioning institution that is immediately below. For example, as argued in preceding chapters, the existence of markets and exchange depends upon the establishment of property rights and systems of contract. By and large, these are enforced and protected by the state. States can exist without markets but the reverse is not true. Hence the state is placed below the market. In turn, the state depends upon a citizenry that is largely reared in families. At a higher level, capitalist firms depend also upon the prior existence of markets or exchange.

In Classical Antiquity, both slavery and markets depended upon the prior existence of the state. But slavery and markets are at the same level in Figure 22.1 – one did not necessarily depend for its existence on the other. However, both slavery and markets were necessary for Classical Antiquity as a whole to function. A similar pattern existed in feudalism. Neither serfdom nor markets necessarily depended for their existence on the other, but both serfdom and markets were necessary for the feudal social formation as a whole to function. In these two cases, markets are an *impurity in parallel* with the prominent provisioning institution. In Antiquity and feudalism respectively, slave and feudal estates were prominent provisioning institutions.

Let us consider one of von Baer's laws in this context. In Reber's (1993, p. 85) version, successful forms 'tend to become fixed and serve as foundations for emerging forms'. Accordingly, the family unit emerged during prehistory and eventually became the foundational unit of all civilised societies. In turn, the state within civilisation eventually provided the legal framework for the growth of contracts, trade, markets and firms.

However, this initial classification is based on relations of prominence and dependence between levels. It does not tell us much about the dominant cultural habits and norms. We turn to this important but secondary issue later.

IMPLICATIONS FOR THE THEORY OF REAL TYPES AND THEORIES OF TRANSITION

One of the most important implications of the analysis above is that a social formation cannot be understood in terms of one or two levels alone. We cannot understand the human mind by focusing solely on its conscious deliberations, or its habits of thought alone, or just its instincts. Although the capacity to reason is a dominant characteristic, it depends on the impurities of habit and instinct. It is likewise with social formations. For example, capitalism cannot be understood adequately by focusing exclusively on markets and capitalist firms.

The mistake of much economic analysis is to treat the social formation as if it was reducible to the modes of calculation and operation pertaining to one type of provisioning institution. The example of Gary Becker's (1976a, 1991) analysis of the family is a regrettable case in point. The family was treated as if it were like a market. Related problems arise in other approaches. Marx (1976) was of course aware of the existence of the family, but because he saw it wrongly as 'a mere money relation' he analysed the capitalist system as though the family did not exist. This is just one example of the more general analytical neglect of the necessary role systemic impurities in *Capital*.

A social formation cannot be adequately defined or understood except in terms of provisioning institutions at every layer. This methodological injunction applies to the analysis of any specific type of socio-economic system, even at the most abstract level possible in this case (namely level four, in Table 21.1). *Consequently, the 'real type' has to embrace impurities.* Although it is not possible to consider everything at once, the constructed real type has to incorporate the impurity principle.

From this standpoint, we may criticise not only Marx and mainstream economics, but also Weber as well. As we have seen in chapter 9, Weber's guidelines for the construction of an ideal type were based on some imprecise and inadequate notions of progressive usefulness or successive approximation in the light of empirical enquiry. The construction of any particular ideal type in Weber's theory is essentially arbitrary. His approach relapses into an instrumentalist interpretation of the ideal type that abandons the question of truth.

The above principles can help to fill this analytical vacuum. For example, the construction of the real type of a capitalist economic system (at level four of analysis in Table 21.1) must involve a layered hierarchy (as in Figure 22.1) with the identification of the prominent and non-prominent layers. The structure of the real type concept is no less than a combination of all the necessary layers within the system.

This formulation has dynamic implications that take us further than Weber or Marx. The dynamic features of the above reformulation of the 'real type' can help overcome a crucial problem outlined in chapter 3, concerning the lack of a theory of transition in Marx's schema of different historical social formations.

The impurity principle is testimony that all systems carry, and to some extent depend upon, a residue of that which precedes them. All systems depend on impurities, and are further obliged to make use of some of those impurities that are bestowed by history. Furthermore, von Baer's principles suggest that provisioning institutions at the more basic layers, with their longer history of adaptive success, change more slowly than the higher, dependent layers.

In this light, we can create evolutionary real types to address the transition between one social formation and another. Consider, for example, the transition from feudalism to capitalism. To address this historical process, static real types for both feudalism and capitalism are first required. These real types must each be multi-layered in character. This multiple layering admits a set of possible transitional links between the elements in one layer in one real type and those of another. The arrows in Figure 22.1 above show some possible transitional links. Accordingly, an evolutionary real type maps the elements of continuity and change in the transition from one layered real type to another.

It must be emphasised that the discussion of dynamic processes here does not imply any preordained 'stages theory' of development. One social formation does not inevitably follow from another. The intention here is to focus on the transitional links involved in a possible – rather than inevitable – path of development.

The transitional links focus on the transformation process between one pro-visioning institution and another, and on the re-layering process in the social formation as a whole. For example, the transition from tribal society to ancient civilisation involved the transformation of the hierarchy of family networks. Within some tribal societies, particularly powerful and high-status families provided the chieftains and priests. These social castes and their practices led to institutions that eventually congealed into a state. Patterns of work and behaviour emerged that were removed from the family structures of tribal society. A new social layer was formed, above the enduring family structures of the subordinate peasantry. While some tribal societies acquired slaves by war or conquest, the institutions of slavery were further developed and enlarged alongside the militaristic prowess of the ancient civilisations.

Consider the example of the development of the capitalist firm. In this case there are transformation processes involving no less than four types of preceding provisioning institution, spanning three layers. There is the primary layer of the preceding feudal order: in the Middle Ages, some firms emerged out of the productive or trading practices of some family units. Regarding the tertiary relations of contract and exchange of the preceding feudal order, legal partner-ships were formed between founding families (Greif, 1996). Trading and legal partnerships depend on an established apparatus of contract law, which had first developed in the mercantile sphere of Ancient Rome. Again concerning the tertiary layer, many of these family firms used hired labour. As we have noted in a preceding chapter, the employment relationship attained and retained the norms and language of feudal relationships of service and duty.

It is not so widely known that the secondary layer of the preceding feudal order – the state – was also involved in the development of the modern capitalist firm. Modern systems of industrial organisation were established in part by imitation of the military hierarchy of the state. The developing factory system was influenced at its origin by the military structures of the time: in Britain during the Napoleonic wars and in the United States around the time of the civil war. The circumstances of war led to militaristic forms of industrial organisation; the hierarchical regimentation of the soldiery had its parallel in the similar organisation of the workforce.[8]

By understanding the particular causal processes involved in these transitional links, the concept of the real type is placed in a broader, evolutionary framework. Generally, it is out of the institutional impurities of a system that new layers

---

8   See McNeill (1980), Mumford (1934), Nef (1950), M. R. Smith (1985) and J. M. Winter (1975).

emerge in succeeding societies. This reinforces the argument that any real type, relating to any kind of social formation, must include and identify the impurities within that type of system. They must be included even at the most abstract level of analysis relating to any type of social formation. In this respect the approaches of Marx and Weber were both deficient.

APPLYING THE PRINCIPLE OF DOMINANCE

We now turn to the principle of dominance, and to the sub-classification of different types of capitalism, feudalism and so on. It is possible that other layers in any system take on the character and hue of the prominent provisioning institutions. If this were the case, then the prominent and dominant layers would coincide. But this is not necessarily the case. For example, the capitalist firm stems from no less than four types of preceding provisioning institution. In different historical contexts, the relative cultural influence of each type of formative provisioning institution can vary. Each social formation is affected by the cultural traits that pervade it. As a result, the capitalist firm can vary in its nature. If the influence of the family on shared habits is greater than elsewhere, then the particular type of capitalism can be described as familial. If the influence of the state is relatively high, then the particular variety of capitalism is *dirigiste*, and so on (Orrù, 1997). The additional varieties or styles of market-led and corporate-dominated capitalism are also relevant.

Japanese capitalism, for example, could be described as feudal-familial, because of the enduring influence of these two types of preceding institution. In contrast, French capitalism has been famously described as *dirigiste*, whereas American capitalism is more corporate-dominated, and British capitalism has for much of its heyday been largely but not completely market-led. Different varieties of capitalism differ not only in the detailed relations between the provisioning institutions but also in the variations in the prevailing social culture.

In all four social formations the cultural influence of the family has relevance for the system as a whole. A striking example of the type of analysis that is relevant to this primary level is Emmanuel Todd's (1985) work on family structures and political or religious ideologies. Based in part on the earlier work of P. G. Frédéric Le Play, Todd identified several types of family structure, depending on such factors as whether there is equality or inequality between brothers, whether there are inheritance rules or not, whether married sons tend to live with their parents, whether marriage is permitted between the children of two brothers, and so on. He associated each type of structure with different norms and values. He was able to explain many prevailing differences of social culture, ideology and religion in these terms. The fact that Todd's argument is challengeable in some of its details, is beyond the central point.[9] The point is

---

9 J. Knight (1992, pp. 164–9) gives evidence of family structures in particular regions at variance with those described by Todd. He also gives historical examples of changing patterns of inheritance law. In particular, more egalitarian modes of property distribution among children have often emerged in response to industrialisation and the growth of employment opportunities.

that there is some evidence of family structures having substantial ideological and historical effects. A refined 'family hypothesis' could form a part of a multi-layered and multi-causal explanation of differences between socio-economic systems. The 'family hypothesis' focuses on the primary layer. Necessarily, theories related to other layers would also be required to complement it.[10]

It is possible, therefore, to create capitalist, feudal or other real types that each contain potential stylistic variation within them, along four principal institutional dimensions and additional cultural dimensions. Hence the theoretical innovation proposed here of a real type that itself contains variation and can thereby encompass a variety of forms. The real type becomes a part of 'population thinking'. Instead of a singular essence, this concept of a real type becomes closer to the concept of 'species' in biology, where variation is inevitable between members of that set.

SOME FURTHER IMPLICATIONS AND CONCLUSIONS

In an earlier attempt to develop 'evolutionary' laws of transition, Marshall Sahlins and Elman Service (1960, p. 97) put forward their 'Law of Evolutionary Potential'. They argued that: 'The more specialized and adapted a form in a given evolutionary stage, the smaller is its potential for passing to the next stage.' This leads to the notion of 'The Phylogenetic Discontinuity of Progress'. By this they mean that 'an advanced form does not normally beget the next stage of advance; that the next stage begins in a different line' (pp. 98–9).

This useful idea breaks with the linear, progressive, step-by-step view of evolution. According to the Sahlins and Service argument, the higher and more adapted layers in a social formation are more specialised in their functions. They contend that these higher and more specialised layers are less able to adapt to new circumstances. Consequently, further socio-economic development may come from elsewhere – from other, less well-adapted societies. There is a 'Local Discontinuity of Progress'. At any given time, the most advanced social formations are not those most likely to give rise to a radically different and possibly more advanced system. As a result, 'if successive stages of progress are not likely to go from one species to its next descendant, then they are not likely to occur in the same locality' (Sahlins and Service, 1960, p. 99). Sahlins and Service argued that two writers 'have come close' to these ideas. First, Thorstein Veblen, in his book *Imperial Germany*, wrote that Britain was

> paying the penalty for having been thrown into the lead and so having shown the way. . . . The shortcomings of this British industrial situation

---

10 Family structures have important effects in the economic development of contemporary low-income countries. See Tinker (1990) for an overview of findings on the effects on economic development of different family structures and the role, status and prosperity of women.

are visible chiefly by contrast with what the British might be doing if it were not for the restraining dead hand of their past achievement.

(Veblen, 1915a, p. 132)

Second, Leon Trotsky in his *History of the Russian Revolution* wrote:

> The privilege of historic backwardness . . . permits, or rather compels, the adoption of whatever is ready in advance of any specified date, skipping a whole series of intermediate stages. Savages throw away their bows and arrows for rifles all at once, without travelling the road which lay between these two weapons in the past. The European colonists in America did not begin history all over again from the beginning. The fact that Germany and the United States have now economically outstripped England was made possible by the very backwardness of their capitalist development.

(Trotsky, 1934, pp. 22–3)

We can recast these ideas within the framework discussed above. Development and specialisation can bring a legacy of rigidity and unadaptability for the future. As a result, the locus of dynamic economic development may shift from one geographical region to another. A social formation that has previously followed and imitated the leaders may develop new and more advanced forms of organisation and technology, and forge ahead of the others at a faster rate. Accordingly, this view of socio-economic development gives prominence to matters of geographic location as well as of historical time. As Sahlins and Service suggested, the ossification of one social formation may mean that a more advanced system may emerge from a different location. This also suggests that exogenous changes and shocks can sometimes be important in overcoming the rigidity of layered institutions.

Historical examples illustrate the importance of exogenous shocks. In England, forces from outside sparked the seventeenth-century revolutions that eventually facilitated the development of the institutional and constitutional foundations of capitalism. The two great English revolutions of the seventeenth century were sparked by the confrontation with Scotland in 1639–41 in the first case, and by the invasion of William of Orange in 1688 in the second. Likewise, the American War of Independence of 1775–83 was endorsed and buttressed by the international Treaty of Paris (1783), involving France as well as Britain. Japan provides even more dramatic illustrations of exogenous shocks: the arrival of American warships in Tokyo Bay led to the Meiji Restoration of 1868 and the abrupt transition from a variety of feudalism to a Western-inspired capitalist society. The occupation of Japan by American troops in 1945 also led to major institutional changes.

Marxists have traditionally underestimated the importance of exogenous influences, seeing the dynamic forces of economic development as coming largely from within. Their concept of a potentially self-sufficient 'pure' capitalism compounds this error.[11]

344

Whether these changes emanate from inside or outside the system, a novel impetus for socio-economic development may come as the result of revolution or war. Some evidence is consistent with the view that institutional disruptions, particularly those resulting from revolution or war, have permitted the construction of new and more advanced institutions, leading to faster rates of economic growth (Olson, 1982; Choi, 1983; Hodgson, 1989, 1991, 1996). The examples of Japanese and German development after 1945 are apposite and widely acknowledged. In both these cases, many social institutions relating to production and distribution were radically rebuilt along modern lines.

Some related considerations pertain to the post-1989 transformation processes in the countries of the former Eastern bloc. Observers have explained that in many of these countries, despite the fall of the Communist party regimes, requisite rules, norms and institutions have been lacking for renewed socio-economic development along capitalist lines (Kozul-Wright and Rayment, 1997; Grabher and Stark, 1997). Furthermore, the building of new institutions has been inhibited by the remnants of the former state bureaucracies. Surviving former practices have thwarted the development of the type of institutional pluralism – from civil society upwards to the state itself – that is necessary for the creation of a dynamic capitalism. Accordingly, Mario Nuti (1996) has argued that these transitional economies must first take a step backwards, to build on lower layers and institutional forms, rather than concentrating on linear, cumulative development from the later institutions at the higher levels.

This is consistent with the biological principle of *paedomorphosis*. The zoologist Walter Garstang coined this word in 1928. It refers to the process by which evolution may, as it were, retrace its steps, to make a new start from an earlier point. Arthur Koestler (1967, p. 194) argued that 'this retracing of steps to escape the dead ends' of development has been widespread in evolution. For the reasons given above, the principle of paedomorphosis may apply also to the evolution of institutions and social formations.

In summary, this chapter has integrated von Baer's principles with the principles of impurity and dominance. The consequence has been to provide a meta-theoretical framework for the analysis of transformation and change in socio-economic systems. It has been argued that this framework is an improvement on those of both Marx and Weber, although it leans greatly on their former achievements. It must be emphasised, however, that a meta-theoretical framework of this kind can only take us so far. A future research programme must consider more specific varieties of social formation (at level five) to guide more detailed historical research.

---

11 A similar criticism can be made of Schumpeter. He defined economic development as involving 'only such changes in economic life as are not forced upon it from without but arise by its own initiative, from within' (Schumpeter, 1934, p. 63). Schumpeter made no secret of the fact that his theory of capitalist development – with its emphasis on the role of endogenous change – was highly influenced by Marx. This is not to undermine the importance of the endogenous factors emphasised by Schumpeter, such as entrepreneurial activity and technological innovation. But Schumpeter should have given due stress to exogenous factors as well.

23

INVENTION IS HELPLESS
WITHOUT TRADITION

The innovating theoretician needs ruthless self-belief. He must
overturn the intellectual dwelling-places of hundreds of people,
whose first instinct will be resistance and revenge. Yet reconstruction
must inevitably use much of the old material. Piety is not only
honourable, it is indispensable. Invention is helpless without
tradition. . . . When a long-accepted view visibly fails to meet the
modern situation, then we pluck up courage and start to dismantle
it. If there must be destruction and clearance of the site for new
architecture, let history herself do some of the demolition.
(George L. S. Shackle, *The Years of High Theory* (1967))

It is a purpose of this final chapter to make some suggestions, in the light of the
argument above, concerning the nature and role of economics as a discipline.
This discussion also leads us to examine the boundaries between economics and
other social sciences. Clearly, it is not possible here to outline particular theories
in detail. Instead, the aim of this book is to raise discussion of the problem of
historical specificity to its proper place in the social sciences. In this chapter some
suggestions are made concerning the place of different types of theoretical
approach, within a meta-theoretical outlook in which the problem is recognised.

WHAT IS ECONOMICS?

Economics, broadly defined, should be the study of the social structures and
institutions governing the production, distribution and exchange of the requisites
of human life. In other words, economics should be the study of all provisioning
institutions. This definition would turn economics into a subject much broader
than it is conceived today. But it would be close to the prevailing conception of
discipline prior to the Second World War. For instance, Alfred Marshall (1949,
p. 1) opened his *Principles* of 1890 with the following words:

Political Economy or Economics is the study of mankind in the ordinary
business of life; it examines that part of individual and social action
which is most closely connected with the attainment and with the use
of the material requisites of wellbeing.

346

Traditionally, 'old' institutionalists have defined economics in a similar and broad way, but given an additional emphasis to institutions. Note, for example, the definition of economics provided by the postwar 'old' American institutionalist, J. Fagg Foster (1981, p. 900): 'Economics, then, is an effort at rational enquiry into those institutions through which man provides himself with the means of life and experience.'[1]

A rare and prominent modern economist, who has continued with a definition of the subject that is almost as broad, is Ronald Coase. With a similar emphasis on institutions, Coase (1977, p. 487) defined economics as the study of 'the working of social institutions which bind the economic system together: firms, markets for goods and services, labour markets, capital markets, the banking system, international trade, and so on'. Although this leaves open the question of what is meant by 'the economic system', Coase's definition of economics is consistent with the idea that the subject involves the study of provisioning institutions. Coase focused on the provisioning institutions of civilised society, particularly firms and markets.

Long ago, in a similar vein to Coase, the German economist Alfred Amonn (1927) argued at length that the scope of economics should be the analysis of the institutions of a market economy. Lionel Robbins (1932, pp. 17–21) rejected this argument on the grounds that underlying the particular problems of a market economy were general 'laws of choice' that applied to every economic system. In the terms of Table 21.1 above, Robbins thus rejected the attempt to base economics on a third or higher level of abstraction, pertaining to civilised human societies with markets, and brought economics down to the second level. Robbins was right to point to the possible existence of universal laws and principles pertaining to the second level of abstraction. But this is no reason to ignore laws or principles at the third, or higher, levels. Nor is it a reason to reject the Amonn–Coase definition of the domain of economics. For reasons already discussed here, Robbins's argument is unconvincing.

On the other hand, although the substance of definitions requires analytical precision, the choice of label involves some degree of flexibility. The choice of labels to attach to a particular type of phenomenon often involves matters such as common usage and understanding. For this reason, at the beginning of the twenty-first century, we face a problem with the common usage of the term 'economics'. In global academic circles, it is Robbins who has had his way. Economics is now narrowly conceived, within most university departments of economics, as 'the science of choice'. Regrettably, the alternative and much broader definitions, by prominent figures such Marshall and Coase, have not prevailed in academia. But outside the college walls, among the lay public and in the bustle of business, there is a commonsense view that economics is, or should be, concerned with the workings of a money and market economy. The tension between these two conceptions of the subject has led to all sorts of havoc and misunderstanding. The definition of economics is under dispute. On the one

---

1 For the definitive discussion of J. F. Foster's economics see Tool (2000).

hand are the academic proponents of 'the science of choice'. On the other are the more worldly practitioners, who would define economics in terms of the study of how real social systems meet the provision of human needs and wants.

The damage that Robbins created by redefining economics as the science of choice will not be easily undone. The minority of dispossessed economists, concerned above all with the study of the provisioning institutions of a market economy, are not contented that their territory and opportunities have been confiscated by the mathematical formalists of abstract choice. Against the hegemonic majority they claim legitimacy for their territorial claim.

But Robbins does not bear the blame alone. The awkward word 'economics' will always have the two irreconcilable connotations of addressing either (a) aspects of real 'economies,' or (b) acts of 'economising' behaviour. Is economics about economies or economising? It is in this congenital linguistic ambiguity that some of the difficulty lies.

THE STUDY OF INSTITUTIONS: *THESMOLOGY*

Sociology too has identity problems of its own. The meaning of 'sociology' has changed since Auguste Comte coined the term in the 1830s. For him, it meant the general study of society, in which political economy was to be a subordinate part. Talcott Parsons (1937a, p. 768) redefined sociology more narrowly as the science concerned with 'the property of common-value integration' in society. The result of the Robbins–Parsons settlement was that economics and sociology were each concerned with an *aspect* of the social system as a whole. 'Sociology' existed, but no science was devoted to the study of the whole society. 'Economics' endured, but no science was devoted to the study of the economy. However, by the end of the twentieth century, the Robbins–Parsons settlement had crumbled, in part because the methodology of rational choice had invaded sociology as well as political science (Coleman, 1990).

One suggestion would be to span the former domains of 'economics' and 'sociology' by creating a discipline devoted to the study of social and economic institutions. In fact, Emile Durkheim (1982, p. 45) proposed in 1901 that 'sociology can then be defined as the science of institutions, their genesis and their functioning.' However, this conception of sociology is no longer prominent. A new discipline devoted to the study of institutions could describe itself as 'institutional science' or *thesmology*, from the Greek word *thesmos*, meaning institution. There are several advantages in focusing on the concept of the institution. First, the subject matter would span the older disciplines of economics and sociology. Second, it would focus on questions of social structure, as well as individuals – their actions and their choices.

The subject matter of 'institutional science' or thesmology would be the nature, formation and evolution of the rules, norms and structures that make up the institutional material of social life. It could take its cue from earlier classic studies of institutions such as by Thorstein Veblen (1899) and later seminal contributions, such as by Peter Berger and Thomas Luckmann (1966), and John Searle (1995).

Part of its task would be to address the general methodology of institutional analysis, as well as the historical transformation of institutions themselves. It would be theoretical and methodological, as well as empirical.

'Institutional science' or thesmology would itself have subdisciplines, each addressing particular types of institution. The study of political institutions would be one such subdiscipline. Another subdiscipline of thesmology would be what is today called 'organisation studies'. Its subject matter would remain the study of business and other organisations, as well as general matters of organisational evolution and ecology (McKelvey, 1982; Nelson and Winter, 1982; Hannan and Freeman, 1989; Aldrich, 1999).

In addition, another crucial subdiscipline of thesmology would address family structures. Existing research into the family is spread across both economics and sociology. Against the 'economic imperialism' of Gary Becker (1991) and others, the key point to recognise is that the family is not a market institution, even if it can be penetrated to some degree by market values. Hence the study of the family cannot use exactly the same theoretical materials as are applied to the study of markets and prices.[2]

THE STUDY OF MARKETS: *AGORALOGY*

Another subdiscipline of thesmology would be concerned with the study of markets. Markets are social institutions. The subdiscipline of *agoralogy* – from the Greek work *agora* meaning marketplace – would devote itself to the study of market institutions, market structures and pricing processes.

There is a sufficiently close historical precedent here, which carries a warning. Richard Whately (1831) was the first to suggest that the word 'catallactics' should be applied to the science that deals with exchange. However, Whately focused primarily on the motives of the participants to the exchange rather than the institution of property and pricing processes. The term thus became associated with the subjectivist theory of value and was later adopted by Austrian school economists such as Ludwig von Mises (1949) and Friedrich Hayek (1982). However, while Whately and his followers had always treated exchange as an interpersonal phenomenon, Mises thoroughly de-institutionalised the term by applying catallactics even to Robinson Crusoe, alone on his island. The individual, Mises argued, carried out an 'exchange with nature'. Catallactics was purged of institutional content by treating the concept of exchange in an individualist, ahistorical and de-institutionalised sense.

This is why agoralogy must be treated as a subdiscipline of thesmology or institutional science. Agoralogy is the study of market *institutions*, not of the

---

2 Feminist economists have rightly observed that an exclusive concentration on pecuniary exchanges and paid work obscures unpaid activities, such as childcare, within the firm (Folbre, 1994). A non-pecuniary calculus of time-use is used in surveys of household labour. Hence the literal economics, relating etymologically to the *oikos* (household), might very much be an economics of time.

strange, universal 'market' of neoclassical or Austrian theory. A market is more than the social space in which individuals interact. It is a social structure, containing institutional rules and norms.

The key phenomena in markets are property, commodities, money, prices and exchange. Accordingly, the central concepts of agoralogy are the same. Money plays a crucial role, except in that subset of markets with barter. Marshall (1949, p. 18) argued that 'money' or 'general purchasing power' is 'the centre around which economic science clusters'. Today, economics has lost this Marshallian analytical centre, being focused instead on the ahistorical generalities of utility and choice. Agoralogy would restore the specific phenomena of markets to their proper place. Crucially, agoralogy does not apply to phenomena where markets, property or exchange are absent. Clearly, we are dealing here with historically specific phenomena.

In chapter 17 a difference was drawn between market and non-market exchange. Exchange, as defined above, involves the transfer of property rights as well as goods or services. Exchange can be a one-off event. What is called 'relational exchange' can be driven by considerations other than pure pecuniary advantage. By contrast, a market is an institution in which a significant number of commodities of a particular type are regularly exchanged, and in which market rules and structures pattern these exchange negotiations and transactions.

In a market, for any given commodity, a foremost canon is its price. Price becomes the supreme measure of potential energy in the market system. Unlike utility, this measure is both observable and indisputably cardinal. Agoralogy restores the study of price and pricing mechanisms their proper place.

Agoralogy is different from catallactics. The focus of catallactics is on an unsatisfactory and ahistorical concept of exchange that does not necessarily involve property, and in which isolated individuals can carry out an 'exchange with nature'. By contrast, agoralogy is focused on the historically specific phenomena of market institutions. Agoralogy does not apply to non-market phenomena.

A fundamental theoretical question within agoralogy is the extent to which phenomena such as property, contracts, exchange and money depend on the existence of a state. It has been argued above that some form of legal apparatus is necessary to sustain these phenomena. But such arguments are matters of legitimate dispute within the discipline of agoralogy.

A major part of the subject matter of agoralogy is the theory of price. What factors influence the prices of commodities? This raises other, controversial questions: is there a historically specific role for a classical, Marshallian or Walrasian theory of price, even if some of these theories were originally cast in a universal and ahistoric role? In a way, this question is well over a century old. As noted already in this book, John Stuart Mill, Walter Bagehot, Alfred Marshall, Max Weber, Werner Sombart and Frank Knight all argued that some form of classical or neoclassical price theory was applicable exclusively to a market economy. Some agoralogists would adopt this broad assumption. Others would argue that none of the existing theories is satisfactory and a new approach to the theory of price is required. Another matter of controversy within agoralogy concerns which type of price theory is to be adopted.

As noted earlier in this volume, the Walrasian approach to price theory has not been successful in dealing with real phenomena such as money and firms. A remaining possibility is some modified version of Marshallian price theory. This would be particularly valuable in more dynamic versions (Souter, 1933b) and in its developments that address product heterogeneity and imperfect competition (Chamberlin, 1933).

One of the fundamental theoretical questions involved here is the conceptualisation of the exchanging agent. It was a relatively neglected issue in classical theory. However, neoclassical theory saw the agent as a utility-maximiser, defined by a preference function. This has been the staple fare of economics for over a century. The approach proposed here would be to follow the example of Weber (1975) and narrow down the concept of rationality to social contexts dominated by pecuniary calculation. In this commercial context, the concept of rationality can gain some meaning, by association with the pecuniary realities of cost, revenue, profit and loss. Indeed, the rise of markets and capitalism coincides with the growing facility for quantification and measurement (Crosby, 1998). By anchoring the concept of rationality to a society dominated by markets and exchange, we avoid the empty universalisation of the concept, by which it can be attached with little meaning to any possible (human or animal) behaviour.

Accepting that some exchange behaviour is dominated by rational and pecuniary calculation, at the same time it is possible to incorporate a notion that habit and routine also pervade behaviour. Indeed, rationality itself functions through acquired habits of calculation and computation (J. M. Clark, 1936, p. 122; Hodgson, 1997, 1998a). Accordingly, habit is the basis of rational choice and has temporal and ontological primacy over it. A neglected project is to develop a habit-based explanation of behaviour related to exchange and markets (Duesenberry, 1949; Becker, 1962; Arrow, 1986).

Other recent models of the agent without utility-maximisation include those of Alan Kirman (1993) and Paul Ormerod (1998). In the Kirman–Ormerod models, agents are assumed to behave in one of three ways: to carry on what they are doing (inertia), to copy others (imitation) or to make different choices (mutation). They can switch from one mode to another at any point in time. Although these models are admittedly crude, there is an element of interactive and imitative behaviour, redolent of Thorstein Veblen's (1899) work. If these models are to be of specific use in the study of markets, then they must be further developed to encompass important features of market institutions and pecuniary behaviour.

Furthermore, it is essential that theoretical developments in the understanding of the behaviour of human agents pay attention to the contribution of psychology (Rabin, 1998). The Parsons–Robbins pact of the 1930s, that diminished the influence of psychology in both sociology and economics, must be ended. The recent revival of approaches akin to the instinct–habit psychology of William James, William McDougall and John Dewey is a valuable and opportune development (Plotkin, 1994; Twomey, 1998). They give a psychological and evolutionary grounding to a habit-based conception of human behaviour.

These habit-based and other alternative theories are consistent with some form of endogenously determined preferences. To be consummated in some adequate theory of price, these lines of enquiry must further resolve the problem of agency and structure in the specific context of market institutions. As Samuel Bowles (1998) has argued, this involves an understanding of the influence of specific pecuniary or market cultures on agent behaviour. This is an area where it may be possible for agoralogy to gain insight from sociology and anthropology as well as economics.

Another – possibly complementary – approach to the study of markets is 'top down' rather than 'bottom up'. Dhananjay Gode and Shyam Sunder (1993) have constructed models where systemic constraints prevail over micro-variations. Gode and Sunder show that experiments with agents of 'zero intelligence' produce predictions that differ little from those with real human traders. As with Becker's (1962) model, the 'accuracy of predictions' criterion for theory selection does not give outright victory to rational choice models. Gode and Sunder further suggest that structural constraints can produce similar outcomes, whatever the objectives or behaviour of the individual agents. Ordered market behaviour can result from the existence of resource and institutional constraints, and may be largely independent of the 'rationality', or otherwise, of the agents. Structural constraints, not individuals, do much of the explanatory work. We thus face the possibility of a study of markets that focuses largely on institutions and structures, to a degree independent of the assumptions made about agents.[3]

Finally, different degrees of market competitiveness have to be considered. Much of the preceding work in the study of pricing in imperfectly competitive markets has been carried out within or close to the institutionalist and Post Keynesian traditions (Chamberlin, 1933; Means, 1938; Hall and Hitch, 1939; Tool, 1991; Lee, 1998). There is a richness of tradition here that is inadequately acknowledged within mainstream economics. The principal modern rival is game theory. Agoralogy is the terrain in which these contested approaches meet.

THE POLITICAL ECONOMY OF CAPITALISM

Another discipline or subdiscipline should be devoted to the study of the institutions and mechanisms of the capitalist social formation. Capitalism is a structured combination of institutions, including markets, capitalist firms, family structures and the state. The study of capitalism as a whole has to draw from the respective studies of these four types of provisioning institution. While Karl Marx's *Capital* can be faulted for focusing on markets and capitalist firms alone, neoclassical economics can also be criticised for attempting to treat all four types of phenomena in a single, ahistorical framework of analysis.

---

3   For discussions of these results see Denzau and North (1994), Mirowski (forthcoming) and Mirowski and Somefun (1998).

What is required is an approach that recognises the importance and necessity of all four types of provisioning institution within the capitalist system as a whole. This was precisely a dominant theme in the German historical school. Gustav von Schmoller, Werner Sombart and others developed an extensive analysis of capitalist institutions, including the state and the family, as well as markets and capitalist firms. The development of the political economy of capitalism requires the rediscovery of ideas from the German historical school and elsewhere.

An adequate general theory of capitalism would have to deal with the structures, incentives and cultures within all four types of provisioning institution. It would show how these structures, incentives and cultures intermesh and interact. Here, it would recognise that the prominent provisioning institution within capitalism is the capitalist firm, while markets are the main means by which the system is co-ordinated. The analyses of commodity production and exchange would be central. However, capitalism can be pervaded by different cultures and exist in different forms. The task here is to develop an analysis of agent–structure interaction that takes into account all these overlapping and interpenetrating institutions and cultures.

The existence of a subdiscipline concerning the political economy of capitalism would recognise the autonomy of what is currently described as macroeconomics. As I have argued elsewhere (Hodgson, 1993a, 1999b), the possibility of a relatively autonomous macroeconomic theory rests in part on the existence of a hierarchical ontology (Whitehead, 1926; Koestler, 1967; Bunge, 1973; Bhaskar, 1979). Accordingly, the macroeconomic level of analysis reveals emergent properties and causal powers, which are not predictable from the analysis of individuals or lower-level institutions. The reductionist attempt to establish macroeconomics on 'sound microfoundations' has failed (Kirman, 1989; Rizvi, 1994a). Reductionist attempts to dispense with macroeconomics are thwarted by the existence of emergent properties at the macroeconomic level.

Long ago the American institutionalists developed an intuitive justification for the existence of a partially autonomous macroeconomics. In his 1924 Presidential Address to the American Economic Association, the institutional economist Wesley Mitchell (1937, p. 26) argued that economists need not begin with a theory of individual behaviour but with the statistical observation of 'mass phenomena'. Mitchell (1937, p. 30) went on: 'The quantitative workers will have a special predilection for institutional problems, because institutions standardize behavior, and thereby facilitate statistical procedure.' Subsequently, Frank Knight's former student, Rutledge Vining (1949, p. 85) noted how 'much orderliness and regularity apparently only becomes evident when large aggregates are observed' and noted the limitations of a reductionist method in economics. Vining's intuition was to develop Knight's (1921a, p. 244) argument that the 'grouping of uncertainties' leads to greater regularities in the aggregate, into the notion that macro-order can emerge from micro-chaos.

Mitchell and his colleagues in the US National Bureau for Economic Research in the 1920s and 1930s played a vital role in the development of national income accounting and suggested that aggregate, macroeconomic phenomena have an ontological and empirical legitimacy. Arguably, this important incursion against reductionism in economics created space for the Keynesian revolution. Through the development of national income accounting the work of Mitchell and his colleagues influenced and inspired Keynes and helped to establish modern macroeconomics and (Mirowski, 1989, p. 307; Colander and Landreth, 1996, p. 141).

A historically grounded economics can make much use of past developments in macroeconomics, particularly from Keynesian macroeconomics. A key difference is that attempts to place these theories on universal microfoundations are rebutted and these insights are based on an understanding of historically specific institutions.

Modern work in this direction can usefully take up some of the insights of complexity theory, particularly concerning the theme of the emergence of order out of randomness (Cohen and Stewart, 1994; Kauffman, 1995; Holland, 1995). But again, this work can only go so far at the general level. To be of substantial value it would have to take on board some of the specific features of the capitalist system.

The research agenda is huge. Fortunately, further work on the political economy of capitalism can draw on a huge amount of existing literature, spanning Marxism, Post Keynesianism, institutionalism, the French *régulation* school and other approaches. Perhaps the last group has done most to integrate the spheres of the state, the firm and the market in a single framework of analysis (Aglietta, 1979; Boyer and Mistral, 1978). In addition, work in the Post Keynesian tradition is important here, as long as it is recognised that the aim is not a general theory, but, at the widest, a general theory of the modern capitalist social formation.

Upon the scaffold of this emerging theory can be constructed the detailed analysis of historically and geographically specific forms of capitalism, from the eighteenth to the twenty-first centuries, and from America to Japan.

REBUILDING THE SOCIAL SCIENCES

There is a great deal of theoretical and empirical material in existence that would be of value in the proposed reconstruction of the social sciences. A small fraction of this material has been mentioned here. The problem, however, is that both economics and sociology have lost their bearings, unable to redefine their role and position within the social sciences as a whole. The argument in this volume is that the development and reorientation of the social sciences can usefully benefit from rediscovering a Lost Continent of problems and ideas. The rehabilitation of historicism and institutionalism is part of this process.

But the rediscovery of old ideas is not a panacea for the theoretical and practical problems of the present. We can learn from tradition but it does not provide all the answers. The reinvigoration of the social sciences requires above all a methodological awareness, particularly concerning the meaning of theoretical explanation and the scope of empirical enquiry. The role of philosophy, as Alfred Whitehead (1926, p. 73) put it in a famous passage, is to help us to see the limits of our own abstractions:

You cannot think without abstractions; accordingly, it is of the utmost importance to be vigilant in critically revising your *modes* of abstraction. It is here that philosophy finds its niche as essential to the healthy progress of society. It is the critique of abstractions. A civilisation which cannot burst through its current abstractions is doomed to sterility after a very limited period of progress.

A task of philosophy is to help provide the meta-theoretical frameworks that can inform and nurture new theories at every level. The creation of historically and geographically sensitive theories depends upon an over-arching framework of guiding methodological principles. One of the aims of this book has been to attempt to learn from the past in the construction of this philosophical scaffolding.

However, it is on this philosophical terrain that the social sciences are currently at their weakest. Philosophy is too frequently omitted from the compulsory curriculum of the social sciences. Many students learn economics and sociology without knowledge of the philosophical problems involved in theory construction and evaluation. It is here too that we can learn from the German historicist tradition. The German universities of the nineteenth century placed philosophy at the apex of all learning. Today, however, there is an alarming degree of philosophical illiteracy among some social scientists that hinders the progress of creative and evaluative intellectual development.

Alongside philosophy, there is a need to re-establish the value and importance of the history of ideas and study of economic history. The reconstitution of the social sciences must proceed with knowledge of both the achievements and errors of the past. Invention is helpless without tradition.

BIBLIOGRAPHY

Abolafia, Mitchel Y. (1996) *Making Markets: Opportunism and Restraint on Wall Street*, Cambridge, MA: Harvard University Press.

Ackerman, Robert (1976) *The Philosophy of Karl Popper*, Amherst, MA: University of Massachusetts Press.

Aglietta, Michel (1979) *A Theory of Capitalist Regulation*, London: NLB.

Åkerman, Johan (1932) *Economic Progress and Economic Crises*, trans. Elizabeth Sprigge and Claude Napier from the Swedish edn (1931) London: Macmillan.

Alchian, Armen A. (1977) 'Some Implications of Recognition of Property Right Transaction Costs', in Brunner, Karl (ed.) (1977) *Economics and Social Institutions: Insights from the Conferences on Analysis and Ideology*, Boston, MA: Martinus Nijhoff, pp. 234–55.

Alchian, Armen A. and Demsetz, Harold (1972) 'Production, Information Costs, and Economic Organization', *American Economic Review*, **62**(4), December, 777–95.

Aldrich, Howard E. (1999) *Organizations Evolving*, London: Sage.

Alexander, Jeffrey C. (1982–3) *Theoretical Logic in Sociology*, 4 vols, Berkeley and London: University of California Press, and Routledge and Kegan Paul.

Alexander, Samuel (1920) *Space, Time and Deity*, 2 vols, London: Macmillan.

Allee, Warder C. (1951) *Cooperation Among Animals: With Human Implications*, New York: Henry Schuman.

Althusser, Louis (1969) *For Marx*, trans. Ben Brewster, from the French edn (1965) London: Allen Lane.

Amonn, Alfred (1927) *Objekt und Grundbegriffe der theoretischen Nationalökonomie*, Leipzig: Deutlicke.

Anderlini, Luca and Felli, Leonardo (1994) 'Incomplete Written Contracts: Undescribable States of Nature', *Quarterly Journal of Economics*, **109**, 1085–124.

Anderlini, Luca and Sabourian, H. (1995) 'Cooperation and Effective Computability', *Econometrica*, **63**, November, 1337–69.

Anderson, Perry (1974) *Passages from Antiquity to Feudalism*, London: NLB.

Aoki, Masahiko (1990) 'Towards an Economic Model of the Japanese Firm', *Journal of Economic Literature*, **26**(1), March, 1–27.

Aoki, Masahiko (forthcoming) *Towards a Comparative Institutional Analysis*, Cambridge, MA: MIT Press.

Aoki, Masahito and Patrick, Hugh (eds) (1994) *The Japanese Main Bank System: Its Relevance for Developing and Transforming Economies*, Oxford: Oxford University Press.

Appel, Michael (1992) *Werner Sombart: Historiker und Theoretiker des modernen Kapitalismus*, Marburg: Metropolis.

Archer, Margaret S. (1995) *Realist Social Theory: The Morphogenetic Approach*, Cambridge: Cambridge University Press.

Arestis, Philip, Dunn, Stephen P. and Sawyer, Malcolm (1999) 'On the Coherence of Post-Keynesian Economics: A Comment on Walters and Young', *Scottish Journal of Political Economy*, **46**(3), August, 339–45.

Argyrous, George and Sethi, Rajiv (1996) 'The Theory of Evolution and the Evolution of Theory: Veblen's Methodology in Contemporary Perspective', *Cambridge Journal of Economics*, **20**(4), July, 475–95.

Aronson, Jerrold L. (1984) *A Realist Philosophy of Science*, Basingstoke: Macmillan.

Arrow, Kenneth J. (1986) 'Rationality of Self and Others in an Economic System', *Journal of Business*, **59**(4.2), October, S385–S399. Repr. in Eatwell, John, Milgate, Murray and Newman, Peter (eds) (1987) *The New Palgrave Dictionary of Economics*, London: Macmillan, vol. 2.

Arrow, Kenneth J. and Hahn, Frank H. (1971) *General Competitive Analysis*, Edinburgh: Oliver and Boyd.

Arthur, W. Brian (1989) 'Competing Technologies, Increasing Returns, and Lock-in by Historical Events', *Economic Journal*, **99**(1), March, 116–31.

Arthur, W. Brian (1994) *Increasing Returns and Path Dependence in the Economy*, Ann Arbor, MI: University of Michigan Press.

Ashby, W. Ross (1952) *Design for a Brain*, New York: Wiley.

Ashby, W. Ross (1956) *An Introduction to Cybernetics*, New York: Wiley.

Ashley, Anne (1932) *William James Ashley: A Life*, London: King.

Ashley, William J. (1891) 'The Rehabilitation of Ricardo', *Economic Journal*, **1**(3), September, 474–89.

Ashley, William J. (1907) 'The Present Position of Political Economy', *Economic Journal*, **17**(4), December, 467–89.

Ashley, William J. (1908) 'The Enlargement of Economics', *Economic Journal*, **18**(2), June, 181–204.

Ashley, William J. (1924) 'Evolutionary Economics', in *Birkbeck College Centenary Lectures: 1823–1923. A Course of Lectures Given at the College in Connection With the Celebration of the Centenary*, with a Preface by J. Ramsay McDonald MP, London: University of London Press, pp. 35–61.

Ashley, William J. (1926) *Business Economics*, London: Longmans, Green.

Aspromourgos, Tony (1986) 'On the Origins of the term "Neoclassical"', *Cambridge Journal of Economics*, **10**(3), September, 265–70.

Augros, Robert and Stanciu, George (1987) *The New Biology: Discovering the Wisdom in Nature*, Boston: Shambhala.

Aumann, Robert J. (1985) 'What is Game Theory Trying to Accomplish?', in Arrow, Kenneth J. and Honkapohja, S. (eds) (1985) *Frontiers of Economics*, Oxford: Blackwell.

Ayres, Clarence E. (1918) *The Nature of the Relationship Between Ethics and Economics*, Chicago: University of Chicago Press.

Ayres, Clarence E. (1921a) 'Instinct and Capacity – I: The Instinct of Belief-in-Instincts', *Journal of Philosophy*, **18**(21), October 13, 561–5.

Ayres, Clarence E. (1921b) 'Instinct and Capacity – II: Homo Domesticus', *Journal of Philosophy*, **18**(22) October 27, 600–6.

Ayres, Clarence E. (1944) *The Theory of Economic Progress*, (1st edn) Chapel Hill, North Carolina: University of North Carolina Press.

Ayres, Clarence E. (1957) 'Review of *Economy and Society* by Talcott Parsons and Neil J. Smelser', *American Economic Review*, **47**(5), September, 686–8.

Ayres, Clarence E. (1958) 'Veblen's Theory of Instincts Reconsidered', in Dowd, Douglas F. (ed.) (1958) *Thorstein Veblen: A Critical Appraisal*, Ithaca, NY: Cornell University Press, pp. 25–37.

Ayres, Clarence E. (1961) *Toward a Reasonable Society: The Values of Industrial Civilization*, Austin: University of Texas Press.

Azzi, Corry and Ehrenberg, Ronald (1975) 'Household Allocation of Time and Church Attendance', *Journal of Political Economy*, **38**(1), 27–56.

Bachelard, Gaston (1953) *Le matérialisme rationnel* (Paris).

Backhaus, Jürgen G. (1985) 'Keynesianism in Germany' in Lawson, Tony and Pesaran, H. (eds) (1985) *Keynes' Economics: Methodological Issues*, London: Croom Helm, pp. 209–53.

Backhaus, Jürgen G. (ed.) (1996) *Werner Sombart (1863–1941) – Social Scientist*, 3 vols, Marburg: Metropolis-Verlag.

Backhaus, Jürgen G. (ed.) (2000) *Karl Bücher: Theory – History – Non Market Economies*, Marburg: Metropolis-Verlag.

Backhaus, Jürgen G. (ed.) (forthcoming) *The History of Evolutionary Thought in Economics*, Cheltenham: Edward Elgar.

Backhouse, Roger E. and Creedy, John (eds) (1999) *From Classical Economics to the Theory of the Firm: Essays in Honour of D. P. O'Brien*, Cheltenham: Edward Elgar.

Bagehot, Walter (1869) *Physics and Politics, or, Thoughts on the Application of the Principles of 'Natural Selection' and 'Inheritance' to Political Society*, New York: Alfred Knopf. Repr. in Norman St. John-Stevas (ed.) (1974) *The Collected Works of Walter Bagehot*, London: The Economist, vol. 7, pp. 15–144.

Bagehot, Walter (1880) *Economic Studies*. Reprinted in Norman St. John-Stevas (ed.) (1978) *The Collected Works of Walter Bagehot*, London: The Economist, vol. 11, pp. 222–394.

Baker, Wayne E. (1984) 'The Social Structure of a National Securities Market', *American Journal of Sociology*, **89**(4), 775–811. Repr. in Swedberg (1996).

Balabkins, Nicholas W. (1988) *Not by Theory Alone . . . The Economics of Gustav von Schmoller and its Legacy to America*, Berlin: Duncker and Humblot.

Balabkins, Nicholas W. (2000) 'Schumpeter's "Creatively Adapted" Innovator', Paper prepared for the 13th Heilbronn Conference on Schumpeter's German Works, June 23–25, 2000, unpublished mimeo.

Baldwin, James Mark (1909) *Darwin and the Humanities*, Baltimore: Review Publishing.

Baron, James N. and Hannan, Michael T. (1994) 'The Impact of Economics on Contemporary Sociology', *Journal of Economic Literature*, **32**(3), September, 1111–46. Repr. in Swedberg (1996).

Bateman, Bradley W. and Kapstein, Ethan B. (1999) 'Between God and the Market: The Religious Roots of the American Economic Association', *Journal of Economic Perspectives*, **13**(4), Fall, 249–58.

Baum, Joel A. C. and Singh, Jitendra V. (eds) (1994) *Evolutionary Dynamics of Organizations*, New York and Oxford: Oxford University Press.

Becker, Gary S. (1962) 'Irrational Behavior and Economic Theory', *Journal of Political Economy*, **70**(1), February, 1–13. Reprinted in Caldwell, Bruce J. (ed.) (1993) *The Philosophy and Methodology of Economics*, vol. 1, Aldershot: Edward Elgar.

Becker, Gary S. (1976a) *The Economic Approach to Human Behavior*, Chicago: University of Chicago Press.

Becker, Gary S. (1976b) 'Altruism, Egoism, and Genetic Fitness: Economics and Sociobiology', *Journal of Economic Literature*, **14**(2), December, 817–26. Repr. in Hodgson (1995a).

Becker, Gary S. (1991) *A Treatise on the Family*, (2nd edn), Cambridge, MA: Harvard University Press.

Becker, Gary S. (1992) 'Habits, Addictions and Traditions', *Kyklos*, **45**, Fasc. 3, 327–46.

Becker, Gary S. (1996) *Accounting for Tastes*, Cambridge, MA: Harvard University Press.

Becker, Gary S. and Posner, Richard A. (1993) 'Cross-Cultural Differences in Family and Sexual Life: An Economic Analysis', *Rationality and Society*, **5**(4), October, 421–31.

Benedict, Ruth (1934) *Patterns of Culture*, New York: New American Library.

Bennett, Charles and Landauer, Rolf (1985) 'The Fundamental Physical Limits of Computation', *Scientific American*, **253**, July, 48–56.

Berger, Peter and Luckmann, Thomas (1966) *The Social Construction of Reality*, Harmondsworth: Penguin.

Berger, Suzanne and Dore, Ronald (eds) (1996) *National Diversity and Global Capitalism*, Ithaca: Cornell University Press.

Bergson, Henri (1911) *Creative Evolution*, translated from the French edition of 1907, New York: Henry Holt.

Bertalanffy, Ludwig von (1950) 'The Theory of Open Systems in Physics and Biology', *Science*, **111**, 23–9.

Bertalanffy, Ludwig von (1971) *General Systems Theory: Foundation Development Applications*, London: Allen Lane.

Bertrand, Joseph (1883) 'Théorie Mathématique de la Richesse Sociale, par L. Walras', *Journal des savants*, pp. 499–508.

Betz, Horst K. (1993) 'From Schmoller to Sombart', *History of Economic Ideas*, **1**(3), 331–56.

Beveridge, William (1960) *The London School of Economics and Its Problems, 1919–1937*, London: Allen and Unwin.

Bhaskar, Roy (1975) *A Realist Theory of Science*, Leeds: Leeds Books.

Bhaskar, Roy (1979) *The Possibility of Naturalism: A Philosophic Critique of the Contemporary Human Sciences*, Brighton: Harvester.

Bicchieri, Cristina (1994) *Rationality and Coordination*, Cambridge and New York: Cambridge University Press.

Biddle, Jeffrey E. and Samuels, Warren J. (1997) 'The Historicism of John R. Commons's *Legal Foundations of Capitalism*', in Koslowski (1997a), pp. 291–318.

Biddle, Jeffrey E. and Samuels, Warren J. (1998) 'John R. Commons and the Compatibility of Neoclassical and Institutional Economics', in Holt, Richard P. F. and Pressman, Steven (1998) *Economics and its Discontents: Twentieth Century Dissenting Economists*, Cheltenham: Edward Elgar, pp. 40–55.

Binmore, Kenneth (1999) 'Why Experiment in Economics?', *Economic Journal*, **109**(2), February, F16–24.

Black, R. D. C., Coats, A. W. and Goodwin, C. (eds) (1973) *The Marginal Revolution in Economics*, Durham: Duke University Press.

Blau, Peter (1964) *Exchange and Power in Social Life*, New York: Wiley.

Blaug, Mark (1992) *The Methodology of Economics: Or How Economists Explain*, (2nd edn) Cambridge: Cambridge University Press.

Blaug, Mark (1999) 'The Formalist Revolution or What Happened to Orthodox Economics After World War II?', in Backhouse and Creedy (1999), pp. 257–80.

Blitch, Charles P. (1995) *Allyn Young: The Prophetic Economist*, London: Macmillan.

Bloch, Marc (1962) *Feudal Society*, trans. L. A. Manyon from the French edn (1939–40) with a foreword by M. M. Postan, London: Routledge and Kegan Paul.

Boettke, Peter J. (1989) 'Evolution and Economics: Austrians as Institutionalists', *Research in the History of Economic Thought and Methodology*, **6**, 73–89.

Böhm-Bawerk, Eugen von (1890) 'The Historical versus the Deductive Method in Political Economy', *Annals of the American Academy of Political and Social Science*, **1**, October, 244–71.

Boland, Lawrence A. (1981) 'On the Futility of Criticizing the Neoclassical Maximization Hypothesis', *American Economic Review*, **71**, 1031–6. Repr. in Boland (1996).

Boland, Lawrence A. (1996) *Critical Economic Methodology: A Personal Odyssey*, London and New York: Routledge.

Bostaph, Samuel (1978) 'The Methodological Debate Between Carl Menger and the German Historicists', *Atlantic Economic Journal*, **6**(3), 3–16.

Boulding, Kenneth E. (1958) 'Review of *Economy and Society* by Talcott Parsons and Neil J. Smelser', *American Journal of Sociology*, **63**(4), January, 427–8.

Bourdieu, Pierre (1977) *Outline of a Theory of Practice*, trans. by Richard Nice, Cambridge and New York: Cambridge University Press.

Bourdieu, Pierre (1990) *The Logic of Practice*, trans. by Richard Nice from the French edn (1980) Stanford and Cambridge: Stanford University Press and Polity Press.

Bowles, Samuel (1998) 'Endogenous Preferences: The Cultural Consequences of Markets and Other Economic Institutions', *Journal of Economic Literature*, **36**(1), March, 75–111.

Boyd, Robert and Richerson, Peter J. (1985) *Culture and the Evolutionary Process*, Chicago: University of Chicago Press.

Boyer, Robert and Mistral, Jacques (1978) *Accumulation, inflation et crises*, Paris: Universitaire de France.

Boylan, Thomas A. and Foley, Timothy P. (1992) *Political Economy and Colonial Ireland: The Propagation and Ideological Function of Economic Discourse in the Nineteenth Century*, London: Routledge.

Boylan, Thomas A. and O'Gorman, Paschal F. (1995) *Beyond Rhetoric and Realism in Economics: Towards a Reformulation of Economic Methodology*, London: Routledge.

Breit, William and Culbertson, William P., Jr (eds) (1976) *Science and Ceremony: The Institutional Economics of C. E. Ayres*, Austin: University of Texas Press.

Brick, Howard (1993) 'The Reformist Dimension of Talcott Parsons's Early Social Theory', in Haskell, Thomas L. and Teichgraeber, Richard F. (eds) (1993) *The Culture of the Market: Historical Essays*, Cambridge: Cambridge University Press, pp. 357–96.

Brocke, Bernhard vom (1996) 'Werner Sombart 1863–1941. Capitalism – Socialism. His Life, Works and Influence', in Backhaus (1996), vol. 1, pp. 19–102.

Bromley, Daniel W. (1989) *Economic Interests and Institutions: Conceptual Foundations of Public Policy*, Oxford: Basil Blackwell.

Brooks, Daniel R. and Wiley, E. O. (1988) *Evolution as Entropy: Toward a Unified Theory of Biology*, (2nd edn) Chicago: University of Chicago Press.

Buchanan, James M. (1969) 'Is Economics the Science of Choice?', in Erich Streissler (ed.) (1969) *Roads to Freedom: Essays in Honour of Friedrich A. von Hayek*, London: Routledge and Kegan Paul, pp. 47–64.

Buchanan, James M. (1976) 'Methods and Morals in Economics: The Ayres–Knight Discussion', in Breit and Culbertson (1976), pp. 164–74.

Bücher, Karl (1893) *Die Entstehung der Volkswirtschaft*, Tübingen: Laupp. Trans. (1901) as *Industrial Evolution*, New York: Henry Holt.

Buckley, Peter J. and Michie, Jonathan (eds) (1996) *Firms, Organizations and Contracts: A Reader in Industrial Organization*, Oxford: Oxford University Press.

Buckley, Walter F. (1967) *Sociology and Modern Systems Theory*, Englewood Cliffs, NJ: Prentice-Hall.

Bunge, Mario A. (1959) *Causality: The Place of the Causal Principle in Modern Science*, Cambridge, MA: Harvard University Press.

Bunge, Mario A. (1973) *Method, Model and Matter*, Dordrecht, Holland: Reidel.

Bunge, Mario A. (1998) *Social Science Under Debate: A Philosophical Perspective*, Toronto: University of Toronto Press.

Burger, Thomas (1987) *Max Weber's Theory of Concept Formation*, Durham, NC: Duke University Press.

Burki, Shavid Javed and Perry, Guillermo E. (1998) *Beyond the Washington Consensus: Institutions Matter*, Washington, DC: World Bank.

Burns, Arthur Edward (1950) 'Review of *Theories of Welfare Economics* by Hla Myint', in *American Economic Review*, **40**(3), June, 422–4.

Burns, Eveline M. (1931) 'Does Institutionalism Complement or Compete with "Orthodox Economics"?', *American Economic Review*, **21**(1), March, 80–7.

Burns, Eveline M. (1949) *The American Social Security System*, Boston: Houghton Mifflin.

Bush, Paul Dale (1983) 'An Exploration of the Structural Characteristics of a Veblen-Ayres-Foster Defined Institutional Domain', *Journal of Economic Issues*, **17**(1), March, 35–66.

Bush, Paul Dale (1986) 'On the Concept of Ceremonial Encapsulation', *The Review of Institutional Thought*, **3**, December, 25–45.

Buss, David M. (1994) *The Evolution of Desire*, New York: Basic Books.

Caldwell, Bruce J. (1982) *Beyond Positivism: Economic Methodology in the Twentieth Century*, London: Allen and Unwin.

Caldwell, Bruce J. (1988) 'Hayek's Transformation', *History of Political Economy*, **20**(4), Winter, 513–41.

Caldwell, Bruce J. (ed.) (1990) *Carl Menger and his Legacy in Economics*, Annual Supplement to *History of Political Economy*, **22**(5), Durham, NC: Duke University Press.

Callinicos, Alex (1999) *Social Theory: A Historical Introduction*, Cambridge: Polity Press.

Callon, Michel (ed.) (1998) *The Laws of the Markets*, Oxford: Blackwell.

Camic, Charles (1986) 'The Matter of Habit', *American Journal of Sociology*, **91**(5), 1039–87.

Camic, Charles (1987) 'The Making of a Method: A Historical Reinterpretation of the Early Parsons', *American Sociological Review*, **52**(4), August, 421–39.

Camic, Charles (1989) '*Structure* After 50 Years: The Anatomy of a Charter', *American Journal of Sociology*, **95**(1), July, 38–107.

Camic, Charles (ed.) (1991) *Talcott Parsons: The Early Essays*, Chicago: University of Chicago Press.

Camic, Charles (1992) 'Reputation and Predecessor Selection: Parsons and the Institutionalists', *American Sociological Review*, **57**(4), August, 421–45.

Campbell, Donald T. (1965) 'Variation, Selection and Retention in Sociocultural Evolution', in Barringer, H. R., Blanksten, G. I. and Mack, R. W. (eds) (1965) *Social Change in Developing Areas: A Reinterpretation of Evolutionary Theory*, Cambridge, MA: Schenkman, pp. 19–49. Repr. in Hodgson (1998c).

Cannan, Edwin (1914) *Wealth*, (3rd edn) London: King.

Carabelli, Anna M. (1991) 'The Methodology of the Critique of Classical Theory: Keynes on Organic Interdependence', in Bateman, Bradley W. and Davis, John B. (eds) (1991) *Keynes and Philosophy: Essays on the Origin of Keynes's Thought*, Aldershot: Edward Elgar, pp. 104–25.

Card, David and Kruger, Alan B. (1995) *Myth and Measurement: The New Economics of the Minimum Wage*, Princeton: Princeton University Press.

Cartier, Kate (1994) 'The Transaction Costs and Benefits of the Incomplete Contract of Employment', *Cambridge Journal of Economics*, **18**(2), April, 181–96.

Cartwright, Nancy (1994) 'Fundamentalism vs the Patchwork of Laws', *Proceedings of the Aristolean Society*, **93**(2), 279–92. Repr. in David Papineau (ed.) (1996) *The Philosophy of Science*, Oxford: Oxford University Press.

Chaloupek, Günther K. (1995) 'Long-Term Economic Perspectives Compared: Joseph Schumpeter and Werner Sombart', *European Journal of the History of Economic Thought*, **2**(1), 127–49.

Chamberlain, Neil W. (1963) 'The Institutional Economics of John R. Commons', in Joseph Dorfman *et al.*, pp. 63–94.

Chamberlin, Edward H. (1933) *The Theory of Monopolistic Competition*, Cambridge, MA: Harvard University Press.

Chamberlin, Edward H. (1957) *Towards a More General Theory of Value*, New York and Oxford: Oxford University Press.

Chandler, Alfred D., Jr (1977) *The Visible Hand: The Managerial Revolution in American Business*, Cambridge, MA: Harvard University Press.

Chang, Ha-Joon, Palma, Gabriel, and Whittaker, D. Hugh (eds) (1998), 'Special Issue on the Asian Crisis', *Cambridge Journal of Economics*, 22(6), November, 649–808.

Cherniak, Christopher (1986) *Minimal Rationality*, Cambridge, MA: MIT Press.

Cheung, Steven N. S. (1983) 'The Contractual Nature of the Firm', *Journal of Law and Economics*, 26(2), April, 1–21.

Chick, Victoria (1986) 'The Evolution of the Banking System and the Theory of Saving, Investment and Interest', *Economies et sociétés*, 20, série Monnaie et Production, 111–26. Reprinted in Chick, Victoria (1991) *On Money, Method and Keynes: Selected Essays by Victoria Chick*, ed. by Philip Arestis and Sheila C. Dow, London: Macmillan.

Choi, Kwang (1983) 'A Statistical Test of Olson's Model', in Mueller, Dennis C. (ed.) (1983) *The Political Economy of Growth*, New Haven: Yale University Press, pp. 57–78.

Clapham, John H. (1922) 'Of Empty Economic Boxes', *Economic Journal*, 22(3), September, 305–14.

Clapham, John H. (1929) *The Study of Economic History: An Inaugural Lecture*, Cambridge: Cambridge University Press.

Clark, Andy (1997a) 'Economic Reason: The Interplay of Individual Learning and External Structure', in Drobak, John N. and Nye, John V. C. (eds) (1997) *The Frontiers of the New Institutional Economics*, San Diego and London: Academic Press, pp. 269–90.

Clark, Andy (1997b) *Being There: Putting the Brain, Body and World Together Again*, Cambridge, MA: MIT Press.

Clark, Charles M. A. (1992) *Economic Theory and Natural Philosophy: The Search for the Natural Laws of the Economy*, Aldershot: Edward Elgar.

Clark, John Bates (1877) 'Unrecognized Forces in Political Economy', *New Englander*, October, 710–24.

Clark, John Bates (1885) *The Philosophy of Wealth: Economic Principles Newly Formulated*, London and New York: Macmillan.

Clark, John Maurice (1936) *Preface to Social Economics: Essays on Economic Theory and Social Economics*, New York: Farrer and Rhinehart. Repr. (1967) New York: Augustus Kelley.

Clark, John Maurice (1957) *Economic Institutions and Human Welfare*, New York: Alfred Knopf.

Clarke, David L. (1987) 'Trade and Industry in Barbarian Europe till Roman Times', in Postan, Michael M. and Miller, Edward (eds) (1987) *The Cambridge Economic History of Europe, Vol II, Trade and Industry in the Middle Ages*, (2nd edn) Cambridge: Cambridge University Press, pp. 1–70.

Clay, Karen (1997) 'Trade Without Law: Private-Order Institutions in Mexican California', *Journal of Law, Economics and Organization*, 13(1), April, 202–31.

Clegg, Stuart R. and Redding, S. Gordon (1990) *Capitalism in Contrasting Cultures*, New York: de Gruyter.

Clemence, Richard V. (ed.) (1951) *Essays on Economic Topics of J. A. Schumpeter*, Port Washington, NY: Kennikat.

Cliff, Tony (1955) *Stalinist Russia: A Marxist Analysis*, London: Michael Kidron. Later reprinted and enlarged as *Russia: A Marxist Analysis*, London: International Socialism, n. d.

Clower, Robert W. (1967) 'A Reconsideration of the Microfoundations of Monetary Theory', *Western Economic Journal*, **6**, 1–9. Repr. in Clower, Robert W. (ed.) (1969) *Monetary Theory*, Harmondsworth: Penguin.

Clower, Robert W. (1994) 'Economics as an Inductive Science', *Southern Economic Journal*, **60**(4), April, 805–14.

Clower, Robert W. (1999) 'Post-Keynes Monetary and Financial Theory', *Journal of Post Keynesian Economics*, **21**(3), Spring, 399–414.

Coase, Ronald H. (1937) 'The Nature of the Firm', *Economica*, **4**, November, 386–405. Repr. in Williamson and Winter (1991).

Coase, Ronald H. (1972) 'The Appointment of Pigou as Marshall's Successor', *Journal of Law and Economics*, **15**, October, 473–85.

Coase, Ronald H. (1977) 'Economics and Contiguous Disciplines', in Perlman Mark (ed.) (1977) *The Organization and Retrieval of Economic Knowledge*, Boulder, CO: Westview Press.

Coase, Ronald H. (1988) 'The Nature of the Firm: Origin, Meaning, Influence', *Journal of Law, Economics, and Organization*, **4**(1), Spring, 3–47. Repr. in Williamson and Winter (1991).

Coase, Ronald H. (1992) 'The Institutional Structure of Production', *American Economic Review*, **82**(4), September, 713–19.

Coats, A. W. (1968) 'Political Economy and the Tariff Reform Campaign of 1903', *Journal of Law and Economics*, **11**, April, 181–229. Repr. in Coats (1992).

Coats, A. W. (1972) 'The Appointment of Pigou as Marshall's Successor: Comment', *Journal of Law and Economics*, **15**, October, 487–95.

Coats, A. W. (1992) *On the History of Economic Thought: British and American Economic Essays, Volume I*, London: Routledge.

Coats, A. W. (1993) *The Sociology and Professionalization of Economics: British and American Economic Essays, Volume II*, London: Routledge.

Cohen, Gerald A. (1978) *Karl Marx's Theory of History: A Defence*, Oxford: Oxford University Press.

Cohen, Jack and Stewart, Ian (1994) *The Collapse of Chaos: Discovering Simplicity in a Complex World*, London and New York: Viking.

Colander, David C. (2000a) *The Complexity Vision and the Teaching of Economics*, Cheltenham: Edward Elgar.

Colander, David C. (2000b) *The Complexity and the History of Economic Thought*, London and New York: Routledge.

Colander, David C. and Landreth, Harry (eds) (1996) *The Coming of Keynesianism to America: Conversations with the Founders of Keynesian Economics*, Aldershot: Edward Elgar.

Coleman, James S. (1990) *Foundations of Social Theory*, Cambridge, MA: Harvard University Press.

Coleman, James S. and Fararo, Thomas (eds) (1990) *Rational Choice Theory: Advocacy and Critique*, Newbury Park: Sage.

Collard, David (1978) *Altruism and Economy: A study in Non-selfish Economics*, Oxford: Martin Robertson.

Collins, Randall (1998) *The Sociology of Philosophies: A Global Theory of Intellectual Change*, Cambridge, MA: Harvard University Press.

Commons, John R. (1893) *The Distribution of Wealth*, (repr. 1963) New York: Augustus Kelley.

Commons, John R. (1897) 'Natural Selection, Social Selection, and Heredity', *The Arena*, **18**, July, 90–7. Repr. in Hodgson (1998c).

Commons, John R. (1924) *Legal Foundations of Capitalism*, New York: Macmillan. (Repr. 1968) Madison: University of Wisconsin Press; (1974) New York: Augustus Kelley, and (1995) with a new introduction by Jeff E. Biddle and Warren J. Samuels, New Brunswick, NJ: Transaction.

Commons, John R. (1927) 'Price Stabilization and the Federal Reserve System', *Annalist*, **29**, 1 April, 459–62.

Commons, John R. (1931) 'Institutional Economics', *American Economic Review*, **21**(4), December, 648–57. Repr. in Samuels (1988), vol. 1.

Commons, John R. (1934a) *Institutional Economics – Its Place in Political Economy*, New York: Macmillan. Repr. (1990) with a new introduction by M. Rutherford, New Brunswick, NJ: Transaction.

Commons, John R. (1934b) *Myself: The Autobiography of John R. Commons*, New York: Macmillan.

Commons, John R. (1950) *The Economics of Collective Action*, ed. K. H. Parsons, New York: Macmillan.

Commons, John R. (1965) *A Sociological View of Sovereignty*, reprinted from the *American Journal of Sociology (1899–1900)*, ed. with introd. by Joseph Dorfman, New York: Augustus Kelley.

Commons, John R. and Perlman, Selig (1929) 'Review of Werner Sombart's *Der moderne Kapitalismus*', *American Economic Review*, **19**(1), March, 78–88.

Commons, John R., Saposs, David J., Sumner, Helen L., Mittleman, H. E., Hoagland, H. E., Andrews, John B. and Perlman, Selig (1918–35) *History of Labor in the United States*, 4 vols, New York: Macmillan.

Comte, Auguste (1853) *The Positive Philosophy of Auguste Comte*, 2 vols, trans. Harriet Martineau from the French volumes of 1830–42, London: Chapman.

Copeland, Morris A. (1927) 'An Instrumental View of the Part–Whole Relation', *Journal of Philosophy*, **24**(4), 17 February, 96–104.

Copeland, Morris A. (1958) 'On the Scope and Method of Economics' in Dowd, Douglas F. (ed.) (1958) *Thorstein Veblen: A Critical Reappraisal*, Ithaca, NY: Cornell University Press, pp. 57–75. Repr. in Hodgson (1995).

Coricelli, Fabrizio and Dosi, Giovanni (1988) 'Coordination and Order in Economic Change and the Interpretative Power of Economic Theory', in Dosi, Giovanni, Freeman, Christopher, Nelson, Richard, Silverberg, Gerald and Soete, Luc (eds) (1988) *Technical Change and Economic Theory*, London: Pinter, pp. 124–47. Repr. in Hodgson (1993b).

Costa, Manuel Luis (1998) *General Equilibrium Analysis and the Theory of Markets*, Cheltenham and Lyme, NH: Edward Elgar.

Cowling, Keith and Sugden, Roger (1993) 'Control, Markets and Firms', in Pitelis, Christos (ed.) (1993) *Transaction Costs, Markets and Hierarchies*, Oxford: Basil Blackwell, pp. 66–76.

Crosby, Alfred W. (1998) *The Measure of Reality: Quantification and Western Society, 1250–1600*, Cambridge: Cambridge University Press.

Cross, Rod (1982) *Economic Theory and Policy in the UK*, Oxford: Martin Robertson.

Cunningham, William (1885) *Politics and Economics: An Essay on the Nature of the Principles of Political Economy, Together with a Survey of Recent Legislation*, London.

Cunningham, William (1887) *Political Economy Treated as an Empirical Science: A Syllabus of Lectures*, Cambridge.

Cunningham, William (1892a) 'The Relativity of Economic Doctrines', *Economic Journal*, **2**(1), March, 1–16.

Cunningham, William (1892b) 'The Perversion of Economic History', *Economic Journal*, **2**(3), September, 491–506.

Cunynghame, Henry (1892) 'Some Improvements in Simple Geometrical Methods of Treating Exchange Value, Monopoly and Rent', *Economic Journal*, **2**(1), March, 35–52.

Currie, Martin and Steedman, Ian (1990) *Wrestling With Time: Problems in Economic Theory*, Manchester: Manchester University Press.

Curti, Merle (1980) *Human Nature in American Thought*, Madison: University of Wisconsin Press.

Cutland, Nigel J. (1980) *Computability: An Introduction to Recursive Function Theory*, Cambridge: Cambridge University Press.

Dahrendorf, Ralf (1995) *LSE: A History of the London School of Economics and Political Science, 1895–1995*, Oxford: Oxford University Press.

Daly, Herman E. (1974) 'The Economics of the Steady State', *American Economic Review (Papers and Proceedings)*, **64**(2), May, 15–21.

Damasio, Antonio R. (1994) *Descartes' Error: Emotion, Reason, and the Human Brain*, New York: Putnam.

Daniel, Glyn (1968) *The First Civilizations: The Archaeology of their Origins*, London: Thames and Hudson.

Darwin, Charles (1859) *On the Origin of Species by Means of Natural Selection, or the Preservation of Favoured Races in the Struggle for Life*, (1st edn) London: Murray. Facsimile reprint 1964 with introduction by Ernst Mayr, Cambridge, MA: Harvard University Press.

Darwin, Charles (1871) *The Descent of Man, and Selection in Relation to Sex*, (1st edn) London: Murray; New York: Hill. Facsimile reprint 1981 with intro. by John T. Bonner and Robert M. May, Princeton, NJ: Princeton University Press.

Daugert, Stanley Matthew (1950) *The Philosophy of Thorstein Veblen*, New York: Columbia University Press.

David, Paul A. (1985) 'Clio and the Economics of QWERTY', *American Economic Review* (Papers and Proceedings), **75**(2), May, 332–7.

David, Paul A. (1994) 'Why are Institutions the "Carriers of History"? Path Dependence and the Evolution of Conventions, Organizations and Institutions', *Structural Change and Economic Dynamics*, **5**(2), 205–20.

Davidson, Paul (1978) *Money and the Real World*, (2nd. edn) London: Macmillan.

Davidson, Paul (1980) 'Post Keynesian Economics', *Public Interest*, Special Edition, 151–73.

Davidson, Paul (1993) 'Austrians and Post Keynesians on Economic Reality: Rejoinder to Critics', *Critical Review*, **7**(2–3), Spring–Summer, 423–44.

Davidson, Paul (1994) *Post Keynesian Macroeconomic Theory: A Foundation for Successful Economic Policies for the Twenty-First Century*, Aldershot: Edward Elgar.

Davidson, Paul (1996) 'What Revolution? The Legacy of Keynes', *Journal of Post Keynesian Economics*, **19**(1), Fall, 47–60. Repr. in Davidson, Louise (ed.) (1999) *Uncertainty, International Money, Employment and Theory: The Collected Writings of Paul Davidson, Volume 3*, London: Macmillan.

Davies, Glyn (1994) *A History of Money: From Ancient Times to the Present Day*, Cardiff: University of Wales Press.

Davis, J. Ronnie (1971) *The New Economics and Old Economists*, Ames, Iowa: Iowa State University Press.

Davis, John B. (1998) 'Davidson, Non-Ergodicity and Individuals', in Arestis, Philip (ed.) (1998) *Method, Theory and Policy in Keynes: Essays in Honour of Paul Davidson, Volume Three*, Cheltenham: Edward Elgar, pp. 1–16.

Davis, M., Sigal, R. and Weyuker, E. (1994) *Computability, Complexity and Languages*, San Diego: Academic Press.

Dawkins, Richard (1983) 'Universal Darwinism', in Bendall, D. S. (ed.) (1983) *Evolution from Molecules to Man*, Cambridge: Cambridge University Press, pp. 403–25.

Dawkins, Richard (1986) *The Blind Watchmaker*, Harlow: Longman.

Day, Richard H. (1987) 'The General Theory of Disequilibrium Economics and of Economic Evolution', in Batten, D., Casti, J. L. and Johansson, B. (eds) (1987) *Economic Evolution and Structural Adjustment*, Berlin: Springer-Verlag, pp. 46–63.

De Vroey, Michel (1998) 'Is the Tâtonnement Hypothesis a Good Caricature of Market Forces?', *Journal of Economic Methodology*, **5**(2), December, 201–22.

Deakin, Simon (1997) 'The Evolution of the Contract of Employment, 1900–1950: The Influence of the Welfare State', in Whiteside, Noel and Salais, Robert (eds) (1998) *Governance, Industry and Labour Markets in Britain and France: The Modernising State in the Mid-Twentieth Century*, London: Routledge, pp. 213–30.

Deaton, Angus (1996) 'Letter from America', *Royal Economic Society Newsletter*, October, p. 13.

Debreu, Gerard (1959) *Theory of Value: An Axiomatic Analysis of General Equilibrium*, New Haven: Yale University Press.

Debreu, Gerard (1974) 'Excess Demand Functions', *Journal of Mathematical Economics*, **1**(1), March, 15–21.

Degler, Carl N. (1991) *In Search of Human Nature: The Decline and Revival of Darwinism in American Social Thought*, Oxford and New York: Oxford University Press.

DeGregori, Thomas R. (1977) 'Ethics and Economic Inquiry: The Ayres–Knight Debate and the Problem of Economic Order', *American Journal of Economics and Sociology*, **36**, 41–50.

Demsetz, Harold (1988) 'The Theory of the Firm Revisited', *Journal of Law, Economics, and Organization*, **4**(1), Spring, 141–62. Repr. Williamson and Winter (1991).

Dennett, Daniel C. (1995) *Darwin's Dangerous Idea: Evolution and the Meanings of Life*, London: Allen Lane.

Denzau, Arthur T. and North, Douglass, C. (1994) 'Shared Mental Models: Ideologies and Institutions', *Kyklos*, **47**, Fasc. 1, 3–31.

Dewey, John (1922) *Human Nature and Conduct: An Introduction to Social Psychology*, (1st edn) New York: Holt.

Dewey, John (1938) *Logic: The Theory of Enquiry*, New York: Holt.

Dewey, John (1939) *Theory of Valuation*, Chicago: University of Chicago Press.

Diamond, Jared (1997) *Guns, Germs and Steel: A Short History of Everybody for the Last 13,000 Years*, London: Jonathan Cape.

Diehl, Carl (1978) *Americans and German Scholarship 1770–1870*, New Haven, CT: Yale University Press.

Dobretsberger, J. (1949) 'Zur Methodenlehre C. Mengers und der österreichischen Schule', *Zeitschrift für Nationalökonomie*, **12**, 78–89.

Doeringer, Peter B. and Piore, Michael J. (1971) *Internal Labor Markets and Manpower Analysis*, Lexington, MA: Heath.

Dopfer, Kurt (1988) 'How Historical is Schmoller's Economic Theory?', *Journal of Institutional and Theoretical Economics*, **144**(3), 552–69. Repr. in Mark Blaug (ed.) (1992) *Gustav Schmoller (1838–1917) and Werner Sombart (1863–1941)*, Aldershot: Edward Elgar.

Dopfer, Kurt (1993) 'On the Significance of Gustave Schmoller's Contribution to Modern Economics', *History of Economic Ideas*, **1**(3), 143–78.

Dopfer, Kurt (1998) 'Causality and Order in Economics: Foundational Contributions by G. Schmoller and W. Eucken', in Fayazmanesh, Sazan and Tool, Marc R. (eds) (1998)

Institutionalist Method and Value: Essays in Honour of Paul Dale Bush, Volume 1, Cheltenham: Edward Elgar, pp. 98–111.

Dore, Ronald (1983) 'Goodwill and the Spirit of Market Capitalism', *British Journal of Sociology,* **34**(4), 459–82.

Dore, Ronald (1987) *Taking Japan Seriously: A Confucian Perspective on Leading Economic Issues,* London: Athlone Press.

Dorfman, Joseph (1934) *Thorstein Veblen and His America,* New York: Viking Press. Repr. 1961, New York: Augustus Kelley.

Dorfman, Joseph (1955) 'The Role of the German Historical School in American Economic Thought', *American Economic Review (Papers and Proceedings),* **45**(2), May, 17–28.

Dorfman, Joseph (1974) 'Walton Hamilton and Industrial Policy' in Hamilton, Walton H. (1974) *Industrial Policy and Institutionalism: Selected Essays,* with introd. by Joseph Dorfman, New York: Augustus Kelley, pp. 5–28.

Dosi, Giovanni, Freeman, Christopher, Nelson, Richard, Silverberg, Gerald and Soete, Luc L. G. (eds) (1988) *Technical Change and Economic Theory,* London: Pinter.

Dow, Alistair, Dow, Sheila C., Hutton, Alan and Keaney, Michael (1998) 'Traditions in Thought: The Case of Scottish Political Economy', *New Political Economy,* **3**(1), 45–58.

Duesenberry, James S. (1949) *Income, Saving and the Theory of Consumer Behavior,* Cambridge MA: Harvard University Press.

Dunbar, Charles (1876) 'Economic Science in America', *North American Review,* **122**, January, 124–54.

Dunn, Stephen P. (2000) 'Whither Post Keynesianism?', *Journal of Post Keynesian Economics,* 22(3), Spring, 343–66.

Dupré, John A. (1993) *The Disorder of Things: Metaphysical Foundations of the Disunity of Science,* Cambridge, MA: Harvard University Press.

Durham, William H. (1991) *Coevolution: Genes, Culture, and Human Diversity,* Stanford: Stanford University Press.

Durkheim, Emile (1982) *The Rules of Sociological Method,* trans. W. D. Halls from the French edn (1901) with introd. by Steven Lukes, London: Macmillan.

Durkheim, Emile (1984) *The Division of Labour in Society,* trans. W. D. Halls from the French edn (1893) with introd. by Lewis Coser, London: Macmillan.

Eatwell, John and Milgate, Murray (eds) (1983) *Keynes' Economics and the Theory of Value and Distribution,* London: Duckworth.

Ebner, Alexander (2000) 'Schumpeter and the "Schmollerprogramm": Integrating Theory and History in the Analysis of Economic Development', *Journal of Evolutionary Economics,* **10**(3), 355–72.

Edgeworth, Francis Y. (1891) 'The British Economic Association', *Economic Journal,* **1**(1), March, 1–2.

Edquist, Charles (ed.) (1997) *Systems of Innovation: Technologies, Institutions and Organizations,* London: Pinter.

Eichner, Alfred S. (ed.) (1979) *A Guide to Post-Keynesian Economics,* London: Macmillan; Armonk, NY: Sharpe.

Eichner, Alfred S. (ed.) (1983) *Why Economics is Not Yet a Science,* Armonk, NY: Sharpe.

Elam, Mark (1997) 'National Imaginations and Systems of Innovation', in Edquist, Charles (ed.) (1997) *Systems of Innovation: Technologies, Institutions and Organizations,* London: Pinter, pp. 157–73.

Ellerman, David P. (1984) 'Arbitrage Theory: A Mathematical Introduction', *SIAM Review,* 26, 241–61.

Ellerman, David P. (1992) *Property and Contract in Economics: The Case for Economic Democracy,* Oxford: Basil Blackwell.

367

Elster, Jon (1982) 'Marxism, Functionalism and Game Theory', *Theory and Society*, **11**(4), 453–82. Repr. in Roemer, John E. (ed.) (1986) *Analytical Marxism*, Cambridge: Cambridge University Press.

Elster, Jon (1985) *Making Sense of Marx*, Cambridge: Cambridge University Press.

Ely, Richard T. (1903) *Studies in the Evolution of Industrial Society*, New York: Macmillan.

Emery, Fred E. (ed.) (1981) *Systems Thinking*, 2 vols, Harmondsworth: Penguin.

Endres, Anthony M. (1997) *Neoclassical Microeconomic Theory: The Founding Austrian Version*, London and New York: Routledge.

Engels, Frederick (1962) *Anti-Dühring: Herr Eugen Dühring's Revolution in Science*, trans. from the 3rd German edn (1894), London: Lawrence and Wishart.

Etzioni, Amitai (1988) *The Moral Dimension: Toward a New Economics*, New York: Free Press.

Eucken, Walter (1950) *Foundations of Economics*, trans. by T. W. Hutchinson, London: Hodge.

Fararo, Thomas (1989) *The Meaning of General Theoretical Sociology: Tradition and Formalization*, Cambridge: Cambridge University Press.

Fayazmanesh, Sasan (1998) 'On Veblen's Coining of the Term "Neoclassical"', in Fayazmanesh, Sazan and Tool, Marc R. (eds) (1998) *Institutionalist Method and Value: Essays in Honour of Paul Dale Bush, Volume 1*, Cheltenham: Edward Elgar, pp. 74–97.

Ferguson, Niall (ed.) (1998) *Virtual History: Alternatives and Counterfactuals*, London: Macmillan.

Fetter, Frank A. (1927) 'Clark's Reformulation of the Capital Concept', in Hollander, Jacob H. (ed.) (1927) *Economic Essays Contributed in Honor of John Bates Clark*, New York: Macmillan, pp. 136–56.

Fetter, Frank A. (1930) 'Capital', in Seligman, Edwin R. A. and Johnson, Alvin (eds) *Encyclopaedia of the Social Sciences*, vol. 3, New York: Macmillan, pp. 187–90.

Field, Alexander J. (1979) 'On the Explanation of Rules Using Rational Choice Models', *Journal of Economic Issues*, **13**(1), March, 49–72. Repr. in Hodgson (1993b).

Field, Alexander J. (1981) 'The Problem with Neoclassical Institutional Economics: A Critique with Special Reference to the North/Thomas Model of Pre-1500 Europe', *Explorations in Economic History*, **18**(2), April, 174–98.

Field, Alexander J. (1984) 'Microeconomics, Norms and Rationality', *Economic Development and Cultural Change*, **32**(4), July, 683–711. Repr. in Hodgson (1993b).

Field, Alexander J. (1991) 'Do Legal Systems Matter?', *Explorations in Economic History*, **28**(1), 1–35.

Finch, John H. (1997) '"Verstehen," Ideal Types and Situational Analysis, and the Problem of Free Will', *Journal of Institutional and Theoretical Economics*, **153**, 737–47.

Finley, Moses I. (ed.) (1962) *Second International Conference of Economic History, Vol. I, Trade and Politics in the Ancient World*, New York: Arno.

Fisher, Franklin M. (1989) 'Games Economists Play: A Noncooperative View', *Rand Journal of Economics*, **20**, 113–24.

Fleetwood, Steven (1995) *Hayek's Political Economy: The Socio-Economics of Order*, London: Routledge.

Flew, Antony G. N. (1959) 'The Structure of Darwinism', *New Biology*, **28**, 25–44.

Folbre, Nancy (1982) 'Exploitation Comes Home: A Critique of the Marxian Theory of Family Labour', *Cambridge Journal of Economics*, **6**(4), December, 317–29.

Folbre, Nancy (1994) *Who Pays for the Kids? Gender and the Structures of Constraint*, London and New York: Routlege.

Foley, Caroline A. (1893) 'Fashion', *Economic Journal*, **3**(3), September, 458–74.

Foss, Nicolai Juul (1994) 'Realism and Evolutionary Economics', *Journal of Social and Evolutionary Systems*, **17**(1), 21–40.

Foss, Nicolai Juul (1996) 'Firms, Incomplete Contracts, and Organizational Learning', *Human Systems Management*, **15**(1), 17–26.

Foster, J. Fagg (1981) 'The Relation Between the Theory of Value and Economic Analysis', *Journal of Economic Issues*, **15**(4), December, 899–905.

Foster, John (1997) 'The Analytical Foundations of Evolutionary Economics: From Biological Analogy to Economic Self-Organisation', *Structural Change and Economic Dynamics*, **8**, 427–51.

Fox, Alan (1974) *Beyond Contract: Work, Power and Trust Relations*, London: Faber and Faber.

Foxwell, Herbert S. (1887) 'The Economic Movement in England', *Quarterly Journal of Economics*, **2**(1), October, 84–103.

Foxwell, Herbert S. (1919) 'Archdeacon Cunningham', *Economic Journal*, **29**(3), September, 382–95.

Frank, Robert H. (1992) 'Melding Sociology and Economics: James Coleman's *Foundations of Social Theory*', *Journal of Economic Literature*, **30**(1), March, 147–70. Repr. in Swedberg (1996).

Freeman, Christopher (1995) 'The "National System of Innovation" in Historical Perspective', *Cambridge Journal of Economics*, **19**(1), February, 5–24.

Friedman, Jeffrey (ed.) (1995) *The Rational Choice Controversy: Economic Models of Politics Reconsidered*, New Haven: Yale University Press.

Friedman, Milton (1953) 'The Methodology of Positive Economics', in Friedman, M., *Essays in Positive Economics*, Chicago: University of Chicago Press, pp. 3–43. Repr. in Caldwell (1984).

Friedman, Milton (1956) *Studies in the Quantity Theory of Money*, Chicago: University of Chicago Press.

Friedman, Milton (1962) *Price Theory*, Chicago: Aldine.

Friess, Horace L. (1930) 'The Progress of German Philosophy in the Last Hundred Years', *Journal of Philosophy*, **27**(15), 17 July, 396–415.

Fullbrook, Edward (1998) 'Caroline Foley and the Theory of Intersubjective Demand', *Journal of Economic Issues*, **32**(3), September, 709–31.

Furubotn, Eirik G. and Pejovich, Svetozar (eds) (1974) *The Economics of Property Rights*, Cambridge, MA: Ballinger.

Furubotn, Eirik G. and Richter, Rudolf (1997) *Institutions in Economic Theory: The Contribution of the New Institutional Economics*, Ann Arbor: University of Michigan Press.

Galbraith, James K. (1996) 'Keynes, Einstein and Scientific Revolution' in Arestis, Philip and Sawyer, Malcolm (eds) (1998) *Keynes, Money and the Open Economy: Essays in Honour of Paul Davidson, Volume One*, Cheltenham: Edward Elgar, pp. 14–21. Adapted from *American Prospect*, Winter 1994, pp. 62–7.

Garcia, Marie-France (1986) 'La construction sociale d'un marché parfait: Le marché au cadran de Fontaines-en-Sologne', *Actes de la Recherche en Sciences Sociales*, **65**, 2–13.

Garnett, Robert F., Jr. (1999) 'Postmodernism and Theories of Value: New Grounds for Institutionalist/Marxist Dialogue?', *Journal of Economic Issues*, **33**(4), December, 817–34.

Garvy, George (1975) 'Keynes and the Economic Activists of Pre-Hitler Germany', *Journal of Political Economy*, **83**(2), April, 391–405.

Georgescu-Roegen, Nicholas (1971) *The Entropy Law and the Economic Process*, Cambridge, MA: Harvard University Press.

Ghiselin, Michael T. (1987) 'Principles and Prospects for General Economy', in Radnitzky and Bernholz (1987), pp. 21–31.

Giddens, Anthony (1981) *A Contemporary Critique of Historical Materialism*, London: Macmillan.

Giddens, Anthony (1984) *The Constitution of Society: Outline of the Theory of Structuration*, Cambridge: Polity Press.

Gide, Charles and Rist, Charles (1915) *A History of Economic Doctrines From the Time of the Physiocrats to the Present Day*, trans. William Smart and R. Richards from the French edn (1913) London: George Harrap.

Giffen, Robert (1880) 'Bagehot as an Economist', *Fortnightly Review*, **27**, 549–67.

Ginsberg, Morris (1932) *Studies in Sociology*, London: Methuen.

Gintis, Herbert (2000) *Game Theory Evolving*, Princeton: Princeton University Press.

Gioia, Vitantonio (1993) 'Causality and Economic Analysis in Gustav Schmoller's Thought', *History of Economic Ideas*, **1**(3), 197–223.

Gloria-Palermo, Sandye (1999) *The Evolution of Austrian Economics: From Menger to Lachmann*, London: Routledge.

Gode, Dhananjay K. and Sunder, Shyam (1993) 'Allocative Efficiency of Markets with Zero-Intelligence Traders: Market as a Partial Substitute for Individual Rationality', *Journal of Political Economy*, **101**(1), February, 119–37.

Goldberg, Victor P. (1980) 'Relational Exchange: Economics and Complex Contracts', *American Behavioral Scientist*, **23**(3), 337–52.

Gonce, R. A. (1996) 'The Social Gospel, Ely, and Commons's Initial Stage of Thought', *Journal of Economic Issues*, **30**(3), September, 641–65.

Gottinger, H. (1982) 'Computational Costs and Bounded Rationality', in Stegmuller, W., Balzer, W. and Spohn, W. (eds) (1982) *Studies in Contemporary Economics*, Berlin: Springer-Verlag, pp. 223–38.

Gould, Stephen Jay (1977) *Ontogeny and Phylogeny*, Cambridge, MA: Harvard University Press.

Gould, Stephen Jay (1985) *The Flamingo's Smile*, New York: Norton.

Gould, Stephen Jay (1989) *Wonderful Life: The Burgess Shale and the Nature of History*, London: Hutchinson Radius.

Glymour, Clark (1980) 'Explanations, Tests, Unity and Necessity', *Nous*, **14**(1), March, 31–50.

Grabher, Gernot and Stark, David (eds) (1997) *Restructuring Networks in Post-Socialism: Legacies, Linkages and Localities*, Oxford: Oxford University Press.

Granovetter, Mark (1985) 'Economic Action and Social Structure: The Problem of Embeddedness', *American Journal of Sociology*, **91**(3), November, 481–510. Repr. in Swedberg (1996).

Granovetter, Mark (1993) 'The Nature of Economic Relationships', in Swedberg, Richard (ed.) (1993) *Explorations in Economic Sociology*, New York: Russell Sage, pp. 3–41.

Gravelle, Hugh and Rees, Ray (1992) *Microeconomics*, (2nd edn) Harlow: Longman.

Green, Donald and Shapiro, Ian (1994) *Pathologies of Rational Choice Theory: A Critique of Applications in Political Science*, New Haven, CT: Yale University Press. (See summary and reviews in *Critical Review*, **9**(1–2), Winter–Spring 1995.)

Greif, Avner (1989) 'Reputations and Coalitions in Medieval Trade: Evidence on the Maghribi Traders', *The Journal of Economic History*, **49**(4), December, 857–82.

Greif, Avner (1993) 'Contract Enforceability and Economic Institutions in Early Trade: The Maghribi Traders' Coalition', *American Economic Review*, **83**(3), June, 525–48.

Greif, Avner (1994a) 'On the Political Foundations of the Late Medieval Commercial Revolution: Genoa During the Twelfth and Thirteenth Centuries', *Journal of Economic History*, **54**(2), June, 271–87.

Greif, Avner (1994b) 'Cultural Beliefs and the Organization of Society: A Historical and Theoretical Reflection on Collectivist and Individualist Societies', *Journal of Political Economy*, **102**(5), October, 912–50.

Greif, Avner (1996) 'The Study of Organizations and Evolving Organizational Forms

Through History: Reflections from the Late Medieval Family Firm', *Industrial and Corporate Change*, **5**(2), 473–501.

Greif, Avner (1998) 'Historical and Comparative Institutional Analysis', *American Economic Review (Papers and Proceedings)*, **88**(2), May, 80–4.

Greif, Avner, Milgrom, Paul and Weingast, Barry R. (1994) 'Coordination, Commitment, and Enforcement: The Case of the Merchant Guild', *Journal of Political Economy*, **102**(4), August, 745–76.

Grierson, Philip (1977) *The Origins of Money*, London: Athlone Press.

Groenewegen, John (1997) 'Institutions of Capitalisms: American, European, and Japanese Systems Compared', *Journal of Economic Issues*, **31**(2), June, 333–47.

Groenewegen, Peter (1995) *A Soaring Eagle: Alfred Marshall 1842–1924*, Aldershot: Edward Elgar.

Grossman, Herschel I. and Noh, Suk Jae (1990) 'A Theory of Kleptocracy with Probabilistic Survival and Reputation', *Economics and Politics*, **2**(2), July, 157–71.

Grossman, Sanford J. and Hart, Oliver D. (1986) 'The Costs and Benefits of Ownership: A Theory of Vertical and Lateral Integration', *Journal of Political Economy*, **94**(4), August, 691–719.

Gruchy, Allan G. (1947) *Modern Economic Thought: The American Contribution*, New York: Prentice Hall.

Haavelmo, Trygve (1997) 'Econometrics and the Welfare State' (Nobel Lecture), *American Economic Review*, **87**(supplement), December, 13–17.

Hahn, Frank H. (1980) 'General Equilibrium Theory', *The Public Interest*, Special Issue, pp. 123–38. Repr. in Hahn, Frank H. (1984) *Equilibrium and Macroeconomics*, Oxford: Basil Blackwell.

Hahn, Frank H. (1984) *Equilibrium and Macroeconomics*, Oxford: Basil Blackwell.

Hahn, Frank H. (1988) 'On Monetary Theory', *Economic Journal*, **98**(4), December, 957–73.

Hahn, Frank H. (1992) 'Autobiographical Notes with Reflections', in Szenberg, Michael (ed.) (1992) *Eminent Economists: Their Life Philosophies*, Cambridge: Cambridge University Press, pp. 160–6.

Hall, Robert L. and Hitch, Charles J. (1939) 'Price Theory and Business Behaviour', *Oxford Economic Papers*, **2**, 12–45. Repr. in Wilson, T. and Andrews, Philip W. S. (eds) (1951) *Oxford Studies in the Price Mechanism*, Oxford: Clarendon Press and in Malcolm Sawyer (ed.) (1988) *Post-Keynesian Economics*, Aldershot: Edward Elgar.

Hamilton, Walton H. (1916) 'The Development of Hoxie's Economics', *Journal of Political Economy*, **24**(9), November, 855–83.

Hamilton, Walton H. (1919) 'The Institutional Approach to Economic Theory', *American Economic Review*, **9**, Supplement, 309–18. Repr. in Hamilton, Walton H. (1974) *Industrial Policy and Institutionalism: Selected Essays*, with introd. by Joseph Dorfman, New York: Augustus Kelley.

Hamilton, Walton H. (1932) 'Institution', in Seligman, Edwin R. A. and Johnson, Alvin (eds) *Encyclopaedia of the Social Sciences*, New York: Macmillan, vol. 8, pp. 84–9. Repr. in Hodgson (1993b).

Hammermesh, Daniel S. and Soss, Neal M. (1974) 'An Economic Theory of Suicide', *Journal of Political Economy*, **82**(1), January–February, 83–98.

Hammond, J. Daniel (1991) 'Alfred Marshall's Methodology', *Methodus*, **3**(1), June, 95–101.

Hampden-Turner, Charles and Trompenaars, Alfons (1993) *The Seven Cultures of Capitalism: Value Systems for Creating Wealth in the United States, Japan, Germany, France, Britain, Sweden, and the Netherlands*, New York: Currency Doubleday.

Hannan, Michael T. and Freeman, John (1989) *Organizational Ecology*, Cambridge, MA: Harvard University Press.

Hansson, Karl-Erik (1952) 'A General Theory of the System of Multilateral Trade', *American Economic Review*, **42**(1), March, 59–68.

Harada, Tetsushi (1997) 'Two Developments of the Concept of Anschauliche Theory (Concrete Theory) in Germany and Japan', in Koslowski (1997a), pp. 375–410.

Harcourt, Geoffrey C. (1982) *Post Keynesianism: Quite Wrong and/or Nothing New*, London: Thames Papers in Political Economy.

Harding, S. G. (ed.) (1976) *Can Theories be Refuted?: Essays on the Duhem–Quine Thesis*, Dordrecht: Reidel.

Harley, C. Knick (1991) 'Substitutions for Prerequisites: Endogenous Institutions and Comparative Economic History', in Sylla, Richard and Toniolo, Gianni (eds) (1991) *Patterns of European Industrialization: The Nineteenth Century*, London: Routledge, pp. 29–43.

Harré, Rom (1986) *Varieties of Realism*, Oxford: Basil Blackwell.

Harré, Rom (1993) *Social Being*, (2nd edn) Oxford: Basil Blackwell.

Harris, Abram L. (1942) 'Sombart and German (National) Socialism', *Journal of Political Economy*, **50**(6), December, 805–35. Repr. in Mark Blaug (ed.) (1992) *Gustav Schmoller (1838–1917) and Werner Sombart (1863–1941)*, Aldershot: Edward Elgar.

Harris, Marvin (1980) *Culture, People, Nature*, New York: Crowell.

Harsanyi, John C. (1966) 'A General Theory of Rational Behavior in Game Situations', *Econometrica*, **34**(3), July, 613–34.

Harsanyi, John C. and Selten, Reinhardt (1988) *A General Theory of Equilibrium Selection in Games*, Cambridge, MA: MIT Press.

Hart, Oliver D. (1988) 'Incomplete Contracts and the Theory of the Firm', *Journal of Law, Economics, and Organization*, **4**(1), Spring, 119–39.

Hartley, James E. (1997) *The Representative Agent in Macroeconomics*, London and New York: Routledge.

Hartman, Heidi I. (1979) 'The Unhappy Marriage of Marxism and Feminism: Towards a More Progressive Union', *Capital and Class*, **8**, Summer, 1–33.

Häuser, Kurt (1988) 'Historical School and "Methodenstreit"', *Journal of Institutional and Theoretical Economics*, **144**, 532–42. Repr. in Mark Blaug (ed.) (1992) *Gustav Schmoller (1838–1917) and Werner Sombart (1863–1941)*, Aldershot: Edward Elgar.

Hausman, Daniel M. (1992) *The Inexact and Separate Science of Economics*, Cambridge and New York: Cambridge University Press.

Hawthorn, Geoffrey (1976) *Enlightenment and Despair: A History of Sociology*, Cambridge: Cambridge University Press.

Hayek, Friedrich A. (ed.) (1935) *Collectivist Economic Planning*, London: George Routledge. Repr. 1975 by Augustus Kelley.

Hayek, Friedrich A. (1946) 'The London School of Economics 1895–1945', *Economica*, **8**(1), 1–31.

Hayek, Friedrich A. (1967) *Studies in Philosophy, Politics and Economics*, London: Routledge and Kegan Paul.

Hayek, Friedrich A. (1982) *Law, Legislation and Liberty*, (3-volume combined edn) London: Routledge and Kegan Paul.

Hearn, William Edward (1863) *Plutology, or, The Theory of the Efforts to Satisfy Human Wants*, Melbourne: George Robertson.

Heiner, Ronald A. (1986) 'Uncertainty, Signal-Detection Experiments, and Modeling Behavior', in Langlois (1986), pp. 59–115.

Hempel, Carl G. (1942) 'The Function of General Laws in History', *Journal of Philosophy*, **39**(2), January, 35–48.

Henderson, Hubert D. (1921) *Supply and Demand*, London: Nisbet.

Henderson, Lawrence J. (1935) *Pareto's General Sociology: A Physiologist's Interpretation*, Harvard: Harvard University Press.

Hennis, Wilhelm (1988) *Max Weber: Essays in Reconstruction*, London: George Allen and Unwin.

Herbst, Jurgen (1965) *The German Historical School in American Scholarship: A Study in the Transfer of Culture*, Ithaca, NY: Cornell University Press.

Heyl, Barbara (1968) 'The Harvard "Pareto Circle"', *Journal of the History of the Behavioral Sciences*, **4**, 316–34.

Hicks, John R. (1939) *Value and Capital: An Inquiry into Some Fundamental Principles of Economic Theory*, (1st edn) Oxford: Oxford University Press.

Hildebrand, Bruno (1863) *Jahrbücher für Nationalökonomie und Statistik*.

Hildenbrand, Werner (1994) *Market Demand: Theory and Empirical Evidence*, Princeton, NJ: Princeton University Press.

Hindess, Barry (1977) *Philosophy and Methodology in the Social Sciences*, Brighton: Harvester.

Hirsch, Paul M., Michaels, Stuart and Friedman, Ray (1987) '"Dirty Hands" Versus "Clean Models": Is Sociology in Danger of Being Seduced by Economics?', *Theory and Society*, **16**(3), May, 317–36. Repr. in Swedberg (1996).

Hirschman, Albert O. (1985) 'Against Parsimony: Three Ways of Complicating Some Categories of Economic Discourse', *Economics and Philosophy*, **1**(1), March, 7–21.

Hirschman, Albert O. (1986) *Rival Views of Market Society and Other Essays*, New York: Viking.

Hirshleifer, Jack (1977) 'Economics from a Biological Viewpoint', *Journal of Law and Economics*, **20**(1), April, 1–52. Repr. in Hodgson (1995).

Hirshleifer, Jack (1985) 'The Expanding Domain of Economics', *American Economic Review*, **75**(6), December, 53–68.

Hirst, Paul Q. and Woolley, Penny (1982) *Social Relations and Human Attributes*, London: Tavistock.

Hobhouse, Leonard T. (1913) *Development and Purpose: An Essay Towards a Philosophy of Evolution*, (1st edn) London: Macmillan.

Hobson, John A. (1902) *The Social Problem: Life and Work*, London: James Nisbet. Repr. 1995 with introd. by James Meadowcroft, Bristol: Thoemmes Press.

Hobson, John A. (1911) *The Science of Wealth*, London: Williams and Norgate.

Hobson, John A. (1914) *Work and Wealth: A Human Valuation*, London: Macmillan.

Hobson, John A. and Ginsberg, Morris (1932) *L. T. Hobhouse: His Life and Work*, London: Chapman and Hall.

Hodges, Richard (1988) *Primitive and Peasant Markets*, Oxford: Basil Blackwell.

Hodgson, Geoffrey M. (1982) *Capitalism, Value and Exploitation: A Radical Theory*, Oxford: Martin Robertson.

Hodgson, Geoffrey M. (1984) *The Democratic Economy: A New Look at Planning, Markets and Power*, Harmondsworth: Penguin.

Hodgson, Geoffrey M. (1988) *Economics and Institutions: A Manifesto for a Modern Institutional Economics*, Cambridge: Polity Press; Philadelphia: University of Pennsylvania Press.

Hodgson, Geoffrey M. (1989) 'Institutional Rigidities and Economic Growth', *Cambridge Journal of Economics*, **13**(1), March, 79–101. Repr. in Hodgson, Geoffrey M. (1991), *After Marx and Sraffa*, Basingstoke: Macmillan.

Hodgson, Geoffrey M. (1991) 'Socio-Political Disruption and Economic Development', in Hodgson, Geoffrey M. and Screpanti, Ernesto (eds) (1991) *Rethinking Economics: Markets, Technology and Economic Evolution*, Aldershot: Edward Elgar, 153–71.

Hodgson, Geoffrey M. (1993a) *Economics and Evolution: Bringing Life Back Into Economics*, Cambridge: Polity Press; Ann Arbor, MI: University of Michigan Press.

Hodgson, Geoffrey M. (ed.) (1993b) *The Economics of Institutions*, Aldershot: Edward Elgar.

Hodgson, Geoffrey M. (ed.) (1995) *Economics and Biology*, Aldershot: Edward Elgar.

Hodgson, Geoffrey M. (1996) 'An Evolutionary Theory of Long-Term Economic Growth', *International Studies Quarterly*, **40**, 393–412.

Hodgson, Geoffrey M. (1997) 'The Ubiquity of Habits and Rules', *Cambridge Journal of Economics*, **21**(6), November, 663–84.

Hodgson, Geoffrey M. (1998a) 'The Approach of Institutional Economics', *Journal of Economic Literature*, **36**(1), March, 166–92.

Hodgson, Geoffrey M. (1998b) 'On the Evolution of Thorstein Veblen's Evolutionary Economics', *Cambridge Journal of Economics*, **22**(4), July, 415–31.

Hodgson, Geoffrey M. (ed.) (1998c) *The Foundations of Evolutionary Economics: 1890–1973*, 2 vols, International Library of Critical Writings in Economics, Cheltenham: Edward Elgar.

Hodgson, Geoffrey M. (1998d) 'The Coasean Tangle: The Nature of the Firm and the Problem of Historical Specificity', in Medema, Steven G. (ed.) (1998), *Coasean Economics: Law and Economics and the New Institutional Economics*, Boston: Kluwer, pp. 23–49. Revised and reprinted in Hodgson (1999b).

Hodgson, Geoffrey M. (1998e) 'Dichotomizing the Dichotomy: Veblen versus Ayres', in Fayazmanesh, S. and Tool, M. (eds) (1998) *Institutionalist Method and Value: Essays in Honour of Paul Dale Bush, Volume 1*, Cheltenham: Edward Elgar, pp. 48–73.

Hodgson, Geoffrey M. (1999a) *Economics and Utopia: Why the Learning Economy is Not the End of History*, London and New York: Routledge.

Hodgson, Geoffrey M. (1999b) *Evolution and Institutions: On Evolutionary Economics and the Evolution of Economics*, Cheltenham: Edward Elgar.

Hodgson, Geoffrey M. (2000) 'What is the Essence of Institutional Economics?', *Journal of Economic Issues*, **34**(2), June, 317–29.

Hodgson, Geoffrey M. (2001a) 'Frank Knight as an Institutional Economist', in Biddle, Jeff E., Davis, John B. and Medema, Steven G. (eds) *Economics Broadly Considered: Essays in Honor of Warren J. Samuels*, London and New York: Routledge, pp. 64–93.

Hodgson, Geoffrey M. (2001b) 'Is Social Evolution Lamarckian or Darwinian?' in Laurent, John and Nightingale, John (eds) *Darwinism and Evolutionary Economics*, Cheltenham: Edward Elgar, pp. 87–118.

Hodgson, Geoffrey M. (2001c) 'Reconstitutive Downward Causation: Social Structure and the Development of Individual Agency', in Fullbrook, Edward (ed.) (2001) *Intersubjectivity in Economics* (forthcoming).

Hodgson, Geoffrey M. (unpublished) 'Darwin, Veblen and the Problem of Causality in Economics', University of Hertfordshire, mimeo.

Hodgson, Geoffrey M., Samuels, Warren J. and Tool, Marc R. (eds) (1994) *The Elgar Companion to Institutional and Evolutionary Economics*, Aldershot: Edward Elgar.

Hofstadter, Richard and Hardy, C. DeWitt (1952) *The Development and Scope of Higher Education in the United States*, New York: Columbia University Press.

Hoksbergen, Roland (1994) 'Postmodernism and Institutionalism: Toward a Resolution of the Debate on Relativism', *Journal of Economic Issues*, **28**(3), September, 679–713.

Holborn, Hajo (1950) 'Wilhelm Dilthey and the Critique of Historical Reason', *Journal of the History of Ideas*, **11**(1), January, 93–118.

Holland, John H. (1995) *Hidden Order: How Adaptation Builds Complexity*, Reading: Helix Books.

Hollingsworth, J. Rogers and Boyer, Robert (eds) (1997) *Contemporary Capitalism: The Embeddedness of Institutions*, Cambridge: Cambridge University Press.

Holmwood, John (1996) *Founding Sociology? Talcott Parsons and the Idea of General Theory*, London and New York: Longman.

Holt, C. (1995) 'Industrial Organization: A Survey of Laboratory Research', in Kagel and Roth (1995).

Holton, Robert J. and Turner, Bryan S. (1989) *Max Weber on Economy and Society*, London: Routledge.

Homan, Paul T. (1932) 'An Appraisal of Institutional Economics', *American Economic Review*, **22**(1), March, 10–17.

Homans, George C. (1961) *Social Behaviour: Its Elementary Form*, London: Routledge and Kegan Paul.

Horgan, John (1995) 'From Complexity to Perplexity', *Scientific American*, June, **272**(6), 104–9.

Howe, John and Mitchell, Richard (1999) 'The Evolution of the Contract of Employment in Australia: A Discussion', *Australian Journal of Labour Law*, **12**, 113–30.

Howey, Ralph S. (1960) *The Rise of the Marginal Utility School*, Lawrence, KA: University of Kansas Press.

Hoxie, Robert F. (1901) 'On the Empirical Method of Economic Instruction', *Journal of Political Economy*, **9**(3), September, 481–526.

Hoxie, Robert F. (1906) 'Historical Method vs. Historical Narrative', *Journal of Political Economy*, **14**, November, 568–72.

Hoxie, Robert F. (1915) *Scientific Management and Labor*, New York: Appleton.

Hsieh, Ching-Yao and Ye, Meng-Hua (1992) *Economics, Philosophy, and Physics*, Armonk, NY: M. E. Sharpe.

Hull, David L. (1973) *Darwin and His Critics: The Reception of Darwin's Theory of Evolution by the Scientific Community*, Cambridge, MA: Harvard University Press.

Hull, David L. (1988) *Science as a Process: An Evolutionary Account of the Social and Conceptual Development of Science*, Chicago: University of Chicago Press.

Hunt, Shelby D. (2000) *A General Theory of Competition: Resources, Competences, Productivity, Economic Growth*, Thousand Oaks, CA and London, UK: Sage.

Hutchison, Terence W. (1938) *The Significance and Basic Postulates of Economic Theory*, London: Macmillan.

Hutchison, Terence W. (1953) *A Review of Economic Doctrines: 1870–1929*, Oxford: Oxford University Press.

Hutchison, Terence W. (1973) 'Some Themes from Investigations into Method', in Hicks, John R. and Weber, Wilhelm (eds) (1973) *Carl Menger and the Austrian School of Economics*, Oxford: Clarendon Press, pp. 15–37.

Hutchison, Terence W. (1981) *The Politics and Philosophy of Economics: Marxians, Keynesians and Austrians*, Oxford: Basil Blackwell.

Hutchison, Terence W. (1988) 'Gustav Schmoller and the Problems of Today', *Journal of Institutional and Theoretical Economics*, **144**(3), 527–31.

Hutchison, Terence W. (1997) 'On the Relations Between Philosophy and Economics. Part II: To What Kind of Philosophical Problems Should Economists Address Themselves?', *Journal of Economic Methodology*, **3**(2), December, 187–213.

Hutchison, Terence W. (1998) 'Ultra-Deductivism from Nassau Senior to Lionel Robbins and Daniel Hausman', *Journal of Economic Methodology*, **5**(1), July, 43–91.

Hüter, Margret (1928) *Die Methodologie der Wirtschaftswissenschaft bei Roscher und Knies*, Jena: Gustav Fischer.

Hutter, Michael (1993) 'Historicist Biologism and Contemporary Evolutionism: Where is the Difference?', *History of Economic Ideas*, **1**(3), 179–96.

Hutter, Michael (1994) 'Organism as a Metaphor in German Economic Thought', in Mirowski, Philip (ed.) (1994) *Natural Images in Economic Thought: Markets Read in Tooth and Claw*, Cambridge and New York: Cambridge University Press, pp. 289–321.

Iannaccone, Laurence R. (1991) 'The Consequences of Religious Market Structure: Adam Smith and the Economics of Religion', *Rationality and Society*, **3**, April, 156–77.

Iannaccone, Laurence R. (1998) 'Introduction to the Economics of Religion', *Journal of Economic Literature*, **36**(3), September, 1465–96.

Imai, Ken-ichi and Itami, Hiroyuki (1984) 'Interpenetration of Organization and Market: Japan's Firm and Market in Comparison with the US', *International Journal of Industrial Organisation*, **6**(4), 285–310.

Ingham, Geoffrey (1996) 'Some Recent Changes in the Relationship Between Economics and Sociology', *Cambridge Journal of Economics*, **20**(2), March, 243–75.

Ingham, Geoffrey (2000) '"Babylonian Madness": On the Historical and Sociological Origins of Money' in Smithin, John (ed.) (2000) *What is Money?*, London: Routledge, pp. 16–41.

Ingram, John K. (1878) 'The Present Position and Prospects of Political Economy', *Report of the British Association for the Advancement of Science*, pp. 641–58. Repr. in Smyth, R. L. (ed.) (1962) *Essays in Economic Method*, London: Duckworth.

Ingram, John K. (1901) *Human Nature and Morals According to Auguste Comte*, London: A. and C. Black.

Ingram, John K. (1915) [1888] *A History of Political Economy*, (2nd edn) New York: Augustus Kelley.

Isard, Walter (1949) 'The General Theory of Location and Space-Economy', *Quarterly Journal of Economics*, **63**(4), November, 476–506.

Jaffé, William (1976) 'Menger, Jevons and Walras De-Homogenized', *Economic Inquiry*, **14**(1), January, 11–24.

James, William (1880) 'Great Men, Great Thoughts, and the Environment', *Atlantic Monthly*, **46**, 441–59. Repr. in James, William (1897) *The Will to Believe and Other Essays in Popular Philosophy*, New York and London: Longmans Green, pp. 216–54.

James, William (1981) *The Principles of Psychology*, repr. in two vols from the 1893 edn, Cambridge, MA: Harvard University Press.

Joas, Hans (1995) 'Communitarianism, Pragmatism, Historicism', in Koslowski (1995), pp. 267–85.

Johnson, Elizabeth S. and Johnson, Harry G. (1978) *The Shadow of Keynes: Understanding Keynes, Cambridge and Keynesian Economics*, Oxford: Basil Blackwell.

Jones, D. G. Brian and Monieson, David D. (1990) 'Early Development of the Philosophy of Marketing Thought', *Journal of Marketing*, **54**, 102–13.

Jones, Trevor W. (1978) 'The Appointment of Pigou as Marshall's Successor: The Other Side of the Coin', *Journal of Law and Economics*, **21**, April, 234–43.

Jorgensen, Elizabeth W. and Jorgensen, Henry I. (1999) *Thorstein Veblen: Victorian Firebrand*, Armonk, NY: M. E. Sharpe.

Kadish, Alon (1989) *Historians, Economists and Economic History*, London: Routledge.

Kadish, Alon and Tribe, Keith (eds) (1993) *The Market for Political Economy: The Advent of Economics in British University Culture, 1850–1905*, London: Routledge.

Kagel, John H. (1995) 'Auctions: A Survey of Experimental Research', in Kagel and Roth (1995).

Kagel, John H., Battalio, Raymond C., Rachlin, Howard and Green, Leonard (1981) 'Demand Curves for Animal Consumers', *Quarterly Journal of Economics*, **96**(1), 1–16.

Kagel, John H., Battalio, Raymond C. and Green, Leonard (1995) *Economic Choice Theory:*

An Experimental Analysis of Animal Behaviour, Cambridge and New York: Cambridge University Press.

Kagel, John H. and Roth, Alvin E. (eds) (1995) *The Handbook of Experimental Economics*, Princeton: Princeton University Press.

Kahn-Freund, O. (1977) 'Blackstone's Neglected Child: The Contract of Employment Law', *Law Quarterly Review*, **93**, 508–28.

Kahneman, Daniel, Slovic, Paul and Tversky, Amos (eds) (1982) *Judgement Under Uncertainty: Heuristics and Biases*, Cambridge and New York: Cambridge University Press.

Kalberg, Stephen (1994) *Max Weber's Comparative-Historical Sociology*, Chicago: University of Chicago Press.

Kalveram, Gertrud (1933) *Die Theorien von den Wirtschaftsstuffen*, Leipzig: Hans Buske.

Kant, Immanuel (1929) *Critique of Pure Reason*, trans. from the 2nd German edn (1787) with introd. by Norman Kemp Smith London: Macmillan.

Kanth, Rajani K. (1992) *Capitalism and Social Theory: The Science of Black Holes*, Armonk, NY: M. E. Sharpe.

Kantor, J. R. (1922) 'An Essay Toward an Institutional Conception of Social Psychology', *American Journal of Sociology*, **27**(5), March, 611–27; **27**(6), May, 758–79.

Kantor, J. R. (1924) 'The Institutional Foundation of a Scientific Social Psychology', *American Journal of Sociology*, **29**(6), May, 674–87.

Katz, Michael L. and Shapiro, Carl (1985) 'Network Externalities, Competition, and Compatibility', *American Economic Review*, **75**(3), June, 424–40.

Katz, Michael L. and Shapiro, Carl (1986) 'Technology Adoption in the Presence of Network Externalities', *Journal of Political Economy*, **94**(4), August, 822–41.

Katz, Michael L. and Shapiro, Carl (1994) 'Systems Competition and Network Effects', *Journal of Economic Perspectives*, **8**(2), Spring, 93–115.

Kauffman, Stuart A. (1993) *The Origins of Order: Self-Organization and Selection in Evolution*, Oxford and New York: Oxford University Press.

Kauffman, Stuart A. (1995) *At Home in the Universe: The Search for Laws of Self-Organization and Complexity*, Oxford and New York: Oxford University Press.

Kay, Neil M. (1982) *The Evolving Firm: Strategy and Structure in Industrial Organisation*, London: Macmillan.

Keesing, Roger (1974) 'Theories of Culture', *Annual Review of Anthropology*, **3**, 73–97.

Kennedy, Paul (1988) *The Rise and Fall of the Great Powers: Economic Change and Military Conflict from 1500 to 2000*, London: Unwin Hyman.

Kenworthy, Lane (1995) *In Search of National Economic Success: Balancing Competition and Cooperation*, Thousand Oaks, CA and London: Sage.

Keynes, John Maynard (1930) *A Treatise on Money, Vol. 1: The Pure Theory of Money, Vol. 2: The Applied Theory of Money*, London: Macmillan.

Keynes, John Maynard (1931) *Essays in Persuasion*, London: Macmillan.

Keynes, John Maynard (1936) *The General Theory of Employment, Interest and Money*, London: Macmillan.

Keynes, John Maynard (1972) *The Collected Writings of John Maynard Keynes, Vol. X, Essays in Biography*, London: Macmillan.

Keynes, John Maynard (1973a) *The Collected Writings of John Maynard Keynes, Vol. XIII, The General Theory and After, Part I: Preparation*, London: Macmillan.

Keynes, John Maynard (1973b) *The Collected Writings of John Maynard Keynes, Vol. XIV, The General Theory and After, Part II: Defence and Development*, London: Macmillan.

Keynes, John Maynard (1981) *The Collected Writings of John Maynard Keynes, Vol. XIX, The Return to Gold and Industrial Policy*, 2 parts, London: Macmillan.

Keynes, John Maynard (1982) *The Collected Writings of John Maynard Keynes, Vol. XXI, Activities 1931–1939: World Crises and Policies in Britain and America*, London: Macmillan.

Keynes, John Neville (1891) *The Scope and Method of Political Economy*, London: Macmillan.

Khalil, Elias L. (1990a) 'Entropy Law and Exhaustion of Natural Resources: Is Nicholas Georgescu-Roegen's Paradigm Defensible?', *Ecological Economics*, **2**(2), June, 163–78.

Khalil, Elias L. (1990b) 'Rationality and Social Labor in Marx', *Critical Review*, **4**(1–2), Winter–Spring, 239–65.

Khalil, Elias L. (1991) 'Entropy and Nicholas Georgescu-Roegen's Paradigm: A Reply', *Ecological Economics*, **3**(1), April, 161–3.

Khalil, Elias L. and Boulding, Kenneth E. (eds) (1996) *Evolution, Order and Complexity*, London: Routledge.

Kim, Il Gon (1995) 'Confucian Culture and Economic Development in East Asia', in Koslowski (1995), pp. 250–62.

Kirman, Alan P. (1983) 'Communication in Markets: A Suggested Approach', *Economics Letters*, **12**, 101–8.

Kirman, Alan P. (1987) 'Graph Theory' in Eatwell, John, Milgate, Murray and Newman, Peter (eds) (1987) *The New Palgrave Dictionary of Economics*, vol. 2, London: Macmillan, pp. 558–9.

Kirman, Alan P. (1989) 'The Intrinsic Limits of Modern Economic Theory: The Emperor Has No Clothes', *Economic Journal (Conference Papers)*, **99**, 126–39.

Kirman, Alan P. (1992) 'Whom or What Does the Representative Individual Represent?', *Journal of Economic Perspectives*, **6**(2), Spring, 117–36.

Kirman, Alan P. (1993) 'Ants, Rationality and Recruitment', *Quarterly Journal of Economics*, February, 137–55.

Kiser, Edgar and Hechter, Michael (1991) 'The Role of General Theory in Comparative-Historical Sociology', *American Journal of Sociology*, **97**(1), July, 1–30.

Kitcher, Philip (1981) 'Explanatory Unification', *Philosophy of Science*, 48, 507–31.

Kitcher, Philip (1989) 'Explanatory Unification and the Causal Structure of the World', *Minnesota Studies in the Philosophy of Science*, **13**, 410–505.

Knapp, Georg F. (1924) [1905] *The State Theory of Money*, trans. from the 4th German edn (1924) London: Macmillan. Repr. (1973) New York: Augustus Kelley.

Knies, Karl (1853) *Politische Ökonomie vom Standpunkt der geschichtlichen Methode* (Political Economy from the Perspective of the Historical Method) Braunschweig: Schwetschke.

Knight, Frank H. (1921a) *Risk, Uncertainty and Profit*, New York: Houghton Mifflin.

Knight, Frank H. (1921b) 'Discussion: Traditional Economic Theory', *American Economic Review*, **11**, Supplement, 143–6.

Knight, Frank H. (1924) 'The Limitations of Scientific Method in Economics', in Tugwell, Rexford G. (ed.) *The Trend of Economics*, New York: Knopf, pp. 229–67. Repr. in Knight, Frank H. (1935) *The Ethics of Competition and Other Essays*, New York: Harper.

Knight, Frank H. (1928a) 'A Suggestion for Simplifying the Statement of the General Theory of Price', *Journal of Political Economy*, **36**(3), June, 353–70.

Knight, Frank H. (1928b) 'Historical and Theoretical Issues in the Problem of Modern Capitalism', *Journal of Economics and Business History*, **1**(1), November, 119–36. Repr. in Knight (1956).

Knight, Frank H. (1933) 'Preface to the Re-Issue', in *Risk, Uncertainty and Profit*, (2nd edn) London: London School of Economics, pp. xi–xxxvi.

Knight, Frank H. (1936) Letter to Talcott Parsons, dated 1 May 1936, Talcott Parsons Papers.

Knight, Frank H. (1952) 'Institutionalism and Empiricism in Economics', *American Economic Review (Papers and Proceedings)*, **42**, May, 45–55.

Knight, Frank H. (1953) 'Theory of Economic Policy and the History of Doctrine', *Ethics*, **63**(4), July, 276–92.

Knight, Frank H. (1956) *On the History and Method of Economics*, Chicago: University of Chicago Press.

Knight, Jack (1992) *Institutions and Social Conflict*, Cambridge: Cambridge University Press.

Koestler, Arthur (1959) *The Sleepwalkers: A History of Man's Changing Vision of the Universe*, London: Hutchinson.

Koestler, Arthur (1967) *The Ghost in the Machine*, London: Hutchinson.

Kohn, David (ed.) (1985) *The Darwinian Heritage*, Princeton: Princeton University Press.

Kontopoulos, Kyriakos M. (1993) *The Logics of Social Structure*, Cambridge: Cambridge University Press.

Koot, Gerard M. (1975) 'T. E. Cliffe Leslie, Irish Social Reform, and the Origin of the English Historical School of Economics', *History of Political Economy*, **7**(3), Fall, 312–36.

Koot, Gerard M. (1987) *English Historical Economics 1870–1926: The Rise of Economic History and Neomercantilism*, Cambridge: Cambridge University Press.

Kornai, Janos (1971) *Anti-Equilibrium: On Economic Systems Theory and the Tasks of Research*, Amsterdam: North-Holland, Repr. 1991, New York: Augustus Kelley.

Koslowski, Peter (ed.) (1995) *The Theory of Ethical Economy in the Historical School: Wilhelm Roscher, Lorenz von Stein, Gustav Schmoller, Wilhelm Dilthey and Contemporary Theory*, Berlin: Springer.

Koslowski, Peter (ed.) (1997a) *Methodology of the Social Sciences, Ethics, and Economics in the Newer Historical School: From Max Weber and Rickert to Sombart and Rothacker*, Berlin: Springer.

Koslowski, Peter (1997b) 'A Philosophy of the Historical School: Erich Rothacker's Theory of the *Geisteswissenschaften* (Human Sciences)', in Koslowski, Peter (1997a), pp. 510–38.

Kozul-Wright, Richard and Rayment, Paul (1997) 'The Institutional Hiatus in Economics in Transition and its Policy Consequences', *Cambridge Journal of Economics*, **21**(5), September, 641–61.

Krabbe, Jacob Jan (1996) *Historicism and Organicism in Economics: The Evolution of Thought*, Dordrecht: Kluwer.

Kregel, Jan A. (1995) 'Neoclassical Price Theory, Institutions and the Evolution of Securities Market Organisation', *Economic Journal*, **105**(2), March, 459–70.

Kroeber, Alfred L. and Kluckhohn, Clyde (1952) 'Culture: A Critical Review of Concepts and Definitions', *Peabody Museum Papers*, pp. 1–223.

Lachmann, Ludwig M. (1971) *The Legacy of Max Weber*, Berkeley: Glendessary Press.

Landa, Janet (1994) *Trust, Ethnicity, and Identity: Beyond the New Institutional Economics of Ethnic Trading Networks, Contract Law, and Gift Exchange*, Ann Arbor, MI: University of Michigan Press.

Landa, Janet (1999) 'Bioeconomics of Some Nonhuman and Human Societies: New Institutional Economics Approach', *Journal of Bioeconomics*, **1**(1), 95–113.

Lane, David A., Malerba, Franco, Maxfield, Robert and Orsenigo, Luigi (1996) 'Choice and Action', *Journal of Evolutionary Economics*, **6**(1), 43–76.

Lange, Oskar R. (1935) 'Marxian Economics and Modern Economic Theory', *Review of Economic Studies*, **2**, 189–201.

Lange, Oskar R. (1938) 'The Rate of Interest and the Optimum Propensity to Consume', *Economica*, **5**(1), February, 12–32.

Lange, Oskar R. (1965) *Wholes and Parts: A General Theory of Systems Behaviour*, London: Pergamon Press.

Lange, Oskar R. and Taylor, Frederick M. (1938) *On the Economic Theory of Socialism*, ed. Benjamin E. Lippincot, Minneapolis: University of Minnesota Press.

Langlois, Richard N. (ed.) (1986) *Economics as a Process: Essays in the New Institutional Economics*, Cambridge: Cambridge University Press.

Langlois, Richard N. (1998) 'Transaction Costs, Production Costs, and the Passage of Time', in Medema, Steven G. (ed.) (1998) *Coasean Economics: Law and Economics and the New Institutional Economics*, Boston: Kluwer, pp. 1–21.

Laszlo, Ervin (1972) *Introduction to Systems Philosophy: Toward a New Paradigm of Contemporary Thought*, New York: Harper and Row.

Laszlo, Ervin (1987) *Evolution: The Grand Synthesis*, Boston, MA: New Science Library – Shambhala.

Latour, Bruno (1987) *Science in Action: How to Follow Scientists and Engineers Through Society*, Cambridge, MA: Harvard University Press.

Lavoie, Marc (1992) *Foundations of Post-Keynesian Economic Analysis*, Aldershot: Edward Elgar.

Lawson, Clive (1996) 'Realism, Theory, and Individualism in the Work of Carl Menger', *Review of Social Economy*, **54**(4), Winter, 445–64.

Lawson, Tony (1997) *Economics and Reality*, London: Routledge.

Lazear, Edward P. (2000) 'Economic Imperialism', *Quarterly Journal of Economics*, **115**(1), February, 99–146.

Leathers, Charles G. (1989) 'New and Old Institutionalists on Legal Rules: Hayek and Commons', *Review of Political Economy*, **1**(3), November, 361–80.

Leathers, Charles G. (1990) 'Veblen and Hayek on Instincts and Evolution', *Journal of the History of Economic Thought*, **12**(2), June, 162–78.

Leathers, Charles G. and Raines, J. Patrick (1992) 'Adam Smith on Competitive Religious Markets', *History of Political Economy*, **24**(2), Summer, 499–513.

Lee, Frederick S. (1998) *Post Keynesian Price Theory*, Cambridge: Cambridge University Press.

Lee, Frederick S. (2001) *Alfred S. Eichner, Joan Robinson and the Founding of Post Keynesian Economics*, Armonk, NY: M. E. Sharpe, forthcoming.

Lenoir, Timothy (1998) 'Revolution from Above: The Role of the State in Creating the German Research System, 1810–1910', *American Economic Review (Papers and Proceedings)*, **88**(2), May, 22–7.

Leontief, Wassily W. (1953) 'Domestic Production and Foreign Trade: The American Capital Position re-Examined', *Proceedings of the American Philosophical Society*, **97**, September, 332–49.

Leslie, Thomas E. Cliffe (1888) [1879] *Essays in Political Economy*, (2nd edn) London: Longmans, Green. Repr. (1969) New York: Augustus Kelley.

Lessnoff, Michael H. (1994) *The Spirit of Capitalism and the Protestant Ethic: An Enquiry into the Weber Thesis*, Aldershot: Edward Elgar.

Levins, Richard and Lewontin, Richard C. (1985) *The Dialectical Biologist*, Cambridge, MA: Harvard University Press.

Levitt, Barbara and March, James G. (1988) 'Organizational Learning', *Annual Review of Sociology*, **14**, 319–40.

Lewin, Shira B. (1996) 'Economics and Psychology: Lessons for Our Own Day from the Early Twentieth Century', *Journal of Economic Literature*, **34**(3), September, 1293–323.

Lewis, A. (1985) 'On Effectively Computable Realization of Choice Functions', *Mathematical Social Sciences*, **10**.

Lewontin, Richard C. (1978) 'Adaptation', *Scientific American*, **239**, 212–30.

Lewontin, Richard C. (1991) 'Facts and the Factitious in Natural Science', *Critical Inquiry*, **18**(1), 140–53.

Lie, John (1997) 'Sociology of Markets', *Annual Review of Sociology*, **23**, 341–60.

Liebowitz, Stanley J. and Margolis, Stephen E. (1990) 'The Fable of the Keys', *Journal of Law and Economics*, **33**(1), April, 1–26.

Liebowitz, Stanley J. and Margolis, Stephen E. (1994) 'Network Externality: An Uncommon Tragedy', *Journal of Economic Perspectives*, **8**(2), Spring, 133–50.

Lilienfeld, Paul von (1873–81) *Gedanken über zur Sozialwissenshaft der Zukunft* (Thoughts on the Social Science of the Future) (Hamburg).

Lindenberg, Siegwert (1990) 'Homo Socio-Oeconomicus: The Emergence of a General Model of Man in the Social Sciences', *Journal of Institutional and Theoretical Economics*, **146**, December, 727–48.

Lippi, Marco (1979) *Value and Naturalism in Marx*, London: NLB.

Lipsey, Richard G. and Lancaster, Kelvin (1956) 'The General Theory of Second Best', *Review of Economic Studies*, **24**(1), December, 11–32.

List, Friedrich (1904) *The National System of Political Economy*, trans. Sampson S. Lloyd from the German edn (1841) with introd. by J. Sheild Nicholson, London: Longmans, Green.

Little, Ian M. D. (1949) 'A Reformulation of the Theory of Consumer's Behaviour', *Oxford Economic Papers*, **1**, 90–9.

Loasby, Brian J. (1998) 'The Organisation of Capabilities', *Journal of Economic Behavior and Organization*, **35**(2), April, 139–60.

Loomes, Graham (1998) 'Probabilities vs Money: A Test of Some Fundamental Assumptions About Rational Decision Making', *Economic Journal*, **108**(1), March, 477–89.

Loomes, Graham (1999) 'Some Lessons from Past Experiments and Some Challenges for the Future', *Economic Journal*, **109**(2), February, F35–45.

Louça, Francisco (1997) *Turbulence in Economics: An Evolutionary Appraisal of Cycles and Complexity in Historical Processes*, Aldershot: Edward Elgar.

Love, J. T. (1991) *Antiquity and Capitalism: Max Weber and the Sociological Foundations of Roman Civilization*, London and New York: Routledge.

Löwe, Adolf (1932) 'Über den Sinn und die Grenzen verstehender Nationalökonomie', *Weltwirtschaftliches Archiv*, **36**, 149–62.

Löwe, Adolf (1935) *Economics and Sociology: A Plea for Co-operation in the Social Sciences*, London: Allen and Unwin.

Lozada, G. A. (1991) 'A Defense of Nicholas Georgescu-Roegen's Paradigm', *Ecological Economics*, **3**(1), April, 157–60.

Luhmann, Niklas (1982) *The Differentiation of Society*, New York: Columbia University Press.

Luhmann, Niklas (1995) *Social Systems*, trans. John Bednarz from the German edn (1984) with a foreword by Eva M. Knodt Stanford: Stanford University Press.

Lundvall, Bengt-Åke (ed.) (1992) *National Systems of Innovation: Towards a Theory of Innovation and Interactive Learning*, London: Pinter.

Lyotard, Jean-François (1984) *The Postmodern Condition: A Report on Knowledge*, trans. G. Bennington and B. Massumi, Minnesota: University of Minnesota Press.

Macaulay, Stewart (1963) 'Non-Contractual Relations in Business: A Preliminary Study', *American Sociological Review*, **28**(1), 55–67. Repr. in Buckley and Michie (1996) and Granovetter and Swedberg (1992).

Machlup, Fritz (1946) 'Marginal Analysis and Empirical Research', *American Economic Review*, **36**(3), September, 519–54.

Machlup, Fritz (1951) 'Schumpeter's Economic Methodology', *Review of Economics and Statistics*, **33**(2), May, 145–51.

Machlup, Fritz (1978) *Methodology of Economics and Other Social Sciences*, London: Academic Press.

Maddison, Angus (1991) *Dynamic Forces in Capitalist Development: A Long-Run Comparative View*, Oxford: Oxford University Press.

Magill, Michael and Quinzii, Martine (1996) *Theory of Incomplete Markets*, 2 vols, Cambridge, MA: MIT Press.

Majumdar, Tapas (1958) *The Measurement of Utility*, London: Macmillan.

Mäki, Uskali (1988a) 'How to Combine Rhetoric and Realism in the Methodology of Economics', *Economics and Philosophy*, 4(1), April, 89–109.

Mäki, Uskali (1988b) 'Realism, Economics, and Rhetoric: A Rejoinder to McCloskey', *Economics and Philosophy*, 4(1), April, 167–9.

Mäki, Uskali (1989) 'On the Problem of Realism in Economics', *Ricerche Economiche*, 43(1–2), gennaio–giugno, 176–98.

Mäki, Uskali (1990a) 'Mengerian Economics in Realist Perspective', in Caldwell (1990) pp. 289–310.

Mäki, Uskali (1990b) 'Scientific Realism and Austrian Explanation', *Review of Political Economy*, 2(3), November, 310–44.

Mäki, Uskali (1992) 'On the Method of Isolation in Economics', in Dilworth, Craig (ed.) (1992) *Idealization IV: Intelligibility in Science*, Amsterdam: Rodopi, pp. 317–51.

Mäki, Uskali (1994) 'Isolation, Idealization and Truth in Economics', *Poznan Studies in the Philosophy of the Sciences and the Humanities*, 38, 147–68.

Mäki, Uskali (1997a) 'The One World and Many Theories', in Salanti, Andrea and Screpanti, Ernesto (eds) (1997) *Pluralism in Economics: New Perspectives in History and Methodology*, Aldershot: Edward Elgar, pp. 37–47.

Mäki, Uskali (1997b) 'Universals and the *Methodenstreit*: A Re-examination of Carl Menger's Conception of Economics as an Exact Science', *Studies in the History and Philosophy of Science*, 28(3), 475–95.

Mäki, Uskali (1998) 'Aspects of Realism About Economics', *Theoria*, 13(2), 301–19.

Mäki, Uskali (forthcoming) 'Explanatory Unification: Double and Doubtful', *Philosophy of the Social Sciences*, forthcoming.

Maloney, John (1985) *Marshall, Orthodoxy and the Professionalisation of Economics*, Cambridge: Cambridge University Press.

Malthus, Thomas Robert (1798) *An Essay on the Principle of Population, as it Affects the Future Improvement of Society, with Remarks on the Speculations of Mr. Godwin, M. Condorcet, and other Writers*, London: Johnson. Repr. 1926 with notes by J. Bonar, London: Macmillan.

Malthus, Thomas Robert (1836) *Principles of Political Economy*, (2nd edn) London: Pickering. Repr. 1986, New York: Augustus Kelley.

Manicas, P. T. (1987) *A History and Philosophy of the Social Sciences*, Oxford: Basil Blackwell.

Mann, Michael (1986) *The Sources of Social Power, Volume 1: A History of Power from the Beginning to A.D. 1760*, Cambridge: Cambridge University Press.

Mantel, Rolf R. (1974) 'On the Characterization of Aggregate Excess Demand', *Journal of Economic Theory*, 12(2), 348–53.

Margolis, Howard (1987) *Patterns, Thinking and Cognition: A Theory of Judgement*, Chicago: University of Chicago Press.

Margolis, Howard (1994) *Paradigms and Barriers: How Habits of Mind Govern Scientific Beliefs*, Chicago: University of Chicago Press.

Marsden, David (1986) *The End of Economic Man? Custom and Competition in Labour Markets*, Brighton: Wheatsheaf Books.

Marshall, Alfred (1885) 'The Present Position of Economics', in Pigou, Arthur C. (ed.) (1925) *Memorials of Alfred Marshall*, London: Macmillan), pp. 152–74.

Marshall, Alfred (1890) *Principles of Economics: An Introductory Volume*, London: Macmillan.

Marshall, Alfred (1892) 'A Reply to "The Perversion of Economic History" by Dr. Cunningham', *Economic Journal*, **2**, 507–19.

Marshall, Alfred (1919) *Industry and Trade*, London: Macmillan.

Marshall, Alfred (1923) *Money, Credit and Commerce*, London: Macmillan.

Marshall, Alfred (1949) [1890] *The Principles of Economics*, (8th edn) London: Macmillan.

Marshall, Alfred and Marshall, Mary Paley (1881) *Economics of Industry*, (2nd edn) London: Macmillan.

Marx, Karl (1971) [1859] *A Contribution to the Critique of Political Economy*, trans. S. W. Ryazanskaya and ed. with introd. by Maurice Dobb London: Lawrence and Wishart.

Marx, Karl (1972) *Theories of Surplus Value: Part Three*, London: Lawrence and Wishart.

Marx, Karl (1973a) *The Revolutions of 1848: Political Writings – Volume 1*, ed. and introd. David Fernbach, Harmondsworth: Penguin.

Marx, Karl (1973b) *Grundrisse: Foundations of the Critique of Political Economy*, trans. M. Nicolaus, Harmondsworth: Penguin.

Marx, Karl (1976) *Capital*, vol. 1, trans. Ben Fowkes from the 4th German edn (1890) Harmondsworth: Pelican.

Marx, Karl (1977) *Karl Marx: Selected Writings*, ed. David McLellan, Oxford: Oxford University Press.

Marx, Karl (1981) *Capital*, vol. 3, trans. David Fernbach from the German edn (1894) Harmondsworth: Pelican.

Marx, Karl and Engels, Frederick (1976) *Karl Marx and Frederick Engels, Collected Works, Vol. 5, Marx and Engels: 1845–47*, London: Lawrence and Wishart.

Marx, Karl and Engels, Frederick (1982) *Karl Marx and Frederick Engels, Collected Works, Vol. 38, Letters 1844–51*, London: Lawrence and Wishart.

Mason, Edward S. and Lamont, Thomas S. (1982) 'The Harvard Department of Economics from the Beginning to World War II', *Quarterly Journal of Economics*, **97**(3), August, 383–433.

Mason, Roger (1995) 'Interpersonal Effects on Consumer Demand in Economic Theory and Marketing Thought, 1890–1950', *Journal of Economic Issues*, **29**(3), September, 871–81.

Mayer, Thomas (1997) 'The Rhetoric of Friedman's Quantity Theory Manifesto', *Journal of Economic Methodology*, **4**(2), December, 199–200.

Mayr, Ernst (1963) *Animal Species and Evolution*, Cambridge, MA: Harvard University Press.

Mayr, Ernst (1964) 'Introduction', in Darwin, C., *On the Origin of Species*, facsimile of the 1st edn, Cambridge, MA: Harvard University Press, pp. vii–xxvii.

Mayr, Ernst (1976) *Evolution and the Diversity of Life: Selected Essays*, Cambridge, MA: Harvard University Press.

Mayr, Ernst (1982) *The Growth of Biological Thought: Diversity, Evolution, and Inheritance*, Cambridge, MA: Harvard University Press.

Mayr, Ernst (1985a) 'How Biology Differs from the Physical Sciences', in Depew, David J. and Weber, Bruce H. (eds) (1985a) *Evolution at a Crossroads: The New Biology and the New Philosophy of Science*, Cambridge, MA: MIT Press, pp. 43–63.

Mayr, Ernst (1985b) 'Darwin's Five Theories of Evolution', in Kohn (1985), pp. 755–72. Repr. in Mayr (1988).

Mayr, Ernst (1988) *Toward a New Philosophy of Biology: Observations of an Evolutionist*, Cambridge, MA and London: Harvard University Press.

Mayr, Ernst (1992) *One Long Argument: Charles Darwin and the Genesis of Modern Evolutionary Thought*, London: Allen Lane.

McCloskey, Donald N. (1985) *The Rhetoric of Economics*, Madison: University of Wisconsin Press.

McCloskey, Donald N. (1988) 'Two Replies and a Dialogue on the Rhetoric of Economics: Mäki, Rappaport, and Rosenberg', *Economics and Philosophy*, **4**(1), April, 150–66.

McCloskey, Donald N. (1991) 'Economic Science: A Search Through the Hyperspace of Assumptions?', *Methodus*, **3**(1), June, 6–16.

McCoy, J. Wynne (1977) 'Complexity in Organic Evolution', *Journal of Theoretical Biology*, **68**, 457–8.

McDougall, William (1929) *Modern Materialism and Emergent Evolution*, London: Methuen.

McKelvey, William (1982) *Organizational Systematics: Taxonomy, Evolution, Classification*, Berkeley, CA: University of California Press.

McNeill, William H. (1980) *The Pursuit of Power: Technology, Armed Force, and Society Since A.D. 1000*, Chicago: University of Chicago Press.

Mead, Margaret (1928) *Coming of Age in Samoa: A Psychological Study of Primitive Youth for Western Civilization*, New York: William Morrow.

Mead, Margaret (1937) *Cooperation and Competition Among Primitive Peoples*, New York: McGraw-Hill.

Means, Gardiner C. (1938) *Patterns of Resource Use*, Washington, DC: Government Printing Office.

Meek, Ronald (1967) *Economics and Ideology and Other Essays: Studies in the Development of Economic Thought*, London: Chapman and Hall.

Ménard, Claude (1995) 'Markets as Institutions versus Organizations as Markets? Disentangling Some Fundamental Concepts', *Journal of Economic Behavior and Organization*, **28**(2), 161–82.

Ménard, Claude (1996) 'On Clusters, Hybrids, and Other Strange Forms: The Case of the French Poultry Industry', *Journal of Institutional and Theoretical Economics*, **152**(1), March, 154–83.

Menger, Carl (1883) *Untersuchungen über die Methode der Sozialwissenschaften und der politischen Ökonomie insbesondere* (Investigations into the Method of the Social Sciences with Special Reference to Economics) Tübingen: Mohr. English translation: Menger (1985).

Menger, Carl (1884) *Die Irrtümer des Historismus in der deutschen Nationalökonomie*, Vienna: Hölder.

Menger, Carl (1892) 'On the Origins of Money', *Economic Journal*, **2**(2), June, 239–55.

Menger, Carl (1909) 'Geld', reprinted in *The Collected Works of Carl Menger, Vol. IV, Schriften über Geldtheorie und Währungspolitik*, London: London School of Economics, 1936), pp. 1–116.

Menger, Carl (1981) *Principles of Economics*, ed. J. Dingwall and trans. B. F. Hoselitz from the German edn (1871) New York: New York University Press.

Menger, Carl (1985) *Investigations into the Method of the Social Sciences with Special Reference to Economics*, published in 1963 as *Problems of Economics and Sociology*, trans. F. J. Nock from the German edn (1883) with 1963 introd. by Louis Schneider and 1985 introd. by Lawrence H. White, New York: New York University Press.

Merchant, Carolyn (1983) *The Death of Nature: Women, Ecology, and the Scientific Revolution*, San Francisco: Harper and Row.

Merton, Robert K. (1949) *Social Theory and Social Structure*, (1st edn) Glencoe, Ill: Free Press.

Merton, Robert K. (1968) *Social Theory and Social Structure*, (3rd (enlarged) edn) Glencoe, Ill: Free Press.

Metcalfe, J. Stanley (1988) 'Evolution and Economic Change', in Silberston, Aubrey (ed.), *Technology and Economic Progress*, Basingstoke: Macmillan, pp. 54–85.

Meyer, Willi (1988) 'Schmoller's Research Programme, His Psychology, and the Autonomy of the Social Sciences', *Journal of Institutional and Theoretical Economics*, **144**, 570–80. Repr. in Blaug, Mark (ed.) (1992) *Gustav Schmoller (1838–1917) and Werner Sombart (1863–1941)*, Aldershot: Edward Elgar.

Milford, K. (1990) 'Menger's Methodology', in Caldwell (1990), pp. 215–39.

Mill, John Stuart (1843) *A System of Logic: Ratiocinative and Inductive, Being a Connected View of the Principles of Evidence and the Methods of Scientific Investigation*, (1st edn), 2 vols, London: Longman.

Mill, John Stuart (1967) 'Leslie and the Land Question', repr. in Robson, J. M. (ed.) *The Collected Works of John Stuart Mill*, vol. IV, Toronto: University of Toronto Press.

Miller, Gary J. (1997) 'The Impact of Economics on Contemporary Political Science', *Journal of Economic Literature*, **35**(3), September, 1173–204.

Miller, James G. (1978) *Living Systems*, New York: McGraw-Hill.

Mills, C. Wright (1959) *The Sociological Imagination*, Oxford and New York: Oxford University Press.

Mirowski, Philip (ed.) (1986) *The Reconstruction of Economic Theory*, Boston: Kluwer-Nijhoff.

Mirowski, Philip (1989) *More Heat Than Light: Economics as Social Physics, Physics as Nature's Economics*, Cambridge: Cambridge University Press.

Mirowski, Philip (1991) 'Postmodernism and the Social Theory of Value', *Journal of Post Keynesian Economics*, **13**(4), Summer, 565–82.

Mirowski, Philip (1994) 'What are the Questions?', in Backhouse, Roger E. (ed.) (1994) *New Directions in Economic Methodology*, London: Routledge, pp. 50–74.

Mirowski, Philip (forthcoming) *Machine Dreams: Economics Becomes a Cyborg Science*, Cambridge: Cambridge University Press.

Mirowski, Philip and Somefun, Koye (1998) 'Markets as Evolving Computational Entities', *Journal of Evolutionary Economics*, **8**(4), 329–56.

Mises, Ludwig von (1933) *Grundprobleme der Nationalökonomie: Untersuchungen über Verfahren, Aufgaben, und Inhalt der Wirtschafts und Gesellschaftslehre*, Jena: Gustav Fischer. English translation: von Mises (1960).

Mises, Ludwig von (1949) *Human Action: A Treatise on Economics*, London: William Hodge.

Mises, Ludwig von (1957) *Theory and History: An Interpretation of Social and Economic Evolution*, New Haven: Yale University Press.

Mises, Ludwig von (1960) *Epistemological Problems of Economics*, trans. George Reisman from the German edn of 1933, New York: Van Nostrand.

Mises, Ludwig von (1978) *Notes and Recollections*, trans. H. F. Sennholz, South Holland, Ill: Libertarian Press.

Mishan, Ezra J. (1952) 'Toward a General Theory of Price, Income, and Money', *Journal of Political Economy*, **60**(6), December, 487–502.

Mitchell, Wesley C. (1910) 'The Rationality of Economic Activity', *Journal of Political Economy*, **18**(2–3), parts I and II, February–March, 97–113; 197–216.

Mitchell, Wesley C. (1937) *The Backward Art of Spending Money and Other Essays*, New York: McGraw-Hill.

Mitchell, Wesley C. (1969) *Types of Economic Theory: From Mercantilism to Institutionalism*, 2 vols, ed. J. Dorfman, New York: Augustus Kelley.

Mixter, Charles W. (1916) 'Review of *Scientific Management and Labor*, by Robert F. Hoxie', *American Economic Review*, **6**(2), June, 373–7.

Moggridge, Donald E. (1992) *Maynard Keynes: An Economist's Biography*, London: Routledge.

Moggridge, Donald E. (1997) 'Method and Marshall', in Koslowsi (1997a), pp. 342–69.

Mommsen, Wolfgang J. (1965) 'Max Weber's Political Sociology and his Philosophy of World History', *International Social Science Journal*, **17**.

Mommsen, Wolfgang J. (1984) *Max Weber and German Politics, 1890–1920*, Chicago: University of Chicago Press.

Mommsen, Wolfgang J. and Osterhammel, Jürgen (eds) (1987) *Max Weber and His Contemporaries*, London: Allen and Unwin.

Montag, Warren (1988) 'What is at Stake in the Debate on Postmodernism?' in Kaplan, E. A. (ed.) (1988) *Postmodernism and its Discontents*, London: Verso.

Montagu, M. F. Ashley (1952) *Darwin, Competition and Cooperation*, New York: Henry Schuman.

Moore, Gregory C. G. (1995) 'T. E. Cliffe Leslie and the English *Methodenstreit*', *Journal of the History of Economic Thought*, **17**(1), Spring, 57–77.

Moore, Gregory C. G. (1996) 'Robert Lowe and the Role of the Vulgar Economist in the English *Methodenstreit*', *Journal of Economic Methodology*, **3**(1), June, 69–90.

Moore, Gregory C. G. (1999) 'John Kells Ingram, the Comtean Movement and the English *Methodenstreit*', *History of Political Economy*, **31**(1), Spring, 53–78.

Morgan, C. Lloyd (1896) *Habit and Instinct*, London and New York: Edward Arnold.

Morgan, C. Lloyd (1927) *Emergent Evolution*, (2nd edn), London: Williams and Norgate.

Morgan, C. Lloyd (1932) 'C. Lloyd Morgan' in Murchison, Carl (ed.) (1932) *A History of Psychology in Autobiography, Volume 2*, New York: Russell and Russell, pp. 253–64.

Morgan, C. Lloyd (1933) *The Emergence of Novelty*, London: Williams and Norgate.

Morgan, Lewis Henry (1877) *Ancient Society*, Chicago: Charles Kerr. Repr. 1964 with introd. by Leslie A. White, Cambridge, MA: Harvard University Press.

Morgan, Mary S. and Rutherford, Malcolm H. (eds) (1998) *The Transformation of American Economics: From Interwar Pluralism to Postwar Neoclassicism, Annual Supplement to Volume 30 of History of Political Economy*, Durham, North Carolina: Duke University Press.

Morishima, Michio (1982) *Why Has Japan 'Succeeded'?: Western Technology and the Japanese Ethos*, Cambridge: Cambridge University Press.

Morishima, Michio and Catephores, George (1988) 'Anti-Say's Law versus Say's Law: A Change in Paradigm', in Hanusch, Horst (ed.) (1988) *Evolutionary Economics: Applications of Schumpeter's Ideas*, Cambridge: Cambridge University Press, pp. 23–53.

Morris-Suzuki, Tessa (1989) *A History of Japanese Economic Thought*, London: Routledge.

Mote, Jonathon (1997) '(Dis)trusting the Tale: Werner Sombart and the Narrative of Economics', in Henderson, James P. (1997) *The State of the History of Economics: Proceedings on the History of Economic Thought*, London: Routledge, pp. 143–56.

Mouzelis, Nicos (1995) *Sociological Theory: What Went Wrong? Diagnosis and Remedies*, London and New York: Routledge.

Mumford, Lewis (1934) *Technics and Civilization*, New York: Harcourt, Brace and World.

Mummery, Albert F. and Hobson, John A. (1889) *The Physiology of Industry*, London: John Murray. Repr. 1989, New York: Augustus Kelley.

Münch, Richard (1981) 'Talcott Parsons and the Theory of Action I: The Structure of the Kantian Core', *American Journal of Sociology*, **86**(4), January, 709–39.

Murphy, James Bernard (1994) 'The Kinds of Order in Society', in Mirowski, Philip (ed.) (1994) *Natural Images in Economic Thought: Markets Read in Tooth and Claw*, Cambridge and New York: Cambridge University Press, pp. 536–82.

Müssigang, Albert (1968) *Die soziale Frage in der historischen Schule der deutschen Nationalökonomie*, Tübingen: J. C. B. Mohr.

Nagel, Ernest (1961) *The Structure of Science*, London and Indianapolis: Routledge and Hackett Publishing.

Nagel, Ernest and Newman, James R. (1959) *Gödel's Proof*, London: Routledge and Kegan Paul.

Nardinelli, Clark and Meiners, Roger E. (1988) 'Schmoller, the Methodenstreit, and the

Development of Economic History', *Journal of Institutional and Theoretical Economics*, **144**(3), June, 543–51.

Nef, John U. (1950) *War and Human Progress: An Essay on the Rise of Industrial Civilization*, Cambridge, MA: Harvard University Press.

Nell, Edward J. (1998) *The General Theory of Transformational Growth: Keynes after Sraffa*, Cambridge: Cambridge University Press.

Nelson, Richard R. (ed.) (1993) *National Innovation Systems: A Comparative Analysis*, Oxford: Oxford University Press.

Nelson, Richard R. and Winter, Sidney G. (1982) *An Evolutionary Theory of Economic Change*, Cambridge, MA: Harvard University Press.

Nicholls, Anthony J. (1994) *Freedom with Responsibility: The Social Market Economy in Germany, 1918–1963*, Oxford and New York: Clarendon Press.

Nicolaides, Phedon (1988) 'Limits to the Expansion of Neoclassical Economics', *Cambridge Journal of Economics*, **12**(3), September, 313–28.

Noppeney, Claus (1997) 'Frank Knight and the Historical School', in Koslowski (1997a), pp. 319–39.

North, Douglass C. (1977) 'Markets and Other Allocation Systems in History: The Challenge of Karl Polanyi', *Journal of European Economic History*, **6**, 703–16. Repr. in Swedberg (1996.

North, Douglass C. (1990) *Institutions, Institutional Change and Economic Performance*, Cambridge: Cambridge University Press.

North, Douglass C. (1991) 'Institutions', *Journal of Economic Perspectives*, **5**(1), Winter, 97–112.

Nozick, Robert (1977) 'On Austrian Methodology', *Synthese*, **36**, 353–92.

Nuti, Domenico Mario (1996) 'Post-Communist Mutations', *Emergo*, **3**(1), Winter, 7–15.

Nutzinger, Hans G. (1976) 'The Firm as a Social Institution: The Failure of the Contractarian Viewpoint', *Economic Analysis and Workers' Management*, **10**, 217–37. Repr. in Hodgson (1993b).

Nyland, Christopher (1996) 'Taylorism, John R. Commons, and the Hoxie Report', *Journal of Economic Issues*, **30**(4), December, 985–1016.

O'Brien, Denis P. (1998) 'Four Detours', *Journal of Economic Methodology*, **5**(1), June, 23–41.

O'Brien, John C. (1987) 'The Social Economics of Hugo Eisenhart Gustav von Schmoller', *International Journal of Social Economics*, **14**, 26–47.

O'Brien, John C. (1989) 'Gustav von Schmoller: Social Economist', *International Journal of Social Economics*, **16**, 17–46.

O'Brien, Roderick (1979) 'One Lawyer's View of Trade with the People's Republic of China', *Australian Journal of Chinese Affairs*, **1**, January, 91–105.

Olson, Mancur, Jr. (1982) *The Rise and Decline of Nations*, New Haven: Yale University Press.

Olson, Mancur, Jr. (1986) 'Toward a More General Theory of Governmental Structure', *American Economic Review (Papers and Proceedings)*, **76**(2), May, 120–5.

Orchard, Lionel and Stretton, Hugh (1997) 'Public Choice', *Cambridge Journal of Economics*, **21**(3), May, 409–30.

Ormerod, Paul (1998) *Butterfly Economics: A New General Theory of Social and Economic Behaviour*, London: Faber and Faber.

Orrù, Marco (1997) 'The Institutionalist Analysis of Capitalist Economies', in Orrù, Marco (ed.) (1997) *The Economic Organization of East Asian Capitalism*, Thousand Oaks, CA: Sage.

Pagano, Ugo (1991) 'Property Rights, Asset Specificity, and the Division of Labour Under Alternative Capitalist Relations', *Cambridge Journal of Economics*, **15**(3), September, 315–42. Repr. in Hodgson (1993b).

Pagano, Ugo (2000) 'The Origin of Organisational Species', in Nicita, A. and Pagano, Ugo (eds) (2000) *The Evolution of Economic Diversity*, London: Routledge.

Pareto, Vilfredo (1935) *The Mind and Society*, 4 vols, trans. A. Bongiorno and A. Livingston from the Italian edn (1923) and ed. A. Livingston, London: Jonathan Cape.

Pareto, Vilfredo (1971) *Manual of Political Economy*, trans. A. S. Schwier from the French edn (1927) and ed. A. S. Schwier and A. N. Page, New York: Augustus Kelley.

Parsons, Talcott (1928) 'Capitalism in Recent German Literature: Sombart and Weber. Part I', *Journal of Political Economy*, **36**, pp. 641–64. Repr. in Camic (1991).

Parsons, Talcott (1929) 'Capitalism in Recent German Literature: Sombart and Weber. Part II', *Journal of Political Economy*, **37**, 31–51. Repr. in Camic (1991).

Parsons, Talcott (1934) 'Some Reflections on "The Nature and Significance of Economics"', *Quarterly Journal of Economics*, **48**(3), May, 511–45. Repr. in Camic (1991).

Parsons, Talcott (1935) 'Sociological Elements in Economic Thought', *Quarterly Journal of Economics*, **49**, 414–53. Repr. in Camic (1991).

Parsons, Talcott (1936) 'Review of *Max Webers Wissenschaftslehre* by Alexander von Schelting', *American Sociological Review*, **1**, 675–81. Repr. in Camic (1991).

Parsons, Talcott (1937a) *The Structure of Social Action*, 2 vols, New York: McGraw-Hill.

Parsons, Talcott (1937b) 'Review of *Economics and Sociology*, by Adolf Löwe', *American Journal of Sociology*, **42**, 477–81. Repr. in Camic (1991).

Parsons, Talcott (1940) 'The Motivation of Economic Activities', *Canadian Journal of Economics and Political Science*, **6**, 187–203.

Parsons, Talcott (1950) 'The Prospects of Sociological Theory', *American Sociological Review*, **15**(1), February, pp. 3–16.

Parsons, Talcott (1951) *The Social System*, New York: Free Press.

Parsons, Talcott (1953), 'Some Comments on the State of the General Theory of Action', *American Sociological Review*, **18**(6), December, 618–31.

Parsons, Talcott (1959) 'A Short Account of My Intellectual Development', *Alpha Kappa Delta*, **29**, Winter, 3–12.

Parsons, Talcott (1964) 'Evolutionary Universals in Society', *American Sociological Review*, June, 339–57.

Parsons, Talcott (1966) *Societies: Evolutionary and Comparative Perspectives*, Englewood Cliffs, NJ: Prentice-Hall.

Parsons, Talcott (1970) 'On Building Social Systems Theory: A Personal History', *Daedalus*, Winter, 826–81.

Parsons, Talcott (1976) 'Clarence Ayres's Economics and Sociology', in Breit and Culbertson (1976), pp. 175–9.

Parsons, Talcott (1977) *The Evolution of Societies*, Englewood Cliffs, NJ: Prentice-Hall.

Parsons, Talcott and Smelser, Neil J. (1956) *Economy and Society: A Study in the Integration of Economic and Social Theory*, Glencoe, IL: Free Press; London: Routledge and Kegan Paul.

Pasinetti, Luigi L. (1981) *Structural Change and Economic Growth: A Theoretical Essay on the Dynamics of the Wealth of Nations*, Cambridge: Cambridge University Press.

Pearson, Heath (1997) *Origins of Law and Economics: The Economists' New Science of Law, 1830–1930*, Cambridge: Cambridge University Press.

Pearson, Heath (1999) 'Was There Really a German Historical School of Economics?', *History of Political Economy*, **31**(2), Summer, 547–62.

Peirce, Charles Sanders (1878) 'How to Make Our Ideas Clear', *Popular Science Monthly*, **12**, January, 286–302. Repr. in Peirce (1958).

Peirce, Charles Sanders (1923) *Chance, Love, and Logic*, ed. Cohen, M. R. New York: Harcourt, Brace.

Peirce, Charles Sanders (1935) *Collected Papers of Charles Sanders Peirce, Volume VI, Scientific Metaphysics*, ed. Hartshorne, C. and Weiss, P. Cambridge, MA: Harvard University Press.

Peirce, Charles Sanders (1958) *Selected Writings (Values in a Universe of Chance)*, ed. with introd. by Philip P. Wiener, New York: Doubleday.

Perlman, Mark and McCann, Charles R. (1998) *The Pillars of Economic Understanding*, Ann Arbor: University of Michigan Press.

Pen, Jan (1952) 'A General Theory of Bargaining', *American Economic Review*, **42**(1), March, 24–42.

Persky, Joseph (2000) 'The Neoclassical Advent: American Economics at the Dawn of the 20th Century', *Journal of Economic Perspectives*, **14**(1), Winter, 95–108.

Pigou, Arthur C. (1903) 'Some Remarks on Utility', *Economic Journal*, **13**(1), March, 58–68.

Pigou, Arthur C. (1910) 'Producers' and Consumers' Surplus', *Economic Journal*, **20**(3), September, 358–70.

Pigou, Arthur C. (1913) 'The Interdependence of Different Sources of Demand and Supply in a Market', *Economic Journal*, **23**(1), March, 19–24.

Pigou, Arthur C. (1914) 'Review of *Business Cycles* by Wesley C. Mitchell', *Economic Journal*, **24**(1), March, 78–81.

Pigou, Arthur C. (ed.) (1925) *Memorials of Alfred Marshall*, London: Macmillan.

Pinker, Steven (1994) *The Language Instinct: The New Science of Language and Mind*, London: Allen Lane; New York: Morrow.

Pirenne, Henri (1937) *Economic and Social History of Medieval Europe*, New York: Harcourt Brace.

Pitelis, Christos (1991) *Market and Non-Market Hierarchies: Theory of Institutional Failure*, Oxford: Basil Blackwell.

Platteau, J.-P. (1994) 'Behind the Market Stage Where Real Societies Exist – Part II: The Role of Moral Norms', *Journal of Development Studies*, **30**(4), 753–817.

Plotkin, Henry C. (1994) *Darwin Machines and the Nature of Knowledge: Concerning Adaptations, Instinct and the Evolution of Intelligence*, Harmondsworth: Penguin.

Polanyi, Karl (1944) *The Great Transformation: The Political and Economic Origins of Our Time*, New York: Rinehart.

Polanyi, Karl (1971) *Primitive and Modern Economics: Essays of Karl Polanyi*, ed. with introd. by George Dalton, Boston: Beacon Press.

Polanyi, Karl (1977) *The Livelihood of Man*, ed. Pearson, Harry W. New York: Academic Press.

Polanyi, Karl, Arensberg, Conrad M. and Pearson, Harry W. (eds) (1957) *Trade and Market in the Early Empires*, Chicago: Henry Regnery.

Polanyi, Michael (1967) *The Tacit Dimension*, London: Routledge and Kegan Paul.

Popkin, Samuel L. (1979) *The Rational Peasant*, Berkeley: University of California Press.

Popper, Karl R. (1960) *The Poverty of Historicism*, London: Routledge and Kegan Paul.

Posner, Richard A. (1980) 'A Theory of Primitive Society, With Special Reference to Law', *Journal of Law and Economics*, **23**(1), 1–53.

Posner, Richard A. (1994) *Sex and Reason*, Cambridge, MA: Harvard University Press.

Potts, Jason (2000) *The New Evolutionary Microeconomics: Complexity, Competence and Adaptive Behaviour*, Cheltenham: Edward Elgar.

Powell, Walter W. and DiMaggio, Paul J. (eds) (1991) *The New Institutionalism in Organizational Analysis*, Chicago and London: University of Chicago Press.

Prendergast, Christopher (1986) 'Alfred Schutz and the Austrian School of Economics', *American Journal of Sociology*, **92**(1), July, 1–26.

Pribram, Karl H. (1983) *A History of Economic Reasoning*, Baltimore, MD: Johns Hopkins University Press.

Priddat, Birger P. (1995) 'Intention and Failure of W. Roscher's Historical Method of National Economics', in Koslowski (1995), pp. 15–34.

Priddat, Birger P. (1998) 'Theory of Subjective Value in German National Economics', *International Journal of Social Economics*, **25**(9), 1509–19.

Prigogine, Ilya and Stengers, Isabelle (1984) *Order Out of Chaos: Man's New Dialogue With Nature*, London: Heinemann.

Prisching, Manfred (1993) 'Schmoller's Theory of Society', *History of Economic Ideas*, **1**(3), 117–42.

Prisching, Manfred (1996) 'The Entrepreneur and His Capitalist Spirit – Sombart's Psycho-Historical Model', in Backhaus (1996), vol. 2, pp. 301–30.

Putterman, Louis (1988) 'The Firm as Association vs. Firm as Commodity: Efficiency, Rights, and Ownership', *Economics and Philosophy*, **4**(2), 243–66.

Quine, Willard van Orman (1951) 'Two Dogmas of Empiricism', *Philosophical Review*, **60**(1), January, 20–43. Repr. in Quine (1953).

Quine, Willard van Orman (1953) *From a Logical Point of View*, Cambridge, MA: Harvard University Press.

Quine, Willard van Orman (1987) *Quiddities: An Intermediate Philosophical Dictionary*, Cambridge, MA: Harvard University Press.

Rabin, Matthew (1998) 'Psychology and Economics', *Journal of Economic Literature*, **36**(1), March, 11–46.

Rader, John Trout (1971) *The Economics of Feudalism*, New York: Gordon and Breach.

Radner, Roy (1968) 'Competitive Equilibrium Under Uncertainty', *Econometrica*, **36**(1), January, 31–58.

Radner, Roy (1996) 'Bounded Rationality, Indeterminacy, and the Theory of the Firm', *Economic Journal*, **106**(5), September, 1360–73.

Radnitzky, Gerard (ed.) (1992) *Universal Economics: Assessing the Achievements of the Economic Approach*, New York: Paragon House.

Radnitzky, Gerard and Bernholz, Peter (eds) (1987) *Economic Imperialism*, New York: Paragon House.

Ramstad, Yngve (1994) 'On the Nature of Economic Evolution: John R. Commons and the Metaphor of Artificial Selection', in Magnusson, Lars (ed.) (1994) *Evolutionary and Neo-Schumpeterian Approaches to Economics*, Boston: Kluwer, pp. 65–121.

Rappaport, Steven (1996) 'Abstraction and Unrealistic Assumptions in Economics', *Journal of Economic Methodology*, **3**(2), December, 215–36.

Rappaport, Steven (1998) *Models and Reality in Economics*, Cheltenham: Edward Elgar.

Rau, Karl H. (1835) 'Ueber den Nutzen, den gegenwärtigen Zustand und die neueste Literatur der Nationalökonomie', in Rau, Karl H. (ed.) (1835) *Archiv der politischen Oekonomie und Polizeiwissenschaft Bd. 1*, Heidelberg: Winter, pp. 1–43.

Reber, Arthur S. (1993) *Implicit Learning and Tacit Knowledge: An Essay on the Cognitive Unconscious*, Oxford: Oxford University Press.

Reheis, Fritz (1996) 'Return to the Grace of God: Werner Sombart's Compromise with National Socialism', in Backhaus (1996), vol. 1, pp. 173–9.

Reinert, Erik S. (2000) 'Karl Bücher and the Geographical Dimensions of Techno-Economic Change: Production-Based Economic Theory and the Stages of Economic Development', in Backhaus (2000), pp. 177–222.

Reinert, Erik S. (forthcoming) 'The Austrians and "The Other Canon": The Austrians Between *Activistic-Idealistic* and *Passivistic-Materialistic* Economics', in Backhaus (forthcoming).

Reinert, Erik S. and Daastøl, Arno Mong (1997) 'Exploring the Genesis of Economic Innovations: The Religious Gestalt-Switch and the Duty to Invent as Preconditions for Economic Growth', *European Journal of Law and Economics*, 4, 233–83.

Reisman, David (1999) *Conservative Capitalism: The Social Economy*, London and New York: Macmillan and St. Martin's Press.

Richardson, George B. (1972) 'The Organisation of Industry', *Economic Journal*, 82, 883–96.

Rickert, Heinrich (1899) *Kulturwissenschaft und Naturwissenschaft*, Freiburg.

Rieß, Rolf (1996) 'Werner Sombart under National Socialism', in Backhaus (1996), vol. 1, pp. 193–204.

Riker, William H. and Ordeshook, Peter C. (1968) 'A Theory of the Calculus of Voting', *American Political Science Review*, 62(1), 25–42.

Ringer, Fritz (1997) *Max Weber's Methodology: The Unification of the Cultural and Social Sciences*, Cambridge, MA: Harvard University Press.

Rizvi, S. Abu Turab (1994a) 'The Microfoundations Project in General Equilibrium Theory', *Cambridge Journal of Economics*, 18(4), August, 357–77.

Rizvi, S. Abu Turab (1994b) 'Game Theory to the Rescue?', *Contributions to Political Economy*, 13, 1–28.

Robbins, Lionel (1932) *An Essay on the Nature and Significance of Economic Science*, (1st edn) London: Macmillan.

Robbins, Lionel (1935) *An Essay on the Nature and Significance of Economic Science*, (2nd edn) London: Macmillan.

Robbins, Lionel (1952) *The Theory of Economic Policy in English Classical Political Economy*, London: Macmillan.

Robbins, Lionel (1998) *A History of Economic Thought: The LSE Lectures*, ed. by Steven G. Medema and Warren J. Samuels, Princeton, NJ: Princeton University Press.

Robinson, Joan (1952) *The Rate of Interest and Other Essays*, London: Macmillan. Repr. and enlarged in 1979 as *The Generalisation of the General Theory and Other Essays*, London: Macmillan.

Robinson, Joan (1964) *Economic Philosophy*, Harmondsworth: Penguin.

Robinson, Joan (ed.) (1973) *After Keynes*, Oxford: Blackwell.

Robinson, Joan (1974) *History versus Equilibrium*, London: Thames Papers in Political Economy.

Robinson, Joan (1979) *Collected Economic Papers – Volume Five*, Oxford: Basil Blackwell.

Roe, Mark J. (1990) 'Political and Legal Restraints on Political Control of Public Companies', *Journal of Financial Economics*, 27, 7–41.

Roe, Mark J. (1994) *Strong Managers, Weak Owners: The Political Roots of American Corporate Finance*, Princeton, NJ: Princeton University Press.

Roemer, John E. (1982) *A General Theory of Exploitation and Class*, Cambridge, MA: Harvard University Press.

Roemer, John E. (1988) *Free to Lose: An Introduction to Marxist Economic Philosophy*, Cambridge, MA: Harvard University Press.

Romanes, George J. (1893) *Darwin and After Darwin*, 2 vols, (2nd edn) London.

Roscher, Wilhelm (1843) *Grundriss zu Vorlesungen über die Staatswirtschaft nach geschichtlicher Methode*, Göttingen.

Roscher, Wilhelm (1849) 'Der gegenwärtige Zustand der wissenschaftlichen Nationalökonomie und die nothwendige Reform desselben', *Deutsche Vierteljahres Schrift*, 45.

Roscher, Wilhelm (1854) *Das System der Volkswirtschaft* (1st edn) Stuttgart: Cotta.

Rosenbaum, Eckehard F. (2000) 'What is a Market? On the Methodology of a Contested Concept', *Review of Social Economy*, 58(4), December, 455–82.

Ross, Dorothy (1991) *The Origins of American Social Science*, Cambridge: Cambridge University Press.

Rosser, J. Barkley, Jr (1991) *From Catastrophe to Chaos: A General Theory of Economic Discontinuities*, Dordrecht: Kluwer.

Rosser, J. Barkley, Jr (1999) 'On the Complexities of Complex Economic Dynamics', *Journal of Economic Perspectives*, **13**(4), Fall, 169–92.

Rothacker, Erich (1938) 'Historismus', in Spiethoff, Arthur (ed.) (1938) *Gustav von Schmoller und die deutsche geschichtliche Volkswirtschaftslehre*, Berlin: Duncker und Humblot, pp. 1–18.

Rubin, Isaac Ilyich (1979) *A History of Economic Thought*, trans. Donald Filtzer from the Russian edn (1929) London: Ink Links.

Rubinstein, Ariel (1991) 'Comments on the Interpretation of Game Theory', *Econometrica*, **59**(4), July, 909–24.

Runciman, Walter G. (1972) *A Critique of Max Weber's Philosophy of Social Science*, Cambridge: Cambridge University Press.

Rutherford, Malcolm H. (1984) 'Thorstein Veblen and the Processes of Institutional Change', *History of Political Economy*, **16**(3), Fall, 331–48. Repr. in Blaug, M. (ed.) (1992) *Thorstein Veblen (1857–1929)*, Aldershot: Edward Elgar.

Rutherford, Malcolm H. (1989) 'Some Issues in the Comparison of Austrian and Institutional Economics', *Research in the History of Economic Thought and Methodology*, **6**, 159–71.

Rutherford, Malcolm H. (1994) *Institutions in Economics: The Old and the New Institutionalism*, Cambridge: Cambridge University Press.

Rutherford, Malcolm H. (1997) 'American Institutionalism and the History of Economics', *Journal of the History of Economic Thought*, **19**(2), Fall, 178–95.

Rutherford, Malcolm H. (ed.) (1998) *The Economic Mind in America: Essays in the History of American Economics*, London and New York: Routledge.

Rutherford, Malcolm H. (1999) 'Institutionalism as "Scientific Economics"', in Backhouse and Creedy (1999), pp. 223–42.

Rutherford, Malcolm H. (2000) 'Institutionalism Between the Wars', *Journal of Economic Issues*, **34**(2), June, 291–303.

Sachs, Jeffrey D. (1993) *Poland's Jump to a Market Economy*, Cambridge, MA: Harvard University Press.

Sahlins, Marshall D. (1972) *Stone Age Economics*, London: Tavistock.

Sahlins, Marshall D. and Service, Elman R. (eds) (1960) *Evolution and Culture*, Ann Arbor, MI: University of Michigan Press.

Salin, Edgar (1927) 'Hochkapitalismus: Eine Studie über Werner Sombart, die deutsche Volkwirtschaftslehre und das Wirtschaftssystem der Gegenwart', *Weltwirtschaftliches Archiv*, **25**, 315–30.

Salin, Edgar (1929) *Geschichte der Volkswirtschaftslehre*, (2nd edn) Berlin: Springer.

Salin, Edgar (ed.) (1948) *Synopsis: Festgabe für Alfred Weber*, Heidelberg: Schneider.

Samuels, Warren J. (1977) 'The Knight–Ayres Correspondence: The Grounds of Knowledge and Social Action', *Journal of Economic Issues*, **11**(3), September, 485–525. Repr. in Blaug, Mark (ed.) (1992) *Wesley Mitchell (1874–1948), John Commons (1862–1945), Clarence Ayres (1891–1972)*, Aldershot: Edward Elgar.

Samuels, Warren J. (ed.) (1988) *Institutional Economics*, 3 vols, Aldershot: Edward Elgar.

Samuels, Warren J. (1989) 'Austrian and Institutional Economics: Some Common Elements', *Research in the History of Economic Thought and Methodology*, **6**, 53–71.

Samuels, Warren J. (ed.) (1998) *The Founding of Institutional Economics: The Leisure Class and Sovereignty*, London: Routledge.

Samuelson, Paul A. (1938) 'A Note on the Pure Theory of Consumer's Behavior', *Economica*, New Series, **5**(1), February, 61–71.

Samuelson, Paul A. (1947) *Foundations of Economic Analysis*, Cambridge, MA: Harvard University Press.

Samuelson, Paul A. (1948) *Economics*, (1st edn) New York: McGraw-Hill.

Saunders, Peter T. and Ho, Mae-Wan (1976) 'On the Increase in Complexity in Evolution', *Journal of Theoretical Biology*, **63**, 375–84.

Saunders, Peter T. and Ho, Mae-Wan (1981) 'On the Increase in Complexity in Evolution II: The Relativity of Complexity and the Principle of Minimum Increase', *Journal of Theoretical Biology*, **90**, 515–30.

Saunders, Peter T. and Ho, Mae-Wan (1984) 'The Complexity of Organisms', in Pollard, J. W. (ed.) (1984) *Evolutionary Theory: Paths into the Future*, London and New York: Wiley.

Saviotti, Pier Paolo (1996) *Technological Evolution, Variety and the Economy*, Aldershot: Edward Elgar.

Sayer, Andrew (1984) *Method in Social Science: A Realist Approach*, London: Hutchinson.

Sayer, Andrew (1995) *Radical Political Economy: A Critique*, Oxford: Basil Blackwell.

Schäffle, Albert (1875–81) *Bau und Leben des socialen Körpers: Encyclopädischer Entwurf einer realen Anatomie, Physiologie und Psychologie der menschlichen Gesellschaft mit besonderer Rücksicht auf die Volkswirtschaft als sozialen Stoffwechsel*, 4 vols (Anatomy and Life of the Social Body) Tübingen: Laupp.

Schank, Jeffrey C. and Wimsatt, William C. (1987) 'Generative Entrenchment and Evolution', in Fine, A. and Machamer, P. (eds) *PSA 1986: Proceedings of the Meeting of the Philosophy of Science Association*, vol. 7, East Lansing, MI: Philosophy of Science Association, pp. 33–60.

Schefold, Bertram (1980) 'The General Theory for a Totalitarian State? A Note on Keynes's Preface to the German Edition of 1936', *Cambridge Journal of Economics*, **4**(2), June, 175–6.

Schefold, Bertram (1995) 'Theoretical Approaches to the Comparison of Economic Systems from a Historical Perspective', in Koslowski (1995), pp. 221–47.

Scherer, Frederick M. (2000) 'The Emigration of German-Speaking Economists After 1933', *Journal of Economic Literature*, **38**(3), 614–26.

Schlicht, Ekkehart (1998) *On Custom in the Economy*, Oxford and New York: Clarendon Press.

Schmoller, Gustav (1883) 'Zur Methodologie der Staats- und Sozialwissenschaften', *Jahrbuch für die Gesetzgebung, Verwaltung und Volkswirtschaft im Deutschen Reich*, **7**.

Schmoller, Gustav (1897) *The Mercantile System and its Historical Significance*, trans. from the German (1884) New York: Macmillan.

Schmoller, Gustav (1898) *Über einige Grundfragen der Sozialpolitik und der Volkswirtschaftslehre*, Munich: Dunker; Leipzig: Humblot.

Schmoller, Gustav (1900) *Grundriss der allgemeinen Volkswirtschaftslehre*, Munich: Duncker; Leipzig: Humblot.

Schneider, Dieter (1993) 'Schmoller and the Theory of the Corporation and of Corporate Control', *History of Economic Ideas*, **1**(3), 357–77.

Schneider, Dieter (1995) 'Historicism and Business Ethics', in Koslowski (1995), pp. 173–202.

Schotter, Andrew R. (1981) *The Economic Theory of Social Institutions*, Cambridge: Cambridge University Press.

Schumpeter, Joseph A. (1908) *Das Wesen und der Hauptinhalt der theoretischen Nationalökonomie*, Munich and Leipzig: Duncker and Humblot.

Schumpeter, Joseph A. (1926) 'Gustav v. Schmoller und die Probleme von heute', *Schmollers Jahrbuch für Gesetzgebung, Verwaltung und Volkwirtschaft im Deutschen Reiche*, **50**, pp. 1–52.

Schumpeter, Joseph A. (1930) 'Mitchell's Business Cycles', *Quarterly Journal of Economics*, **45**(1), November, 150–72. Repr. in Clemence (1951).

Schumpeter, Joseph A. (1934) [1911] *The Theory of Economic Development: An Inquiry into Profits, Capital, Credit, Interest, and the Business Cycle*, trans. Redvers Opie from the 2nd German edn (1926) Cambridge, MA: Harvard University Press. Repr. 1989 with new introd. by John E. Elliott, New Brunswick, NJ: Transaction.

Schumpeter, Joseph A. (1936) 'Review of *The General Theory of Employment, Interest and Money* by John Maynard Keynes', in *Journal of the American Statistical Association*, **31**(196) December, 791–5. Repr. in Clemence (1951).

Schumpeter, Joseph A. (1946) 'John Maynard Keynes 1883–1946', *American Economic Review*, **36**(4), September, 495–518.

Schumpeter, Joseph A. (1951) 'The Historical Approach to the Analysis of Business Cycles', in Clemence, Richard V. (ed.) (1951) *Essays on Economic Topics of J. A. Schumpeter*, Port Washington, NY: Kennikat, pp. 308–15.

Schumpeter, Joseph A. (1954) *History of Economic Analysis*, New York: Oxford University Press.

Schumpeter, Joseph A. (1976) [1942] *Capitalism, Socialism and Democracy*, (5th edn) London: George Allen and Unwin.

Schumpeter, Joseph A. (1991) *The Economics and Sociology of Capitalism*, ed. R. Swedberg, Princeton: Princeton University Press.

Schutz, Alfred (1967) *The Phenomenology of the Social World*, trans. from German edn (1932) Evanston, Ill: Northwestern University Press.

Schweitzer, Arthur (1975) 'Frank Knight's Social Economics', *History of Political Economy*, **7**(3), Fall, 279–92. Repr. in Blaug, Mark (ed.) (1992) *Frank Knight (1885–1972), Henry Simons (1899–1946), Joseph Schumpeter (1883–1950)*, Aldershot: Edward Elgar.

Screpanti, Ernesto (2001) *The Fundamental Institutions of Capitalism*, London and New York: Routledge.

Screpanti, Ernesto and Zamagni, Stefano (1993) *An Outline of the History of Economic Thought*, Oxford: Clarendon Press.

Seager, H. R. (1893) 'Economics at Berlin and Vienna', *Journal of Political Economy*, **1**(2), 236–62.

Searle, John R. (1995) *The Construction of Social Reality*, London: Allen Lane.

Sekine, Thomas T. (1975) '*Uno-Riron*: A Japanese Contribution to Marxian Political Economy', *Journal of Economic Literature*, **8**(4), December, 847–77.

Seligman, Benjamin B. (1962) *Main Currents in Modern Economics: Economic Thought Since 1870*, New York: Macmillan.

Seligman, Edwin R. A. (1925) *Essays in Economics*, New York: Macmillan.

Sen, Amartya K. (1973) 'Behaviour and the Concept of Preference', *Economica*, **40**, 241–59. Repr. in Elster, Jon (ed.) (1986) *Rational Choice*, Oxford: Basil Blackwell.

Sened, Itai (1997) *The Political Institution of Private Property*, Cambridge: Cambridge University Press.

Shackle, George L. S. (1967) *The Years of High Theory: Invention and Tradition in Economic Thought 1926–1939*, Cambridge: Cambridge University Press.

Shannon, Claude E. (1950) 'Programming a Computer to Play Chess', *Philosophical Magazine*, **41**(7), 256–75.

Shaper, Colin F. (2000) 'Preferences, Choice and Explanation: "The Economic Approach" – A Case Study', PhD Thesis, University of Cambridge.

Shionoya, Yuichi (1990) 'Instrumentalism in Schumpeter's Economic Methodology', *History of Political Economy*, **22**(2), Summer, 187–222.

Shionoya, Yuichi (1991) 'Schumpeter on Schmoller and Weber: A Methodology of Economic Sociology', *History of Political Economy*, **23**(2), Summer, 193–219.

Shionoya, Yuichi (1995) 'A Methodological Appraisal of Schmoller's Research Program', in Koslowski (1995), pp. 57–78.

Shionoya, Yuichi (1997) *Schumpeter and the Idea of Social Science: A Metatheoretical Study*, Cambridge and New York: Cambridge University Press.

Shove, Gerald F. (1942) 'The Place of Marshall's *Principles* in the Development of Economic Theory', *Economic Journal*, **52**(4), December, 294–329.

Siakantaris, Nikos (2000) 'Experimental Economics Under the Microscope', *Cambridge Journal of Economics*, **24**(3), May, 267–81.

Simon, Herbert A. (1957) *Models of Man: Social and Rational. Mathematical Essays on Rational Human Behavior in a Social Setting*, New York: Wiley.

Skidelsky, Robert (1983) *John Maynard Keynes: Volume One: Hopes Betrayed, 1883–1920*, London: Macmillan.

Skidelsky, Robert (1992) *John Maynard Keynes: Volume Two: The Economist as Saviour, 1920–1937*, London: Macmillan.

Slichter, Sumner H. (1924) 'The Organization and Control of Economic Activity', in Rexford G. Tugwell (ed.) *The Trend of Economics*, New York: Alfred Knopf, pp. 301–56.

Slichter, Sumner H. (1931) *Modern Economic Society*, New York: Holt.

Slovic, Paul and Lichtenstein, Sarah (1983) 'Preference Reversals: A Broader Perspective', *American Economic Review*, **73**(4), September, pp. 596–605.

Smith, Adam (1976) [1776] *An Inquiry into the Nature and Causes of the Wealth of Nations*, 2 vols, ed. Campbell, R. H. and Skinner, A. S. London: Methuen.

Smith, Barry (1990) 'Aristotle, Menger, Mises: An Essay in the Metaphysics of Economics', in Caldwell (1990), pp. 263–88.

Smith, Merritt R. (ed.) (1985) *Military Enterprise and Technological Change*, Cambridge, MA: MIT Press.

Smith, Vernon L. (1982) 'Microeconomic Systems as an Experimental Science', *American Economic Review*, **72**(5), December, 923–55. Repr. in Smith, Vernon L. (1992) *Papers in Experimental Economics*, Cambridge: Cambridge University Press.

Sober, Elliott (1985) 'Darwin on Natural Selection: A Philosophical Perspective', in Kohn, David (ed.) (1985) *The Darwinian Heritage*, Princeton: Princeton University Press, pp. 867–99.

Sofianou, Evanthia (1995) 'Post-Modernism and the Notion of Rationality in Economics', *Cambridge Journal of Economics*, **19**(3), June, 373–89.

Solow, Robert M. (1985) 'Economic History and Economics', *American Economic Review (Papers and Proceedings)*, **75**(2), May, 328–31.

Sombart, Werner (1894) 'Zur Kritik des ökonomischen Systems vom Karl Marx', *Archiv für soziale Gesetzgebung und Statistik*, **7**, 555–94.

Sombart, Werner (1902) *Der moderne Kapitalismus: Historisch-systematische Darstellung des gesamteuropäischen Wirtschaftslebens von seinen Anfängen bis zur Gegenwart*, (1st edn), 2 vols, Munich and Leipzig: Duncker and Humblot.

Sombart, Werner (1913a) *Der Bourgeois: zur Geistesgeschichte des modernen Wirtschafts-menschen*, Munich and Leipzig: Duncker and Humblot.

Sombart, Werner (1913b) *Krieg und Kapitalismus*, Munich and Leipzig: Duncker and Humblot.

Sombart, Werner (1916–27) *Der moderne Kapitalismus: Historisch-systematische Darstellung des gesamteuropäischen Wirtschaftslebens von seinen Anfängen bis zur Gegenwart*, (2nd edn), 4 vols, Munich and Leipzig: Duncker and Humblot.

Sombart, Werner (1929) 'Economic Theory and Economic History', *European History Review*, 2(1), January, 1–19.

Sombart, Werner (1930a) *Die drei Nationalökonomien: Geschichte und System der Lehre von der Wirtschaft*, Munich and Leipzig: Duncker and Humblot.

Sombart, Werner (1930b) 'Capitalism', in Seligman, Edwin R. A. and Johnson, Alvin (eds) *Encyclopaedia of the Social Sciences*, New York: Macmillan, vol. 3, pp. 195–208.

Sombart, Werner (1956) *Noö-Soziologie*, Berlin: Duncker and Humblot.

Sonnenschein, Hugo F. (1972) 'Market Excess Demand Functions', *Econometrica*, 40(3), 549–63.

Sonnenschein, Hugo F. (1973a) 'Do Walras's Identity and Continuity Characterize the Class of Community Excess Demand Functions?', *Journal of Economic Theory*, 6(4), 345–54.

Sonnenschein, Hugo F. (1973b) 'The Utility Hypothesis and Market Demand Theory', *Western Economic Journal*, 11(4), 404–10.

Souter, Ralph W. (1930) 'Equilibrium Economics and Business Cycle Theory: A Commentary', *Quarterly Journal of Economics*, 45(1), November, 40–93.

Souter, Ralph W. (1933a) '"The Nature and Significance of Economic Science" in Recent Discussion', *Quarterly Journal of Economics*, 47, 377–413.

Souter, Ralph W. (1933b) *Prolegomena to Relativity Economics: An Elementary Study in the Mechanics and Organics of an Expanding Economic Universe*, New York: Columbia University Press.

Spear, S. E. (1989) 'Learning Rational Expectations Under Computability Constraints', *Econometrica*, 57, 889–910.

Spencer, Herbert (1851) *Social Statics*, London: Chapman.

Spencer, Herbert (1855) *The Principles of Psychology*, London: Williams and Norgate.

Spencer, Herbert (1862) *First Principles*, (1st edn) London: Williams and Norgate.

Spencer, Herbert (1880) *The Study of Sociology*, London: Williams and Norgate.

Spencer, Herbert (1894) *The Principles of Biology* (2 vols) London: Williams and Norgate.

Spencer, Herbert (1969) [1876–96] *Principles of Sociology*, ed. Andreski, S. London: Macmillan.

Sperry, Roger W. (1991) 'In Defense of Mentalism and Emergent Interaction', *Journal of Mind and Behavior*, 12(2), pp. 221–46.

Spiethoff, Arthur (1932) 'Die Allgemeine Volkswirtschaftslehre als geschichtliche Theorie, Die Wirtschaftsstile', *Schmollers Jahrbuch für Witschaftsgeschichte*, 56(2), 50–85.

Spiethoff, Arthur (1952) 'The "Historical" Character of Economic Theories', *Journal of Economic History*, 12(2), Spring, 131–9.

Sraffa, Piero (1960) *Production of Commodities by Means of Commodities: Prelude to a Critique of Economic Theory*, Cambridge: Cambridge University Press.

Starmer, Christopher (1999a) 'Experimental Economics: Hard Science or Wasteful Tinkering?', *Economic Journal*, 109(2), February, F5–15.

Starmer, Christopher (1999b) 'Experiments in Economics: Should We Trust the Dismal Scientists in White Coats?', *Journal of Economic Methodology*, 6(1), March, 1–30.

Stebbins, G. Ledyard (1969) *The Biological Basis of Progressive Evolution*, Chapel Hill, NC: University of North Carolina Press.

Steiner, Philippe (1995) 'Economic Sociology: A Historical Perspective', *The European Journal of the History of Economic Thought*, 2(1), Spring, 175–95.

Stigler, George J. (1987) *The Theory of Price*, (4th edn) New York and London: Macmillan.

Stiglitz, Joseph E. (1987) 'The Causes and Consequences of the Dependence of Quality on Price', *Journal of Economic Literature*, **25**(1), March, 1–48.

Stiglitz, Joseph E. (1994) *Whither Socialism?* Cambridge, MA: MIT Press.

Stinchcombe, Arthur L. (1965) 'Social Structure and Organizations', in March, James G. (ed.) *Handbook of Organizations*, Chicago: Rand McNally, pp. 142–93.

Streissler, Erich W. (1972) 'To What Extent was the Austrian School Marginalist?', *History of Political Economy*, **4**(2), Fall, 426–41.

Streissler, Erich W. (1990) 'Menger, Böhm-Bawerk and Wieser: The Origin of the Austrian School', in Hennings, Klaus and Samuels, Warren J. (eds) *Neoclassical Economic Theory, 1870 to 1930*, Boston: Kluwer, pp. 151–89.

Streissler, Erich W. (1994) 'The Influence of German and Austrian Economics on Joseph A. Schumpeter', in Shionoya, Yuichi and Perlman, Mark (eds) *Schumpeter in the History of Ideas*, Ann Arbor, MI: University of Michigan Press.

Sugden, Robert (1991) 'Rational Choice: A Survey of Contributions from Economics and Philosophy', *Economic Journal*, **101**(4), July, 751–85.

Swedberg, Richard (1989) 'Joseph A. Schumpeter and the Tradition of Economic Sociology', *Journal of Institutional and Theoretical Economics*, **145**, 508–24.

Swedberg, Richard (1991) *Joseph A. Schumpeter: His Life and Work*, Cambridge: Polity Press.

Swedberg, Richard (ed.) (1996) *Economic Sociology*, Aldershot: Edward Elgar.

Swedberg, Richard (1998) *Max Weber and the Idea of Economic Sociology*, Princeton, NJ: Princeton University Press.

Sweet, Paul R. (1980) *Wilhelm von Humboldt: A Biography. Volume Two: 1808–1835*, Columbus, OH: Ohio State University Press.

Taylor, Frederick Winslow (1911) *The Principles of Scientific Management*, New York: Harper.

Thagard, Paul (1978) 'The Best Explanation: Criteria for Theory Choice', *Journal of Philosophy*, **75**, 76–92.

Thomas, Brinley (1991) 'Alfred Marshall on Economic Biology', *Review of Political Economy*, **3**(1), January, 1–14. Repr. in Hodgson (1995).

Tilman, Rick (1992) *Thorstein Veblen and His Critics, 1891–1963: Conservative, Liberal, and Radical*, Princeton: Princeton University Press.

Tilman, Rick (1996) *The Intellectual Legacy of Thorstein Veblen: Unresolved Issues*, Westport, Connecticut: Greenwood Press.

Tinker, Irene (ed.) (1990) *Persistent Inequalities: Women and World Development*, Oxford and New York: Oxford University Press.

Todd, Emmanuel (1985) *The Explanation of Ideology: Family Structures and Social Systems*, Oxford: Basil Blackwell.

Toner, Phillip (1999) *Main Currents in Cumulative Causation: The Dynamics of Growth and Development*, London: Macmillan.

Tool, Marc R. (1991) 'Contributions to an Institutionalist Theory of Price Determination', in Hodgson, Geoffrey M. and Screpanti, Ernesto (eds) *Rethinking Economics: Markets, Technology and Economic Evolution*, Aldershot: Edward Elgar, pp. 19–39. Repr. in Tool, Marc R. (1995) *Pricing, Valuation and Systems: Essays in Neoinstitutional Economics*, Aldershot: Edward Elgar.

Tool, Marc R. (2000) *Value Theory and Economic Progress: The Institutional Economics of J. Fagg Foster*, Boston: Kluwer.

Toynbee, Arnold (1894) *Lectures on the Industrial Revolution in England*, London: Longman.

Tribe, Keith (1988) *Governing the Economy: The Reformation of German Economic Discourse, 1750–1840*, Cambridge: Cambridge University Press.

Tribe, Keith (1995) *Strategies of Economic Order: German Economic Discourse, 1750–1950*, Cambridge: Cambridge University Press.

Tribe, Keith (2000) 'The Cambridge Economics Tripos 1903–55 and the Training of Economists', *Manchester School*, **68**(2), March, 222–48.

Trotsky, Leon (1934) *The History of the Russian Revolution*, London: Gollancz.

Tullock, Gordon (1994) *The Economics of Non-Human Societies*, Tucson, Arizona: Pallas Press.

Twomey, Paul (1998) 'Reviving Veblenian Economic Psychology', *Cambridge Journal of Economics*, **22**(4), July, 433–48.

Tylor, Sir Edward Burnett (1871) *Primitive Culture: Researches into the Development of Mythology, Philosophy, Religion, Language, Art, and Custom*, 2 vols, London: John Murray. Repr. 1958, New York: Harper.

Udéhn, Lars (1992) 'The Limits of Economic Imperialism', in Himmelstrand, Ulf (ed.) (1992) *Interfaces in Economic and Social Analysis*, London: Routledge, pp. 239–80.

Udéhn, Lars (1996) *The Limits of Public Choice: A Sociological Critique of the Economic Theory of Politics*, London: Routledge.

Uno, Kozo (1980) *Principles of Political Economy: Theory of a Purely Capitalist Society*, trans. Thomas T. Sekine from the Japanese edn (1964) Brighton: Harvester.

Van den Berg, Axel (1997) 'Is Sociological Theory Too Grand for Social Mechanisms?', in Hedström, Peter and Swedberg, Richard (eds) (1997) *Social Mechanisms: An Analytical Approach to Social Theory*, Cambridge: Cambridge University Press, pp. 204–37.

Van den Berg, Axel (1998) 'Out of Habit: Notes Toward a General Theory of Deliberate Action', *Amsterdam Sociologisch Tijdschrift*, **25**(3), October, 429–63.

Van Eeghen, Piet-Hein (1996) 'Towards a Methodology of Tendencies', *Journal of Economic Methodology*, **3**(2), December, 261–84.

Vanberg, Viktor J. (1986) 'Spontaneous Market Order and Social Rules: A Critique of F. A. Hayek's Theory of Cultural Evolution', *Economics and Philosophy*, **2**(1), April, 75–100. Repr. in Vanberg, Viktor J. (1994) *Rules and Choice in Economics*, London: Routledge.

Vanek, Jaroslav (1966) 'Towards a More General Theory of Growth with Technological Change', *Economic Journal*, **76**(4), December, 841–54.

Vanek, Jaroslav (1970) *The General Theory of Labor-Managed Market Economies*, Ithaca, NY: Cornell University Press.

Veblen, Thorstein B. (1896) 'Review of *Socialisme et Science Positive* by Enrico Ferri', in *Journal of Political Economy*, December, 98–103. Repr. in Veblen (1973).

Veblen, Thorstein B. (1897a) 'Review of *Essais sur la conception matérialiste de l'histoire* by Antonio Labriola', in *Journal of Political Economy*, **5**(3), June, 390–1. Repr. in Veblen (1973).

Veblen, Thorstein B. (1897b) 'Review of *Die Marxistische Socialdemokratie* by Max Lorenz', in *Journal of Political Economy*, **6**(1), December, 136–7. Repr. in Veblen (1973).

Veblen, Thorstein B. (1898) 'Why Is Economics Not an Evolutionary Science?', *Quarterly Journal of Economics*, **12**(3), July, 373–97. Repr. in Veblen (1919).

Veblen, Thorstein B. (1899) *The Theory of the Leisure Class: An Economic Study in the Evolution of Institutions*, New York: Macmillan. Republished 1961, New York: Random House.

Veblen, Thorstein B. (1901) 'Gustav Schmoller's Economics', *Quarterly Journal of Economics*, **16**(1), November, 69–93. Repr. in Veblen (1919).

Veblen, Thorstein B. (1903) 'Review of *Der moderne Kapitalismus* by Werner Sombart', *Journal of Political Economy*, **11**(2), March, 300–5. Repr. in Veblen (1973).

Veblen, Thorstein B. (1904) *The Theory of Business Enterprise*, New York: Charles Scribners. Repr. 1975 by Augustus Kelley.

Veblen, Thorstein B. (1914) *The Instinct of Workmanship, and the State of the Industrial Arts*, New York: Macmillan. Repr. 1990 with new introd. by Murray G. Murphey and 1964 introductory note by J. Dorfman, New Brunswick, NJ: Transaction Books.

Veblen, Thorstein B. (1915a) *Imperial Germany and the Industrial Revolution*, New York: Macmillan. Repr. 1964 by Augustus Kelley.

Veblen, Thorstein B. (1915b) 'Review of *Der Bourgeois: zur Geistesgeschichte des modernen Wirtschaftsmenschen* by Werner Sombart', in *Journal of Political Economy*, **23**(8), October, 846–8. Repr. in Veblen (1973).

Veblen, Thorstein B. (1919) *The Place of Science in Modern Civilisation and Other Essays*, New York: Huebsch. Repr. 1990 with new introd. by W. J. Samuels, New Brunswick, NJ: Transaction.

Veblen, Thorstein B. (1934) *Essays on Our Changing Order*, ed. Leon Ardzrooni, New York: The Viking Press.

Veblen, Thorstein B. (1973) *Essays, Reviews and Reports*, ed. with introd. by Joseph Dorfman, New York: Augustus Kelley.

Velupillai, Kumaraswamy (1996) 'The Computable Alternative in the Formalization of Economics: A Counterfactual Essay', *Kyklos*, **49**(3), 251–72.

Veysey, Laurence R. (1965) *The Emergence of the American University*, Chicago: University of Chicago Press.

Vickers, Douglas (1995) *The Tyranny of the Market: A Critique of Theoretical Foundations*, Ann Arbor: University of Michigan Press.

Vining, Rutledge (1949) 'Methodological Issues in Quantitative Economics', *Review of Economics and Statistics*, **31**(2), May, 77–86.

Voigt, Andreas (1912–13) 'Die wirtschaftlichen Güter als Rechte', *Archiv für Rechts- und Wirtschaftspolitik*, **6**, 304–16.

Walbank, Frank William (1987) 'Trade and Industry under the Later Roman Empire in the West', in Postan, Michael M. and Miller, Edward (eds) (1987) *The Cambridge Economic History of Europe, Vol II, Trade and Industry in the Middle Ages*, (2nd edn) Cambridge: Cambridge University Press, pp. 74–131.

Wald, Abraham (1947) 'Foundations of a General Theory of Sequential Decision Functions', *Econometrica*, **15**(4), October, 279–313.

Walters, B. and Young, David (1997) 'On the Coherence of Post-Keynesian Economics', *Scottish Journal of Political Economy*, **44**(3), August, 329–49.

Watson, John B. (1919) *Psychology from the Standpoint of a Behaviorist*, Philadelphia: J. B. Lippincott. Repr. 1994 with introd. by Robert H. Wozniak, London: Routledge/Thoemmes.

Wearne, Bruce C. (1989) *The Theory and Scholarship of Talcott Parsons to 1951: A Critical Commentary*, Cambridge: Cambridge University Press.

Weber, Max (1904) 'Die "Objektivität" sozialwissenschaftlicher und sozialpolitischer Erkenntnis' ('"Objectivity" in Social Science and Social Policy'), *Archiv für Sozialwissenschaft und Sozialpolitik*, 19. Translated in Weber (1949), pp. 49–112.

Weber, Max (1927) *General Economic History*, trans. Frank H. Knight from the German edn (1923) London: Allen and Unwin. Repr. 1981 with introd. by Ira J. Cohen, New Brunswick, NJ: Transaction Books.

Weber, Max (1930) [1904–5] *The Protestant Ethic and the Spirit of Capitalism*, London: Allen and Unwin.

Weber, Max (1947) *The Theory of Social and Economic Organization*, ed. with introd. by Talcott Parsons, New York: Free Press.

Weber, Max (1949) *Max Weber on the Methodology of the Social Sciences*, trans. and ed. Edward A. Shils and Henry A. Finch, Glencoe, IL: Free Press.

Weber, Max (1968) *Economy and Society: An Outline of Interpretative Sociology*, 2 vols, trans. G. Roth and C. Wittich from the German edn (1921–1922) Berkeley: University of California Press.

Weber, Max (1975) 'Marginal Utility Theory and "The Fundamental Laws of Psychophysics', trans. from the German publication of 1908, *Social Science Quarterly*, **56**(1), June, 21–36.

Weber, Max (1978) *Max Weber: Selections in Translation*, ed. and introd. by W. G. Runciman, Cambridge: Cambridge University Press.

Wedderburn, Kenneth W. (1971) *The Worker and the Law*, (2nd edn) Harmondsworth: Penguin.

Weingart, Peter, Mitchell, Sandra D., Richerson, Peter J. and Maasen, Sabine (eds) (1997) *Human By Nature: Between Biology and the Social Sciences*, Mahwah, NJ: Lawrence Erlbaum Associates.

Weingartner, Rudolph H. (1961) 'The Quarrel About Historical Explanation', *Journal of Philosophy*, **58**(2), January, 29–45.

Western, John R. (1972) *Monarchy and Revolution: The English State in the 1680s*, London: Blandford.

Whalen, Charles J. (1993) 'Saving Capitalism By Making it Good: The Monetary Economics of John R. Commons', *Journal of Economic Issues*, **27**(4), December, 1155–79.

Whately, Richard (1831) *Introductory Lectures on Political Economy*, (1st edn) London: Fellowes.

Wheeler, William M. (1930) *Social Life Among the Insects*, New York: Harcourt.

Whitaker, John K. (ed.) (1996) *The Correspondence of Alfred Marshall*, 3 vols, Cambridge: Cambridge University Press.

White, Harrison C. (1992) *Identity and Control: A Structural Theory of Social Action*, Princeton, NJ: Princeton University Press.

Whitehead, Alfred N. (1926) *Science and the Modern World*, Cambridge: Cambridge University Press.

Whitley, Richard (1992) *Business Systems in East Asia: Firms, Markets and Societies*, London: Sage.

Whitley, Richard (1999) *Divergent Capitalisms: The Social Structuring and Change of Business Systems*, Oxford and New York: Oxford University Press.

Wicksell, Knut (1934) *Lectures on Political Economy: Volume One – General Theory*, trans. E. Classen from the 3rd Swedish edn (1928) and ed. with introd. Lionel Robbins, London: George Routledge.

Wicksteed, Philip H. (1933) [1910] *The Commonsense of Political Economy*, ed. Lionel Robbins, London: George Routledge.

Wilber, Charles K. and Harrison, Robert S. (1978) 'The Methodological Basis of Institutional Economics: Pattern Model, Storytelling, and Holism', *Journal of Economic Issues*, **12**(1), March, 61–89. Repr. in Samuels (1988), vol. 2.

Willey, Malcolm M. (1929) 'The Validity of the Culture Concept', *American Journal of Sociology*, **35**(2), September, 204–19.

Williams, George C. (1966) *Adaptation and Natural Selection*, Princeton, NJ; Princeton University Press.

Williamson, Oliver E. (1975) *Markets and Hierarchies: Analysis and Anti-Trust Implications: A Study in the Economics of Internal Organization*, New York: Free Press.

Williamson, Oliver E. (1983) 'Credible Commitments: Using Hostages to Support Exchange', *American Economic Review*, **74**(3), September, 519–40.

Williamson, Oliver E. (1985) *The Economic Institutions of Capitalism: Firms, Markets, Relational Contracting*, London: Macmillan.

Williamson, Oliver E. (1991) 'Comparative Economic Organization: The Analysis of Discrete Structural Alternatives', *Administrative Science Quarterly*, **36**, 269–96.

Williamson, Oliver E. (1999) 'Strategy Research: Governance and Competence Perspectives', *Strategic Management Journal*, **20**, 1087–108.

Williamson, Oliver E. and Winter, Sidney G. (eds) (1991) *The Nature of the Firm: Origins, Evolution, and Development*, Oxford and New York: Oxford University Press.

Wiltshire, David (1978) *The Social and Political Thought of Herbert Spencer*, Oxford: Oxford University Press.

Wimsatt, William C. (1986) 'Developmental Constraints, Generative Entrenchment, and the Innate-Acquired Distinction', in Bechtel, W. (ed.) (1986) *Integrating Scientific Disciplines*, Dordrecht, Holland: Martinus-Nijhoff, pp. 185–208.

Winch, Donald (1969) *Economics and Policy: A Historical Study*, London: Hodder and Stoughton.

Winslow, Edward A. (1989) 'Organic Interdependence, Uncertainty and Economic Analysis', *Economic Journal*, **99**(4), December, 1173–82.

Winter, J. M. (ed.) (1975) *War and Economic Development*, Cambridge, MA: Harvard University Press.

Winter, Sidney G., Jr (1964) 'Economic "Natural Selection" and the Theory of the Firm', *Yale Economic Essays*, **4**(1), 225–72. Repr. in Hodgson (1998c).

Wong, Stanley (1978) *The Foundations of Paul Samuelson's Revealed Preference Theory: A Study by the Method of Rational Reconstruction*, London: Routledge and Kegan Paul.

Woo, Henry K. H. (1992) *Cognition, Value and Price: A General Theory of Value*, Ann Arbor, MI: University of Michigan Press.

Woodham-Smith, Cecil (1962) *The Great Hunger: Ireland 1845–1849*, London: Hamish Hamilton.

Worswick, George D. N. (1957) 'Review of *Economy and Society* by Talcott Parsons and Neil J. Smelser', *Economic Journal*, **67**(4), December, 700–2.

Wynarczyk, Peter (1992) 'Comparing Alleged Incommensurables: Institutional and Austrian Economics as Rivals and Possible Complements?', *Review of Political Economy*, **4**(1), January, 18–36.

Yagi, Kiichiro (1997) 'Carl Menger and the Historicism in Economics', in Koslowski (1997a), pp. 231–58.

Yonay, Yuval P. (1998) *The Struggle Over the Soul of Economics: Institutionalist and Neo-classical Economists in America Between the Wars*, Princeton, NJ: Princeton University Press.

Yonay, Yuval P. (2000) 'An Ethnographer's Credo: Methodological Reflections Following an Anthropological Journey Among the Econ', *Journal of Economic Issues*, **34**(2), June, 341–56.

Young, Allyn A. (1911) 'Some Limitations of the Value Concept', *Quarterly Journal of Economics*, **25**(3), 409–28.

Young, Allyn A. (1927) 'Economics as a Field of Research', *Quarterly Journal of Economics*, **42**(1), November, 1–25.

Young, Allyn A. (1928) 'Increasing Returns and Economic Progress', *Economic Journal*, **38**(4), December, 527–42.

Young, Allyn A. (1929) 'Economics', in Gee, Wilson (ed.) *Research in the Social Sciences: Its Fundamental Methods and Objectives*, New York: Macmillan, pp. 53–80.

Young, H. Peyton (1996) 'The Economics of Convention', *Journal of Economic Perspectives*, **10**(2), Spring, 105–22.

Zaret, David (1980) 'From Weber to Parsons and Schultz: The Eclipse of History in Modern Social Theory', *American Journal of Sociology*, **85**(5), March, 1180–201.

Zecchini, Salvatore (ed.) (1997) *Lessons from the Economic Transition in Central and Eastern Europe in the 1990s*, Boston: Kluwer.

Zelizer, Viviana A. (1988) 'Beyond the Polemics on the Market: Establishing a Theoretical and Empirical Agenda', *Sociological Forum*, **3**(4), 614–34. Repr. in Swedberg (1996).

Zelizer, Viviana A. (1993) 'Making Multiple Monies', in Swedberg, Richard (ed.) *Explorations in Economic Sociology*, New York: Russell Sage, pp. 193–212.

Zinn, M. K. (1927) 'A General Theory of the Correlation of Time Series of Statistics', *Review of Economic Statistics*, **9**(4), October, 184–97.

Zouboulakis, Michel S. (1999) 'Walter Bagehot on Economic Methodology: Evolutionism and Realisticness', *Journal of Economic Methodology*, **6**(1), March, 79–94.

INDEX